# TAKEOVERS, RESTRUCTURING, AND CORPORATE GOVERNANCE

## SECOND EDITION

### J. Fred Weston

*The Anderson School*
*University of California, Los Angeles*

### Kwang S. Chung

*College of Business Administration*
*Chung-Ang University, Seoul*

### Juan A. Siu

*The Anderson School*
*University of California, Los Angeles*

 Prentice Hall, Upper Saddle River, New Jersey 07458

# To Bernadine

*Acquisitions Editor:* Paul Donnelly
*Assistant Editor:* Gladys Soto
*Editorial Director:* James Boyd
*Marketing Manager:* Patrick Lynch
*Production Editor:* Mollie Pfeiffer
*Associate Managing Editor:* David Salierno
*Managing Editor:* Dee Josephson
*Production Coordinator:* Carol Samet
*Manufacturing Buyer:* Diane Peirano
*Manufacturing Supervisor:* Arnold Vila
*Manufacturing Manager:* Vincent Scelta
*Cover Design:* Rosemarie Votta
*Cover Design Manager:* Jayne Conte
*Cover Art:* © Peter B. Kaplan
*Composition:* Omegatype Typography, Inc.

**Library of Congress Cataloging-in-Publication Data**

Weston, J. Fred (John Fred)
   Takeovers, restructuring, and corporate governance / J. Fred
Weston, Kwang S. Chung, Juan A. Siu.—[2nd ed.]
     p.    cm.
   Rev. ed. of: Mergers, restructuring, and corporate control. 1990.
   Includes bibliographical references and index.
   **ISBN 0-13-889163-X**
   1. Consolidation and merger of corporations—United States—
Finance.   2. Consolidation and merger of corporations—United
States—Management.   I. Chung, Kwang S.   II. Siu, Juan
A.   III. Weston, J. Fred (John Fred).   Mergers,
restructuring, and corporate control.
HG4028.M4W47   1997
338.8'3'0973—dc21                         97-31325
                                                  CIP

Prentice-Hall International (UK) Limited, London
Prentice-Hall of Australia Pty. Limited, Sydney
Prentice-Hall Canada, Inc., Toronto
Prentice-Hall Hispanoamericana, S.A., Mexico
Prentice-Hall of India Private Limited, New Delhi
Prentice-Hall of Japan, Inc., Tokyo
Simon & Schuster Asia Pte. Ltd., Singapore
Editora Prentice-Hall do Brasil, Ltda., Rio de Janeiro

Printed in the United States of America

10  9  8  7

# Overview

# Contents

## Cases in Text

---------------
# Preface

## MERGER ACTIVITY CONTINUES TO REACH HIGHER LEVELS

After peaking in 1988 and then declining to a low in 1991, merger activity increased to new highs from 1995 to 1997. These resurgent mergers and acquisitions (M&As) have been called *strategic mergers,* a phrase that conveys that firms are using M&As as well as internal new product and project programs to realign themselves to their changing environments. Some powerful forces have been unleashed. Global competition has intensified. Technological change has impacted telecommunications and a wide range of media businesses. Deregulation has impacted the airlines, banking, telecommunications, and even the traditional public utility industries. Computers and the Internet are changing the way businesses are conducted. Business enterprises find that they must adjust to massive changes in their environments and in the nature of competition as well as in their relations with suppliers, workers, consumers, and other stakeholders. These forces are not likely to diminish in the years ahead. The M&A subject, therefore, takes on even greater importance.

Dramatic events in mergers, takeovers, restructuring, and corporate control fill the newspaper headlines almost daily. Mergers, takeovers, restructuring, and corporate control issues have become central public- and corporate-policy issues. To some, M&As, restructuring, and corporate control activities represent a new industrial force that will lead the United States and other economies that practice these arts to new heights of creativity and productivity. To others, these same activities are regarded as a blight on our economy—a symptom of the larger malaise of greed and gambling that is rotting the core of American society. M&As are increasingly used in China to attempt to improve the performance of the state-owned enterprises. Regardless of which view is held, M&As, restructuring, and corporate control represent major forces in the modern financial and economic environments. These are areas with potential for both good and harm.

Merger and aquisition activity has continued to stimulate a veritable deluge of published materials. Compact summaries of these materials or synthesis articles cannot cover the material adequately. This book seeks to provide a more complete treatment of the leading topics related to mergers, takeovers, restructuring, and corporate control. In the future, shifts in the levels of these activities may occur with fluctuations in the economy and with changing regulatory environments. However, takeovers, restructuring, and leveraged buyouts will continue to be major forces in the economy. Additionally, to analyze takeovers and restructuring, some key topics such as valuation, cost of capital, and strategic financial planning—essential to the subject of financial economics—are involved. Therefore, important analytical concepts must be mastered.

## POINT OF VIEW

We try to be objective in our analysis of M&A activity. We see some positive benefits from increased emphasis on financial strategy and restructuring. Undoubtedly, there have been excesses as typically occur in waves in exploding markets. We have to separate the good from the bad. We come not to praise, criticize, or condemn, but to increase understanding. Our central aim is to provide a conceptual framework that will help the reader put into perspective and increase his or her understanding of events that are headlined almost daily in the financial and general press.

The main audience we have in mind is the academic user. Increasingly, M&A courses deal with all or part of the subject matter of this book. For that reason, we have included end-of-chapter questions to stimulate discussion and to focus the key subject matter. We have also kept in mind two other audiences—the businessperson and the general public, including legislators and other policy makers. We have tried to keep the level of treatment accessible by avoiding excessive jargon. We have tried to develop the technical materials from the ground level up so that both the academic reader and the general reader will be able to master the material and, we hope, experience intellectual growth in the process.

What we think will be of value to academics and for businesspeople is the ability to answer natural and practical questions that arise. For the bidding firm, how much will my early investment in the target increase in value if I use cash versus stock as a method of payment? For the target, what is a reasonable premium for me to expect from a bidder? How much will my firm increase in value if I engage in a sell-off or divestiture? What will be the effect on a firm's share price on average if it engages in stock repurchase? What will be the impact of my firm's share price if it makes a stock or debt issue? What will the share price effect be if a proxy contest is started? What will be the effect of paying greenmail? What value changes take place with going private, particularly through a leveraged buyout? If my firm establishes two classes of stock, which one will have the greater value—the one that pays more income or the one that has more voting power?

There is a rich body of empirical material that can provide a basis for answering such questions. This book attempts to bring that empirical material together in a systematic way. At the same time it tries to lay bare the theory or principles and the logical analysis that give meaning to the empirical findings. These and related materials will provide the general reader with a basis for understanding and judgment about the continued flow of proposals to alter public policy toward M&As and corporate restructuring that are introduced into every session of Congress.

## CHANGES IN THE SECOND EDITION

We have reduced the length of the book while adding new material. In reorienting the book, we have eliminated treatment of abstract theoretical models. We believe that such material is more appropriate in books aimed mainly at doctoral students. We seek to utilize the implications of these models developed fully in the first edition, but do not attempt to repeat the extended discussions that are still available in the first edition.

We have updated the text with new empirical data and literature. In some cases, we have summarized groups of articles into their main findings. In other cases, where individual articles develop their own distinct new findings, we discuss them individually. We have been striving to tighten the conceptual framework that provides perspective on groups of articles in individual subject areas.

We have streamlined the valuation material, orienting it more fully to M&A decisions and case studies, by introducing many more cases in the text and as end-of-chapter exercises. We plan to continue to do more along these lines in the *Study Guide to Takeovers, Restructuring, and Corporate Governance* and in future editions.

In this second edition, at least 70% of the material is new or rewritten. We have class-tested the manuscript with gratifying results. Students have requested permission to make copies for friends who are doing corporate internships before taking their M&A course. Students and practitioners have told us that reading the materials has improved the breadth and maturity of their understanding of the M&A field.

This book applies materials from business finance and financial economics, business economics, strategy, accounting, and law. It demonstrates the application of a wide range of concepts from diverse fields. A framework for performing M&A analysis is provided. Many applications are developed through case studies and examples. The book helps develop the intellectual maturity for sound judgments on M&A analysis and decisions.

## SUPPLEMENTARY MATERIALS

An important companion piece to this text is the related *Study Guide* to *Takeovers, Restructuring, and Corporate Governance.* Our *Study Guide* contains outlines that provide an overview of the subject matter of each chapter and illustrative problems and solutions that seek to help the student understand how to apply the main ideas contained in the book itself. The main goal of the *Study Guide* is to help students develop a conceptual framework for analyzing the subject matter of the M&A field.

A comprehensive *Instructor's Manual* contains six parts: suggestions for teaching the M&A course; solutions to end-of-chapter questions, problems, and cases; 10 true–false questions per chapter; illustrative examinations; and a sample chapter of our PowerPoint Presentation Graphics, which shows a chapter outline and includes transparency masters.

We also supply a disk in which we have formulated key analytical models contained in our book. These computer models enable the user of the book to study a wide range of alternative concepts, assumptions, or company characteristics.

## APPRECIATION

We are grateful to the following people for their helpful comments on the first edition: Nickolaos Travlos, Boston College; Michael J. Sullivan, Florida State University; Kenneth W. Wiles, University of Texas at Austin; George J. Papaioannou, Hofstra University; Douglas V. Austin, University of Toledo; Maclyn L. Clouse, University of Denver; Matthew Spiegel and Michael Salinger, Columbia University; Nikhil P. Varaiya, Southern Methodist University; Robert F. Bruner, University of Virginia; and Ralph A. Walkling, Ohio State University.

For help on the second edition, we thank: Michael F. Toyne, La Salle University; Kent Hickman, Gonzaga University; and Yun W. Park, Saint Mary's University.

We extend our appreciation also to the many scholars whose writings have enriched the literature on M&As and corporate control. They are listed in the Author Index, and those with multiple citations deserve our special gratitude. We were also helped by scholars whose writings and discussions have stimulated our thinking: Armen Alchian, Edward Altman, Antonio Bernardo, Michael Brennan, Bhagwan Chowdhry,

Bradford Cornell, Harry DeAngelo, Jack Farrell, David Hirshleifer, Patricia Hughes, John Matsusaka, Jeff Pontiff, Richard Roll, Eduardo Schwartz, James Seward, and Ivo Welch. Particular thanks to Matthias Kahl for his corrections and many penetrating comments.

We received assistance from associates in our M&A Research Program at The Anderson School at UCLA. They include Susan Chiu, Scott Ho, Jonathan Howe, Piotr Jawien, Scott Miller, Mike Riela, Carlos Sagasta, Gaurav Trehan, and David Wessels. Marilyn McElroy helped on so many aspects of the development of the book that she was virtually a coauthor. Allen Latta deserves special mention for his contributions.

We appreciate the complete cooperation of the people at Prentice Hall, particularly Paul Donnelly, Senior Editor of Finance, and his associates, MaryBeth Sanok, Gladys Soto, David Salierno, and Mollie Pfeiffer.

This subject is so dynamic and the flow of articles and other materials is so voluminous that there will be need for future updating. We invite reactions, comments, and suggestions from our readers.

J. Fred Weston
Kwang S. Chung
Juan A. Siu

The Anderson School at UCLA
Los Angeles, CA 90095-1481
(310) 825-2200

C H A P T E R

$$\boxed{1}$$

# The Takeover Process

## PATTERNS OF MERGER ACTIVITY

Table 1.1 shows that after declining during the years 1990–1992, takeover and merger activity in 1995 increased to $356 billion, exceeding the earlier peak year 1988 figure of $247 billion (Houlihan Lokey Howard and Zukin, 1997). In constant 1992 dollars, the 1995 amount is $331 billion, still larger than the 1988 amount of $287 billion. The daily newspapers continue to be filled with case studies of mergers and acquisitions (M&As), tender offers (both friendly and hostile), spin-offs and divestitures, corporate restructuring, changes in ownership structures, and struggles for corporate control. The Securities and Exchange Commission (SEC) is active in pursuing insider trading cases. In recent years, leverage ratios for some companies have increased and newer forms of financing have proliferated, including an increase in the use of bonds with ratings below the first four grades (below Baa3 by Moody's or BBB− by Standard and Poor's, referred to as high yield or "junk bonds"). Thus, the traditional subject matter of M&As has been expanded to include takeovers and related issues of corporate restructuring, corporate control, and changes in the ownership structure of firms. For brevity, we refer to these and related activities as M&As.

Examples of the announcement of large transactions since 1994 are presented in Table 1.2. Other large transactions in earlier years are listed in Table 1.3. What do the lists of company names in these two tables tell us? Many of these companies are household names: Disney, Wells Fargo, Chemical Bank, Time Warner, Westinghouse, etc. They cut across a wide range of industries. Although the 1980s were considered the decade of increased merger activity, many large transactions have occurred since 1994.

Mergers and industrial restructuring activities have raised important issues both for business decisions and for public policy formulation. No firm is regarded safe from a takeover possibility. Mergers and acquisitions may be critical to the healthy expansion of business firms as they evolve through successive stages of growth and development. Both internal and external growth may be complementary in the long-range evolution of firms. Successful entry into new product markets and into new geographic markets by a firm may require M&As at some stage in the firm's development. Successful competition in international markets may depend on capabilities obtained in a timely and efficient fashion through M&As. Some have argued that mergers increase value and efficiency and move resources to their optimal uses, thereby increasing shareholder value (Jensen, 1984).

Others are skeptical. They argue that acquired companies are already efficient and that their subsequent performance after acquisition is not improved (Magenheim

**TABLE 1.1**   Merger Activity: The Mergerstat Series

| Year | (1)<br>Total Dollar Value Paid<br>($ Billion) | (2)<br>1992 Constant-Dollar<br>Consideration ($ Billion) |
|------|------|------|
| 1968 | 43.6 | 157.4 |
| 1969 | 23.7 | 81.7 |
| 1970 | 16.4 | 53.6 |
| 1971 | 12.6 | 39.3 |
| 1972 | 16.7 | 49.9 |
| 1973 | 16.7 | 47.2 |
| 1974 | 12.4 | 32.2 |
| 1975 | 11.8 | 28.0 |
| 1976 | 20.0 | 44.8 |
| 1977 | 21.9 | 46.1 |
| 1978 | 34.2 | 67.2 |
| 1979 | 43.5 | 78.7 |
| 1980 | 44.3 | 73.3 |
| 1981 | 82.6 | 125.0 |
| 1982 | 53.8 | 76.6 |
| 1983 | 73.1 | 99.9 |
| 1984 | 122.2 | 161.0 |
| 1985 | 179.6 | 228.5 |
| 1986 | 173.1 | 214.8 |
| 1987 | 163.7 | 197.0 |
| 1988 | 246.9 | 286.8 |
| 1989 | 221.1 | 246.5 |
| 1990 | 108.2 | 115.6 |
| 1991 | 71.2 | 73.2 |
| 1992 | 96.7 | 96.7 |
| 1993 | 176.4 | 171.9 |
| 1994 | 226.7 | 215.9 |
| 1995 | 356.0 | 330.9 |
| 1996 | 492.9 | 446.9 |

*Source:* Houlihan Lokey Howard & Zukin, *Mergerstat Review, 1997,* Los Angeles, CA; GDP deflator: *Economic Report of the President* (Table B-3) February 1996.

and Mueller, 1988; Ravenscraft and Scherer, 1988). Others aver that the gains to shareholders merely represent a redistribution away from labor and other stakeholders (Shleifer and Summers, 1988). Another view is that the M&A activity represents the machinations of speculators who reflect the frenzy of a "Casino Society." This speculative activity is said to increase debt unduly and to erode equity, resulting in an economy highly vulnerable to economic instability (Rohatyn, 1986).

Even individual businesspeople have expressed skepticism of the power of mergers. Warren Buffett (1981, pp. 4–5) observed:

Many managements apparently were overexposed in impressionable childhood years to the story in which the imprisoned handsome prince is released from a toad's body by a kiss from a beautiful princess. Consequently, they are certain their managerial kiss will do wonders for the profitability of Company T[arget]. . . . Investors can always buy toads at the going price for toads. If investors instead bankroll princesses who wish to pay double for the right to kiss the toad, those kisses had better pack some real dynamite. We've observed many kisses but very few miracles. Nevertheless, many managerial princesses remain serenely confident about the future potency of their kisses—even after their corporate backyards are knee-deep in unresponsive toads . . .

We have tried occasionally to buy toads at bargain prices with results that have been chronicled in past reports. Clearly our kisses fell flat. We have done well with a couple of princes—but they were princes when purchased. At least our kisses didn't turn them into toads. And, finally, we have occasionally been quite successful in purchasing fractional interests in easily identifiable princes at toadlike prices.

In this volume, we seek to sort out these opposing views. We offer guidelines for such practical matters as M&A planning by firms and the valuation of combining firms. [Further, the theory and empirical evidence have implications for social and economic policies toward mergers.] Thus, this work provides a framework to evaluate alternative business and social policies involving M&As.

In this chapter, we provide a framework for understanding the many aspects of mergers and takeovers. We cover the topics of merger and tender offer terminology, types of mergers from an economic standpoint, mergers in a legal framework, and the nature of tender offers.

**TABLE 1.2**   Illustrative Large Transactions Announced in 1994 or 1995

| Buyer (or Surviving Entity) | Seller (or Merger Partner or Product Line Sold) | Value of Deal ($ Billion) |
|---|---|---|
| Disney | Capital Cities/ABC | 19.0 |
| Wells Fargo | First Interstate | 10.3 |
| Chemical Bank | Chase Manhattan Bank | 10.0 |
| Martin Marietta | Lockheed | 10.0 |
| Kimberly-Clark | Scott Paper | 9.4 |
| American Home Products Corp. | American Cyanamid Co., Inc. | 9.2 |
| National Amusements Inc. | Blockbuster Entertainment Corp. | 8.4 |
| Time Warner | Turner Broadcasting System | 7.5 |
| Westinghouse | CBS | 5.4 |
| Roche Holding Ltd. | Syntex Corp. | 5.3 |
| Federated Department Stores Inc. | R.H. Macy & Co., Inc. | 4.1 |
| Lilly (Eli) & Co. | McKesson Corp./PCS Health Systems Inc. | 4.0 |
| Burlington Northern Inc. | Santa Fe Pacific Corp. | 3.9 |
| Sandoz AG | Gerber Products Co., Inc. | 3.7 |
| Columbia/HCA Healthcare Corp. | Health Trust Inc.—The Hospital Company | 3.5 |
| SmithKline Beecham PLC | Eastman Kodak Co./Sterling Drug | 2.9 |

**TABLE 1.3** Other Large M&A Announcements

| Buyer | Seller | Price ($ Billion) | Year Announced |
|---|---|---|---|
| Kohlberg Kravis Roberts | RJR Nabisco | 24.6 | 1988 |
| *Beecham Group PLC—U.K. | SmithKline Beckman Corp. | 16.1 | 1989 |
| Chevron Corp. | Gulf Corp. | 13.2 | 1984 |
| Philip Morris Companies Inc. | Kraft Inc. | 13.1 | 1988 |
| American Telephone & Telegraph Co. | McCaw Cellular Communications Co. | 12.6 | 1993 |
| Bristol-Myers Co. | Squibb Corp. | 12.0 | 1989 |
| Time Inc. | Warner Communications Inc. | 11.7 | 1989 |
| Texaco Inc. | Getty Oil Co. | 10.1 | 1984 |
| National Amusement Inc. | Paramount Communications Inc. | 10.0 | 1993 |
| E.I. du Pont de Nemours & Co. | Conoco Inc. | 8.0 | 1981 |
| *KeyCorp | Society Corp. | 7.8 | 1993 |
| British Petroleum Co.—U.K. | Standard Oil Co.—REM 45.0% | 7.8 | 1987 |
| American Telephone & Telegraph Co. | NCR Corp. | 7.4 | 1990 |
| U.S. Steel Corp. | Marathon Oil Corp. | 6.6 | 1981 |
| Matsushita Electric Industrial Co. | MCA Inc. | 6.6 | 1990 |
| Campeau Corp.—Canada | Federated Department Stores Inc. | 6.5 | 1988 |
| GTE Corp. | Contel Corp. | 6.4 | 1990 |
| Merck & Co., Inc. | Medco Containment Services Inc. | 6.0 | 1993 |
| General Electric Corp. | RCA Corp. | 6.0 | 1985 |
| Mobil Corp. | Superior Oil Co. | 5.7 | 1984 |
| *Columbia Healthcare Corp. | HCA—Hospital Corp. of America | 5.7 | 1993 |
| Grand Metropolitan PLC—U.K. | Pillsbury Co. | 5.6 | 1988 |
| Philip Morris Companies Inc. | General Foods Corp. | 5.6 | 1985 |

*Statutory merger.

## MERGER AND TENDER OFFER TERMINOLOGY

The words **merger** and **tender offer** are frequently used but the distinctions are not precise. In general, mergers refer to negotiated deals that meet certain technical and legal requirements. Tender offers usually convey that one firm or person is making an offer directly to the shareholders to sell (tender) their shares at specified prices. In one sense, the word merger refers to negotiations between friendly parties who arrive at a mutually agreeable decision to combine their companies. However in practice, one firm in a merger may be stronger and may dominate the transaction. Similarly, tender offers can be friendly or hostile. In either mergers or tender offers, the negotiations could start out friendly and become hostile. Conversely, negotiations could start out hostile and become friendly. In addition, there could be wide variations in attitudes in either direction as negotiations proceed. However, mergers are mostly "friendly." Some tender offers are "hostile" in the sense that an offer is made to the shareholders without the approval of the board of directors.

As a practical matter, it is useful to have some language to describe the M&A activities. Definitions are arbitrary but useful. In general, mergers reflect various forms of combining companies through some mutuality of negotiations. In tender offers the bidder directly contacts shareholders, inviting them to sell (tender) their shares at an offer price. The directors of the company may or may not have endorsed the tender offer proposal. These distinctions are reflected in a practical way in business practice. That segment of investment banking firms engaged in providing advice on these activities is usually referred to as the Mergers and Acquisitions (M&A) Department. In this sense, mergers and tender offers are two forms of **takeovers.** It is appropriate, therefore, to refer to these activities interchangeably as takeovers or M&As or M&A activity.

With the above as background, we describe some characteristics of mergers, and then follow with a section in which some technical aspects of tender offers are discussed. Then we discuss the concept of restructuring, which involves changes in organizations or policies to alter the firm's approach to achieving its long-term objectives. Describing the activities related to the words and concepts conveys a practical understanding of their meaning. With experience, a judgmental feel for or understanding of how these terms are used is developed. They provide some useful handles for organizing data and studying some important phenomena. However, the terms should be used thoughtfully and not in a mechanical way.

## TYPES OF MERGERS FROM AN ECONOMIC STANDPOINT

Economists have grouped mergers based on whether they take place at the same level of economic activity—exploration, production or manufacturing, wholesale distribution, or retail distribution to the ultimate consumer. The element of relatedness is also important in defining economic categories of mergers.

### Horizontal Mergers

A horizontal merger involves two firms operating and competing in the same kind of business activity. Thus, the acquisition in 1987 of American Motors by Chrysler represented a horizontal combination or merger. Forming a larger firm may have the benefit of economies of scale. The argument that horizontal mergers occur to realize economies of scale is, however, not sufficient to be a theory of horizontal mergers. Although these mergers would generally benefit from large-scale operation, not all small firms merge horizontally to achieve economies of scale. Further, why do firms decide to merge at a particular time? Why do they choose a merger rather than internal growth? Because a merger theory should have implications on these aspects, it must be more than a theory of large firm size or a theory of horizontally integrated operations.

Horizontal mergers are regulated by the government for their potential negative effect on competition. They decrease the number of firms in an industry, possibly making it easier for the industry members to collude for monopoly profits. Some believe that horizontal mergers potentially create monopoly power on the part of the combined firm, enabling it to engage in anticompetitive practices. It remains an empirical question whether horizontal mergers take place to increase the market power of the combined firm, or to seek to augment the firm's capabilities to become a more effective competitor.

### Vertical Mergers

Vertical mergers occur between firms in different stages of production operation. In the oil industry, for example, distinctions are made between exploration and production, refining, and marketing to the ultimate consumer. In the pharmaceutical industry one could distinguish between research and the development of new drugs, the production of drugs, and the marketing of drug products through retail drugstores.

There are many reasons why firms might want to be vertically integrated between different stages. There are technological economies such as the avoidance of reheating and transportation costs in the case of an integrated iron and steel producer. Transactions within a firm may eliminate the costs of searching for prices, contracting, payment collecting, and advertising, and may also reduce the costs of communicating and of coordinating production. Planning for inventory and production may be improved due to more efficient information flow within a single firm. When assets of a firm are specialized to another firm, the latter may act opportunistically. Expropriation can be accomplished by demanding supply of a good or service produced from the specialized assets at a price below its average cost. To avoid the costs of haggling that arise from expropriation attempts, the assets are owned by a single vertically integrated firm. Divergent interests of parties to a transaction can be reconciled by common ownership.

The efficiency and affirmative rationale of vertical integration rests primarily on the costliness of market exchange and contracting. The argument, for instance, that uncertainty over input supply is avoided by backward integration reduces to the fact that long-term contracts are difficult to write, execute, and police.

## Conglomerate Mergers

Conglomerate mergers involve firms engaged in unrelated types of business activity. Thus, the merger between Mobil Oil and Montgomery Ward was generally regarded as a conglomerate merger. Among conglomerate mergers, three types have been distinguished. Product-extension mergers broaden the product lines of firms. These are mergers between firms in related business activities and may also be called concentric mergers. A geographic market-extension merger involves two firms whose operations have been conducted in nonoverlapping geographic areas. Finally, the other conglomerate mergers that are often referred to as pure conglomerate mergers involve unrelated business activities. These would not qualify as either product-extension or market-extension mergers.

By contrasting four categories of companies, the economic functions of conglomerate mergers may be illuminated. Investment companies can be compared with three categories of multi-industry firms to highlight their characteristics. A fundamental economic function of investment companies is to reduce risk by diversification. Combinations of securities whose returns are not perfectly correlated reduce portfolio variance for a target rate of return. Because investment companies combine resources from many sources, their power to achieve a reduction in variance through portfolio effects is greater than that of individual investors. In addition, the managements of investment companies provide professional selection from among investment alternatives.

Conglomerate firms differ fundamentally from investment companies in that they control the entities to which they make major financial commitments. Two important characteristics define a conglomerate firm. First, a conglomerate firm controls a range of activities in various industries that require different skills in the specific managerial functions of research, applied engineering, production, marketing, and so on. Second, the diversification is achieved mainly by external acquisitions and mergers, not by internal development.

## Financial Conglomerates

Within this broader category, two types of conglomerate firms can be distinguished. Financial conglomerates provide a flow of funds to each segment of their operations, exercise control, and are the ultimate financial risk takers. In theory, financial conglomerates undertake strategic planning but do not participate in operating decisions. Management conglomerates not only assume financial responsibility and control, but also play a role in operating decisions and provide staff expertise and staff services to the operating entities.

The characteristics of financial conglomerates may be further clarified by comparisons with investment companies. The financial conglomerate serves at least five distinct economic functions. First, like investment companies, it improves risk/return ratios through diversification. Second, it avoids "gambler's ruin" (an adverse run of losses that might cause bankruptcy). If the losses can be covered by avoiding gambler's ruin, the financial conglomerate maintains the viability of an economic activity with long-run value. Without this form of risk reduction or bankruptcy avoidance, the assets of the operating entity might be shifted to less productive uses because of a run of losses at some point in its development.

Third, a potential contribution by financial conglomerates derives from their establishing programs of financial planning and control. Often, these systems improve the quality of general and functional managerial performance, thereby resulting in more efficient operations and better resource allocation for the economy.

Fourth, if management does not perform effectively but the productivity of assets in the market is favorable, the management is changed. This reflects an effective competitive process because assets are placed under more efficient managements to assure more effective use of resources. A contribution to improved resource allocation is thereby made.

Fifth, in the financial planning and control process, a distinction is made between performance based on underlying potentials in the product-market area and results related to managerial performance. Thus, adverse performance does not necessarily indicate inadequate management performance. If management is competent but product-market potentials are inadequate, executives of the financial conglomerate will seek to shift resources by diverting internal cash flows from the unfavorable areas to areas more attractive from a growth and profitability standpoint. From the standpoint of the economy as a whole, resource allocation is improved.

## Managerial Conglomerates

Managerial conglomerates carry the attributes of financial conglomerates still further. By providing managerial counsel and interactions on decisions, managerial conglomerates increase the potential for improving performance. One school of management theory holds that the generic management functions of planning, organizing, directing, and controlling are readily transferable to all types of business firms. Those managers who have the experience and capability to perform general management functions can perform them in any environment.

This theory argues for management transferability across a wide variety of industries and types of organizations, including government, nonprofit institutions, and military and religious organizations. To the extent that this proposition is valid, it provides a basis for the most general theory of mergers. When any two firms of unequal management competence are combined, the performance of the combined firm will benefit from the impact of the superior management firm, and the total performance of the combined firm will be greater than the sum of the individual parts. This interaction defines **synergy** in its most general form. In the managerial conglomerate, these economic benefits are achieved through corporate headquarters that provide the individual operating entities with expertise and counsel on the generic management functions.

### Concentric Companies

The difference between the managerial conglomerate and the concentric company is based on the distinction between the general and specific management functions. If the activities of the segments brought together are so related that there is carryover of specific management functions (research, manufacturing, finance, marketing, personnel, and so on) or complementarity in relative strengths among these specific management functions, the merger should be termed concentric rather than conglomerate. This transferability of specific management functions across individual segments has long been exemplified by the operations of large, multiproduct, multiplant firms in the American economy. The characteristic organizational structure of these firms has included senior vice presidents who perform as staff specialists to corresponding functional executives in operating departments.

Definitions are inherently arbitrary. Is there any reason to distinguish between managerial conglomerates and concentric companies? The two types have in common a basic economic characteristic. Each transfers general management functions over a variety of activities, using the principle of spreading a fixed factor over a larger number of activities to achieve scale economies and to lower the cost function for the output range. Concentric companies achieve these economic gains in specific management functions as well as in general management functions. A priori, the potential economies for the concentric companies might be expected to be larger. But the magnitude of economies gained in general rather than specific management functions may vary by industry and by industry mix. Further, in the multiproduct, multiplant firms that have achieved economies of carryover of both specific and general management functions, the interactions may be so great that it is impossible to differentiate between the two.

Similarly, a managerial conglomerate that originally provided expertise on general management functions may increasingly act on specific management functions as its executives become more familiar with the operations of the individual entities. Financial conglomerates also may increasingly provide staff service for both general and specific management functions.

Additional illustrations will clarify these concepts and their economic implications. If one company has competence in research, manufacturing, or marketing that can be applied to the product problems of another company that lacks that particular competence, a merger will provide the opportunity to lower cost functions. For example, firms seeking to diversify from advanced technology industries may be strong on research but weaker on production and marketing capabilities than firms in industries with less advanced technology.

To this point we have described the different kinds of mergers and explained some of the reasons why they appear to take place. In the following section we look at mergers within a legal framework.

## MERGERS IN A LEGAL FRAMEWORK

From a legal standpoint, the **statutory merger** is the basic form of transaction. The transaction is governed by the statutory provisions of the state or states in which the parties to the merger are chartered. The main elements of a statutory merger are the percentage vote required for approval of the transaction, who is entitled to vote, how the votes are counted, and the rights of the voters who object to the transaction or its terms.

The Delaware statute is typical of the merger provisions found in most states. After the boards of directors have approved the transaction, it is submitted for ratification to the shareholders of the respective corporations. Prior to the 1960s, most states required approval by two-thirds of the shareholders who possessed the right to vote. In 1962 the model Business Corporation Act provided for a majority vote. In 1967 the state of Delaware adopted the majority vote provision. Other states that provide for a majority vote include California, Michigan, and New Jersey. The state of New York, in contrast, still requires a two-thirds majority for approval of a takeover proposal. In a merger, the traditional legal doctrine was that the minority must agree to the terms approved by the majority. The minority still has the right to sue on a number of issues such as the fairness of the pricing of ownership interests.

After approval by the majority of those with voting rights, the act of "merger" takes place upon the filing of appropriate documents with the states in which the participant companies are chartered. One corporation survives, the others go out of existence. The surviving company assumes the assets and liabilities of the merging firms. When the Nabisco Corporation merged with Standard Brands, Standard Brands was dissolved and Nabisco survived. Nabisco itself was subsequently acquired by the RJ Reynolds tobacco company to form RJR Nabisco. In some combinations, a new entity is created. For example, when Burroughs and Sperry combined in May 1986, the new company adopted the name of Unisys, a name completely unrelated to the former names of the merging companies.

The law also makes provision for a **short-form merger.** The legal procedures are streamlined and shareholder approval is not required. In such a transaction, the ownership of the corporation is concentrated in the hands of a small group, usually referred to as insiders. The threshold ownership requirement is usually 90%.

Sometimes the identity of one of the companies in the merger transaction is preserved. For example, when General Motors bought Electronics Data Systems (EDS) from Ross Perot, EDS was a subsidiary of General Motors. In 1995 General Motors announced that it was going to spin off or divest its EDS subsidiary.

Futhermore, when one firm controls a number of other firms held in the form of subsidiaries, the parent firm is referred to as a holding company. Each of the subsidiaries remains a separate legal entity. In a holding company system, the parent has a controlling interest in each of the subsidiaries.

The percentage of ownership required for a controlling interest varies. If a target has widely dispersed ownership, holdings of 10 to 20% probably gives the parent effective control. Ownership of more than 50% conveys certain control. If a parent owns 80% or more of the shares of its subsidiary, the financial results of the subsidiary can be consolidated for income tax purposes.

The above discussion conveys much of the terminology of the legal rules governing merger transactions. Many of the same principles apply to tender offers.

## THE NATURE OF TENDER OFFERS

In a tender offer, the bidder typically seeks the approval of the company management and board of directors of the target company, but makes an offer directly to shareholders of the target firm. The bidder's obtaining 50% or more of the shares of the target firm is equivalent to having received shareholder approval. In this case, the shareholders have voted with their pocketbooks.

In a merger, the traditional legal doctrine held that the minority must agree to the terms negotiated. In a tender offer, the offer is extended to the individual shareholders so that management and the board of directors can be bypassed. The law is still not clear on whether merger doctrine applies. In some cases, after the bidder has obtained control, the terms may be "crammed down" on the minority. Sometimes the acquirer may decide not to complete the buyout. In this case, there is a "freeze-in" problem in that the minority is subject to the decisions of the majority holders. The minority always has the right to bring legal action if it feels that it has been treated inequitably.

There are different kinds of tender offers with different kinds of provisions. The financial press from time to time reports detailed tender offers summarizing the provisions of the documents sent directly to shareholders. These, in effect, are public notices of the proposals mailed to the shareholders. The tender offer may be conditional or unconditional. For example, the offer may be contingent on obtaining 50% of the shares of the target. The tender offer may be restricted versus unrestricted. A restricted tender offer prespecifies the number or percentage of shares the bidder will take. An "any-or-all" tender offer is both unconditional and unrestricted.

If the tender offer is restricted, oversubscription may result in prorationing by the bidder. For example, assume that the bidder tenders for 60% of a target company's 1,000 shares of stock, and that 80% of the total shares are offered. The bidder may decide to accept all 800 or to accept only 600 shares, which are 75% of the amount tendered by each shareholder. For example, if shareholder A offered 100 shares, the bidder would buy only 75.

The law requires a 20-day waiting period during which the target company shareholders may make their decision to offer their shares for sale. So the bidder would have to wait until after the 20-day waiting period to calculate the proration percentage. If the bidder decides to extend the offer, the proration period is also automatically extended.

Another complication arises when other bidders compete with the first bidder—a contested offer. The law requires that when a new tender offer is made, the stockholders of the target company must have 10 business days to consider that new offer. The effect is to extend the initial offer period. For example, suppose 18 days have elapsed since the first offer. If a second bid is made, the shareholders have an additional 10 days, which is equivalent to 28 days on the first bid and 10 days on the second bid. If the second bid occurred five days after the first bid was made, the original 20-day waiting period is not extended because 5 + 10 is less than the original 20-day waiting period.

Another variation is the use of a two-tier tender offer. The first tier, typically for cash, is to obtain 50% or more of the target's stock to obtain control. In the second tier, a smaller value may be offered because control has already been established. The second tier is often paid in securities such as debt rather than cash or equity of the bidder.

A variation of the two-tier offer is the "three-piece-suitor." The three steps are (1) an initial toehold; (2) a tender offer to obtain control; and (3) after control and a majority of shareholders have tendered, a freeze-out purchase of the minority shareholders.

The above by no means describes all of the different types of tender offers or merger patterns, nor does it cover the multitude of legal issues that may become involved. We simply convey the general patterns. The details would require legal and accounting expertise of a very high order.

## RISK ARBITRAGE IN M&A ACTIVITY

Arbitrage is defined as purchasing in one market for immediate sale in another at a higher price. Thus, arbitragers take advantage of temporary price discrepancies between markets. By their actions, the differences are eliminated, driving prices up by their purchases in one market, and driving prices down by their sales in the other.

Arbitragers may take offsetting positions in one security in two markets, or in equivalent securities in one or two markets, to make profits without assuming any risk under the theory of pure arbitrage.

In the area of mergers and acquisitions, risk arbitrage refers to the practice of purchasing (speculating in) the stock of takeover targets for short-term (though not immediate) resale at a higher price. Recall that, on average, target shareholders earn excess returns in the range of 20% in successful takeovers. By taking a position in the stock of target firms, risk arbitragers are, in effect, betting on the outcome of contests for corporate control. Thus, the term *risk arbitrage* is used differently from the true or original concept of arbitrage.

## Illustrative Example

An example will illustrate the arbitrage operation. When a tender is announced, the price will rise toward the offer price. For example, B selling at $100 may offer $60 for T now selling at $40 (a 50% premium). After the offer is announced, the arbitrage firm (A) may short B and go long in T. The position of the hedge depends on price levels after the announcement. Suppose B goes to $90 and T to $55. If the arbitrage firm (A) shorts B and goes long on T, the outcome depends on a number of alternatives. If the tender succeeds at $60, the value of B may not change or fall further, but T will rise to $60, resulting in a profit of at least $5 per T share for (A). If the tender fails, T may fall in price but not much if other bids are made for T; the price of B may fall because it has "wasted" its search and bidding costs to acquire T. Thus, (A) may gain whether or not the bid succeeds. If the competition of other bidders causes B to raise its offer further, (A) will gain even more because T will rise more and B will fall. (Remember that (A) is short on B and long on T.)

During the stock market crash of October 1987, it was reported that the arbitrage departments of most investment banking firms suffered large losses. The prices of both B and T decreased. It was likely that T fell more than B, because B was likely to reduce or withdraw its offer and acquisition activity dried up in the initial general uncertainty following the market crash. If the arbitrage department (A) was not hedged, but simply long on T, its losses would be even larger.

The increased incidence of hostile takeover activity via cash tender offers in the late 1970s created more opportunities for risk arbitrage and led to dramatic growth of the industry, from about 24 participants in 1976 to about 300 by the end of 1986 (Garcia and Anders, 1986, p. 6). These participants include both freestanding arbitrage funds and partnerships as well as the arbitrage departments now found in most brokerage houses, investment banks, and many other financial institutions. Ivan Boesky's famous (now infamous) arbitrage fund was started in 1975 with an initial investment of $700,000, grown to over $1 billion by November 1986, for a compound annual growth rate of 93.6%. Citicorp, one of the most recent entrants, started up its arbitrage unit in the summer of 1986.

## The Nature of the Arbitrage Business

Traditionally, arbitragers have responded to announced takeover bids. They evaluate the offer and assess its probability of success relative to the value of the target. They must consider the likelihood and consequences of a bidding war between alternative potential acquirers, various takeover defenses, a white knight, and so on. However, the arbitragers do not have the luxury of time to perform their analyses; they must act early enough to capture the gains inherent in the transaction. Numerous empirical studies document that target firm stock prices begin to rise even before the first public announcement of a takeover bid.

Information is the principal raw material in the arbitrage business. The vast majority of this information comes from careful analysis of publicly available documents, such as financial statements, and filings with the SEC and/or regulatory agencies. They buy expert advice from lawyers and industry specialists. They may hire investment bankers to assist in their assessment of the offer. In some cases, the investment bankers involved in the transaction may double-check their own assessment of valuation against that of the arbitragers. They attempt to get all available information from the investment bankers representing the target and bidding firms, and from the participants themselves. This phase of information gathering may perhaps cross over the boundary into the gray area of insider trading if the pursuit is too vigorous.

With the increased pace in recent years, arbitragers have, in some cases, attempted to anticipate takeover bids to establish their stock positions in advance of any public announcement, thus increasing their potential return. To do so, they try to identify undervalued firms that would make attractive targets, and to track down rumors of impending bids; they may monitor price increases that might signal someone is accumulating stock in a particular company to ferret out potential bidders before the 5% disclosure trigger at which the purchaser has to announce his or her intentions. The risk of taking a position based upon this type of activity is clearly greater. Also, if one firm in an industry is acquired, other firms in the industry may be expected to become targets.

### Arbitrage Funds

The use of an arbitrage approach in a merger fund has been described in some detail by Welling (1996), who interviewed Bonnie Smith, the copartner of an asset management fund. The basic philosophy of an arbitrage fund is to eliminate market risk by arbitrage positions in connection with merger and takeover transactions. It does prior intensive research in order to mitigate deal risk and does not invest in rumors. The firm takes a position when there has been a public announcement that two firms are likely to sign a definitive merger agreement. At this point it is likely that there has been some rise in the market price of the target and some decline in the market price of the bidder. As long as the terms of the merger agreement make it likely that the market price of one merger partner is out of line with the other, an arbitrage position can profitably be taken. The main risk is whether the deal is completed and on a timely basis. Investing in 10 to 20 transactions at a given time, plus the prior research, reduces the unfavorable impact if a particular deal is not completed. For this particular fund, 95% of the deals in recent years had gone through. The goal of the fund is to generate 10 to 15% annual returns in all market environments. The fund has actually averaged 12 to 13%. In 1995, an active M&A year, the fund gained 14.2%. It is clear from the interview that the operations of this fund were quite different from the aggressive positions in individual transactions taken by some of the well-known arbitrage firms in the 1980s.

--------------------------------------------------------------------------------

## Summary

This chapter has summarized some basic terminology and concepts, providing a foundation for developing further knowledge and understanding of M&As. In tender offers, the bidder directly contacts shareholders, inviting them to sell (tender) their shares at an offer price. Mergers usually involve some mutuality of negotiations. In practice, the acquiring company may make a successful tender offer for the target followed by a formal merger of the two companies. From an economic standpoint, different types of mergers or tender offers are grouped on the basis of the stage of economic activity and the degree of relatedness of the firms. Horizontal mergers involve firms operating in the same kinds of business activity. Vertical mergers take place between firms in different stages of production operations. Pure conglomerate mergers involve firms engaged in unrelated types of business activity. Financial conglomerates develop financial planning and control systems for groups of segments that may be otherwise unrelated from a business standpoint. Financial conglomerates operate as an internal capital market in assigning funds to segments. Future allocations of funds will depend on the performance of the segments. Managerial conglomerates provide managerial counsel and interactions with its segments. Concentric companies carry the idea further in having staff expertise in specific managerial functions such as production, marketing, and finance.

Statutory mergers meet the formal legal requirements of the state or states in which the parties to the merger are chartered. After the approval of the tender offer followed by a merger agreement or approval of a merger directly, the act of merger takes place upon the filing of appropriate documents with the states. Tender offers may have various types of conditions or restrictions.

Risk arbitrage in connection with M&As is the practice of making short-term gains from the relationship between the takeover bid price and the relative price of the bidder's and target's stock. The announcement of a merger or tender offer causes the stock price of the target to rise because the bidder pays a premium. On average, in recent years, the bidder pays too much and its price falls. Arbitragers generally will take a long position in the target stock and a short position in the bidder stock, especially if they are out of line. For example, if the bidder offers to trade 1.5 shares for 1 share of the target and, net of commissions, the bidder stock sells for $10 and the target stock sells for $14.25, the arbitrager can lock in a $0.75 gain by shorting 1.5 shares of the bidder and going long on one share of the target stock. If the deal is completed, the arbitrager has made a substantial return on the investment. If anything, the spread is likely to move in favor of the arbitrager. The big risk is that the deal is not successful. The arbitragers attempt to establish their stock positions before the runup of the target's stock price by trying to anticipate takeover announcements through careful research.

## Questions

1.1 What is the difference between a merger and a tender offer?

1.2 What are some of the potential synergy advantages of horizontal mergers?

1.3 How do the economic advantages of vertical mergers differ from those of horizontal mergers?

1.4 Are there valid distinctions between pure conglomerates, managerial conglomerates, and a concentric company?

1.5 An arbitrage firm (A) notes that a bidder (B) whose stock is selling at $30 makes an offer for a target (T) selling at $40 to exchange 1.5 shares of B for 1 share of T. T rises to $44; B stays at $30. A sells 1.5 B short for $45 and goes long on T at $44. One month later the deal is completed with B at $30 and T at $45. What is A's dollar and percentage annualized gain, assuming a required 50% margin on both transactions?

-------------------------------------------------------------------------------

## References

Buffett, Warren E., Berkshire Hathaway Inc., *1981 Annual Report,* pp. 4–5.

Garcia, Beatrice E., and George Anders, "In Arbitrage, Risks are Burgeoning Along with Profits," *Wall Street Journal,* December 23, 1986, p. 6.

Houlihan Lokey Howard & Zukin, *Mergerstat Review,* Los Angeles, CA., 1996, 1997.

Jensen, Michael C., "Takeovers: Folklore and Science," *Harvard Business Review,* 62, November-December 1984, pp. 109–120.

Magenheim, Ellen B., and Dennis C. Mueller, "Are Acquiring-Firm Shareholders Better Off After an Acquisition?" Chapter 11 in John C. Coffee, Jr., Louis Lowenstein, and Susan Rose-Ackerman, eds., *Knights, Raiders, and Targets,* New York: Oxford University Press, 1988, pp. 171–193.

Ravenscraft, David J., and F. M. Scherer, "Mergers and Managerial Performance," Chapter 12 in John C. Coffee, Jr., Louis Lowenstein, and Susan Rose-Ackerman, eds., *Knights, Raiders, and Targets,* New York: Oxford University Press, 1988, pp. 194–210.

Rohatyn, Felix G., "Needed: Restraints on the Takeover Mania," *Challenge,* 29, May–June 1986, p. 30.

Shleifer, Andrei, and Lawrence H. Summers, "Breach of Trust in Hostile Takeovers," Chapter 2 in Alan J. Auerbach, ed., *Corporate Takeovers: Causes and Consequences,* Chicago: University of Chicago Press, 1988.

Welling, Kathryn M., "Arb-Firm—and Its Mutual Fund," *Barron's,* February 5, 1996, pp. 24–28.

# 2

# The Legal
# and Regulatory
# Framework

This chapter discusses the laws and rules or regulations promulgated to cover securities trading and takeover activity. We discuss securities trading generally as well as takeover activity, the central focus of this book, because the two are so interlinked that they really cannot be separated. Indeed, the laws that were enacted to regulate takeover activity were made a part of the original securities acts enacted in the early 1930s. We also examine the leading cases related to the laws we cover because they give more explicit content to the nature of the law and its intent.

Violations of the security trading laws continue to make news. For example, a *Wall Street Journal* story of May 10, 1996, described the settlement of insider trading charges related to Microsoft's unsuccessful 1994 bid to acquire Intuit. The SEC accused the wife of Intuit's chief financial officer of telling relatives about Microsoft's offer (later called off) for Intuit. To settle the SEC complaint, the six defendants agreed to pay a total of $472,342 in "disgorgement and penalties," without admitting or denying the allegations. The SEC has continually investigated a rise in predeal trading activity. This chapter describes in detail the rules of the game with regard to securities trading and takeover activity.

## THE MAIN SECURITIES LAWS

Because wide price fluctuations are likely to be associated with merger and acquisition activity, public policy has been concerned that investors be treated fairly. Legislation and regulations have sought to carry over to the takeover activity of recent decades the philosophy of the securities acts of the 1930s. The aim is prompt and full disclosure of relevant information in the effort to achieve a fair "playing field" for all participants. Some of the earlier legislation is fully applicable, but it has been augmented with additional statutes since the late 1960s.

Because the takeover laws are so closely interlinked with securities laws generally, we begin with a summary of the major securities laws. This provides a framework to which we can relate the laws, rules, and regulations governing takeover activity.

### Federal Securities Laws

The federal securities laws are mainly seven statutes, six of which were enacted between 1933 and 1940. The seven statutes are:

> Securities Act of 1933 (SA)
>
> Securities Exchange Act of 1934 (SEA)
>
> Public Utility Holding Company Act of 1935 (PUHCA)
>
> Trust Indenture Act of 1939 (TIA)
>
> Investment Company Act of 1940 (ICA)
>
> Investment Advisers Act of 1940 (IAA)
>
> Securities Investor Protection Act of 1970 (SIPA)

We first summarize what each of the laws covers to provide an overview of the pattern of legislation. We then develop some of the more important provisions in greater detail. As we have noted, six of the seven major acts were enacted beginning in 1933. There is a reason for the timing. The stock market crash of 1929 was followed by continued depressed markets for several years. Because so many investors lost money, both houses of Congress conducted lengthy hearings to find the causes and the culprits. The hearings were marked by sensationalism and wide publicity. The securities acts of 1933 and 1934 were the direct outgrowth of the congressional hearings.

The Securities Act of 1933 regulates the sale of securities to the public. It provides for the registration of public offerings of securities to establish a record of representations. All participants involved in preparing the registration statements are subject to legal liability for any misstatement of facts or omissions of vital information.

The Securities Exchange Act of 1934 established the Securities and Exchange Commission (SEC) to administer the securities laws and to regulate practices in the purchase and sale of securities.

The purpose of the Public Utility Holding Company Act of 1935 was to correct abuses in the financing and operation of electric and gas public utility holding company systems and to bring about simplification of the corporate structures and physical integration of the operating properties. The SEC's responsibilities under the act of 1935 were substantially completed by the 1950s.

The Trust Indenture Act of 1939 applies to public issues of debt securities with a value of $5 million or more. Debt issues represent a form of promissory note associated with a long document setting out the terms of a complex contract and referred to as the **indenture.** The 1939 act sets forth the responsibilities of the indenture trustee (often a commercial bank) and specifies requirements to be included in the indenture (bond contract) for the protection of the bond purchasers. In September 1987, the SEC recommended to Congress a number of amendments to establish new conflict of interest standards for indenture trustees and to recognize new developments in financing techniques.

The Investment Company Act of 1940 regulates publicly owned companies engaged in the business of investing and trading in securities. Investment companies are subject to rules formulated and enforced by the SEC. The act of 1940 was amended in 1970 to place additional controls on management compensation and sales charges.

The Investment Advisers Act of 1940, as amended in 1960, provides for registration and regulation of investment advisers, as the name suggests.

The Securities Investor Protection Act of 1970 established the Securities Investor Protection Corporation (SIPCO). This corporation is empowered to supervise the liquidation of bankrupt securities firms and to arrange for payments to their customers.

The Securities Act Amendments of 1975 were passed after four years of research and investigation into the changing nature of securities markets. The study recommended the abolition of fixed minimum brokerage commissions. It called for increased automation of trading by utilizing data processing technology to link markets. The SEC was mandated to work with the securities industry to develop an effective national market system to achieve the goal of nationwide competition in securities trading with centralized reporting of price quotations and transactions. It proposed a central order routing system to find the best available price.

In 1978 the SEC began to streamline the securities registration process. Large, well-known corporations were permitted to abbreviate registration statements and to disclose information by reference to other documents that had already been made public. Before these changes, the registration process often required at least several weeks. After the 1978 changes, a registration statement could be approved in as short a time as two days.

In March 1982 Rule 415 provided for shelf registration. Large corporations can register the full amount of debt or equity they plan to sell over a two-year period. After the initial registration has been completed, the firm can sell up to the specified amount of debt or equity without further delay. The firm can choose the time when the funds are needed or when market conditions appear favorable. Shelf registration has been actively used in the sale of bonds, with as much as 60% of debt sales utilizing shelf registration. Less than 10% of the total issuance of equities has employed shelf registration.

## THE OPERATION OF THE SECURITIES ACTS

The Securities Act of 1933 has primary responsibility for recording information. Section 5 prevents the public offering and sale of securities without a registration statement. Section 8 provides for registration and permits the statement to automatically become effective 20 days after it is filed with the SEC. However, the SEC has the power to request more information or to issue a stop order, which delays the operation of the 20-day waiting period.

It is the Securities Exchange Act of 1934 (SEA) that provides the basis for the amendments that were applicable to takeover activities. Section 12(j) empowers the SEC to revoke or suspend the registration of a security if the issuer has violated any provisions of the 1934 act. The SEC imposes periodic disclosure requirements under Section 13. The basic reports are (1) Form 10-K, the annual report; (2) Form 10-Q, the quarterly report; and (3) Form 8-K, the current report for any month in which specified events occur.

Section 14 governs proxy solicitation. Prior to every meeting of its security holders, they must be furnished with a proxy statement containing information specified. The SEC provides procedural requirements for proxy contests. Under SEA Rule 14a-8, any security holder may require management to include his or her proposal for action in the proxy statement. If management opposes the proposal, it must include in the proxy material a statement by the security holder not more than 200 words in length in support of his or her proposal.

## TENDER OFFER REGULATION—THE WILLIAMS ACT

Prior to the late 1960s, most intercorporate combinations were represented by mergers. This typically involved "friendly" negotiations by two or more firms. When they mutually agreed, combination of some form might occur. During the conglomerate merger movement of the 1960s, corporate takeovers began to occur. Some were friendly and not much different from mergers. Others were hostile and shook up the business community.

In October 1965 Senator Harrison Williams introduced legislation seeking to protect the target companies. These initial efforts failed, but his second effort initiated in 1967 succeeded. The Williams Act, in the form of various amendments to the Securities Exchange Act of 1934, became law on July 29, 1968. Its stated purpose was to protect target shareholders from swift and secret takeovers in three ways: (1) by generating more information during the takeover process that target shareholders and management could use to evaluate outstanding offers; (2) by requiring a minimum period during which a tender offer must be held open, thus delaying the execution of the tender offer; and (3) by explicitly authorizing targets to sue bidding firms.

## Section 13

Section 13(d) of the Williams Act of 1968 required that any person who had acquired 10% or more of the stock of a public corporation must file a Schedule 13D with the SEC within 10 days of crossing the 10% threshold. The act was amended in 1970 to increase the SEC powers and to reduce the trigger point for the reporting obligation under Section 13(d) from 10 to 5%. Basically, Section 13(d) provides management and the shareholders with an early warning system.

The filing requirement does not apply to those persons who had purchased less than 2% of the stock within the previous 12 months. Due to this exemption, a substantial amount of stock can be accumulated over years without having to file Schedule 13D. Institutional investors (registered brokers and dealers, banks, insurance companies, and so forth) can choose to file Schedule 13G instead of Schedule 13D if the equity securities were acquired in the ordinary course of business. Schedule 13G is an abbreviated version of Schedule 13D.

More recently, the insider trading scandals of the late 1980s produced calls for a reduction below 5% and a shortening of the 10-day minimum period for filing. However, shortening the period would not stop the practice of "parking" violations that was uncovered in the Boesky investigation. Under parking arrangements, traders attempt to hide the extent of their ownership to avoid the 5% disclosure trigger by "parking" purchased securities with an accomplice broker until a later date. A related practice is to purchase options on the stock of the target; this is equivalent to ownership because the options can be exercised whenever the holder wishes to take actual ownership.

Schedule 13D identifies the acquirer, his or her occupation and associates, sources of financing, and purpose of the acquisition. If the purpose of the acquisition is to take over the target, the acquirer's business plans for the target must be revealed. That is, does the acquirer plan to liquidate the target, merge it with another firm, or otherwise change its basic corporate structure in a material way? Copies of the 13D must be provided to the target and to all the exchanges on which the stock is traded. Any material changes in the information provided in the 13D must be disclosed promptly in an amended schedule with the same notification requirements. Although these requirements seem fairly specific and straightforward, the language used to respond to them is kept as broad as possible so as to maintain flexibility.

Section 13(g), which requires the filing of Schedule 13G, was added to the act in 1972 to apply to all 5% owners, regardless of how the 5% threshold was reached. Obviously, in the case of takeover contests, the 5% interest is amassed fairly quickly; the purpose of adding Section 13(g) was to alert targets to creeping acquisitions over time. The timing requirements for filing 13G are generous. Acquirers have until 45 days from the end of the year during which they reached the 5% position, a possible 410-day lag versus only 10 days for the 13D. If their large block acquisitions push them to a 10% ownership interest, they have 10 days following the end of the month during which this level was reached to file the 13G with the SEC (a possible 40-day lag).

### Section 14

Sections 13(d) and 13(g) of the Williams Act apply to any large stock acquisitions, whether public or private (an offering to less than 25 people). Section 14(d) applies only to public tender offers, but applies whether the acquisition is small or large so its coverage is broader. The 5% trigger rule also applies under Section 14(d). Thus, any group making solicitations or recommendations to a target group of shareholders that would result in owning more than 5% of a class of securities registered under Section 12 of the Securities Act must first file a Schedule 14D with the SEC. So, an acquiring firm must disclose in a Tender Offer Statement (Schedule 14D-1) its intentions and business plans for the target, as well as any relationships or agreements between the two firms. The schedule must be filed with the SEC "as soon as practicable on the date of the commencement of the tender offer"; copies must be hand-delivered to the target firm and to any competitive bidders; the relevant stock exchanges (or the National Association of Securities Dealers for the over-the-counter stocks) must be notified by telephone (followed by a mailing of the schedule).

Note, however, that the language of Section 14(d) refers to *any* group making recommendations to target shareholders. This includes target management, which is prohibited from advising target shareholders as to how to respond to a tender offer until it too has filed with the SEC. Until target management has filed a Schedule 14D-9, a Tender Offer Solicitation/Recommendation Statement, they may only advise shareholders to defer tendering their shares while management considers the offer. Companies who consider themselves vulnerable often take the precaution of preparing a fill-in-the-blanks schedule left with an agent in Washington, to be filed immediately in the event of a takeover attempt, allowing target management to respond swiftly in making public recommendations to shareholders. Thus, Section 14(d)-1 provides both the early warning system and information that will help target shareholders determine whether or not to tender their shares. SEA Sections 14(d) (4)–(7) regulate the terms of a tender offer, including the length of time the offer must be left open (20 trading days), the right of shareholders to withdraw shares that they may have tendered previously, the manner in which tendered shares must be purchased in oversubscribed offers, and the effect of the bidder changing the terms of the offer. The delay period, of course, also gives shareholders time to evaluate the offer, but more importantly enables management to seek out competing bids.

Also, SEA Section 14(e) prohibits misrepresentation, nondisclosure, or any fraudulent, deceptive, or manipulative acts or practices in connection with a tender offer.

## INSIDER TRADING OVERVIEW

The SEC adopted Rule 14e-3 to apply to insider trading, specifically within the context of tender offers. Table 2.1 summarizes the SEC regulations used to prosecute insider

**TABLE 2.1**    SEC Regulation of Insider Trading

RULE 10b-5: "It shall be unlawful . . . by the use of any means or instrumentality of interstate commerce, or of the mails, or of any facility of any national securities exchange,
> (1) to employ any device, scheme, or artifice to defraud,
> (2) to make any untrue statement of a material fact or to omit to state a material fact necessary . . . or
> (3) to engage in any act . . . which operates . . . as a fraud or deceit . . . in connection with the purchase or sale of any security."

RULE 14e-3: Prohibits "transactions in securities on the basis of material, nonpublic information in the context of tender offers." Once a tender offer has commenced (substantial steps toward the commencement of a tender offer are sufficient), this rule prohibits trading by any person on the basis of material information that he knows or has reason to know is nonpublic, and which he knows or has reason to know was acquired directly or indirectly from the offering person, the issuer of the securities sought, any officer, director, partner, employee, or any other person acting on behalf of the offeror or the issuer. Trading is prohibited until a reasonable time after the public release of such information.

INSIDER TRADING SANCTIONS ACT OF 1984: Those who trade on information not available to the general public can be made to give back their illegal profits and pay a penalty of three times as much as their illegal activities produced.

trading cases. To date, the term **insider trading** has not been defined by the SEC. Thus, the SEC now has three broad categories under which insider trading, fraud, or illegal profits can be attacked. Rule 10b-5 has an emphasis on fraud or deceit. Rule 14e-3 applies more directly to tender offers. The Insider Trading Sanctions Act of 1984 applies to insider trading more generally. The very ambiguity of the three sources of power that may be used by the SEC in the regulation of insider trading gives the SEC considerable discretion in its choice of practices and cases to prosecute.

It should be noted also that the traditional regulation of insider trading was provided for under SEA Sections 16(a) and 16(b). Section 16(a) applies to officers, directors, and any persons who own 10% or more of any class of securities of a company. Section 16(a) provides that these corporate insiders must report to the SEC all transactions involving their purchase or sale of the corporation's stock on a monthly basis. Section 16(a) is based on the premise that a corporate insider has an unfair advantage by virtue of his or her knowledge of information that is generated within the corporation. This information is available on a privileged basis because he or she is an officer, director, or a major security holder who is presumed to have privileged communications with top officers in the company. Section 16(b) provides that the corporation or any of its security holders may bring suit against the offending corporate insider to return the profits to the corporation because of insider trading completed within a six-month period.

### The Racketeer Influenced and Corrupt Organizations Act of 1970 (RICO)

The Racketeer Influenced and Corrupt Organizations Act of 1970 (RICO) was originally aimed at unions. It provides for triple damages, as do the antitrust laws. It has also been applied to securities trading in famous cases such as the legal action against

Michael Milken. Its requirements are simple: (1) conspiracy and (2) repeated transactions. If more than one person is involved, it is a conspiracy. If, in addition, repeated acts occur, the two requirements for the applicability of RICO have been met. Its provisions are truly draconian.

The act is now aimed at companies that engage in acts that defraud consumers, investors, or public bodies such as cities or states, and authorizes triple damages for winning plaintiffs. Furthermore, in a criminal suit brought by any representative of the Department of Justice, RICO permits the court to order that all of the assets of the accused be seized while the case is still being tried. This gives the prosecutor tremendous power. From a practical standpoint, it means that the mere accusation brought under RICO can bring the business of any accused to a halt. If its assets are seized, particularly if it is engaged in securities transactions, it no longer has the means of conducting business. Hence, whether the accused is guilty or not, there is tremendous pressure to settle, because the alternative is to have its business disrupted. And even if after months and months of trial, the accused is found innocent, it is small solace, because the disruption may have resulted in irreparable damage to its business.

We have thus brought together in one place the whole array of laws, rules, and regulations that apply to securities trading including the takeover process. For convenience of reference, we summarize them briefly in Table 2.2.

**TABLE 2.2**   Summary of Securities Laws and Regulations

| | |
|---|---|
| *Rule 10b-5* | Prohibits fraud, misstatements, or omission of material facts in connection with the purchase or sale of any security. |
| *Section 13(d)* | Provides early warning to target firms of acquisitions of their stock by potential acquirers: 5% threshold, 10-day filing period. Applies to all large stock acquisitions. |
| *Section 14(d) (1)* | Requirements of Section 13(d) extended to *all public tender offers*. Provides for full disclosure to SEC by any group making recommendations to target shareholders. |
| *Section 14(d) (4)–(7)* | Regulates terms of tender offers. Length of time offer must be held open (20 days), right of shareholders to withdraw tendered shares, and so on. |
| *Section 14(e)* | Prohibits fraud, misrepresentation in context of tender offers. Rule 14e-3 prohibits trading on nonpublic information in tender offers. |
| *Section 16(a)* | Provides for reporting by corporate insiders on their transactions in their corporations' stocks. |
| *Section 16(b)* | Allows the corporation or its security holders to sue for return of profits on transactions by corporate insiders completed within a six-month period. |
| *Insider Trading Sanctions Act of 1984* | Provides for triple damages in insider trading cases. |
| *Racketeer Influenced and Corrupt Organizations Act of 1970 (RICO)* | Provides for seizure of assets upon accusation and triple damages upon conviction for companies that defraud consumers, investors, and so on. |

## COURT CASES AND SEC RULES

To this point we have described the main statutory provisions that specify the various elements of fraud and insider trading in connection with trading in securities and takeover activities. The full meaning of these statutes is brought out by the subsequent court interpretations and SEC rules implementing the powers granted the SEC by the various statutes.

### Liability Under Rule 10b-5 of the 1934 Act

As we have indicated, Rule 10b-5, issued by the Securities and Exchange Commission under the powers granted to it by the 1934 act, is a broad, powerful, and general securities antifraud provision. In general, for Rule 10b-5 to apply, a security must be involved. Technical issues have arisen as to what constitutes a security. If securities are involved, all transactions are covered, whether on one of the securities exchanges or over the counter. A number of elements for a cause of action have been set forth in connection with Rule 10b-5, as follows.

1. There must be fraud, misrepresentation, a material omission, or deception in connection with the purchase or sale of securities.
2. The misrepresentation or omission must be of a fact as opposed to an opinion. However, inaccurate predictions of earnings may be held to be misrepresentations, and failure to disclose prospective developments may be challenged.
3. The misrepresentation or omission must be material to an investor's decision in the sense that there was a substantial likelihood that a reasonable investor would consider the fact of significance in his or her decision.
4. There must be a showing that the plaintiff actually believed the misrepresentation, relied upon it, and that it was a substantial factor in his or her decision to enter the transaction.
5. The plaintiff must be an actual purchaser or an actual seller to have standing.
6. Defendant's deception or fraud must have a sufficiently close nexus to the transaction so that a court could find that the defendant's fraud was "in connection with" the purchase or sale by plaintiff.
7. Plaintiff must prove that the defendant had "scienter." Scienter literally means knowingly or willfully. It means that the defendant had a degree of knowledge that makes the individual legally responsible for the consequences of his or her act and that he or she had an actual intent to deceive or defraud. Negligence is not sufficient.

These elements represent requirements for a successful suit under Rule 10b-5. Some of the elements were developed in a series of court decisions. The main thrust of Rule 10b-5 is fraud or deceit. The Supreme Court set forth the scienter requirement in two cases: *Ernst and Ernst v. Hochfelder,* 425 US 185 (1976); and *Aaron v. SEC,* 446 US 680 (1980).

In addition to its use in fraud or deceit cases, a number of interesting cases have brought out the meaning and applicability of Rule 10b-5 in connection with insider trading. For the present, we refer to insider trading merely as purchases or sales by persons who have access to information that is not available to those with whom they deal or to traders generally. However, there are many court decisions about what constitutes insider trading and a continued stream of proposals in Congress to clarify the meaning of the term.

An early case was *Cady, Roberts & Co.,* 40 SEC 907 (1961). In this case, a partner in a brokerage firm received a message from a director of the Curtiss-Wright

Corporation that the board of directors had voted to cut the dividend. The broker immediately placed orders to sell the Curtiss-Wright stock for some of his customers. The sales were made before news of the dividend cut was generally disseminated. The broker who made the transactions was held to have violated Rule 10b-5.

The Texas Gulf Sulphur Corp. case of 1965 was classic *(SEC v. Texas Gulf Sulphur Company,* 401 F. 2d 833 (2d Cir. (1968)). A vast mineral deposit consisting of millions of tons of copper, zinc, and silver was discovered in November 1963. However, far from publicizing the discovery, the company took great pains to conceal it for over five months, to the extent of issuing a false press release in April 1964 labeling proliferating rumors as "unreliable . . . premature and possibly misleading." Meanwhile, certain directors, officers, and employees of Texas Gulf Sulphur who knew of the find bought up quantities of the firm's stock (and options on many more shares) before any public announcement. The false press release was followed only four days later by another finally revealing publicly the extent of the find. In the company's defense, it was alleged that secrecy was necessary to keep down the price of neighboring tracts of land that they had to acquire in order to fully exploit the discovery. However, the SEC brought and won a civil suit based on Rule 10b-5.

The next case is *Investors Management Co.* (44 SEC 633 (1971)). An aircraft manufacturer disclosed to a broker-dealer, acting as the lead underwriter for a proposed debenture issue, that its earnings for the current year would be much lower than it had previously publicly announced. This information was conveyed to the members of the sales department of the broker-dealer and passed on in turn to major institutional clients. The institutions sold large amounts of the stock before the earnings revisions were made public. Again the SEC won the suit.

In the next two cases we cover, the SEC lost. The first case involved one of the leading investment banking corporations, Morgan Stanley. The Kennecott Copper Corporation was analyzing whether or not to buy Olinkraft, a paper manufacturer. Morgan Stanley began negotiations with Olinkraft on behalf of Kennecott. Later, Kennecott decided it did not wish to purchase Olinkraft. The knowledge that Morgan Stanley had gained in its negotiations led it to believe that one of its other clients, Johns-Manville, would find Olinkraft attractive. In anticipation of this possibility, Morgan Stanley bought large amounts of the common stock of Olinkraft. When Johns-Manville subsequently made a bid for Olinkraft, Morgan Stanley realized large profits. A suit was brought against Morgan Stanley. However, the court held that Morgan Stanley had not engaged in any improper behavior under Rule 10b-5.

In the next case, Raymond Dirks was a New York investment analyst who was informed by a former officer of Equity Funding of America that the company had been fraudulently overstating its income and net assets by large amounts. Dirks conducted his own investigation which corroborated the information he received. He told the SEC and a reporter at the *Wall Street Journal* to follow up on the situation and advised his clients to sell their Equity Funding shares. The SEC brought an action against Dirks on grounds that if a tippee has material information knowingly obtained from a corporate insider, he or she must either disclose it or refrain from trading. However, the U.S. Supreme Court found that Dirks had not engaged in improper behavior *(Dirks v. SEC,* 463 US 646 (1983)). In Texas Gulf Sulphur, the law made it clear that trading by insiders in shares of their own company using insider knowledge is definitely illegal. But the court held that it was not illegal for Raymond Dirks to cause trades to be made on the basis of what he learned about Equity Funding because the officer who conveyed the information was not breaching any duty, and Dirks did not pay for the information.

So the first principle is that it is illegal for insiders to trade on the basis of inside information. A second principle that has developed is that it is illegal for an outsider to trade on the basis of information which has been "misappropriated." The misappropriation doctrine began to develop in the famous Chiarella case (*Chiarella v. United States,* 445 US 222 (1980)). *United States v. Chiarella* was a criminal case. Vincent Chiarella was the "markup man" in the New York composing room of Pandick Press, one of the leading U.S. financial printing firms. In working on documents, he observed five announcements of corporate takeover bids in which the targets' identities had presumably been concealed by blank spaces and false names. But Chiarella made some judgments about the names of the targets, bought their stock, and realized some profits. Chiarella was sued under Rule 10b-5 on the theory that like the officers and directors of Texas Gulf Sulphur, he had defrauded the uninformed shareholders whose stock he had bought. Chiarella had been convicted in the lower courts and his case was appealed to the Supreme Court. In arguing its case before the Supreme Court, the government sought to strengthen its case. It argued that even if Chiarella did not defraud the persons with whom he traded, he had defrauded his employer, Pandick Press, and its clients, the acquiring firms in the documents he had read. He had misappropriated information that had belonged to Pandick Press and its clients. As a result he had caused the price of the targets' stock to rise, thereby injuring his employer's clients and his employer's reputation for reliability. The Supreme Court expressed sympathy with the misappropriation theory, but reversed Chiarella's conviction because the theory had not been used in the lower court.

However, in the next case that arose, the SEC used its misappropriation theory from the beginning and won in a criminal case. A stockbroker named Newman was informed by friends at Morgan Stanley and Kuhn Loeb about prospective acquisitions. He bought the targets' shares and split the profits with his friends who had supplied the information. He was convicted under the misappropriation theory on grounds that he had defrauded the investment banking houses by injuring their reputation as safe repositories of confidential information from their clients. He had also defrauded their clients because the stock purchases based on confidential information had pushed up the prices of the targets.

The misappropriation theory also won in a case very similar to Chiarella. Materia was a proofreader at the Bowne Printing firm. Materia figured out the identity of four takeover targets and invested in them. This time the SEC applied the misappropriation theory from the start and won (*SEC v. Materia,* 745 F. 2d 197 (2d Cir. (1984)).

The SEC also employed the misappropriation theory in its criminal case against the *Wall Street Journal* reporter, R. Foster Winans, the author of the newspaper's influential "Heard on the Street" column. Along with friends, Winans traded on the basis of what they knew would appear in the paper the following day. While his conviction was upheld by the Supreme Court, the four–four vote could not be mistaken for a resounding affirmation of the misappropriation doctrine, and there are those who suspect that without the mail and wire fraud involved in the Winans case, the outcome might have been different. Rulings in later cases strengthened the misappropriation doctrine.

## OTHER DISCLOSURE REQUIREMENTS

Regulations and legislation have been applied to all phases of trading activity generally. We next describe some additional aspects of disclosure including interpretation and implementation of the regulations.

## Disclosure by Insiders—Section 16 of SEA

Section 16 of the Securities Exchange Act of 1934 was designed to curb insider trading by requiring designated insiders to report all securities transactions and prohibiting insiders from retaining the profits on any purchase and sale (or sale and purchase) of their corporations' stocks within a six-month period. Voluntary changes in stock ownership must be disclosed by the tenth day following the end of the month in which the transaction took place.

An American Bar Association task force has made a number of proposals to modify Section 16 (Grass, 1987). One is to reduce the reporting period to two business days following the transaction, with monetary penalties for late filings. Another is shortening the short-swing trading period from six months to something less, given the almost instantaneous dissemination of corporate information in today's markets. The task force has recommended more specific definitions of such terms as *insider, officer, director,* as well as *beneficial ownership* and *equity security* (in view of the wide range of hybrid securities now available).

## Disclosure Requirements of Stock Exchanges

In addition to the disclosure and notification requirements of federal and state securities regulation, the various national and regional stock exchanges have their own internal disclosure requirements for listed companies. In general, these amount to notifying the exchanges promptly (that is, by telephone) of any material developments that may significantly affect the trading volume and/or price of the listed firm's stock.

The exchanges are naturally reluctant to halt trading in a stock, particularly because institutional investors may continue to trade in the "third market" during a halt. However, it sometimes does so to allow the public time to digest important information that would otherwise result in an order imbalance. A listed company may also request a trading halt. Target companies have sometimes requested halts as a defensive strategy to buy time to find another bidder (a white knight), or to force the initial bid higher. As a result, the NYSE has implemented a policy to limit the length of such voluntary halts. Once a halt is requested, a company has 30 minutes to disclose its news, after which the exchange, not the company, decides when to reopen trading.

## Disclosure of Merger Talks

On April 4, 1988, the Supreme Court ruled by a 6–0 vote (three justices not participating) that investors may claim damages from a company that falsely denied it was involved in negotiations that resulted in a subsequent merger. Such denials would represent misleading information about a pending merger, which would provide investors who sold stock during the period with a basis for winning damages from the company officers.

The case involved the acquisition by Combustion Engineering of Basic Inc. Executives of Combustion Engineering began talks with Basic officers in 1976. The talks continued through 1977 and into early 1978 when Basic stock was selling for less than $20 per share. The stock began to rise in price, and in response to rumors of a merger, Basic issued three public statements denying that its officers knew of any reason for the rise in the price of its stock. It issued a denial as late as November 6, 1978.

On December 19, 1978, Basic's board voted to approve the sale of the company to Combustion at $46 per share. Some shareholders filed suit against Basic's board claiming that they were misled into selling their stock at the low, premerger price. A district court judge in Cleveland rejected their suit, but a federal appeals court reinstated the suit in 1986 on grounds that the statements made were both significant and misleading. The Supreme Court returned the case to the district court judge for trial. The Supreme Court decision written by Justice Blackmun stated that federal securities laws require that investors be informed about "material developments." What is "material" depends on the facts of the case, but corporate boards may not deny merger talks that reach the point of board resolutions, instructions to investment bankers, and actual negotiations between principals (Savage, 1988).

In a footnote, Justice Blackmun appeared to suggest that refusing to comment might shield a board. Apparently silence is not misleading under Rule 10b-5 of the Securities Exchange Act. This has been interpreted as saying that either the board must put a sufficiently tight lid on any information about mergers so that no rumors get started, or if there are leaks, the board must issue accurate statements of information. The decision appeared to be consistent with the spirit of federal laws and regulations governing securities transactions. Mergers simply represent an area of particular importance because of the large price fluctuations frequently associated with such activity.

## REGULATION OF TAKEOVER ACTIVITY BY THE STATES

Before the Williams Act of 1968, there was virtually no state regulation of takeover activity. Even by 1974 only seven states had enacted statutes in this area. This is surprising because states are the primary regulators of corporate activity. The chartering of corporations takes place in individual states. State law has defined a corporation as a legal person subject to state laws. Corporate charters obtained from states define the powers of the firm and the rights and obligations of its shareholders, boards of directors, and managers. However, states are not permitted to pass laws that impose restrictions on interstate commerce or that conflict with federal laws regulating interstate commerce.

Early state laws regulating hostile takeovers were declared illegal by the courts. For example, in 1982 the U.S. Supreme Court declared illegal an antitakeover law passed by the state of Illinois. The courts held that the Illinois law favored management over the interests of shareholders and bidders. The Illinois law was also found to impose impediments on interstate commerce and was therefore unconstitutional.

### Recent Developments

To the surprise of most observers, the Supreme Court in April 1987 upheld the Indiana Act. The Indiana Act provides that when an acquiring entity or bidder obtains shares that would cause its voting power to reach specified threshold levels, the bidder does not automatically obtain the voting rights associated with those shares. The transfer of voting rights must receive the approval of a majority of shareholders, not including the shares held by the bidder or insider directors and officers of the target company. A bidder can request a special shareholders meeting that must be held within 50 days of the request with the expenses of the meeting to be borne by the bidder.

Critics of the Indiana Act regard it as a delaying tactic that enables the target to delay the process by at least 50 days. The special requirements in connection with voting make the outcome of the tender offer much more uncertain. The Indiana Act was tested in a case brought by Dynamics Corporation of America chartered in Connecticut. It announced a tender offer to increase its holdings of CTS Corporation (incorporated in Indiana) from 9.6 to 27.5%. CTS invoked the Indiana Act. Dynamics would not be able to vote either the additional shares or the initial 9.6%. Dynamics filed suit arguing that the Indiana Act was preempted by the Williams Act and violated the interstate commerce clause. Dynamics won in the U.S. district court and in the appeals court, but was reversed in the U.S. Supreme Court.

Other states passed acts more moderate than the Indiana Act. The New York–New Jersey pattern provides for a five-year moratorium preventing hostile bidders from doing a second-step transaction such as merging a newly acquired company with another (Veasey, 1988).

A Delaware law was enacted in early 1988. It followed the New York–New Jersey model. The Delaware moratorium on second-step transactions is only for three years; nor does it apply if the hostile bidder buys virtually all of the stock of the target company. A hostile bidder can also obtain the approval of the board of the target company and a two-thirds vote of the other stockholders for the transaction to proceed. The board of a Delaware corporation may also vote to "opt out" of the statute within 90 days of its effective date (Veasey, 1988).

The Delaware statute was regarded with great significance because more than half of the Fortune 500 companies are incorporated in Delaware. Also, Delaware's statutes and regulations of corporations are widely regarded as a national model. But in this instance it is argued that Delaware acted because the Delaware state legislators "apparently feared an exodus of companies in search of protection elsewhere" (Bandow, 1988, p. 2).

## Issues with Regard to State Takeover Laws

One reason put forth for state takeover laws is to permit shareholders a more considered response to two-tier and partial tender offers. The other argument is that the Williams Act provides that tender offers remain open for only 20 days. It is argued that a longer time period may be needed where the target is large to permit other bidders to develop information to decide whether or not to compete for the target.

However, in practice it has been found that 70% of the tender offers during the years 1981–1984 were for all outstanding shares. The other 30% of the offers were split between two-tier and partial offers. The proportion of two-tier offers declined over the period of the study (Office of the Chief Economist, SEC, April 1985).

Furthermore, many companies have adopted fair price amendments that require the bidder to pay a fair price for all shares acquired. Under Delaware, Massachusetts, and certain other state laws, dissenting shareholders may request court appraisal of the value of their shares. To do so, however, they must file a written demand for appraisal before the shareholders meeting to vote on the merger. Tendering shareholders must not vote for the merger if they wish to preserve the right to an appraisal.

Critics also point out that state antitakeover laws have hurt shareholders. Studies by the Office of the Chief Economist of the SEC found that when in 1986 New Jersey placed restrictions on takeovers, the prices for 87 affected companies fell by 11.5% (Bandow, 1988). Similarly, an SEC study found that stock prices for 74 companies chartered in Ohio declined an average of 3.2%, a $1.5 billion loss after that state passed restrictive legislation. Another study estimated that the New York antitakeover rules reduced equity values by 1%, costing shareholders $1.2 billion (Bandow, 1988).

For these reasons, critics argue that the state laws protect parochial state interests rather than shareholders. They argue that the states act to protect employment and increase control over companies in local areas. Furthermore, they argue that state laws are not needed. If more shareholder protection were needed, all that would be required would be to amend the Williams Act, by extending the waiting period from 20 to 30 days, for example. It is argued further that securities transactions clearly represent interstate commerce. Thus, it is difficult to argue that the state laws are not unconstitutional. By limiting securities transactions, they impede interstate commerce.

The goal is to achieve a balance. Certainly it is desirable to protect the interests of shareholders. However, it must be recognized that two-tier offers and partial offers are used to prevent free-riding. In the absence of two-tier pricing and post-takeover dilution, shareholders know that their shares will not decline in value if the takeover succeeds. So individual small shareholders will wait until after the takeover in hopes that the changes made by the acquirer will increase the value of the stock. Most individual shareholders may behave this way. Then this "free-rider" behavior will prevent takeovers from being accomplished.

Similarly, if states make takeovers more difficult, the advantage is that time can be extended so that competing bids may be made. The data show that competing bids lead to higher prices for target shareholders. On the other hand, if the impediments to takeover are increased too greatly, bidders will be discouraged from even making the effort. In this case target shareholders will lose all benefits. The argument then concludes that state takeover laws are unnecessary. Applicable federal laws should seek to strike a balance between protecting shareholders and stimulating reasonable competing bidding activity, but not to the point where all bidding activity is discouraged.

It has also been argued that federal laws should prevent "abusive takeovers" where "speculative financing" may be involved. But the critical concepts are ambiguous. What is regarded as abusive or speculative varies with the viewpoints of different decision makers. There may, however, be legitimate concerns that rising debt ratios, whether or not associated with takeovers or restructuring, may amplify financial problems when a future economic downturn takes place.

## ANTITRUST POLICIES

In almost two full pages, the *New York Times* business section of April 25, 1996, discussed recent developments in antitrust rules and regulations that influence merger activity (Gilpin, 1996). One article was entitled, "F. T. C. Gets New Teeth (Fangs to Some)" (Meier, 1996). The articles reviewed three recent decisions of the Federal Trade Commission (FTC) in which proposed mergers were "stopped in their tracks." Three cases were cited. In one, the Sara Lee Corp. had bought the Griffin Shoe Polish business from a British company for $26 million in 1991. Under the Hart-Scott-Rodino merger act of 1976, any acquisition of a company with a value of net sales or total assets of $10 million or more acquired by a firm with sales or total assets of $100 million or more must obtain the approval of the FTC or the Department of Justice. Sara Lee is said to have used questionable asset valuations to avoid submitting the deal to the Hart-Scott-Rodino review. It is alleged that Sara Lee wanted to avoid the review because of concern that the deal would be blocked because the shoe polish sales of Sara Lee already accounted for 90% of the U.S. market. The FTC required that Sara Lee sell both Griffin and Esquire shoe polish lines in 1994 and Sara Lee agreed in February 1996 to pay a $3.1 million fine (without admitting wrongdoing).

In a second action, Questar had entered into an agreement to buy from Tenneco a half interest in the Wyoming to California Kern River Natural Gas Pipe Line for $475 million in 1995. The FTC objected that this transaction would have eliminated Tenneco as a potential competitor in natural gas transmission to Utah. To avoid litigation with the FTC in the courts, Questar and Tenneco called off the transaction in December 1995.

A third transaction involved the acquisition by the Rite Aid drug chain for Revco D.S. for $1.8 billion in 1995. The following chronology conveys the nature of the issues that were raised.

## Chronology of Rite Aid Tender Offer for Revco

11/30/85   Rite Aid offers to buy Revco for $1.8 billion, creating a chain of more than 4,500 drug stores with sales of $11 billion.

12/28/95   FTC requests more information, and the deadline for the tender offer is extended.

2/8/96   FTC states that Rite Aid and Revco both violated consent decrees requiring them to sell specified stores from previous acquisitions.

2/20/96   Merck & Co. files an antitrust lawsuit against Rite Aid and other retail pharmacies. Merck alleged that these pharmacies joined a conspiracy to boycott a contract for its Medco unit to administer the prescription drug benefit program for employees of the state of Maryland. Merck lost the contract after more than half the state's pharmacies refused to fill prescriptions using Medco.

4/17/96   FTC votes to block the Rite Aid–Revco merger, citing concerns about higher prices to consumers and buying groups.

4/22/96   Rite Aid offers to sell 340 stores (about 8% of the combined total).

4/23/96   FTC rejects the settlement proposal and demands that the combined company hold no more than 35% of the market in any given area. Rite Aid proposed to meet the requirement, but the FTC demanded that Rite Aid sell all Revco stores in Ohio, West Virginia, and South Carolina. The chairman of Rite Aid characterized this new demand by the FTC as changing the rules of the game again and as "extortion."

4/24/96   Rite Aid drops its tender offer for Revco. Rite Aid shares dropped $1.75 closing at $29.875; Revco stock dropped $1.875 closing at $24.125.

After discussing these three cases, the *New York Times* articles point out that in the 1995 fiscal year the FTC and the Department of Justice challenged or threatened to challenge 45 proposed mergers as compared with 15 in the 1992 fiscal year. Will these actions stop the merger movement? For perspective, recall that in 1995 the dollar values of M&A announcements were $356 billion, representing 424% of the average levels of 1991–1992. The total number of transactions was 3,510 representing 158% of the 2,225 average for 1991–1992. In 1995, 462 transactions were more than $100 million and 74 were more than $1 billion each. This puts the expected 45 transactions that may be challenged into perspective as a relatively moderate number. Robert Pitofsky, the chairman of the Federal Trade Commission, has acknowledged that antitrust policies must take into account the realities of global competition. He also pointed out that the M&A activity of the 1990s involved "industries that are reinventing themselves."

Newspaper articles on May 7 and 8, 1996, reported that the staff of the FTC was recommending that the Time Warner–Turner merger would concentrate too much power in the cable industry (Landler, 1996). After imposing some restrictive conditions, the FTC finally approved the merger on July 17, 1996.

The foregoing review of 1996 developments in antitrust reflects two opposing philosophies toward M&A activity. Some view M&A activity with great concern. They hold that competition will be decreased, efficiency reduced, and financial instability increased. Others see merger activity as a natural expression of market forces. Mergers and the market for control according to this second view will discipline managers to be efficient and will move resources to their most productive uses. The results will be increased efficiency and an improvement in the ability of business firms to cope with increased international competition (Weston, 1953, 1978, 1980a,b, 1982).

## THE BASIC ANTITRUST STATUTES

The U.S. antitrust laws can be grouped into three major areas:

### Sherman Act of 1890

Section 1 prohibits mergers that would tend to create a monopoly or market control. For example, a proposed merger between GM, Ford, and Chrysler would undoubtedly cause the government to sue under Section 1. Section 2 is directed against firms that had already become dominant in the view of the government. Under Section 2, IBM earlier was sued for being a dominant firm, and in the mid-1990s Microsoft is vulnerable to the same allegation.

### Clayton Act, Section 7, 1914

The original act made it illegal for a company to acquire the stock of another company if competition could be adversely affected. Companies made asset acquisitions to avoid the prohibition against acquiring stock. The 1950 amendment gave the FTC the power to block asset purchases as well as stock purchases. The amendment also added an incipiency doctrine. The FTC can block mergers if it judged trends of a tendency toward increased concentration—that the share of industry sales of the largest firms appeared to be increasing.

### Hart-Scott-Rodino Act of 1976

Title I expands Department of Justice (DOJ) power to issue civil investigative demands (CIDs) in antitrust investigations. Title II is a premerger notification provision. Information must be submitted to the DOJ and the FTC for review. Before the takeover can be completed, a 30-day waiting period for mergers, and 15 days for tender offers, is required to enable the agencies to render an opinion on legality. Either agency may request a 20-day extension of the waiting period for mergers and 10 days for tender offers. This prenotification applies to all acquisitions of 15% or more of voting stock or assets of the target company. Title III is the Parens Patriae Act. This means each state is the parent or protector of consumers and competitors. It expands the powers of state attorneys general to initiate triple damage suits on behalf of persons (in their states) injured by violations of the antitrust laws. The state itself does not need to be injured by the violation.

## THE ANTITRUST GUIDELINES

In the merger guidelines of 1982, and successively in 1987, 1992, and 1996, the spirit of the regulatory authorities is altered. In the merger guidelines of 1968, concentration tests were applied somewhat mechanically. With the recognition of the internationalization of competition and other economic realities, the courts and the antitrust agencies began to be less rigid in their approach to antitrust. In addition to the concentration measures, the economics of the industry were taken into account. For example, in its July 8, 1995 issue, the *Economist* had a lead article entitled, "How Dangerous Is

Microsoft?" (pp. 13–14). In an article on antitrust in the same issue, the *Economist* commented that Microsoft held 80% of its market but advised that the trust busters should analyze the economics of the industry.

The guidelines sought to assure business firms that the older antitrust rules that emphasize various measures of concentration would be replaced by consideration of the realities of the marketplace. Nevertheless, the guidelines start with measures of concentration. For many years, the antitrust authorities, following the academic literature, looked at the share of sales or value added by the top four firms. If this share exceeded 20% (in some cases even lower), it might trigger an antitrust investigation.

Beginning in the 1982 guidelines the quantitative test shifted to the Herfindahl-Hirschman Index (HHI), which is a concentration measure based on the market shares of all firms in the industry. It is simply the sum of the squared market shares of each firm in the industry. For example, if there were 10 firms in the industry and each held a 10% market share, the HHI would be 1,000%. If one firm held a 90% market share, and the nine others held a 1% market share, the HHI would be 8,109 ($90^2 + 9 \times 1$). Notice how having a dominant firm greatly increases the HHI. The HHI is applied as indicated by Table 2.3.

A merger in an industry with a resulting HHI of less than 1,000 is unlikely to be investigated or challenged by the antitrust authorities. A HHI between 1,000 and 1,800 is considered to represent moderate concentration. Investigation and challenge depend on the amount by which the HHI increased over its premerger level. An increase of 100 or more may invite an investigation. An industry with a postmerger HHI above 1,800 is considered a concentrated market. Even a moderate increase over the premerger HHI is likely to result in an investigation by the antitrust authorities.

But the guidelines beginning in 1982 had already recognized the role of market characteristics. Particularly important is the ability of existing and potential competitors to expand the supply of a product if one firm tries to restrict output. On the demand side, it is recognized that there are usually close substitutes for any product so that a high market share of the sales of one product does not give the ability to elevate price. Quality differences, the introduction of new products, and technological change result in product proliferation and close substitutes. The result is usually fluctuating market shares. For these reasons, concentration measures alone are not a reliable guide to measure the competitiveness of an industry.

### Other Market Characteristics

Most important is whether entry is easy or difficult. If output can be increased by expansion of noncooperating firms already in the market or if new firms can construct new facilities or convert existing ones, an effort by some firms to increase price would not be profitable. The expansion of supply would drive prices down. Conditions of entry or other supply expansion potentials determine whether firms can successfully collude regardless of market structure numbers.

**TABLE 2.3**   Critical Concentration Levels

| *Postmerger HHI* | *Antitrust Challenge to a Merger?* |
|---|---|
| Less than 1,000 | No challenge—industry is unconcentrated |
| Between 1,000 and 1,800 | If HHI increased by 100, investigate |
| More than 1,800 | If HHI increased by 50, challenge |

Next considered is the ease and profitability of collusion because there is less like-lihood that firms will attempt to coordinate price increases if collusion is difficult or impossible. Here the factors to consider are product differences (heterogeneity), fre-quent quality changes, frequent new products, technological changes, contracts that involve complicated terms in addition to price, cost differences among suppliers, and so on. Also, DOJ challenges are more likely when firms in an industry have colluded in the past or use practices such as exchange of price or output information.

## Nonhorizontal Mergers

The guidelines also include consideration of nonhorizontal mergers. Nonhorizontal mergers include vertical and conglomerate mergers. Much of the discussion of horizon-tal mergers is applicable to nonhorizontal mergers. These include market definition, measurement of market concentration, the role of ease of entry, and all the other fac-tors discussed previously. The guidelines express the view that while nonhorizontal mergers are less likely than horizontal mergers to create competitive problems, "they are not invariably innocuous."

The principal theories under which nonhorizontal mergers are likely to be chal-lenged are then set forth. Concern is expressed over the elimination of potential entrants by nonhorizontal mergers. The degree of concern is greatly influenced by whether conditions of entry generally are easy or difficult. If entry is easy, effects on potential entrants are likely to be small. If entry is difficult, the merger will be examined more closely.

The guidelines set forth three circumstances under which vertical mergers may facilitate collusion and therefore be objectionable: (1) If upstream firms obtain a high level of vertical integration into an associated retail market, this may facilitate collusion in the upstream market by monitoring retail prices. (2) The elimination by vertical merger of a disruptive buyer in a downstream market may facilitate collusion in the upstream market. (3) Nonhorizontal mergers by monopoly public utilities may be used to evade rate regulation.

## Private Antitrust Suits

The attitudes of business competitors have always had a strong influence on antitrust policy. Writers have pointed out that even when government was responsible for most antitrust actions, the investigations usually followed complaints that had been lodged by competitors against the behavior of other firms that were making life difficult for them in the marketplace (Ellert, 1975, 1976).

But it is also argued that the private lawsuit has always been a temptation to lawyers. The cost of litigation is so high that the threat of a private lawsuit can some-times be used as blackmail to pressure the prospective defendant to make a cash settle-ment (Grundman, 1987). Some basic statistics on private antitrust cases were developed under the auspices of the Georgetown Law School (Pitofsky, 1987; White, 1988). Most private antitrust cases are Sherman Act cases in which plaintiffs challenge cartel behav-ior. The average private triple damage case takes about 1.5 years to complete compared with nine months for the average civil case including relatively minor court cases. The median award in private antitrust cases is $154,000, about the same as the median award in civil litigation.

## State Antitrust Activity

Another development said to be stimulated by the changed policies of the federal antitrust agencies has been an increase in state activity. The arguments here are also complex and require careful analysis. In the first place the increased power of the states was granted in the Hart-Scott-Rodino (HSR) Act of 1976 described earlier in this chapter. This was four years before antitrust policies by the federal agencies began to change in 1980. In addition, the federal government gave $10 million to the states to increase their antitrust enforcement efforts under HSR. The Department of Justice reported that during the grant period the number of state actions increased from 206 in 1977 to over 400 in 1979 (Ewing, 1987). Again all of this increase in activity was before the change in policies by the federal antitrust agencies after 1980.

The activity of the states has been increasing. The state attorneys general have formed the National Association of Attorneys General (NAAG), which has published both merger and vertical restraint guidelines. In addition, it is developing a legislative program to change by statute the content of the federal antitrust laws.

Although the state attorneys general have been cooperating, there is potential chaos in having 50 different antitrust laws to which business operations may be subject. While cooperation between the state attorneys general may mitigate this problem, some risk remains. Whenever jobs are threatened in any locality by either the functioning of active free markets or by merger activity, there is a risk that parochial views will dominate what is best for the national economy (Ewing, 1987).

# REGULATION BY PUBLICITY

Three in-depth studies (DeAngelo, DeAngelo, and Gilson (DDG), 1994, 1996; DeAngelo and DeAngelo (DD), 1996) document some propositions developed by Michael Jensen on the politics of finance (1979, 1991, 1993).

## Seizure of the First Executive Corporation and First Capital Life

In their 1994 study, DDG described the experience of the First Executive Corporation (FE) and its main subsidiary, the Executive Life Insurance Company (ELIC). In 1974 Fred Carr took over as chief executive officer of FE. Under his direction, ELIC's total assets grew from 355th in rank to 15th in 1988. Measured by insurance in force FE grew from $700 million in 1974 to $60 billion in 1989.

This spectacular growth came from two major sources. One was innovative products such as single premium deferred annuities. Another important innovation was interest-sensitive whole life products that put competitive pressure on traditional insurers locked into long-term and low-risk assets with low returns. On the management side, FE and ELIC followed some innovative cost-reducing methods. The other major competitive advantage developed was to invest in higher yielding junk bonds, which grew to 65% of the assets of ELIC. Until January 1990, ELIC enjoyed an AAA rating from Standard & Poor's with comparable ratings from Moody's and Best.

Carr was a tough competitor. His letters to stockholders criticized his competitors for their stodginess and refusal to mark assets to market values. The aggressive behavior by Carr was especially inflammatory because it was accompanied by a substantial increase in market share.

In 1989, when Milken and the Drexel Company became the target of regulatory and legal actions, the junk bond market in its entirety was unfavorably impacted. In 1989 the Congressional enactment of the Financial Institutions Reform Recovery and Enforcement Act (FIRREA) essentially forced the S&Ls to dispose of their junk bonds and caused the junk bond market to collapse. Although Carr had been calling for "mark-to-market" accounting in his letters to shareholders for many years, the timing of the enactment of the legislation made what otherwise might have been a minor adjustment a major collapse.

The competitors to ELIC publicized these adverse developments and encouraged the policyholders of FE and ELIC to cash in their policies, resulting in the equivalent of a bank run. The financial press ran numerous feature articles dramatizing the difficulties of FE. This adverse publicity gave John Garamendi, the insurance commissioner of California, a basis for placing ELIC in a conservatorship on April 11, 1991. This seizure caused further policy surrender requests. Ultimately, in March 1992, California regulators sold $6.13 billion (par value) of ELIC's junk bonds for $3.25 billion; this was a price at least $2 billion below their then current value.

Ironically, the more traditional insurers experienced declines in their real estate portfolios that were 2.5 times the decline in junk bonds. Furthermore, while junk bonds, real estate, and mortgages bottomed out toward the end of 1990, the value of junk bonds increased in value by almost 60% by July 1992, while real estate and mortgages had recovered by less then 20%. Without regulatory intervention, FE and ELIC would have been fully solvent within a year-and-a-half after the junk bond market bottomed. Insurance companies and S&Ls with heavy investments in real estate and mortgages experienced continued difficulties.

The story of First Capital Life is similar (DDG, 1996). The seizure of First Capital Life and its parent First Capital Holdings was related to the investment of 40% of its portfolio in junk bonds. DDG state that their evidence suggests that regulatory seizure reflected the targeting of insurers that had invested in junk bonds. But these companies did not experience differentially poorer financial positions compared with other insurers.

### The Hostile Takeover of the Pacific Lumber Company

In 1986 the Pacific Lumber Company (PL), the largest private owner of old redwood trees, was acquired in a leveraged hostile takeover by the MAXXAM Group headed by Charles Hurwitz, regarded as a corporate raider. The event resulted in a dramatic barrage of negative media coverage, linking junk bonds and takeover greed to the destruction of the redwoods.

In their careful analysis of the facts, DD (1996) reach a more balanced conclusion. They point out that basic timber economics explains the behavior of MAXXAM and the predecessor owners of PL. Timber economics predict that old growth forests will be harvested first because they will yield virtually no further growth in harvestable timber volume. Timber economics principles predict that under any private ownership, old growth forests will be harvested, a process that had been taking place for at least 100 years before the 1986 takeover of PL. Their study presents evidence that shows that 91% of PL's old growth redwoods had already been logged by the time of the takeover and that both the old and new managements had similar timetables for the remaining acreage. Junk bonds and takeovers would have little effect on these timetables. DD outline the correct policies for saving the redwoods. One is to raise funds to purchase for public holding the old growth acreage. The other is to raise funds to purchase previously logged land to grow new redwood forests. These eminently sensible prescriptions were lost in the hysteria over the change of ownership of the Pacific Lumber Company.

### Regulation by the Politics of Finance

The clinical studies of ELIC, First Capital Life, and PL illustrate how the use of junk bonds resulted in regulation by the politics of finance. The ultimate explanation for the bad reputation of junk bonds is that potentially they could finance the takeover of any firm that was not performing up to its potential. Thus, junk bonds became a vigilant monitoring instrument to pressure managements to achieve a high level of efficiency in the companies under their stewardship. The junk bond takeover threat was unsettling to the managers of the leading companies in the United States. Widespread animosity toward the use of junk bonds developed. Junk bonds filled an important financing gap for new and risky growth companies. Their use in takeovers led to value enhancement for shareholders. But these three case studies illustrate how junk bond use became a lightning rod for widespread hysteria, animosity, and pressures on government regulators to limit and penalize their use.

---

## Summary

Regulation of securities trading is closely related to regulation of merger and acquisition activity, because takeovers are carried out by means of the securities markets. Special characteristics of securities that make them vulnerable to being used fraudulently mandate regulation to increase public confidence in securities markets. The earliest securities legislation in the 1930s grew out of the collapse of confidence following the stock market crash of 1929. The Securities Act of 1933 called for registration of public offerings of securities. The Securities Exchange Act of 1934 established the Securities and Exchange Commission to regulate securities market practices; it also specified disclosure requirements for public companies (Section 13) and set out the procedural requirements for proxy contests. A number of other securities laws in the late 1930s and 1940s applied to public utilities, bond indenture trustees, and investment companies.

The Securities Act of 1933 and Securities Exchange Act of 1934 provided the framework for subsequent regulation. Most of the more recent legislation has been in the form of amendments to these two acts. The Williams Act of 1968 amended the 1934 act to regulate tender offers. Two main requirements were a filing with the SEC upon obtaining 5% ownership and a 20-day waiting period after making a tender offer. The disclosure requirements aim to give the target shareholders information that will enable them to receive more of the gains associated with the rise in the share price of the takeover target. The 20-day waiting period gives the target more time to evaluate the offer and/or to tailor a defense or seek multiple bids. Empirical studies on the impact of tender offer regulation on shareholder returns almost universally document significantly higher returns for target shareholders and lower (or negative) returns for bidder shareholders. To the extent that successful tender offers continue to take place, the legislation has achieved its goal of benefiting target shareholders. The risk, however, is that reductions in the returns to bidding firms reduce their incentives to engage in the kind of information-producing activities that lead to beneficial takeovers; thus, the lot of target shareholders in those tender offers that *might* have taken place is not improved.

Historically, insider trading has little to do with M&A activity; it refers to the trading in their own companies' stock by corporate officers, directors, and other insiders. It is largely controlled by Section 16 of the Securities Exchange Act, which requires insiders to report such transactions to the SEC on a regular basis. However, the volatility of stock price changes in connection with M&As creates opportunities for gains by individuals who may not fit the traditional definition of insiders. Rule 10b-5 is a general prohibition of fraud and deceit in the purchase or sale of securities. Rule 14e-3 applies to insider trading particularly in connection with tender offers. The Insider Trading

Sanctions Act of 1984 provides for triple damage penalties in insider trading cases, as does the Racketeer Influenced and Corrupt Organizations Act of 1970 (RICO), which also allows immediate seizure of assets and which is invoked in some of the more notorious cases of insider trading. The SEC rules are somewhat ambiguous, but it is illegal to trade on inside information, whether obtained as a result of one's fiduciary relationship to a firm or through misappropriation.

In addition to federal regulation of M&A activity, a number of states have enacted legislation to protect corporations headquartered within their boundaries. States are the primary regulators of corporate activities. However, there are problems in state regulation of takeovers. Securities markets represent interstate commerce, and state regulations that interfere with interstate commerce are, by definition, unconstitutional. Others argue that state regulations are not necessary, that federal regulations and corporate antitakeover amendments provide sufficient protection. There is even evidence that shareholders are damaged by restrictive state legislation that limits takeovers.

It is unlikely, however, that antitrust policy in the United States will go back to the narrow approach that dominated policy through most of the three decades from 1950 through the late 1970s. Some of the fundamental economic factors have changed:

1. International competition has clearly increased and many of our important industries are now international in scope. Concentration ratios must take into account international markets and will be much lower than when measured on the assumption of purely domestic markets.

2. The pace of technological change has increased and the pace of industrial change has increased substantially. This requires more frequent adjustments by business firms, including many aspects of restructuring that include acquisitions and divestitures.

3. Deregulation in a number of major industries requires industrial realignment and readjustments. These require greater flexibility in government policy.

4. New institutions particularly among financial intermediaries represent new mechanisms for facilitating the restructuring processes that are likely to continue.

Thus, while different political administrations may reinstitute some of the historical challenges to merger and acquisition activity, the extreme standards of the earlier structural theory are not likely to be applied. However, such a position must be expressed with qualification because the various guidelines issued by the NAAG represent the same type of philosophy as was reflected in the structural theory. Thus, the possibility remains of a return to tough antimerger policies in the future. It was these considerations that stimulated many mergers and acquisitions in 1988.

---

## Questions

2.1. What is the rationale for tender offer regulation?

2.2. Discuss the pros and cons of trading halts as a measure to deal with significant information about a listed firm.

2.3. Discuss the pros and cons of *state* regulation of mergers and tender offers.

2.4. List and briefly explain the product characteristics and/or management decision variables that make collusion within an industry more difficult.

2.5. What other factors are considered along with the Herfindahl-Hirschman Index in the government's decision to initiate an antitrust case?

--------------------------------- C A S E  2-1 ---------------------------------

# Broader Board Responsibilities

An area of great practical importance to directors involved in the sale of their company is the obligation to prove that they received the best possible price for their shareholders. One reason this problem arises is that a target may receive a very attractive proposal from a bidder. The board of the target and some of its key shareholders may believe the offer is a very attractive one. To prove to other shareholders that the offer is the best that could be achieved, the board of the target might test the market (shop around) for other possible bidders. Or they might hire an investment banker or some other financial intermediary to test the market or even to conduct an auction.

But one risk is that if the market feels that the target is being shopped, this may reflect some weakness and potential problems at the target. If no other offers are forthcoming or if other offers come in at much lower prices, the first bidder may lower his offer because his position has been clearly strengthened. Another possibility is that the initial bidder may drop out as soon as the target checks other alternatives rather than continue to incur the additional expenses required to investigate and evaluate the deal with the target.

The basic problem is that if bidding is costly, the decision of the potential bidder to make an investigation is influenced by the probability that the investigation investments will be profitable. There are advantages to the target to encourage bids by reducing the investment risk of potential acquirers. Four types of techniques have been used to provide this kind of encouragement (Gilson and Black, 1995, pp. 1020–1023). One is a *no-shop* agreement by the target. This prohibits the target from seeking other bids or providing nonpublic information to third parties. A related agreement commits the target management to use its best efforts to secure shareholder approval of the offer by the bidder. These protections to the acquirer are subject to a **fiduciary out** when the target receives a legal opinion that the fiduciary duty of the target board requires it to consider competitive bids.

Another protection is the payment of a **breakup or termination fee** to the initial bidder if the target is ultimately acquired by another bidder. For example, the termination fee Paramount Communications agreed to pay to Viacom, the favored acquirer, was $100 million. The termination fee reflects investigation expenses and the executive time involved in formulating an offer as well as opportunity costs of alternative investment options not pursued.

Another protection to a bidder is a *stock lockup* such as an option to buy the target's stock at the first bidder's initial offer when a rival bidder wins. This technique was used in the bidding contest between U.S. Steel (later USX) with Mobil Oil for the acquisition of Marathon Oil. In this case, Mobil had made an initial hostile bid. Marathon granted USX the right to purchase 10 million newly issued Marathon shares for $90 per share, which was the competing offer by USX. If Mobil or some other firm ultimately acquired Marathon for $95 per share, for example, the gain to USX would have been $5 times 10 million shares or $50 million.

Still another method of encouraging the initial bidder is to grant a *crown jewels lockup*. USX was also granted an option to purchase for $2.8 billion Marathon's 48% interest in the oil and mineral rights to the Yates Field in west Texas, one of the richest domestic oil wells ever discovered.

-----------------------------------------------------------

--------------------------------- C A S E  2-2 ---------------------------------

# Van Gorkom

The creation of techniques to favor an early bidder plus the economic environment of competitive bids raise practical and legal issues. How does the board of directors of the target demonstrate that it obtained the best price? A series of court cases illustrate the nature of the issues involved. The lead case in this area is *Smith v. Van Gorkom,* 488 A.2d 858 (Del. (1985)). The plaintiff Smith represented a class action brought by the shareholders of the Trans Union Corporation (Trans Union). Van Gorkom had been an officer of Trans Union for 24 years during most of which he was either chief executive officer (CEO) or chairman of the board. Trans Union was a diversified company but most of its profits came from its rail car leasing business. The company had difficulty generating sufficient taxable income to offset increasingly large investment tax credits (ITCs). Trans Union beginning in the late 1960s followed a program of acquiring many companies to increase available taxable income. A 1980 report considered still further alternatives to deal with the ITC problem. Van Gorkom was approaching 65 years of age and mandatory retirement.

One of the alternatives was a leveraged buyout. The chief financial officer (CFO) of Trans Union ran some numbers at $50 a share and $60 a share to check whether the prospective cash flows could service the debt in a leveraged buyout (LBO). The numbers indicated that $50 would be easy but that $60 would be difficult. Van Gorkom took a midway $55 price and met with Jay Pritzker, a well-known takeover investor and social acquaintance. Van Gorkom explained to Pritzker that the $55 share price represented a substantial premium and would still enable the buyer to pay off most of the loan in the first five years. Van Gorkom stated that to be sure the $55 was the best price obtainable, Trans Union should be free to accept any better offer. Pritzker stated that his organization would serve as a "stalking horse" for an "auction contest" only if Trans Union would permit Pritzker to buy 1.75 million shares at (the current) market price, which Pritzker could then sell to any higher bidder. After many discussions and negotiations, Salomon Brothers over a three-month period ending January 21, 1981 tried to elicit other bids. GE Credit was interested but was unwilling to make an offer unless Trans Union first rescinded its merger agreement with Pritzker. Kohlberg Kravis Roberts (KKR) had also made an offer but had withdrawn it.

Ultimately the Pritzker offer was submitted to the vote of shareholders. Of the outstanding shares, 69.6% voted in favor of the merger; 7.55% voted against; 22.85% were not voted. The class action suit was then brought. The defendants argued that the $55 represented a 60% premium and established the most reliable evidence possible, a marketplace test that the price was more than fair. Nevertheless, the court concluded that the directors of Trans Union had breached their fiduciary duty to their stockholders on two counts: (1) their failure to inform themselves of all information relevant to the decision to recommend the Pritzker merger, and (2) their failure to disclose all material information that a reasonable stockholder would consider important in evaluating the Pritzker offer. Interestingly enough, the court's measure of damages was the amount by which the fair value of the transaction exceeds $55 per share, and the case was ultimately settled for about $23.5 million.

Within a few months after the Trans Union decision, the Delaware legislature amended the Delaware general corporate law to provide directors with more protection in connection with a transaction such as the Trans Union. The new law made three points: (1) Once it was recognized that a company was "in play," meaning it was going to be sold, the directors had the responsibility to get the best price for shareholders. (2) The directors should be equally fair to all bidders. (3) The decision should not be tainted by the self-interest of management or directors.

It was in the same year, 1985, that the Delaware Supreme Court was confronted with the issues of *Unocal v. Mesa.* In the Unocal case the directors paid a large special dividend to all shareholders except Mesa. The court distinguished Unocal as a case in which the directors were seeking to preserve the company. To do this, the court held that the directors had the right to take defensive actions in the face of a hostile takeover attempt. In particular, the court held that Mesa had made a two-tier offer with a second-tier price less than the first tier, so that it was coercive.

---

## C A S E  2-3

# ⚡ Revlon Inc. v. Pantry Pride

The defendant in the Revlon case was technically MacAndrews & Forbes Holdings, which was the controlling stockholder of Pantry Pride, 506 A.2d 173 (Del. (1986)). Ronald O. Perelman, chairman and CEO of Pantry Pride, met with the head of Revlon in June 1985 to suggest a friendly acquisition of Revlon.

Perelman indicated that Pantry Pride (PP) would offer $45 per share. Revlon's investment banker (in August 1985) advised that $45 was too low and that Perelman would use junk bond financing followed by a bust-up of Revlon, which would bring as much as $70 a share. As defenses Revlon was advised to repurchase at least one-sixth of its shares and to adopt a poison pill.

In October, Revlon received a proposal from Forstmann Little and the investment group Adler & Shaykin. The directors agreed to a LBO plan. Each shareholder would receive $56 cash per share and management would receive a substantial stock position in the new company by the exercise of their Revlon golden parachutes. Some initial bids and counterbids by Pantry Pride and Forstmann took place. At this point the court observed that the duty of the board had changed from the preservation of Revlon as a corporate entity to getting the best price for the shareholders. This made the case different from Unocal. The Revlon board had (1) granted Forstmann a lockup option to purchase certain Revlon assets, (2) a no-shop provision to deal exclusively with Forstmann, and (3) a termination fee of $25 million. The Delaware Supreme Court concluded that it agreed with the Court of Chancery that the Revlon defensive measures were inconsistent with the director's duties to shareholders.

---

## CASE 2–4

# ✶ Maxwell Communications v. Macmillan

Macmillan was a large publishing company. In May 1987 Robert Maxwell had made a hostile bid for another publishing company, Harcourt Brace Jovanovich, Inc., which was defeated by a leveraged recap. Fearing that Maxwell would make a hostile bid, the management of Macmillan decided to restructure the company so that it would increase its share of stock ownership to block a Maxwell takeover.

On October 21, 1987, the Bass Group of Texas announced that it had acquired 7.5% of Macmillan's stock. At a special board meeting, management painted an uncomplimentary picture of the Bass Group. Offers and counteroffers took place. On July 20, 1988, Maxwell intervened in the Bass-Macmillan bidding contest with an all-cash offer of $80 per share. Macmillan did not respond but instead started negotiations for Kohlberg Kravis Roberts (KKR) to do an LBO of Macmillan. In the subsequent offers and counteroffers, Macmillan gave preferential treatment to KKR in a number of ways. KKR asked for a "no-shop rule" and a lockup option to purchase eight Macmillan subsidiaries for $950 million. Maxwell countered by stating that he would always top whatever bid was made by KKR. Maxwell sued, requesting an injunction against the lockup option. A lower court denied the injunction.

The Supreme Court of Delaware concluded that the Macmillan board had not been neutral. To conduct a fair auction to get the best price for shareholders, fairness to all bidders must be achieved. The higher court reversed the lower court's decision, denying Maxwell's motion for a preliminary injunction. This blocked the sale of the eight Macmillan subsidiaries to KKR. Maxwell succeeded in acquiring Macmillan in 1988 for $2,335 million.

---

## CASE 2–5

# Paramount v. Time

In *Paramount Communications, Inc. v. Time, Inc.,* Fed.Sec.L. Rep. (CCH) ¶94,514 (Del.Ch. (1989)) and 571 A.2d 1140 (Del. (1990)), the Revlon and Macmillan case issues were visited again. The Supreme Court of Delaware reached a different decision. The court held that Time did not expressly resolve to sell the company. The exchange of stock between Time and Warner did not contemplate a change in corporate control. Although the Paramount offer had a higher dollar value, the Time board argued that it was follow-ing a program of long-term share value maximization for its shareholders. The court, therefore, upheld the right of the Time board to not accept the Paramount offer.

---

## CASE 2-6

# Paramount v. QVC Network

This case is cited as 637 A.2d 34 (Del. (1993)). Paramount had a strategic vision in trying to acquire Time. It would have given Paramount entry into the cable television industry. Failing to acquire Time, Paramount negotiated an acquisition of Viacom. The form of the transaction sought to avoid any implica-tion of a change in control of Paramount. Paramount tried to avoid the Revlon trigger, and sought to take advantage of that avoidance by providing Viacom with important lockups. Viacom was controlled by Sumner Redstone, who essentially owned about 90% of the company. Viacom's equity coinvestors in the Paramount-Viacom transaction included NYNEX and Blockbuster Entertainment Corporation.

After some preliminary negotiations, on September 12, 1993 the Paramount board approved a merger agreement. It was understood that Martin Davis, the head of Paramount, would be the CEO of the combined company and Redstone would be its controlling stockholder. The merger agreement included a no-shop provision. It provided a termina-tion fee to Viacom of $100 million. It granted Viacom an option to purchase about 20% of Paramount's outstanding common stock at $69.14 per share if any of the triggering events related to the termination fee occurred.

Despite the attempts to discourage a competing bid, Barry Diller, the chairman and CEO of QVC, along with several equity coinvestors including Bell South and Comcast, proposed a merger paying $30 in cash and about 0.9 shares of QVC common to total $80 per share. This started counterbids by Viacom and fur-ther bids by QVC. In their final offers, the Paramount management disparaged some aspects of the QVC bid but failed to mention that it was $1 billion higher than the best Viacom offer. The Supreme Court of Delaware held that the directors of Paramount had breached their fiduciary duty in not getting the best possible price. Rather than seizing opportunities to get the highest price, the Paramount directors walled themselves off from material information and refused to negotiate with QVC or to seek other alternatives. The bidding war continued, but ultimately Viacom became the successful buyer of Paramount.

---

## CASE 2-7

# Sandoz–Gerber

We have seen legal subtleties weave their way through a number of major merger transactions. The decisions of the court seem inconsistent to some. To others each of the court decisions had a valid factual basis for distinguishing between distinct and different circumstances. To wrap up this story, when Gerber Products was acquired by Sandoz in May 1994, there were no stock option lockups (Steinmetz, 1994). It was generally recognized that the Paramount deci-sion had an impact. It was pointed out that the pur-chase by Roche Holdings of Syntex for $5.4 billion had no option agreements whatsoever. In the

Sandoz–Gerber deal, there was a $70 million breakup fee. Takeover lawyers have commented that as long as the compensation of stock options and breakup fees were under 2.5% of the deal's value, the courts probably would not find preferential treatment. The $70 million Sandoz breakup fee represented 1.9% of the $3.7 billion deal value.

--------------------------------------------------------

## Questions on Case Studies C2.1–C2.7

C2.1  What are the four techniques used to encourage bidders?

C2.2  On what basis did the courts conclude that the directors of Trans Union had breached their fiduciary duty to their stockholders?

C2.3  What was the reasoning of the court in *Revlon v. Pantry Pride?*

C2.4  What was the reasoning in the Macmillan decision?

C2.5  On what basis did the court uphold the right of the Time board not to accept the Paramount offer?

C2.6  What was the reasoning of the court in the *Paramount v. QVC* decision? How did that affect Viacom?

C2.7  How did the previous court decisions affect the size of the breakup fee in the acquisition of Gerber Products by Sandoz?

## References

Bandow, D., "Curbing Raiders Is Bad for Business," *New York Times,* February 7, 1988, p. 2.

DeAngelo, Harry, and Linda DeAngelo, "Ancient Redwoods, Junk Bonds, and the Politics of Finance: A Study of the Hostile Takeover of the Pacific Lumber Company," ms., University of Southern California, April 1996.

———, and Stuart C. Gilson, "The Collapse of First Executive Corporation Junk Bonds, Adverse Publicity, and the 'Run on the Bank' Phenomenon," *Journal of Financial Economics,* 36, 1994, pp. 287–336.

———, "Perceptions and the Politics of Finance: Junk Bonds and the Regulatory Seizure of First Capital Life," *Journal of Financial Economics,* 41, 1996, pp. 475–511.

*Economist,* "How Dangerous Is Microsoft?" July 8, 1995, pp. 13–14.

———, "Thoroughly Modern Monopoly," July 8, 1995, p. 76.

Ellert, J. C., "Antitrust Enforcement and the Behavior of Stock Prices," Ph.D. dissertation, Graduate School of Business, University of Chicago, June 1975, pp. 66–67.

———, "Mergers, Antitrust Law Enforcement and Stockholder Returns," *Journal of Finance,* 31, 1976, pp. 715–732.

Ewing, Ky P., Jr., "Current Trends in State Antitrust Enforcement: Overview of State Antitrust Law," *Antitrust Law Journal,* 56, April 1987, pp. 103–110.

Gilpin, Kenneth N., "Rite Aid Drops Revco Bid After Regulatory Opposition," *New York Times,* April 25, 1996, pp. C1, C2.

Gilson, Ronald J., and Bernard S. Black, *The Law and Finance of Corporate Acquisitions,* 2nd ed., Westbury, NY: The Foundation Press, Inc., 1995.

Grass, A., "Insider Trading Report Addresses Reform of Section 16," *Business Lawyer Update,* July/August 1987, p. 3.

Grundman, V. Rock, Jr., "Antitrust: Public vs. Private Law," *Restructuring and Antitrust,* The Conference Board Research Bulletin No. 212, 1987, pp. 5–13.

Jensen, Michael C., "Toward a Theory of the Press," in Karl Brunner, ed., *Economics and Social Institutions,* Boston, MA: Martinus Nijhoff Publishing, 1979, pp. 267–287.

———, "Corporate Control and the Politics of Finance," *Journal of Applied Corporate Finance,* 4, 1991, pp. 13–33.

———, "The Modern Industrial Revolution, Exit, and the Failure of Internal Control Systems, *Journal of Finance,* 48, 1993, pp. 831–880.

Landler, Mark, "Time Warner-Turner Deal Said to Face F.T.C. Resistance," *New York Times,* May 8, 1996, pp. C1, C5.

Meier, Barry, "F.T.C. Gets New Teeth (Fangs to Some)," *New York Times,* April 25, 1996, pp. C1, C2.

Office of the Chief Economist, Securities and Exchange Commission, "The Economics of Any-or-All, Partial, and Two-Tier Tender Offers," April 1985.

Pitofsky, Robert, "Antitrust: Public vs. Private Law," *Restructuring and Antitrust,* The Conference Board Research Bulletin No. 212, 1987, pp. 5–13.

Savage, D. G., "Justices Say Firm Can't Lie About Merger Talks," *Los Angeles Times,* March 8, 1988, pp. 1, 17.

Steinmetz, Greg, "Stock-Option Lockups Are Absent From Takeover Deals," *Wall Street Journal,* May 24, 1994, pp. C1, C21.

U.S. Department of Justice, "1985 Vertical Restraints Guidelines," *The Journal of Reprints for Antitrust Law and Economics,* 16, 1986, pp. 3–57.

———, "1984 Department of Justice Merger Guidelines," *The Journal of Reprints for Antitrust Law and Economics,* 16, 1986, pp. 61–115.

———, "1982 Department of Justice Merger Guidelines," *The Journal of Reprints for Antitrust Law and Economics,* 16, 1986, pp. 119–165.

———, "1982 Federal Trade Commission Horizontal Merger Guidelines," *The Journal of Reprints for Antitrust Law and Economics,* 16, 1986, pp. 169–185.

———, "1980 Antitrust Guide Concerning Research Joint Ventures," *The Journal of Reprints for Antitrust Law and Economics,* 16, 1986, pp. 189–303.

———, "1977 Antitrust Guide for International Operations," *The Journal of Reprints for Antitrust Law and Economics,* 16, 1986, pp. 307–375.

———, "1977 Guidelines for Sentencing Recommendations in Felony Cases Under the Sherman Act," *The Journal of Reprints for Antitrust Law and Economics,* 16, 1986, pp. 379–397.

———, "1968 Department of Justice Merger Guidelines," May 30, 1968, p. 12.

Veasey, N., "A Statute Was Needed to Stop Abuses," *New York Times,* February 7, 1988, p. 2.

Weston, J. Fred, *The Role of Mergers in the Growth of Large Firms,* Berkeley: University of California Press, 1953.

———, *Concentration and Efficiency: The Other Side of the Monopoly Issue,* Special Issues in the Public Interest No. 4, New York: Hudson Institute, 1978.

———, "Section 7 Enforcement: Implementation of Outmoded Theories," *Antitrust Law Journal,* 49, August 1980a, pp. 1411–1450.

———, "International Competition, Industrial Structure and Economic Policy," Chapter 10 in I. Leveson and J. W. Wheeler, eds., *Western Economies in Transition,* Hudson Institute, Boulder, CO: Westview Press, 1980b.

———, "Trends in Anti-Trust Policy," *Chase Financial Quarterly,* 1, Spring 1982, pp. 66–87.

———, and Stanley I. Ornstein, *The Impact of the Large Firm on the U.S. Economy,* Lexington, MA: Heath Lexington Books, January 1973.

White, Lawrence J., ed., *Private Antitrust Litigation,* in Richard Schmaler, ed., *Regulation of Economics Series,* Cambridge, MA: MIT Press, 1988.

# C H A P T E R

# 3

# Pooling Versus
# Purchase Accounting

The analysis of M&As and restructuring must begin with the accounting numbers. This is a necessary first step if only to get behind the numbers to see what is really going on. The rules follow the recommendations of professional accounting organizations. Securities and Exchange Commission (SEC) approval is required in connection with financial statements issued to investors.

## HISTORICAL BACKGROUND

On August 2, 1970, the 18-member Accounting Principles Board (APB) of the American Institute of Certified Public Accountants issued Opinion 16 dealing with guidelines for corporate mergers and Opinion 17 dealing with goodwill arising from mergers. The recommendations, which became effective October 31, 1970, modify and elaborate previous pronouncements on the pooling of interests and purchase methods of accounting for business combinations. These 1970 rules still prevail, although discussion memoranda and related statements have been issued periodically.

In recent decades, the formulation of accounting principles has been the primary responsibility of the Financial Accounting Standards Board (FASB) of the Financial Accounting Foundation. On August 19, 1976, FASB issued a lengthy "Discussion Memorandum on Accounting for Business Combinations and Purchased Intangibles." It consisted of 178 pages of text plus Appendices A through J consisting of an additional 154 pages. Later FASB publications dealt with rules for preparing consolidated statements, for example, "Statement of Financial Accounting Standards No. 94, Consolidation of All Majority-Owned Subsidiaries, an amendment of ARB No. 51, with related amendments to APB Opinion No. 18 and ARB No. 43, Chapter 12." On August 26, 1994, in the Financial Accounting Series, FASB published "Preliminary Views, Consolidation Policy," No. 140-B. Comprehensive item-by-item comparisons of the Generally Accepted Accounting Principles (GAAP) in Canada, Mexico, and the United States were published in the Financial Accounting Series in December 1994 as No. 144-B entitled, "Financial Reporting in North America, Highlights of a Joint Study." The GAAP for business combinations as well as consolidation and equity accounting followed the earlier rules adopted in 1970.

In a business combination, one company will usually be the "acquiring firm" with the other company being described as the acquired or "target firm." Although there are

Much appreciation to Professors Jack Farrell, Patricia Hughes, and Bruce Miller of the accounting department at The Anderson School, University of California, Los Angeles, for considerable assistance on this chapter.

many ways to structure a business combination, one board of directors and one CEO usually end up with control over the combined operations. When the operations of two companies are placed under a common control through any form of business combination, financial reporting rules require that financial statements (at the date of combining) present numbers from the combining of two accounting systems.

Accounting Principles Board Opinion No. 16, "Accounting for Business Combinations," prescribes two accounting methods for recording the acquisition of a "target" company by an "acquiring" company:

*Blended*

1. The pooling of interests method of accounting, which requires that the original "historical cost" basis of the assets and liabilities of the target company be carried forward.
2. The purchase method of accounting, which requires that a new "historical cost" basis be established for the assets and liabilities of the target company.

A second major difference between the two methods has to do with the reporting of earnings:

1. The pooling of interests method of accounting, in which earnings of the combined entities are combined for any reporting periods. If in a subsequent financial report data for a prior year are included, it would reflect the accounting for a pooling of interests combination.
2. The purchase method of accounting, in which earnings of the acquired company are reported by the acquirer only from the date of acquisition forward.

In its status report of April 22, 1997, FASB described its project to reconsider the 1970 APB Opinions No. 16 and No. 17. It stated that more than 50 issues related to business combinations and tangible assets had been considered by its Emerging Issues Task Force (EITF). A *Wall Street Journal* article at about the same time (April 15, 1997) commented that business firms were seeking to have the rules changed to make it easier to use pooling accounting, but that the FASB was considering proposals to restrict more narrowly the use of pooling. One objection to pooling is that it ignores the new market values that have been established by the merger or acquisition transaction itself. Another criticism is that in a pooling, the financial statements do not record what the buyer paid. Yet companies have been seeking to use pooling to avoid recording goodwill. Since 1992 in deals valued at over $100 million, 357 have been recorded as poolings versus 36 purchase acquisitions. The analysis in this chapter seeks to provide background for evaluating the proposals to restrict the use of pooling versus those seeking the expansion of the use of pooling.

## POOLING OF INTERESTS

Twelve criteria are prescribed to determine whether the conditions for the pooling of interests treatment are satisfied. If all of them are met, the combination is, in theory, a merger between companies of comparable size, and the **pooling of interests** method must be employed. In practice, comparable size is not a compelling requirement. Accounting practice with SEC approval permits flexibility. Six important tests are:

1. The acquired firm's stockholders must maintain an ownership position in the surviving firm.
2. The basis for accounting for the assets of the acquired entity must remain unchanged.
3. Independent interests must be combined. Each entity must have had autonomy for two years prior to the initiation of the plan to combine, and no more than 10% ownership of voting common stock can be held as intercorporate investments.

4. The combination must be effected in a single transaction; contingent payouts are not permitted in poolings but can be used in purchases.

5. The acquiring corporation must issue only common stock in exchange for substantially all the voting common stock of the other company (*substantially* is defined as 90%).

6. The combined entity must not intend to dispose of a significant portion of the assets of the combining companies within two years after the merger.

## PURCHASE ACCOUNTING

In purchase accounting, an acquiring corporation should allocate the cost of an acquired company to the assets acquired and liabilities assumed. All identifiable assets acquired and liabilities assumed in a business combination, whether or not shown in the financial statements of the acquired company, should be assigned a portion of the cost of the acquired company, normally equal to their fair values at date of acquisition. Assuming a taxable transaction, the new stepped-up basis is depreciable for tax accounting.

The excess of the cost of the acquired company over the sum of the amounts assigned to identifiable assets acquired less liabilities assumed should be recorded as goodwill. This goodwill account is required to be written off, for financial reporting, over some reasonable period, but no longer than 40 years. This requires a write-off of at least 2.5% a year of the amount of goodwill arising in purchase accounting.

Under a 1993 tax law change, if an acquisition is made by the purchase of the assets of the acquired company, any resulting goodwill can be amortized over 15 years for tax accounting. The intention of the 1993 tax law change was to match the tax deductibility of goodwill write-offs provided by foreign countries such as Japan, Switzerland, and Germany. In some countries, goodwill can be written off directly to shareholders' equity for financial reporting (bypassing the income statement); under some circumstances the total of goodwill can be written off in the year of the acquisition, which maximizes the tax shelter benefits on cash flows.

As we demonstrate below, when purchase accounting is employed, reported net income is usually lower than under pooling of interests accounting. This is because of an increased depreciation charge or amortization of goodwill. However, cash flows will be higher under purchase accounting if any of the depreciation or amortization is tax deductible.

Previous to the issuance of APB Opinion 16, a stimulus to pooling was the opportunity to dispose of assets acquired at depreciated book values, selling them at their current values and recording subsequent profits on sales of assets. Opinion 16 attempted to deal with this practice by the requirement that sales of major portions of assets not be contemplated for at least two years after the merger has taken place. For example, suppose firm A buys firm B, exchanging stock worth $100 million for assets worth $100 million but carried at $25 million. After the merger, A could, before the change in rules, sell the acquired assets and report the difference between book value and the purchase price, or $75 million, as earned income. Thus, pooling could be used to manipulate accounting measures of net income.

## ACCOUNTING FOR POOLING VERSUS PURCHASE

We now illustrate the different accounting treatments under pooling versus purchase. Our treatment focuses on the central financial and economic implications of the alternative treatments, and does not include some of the fine points of the accounting treatments found in advanced accounting texts (e.g., Pahler and Mori, 1997) or the technicalities covered in case books on the legal aspects of pooling versus purchase (e.g., Gilson and Black, 1995).

We shall use a case example starting with the financial statements of the acquiring firm (A) and target firm (T) as shown in Table 3.1. We choose to use the same set of data to illustrate both pooling and purchase to highlight the contrasts. The spirit of the accounting regulations for pooling is that the acquiring firm and target firm would be approximately the same size. Thus, the combined firm would reflect a continuity of the influence of both companies. In a purchase, the target firm would be much smaller and be absorbed into the operations of the acquiring firm.

But the choice of purchase versus pooling has some judgmental factors involved. For example, AT&T succeeded in having its acquisition of NCR treated as a pooling of

**TABLE 3.1**   Initial Financial Data for Merging Firms

| *Initial Balance Sheets* | | *Acquiring Firm* | | | *Target Firm* | |
|---|---|---|---|---|---|---|
| Current assets | | | $210,000 | | | $110,000 |
| Land | | | 50,000 | | | 20,000 |
| Plant and equipment | | 200,000 | | | 100,000 | |
|    Less: accumulated depr. | | 60,000 | | | 30,000 | |
| Net plant and equipment | | | 140,000 | | | 70,000 |
| Goodwill | | | | | | |
| Total assets | | | $400,000 | | | $200,000 |
| | | | | | | |
| Interest-bearing debt | | 40,000 | | | 20,000 | |
| Other current liabilities | | 60,000 | | | 30,000 | |
| Long-term debt | | 60,000 | | | 30,000 | |
| Total liabilities | | | 160,000 | | | 80,000 |
| | | | | | | |
| Common stock | (Par $4) | 80,000 | | (Par $2) | 40,000 | |
| Paid-in capital | | 100,000 | | | 50,000 | |
| Retained earnings | | 60,000 | | | 30,000 | |
| Shareholders' equity | | | $240,000 | | | $120,000 |
| | | | | | | |
| Total claims on assets | | | $400,000 | | | $200,000 |

| *Initial Income Statements* | | | |
|---|---|---|---|
| Sales | | $800,000 | $400,000 |
| Operating costs less depr. and amort. | | 703,333 | 351,667 |
| EBITDA* | | 96,667 | 48,333 |
| Depreciation (D)** | | 20,000 | 10,000 |
| Amortization of goodwill (A) | | | |
| Net operating income (NOI) = EBIT | | 76,667 | 38,333 |
| Interest cost @ 10% | | 10,000 | 5,000 |
| Earnings before taxes | | 66,667 | 33,333 |
| Taxes @ 40% | | 26,667 | 13,333 |
| Net income | | $40,000 | $20,000 |

*Earnings before interest, taxes, depreciation and amortization.

**Ten-year life, so 10% of the gross plant and equipment account.

interests. At the time of its unsolicited bid for NCR on December 2, 1990, AT&T was six times larger with a 1989 revenue of $36 billion vs. $6 billion for NCR. Observing the differences in revenues and in stock market values, the *Wall Street Journal* commented that AT&T "could swallow NCR with barely a gulp" (December 3, 1990, p. A3). Nevertheless, AT&T succeeded in obtaining SEC approval to have the acquisition treated as a pooling.

Its market value was $11 billion when Chevron bought Gulf in 1984 for $13.3 billion. Yet Chevron treated the acquisition as a purchase. Because accounting rules and the SEC permit discretion in choice of pooling versus purchase, it is convenient to use the same set of input data to illustrate the two methods.

The illustrative data in our example in Table 3.1 show A to be roughly double the size of T. A has net income of $40,000; T of $20,000. Each firm has 20,000 shares outstanding, so A has earnings per share of $2 versus $1 for T. We postulate that the price earnings ratio for A is 15 and for T it is 20. Hence, the indicated market price per share of A is $30 and $20 for T. The book value per share of A is $240,000 divided by 20,000, which is $12, versus $6 for the target. The market to book ratio for the acquiring firm is ($30/$12) = 2.5 times; for the target it is ($20/$6) = 3.3 times.

## Illustration of Pooling Accounting

For illustrative purposes, let us assume further that A buys T by exchanging one share of its stock for one share of the target stock. This represents a 50% premium to T in market value reflecting its higher growth prospects implied by its higher valuation multiple. In Table 3.2, we present balance sheets to illustrate pooling of interests accounting for this combination. Under a pooling of interests, the accounting treatment is simply to combine the balance sheets of the two companies. The target firm shows common stock with a total par value of $40,000 (20,000 shares with a par value of $2 per share). Thus,

**TABLE 3.2**   Balance Sheets to Illustrate Pooling of Interests Accounting for a Combination*

| | Acquiring Firm | | Target Firm | | Adjustment Pooling | | Consolidated Pooling |
|---|---|---|---|---|---|---|---|
| | | | | | Debit | Credit | |
| Current assets | | $210,000 | | $110,000 | | | $320,000 |
| Net fixed assets | | 190,000 | | 90,000 | | | 280,000 |
| Total assets | | $400,000 | | $200,000 | | | $600,000 |
| | | | | | | | |
| Current liabilities | | $100,000 | | $50,000 | | | $150,000 |
| Long-term debt | | 60,000 | | 30,000 | | | 90,000 |
| | | | | | | | |
| Common stock | 80,000 | | 40,000 | | | $40,000 $^{(1)}$ | 160,000 |
| Paid-in capital | 100,000 | | 50,000 | | $40,000 $^{(1)}$ | | 110,000 |
| Retained earnings | 60,000 | | 30,000 | | | | 90,000 |
| Shareholders' equity (SHE) | | 240,000 | | 120,000 | | | 360,000 |
| | | | | | | | |
| Total claims on assets | | $400,000 | | $200,000 | $40,000 | $40,000 | $600,000 |

*Accounting texts and practice use an investment account among other intermediate steps. The final result is as shown here.

$^{(1)}$ Issued 20,000 shares at $4 par to buy the target firm to give a total of 40,000 shares at par of $4, totaling $160,000. Summing the common stock accounts of A and T gives $120,000, so an additional credit of $40,000 is required. The offsetting debit is to the paid-in capital account (i.e., paid-in capital serves as the "plug").

the acquiring firm issues 20,000 additional shares with a par of $4 per share or a book total of $80,000 in acquiring T. When added to the original $80,000 par value of the acquiring firm, the consolidated book total under pooling will be $160,000. To obtain this amount, a credit of $40,000 to the common stock account is required to add to the sum of the existing $80,000 for A and the existing $40,000 for T. The offsetting debit of $40,000 is to the combined paid-in capital. So the consolidated total paid-in capital is reduced from $150,000 to $110,000.

Retained earnings are simply added to obtain $90,000 for the combined companies. This illustrates one of the advantages of pooling. If the target company shows a large amount in retained earnings, and if the acquiring firm wished to strengthen the retained earnings account, it could do so by using the pooling method. This is one of the reasons given for AT&T's strong preference for the use of pooling in its acquisition of NCR (Lys and Vincent, 1995).

In summary, we see from Table 3.2 that pooling is simply adding the individual asset and liability amounts. There is no change in the historical cost basis of either company. Additional shares of common stock issued by the acquiring firm may cause the consolidated common stock account to be different than the simple sum for the A firm and T firm accounts, so a credit or debit may be required. The offsetting credit or debit will be to the paid-in capital account. Usually retained earnings will be the sum of the two or more companies involved in the merger or acquisition. It is possible that if a debit were required to the paid-in capital account that exhausted the total, any remaining debit would be made to the retained earnings account.

### Illustration of Purchase Accounting

The nature of purchase accounting is shown in Table 3.3. We illustrate a taxable transaction in which one or more of the 12 criteria for the use of pooling of interests accounting are not met. As before, A buys T for 20,000 shares of A with a market value of $30 per share, a total value of $600,000. This cost of the acquired company is assigned to the assets acquired and liabilities assumed. If the cost of the acquired company exceeds the amounts assigned to identifiable assets less liabilities assumed, this difference is recorded as goodwill. In practice, it is likely that some of the excess of the amount paid over the net worth of the acquired firm would be assigned to identifiable assets. To illustrate the different consequences of pooling versus purchase accounting, we analyze the extreme cases: (1) all of the excess assigned to identifiable and depreciable assets; and (2) none is so assigned, so that the excess is entirely goodwill. We first discuss the case in which all of the excess is assigned to depreciable assets, as shown in Table 3.3.

The adjustments in purchase consolidation accounting designated by (1) in Table 3.3 represent the elimination of the net worth accounts of the target by debits totaling $120,000. The difference between the market value of $600,000 paid and the elimination of the net worth accounts of the target is $480,000. In note (2) in Table 3.3, the gross plant and equipment account is debited $480,000 and the accumulated depreciation account for the target is eliminated by a debit of $30,000. In the consolidated column, gross plant and equipment is A's $200,000 plus T's $100,000 plus the net step-up of $450,000, totaling $750,000. The accumulated depreciation is only that of the acquiring firm in the amount of $60,000. The consolidated net plant and equipment is, therefore, $690,000 as shown.

The common stock account of A was 20,000 shares with a par value of $4, totaling $80,000. Table 3.3 shows a credit to the common stock account of $80,000. This represents the 20,000 new shares of A issued to buy T. Because these 20,000 shares have a par value of $4 each, the credit [(3) in Table 3.3] to the book common stock account is

**TABLE 3.3**  Consolidated Balance Sheet, Purchase Accounting All "Excess" to Depreciable Assets

| | Acquiring Firm | Target Firm | Adjustment Purchase Debit | Adjustment Purchase Credit | Consolidated Purchase (All "Excess" to Depreciable Assets) |
|---|---|---|---|---|---|
| Current assets | $210,000 | $110,000 | | | $ 320,000 |
| Land | 50,000 | 20,000 | | | 70,000 |
| Plant and equipment | 200,000 | 100,000 | 480,000 (2) | 30,000 (2) | 750,000 |
| Less: accumulated depr. | 60,000 | 30,000 | 30,000 (2) | | 60,000 |
| Net plant and equipment | 140,000 | 70,000 | | | 690,000 |
| Goodwill | | | | | |
| Total assets | $400,000 | $200,000 | | | $1,080,000 |
| | | | | | |
| Interest-bearing debt | 40,000 | 20,000 | | | 60,000 |
| Other current liabilities | 60,000 | 30,000 | | | 90,000 |
| Long-term debt | 60,000 | 30,000 | | | 90,000 |
| Total liabilities | 160,000 | 80,000 | | | 240,000 |
| | | | | | |
| Common stock | 80,000 | 40,000 | 40,000 (1) | 80,000 (3) | 160,000 |
| Paid-in capital | 100,000 | 50,000 | 50,000 (1) | 520,000 (4) | 620,000 |
| Retained earnings | 60,000 | 30,000 | 30,000 (1) | | 60,000 |
| Shareholders' equity (SHE) | 240,000 | 120,000 | | | 840,000 |
| | | | | | |
| Total claims on assets | $400,000 | $200,000 | $630,000 | $630,000 | $1,080,000 |

(1) Paid $30 each for 20,000 shares = $600,000. Eliminate SHE of target of $120,000. The $600,000 less $120,000 equals $480,000 to asset write-ups or to goodwill or some combination of the two.

(2) The difference between the market value of $600,000 paid and the elimination of the net worth accounts of the target is $480,000. The gross plant and equipment account is debited $480,000 and the accumulated depreciation account for the target is eliminated by a debit of $30,000 with an offsetting credit of $30,000. In the consolidated column, gross plant and equipment is $200,000 plus $100,000 plus a net $450,000, totaling $750,000. The accumulated depreciation is only that of the acquiring firm in the amount of $60,000. Net plant and equipment is, therefore, $690,000.

(3) The common stock account of the acquiring firm (A) was 20,000 shares with a par value of $4, totaling $80,000. A issued 20,000 new shares at a par of $4 to buy T. The consolidated common stock account, therefore, would be $160,000, shown in the column for the consolidated company.

(4) The total debits were $600,000. A credit of $80,000 was made to the common stock account. So it is necessary to make an additional credit of $520,000 to the paid-in capital account.

$80,000. For the combined company, there are now 40,000 shares of stock outstanding, the 20,000 original shares of A and the additional 20,000 shares it issued to buy T. With a par value of $4, the book total of common stock is, therefore, $160,000 for the combined company. The difference between the $600,000 and the $80,000 credit to the common stock is $520,000 representing the additional credit [(4) in Table 3.3] that must be made to the paid-in capital account for the combined company.

Recall that in Table 3.2, for pooling accounting the total assets were simply the sum of the total assets of the combining companies of $600,000. In Table 3.3, under purchase accounting, the total consolidated assets for the combined companies is $1,080,000. This new total represents the total under pooling accounting of $600,000 plus $480,000 representing the excess of the total value paid less the book value of net worth purchased.

In Table 3.4, we show the balance sheet effects of assigning all of the excess to goodwill rather than to depreciable assets as was done in Table 3.3. The excess of $480,000 is assigned to a goodwill account rather than to depreciable assets. The accumulated depreciation account of the target firm is eliminated. The combined net plant and equipment is $210,000.

### Effects of Pooling Versus Purchase on Income Measurement

We now consider the effects of pooling versus purchase on the consolidated income statements. The first two columns of Table 3.5 repeat the information for A and T from the statement of facts presented in Table 3.1. The consolidated income statement *under pooling* shown in column 3 would be the summation item by item of each account in the income statement except for the per share figures. Earnings per share for the combined company would be the initial combined net income of $60,000 divided by the 40,000 shares now outstanding, which gives $1.50 for earnings per share.

**TABLE 3.4**   Consolidated Balance Sheet, Purchase Accounting All "Excess" to Goodwill

| | Acquiring Firm | | Target Firm | | Adjustment Purchase Debit | Adjustment Purchase Credit | Consolidated Purchase (All "Excess" to Goodwill) |
|---|---|---|---|---|---|---|---|
| Current assets | | $210,000 | | $110,000 | | | $ 320,000 |
| Land | | 50,000 | | 20,000 | | | 70,000 |
| Plant and equipment | 200,000 | | 100,000 | | | 30,000 (2) | 270,000 |
| Less: accumulated depr. | 60,000 | | 30,000 | | 30,000 (2) | | 60,000 |
| Net plant and equipment | | 140,000 | | 70,000 | | | 210,000 |
| Goodwill | | | | | 480,000 (1) | | 480,000 |
| Total assets | | $400,000 | | $200,000 | | | $1,080,000 |
| | | | | | | | |
| Interest-bearing debt | 40,000 | | 20,000 | | | | 60,000 |
| Other current liabilities | 60,000 | | 30,000 | | | | 90,000 |
| Long-term debt | 60,000 | | 30,000 | | | | 90,000 |
| Total liabilities | | 160,000 | | 80,000 | | | 240,000 |
| | | | | | | | |
| Common stock | 80,000 | | 40,000 | | 40,000 (1) | 80,000 (3) 160,000 | |
| Paid-in capital | 100,000 | | 50,000 | | 50,000 (1) | 520,000 (4) 620,000 | |
| Retained earnings | 60,000 | | 30,000 | | 30,000 (1) | | 60,000 |
| Shareholders' equity (SHE) | | 240,000 | | 120,000 | | | 840,000 |
| | | | | | | | |
| Total claims on assets | | $400,000 | | $200,000 | $630,000 | $630,000 | $1,080,000 |

(1) Paid $30 for 20,000 shares = $600,000. Eliminate SHE of target of $120,000. The $600,000 less $120,000 equals $480,000 to goodwill.

(2) The accumulated depreciation account of the target firm is eliminated by a debit with an offsetting credit of $30,000.

(3) The common stock account of the acquiring firm (A) was 20,000 shares with a par value of $4, totaling $80,000. A issued 20,000 new shares at a par of $4 to buy T. The consolidated common stock account, therefore, would be $160,000, shown in the column for the consolidated company.

(4) Total of $600,000 debits less credit of $80,000, requires a credit of $520,000 to paid-in capital.

**TABLE 3.5**    Income Statements for Pooling vs. Purchase

| | Acquiring Firm (1) | Target Firm (2) | Consolidated, Pooling Accounting (3) | All "Excess" to Depreciable Assets (4) | CONSOLIDATED, PURCHASE ACCOUNTING* — All "Excess" to Goodwill — Depreciable Over 15 Years (5) | Nondeductible (6) |
|---|---|---|---|---|---|---|
| Sales | $800,000 | $400,000 | $1,200,000 | $1,200,000 | $1,200,000 | $1,200,000 |
| Operating cost | 703,333 | 351,667 | 1,055,000 | 1,055,000 | 1,055,000 | 1,055,000 |
| EBITDA | 96,667 | 48,333 | 145,000 | 145,000 | 145,000 | 145,000 |
| Depreciation | 20,000 | 10,000 | 30,000 | 75,000 | 30,000 | 30,000 |
| Amortization (deductible) | | | | | 32,000 | |
| EBIT | 76,667 | 38,333 | 115,000 | 70,000 | 83,000 | 115,000 |
| Interest cost @ 10% | 10,000 | 5,000 | 15,000 | 15,000 | 15,000 | 15,000 |
| Earnings before taxes | 66,667 | 33,333 | 100,000 | 55,000 | 68,000 | 100,000 |
| Taxes @ 40% | 26,667 | 13,333 | 40,000 | 22,000 | 27,200 | 40,000 |
| Amortization (not deduct.) | | | | | | 12,000 |
| Net income | $40,000 | $20,000 | $60,000 | $33,000 | $40,800 | $48,000 |
| Earnings per share | $2.00 | $1.00 | $1.50 | $0.83 | $1.02 | $1.20 |
| | | | | | | |
| Cash flows** | $60,000 | $30,000 | $90,000 | $108,000 | $102,800 | $90,000 |
| Cash flows per share | $3.00 | $1.50 | $2.25 | $2.70 | $2.57 | $2.25 |

*This assumes that the purchase was completed on the first day of the fiscal year. In column 4, the depreciation charge is the new gross plant and equipment total of $750,000 times 10%. In column 5, the amortization of goodwill on the tax return is shown as a tax deduction amortized over 15 years. In column 6, the depreciation charge of $30,000 is composed of the $20,000 in the $200,000 gross assets of A and one-seventh (the remaining life of the assets of T is 7 years) of $70,000, which is the postacquisition gross and net value of the target's depreciable assets now owned by the combined company; 40 years is the period for the nondeductible amortization.

**Cash flows are defined as net income plus depreciation and amortization. The cash flows in purchase accounting exceed the cash flows in pooling by the tax shield of 0.4($45,000) = $18,000 for column 4 and 0.4($32,000) = $12,800 for column 5.

Shareholders of T, who are now shareholders of the combined firm, now have a claim on earnings per share that is increased by 50% over the dollar per share earnings before the acquisition. This is because T shareholders had a 100% claim to $20,000 earnings prior to the combination. With 20,000 shares outstanding, this was earnings per share (EPS) of $1. After the combination, the former T shareholders have a 50% claim to $60,000. For the 20,000 shares of the combined company they now own, this represents $1.50 per share. In this example, T shareholders have earnings accretion of 50¢ per share while the A shareholders have earnings dilution of 50¢ per share. This results from the facts of this particular example. More generally, the earnings accretion per share need not be exactly equal to the earnings dilution per share of the lower price-to-earnings (P/E) ratio company. Many different patterns are observed in practice.

The next three columns, 4, 5, and 6, analyze the income statement effects of purchase accounting under alternative assumptions. In column 4, all of the excess of the purchase price over the book net worth acquired is assigned to depreciable assets. In Table 3.3, the balance sheet under purchase accounting showed the net $450,000 excess added to the gross plant and equipment accounts, resulting in a total gross plant and equipment of $750,000. Because the 10-year life assumption is continued from

Table 3.1, the tax deductible depreciation will be 10% of the $750,000 or $75,000 as shown. We then calculate net income and cash flows in total and on a per share basis.

In column 5, all of the excess is assigned to goodwill and qualifies for the 15-year write-off permitted by the tax law change of 1993. Hence, the depreciation charge continues at $30,000. In addition, the $480,000 goodwill is amortized over 15 years representing $32,000 as shown. We calculate EPS and cash flow per share.

If all of the excess were assigned to goodwill and it did not qualify for tax deductibility, we have column 6. The depreciation expenses are 10% of $20,000 plus one-seventh of the gross value and net value of the plant and equipment acquired from the target firm. EBIT would become $115,000 and earnings before taxes $100,000. After deduction of $40,000 for taxes and $12,000 for amortization of goodwill, the reported net income would be $48,000 or $1.20 per share. Cash flows would be $90,000 (net income of $48,000 plus depreciation of $30,000 and amortization of $12,000) or $2.25 per share. The cash flows per share would be the same as in column 3 under pooling because both lack the tax shelter benefit of the amortization of goodwill.

These results illustrate the generalization we presented at the beginning of the analysis. In every case, net income is lower under purchase accounting than under pooling accounting. This is because of the deductions made for amortization of goodwill or increased depreciation expenses. However, when amortization or increased depreciation are deductible for tax purposes, they shelter cash flows. In columns 4 and 5, where purchase accounting provides for increased tax shelter, cash flows are larger than under pooling accounting. In column 6, where the goodwill amortization is not tax deductible, cash flows are the same as under pooling accounting.

Intermediate cases in which part of the excess is assigned to depreciable assets and part to goodwill, would follow the patterns developed in Table 3.5. Because the results would fall between the cases we have analyzed, they can be pursued as problem exercises.

## EFFECTS ON LEVERAGE

In pooling, because assets and claims on assets are simply added, total assets and total claims on assets are the sum of the individual component firms. Leverage measured by debt-to-equity at book values would remain unchanged. For the example in Table 3.2, the ratio of debt-to-equity for the component firms and for the combined firm is two-thirds or 67%.

In purchase accounting when stock is used, the result is shown in Table 3.3. The debt-to-equity ratio for the component firms is again two-thirds or 67%. In the consolidated firm, the debt-to-equity ratio is 240/840, which is 29%. Thus, in a purchase when stock is used as the medium of payment, the leverage ratio declines. The intuition behind this is that the net worth of the combined firm is increased by the actual market value of the purchase price of the target firm less the debt of the book net worth accounts of the target firm. As shown in Table 3.3, the difference between the purchase price of $600,000 and the credit of $80,000 to the common stock account is $520,000, which is added to the paid-in capital account increasing the net worth in the combined firm. This causes the debt-to-equity ratio to decline.

The Time Warner acquisition of the Turner Broadcasting System provides an example. On page 113 of the September 6, 1996 proxy statement issued by Time Warner in connection with the Turner acquisition, a pro forma consolidated balance sheet is presented. It shows that as a result of the transaction, goodwill was increased by $6.4

billion. The Turner shareholders' equity of $500 million was eliminated. Paid-in capital in the combined accounts was increased by $6.4 billion. As a result of the transaction, the shareholders' equity of Time Warner increased from $3.8 billion to $9.9 billion resulting from the large credit to the paid-in capital account to offset the debit of $6.4 billion to the goodwill account in the "New Time Warner" pro forma balance sheet of June 30, 1996.

If the method of payment in a purchase is cash, leverage is increased rather than decreased. This is shown in the simple example in Table 3.6. The acquiring firm has $25 excess cash. The debt-to-equity ratio of the acquirer was the debt (net of excess cash) of $25 divided by the $50 equity or 50%. It acquires for $25 a target firm with a net worth of $10. In the adjustments, the shareholders' equity of the target ($10) is eliminated. The cash used to make the transaction is credited. A debit of $15 is made either to depreciable assets or to a goodwill account. The new total assets are $110. The new debt-to-equity ratio is 60/50 which is 120%, a rise from 50%.

## DYNAMIC VERSUS STATIC EFFECTS OF POOLING VERSUS PURCHASE

The foregoing examples bring out the main differences between pooling versus purchase accounting. Our presentation compresses some details of financial accounting. But these minor technical differences are much less important than the more dynamic aspects of merger and acquisition transactions. Over a longer term the total earnings of the combined company should be greater than the sum of the parts. The purpose of combining the companies was to achieve improvements that the individual companies could not have achieved alone. If the merger was soundly conceived and effectively implemented, the combined cash flows should be greater than the simple sum of the constituent firms. Conversely, a combination that did not make sense from an economic standpoint or that was not implemented effectively could result in combined cash flows less than the sum for the individual companies.

In this longer-term perspective, even if an acquisition results in initial dilution in earnings per share for the stockholders of one of the companies, the merger still may make business and economic sense. The initial dilution can be regarded as an investment that will have a payoff in future years in the form of magnified cash flows for the combined company.

**TABLE 3.6**   Effect on Leverage of a Cash Purchase

|  | Acquirer | Target | Adjustments Debit | Adjustments Credit | Combined Firm |
|---|---|---|---|---|---|
| Excess cash | $ 25 | | | $25 | $ 0 |
| Other assets | 75 | $20 | | | 95 |
| Goodwill | | | $15 | | 15 |
| Total assets | $100 | $20 | | | $110 |
| Total debt | 50 | 10 | | | 60 |
| Shareholders' equity | 50 | 10 | 10 | | 50 |
| Total claims | $100 | $20 | $25 | $25 | $110 |

Other differences between purchase and pooling are more technical in nature. For example, in contrasting Canadian and U.S. financial reporting, FASB gives a case example (*Financial Accounting Series,* No. 144-B, December 1994, p. 18). During 1991 the Bema Gold Corporation (Bema) acquired 100% of Norgold Resources Inc. (Norgold) by a share exchange. The acquisition was treated as a purchase under Canadian GAAP. But because it was a stock-for-stock exchange and met other U.S. pooling criteria, it would have been treated as a pooling under U.S. GAAP. Two differences from purchase accounting were noted. Under pooling, Bema would have reported Norgold's operating loss for the entire year, rather than only from the date of acquisition. Also, Bema would have been required to expense the legal fees and other expenses of the acquisition. The additional expenses would have totaled C$328,867 (Canadian dollars), about a 10% difference.

# EMPIRICAL STUDIES OF EFFECTS OF POOLING VERSUS PURCHASE ON STOCK PRICES

The rules for accounting treatment of pooling versus purchase involve two significant dates. Before 1970, when Accounting Principles Board (APB) 16 was passed, companies had relatively complete freedom in their choice between pooling vs. purchase accounting. APB 16 required that 12 tests had to be met before pooling accounting could be used. The Omnibus Budget Reconciliation Act (OBRA) of 1993 provided that if an acquisition represented an asset purchase, goodwill could be amortized over 15 years and deductible for tax purposes. Because nontaxable transactions must represent stock-for-stock exchanges, they are likely to employ pooling accounting and no goodwill is recorded. Thus, OBRA appears to apply to combinations that are taxable. These are also likely to involve purchase accounting.

## Hong, Kaplan, Mandelker, 1978

The first empirical study of pooling versus purchase was by Hong, Kaplan, and Mandelker (HKM) (1978). They studied monthly price movements of 122 pooling and 37 purchase method combinations for the period 1954–1964. So these combinations occurred before the enactment of APB 16 in 1970. To be admitted into their sample the merger had to take place by an exchange of shares. This criterion excluded cash acquisitions, which even during that period were not accounted for as poolings. They observed that it also virtually ruled out taxable mergers (p. 35). All of the 122 pooling firms involved an acquisition price in excess of book value. Eighty percent of the acquisitions involved goodwill of 20% or more. Firms using purchase accounting reported higher depreciation and amortization charges and lower net income than pooling firms.

The stock prices of firms using the pooling method did not exhibit abnormal behavior over the 120 months centered on the effective date of the merger. For their small sample of 37 purchase firms, significantly positive abnormal returns were observed. But they all occurred during the 12 months preceding the effective date of the merger with a cumulative abnormal residual (CAR) of about 9%.

The results are surprising in that reported net income is likely to be higher under pooling than under purchase. The positive abnormal returns were especially strong in months −12 to −9 and −4 to the month in which the effective date of the merger took place. They observe that firms that chose the purchase method did so because their strong performance enabled them to "afford the lower earnings caused by the use of the purchase method." They noted also that pooling firms generally made larger acquisitions than the purchase firms.

The authors use the effective date of the merger as the "event around which the stock price returns were calculated." They also use monthly data. Subsequent studies have used daily data and an estimate of the announcement date. The data show a considerable runup in prices in the 5- to 10-day period before the announcement date and leakage runups beginning as much as 40 days before the event. So their use of the effective date of the merger was, on average, six to eight months after the announcement date used in subsequent studies. Nevertheless, they looked at CARs for 60 months before and after the effective date of the merger. They performed statistical tests on the CARs for 12 months before and after the effective date. Thus, in their tables and graphs of the monthly movements in the CARs, they were able to pick up what happened around the true announcement date even though they did not know when it actually occurred.

### Robinson and Shane, 1990

In January 1990 Robinson and Shane (RS) (pp. 25–48) investigated another dimension of the HKM study. Their sample consisted of 36 purchases and 59 poolings for the period 1972–1982 taken from the Compustat Industrial Research file. They analyzed the association between accounting method and bid premiums for target firms. They observe reasons why pooling may be preferred by management when a premium is paid. Management compensation may be based on accounting measures. They also mention their concern that stock prices might react negatively to lower reported net earnings. They also cite data that in a substantial number of acquisitions the proxy to shareholders states that the use of pooling was a condition of the merger.

The authors find that the mean bid premium in poolings was 64% and only 42% in purchases. The target CARs were 28% in poolings and 17% in purchases. They also examined the influence of other variables on the size of premium paid. These were liquidity, leverage, market to book ratios, relative size of the target to the bidder, and initial holdings, the first three industry adjusted.

They observe that poolings involve higher average bid premiums than acquisitions treated as purchases. Their explanation is that the higher bid premiums for mergers accounted for as poolings represent an additional amount that bidders are willing to pay for the advantages of that accounting method. They acknowledge that an equally plausible alternative is that when higher bid premiums are paid, the underlying real reasons may be associated with target characteristics.

### Davis, 1990

The Davis study (1990) represented a sample of 108 poolings and 69 purchase transactions during the period 1971–1982. He used weekly data. Purchase firms had statistically significant positive CARs for time segments between 26 weeks and the announcement date. The CARs were positive and significant for 11 days before the announcement period and for four days before the announcement period as well. For pooling firms, the CAR was positive and significant only for the full −26 days through the announcement date.

He considered whether other nonmerger-omitted variables might influence the results. He tested whether price-earnings ratios, firm size, earnings surprise, leverage, or preannouncement period estimates of alpha and beta might explain the difference in results for poolings versus purchase. Only leverage for the purchase method was significantly different (higher) than for the pooling method. He concludes that the larger the premium paid the more likely that pooling of interest accounting will be used. He observes that in pooling, the average premium paid was nearly three times that paid by the purchase firms.

### Davis, 1996

A summary of the literature is developed by Davis in a later article (1996). Davis begins by listing the proportion of poolings versus purchases since the passage of APB 16 in 1970. For the period 1970–1978, 68% of transactions were treated as purchases. After 1979, 91% of the transactions were treated as purchases. Davis summarizes the findings from the earlier studies of little market reaction to pooling mergers, but strong and statistically significant positive stock price movements for the purchases. He states that there is no evidence that companies with managerial compensation contracts tied to reported earnings are more likely to use pooling. He finds that the average premium over book value was about three times as large for pooling firms as for purchase firms. He concludes that the larger premiums represent what the firms are willing to pay to avoid using the purchase method. He suggests that the stock returns of pooling firms are lower because they pay extra to avoid using the purchase method.

But the explanation could well be that in the poolings the acquirer simply overpaid. Why they overpaid is another question. If they overpaid, the returns to the acquirers would be small or negative. Statistically it would be interesting to observe what the total value effects were. Because the surviving firm has positive gains in the purchase transactions, the total gains from the merger will be positive because the target always gains. For poolings, the returns to acquirers can be negative. Thus, the poolings sample should be divided between those with a total value increase (good mergers) and transactions with a total value decrease (unsound transactions).

Other studies show a positive relationship between the firm's value and either the acquisition premium or reported goodwill. Davis states, "In other words, as the acquisition premium or reported goodwill increases, the market value of the firm increases" (p. 57). This statement implies a causation. What is more likely is that the acquisition premium reflects the magnitude of positive contributions to value.

Davis also reviews studies of acquisitions by foreign firms. One found a positive relationship between size of premiums and the ability to avoid booking and amortizing goodwill. Another study found that when the country's laws permit a firm to deduct amortized goodwill for tax purposes, stock price returns are larger.

The article concludes by stating a puzzle. The data show that foreign firms, on average, pay higher premiums for U.S. firms than the size of premiums paid by U.S. firms in buying other U.S. firms. Why the higher premium? One possible explanation is that the U.K. firms do not have to write off the goodwill. Davis comments that it is foolish to overpay to avoid writing off goodwill. Cash flows are not affected and this is simply a change in accounting measurements.

His final conclusions can be briefly stated. First, the market does not reward firms for using pooling. Therefore, it is not rational for a firm to pay to use pooling. Second, both recorded and purchased goodwill are valued positively by the market treating them like other valuable assets such as plant and equipment.

In our judgment, what is really critical is whether the sum of bidder and target gains is positive. If so, the market judges this to be a good merger. If the sum is negative, it is a bad merger. Whether purchase or pooling is used is cosmetic. If goodwill is not tax deductible, cash flows will be the same, so market values and market returns will be the same. If goodwill is deductible for tax purposes, purchase accounting firms will benefit from the additional tax shield. Because their after-tax cash flows are higher, their values and market returns will be higher.

The earlier studies found that purchase firms had significantly higher market returns. One plausible explanation can be that there were higher returns to the acquiring firms in purchases, on average, because the bidders did not overpay. Our hypothesis is that in purchase accounting, on average, the sum of bidder and target returns would be positive. In pooling firms, either total value was reduced or the bidder paid too much.

### Further Research

Three motivations for further research can be stated. One, previous work could be replicated, but the sample data could be divided into transactions in which total value was increased and those in which total value was decreased.

Two, both of the papers published in 1990 cover data only to 1982. Merger activity really took off in 1983. It is possible that in the 1980s acquiring firms did not pay higher premiums to use pooling accounting. A possible confounding effect is that the defenses against takeovers increased by a substantial magnitude from 1983 on.

Three, because OBRA 1993 provided for tax deductibility for the goodwill write-off, we would predict that, in years after 1993, purchase accounting would be associated with higher returns to bidders than would the use of pooling accounting.

For points two and three, the dichotomy of value increasing and value decreasing transactions should be continued.

---

## Summary

The use of the purchase method in financial accounting results in lower reported net income. When the excess of the price paid over the target net worth is assigned to depreciable assets or to deductible amortization of goodwill, cash flows will be higher by the tax shelter effects of the increased depreciation or amortization of goodwill. When all of the excess paid in purchase accounting is assigned to goodwill whose amortization is not tax deductible, the cash flows are the same under both pooling and purchase accounting.

---

## Questions

3.1 Why is reported net income lower under purchase accounting than under pooling of interests accounting?

3.2 Are actual cash flows different in financial accounting for pooling versus purchase if the 40-year write-off period for nontax-deductible amortization of goodwill is used?

3.3 Why are cash flows higher under purchase accounting when the amortization of goodwill is deductible for tax purposes under the conditions of the 1993 law changes?

3.4 Summarize the literature review on the effects of pooling versus purchase on stock prices.

3.5 Rework Table 3.3 when the terms of the merger are 0.9 shares of the acquirer (A) for one share of target (T).

---------------------------------- C A S E   3–1 ----------------------------------

# AT&T's Acquisition of NCR

In 1991, after about six months of offers by AT&T and resistance by NCR, NCR agreed to be acquired for $7.5 billion in a stock-for-stock transaction. During the negotiations, the market value of AT&T stock declined by between $3.9 billion and $6.5 billion. The purchase price at $111 per share was regarded as a substantial overpayment. On November 7, 1990, the day before a *Wall Street Journal* article reported a rumor of AT&T's interest in acquiring NCR, NCR closed at $48 per share. When AT&T made its initial bid of $90 on December 3, 1990, NCR called the offer "grossly inadequate," but stated that it would "carefully consider a financially sound proposal."

AT&T paid a documented $50 million and possibly as much as $500 million to satisfy the requirements of pooling accounting. By using the pooling method, earnings per share were about 17% higher than under purchase accounting, but cash flows were unchanged. For further details, see the *Wall Street Journal,* December 3, 1990, "AT&T Makes Unsolicited $6.03 Billion Bid For NCR After Merger Discussion Stall" (also see Lys and Vincent, 1995).

---

## Questions on Case Study C3.1

C3.1.1  Why did AT&T persist in its efforts to acquire NCR for about six months and continue to raise its bid price when "the market" reaction predicted that it was an unsound acquisition with negative synergies?

C3.1.2  Why would AT&T go to extra expenses of over $50 million to use pooling accounting rather than purchase accounting even though the method of accounting had no effect on cash flows?

---------------------------------- C A S E   3–2 ----------------------------------

# Wells Fargo Acquisition of First Interstate Bancorporation

On October 17, 1995, Wells Fargo Bank (WF) made an unsolicited bid for the First Interstate Bancorporation (FIB), both operating mainly in California. First Interstate Bancorporation rejected the bid as inadequate. It solicited a second bidder (white knight), the First Bank System (FBS) of Minneapolis, Minnesota, with branches in that area. The wealth effects of the WF initial bid are shown in Part A.

| *Part A—Wells Fargo Initial Bid* | WF | FIB | FBS |
|---|---|---|---|
| 1.  10/3/95—Preannouncement (1) prices | $207 | $105 | $51 |
| 2.  Number of shares (millions) | 47 | 76 | 127 |
| 3.  Total market value (billions) (1 × 2) | $9.7 | $8.0 | $6.5 |
| 4a. 10/17/95—Initial WF offer | 0.625/FIB | | |
| 4b. Dollar value to FIB (1 × 4a) | | $129.375/sh | |
| 5.  After announcement prices | $229 | $140 | |
| 5a. Price change per share (5 − 1) | $22 | $35 | |
| 5b. Shareholder wealth effect (billions) (2 × 5a) | $1.03 | $2.66 | |
| 5c. New total market value (billions) (2 × 5) | $10.76 | $10.64 | |

The results of the white knight bid by FBS on 11/6/95 are shown in Part B.

| Part B—FBS Bid | WF | FIB | FBS |
|---|---|---|---|
| 6. 11/6/95—FBS merger agreement | | | 2.6/FIB |
| 6a. After announcement (2) prices | $211 | $127 | $51 |
| 6b. Implied dollar value of FIB | | FBS Offer: 2.6($51) = $132.60/sh | |
| 6c. WF counteroffer | | WF Offer: 0.625($211) = $131.88/sh | |

Further bids by WF are shown in Part C.

| Part C—WF Further Bids | WF | FIB | FBS |
|---|---|---|---|
| 7a. 11/6/95—WF raises offer to 0.65 | | 0.65($211) = $137.15/sh | |
| 7b. 11/13/95—WF raises offer to 0.667 | | 0.667($211) = $140.74/sh | |

On January 19, 1996 the SEC ruled that FBS could not use pooling accounting because its share repurchase program violated one of the conditions for use of pooling. The price effects are shown in Part D.

| Part D—SEC Rules that FBS Cannot Use Pooling | WF | FIB | FBS |
|---|---|---|---|
| 8. 1/19/96—SEC ruling | | | |
| 9. From 1/17/96 to 1/23/96—Stock price movements | $215 to $229 | $136.75 to $149.25 | $48.25 to $50.50 |

The wealth effects of WF's winning bid on 1/24/96 are shown in Part E.

| Part E—WF Winning Bid | WF | FIB | FBS |
|---|---|---|---|
| 10. 1/24/96—WF and FIB agree to merge | | | $51.75 |
| 10a. Value of FIB | | 0.667($229) = $152.74/sh | |
| 11. 1/24/96—Prices less initial prices | $229 − $207 = $22/sh | $149.25 − $105 = $44.25/sh | $51.75 − $51 = $0.75/sh |
| 12. Deflate by 6% rise in NASDAQ Bank stock index (10/3/95 to 1/24/96) | $229/1.06 = $216/sh | $149.25/1.06 = $140.80/sh | $51.75/1.06 = $48.82/sh |
| 12a. Price change based on deflated prices | $216 − $207 = $9/sh | $140.80 − $105 = $35.80/sh | $48.82 − $51 = −$2.18/sh |
| 13a. Wealth effect—nominal (millions) | 47($22)= $1,034 | 76($44.25) = $3,363 | 127($0.75) = $95.25 |
| 13b. Wealth effect—deflated (millions) | 47($9) = $423 | 76($35.80) = $2,720.8 | 127(−$2.18) = −$276.86 |

Wells Fargo estimated that they could save at least a billion dollars a year by combining overlapping offices. This was not possible for FBS because it was located in a different geographic area. One attraction of FIB was that its average interest cost on deposits in the first half of 1995 was 2.49% annualized, the lowest of 42 big regional banks. Wells Fargo's cost of funds was 3.14% and for FBS 3.71%. For FBS, the inexpensive deposits of FIB were especially attractive because FBS was "an aggressive lender hungry for funds" (Tom Petruno, "Suitors Covet First Interstate's Low-Cost Deposits," *Los Angeles Times*, November 10, 1995, pp. D1, D12).

The offers by both WF and FBS were exchanges of stock. In the attempt to make its stock exchange offer more attractive, FBS had embarked on an open market share repurchase program of 73 million shares. But FBS was planning to treat the acquisition as a pooling of interests transaction for financial accounting purposes. It was announced on January 20, 1996 that the SEC ruled that to qualify for a pooling accounting FBS could not buy back its own stock for two years (Saul Hansell, "S.E.C. Deals a Blow to First Bank's Bid for First Interstate," the *New York Times,* January 20, 1996, pp. 17, 31).

On January 25, 1996, it was announced that WF and FIB had agreed to merge on the terms described in the chronology above. Wells Fargo planned to use purchase accounting that involved a write-off of goodwill, reducing reported net income by $400 million per year. First Interstate Bancorporation had contracted to pay FBS a $200 million fee if their agreement was not consummated. In the early stages of counterbidding, WF sued to have this agreement declared illegal. After its merger agreement with FIB, WF paid the $200 million to FBS in two installments.

For additional background, see the *Wall Street Journal,* the *New York Times,* and the *Los Angeles Times* from October 3, 1995 to March 5, 1996 and the following journal articles:

Davis, Michael L, "The Purchase vs. Pooling Controversy: How the Stock Market Responds to Goodwill," *Journal of Applied Corporate Finance,* 9, Spring 1996, pp. 50–59.

Houston, Joel F., and Michael D. Ryngaert, "The Value Added by Bank Acquisitions: Lessons From Wells Fargo's Acquisition of First Interstate," *Journal of Applied Corporate Finance,* 9, 1996, pp. 74–82.

-------------------------------------------------------------------

## Questions on Case Study C3.2

C3.2.1   Why were greater savings available to WF as compared with FBS?

C3.2.2   Compare the two methods of accounting that FBS and WF planned to use.

C3.2.3   What were the wealth effects of the transaction and what are their implications?

-------------------------------------------------------------------

## References

Davis, Michael L., "Differential Market Reaction to Pooling and Purchase Methods," *The Accounting Review,* 65, July 1990, pp. 696–709.

———, "The Purchase vs. Pooling Controversy: How the Stock Market Responds to Goodwill," *Journal of Applied Corporate Finance,* 9, Spring 1996, pp. 50–59.

Financial Accounting Standards Board, "Financial Accounting Series," No. 172-A, April 22, 1997, "Status Report," No. 287, p. 3.

Gilson, Ronald J., and Bernard S. Black, *The Law and Finance of Corporate Acquisitions,* New York: The Foundation Press, Inc., 1995.

Hong, Hai, Robert S. Kaplan, and Gershon Mandelker, "Pooling vs. Purchase: The Effects of Accounting for Mergers on Stock Prices," *The Accounting Review,* 53, January 1978, pp. 31–47.

Lys, Thomas, and Linda Vincent, "An Analysis of Value Destruction in AT&T's Acquisition of NCR," *Journal of Financial Economics,* 39, 1995, pp. 353–378.

McDonald, Elizabeth, "Merger-Accounting Method Under Fire," *The Wall Street Journal,* April 15, 1997, pp. A2, A9.

Pahler, Arnold J., and Joseph E. Mori, *Advanced Accounting,* Fort Worth, TX: The Dryden Press, 1997.

Robinson, John R., and Philip B. Shane, "Acquisition Accounting Method and Bid Premia for Target Firms," *The Accounting Review,* 65, January 1990, pp. 25–48.

# 4

# Tax Planning Options

A considerable literature has been produced on the relationship between taxes and takeovers. This chapter provides a synthesis and assesses the results of the studies to date. The following topics are covered: taxable versus nontaxable or tax-deferred acquisitions, the Tax Reform Act of 1986, do tax gains cause acquisitions?, early empirical tests of tax effects, later empirical studies of tax effects, and taxes and LBOs.

## TAXABLE VERSUS NONTAXABLE
## OR TAX-DEFERRED ACQUISITIONS

The basic tax rule is simple. If the merger or tender offer involves the stock of one company for the stock of the other, it is a nontaxable transaction. If cash or debt is used, it is a taxable transaction. In practice, many complications exist.

The Internal Revenue Code makes a technical distinction between three types of "acquisitive tax-free reorganizations" defined in Section 368 of the code. The sections are referred to as types A, B, and C reorganizations. The type A reorganization is a statutory merger or consolidation. In a merger, target firm shareholders exchange their target stock for shares in the acquiring firm; in consolidations, both target and acquiring firm shareholders turn in their shares and receive stock in the newly created company.

Type B reorganizations are similarly stock-for-stock exchanges. Following a type B reorganization, the target may be liquidated into the acquiring firm or maintained as an independent operating entity.

Type C reorganizations are stock-for-asset transactions with the requirement that at least 80% of the fair market value of the target's property be acquired. Typically, the target firm "sells" its assets to the acquiring firm in exchange for acquiring firm voting stock; the target then dissolves, distributing the acquiring firm stock to its shareholders in return for their (now-canceled) target stock. In general, types A and B reorganizations use the pooling of interests method of accounting, while type C reorganizations use the purchase method.

In practice, a three-party acquisition technique is employed. The parent creates a shell subsidiary. The shell issues stock, all of which is bought by the parent with cash or its own stock. The target as the third party is bought with the cash or stock of the parent held by the subsidiary. The advantage of creating the subsidiary as an intermediary is that the parent acquires control of the target through the subsidiary without incurring separate liability for the debt of the target. The transaction still qualifies as an A reorganization. The target firm may remain in existence if the stock of the parent is used in the acquisition. Because the parent-acquirer shareholders are not directly involved, they are denied voting and appraisal rights in the transaction. In a reverse three-party merger, the subsidiary is merged into the target. The parent stock held by the subsidiary is distributed to the target's shareholders in exchange for their target stock. This is equivalent to a B reorganization.

The "tax-free" reorganization actually represents only tax deferral for the target firm shareholders. If the target shareholder subsequently sells the acquiring firm's stock received in the transaction, a capital gains tax becomes payable. The basis for the capital gains tax is the original basis of the target stock held by the target shareholder. If the former target shareholder dies without selling the acquiring firm's stock, the estate tax laws establish the tax basis as the value at time of death.

In Table 4.1, the main implications of nontaxable vs. taxable acquisitions are summarized. In a nontaxable (tax-deferred) reorganization, the acquiring firm can generally use the net operating loss (NOL) carryover and unused tax credits of the acquired firm. However, even though the value of the shares paid may be greater than the net book values of the assets acquired, no write-up or step-up of the depreciable values of the assets acquired can be made. For the shareholders of the target firm, taxes are deferred until the common shares received in the transaction are sold. Thus, the shareholders can defer the taxes. If the shares are held until death, a surviving spouse would be able to step up the tax basis of the shares to their value as of the date of death. However, if the spouse subsequently bequeaths these assets, their full value at her subsequent death would be subject to estate taxes, which start at almost 50% and rise rapidly. However, techniques can be used for deferring these taxes through several generations by various forms of "pass-through" trusts.

In taxable acquisitions, the acquiring firm may assign the excess of purchase price over the book value of equity acquired to depreciable assets, as described under purchase accounting. The acquiring firm, however, is unable to carry over the NOLs and tax credits. The shareholders of the target firm in a taxable acquisition must recognize the gain over their tax basis in the shares. If, in addition, the target firm has used accelerated depreciation, a portion of any gain that is attributable to excess depreciation deductions will be recaptured to be taxed as ordinary income rather than capital gains, the amount of recapture depending on the nature of the property involved.

# THE TAX REFORM ACT OF 1986

The Tax Reform Act of 1986 (TRA 1986) made many fundamental amendments to the prevailing 1954 code. It had a number of impacts on merger and acquisition transactions. (1) It severely restricted the use of net operating loss carryovers. (2) The preferential rate on corporate capital gains was repealed. (3) A minimum tax was imposed on corporate profits. (4) The General Utilities doctrine was repealed. (5) Greenmail payments could not be deducted.

## Net Operating Loss (NOL) Carryovers

The Tax Reform Act of 1986 provides that if there is greater than a 50% ownership change in a loss corporation within a three-year period, an annual limit on the use of NOLs will be imposed. The amount of an NOL that may be used to offset earnings is limited to the value of the loss corporation at the date of ownership change multiplied by the long-term tax-exempt bond rate. For example, assume a loss corporation is worth $10 million immediately before an ownership change, the tax-exempt bond rate is 7%, and the corporation has a $5 million loss carryforward. Then $700,000 ($10 million × 7%) of the NOL can be used annually to offset the acquiring firm's taxable income.

| | *Acquiring Firm* | *Target Firm* |
|---|---|---|
| A. Nontaxable reorganizations | NOL carryover  Tax-credit carryover  Carryover asset basis *(cant step up)* | Deferred gains for shareholders |
| B. Taxable acquisitions | Stepped-up asset basis  Loss of NOLs and tax credits | Immediate gain recognition by target shareholders *Capital gains*  Depreciation recapture of income |

**TABLE 4.1**   Nontaxable vs. Taxable M&As

In addition, a loss corporation may not utilize NOL carryovers unless it continues substantially the same business for two years after the change in ownership. If this requirement is not met, all of the losses generally are disallowed (Curtis, 1987).

### Corporate Capital Gains Tax

The corporate capital gains tax rate had been 28%. For taxable years beginning on or after July 1, 1987, long-term as well as short-term corporate capital gains are taxed as ordinary income subject to the maximum corporate tax rate of 34%. Because many individuals will be taxed at less than the top corporate rate of 34%, this could stimulate more acquisitions through master limited partnerships (MLPs) or through use of S corporations. The use of MLPs or S corporations enables profits to flow directly to the partners or to the S corporation shareholders. This achieves a lower tax rate and avoids double taxation on both earnings and dividends.

### Minimum Tax on Corporate Profits

Before the Tax Reform Act of 1986, a corporation paid a minimum tax on specific tax preferences in addition to its regular tax. The old add-on minimum tax is replaced by an alternative minimum tax with a flat rate of 20%. Thus, corporations pay taxes to at least 20% of their income above the exemption amount. This has a negative impact on leveraged buyouts and acquisitions of mature companies for which effective tax rates are below 20%.

### General Utilities Doctrine

Under the General Utilities case decided in the 1930s and incorporated in later code sections, corporations did not recognize gains when they sold assets in connection with a "complete liquidation" in the sense of legal technicalities. This required adoption of a plan of liquidation and sale with distribution of assets within a 12-month period. Distribution of assets in kind in liquidation also was not subject to tax. The provisions were repealed by the TRA of 1986. Most of the exemptions from the new rules are for relatively small and closely held corporations or provide for limited transitional periods (Wood, 1987).

### Greenmail

The Tax Reform Act of 1986 also limited the extent to which amounts paid as greenmail to corporate raiders could be deducted for tax purposes. This change and the others listed previously move in the direction of being less favorable to merger and acquisition activity.

## DO TAX GAINS CAUSE ACQUISITIONS?

Gilson, Scholes, and Wolfson (GSW) (1988) make the most comprehensive analysis of the possibility that acquisitions are fostered by the tax system. Another way of posing the issue is whether acquisitions represent the best method of achieving tax gains. They present a lengthy discussion of a number of possibilities. We will greatly compress their highly sophisticated analysis.

Gilson, Scholes, and Wolfson (1988) focus on three main types of tax gains from acquisitions under the pre-1986 tax code: increased leverage, net operating loss carryforwards (NOLs), and the basis increase on acquired assets. Leverage can be easily disposed of because there is no clear reason why a company cannot leverage itself without an acquisition, for example, by issuing debt and repurchasing stock.

Net operating losses could be utilized under perfect markets by issuing equity and buying taxable debt. The NOLs could be used to offset the taxable interest income. Gilson, Scholes, and Wolfson (1988) indicate that various types of transaction costs may prevent this simple utilization of NOLs but also inhibit acquisitions. Because some NOLs expire unused, this is evidence that the transaction costs of utilizing NOLs either by acquisitions or other transactions are substantial. Again, under perfect markets (no information costs and no transaction costs), a firm could sell assets and then buy them to achieve the basis step-up, or sale and leaseback transactions could be used. However, if acquisitions are motivated primarily by efficiency considerations, the basis step-up simply adds to the gains from acquisition. Thus, if the acquisition is efficiency improving, any subsidy involved in the tax gains may be socially efficient.

## EARLY EMPIRICAL TESTS OF TAX EFFECTS

Empirical studies of the effects of taxes on the merger decision were reported by Auerbach and Reishus in three related papers (1988a, 1988b, 1988c).

### NOLs and Tax Credits

Potential NOL benefits and tax credits are present in about one-fifth of the mergers studied. One-third of the NOL mergers had benefits in excess of 10% of the acquired firm's market value, representing about 6.5% of the total sample. Auerbach and Reishus conclude that NOLs and tax credits could have been important only in a small fraction of their sample.

### Basis Step-Up

The basis step-up benefits they found were smaller than the NOLs and tax credit benefits. Of the 275 firms studied, only seven produced gains from a basis step-up greater than 5% of the target firm's value. Of the 40 cases where the target also had unused credits and losses, the basis step-up was only 2%.

### Leverage

The authors looked at the debt ratio two years before a merger and two years after a merger to determine the company's long-run debt/equity ratio. Equity was defined as the year-end market value of common stock. Debt was calculated from the book value of long-term debt. Long-term debt as a percentage of debt plus equity increases from an average of 30 to 32%, a weighted increase of 25.4 to 26.7%. These changes in the sample are not statistically significant.

The combined debt ratios of merged firms with a target market value between 25 and 50% of the parent's was unchanged at 39% and experienced a decrease in the weighted debt ratio from 40.4 to 38.3%. With an acquired firm's market value greater than 50% of the parent's, the debt market value ratio increased from 30.0 to 35.4%, unweighted, and from 32.1 to 35.3%, weighted.

The main implication of the Auerbach-Reishus studies is that tax factors, mainly NOLs and tax credits, could have had a significant effect on takeovers in only a small percentage (6.5%) of their total samples. This is consistent with individual case studies in which major tax considerations appear to be involved, but not the main motivation for mergers or takeovers (Ginsburg, 1983, 1988).

In his comment on the Auerbach and Reishus paper, Poterba (1988) observes that the presence of NOLs may signal a number of things. Among others it indicates that a firm with accumulated losses has probably experienced business problems. This may reflect inefficient management. In addition, Poterba observes that NOL companies "have typically faced tight cash flow constraints in the recent past, and they may have postponed high-return investment projects because of this" (p. 186). Thus, the presence and size of NOLs may have less significance for the tax influence than for other real business effects. If so, the statistical studies using NOLs may overstate the role of taxes.

## LATER EMPIRICAL STUDIES OF TAX EFFECTS

Carla Hayn (1989) developed evidence on the role of tax factors versus nontax factors in different types of mergers and acquisitions. Her sample was 640 target firms. By tax status, 54% were taxable and the remaining 46% were either tax-free or partially taxable, which she states were essentially tax-free also. Most of the tax-free acquisitions were mergers in which the method of payment was common stock (pooling likely). Most of the taxable acquisitions were tender offers in which cash is the method of payment (purchase accounting is likely). Note that more than 50% of the transactions were taxable, so taxes could not be the main motive for takeovers.

Table 4.2 presents the announcement period returns. For target firms, taxable acquisitions result in abnormal returns about 10 percentage points higher than tax-free acquisitions. So, a tax influence is supported. Within a tax status group, returns for tender offers are 5 to 8 percentage points higher than for mergers. This indicates that other influences are also operating such as whether the method of payment is cash or stock.

**TABLE 4.2**   Cumulative Abnormal Returns in 640 Successful Acquisitions, 1970–1985 (measured during the period –9 to +5 relative to the announcement date)

| | CUMULATIVE ABNORMAL RETURNS (%) | | | |
| | *Taxable* | | *Tax-Free* | |
| | *Tender Offers* | *Mergers* | *Tender Offers* | *Mergers* |
|---|---|---|---|---|
| Target firms | 31.1 | 23.4 | 19.2 | 15.2 |
| Acquiring firms | 3.5 | 2.9 | 3.4 | 1.7* |

*Significant at 10% level; all others significant at 5% level.

*Source:* Hayn, 1989, p. 138.

Returns to acquiring firms follow the same patterns as for target firms except that the magnitude of the abnormal returns are about 10% of the abnormal returns to the target firms. Some studies show that acquiring firms are 10 times larger, on average, than target firms. This would imply that the *absolute* magnitude of positive returns from the transactions are about equally divided between target and bidder firms.

Hayn also presented data on the materiality of tax effects. The NOLs in tax-free transactions represented about 3 to 5% of target equity values and about 1 to 2% of acquiring firm equity values. The magnitude of step-up and capital gains variables in taxable transactions could be as high as 24% for targets and 4 to 6% for acquiring firms. So, these tax benefits had a substantial potential for an impact on the premiums observed in takeovers.

In the regression studies, Hayn also included some nontax variables that other studies had found to influence announcement period returns. She found that the relative size of bidder and target, type of acquisition (tender or merger), and resistance by management all had significant and positive influences on announcement period returns. This demonstrated that the tax variables alone did not fully explain the size of premiums paid in an acquisition or the magnitude of the price changes that took place around the announcement date of the tender offer or merger.

Hayn also studied another possible measure of tax effects. In January 1986 the IRS passed a regulation that would have retroactively abolished the tax benefit of a step-up in purchases. This ruling was repealed by the IRS in April 1986. Hayn studied the impact on acquisition transactions of the new regulation and its repeal. Her analysis suggested a tax impact on acquisitions.

Hayn's conclusions are similar to those in previous studies. Tax benefits do have an influence on tender offer and merger transactions, but the magnitude of the influence does not explain the size of premiums that are paid nor is it likely that taxes generally are the motivating force behind acquisition decisions.

## TAXES AND LBOs

Kaplan (1989) found that tax benefits can influence the gains and premiums paid in management buyouts (MBOs). The tax savings had an upper bound of 143% and a lower bound of 21% of the premium. This calculation was based on potential gains to a sample of 76 MBOs from 1980 to 1986. The actual tax paying experiences of 48 of these substantiate the findings. The gains were mainly (130% of premium upper bound) from increased leverage. However, Kaplan did not address the critique of GSW (1988) that takeovers (or MBOs) were not necessary to achieve leverage-induced tax savings.

Furthermore, there are more dimensions to the analysis. Jensen, Kaplan, and Stiglin (1989) considered a broader range of effects on LBOs on tax revenues of the U.S. Treasury. They listed five sources of incremental tax revenues. First, capital gains taxes are paid on the realized capital gains of shareholders. Second, the LBO may sell off assets, realizing taxable capital gains. Third, the interest income from the LBO debt payments is subject to tax. Fourth, the LBO increases operating income, which gives rise to incremental taxes. Fifth, by using capital more efficiently additional taxable revenues are generated in the economy. The negative effects are the increased tax deductions from the additional debt and the lower tax revenues because LBOs pay little or no dividends.

Jensen, Kaplan, and Stiglin (1989) drew on the data in Kaplan (1989), which covered 48 of the 76 LBOs greater than $50 million announced during the years 1979 to 1985. They developed the tax revenue implications of the average LBO based on Kaplan's study. They concluded that, on average, LBOs generated tax increases that were almost 200% of the tax losses they created. They estimated that the average LBO involved a purchase of $500 million, which generated $227 million in present value (using a 10% discount factor) of tax revenue increases versus $117 million in present value of tax losses to the treasury.

They made similar estimates for the RJR-Nabisco leveraged buyout. They estimated that in present value terms the increased revenue to the treasury was $3.76 billion. They observed that these payments were more than eight times the $370 million in federal taxes paid by RJR-Nabisco in 1987 (Jensen, Kaplan, and Stiglin, 1989, p. 733). A *Fortune* magazine article (Newport, 1988) obtained similar results from their analysis of the tax effects of LBOs.

## Summary

Tax considerations affect the planning and structuring of corporate combinations. Even in M&As undertaken for other motives, transactions are structured to maximize tax benefits while complying with internal revenue code regulations. In some individual instances, the tax benefits may have been substantial and have had a major impact. Unfavorable tax rulings by the IRS have also led to the abandonment of some proposed M&As. But tax effects are not the dominant influence in merger and acquisition decisions.

In LBOs, taxes could have a significant influence resulting from the higher leverage employed. But such leverage increases could also have been accomplished without LBOs. Furthermore, LBOs reduce leverage from cash flows and from subsequent public offerings of equity. As will be shown in chapter 13 on LBOs, leverage is used as a device to increase the ownership position and to motivate key managers.

In addition, when broader aspects of the tax effects of LBOs are taken into account, the tax benefits appear to go to the U.S. Treasury. Studies of LBOs also demonstrate that there are always important elements of a "business turnaround" informing the LBO. Empirical studies of LBOs demonstrate substantial improvements in operating performance. The lasting gains from LBOs result from improving performance rather than from tax benefits alone.

## Questions

4.1 How can personal taxation affect mergers?

4.2 Discuss the advantages and disadvantages of stock-for-stock versus cash-for-stock transactions from the viewpoint of acquired and acquiring firm shareholders.

4.3 How do a firm's growth prospects affect its potential for being involved in a tax-motivated merger?

------------------------------------------------------------------------

## References

Auerbach, A. J., and D. Reishus, "Taxes and the Merger Decision," Chapter 19 in J. C. Coffee, Jr., L. Lowenstein, and S. Rose-Ackerman, eds., *Knights, Raiders, and Targets,* New York: Oxford University Press, 1988a, pp. 300–313.

_____, "The Impact of Taxation on Mergers and Acquisitions," Chapter 4 in A. J. Auerbach, ed., *Mergers & Acquisitions,* Chicago: University of Chicago Press, 1988b, pp. 69–85.

_____, "The Effects of Taxation on the Merger Decision," Chapter 6 in A. J. Auerbach, ed., *Corporate Takeovers: Causes and Consequences,* Chicago: University of Chicago Press, 1988c, pp. 157–183.

Curtis, M. R., "Tempered Benefits on NOLs and Capital Gains," *Mergers & Acquisitions,* 21, January/February 1987, pp. 48–49.

Gilson, R. J., M. S. Scholes, and M. A. Wolfson, "Taxation and the Dynamics of Corporate Control: The Uncertain Case for Tax-Motivated Acquisitions," Chapter 18 in J. C. Coffee, Jr., L. Lowenstein, and S. Rose-Ackerman, eds., *Knights, Raiders, and Targets,* New York: Oxford University Press, 1988, pp. 271–299.

Ginsburg, M. D., "Taxing Corporate Acquisitions," *Tax Law Review,* 38, 1983, pp. 177–319.

_____, "Comment," Chapter 24 in J. C. Coffee, Jr., L. Lowenstein, and S. Rose-Ackerman, eds., *Knights, Raiders, and Targets,* New York: Oxford University Press, 1988, pp. 366–367.

Hayn, C., "Tax Attributes as Determinants of Shareholder Gains in Corporate Acquisitions," *Journal of Financial Economics,* 23, 1989, pp. 121–153.

Jensen, M., S. Kaplan, and L. Stiglin, "The Effects of LBO's on Tax Revenues," *Tax Notes,* February 6, 1989, pp. 727–733.

Kaplan, S., "Management Buyouts: Evidence on Taxes as a Source of Value," *Journal of Finance,* 44, July 1989, pp. 611–632.

Newport, J. P., Jr., "Why the IRS Might Love Those LBOs," *Fortune,* December 5, 1988, pp. 145–152.

Poterba, J. M., "Comment on Auerbach and Reishus, The Effects of Taxation on the Merger Decision," Chapter 6 in A. J. Auerbach, ed., *Corporate Takeovers: Causes and Consequences,* Chicago: University of Chicago Press, 1988, pp. 183–187.

Wood, R. W., "General Utilities Repeal: Injecting New Levies Into M&A," *Mergers & Acquisitions,* 21, January/February 1987, pp. 44–47.

C H A P T E R

# 5

# Theories of Mergers and Tender Offers

Almost every week the *Wall Street Journal, Business Week,* and other financial publications report major merger and takeover events. Some are alarmed by all this activity. Others see resources being redeployed to their highest value uses. This chapter explains the reasons for merger and takeover activity.

## ORGANIZATION LEARNING AND ORGANIZATION CAPITAL

With the purpose of explaining theories of mergers, we first examine the concept of **organization capital.** Second, a model of the firm with organization capital as a factor of production is presented, in which the firm may earn economic rents from its organization capital (or positive economic profits) under competition. **Investment opportunities** are defined in this context and mergers are hypothesized to represent a process of reallocating resources across activities or industries in the firms' efforts to internalize investment opportunities, that is, to earn rents from their organization capital.

Organization capital is accumulated through experience within an organization called a firm. To avoid any confusion that may exist in the literature on the concept and role of organization capital and to sharpen the theoretical exposition, we introduce a separate concept that we call **organization learning** and define it as improvement in the skills and abilities of individual employees through learning by experience within the firm.

We distinguish three types of organization learning. Rosen (1972), in explaining what could constitute "production knowledge," suggested that one case of learning is in the area of entrepreneurial or managerial ability to organize and maintain complex production processes economically. A useful dichotomy of this managerial learning is between general and industry-specific experiences. The first form of organization learning may be termed raw managerial experience, which refers to the capabilities developed in generic management functions of planning, organizing, directing, controlling, and so on, as well as in financial planning and control.[1] The second form consists of industry-specific managerial experience, which refers to the development of capabili-

---

[1]While finance is a specific management function, its role in the generic functions of planning and control and the broad generality of its applications suggest its treatment as a general management function as well.

ties in specific management functions related to the characteristics of production and marketing in particular industries. The third type of organization learning is in the area of nonmanagerial labor input. The level of skills of the production workers will improve over time through learning by experience.

The stock of organization learning in the three areas—generic managerial, industry specific, and nonmanagerial—has no significance by itself in the theory of the firm. This is because we identify organization learning with improvements in individual ability through experience in the firm, and each individual thus will be free to move to another firm. Organization learning becomes significant, however, when it is combined with firm-specific information or organization capital and thus *cannot be transferred freely to other firms through the labor market.*

The most detailed discussion of organization capital has been provided by Rosen (1972) and by Prescott and Visscher (1980). The first type of organization capital is firm-specific information embodied in individual employees and is called **employee-embodied information.** This information is obtained when employees become familiar with the firm's particular production arrangements, management and control systems, and other employees' skills, knowledgeability, and job duties in the firm.

The second and third types of organization capital may be termed **team effects.** That is, the role of information here is to allow the firm to organize efficient managerial and production teams within the firm. The second type consists of information on employee characteristics, allowing an efficient match between workers and tasks to the extent that some tasks are better fulfilled by particular talents and skills. In the formulation of Prescott and Visscher, new employees are initially assigned to a screening job that can be performed equally well by workers with different talents. After information on characteristics is obtained, workers are assigned to jobs that can be better implemented by workers with particular characteristics. The precision of the information will depend on the length of time that workers spend on the screening job.

The third type of information is used in the matching of workers to workers, because how well the characteristics of an individual mesh with those of others performing related duties is important to the overall performance of the team.

The types of information that we have included in organization capital are likely to be firm specific. Information on workers that gives rise to team effects may be better known to the firm's owners (managers) than to the workers themselves. It would be transferred to other firms only with difficulty and subject to transactions costs. Employee-embodied information is firm specific by definition, because it is information on workers and systems that are components of the firm.

To an extent, organization capital is a joint product that does not involve extra costs in production. Greater investment and production activity in one period will therefore lead to a greater amount of organization capital in the next period. However, because it can be preserved in the firm into the future and its value in future production will be positive, it is in the firm's interest to produce the firm-specific assets at its own cost. For example, new employees often receive on-the-job training that is specialized to the firm. Also, management spends real resources to organize efficient production and managerial teams. However organization capital is obtained, the important point is that it increases and accumulates within the firm over time, at least until its depreciation becomes fast enough, if it ever does, to offset the additions.

The concepts used to this point are summarized in Table 5.1, which lists the elements of organization learning and organization capital. This provides a framework for discussing the combination of organization learning and organization capital that follows.

| **TABLE 5.1**   Organization Learning and Organization Capital |
|---|

   I. *Organization learning*—Improvement in skills and abilities through learning within firm
      A. Generic managerial
      B. Industry-specific managerial
      C. Nonmanagerial
  II. *Organizational capital*—Firm-specific informational assets
      A. Employee-embodied
      B. Match between worker and job (team effect)
      C. Match between worker and other workers (team effect)
 III. *Combination of organization learning and organization capital*
      A. Generic managerial capabilities ($C_1$)
      B. Industry-specific managerial capabilities ($C_2$)
      C. Firm-specific nonmanagerial human capital ($C_3$)
 IV. *Transfer through mergers*
      A. $C_1$ = Transferable to most other industries
      B. $C_2$ = Transferable only to related industries
      C. $C_3$ = Difficult to transfer even to other firms in the same industry

The final human capital resources available to the firm as inputs for production are the output resulting from the combination of organization learning and organization capital. The first of these human capital resources may be termed **generic managerial capabilities** to represent the combination of organization learning in the generic managerial functions and the relevant organization capital. The second is called **industry-specific managerial capabilities.** Finally, the third includes all others and can be called **nonmanagerial human capital.**

Given that the three types of human resources are specialized to the firm to some extent, we need to examine the implications and degrees of their specificity. The jobs of nonmanagerial production workers are specified according to the details of the production facility. Once a team of workers is organized with each worker assigned to a different job based on specific information on their characteristics, the team is specialized to the facility. Therefore, it is specialized to the firm's production establishment or can at best be transferred to a similar establishment. A merger between firms even in related industries will therefore not include the transfer of nonmanagerial human capital between the firms. Its transfer between firms is only feasible in horizontal mergers.

The industry-specific managerial capabilities can be transferred to other firms in related industries without impairing the team effect, as they are not identified with a particular establishment. The requirement that managers should be transferred as a team is met by a merger initiated to carry over industry-specific managerial capabilities. The team-effect portion of organization capital will be preserved through a merger, although the other type of organization capital (that is, employee-embodied firm-specific information) has to be reacquired for the new setting of the acquired or combined firm. Mergers between firms therefore are more efficient than the movements through the labor market of individual managers in transferring these capabilities. Mergers thus cause the supply of managerial capabilities in the market to be more elastic.

The generic managerial capabilities can, of course, be carried over through a merger with a firm even in an unrelated industry. Again, to the extent that team effects are important, a merger which can preserve these effects is more efficient than inter-firm movements of managers as individuals. However, there are reasons to believe that invoking a merger to acquire or to carry over generic managerial resources will not be as compelling as in the case of industry-specific resources. First, the team size to produce generic managerial service is in general smaller than that for managerial resources related to production and marketing. Thus, the organization of a managerial team for control, coordination, and planning requires less time than the organization of a team for other managerial capabilities. Second, information on top-level managers who perform the control and coordination functions may be more public than on lower-level managers for the production and marketing functions. This also makes team organization more expedient. Third, managers for generic functions can come from even remotely related industries, whereas managers in specific function areas should have experience in closely related industries. Thus, the supply of the former type of managers is more elastic than that of the latter. Assuming that these are empirically valid observations, the case for a merger for the purpose of transferring generic managerial resources would seem weaker than for the transfer of industry-specific resources.

### Investment Opportunities

Investment (or growth) opportunities exist for a firm if the present value of an investment project is positive. Given this definition, a value-maximizing firm will attempt to internalize whatever investment opportunities it can find. The literature has not been clear, however, on what factors in general give rise to investment opportunities in competitive industries. Miller and Modigliani (1961, p. 416) gave only a cursory hint:

> [Investment] opportunities, frequently termed the "good will" of the business, may arise, in practice, from any of a number of circumstances (ranging all the way from special locational advantages to patents or other monopolistic advantages).

Further insights on the nature of investment opportunities can be provided by treating organization capital as a factor of production, as in Rosen (1972). Recall that organization capital is defined as firm-specific informational assets. Then we can envisage a simple production process having organization capital and investments as the only two input variables.

Given the short-run fixity of organization capital as a factor of production and the elastic supply of capital, any adjustment in the output quantity occurs by changing the amount of capital investments. But in general as investments are increased, output is increased only at a decreasing rate. That is, investments are subject to diminishing returns in the short run.

## MODELS OF THE TAKEOVER PROCESS

Many factors can potentially influence the structure of formal models of the merger and takeover processes. These are listed in Table 5.2.

An infinite number of models could be constructed by selecting alternative combinations of the variables or assumptions in Table 5.2. We illustrate the kinds of models that can be constructed, but we cover only a small sample of the models published and described in working papers. We have selected those aspects of models that can most readily be communicated to nonspecialists in the literature of bargaining, games, and auctions. Other aspects are so technical that their study is most appropriate in courses and writings for specialized study of such subjects.

| **TABLE 5.2**   Variables in Models of the Merger and Takeover Processes |
| --- |

1. Choice of model: (a) microeconomics—competition or market power; (b) bargaining; (c) game theory; (d) auctions.
2. Form of auction: English, Dutch, or other.
3. Form of game.
4. Bargaining: (a) Does it take place?; (b) If so, what forms or types?
5. Form of equilibrium: pooling, separating, sequential?
6. Incentives of shareholders, managers, and bidders.
7. Friendly (merger) or unfriendly (tender).
8. Form of tender: (a) unconditional bid for any and all shares; (b) conditional bid on acquiring a specified number, percentage, or control.
9. Form of two-part bids: (a) front- and back-end bids revealed in bid; (b) only front end revealed; (c) competition from multiple bidders.
10. Degree to which bids provide information or signal to shareholders, managers, and bidders.
11. Atomistic versus finite shareholders.
12. If finite shareholders, how did they acquire their position?
13. Kinds and amounts of transactions costs in multiple or successive bids.
14. Investigation costs of first bidder and subsequent bidders.
15. Legislative, regulatory, and other rules of the game as they affect transactions, investigation, and other aspects of bargaining, games, or auctions.
16. Degree of synergy between target and bidder and potential bidders.
17. Reservation values of target and explanations of how established.
18. Degree to which target could restructure without another firm.
19. Amount, kinds, and values of information provided by target to some or all bidders.
20. Private information of target about its value; private information of bidder on the profitability of takeover.
21. Effects of taxes on the forms of transactions included in the models.
22. Effects of costs of investigation on actions of bidders.
23. Disadvantages or advantages to target and bidders of eliminating some bidders, and circumstances under which elimination can be accomplished, if ever.
24. Influence of method of financing: cash, securities. If securities, what forms of debt and equity, and combinations, are used.
25. Degree to which prices paid incorporate earn-outs and bonuses.

# FREE-RIDER PROBLEM, INITIAL SHAREHOLDING, AND THE EQUILIBRIUM BID

In a diffusely held corporation, it may not pay a small shareholder to make expenditures on monitoring the performance of its management. The reason for this is that shareholders could simply free-ride on the monitoring efforts of other shareholders and share in the resulting improvements of the firm's performance.

Grossman and Hart (1980) argue that this free-rider problem also reduces the incentives of outsiders without any shareholdings to be engaged in a costly takeover of the diffusely held firm in order to improve its performance. The small ("atomistic") shareholders will not accept any offer price below the new revised price that should obtain as a result of the improvement. They reason that their individual decision to accept or reject the tender offer does not affect the success of the offer and that, if the offer succeeds, they will fully share in the improvement brought about by the takeover.

One solution to the free-rider problem is to allow the bidder to dilute the value of the remaining, nontendered shares of the target firm after takeover. The dilution could be allowed explicitly by limiting the rights of minority shareholders through a corporate charter amendment (Grossman and Hart, 1980). Or the bidder might be able to effect dilution by supplying overpriced inputs to the target or buying underpriced products or other assets from the target. The anticipated dilution induces shareholders to tender their shares at a price below that reflecting the post-takeover improvements. The bidder will be able to profit from the takeover if dilution is possible.

Another method used to avoid the free-rider problem and theoretically equivalent to dilution is to announce a two-tier offer. In such an offer, the bidder will buy target shares up to a certain percentage of the firm at a first-tier price and, after the takeover, the remaining shares at a lower, second-tier price (for a follow-up merger). The second tier price will be lower than the value of the target shares under the anticipated improvements so that the takeover will be profitable for the bidder. However, the average price paid may represent a division (equitable) of the improvement in value that conceivably might have been contained in a single price offer were it not for the free-rider problem.

In a study critical of the atomistic-stockholder models that emphasize the free-rider problem, Bagnoli and Lipman (1988) argue that when there are finitely many stockholders, the bidder can overcome the free-rider problem. They show that when there is a finite number of stockholders, some stockholders must be pivotal in the sense that they do recognize that they may affect the outcome of the bid. In their model, making some stockholders pivotal is crucial because it forces them to choose whether or not the bid succeeds. Hence, they cannot free-ride, so exclusionary devices such as dilution and two-tier offers are not necessary for successful takeovers.

A third way of avoiding the free-rider problem, which does not require dilution, is for a large shareholder (or an outsider after "secretly" accumulating a large fraction of the equity) to make a tender offer. This is the subject of the analysis by Shleifer and Vishny (1986), Hirshleifer and Titman (1990), and Chowdhry and Jegadeesh (1994).

## A FRAMEWORK

In addition to the broad models discussed in the previous sections, many individual theories or explanations for mergers and takeovers have been formulated. They can be summarized into three major categories as shown by Table 5.3 (Berkovitch and Narayanan (BN), 1993). The first column of Table 5.3 lists the three major motives for mergers and takeovers on the basis of whether value changes are positive, zero, or negative. The value changes refer to movements in the prices of the securities of companies as a result of mergers, takeovers, divestitures, spin-offs, share repurchases, or other significant developments affecting the outlook for a firm. The gains can be measured as percentage returns or in absolute dollar amounts. How these "event returns" are measured is described in Appendix A to this chapter.

Total gains can be positive because of efficiency improvements, synergy, or increased market power. The hubris theory (Roll, 1986) postulates that total gains are zero and that acquiring firms overpay. Total gains are negative as the result of agency problems or mistakes. When agency factors motivate an acquisition or merger, managers take the action in their own self-interest even to the detriment of the company.

**TABLE 5.3**   Pattern of Gains Related to Takeover Theories

|  | *(1)*<br>Total Gains | *(2)*<br>Gains to<br>Target | *(3)*<br>Gains to<br>Acquirer |
|---|---|---|---|
| I.   Efficiency or synergy | + | + | + |
| II.   Hubris (winner's curse, overpay) | 0 | + | − |
| III.   Agency problems or mistakes | − | + | − |

By definition, then, total gains are positive for synergy, zero for hubris, and negative for agency problems. Column 2 of Table 5.3 lists gains to targets. All empirical studies show positive gains for groups of targets. For each of the three categories of theories, the entry would be a plus. We next consider the gains to the acquirer. With synergy or efficiency, the total gains from the merger are positive. If the value increases are shared to any degree, the gains to both the target and the bidder would be positive. Of course, when the total gains are positive, it is possible that the premium paid by the bidder could be greater than the total gains, resulting in negative gains to the bidder. But overpaying puts us in the second category of hubris in which gains to targets are positive but the gains to bidders are negative. In the third category of agency problems or mistakes, total gains are negative. Because gains to targets are positive, the returns to the acquirer or bidding firm would necessarily be negative.

Table 5.3 provides a beginning framework for analyzing the reasons for mergers and takeovers. It centers attention on the very important issue of whether the total gains are positive, negative, or negligible. But some redistribution elements are not encompassed by it. A full overview of theories of M&As is presented in Table 5.4.

## SOURCES OF VALUE INCREASES FROM M&AS

We shall discuss each of the four major sections of Table 5.4. We begin with the sources of total value increases.

**TABLE 5.4**   Theories of M&As

I.  Total value increased
   1. Efficiency increases
   2. Operating synergy
   3. Diversification
   4. Financial synergy
   5. Strategic realignments
   6. The q-ratio
   7. Information
   8. Signaling
II.  Hubris—acquirer overpays for target
III.  Agency—managers make value-decreasing mergers to increase size of firm
IV.  Redistribution
   1. Taxes—redistribution from government
   2. Market power—redistribution from consumers
   3. Redistribution from bondholders
   4. Labor—wage adjustments
   5. Pension reversions

### Efficiency Increases

Efficiency improvements can result from combining firms of unequal managerial capabilities. A relatively efficient bidder may acquire a relatively inefficient target. Value can be increased by improving the efficiency of the target. Or the bidder may seek a merger with a target firm because the management of the target firm can improve the efficiency of the bidder. The target firm may have relatively better growth opportunities than the bidder or vice versa. Sometimes the combination will achieve a more efficient critical size mass. The investments in expensive specialized machinery may be large. Combining firms may achieve better utilization of large fixed investments. Plants that have old or inefficient-sized equipment may be shut down after the merger.

### Operating Synergy

The theory based on operating synergy assumes that economies of scale do exist in the industry and that prior to the merger, the firms are operating at levels of activity that fall short of achieving the potentials for economies of scale. Economies of scale arise because of indivisibilities, such as people, equipment, and overhead, which provide increasing returns if spread over a large number of units of output. Thus, in manufacturing operations, heavy investments in plant and equipment typically produce such economies. For example, costly machinery such as the large presses used to produce automobile bodies requires optimal utilization. The research and development departments of chemical and pharmaceutical companies often must have a large staff of highly competent scientists who, if given the opportunity, could develop and oversee a larger number of product areas. In marketing, having one organization cover the entire United States may yield economies of scale because of the increase in the ratio of calling-on-customer time to traveling time, which in turn is due to the higher density of customers who can be called on by the same number of salespeople.

One potential problem in merging firms with existing organizations is the question of how to combine and coordinate the good parts of the organizations and eliminate what is not required. Often the merger announcement will say that firm A is strong in research and development but weak in marketing, while firm B is strong in marketing but weak in research and development, and the two firms combined will complement each other. Analytically, this implies underutilization of some existing factors and inadequate investment in other factors of production. (Because the economies are jointly achieved, the assignment of the contributions of each firm to the merger is difficult both in theory and in practice.)

Managerial economies in production, research, marketing, or finance are sometimes referred to as economies in the specific management functions. It has also been suggested that economies may be achieved in generic management activity such as the planning and control functions of the firm. It is argued that firms of even moderate size need at least a minimum number of corporate officers. The corporate staff with capabilities for planning and control is therefore assumed to be underutilized to some degree. Acquisitions of firms just approaching the size where they need to add corporate staff would provide for fuller utilization of the corporate staff of the acquiring firm and avoid the necessity of adding such staff for the other firm.

Another area in which operating economies may be achieved is in vertical integration. Combining firms at different stages of an industry may achieve more efficient coordination of the different levels. The argument here is that costs of communication and various forms of bargaining can be avoided by vertical integration (Arrow, 1975; Klein, Crawford, and Alchian, 1978; Williamson, 1975).

Economies of scope are another form of operating synergy. Because a firm has developed capabilities to produce some products, this capability can be extended to related products. For example, a pharmaceutical company that is producing antibiotics has the experience to do research, production, and marketing of related drug products that use the same or similar facilities.

## Diversification Motives

Diversification may be sought by managers and other employees for preservation of organizational and reputational capital and for financial and tax advantages.

First, in contrast to the position of shareholders who can diversify across firms in the capital market, employees of the firm have only a limited opportunity to diversify their labor income sources. In general, employees need to make firm-specific investments. Most of their knowledge acquired while working for the firm may be valuable to the firm but not to others. Typically employees are more productive in their current job than in other firms because of their specialized knowledge. They are compensated for these firm-specific investments. Thus, they value stability in their job and greater opportunity to acquire specialized knowledge and to get higher pay. This latter opportunity normally comes with promotion in the firm. Diversification of the firm can provide managers and other employees with job security and opportunities for promotion and, other things being equal, results in lower labor costs.

This diversification argument also applies to an owner-manager whose wealth is concentrated in his or her firm. The owner-manager may not want to sell ownership shares in the firm for reasons of corporate control. An undiversified owner will require a higher risk premium in investments and make smaller investments than otherwise optimal (Fama and Jensen, 1985). Thus, diversification at the firm level (that is, diversification of the firm itself) is valuable for such an owner-manager or, in general, for shareholders who hold a controlling interest and are undiversified.

Second, in the modern theory of the firm, information on employees is accumulated within the firm over time. This information is firm specific to the extent that its transfer to outside firms or the market is not feasible or is done with difficulty. The information is used for efficient matching of employees and jobs or of employees themselves for a particular job. This implies that managerial and other teams are formed in the firm. When a firm is liquidated, these teams are destroyed and the value of the organization is lost. If the firm is diversified, these teams can be transferred from unprofitable business activities to growing and profitable activities. Diversification may ensure smooth and efficient transition of the firm's activities and the continuity of the teams and the organization.

Third, firms have reputational capital that customers, suppliers, and employees utilize in establishing their relationships with the firm. Reputation is acquired over time through firm-specific (and thus nonsalvageable) investments in advertising, research and development, fixed assets, personnel training, organizational development, and so on. Diversification can help preserve the firm's reputational capital, which will cease to exist if the firm is liquidated.

Fourth, as in the discussion of financial synergy and tax effects, diversification can increase corporate debt capacity and decrease the present value of future tax liability. These effects are a result of the decrease in cash flow variability due to the merger.

Diversification can be achieved through internal growth as well as mergers. However, mergers may be preferred to the internal growth avenue to diversification under certain circumstances. The firm may simply lack internal growth opportunities for lack of requisite resources or due to potential excess capacity in the industry. Timing may be important and mergers can provide diversification more quickly. There may exist many firms in pursuit of diversification at any given time.

## Financial Synergy

One source of financial synergy is the lower costs of internal financing versus external financing. Firms with large internal cash flows and small investment opportunities have excess cash flows. Firms with low internal funds generation and large growth opportunities have needs for additional financing. Combining the two may result in advantages from the lower costs of internal funds availability.

Previous empirical findings appear to support this internal funds effect. Nielsen and Melicher (1973) found that the rate of premium paid to the acquired firm as an approximation to the merger gain was greater when the cash flow rate of the acquiring firm was greater and that of the acquired firm was smaller. This implied that there was redeployment of capital from the acquiring to the acquired firm's industry. The investment literature also indicates that internal cash flows affect the rate of investment of firms (Nickell, 1978).

Another proposition is that the debt capacity of the combined firm can be greater than the sum of the two firms' capacities before their merger, and this provides tax savings on investment income. Still another possible dimension is economies of scale in flotation and transaction costs of securities (Levy and Sarnat, 1970). Changes in the economic and financial environments may permit higher levels of debt than employed historically. Debt ratios increased during the 1980s in an economy of sustained growth and large tax advantages to debt. Tax law changes after 1986 and the recession of 1989–1990 resulted in more equity financing and a reduction in book leverage ratios.

## Strategic Realignments

The increased merger activity of 1992–1996 was said to be motivated by strategic considerations. Here the emphasis is on acquiring new management skills to augment the capabilities of the firm in relation to new growth areas or to meet new competitive threats. New capabilities and new markets could be developed internally. However, the speed of adjustment can be improved through merger activity.

## The q-Ratio

The q-ratio is defined as the ratio of the market value of the firm's securities to the replacement costs of its assets. One frequently discussed reason that firms stepped up acquisition programs in the late 1970s was that entry into new product market areas could be accomplished on a bargain basis. Inflation had a double-barreled impact. For various reasons, including inflation, stock prices were depressed during the 1970s and did not recover until the latter part of 1982 as the level of inflation dropped and business prospects improved. The second impact of inflation was to cause current replacement costs of assets to be substantially higher than their recorded historical book values. These twin effects resulted in a decline of the q-ratio, because the market value of the firm's securities fell and the replacement costs of its assets increased.

In the late 1970s and early 1980s the q-ratio had been running between 0.5 and 0.6. If a company wished to add to capacity in producing a particular product, it could acquire the additional capacity more cheaply by buying a company that produced the product rather than building brick-and-mortar from scratch. If firm A sought to add capacity, this implied that its marginal q-ratio was greater than 1. But if other firms in its industry had average q-ratios of less than 1, it was efficient for firm A to add capacity by the purchase of other firms. For example, if the q-ratio was 0.6 and if in a merger the premium paid over market value was even as high as 50%, the resulting purchase price was 0.6 times 1.5, which equals 0.9. Thus, the average purchase price would still be 10% below the current replacement costs of the assets acquired. This potential advantage would provide a broad basis for the operation of the undervaluation theory in years when the q-ratio was low.

## Information

The shares of the target firm in a tender often experience upward revaluation even if the offer turns out to be unsuccessful (Bradley, 1980; Dodd and Ruback, 1977). A hypothesis based on this empirical observation posits that new information is generated as a result of the tender offer and the revaluation is permanent. Two forms of this information hypothesis can be distinguished. One is that the tender offer disseminates information that the target shares are undervalued and the offer prompts the market to revalue those shares. No particular action by the target firm or any others is necessary to cause the revaluation. This has been called the "sitting-on-a-gold-mine" explanation (Bradley, Desai, and Kim, 1983). The other is that the offer inspires target firm management to implement a more efficient business strategy on its own. This is the "kick-in-the-pants" explanation. No outside input other than the offer itself is required for the upward revaluation.

An opposing view holds that the increase in share value of the target firm involved in an unsuccessful offer is due to the expectation that the target firm will subsequently be acquired by another firm. The latter would have some specialized resources to apply to the target resources. Bradley, Desai, and Kim (1983, 1988) examined the data to determine whether the information hypothesis or the latter (synergy) explanation is acceptable. They found that the share prices of the target firms that did not subsequently receive acquisition offers within five years of the initial unsuccessful offer fell back to their preoffer level. The share prices of those targets that received a subsequent bid increased further. They interpret this result as indicating that the information hypothesis is not valid. A permanent revaluation of the target shares occurs when the target resources are combined with the resources of an acquiring firm, or at least when the control of the target resources is transferred to the acquiring firm.

But Roll (1987, pp. 74–91) suggested that the data were equally consistent with an information explanation. He observed that the appearance of a rival bid increased the probability that there existed positive nonpublic information about the target firm. It also decreased the probability that the initial bidder had exclusive possession of the information.

## Signaling

A distinction may be drawn between information and signaling. When a firm receives a tender offer, this conveys information to the market that a bidder sees value in the firm greater than its prevailing market price. The information conveyed to the market by the bid did not represent the motive of the bidder, which was to make an advantageous purchase. On the other hand, in a share repurchase when management holds a significant proportion of the stock and does not tender stock at the premium in the repurchase price, it is signaling that the company's shares are undervalued. In the original theory of signaling by Spence (1973, 1974), higher quality labor in terms of intelligence or aptitudes would receive greater returns from education and training than lower quality labor. Hence, the level of education of a laborer was a signal not only of more training but of higher innate abilities as well. Lower quality labor would have negative returns on investment in education and training. Thus, it was advantageous for some to signal but disadvantageous for others. As a result, the signal would convey meaningful and correct information. In a share repurchase, firms with undervalued stock are signaling. It would not be advantageous for the control group of companies with overvalued stock to pay a premium in a share repurchase because it would not recoup the premium paid.

## WINNER'S CURSE AND HUBRIS

The winner's curse concept has a long history in the literature on auctions. When there are many bidders or competitors for an object of highly uncertain value, a wide range of bids is likely to result. For example, suppose that many oil companies are bidding on the drilling rights to a particular parcel of land. Given the difficulty of estimating the actual amount of oil in the land, the estimates of the oil companies will vary greatly. The highest bidder will bid and typically pay in excess of the expected value of the oil on the property. The winning bidder is, therefore, "cursed" in the sense that its bid exceeds the value of the tract, so the firm loses money. Capen, Clapp, and Campbell (1971), based on their analysis of sealed-bid competitive lease sales, presented a diagram that depicted the ratio between the high estimate to true value as a function of the degree of uncertainty and the number of bidders. For example, with 10 bidders for leases on a large-uncertainty oil project (Arctic), the ratio of high estimate (bid) to true value was about 3.5 times.

Roll (1986) analyzed the effect in takeover activity. Postulating strong market efficiency in all markets, the prevailing market price of the target already reflected the full value of the firm. The higher valuation of the bidders (over the target's true economic value), he states, resulted from hubris—their excessive self-confidence (pride, arrogance). Hubris is one of the factors that caused the winner's curse phenomenon to occur.

Even if there were synergies, competition between bidders was likely to result in paying too much. Even when there was a single bidder, the potential competition of other bidders may cause the winning bidder to pay too much. And even without competition, Roll (1986) hypothesized that managers committed errors of overoptimism in evaluating merger opportunities due to hubris.

## AGENCY PROBLEMS

Jensen and Meckling (1976) formulated the implications of agency problems. An agency problem arises when managers own only a fraction of the ownership shares of the firm. This partial ownership may cause managers to work less vigorously than otherwise and/or to consume more perquisites (luxurious offices, company cars, memberships in clubs) because the majority owners bear most of the cost. Furthermore, the argument goes, in large corporations with widely dispersed ownership, there is not sufficient incentive for individual owners to expend the substantial resources required to monitor the behavior of managers.

Agency problems arise basically because contracts between managers (decision or control agents) and owners (risk bearers) cannot be costlessly written and enforced. Resulting (agency) costs include (1) costs of structuring a set of contracts, (2) costs of monitoring and controlling the behavior of agents by principals, (3) costs of bonding to guarantee that agents will make optimal decisions or principals will be compensated for the consequences of suboptimal decisions, and (4) the residual loss, that is, the welfare loss experienced by principals, arising from the divergence between agents' decisions and decisions to maximize principals' welfare. This residual loss can arise because the costs of full enforcement of contracts exceed the benefits.

## Takeovers as a Solution to Agency Problems

The agency problems may be efficiently controlled by some organizational and market mechanisms. Fama and Jensen (1983) hypothesize that, when a firm is characterized by separation of ownership and control, decision systems of the firm separate decision management (initiation and implementation) from decision control (ratification and monitoring) in order to limit the power of individual decision agents to expropriate shareholders' interests. Control functions are delegated to a board of directors by the shareholders, who retain approval rights on important matters including board membership, mergers, and new stock issues.

Compensation arrangements and the market for managers may also mitigate the agency problem (Fama, 1980). Compensation can be tied to performance through such devices as bonuses and executive stock options. Managers carry their own reputation and the labor market sets their wage levels based on performance reputation.

The stock market gives rise to an external monitoring device because stock prices summarize the implications of decisions made by managers. Low stock prices exert pressure on managers to change their behavior and to stay in line with the interests of shareholders (Fama and Jensen, 1983).

When these mechanisms are not sufficient to control agency problems, the market for takeovers provides an external control device of last resort (Manne, 1965). A takeover through a tender offer or a proxy fight enables outside managers to gain control of the decision processes of the target while circumventing existing managers and the board of directors. Manne emphasized mergers as a threat of takeover if a firm's management lagged in performance either because of inefficiency or because of agency problems.

## Managerialism

In contrast to the view that mergers occur to control agency problems, some observers consider mergers as a manifestation of agency problems rather than as a solution. The managerialism explanation for conglomerate mergers was set forth most fully by Mueller (1969). Mueller hypothesized that managers are motivated to increase the size of their firms. He assumes that the compensation to managers is a function of the size of the firm, and he argues, therefore, that managers adopt a lower investment hurdle rate. But in a study critical of earlier evidence, Lewellen and Huntsman (1970) present findings that managers' compensation is significantly correlated with the firm's profit rate, not its level of sales. Thus, the basic premise of the Mueller theory may not be valid.

The managerialism theory argues that the agency problem is not solved, and the merger activity is a manifestation of the agency problems of inefficient, external investments by managers. An alternative view of the firm takes the opposite position on the role of mergers.

The modern theory of the firm suggests that firms exist because the market is not frictionless. Economies of scale arise out of indivisibilities. Managements are organized as teams based on firm-specific information on individual characteristics. Firm reputation is valuable because information is costly. Certain transaction costs lead to integration of operations. The existence of these imperfections (indivisibilities, information costs, and transaction costs) make it inefficient to have individual productive inputs move individually and separately across firms. Takeovers and mergers may be one means of efficiently redeploying corporate resources across firms while minimizing transaction costs and preserving organizational values. Product and labor market efficiency would not automatically obtain in changing market conditions and would require reallocation of resources across economic activities. Mergers and takeovers may represent one of the processes necessary to maintain or restore efficiency.

### The Free Cash Flow Hypothesis (FCFH)

The problem of agency costs discussed in the preceding section also gives rise to the free cash flow hypothesis. Michael Jensen (1986, 1988) considered the agency costs associated with conflicts between managers and shareholders over the payout of free cash flow to be a major cause of takeover activity. According to Jensen, shareholders and managers (who are their agents) had serious conflicts of interest over the choice of corporate strategy. Agency costs resulted from these conflicts of interest that could never be resolved perfectly. When these costs were large, takeovers could help reduce them, according to Jensen.

Jensen's free cash flow hypothesis (FCFH) is that the payout of free cash flow can serve an important role in dealing with the conflict between managers and shareholders. Jensen defines free cash flow as cash flow in excess of the amounts required to fund all projects that have positive net present values when discounted at the applicable cost of capital. He states that such free cash flow must be paid out to shareholders if the firm is to be efficient and to maximize share price. The payout of free cash flow (FCF) reduces the amount of resources under the control of managers and thereby reduces their power. In addition, they are then more likely to be subject to monitoring by the capital markets when they seek to finance additional investments with new capital.

In addition to paying out the current amount of excess cash, Jensen considers it important that managers bond their promise to pay out future cash flows. An effective way to do this is by debt creation without retention of the proceeds of the issue. Jensen argues that by issuing debt in exchange for stock, for example, managers bond their promise to pay out future cash flows more effectively than any announced dividend policy could achieve. Jensen emphasizes that the control function of debt is most important in organizations that generate large cash flows, but whose outlook involves low growth or an actual reduction in size.

He recognizes that increased leverage involves costs. It increases the risks of bankruptcy costs. There are agency costs of debt as well. One is for the firm to take on highly risky projects that benefit shareholders at the expense of bondholders. He defines an optimal debt/equity ratio where the marginal costs of debt equal the marginal benefits of debt.

For evidence Jensen began with a review of a wide range of financial transactions. He cited an earlier study by Smith (1986a, 1986b) of 20 studies of stock price changes at announcements of transactions that involved a change of capital structure or dividend behavior. In a preliminary to a review of the evidence, he restated the prediction of the FCFH. For firms with positive FCF, stock prices will increase with unexpected increases in payouts and decrease with unexpected decreases in payouts to shareholders. The hypothesis predicts further that increasing tightness of the constraints requiring the payout of future FCF will also increase stock prices.

Jensen argued that in virtually all of the 32 cases he summarized, the direction of the effect on share price agreed with the predictions of the free cash flow hypothesis. Jensen stated that his predictions did not apply to firms that had more profitable projects than cash flow to fund them. Nor did the theory apply to growth firms, only to firms that should be exiting some of their activities. Similarly, Jensen argued that in leveraged buyouts the high debt ratios taken on caused the increase in share price. But successful LBOs usually involved a turnaround—an improvement in company performance (Kaplan, 1989). Also, in LBOs the executive group was provided with a large ownership stake in the company, which would have substantial value if the LBO succeeded. It was possible that the incentives provided by the strong ownership stake and other characteristics of LBO situations accounted for the rise in value rather than the bonding effect of the high debt ratios.

# REDISTRIBUTION

The Berkovitch and Narayanan (BN) framework reflected in Table 5.3 does not fully encompass forms of redistribution such as taxes and market power as well as breach of trust (redistribution) with respect to bondholders and labor.

## Tax Gains

Tax savings may be another motive for mergers, representing a form of redistribution from the government or public at large. In chapter 4, we discussed how mergers may be used to substitute capital gains for ordinary income. We discussed the role of the carryover of net operating losses and the value of tax credits that would otherwise be unused. We also discussed the use of a stepped-up tax basis for assets after a merger.

The empirical evidence establishes that tax benefits from a merger may be substantial. However, the evidence also establishes that tax advantages are not likely to be the major reason. Successful mergers are based on sound business and economic principles. Taxes are likely to be a reinforcing influence rather than the major force in a sound merger.

## Market Power

An objection that is often raised to permitting a firm to increase its market share by merger is that the result will be "undue concentration" in the industry. The argument in brief is that if four or fewer firms account for a substantial percentage of an industry's sales, these firms will recognize the impact of their actions and policies upon one another. This recognized interdependence will lead to a consideration of actions and reactions to changes in policy that will tend toward "tacit collusion." As a result, the prices and profits of the firms will contain monopoly elements. Thus, if economies from mergers cannot be established, it is assumed that the resulting increases in concentration may lead to monopoly returns. If economies can be demonstrated, then a comparison of efficiencies versus the effects of increased concentration must be made.

While some economists hold that high concentration, however measured, causes some degree of monopoly, other economists hold that increased concentration is generally the *result* of active and intense competition. They argue further that the intense competition continues among large firms in concentrated industries because the dimensions of decision making over prices, outputs, types of product, quality of product, service, and so on are so numerous and of so many gradations that neither tacit nor overt collusion could be possible to achieve.

When the antitrust authorities determine a merger to be anticompetitive in some sense, they can block the merger, as discussed in chapter 2. They can block the merger or approve only if certain conditions are met, such as selling off part of the assets acquired.

## Redistribution from Bondholders

Most of the studies find no evidence that shareholders gain in mergers and tender offers at the expense of bondholders (Asquith and Kim, 1982; Dennis and McConnell, 1986; Kim and McConnell, 1977). Even in debt for common stock exchanges, most of the evidence indicates that there is no negative impact on bondholders even though leverage has been increased. However, in leveraged buyouts in which debt is increased by very high orders of magnitude, there is evidence of negative impacts on bondholders (McDaniel, 1986; Warga and Welch, 1993). There is also dramatic evidence of negative effects on bondholders in individual cases and in patterns of downgrading (the *Wall Street Journal,* October 25, 1988). But the losses to bondholders, on average, represent only a small fraction of the gains to shareholders.

## Redistribution from Labor

Redistribution from labor to shareholders has also received attention (Shleifer and Summers, 1988). The problem has been formalized by Williamson (1988). The issues can be delineated by a case example based on the TWA-Icahn study outlined by Shleifer and Summers and covered in some detail in the press. The stylized facts can be summarized as shown in Table 5.5.

The original annual salary levels of the pilots, machinists, and flight attendants are shown in column 3. When these are multiplied by the number of employees shown in column 2 we obtain the total annual wage bill shown in column 4. Column 5 is a stylized estimate of the salary cuts achieved by Icahn after he obtained control of TWA. They represent the percentage rate reductions in the annual compensation rates shown in column 3. Applying the rate reductions to the total annual wage bill yields the annual savings shown in column 6. The total annual savings appear to be roughly $200 million per year. The gains from the savings are shown in Table 5.6.

Before the takeover, TWA had 33 million shares of common stock outstanding, whose market price was $8 per share giving a total market value of $264 million. The final block of shares obtained in the takeover were priced at $24. The gains to the participants can, therefore, be calculated. For the roughly 6.5 million shares Icahn purchased at an average price of $12, his gain would be the difference between $24 and $12, or $12 per share. For the 6.5 million shares Icahn purchased at $18, his gain would be $6 per share. The total gains to Icahn would, therefore, be $117 million. Similarly, the gains to the original shareholders are shown in column 3. The gains per share represent the

**TABLE 5.5**   Labor Cost Savings in the TWA Takeover (M = $ Million)

| *(1)* Category | *(2)* Number of Employees | *(3)* Annual Wage Rates | *(4)* Total Annual Wage Bill | *(5)* Rate Reductions | *(6)* Annual Savings |
|---|---|---|---|---|---|
| Pilots | 3,000 @ | $90,000 = | $270M | 33% | $ 90M |
| Machinists | 9,000 @ | 38,000 = | 342M | 15% | 50M |
| Flight attendants | 6,000 @ | 35,000 = | 210M | 28.5% | 60M |
| | | | | Total savings | $200M |

**TABLE 5.6**   Gain from Savings (M = $ Million)

| *(1)* | *(2)* | *(3)* |
|---|---|---|
| *ICAHN Purchases* | *Gains to ICAHN* | *To Original Shareholders* |
| 6.5 @ 12 | $12 × 6.5 = $ 78M | $ 4 × 6.5 = $ 26M |
| 6.5 @ 18 | 6 × 6.5 =   39M | 10 × 6.5 =   65M |
| 20.0 @ 24 | 0M | 16 × 20 =   320M |
|  | $117M | $411M |
|  |  | 117M |
| Total |  | $528M |
|  |  | Original Value  264M |
|  |  | Total Value $792M |

difference between the $8 price and the Icahn purchase price. The gains to the original shareholders total $411 million. When these gains are added to the original value of the company, we obtain a total value for TWA after the takeover of $792 million.

Whether "breach of trust" or redistribution occurs depends on a number of variables shown in Table 5.7. The labor costs that were subsequently reduced could have reflected union power, the firm-specific productivity of the employees, or a form of management inefficiency. Another set of variables that influences the interpretation of the case is whether the product markets in which airline services were being sold were competitive, monopolized, or operated under government regulation. A third set of variables to consider is whether, as a consequence of the takeover, the quality of the product-services sold went down, up, or remained the same.

In their analysis of the case, Shleifer and Summers (1988) gave emphasis to the interpretation that the high labor costs may have reflected the firm-specific productivity developed by the employees. With deregulation, new airline entrants hired employees at much lower rates than unionized airlines such as TWA were paying. But if the unionized employees at TWA were more efficient because of their firm-specific skills, the real cost of labor would not necessarily be any higher in TWA than in its nonunionized rivals. Under this scenario, Shleifer and Summers observed that a breach of trust is involved. This says that as a consequence of the takeover, investments made by employees to develop firm-specific skills are not paid their full value when previous labor contracts are broken by the new control group. If breach of trust is involved, then employees would take this into account in writing contracts in the future. It would affect their supply price. The consequence would be that labor costs in the airline industry would rise and prices to airline passengers and other users would be increased in the long run.

**TABLE 5.7**   Alternative Sources of Increases in Value

| *Labor Costs* | *Product Market* | *Product Quality* |
|---|---|---|
| Union power | Regulated | Down |
| Firm-specific productivity | Monopoly | Same |
| Management inefficiency | Competitive | Up |

Another possible scenario is that the higher union wages at TWA reflect the previous period of regulation. One theory holds that in a regulated industry, employees, whether unionized or not, are able to extract wage increases. It is argued that either management will be soft on wage demands or that the pressure of regulatory bodies will cause management to accept higher wages, which, in turn, the regulator permits to be passed on in higher prices. With subsequent deregulation, the competition of new entrants with lower costs will result in lower product and service prices. The lower prices of competitors pressure firms with high-wage unionized employees to force wage reductions if they are to stay in business. To meet the lower prices of competitors requires a reduction of monopoly rents that formerly had been paid to unionized labor. Under this scenario, lower employee compensation rates would not represent a breach of trust but a restoration of more competitive conditions. It could be argued that the rise in share prices then simply enables shareholders to earn competitive returns on their investments. Consumers benefit from the lower competitive prices. The degree of the benefit to consumers and the extent to which the returns to shareholders are competitive depend on whether full competitive conditions are achieved in the airline industry. There appear to be some elements of regulation and supply restriction in space allocations at airport terminals. This would prevent the full realization of the competitive assumptions of the present scenario.

Still a third scenario, in addition to the "breach of trust" and the "end of regulation" theories, is the management inefficiency explanation. In this scenario the problem is that one of the manifestations of managerial inefficiency is the failure to bargain effectively with labor. The new competition with deregulation stimulates takeovers to provide new and efficient management. If the new management efficiencies include bargaining employee compensation down to competitive levels, shareholders should earn competitive rates of return and prices to consumers should be reduced to competitive levels. The price reductions might be expressed to some degree in the form of improved product quality.

Thus, whether the value increases associated with mergers and takeovers represent redistribution, particularly from labor, depends on which scenario is correct. If union power is reflected in monopoly rents to employees, then the employee cost reductions do not represent a breach of trust. They represent a movement from monopoly elements to competitive elements in the industry. If management inefficiency is involved, the introduction of efficient managers moves the industry from inefficiency to efficiency gains. Thus, whether breach of contract or other forms of expropriation are involved depends on the facts of individual industry circumstances.

### Pension Fund Reversions

Pontiff, Shleifer, and Weisbach (PSW) (1990) studied another aspect of breach of trust. Their sample of 413 successful tender offers executed from March 1981 through May 1988 was taken from Jarrell (1988). This sample was matched to a list of pension-plan reversions over $1 million from the Pension Benefit Guarantee Corporation (PBGC). In the two years following hostile takeovers, 15.1% of acquirers executed pension asset reversions compared with 8.4% in friendly takeovers.

Reversions occurred mostly in unit-benefit plans in which pension benefits are based on final wages (a pension bond). Reversions are less likely in flat-benefit plans based on number of years worked (no pension bond). Viewing the pension plan agreement as an implicit contract, terminations or returning excess funding to the firm benefits shareholders, and workers lose. Event return analysis finds positive returns to shareholders at the announcement of a pension plan termination. Pontiff, Shleifer, and Weisbach (1990) suggest that the stock market is surprised by this transfer of cash to the shareholders and expects that the funds will be used in positive net present value (NPV) projects. Similarly, share prices rise on reversion announcements, indicating that the market expects the funds to be used more in the shareholders' interest. Reversions, on average, account for about 11% of the takeover premium in cases in which they actually occurred. Pontiff, Shleifer, and Weisbach conclude that reversions are not a major source of takeover gains.

## Summary

Many theories have been advanced to explain why mergers and other forms of restructuring take place. Efficiency theories imply social gains from M&A activity in addition to the gains for participants. The **differential efficiency** theory says that more efficient firms will acquire less efficient firms and realize gains by improving their efficiency; this implies excess managerial capabilities in the acquiring firm. Differential efficiency would be most likely to be a factor in mergers between firms in related industries where the need for improvement could be more easily identified. The related **inefficient management** theory suggests that target management is so inept that virtually any management could do better, and thus could be an explanation for mergers between firms in unrelated industries.

The **operating synergy** theory postulates economies of scale or of scope and that mergers help achieve levels of activities at which they can be obtained. It includes the concept of complementarity of capabilities. For example, one firm might be strong in R&D but weak in marketing while another has a strong marketing department without the R&D capability. Merging the two firms would result in operating synergy. The **financial synergy** theory hypothesizes complementarities between merging firms, not in management capabilities, but in matching the availability of investment opportunities and internal cash flows. A firm in a declining industry will produce large cash flows because there are few attractive investment opportunities. A growth industry has more investment opportunities than cash with which to finance them. The merged firm will have a lower cost of capital due to the lower cost of internal funds as well as possible risk reduction, savings in flotation costs, and improvements in capital allocation.

Diversification as a motive for mergers differs from shareholder portfolio diversification. Shareholders can efficiently spread their investments and risk among industries, so there is no need for firms to diversify for the sake of their shareholders. Managers and other employees, however, are at greater risk if the single industry in which their firm operates should decline; their firm-specific human capital is not transferable. Therefore, firms may diversify to encourage firm-specific human capital investments that make their employees more valuable and productive, and to increase the probability that the organization and reputation capital of the firm will be preserved by transfer to another line of business owned by the firm in the event its initial industry declines.

The theory of **strategic alignment to changing environments** says that mergers take place in response to environmental changes. External acquisitions of needed capabilities allow firms to adapt more quickly and with less risk than developing capabilities internally.

The **undervaluation** theory states that mergers occur when the market value of target firm stock for some reason does not reflect its true or potential value or its value in the hands of an alternative management. The q-ratio is also related to the undervaluation theory. Firms can acquire assets for expansion more cheaply by buying the stock of existing firms than by buying or building the assets when the target's stock price is below the replacement cost of its assets. Some bidders seek targets with high q's.

The **information** theory attempts to explain why target shares seem to be permanently revalued upward in a tender offer whether or not it is successful. The information hypothesis says that the tender offer conveys information to the market that the target shares are undervalued. Alternatively, the tender offer sends information to target management that inspires them to implement a more efficient strategy on their own. Another school holds that the revaluation is not really permanent, but only reflects the likelihood that another acquirer will materialize for a synergistic combination.

Positive valuation errors in bidding for companies represent the winner's curse. Roll (1986) analyzes the effect in takeover activity. Postulating strong market efficiency in all markets, the prevailing market price of the target already reflects the full value of the firm. The higher valuation of the bidders (over the target's true economic value), he states, results from hubris—their excessive self-confidence (pride, arrogance). Hubris is one of the factors that causes the winner's curse phenomenon to occur in takeover bids.

**Agency problems** may result from a conflict of interest between managers and shareholders or between shareholders and debt holders. A number of organization and market mechanisms serve to discipline self-serving managers, and takeovers are viewed as the discipline of last resort. **Managerialism,** on the other hand, views takeovers as a manifestation of the agency problem rather than its solution. It suggests that self-serving managers make ill-conceived combinations solely to increase firm size and their own compensation. The hubris theory is another variant on the agency cost theory; it implies acquiring firm managers commit errors of overoptimism (winner's curse) in bidding for targets.

Jensen's **free cash flow** hypothesis says that takeovers take place because of the conflicts between managers and shareholders over the payout of free cash flows. The hypothesis posits that free cash flows (that is, in excess of investment needs) should be paid out to shareholders, reducing the power of management and subjecting managers to the scrutiny of the public capital markets more frequently. Debt-for-stock exchange offers are viewed as a means of bonding the managers' promise to pay out future cash flows to shareholders.

Another theory of the value increases to shareholders in takeovers is that the gains come at the expense of other stakeholders in the firm. Expropriated stakeholders under the **redistribution** hypothesis may include bondholders, the government (in the case of tax savings), and employees.

**Tax effects** can be important in mergers, although they do not play a major role in explaining M&A activity overall. Carryover of net operating losses and tax credits, stepped-up asset basis, and the substitution of capital gains for ordinary income (less important after the Tax Reform Act of 1986) are among the tax motivations for mergers. Looming inheritance taxes may also motivate the sale of privately held firms with aging owners.

The **market power** theory holds that merger gains are the result of increased concentration leading to collusion and monopoly effects. Empirical evidence on whether industry concentration causes reduced competition is not conclusive. There is much evidence that concentration is the result of vigorous and continuing competition, which causes the composition of the leading firms to change over time.

## Questions

5.1  Briefly explain how the various efficiency theories of mergers differ and how they are alike.

5.2  Explain the differences between managerial synergy, operating synergy, and financial synergy, and their relationships to different types of mergers.

5.3  How are agency problems and managerialism related? What is the hypothesized effect of each on merger activity?

5.4  Discuss the hubris hypothesis in terms of efficiency theories of mergers.

5.5  What is the rationale for the use of such measures as the four-firm concentration ratio and the Herfindahl index?

5.6  How do tax considerations affect mergers and their structuring?

5.7  What is the "breach of trust" theory of merger gains?

5.8  Using option pricing theory, why is leverage likely to increase after two firms with uncorrelated cash flow streams combine?

------------------------------------ C A S E   5–1 ------------------------------------
# Boeing's Acquisition of McDonnell Douglas

On December 16, 1996, Boeing agreed to acquire McDonnell Douglas by paying 0.65 shares of Boeing for each share of McDonnell Douglas. The deal was valued at $13.3 billion. It was stated that the combined employment of 200,000 was not expected to be reduced, although a redeployment of workers would take place. In 1995 Boeing had commercial aircraft sales of about $14 billion and $5.6 billion in defense and space. McDonnell Douglas had commercial aircraft revenues of about $4 billion with about $10 billion in military aircraft and other defense. St. Louis would be the headquarters for the defense operations; Seattle would be the headquarters for the commercial.

It was stated that this acquisition would enable Boeing to develop a better balance in its mix between commercial and defense business. The executives judged that they would be stronger competitors in the world commercial aviation business. Seventy percent of Boeing's commercial business was outside the United States; 50% for McDonnell Douglas. Savings of at least a billion dollars a year would be achieved by combining the defense operations. Employment in research and development (R&D) was expected to increase rather than decrease.

On the day of the announcement of the acquisition (December 16, 1996), the common stock of Boeing rose by about $6 per share and the price of McDonnell Douglas stock rose by about $10 a share. The number of common shares of Boeing outstanding was about 344 million. For McDonnell Douglas the number of shares was 223.6 million.

## Questions on Case Study C5.1

C5.1.1  By how much did the market value of the two companies increase on the announcement date?

C5.1.2  Why did "the market" evaluate this combination as value increasing?

## References

Arrow, K. J., "Vertical Integration and Communication," *Bell Journal of Economics,* 6, Spring 1975, pp. 173–183.

Asquith, P., and E. H. Kim, "The Impact of Merger Bids on the Participating Firms' Security Holders," *Journal of Finance,* 37, 1982, pp. 1209–1228.

Bagnoli, Mark, and Barton Lipman, "Successful Takeovers without Exclusion," *Review of Financial Studies,* 1, 1988, pp. 89–110.

Berkovitch, Elazar, and M. P. Narayanan, "Motives for Takeovers: An Empirical Investigation," *Journal of Financial and Quantitative Analysis,* 28, September 1993, pp. 347–362.

Bradley, M., "Interfirm Tender Offers and the Market for Corporate Control," *Journal of Business,* 53, October 1980, pp. 345–376.

——, A. Desai, and E. H. Kim, "The Rationale Behind Interfirm Tender Offers: Information or Synergy?" *Journal of Financial Economics,* 11, April 1983, pp. 183–206.

——, "Synergistic Gains from Corporate Acquisitions and Their Division Between the Stockholders of Target and Acquiring Firms," *Journal of Financial Economics,* 21, 1988, pp. 3–40.

Capen, E. C., R. V. Clapp, and W. M. Campbell, "Competitive Bidding in High-Risk Situations," *Journal of Petroleum Technology,* 23, June 1971, pp. 641–653.

Chowdhry, Bhagwan, and Narasimhan Jegadeesh, "Pre-Tender Offer Share Acquisition Strategy in Takeovers," *Journal of Financial and Quantitative Analysis,* 29, 1994, pp. 117–129.

Dennis, Debra K., and John J. McConnell, "Corporate Mergers and Security Returns," *Journal of Financial Economics,* 16, 1986, pp. 143–187.

Dodd, P., and R. Ruback, "Tender Offers and Stockholder Returns: An Empirical Analysis," *Journal of Financial Economics,* 5, December 1977, pp. 351–374.

Fama, E. F., "Agency Problems and the Theory of the Firm," *Journal of Political Economy,* 88, April 1980, pp. 288–307.

——, and M. C. Jensen, "Separation of Ownership and Control," *Journal of Law and Economics,* 26, 1983, pp. 301–325.

——, "Organizational Forms and Investment Decisions," *Journal of Financial Economics,* 14, 1985, pp. 101–119.

Grossman, S. J., and O. D. Hart, "Takeover Bids, the Free-Rider Problem and the Theory of the Corporation," *Bell Journal of Economics,* 11, Spring 1980, pp. 42–64.

Hirshleifer, David, and Sheridan Titman, "Share Tendering Strategies and the Success of Hostile Takeover Bids," *Journal of Political Economy,* 98, 1990, pp. 295–324.

Jarrell, G. A., Testimony in the Case of *RP Acquisition Corp.* v. *Staley Continental and Michael Harkins.* Testimony in the United States District Court for the District of Delaware. (Civil Action No. 88-190), 1988.

——, and A. Poulsen, "Stock Trading Before the Announcement of Tender Offers: Insider Trading or Market Anticipation," *Journal of Law, Economics and Organization,* 5, 1989, pp. 225–248.

Jensen, M. C., "Agency Costs of Free Cash Flow, Corporate Finance and Takeovers," *American Economic Review,* 76, May 1986, pp. 323–329.

——, "The Takeover Controversy: Analysis and Evidence," Chapter 20 in J. C. Coffee, Jr., L. Lowenstein, and S. Rose-Ackerman, eds., *Knights, Raiders, and Targets,* New York: Oxford University Press, 1988.

——, and W. Meckling, "Theory of the Firm: Managerial Behavior, Agency Costs and Ownership Structure," *Journal of Financial Economics,* 3, October 1976, pp. 305–360.

Kaplan, Steven, "The Effects of Management Buyouts on Operating Performance and Value," *Journal of Financial Economics,* 24, 1989, pp. 217–254.

Kim, E. H., and J. McConnell, "Corporate Merger and the Coinsurance of Corporate Debt," *Journal of Finance,* 32, 1977, pp. 349–365.

Klein, B., R. Crawford, and A. Alchian, "Vertical Integration, Appropriable Rents, and the Competitive Contracting Process," *Journal of Law and Economics,* 21, October 1978, pp. 297–326.

Levy, H., and M. Sarnat, "Diversification, Portfolio Analysis and the Uneasy Case for Conglomerate Mergers," *Journal of Finance,* September 1970, pp. 795–802.

Lewellen, W. G., and B. Huntsman, "Managerial Pay and Corporate Performance," *American Economic Review,* 60, September 1970, pp. 710–720.

Manne, H. G., "Mergers and the Market for Corporate Control," *Journal of Political Economy,* 73, April 1965, pp. 110–120.

McDaniel, Morey W., "Bondholders and Corporate Governance," *The Business Lawyer,* 41, February 1986, pp. 413–460.

Miller, M., and F. Modigliani, "Dividend Policy, Growth and the Valuation of Shares," *Journal of Business,* 34, October 1961, pp. 411–433.

Mueller, D. C., "A Theory of Conglomerate Mergers," *Quarterly Journal of Economics,* 83, 1969, pp. 643–659.

Nickell, S. J., *The Investment Decisions of Firms,* Oxford, England: Cambridge University Press, 1978.

Nielsen, J. F., and R. W. Melicher, "A Financial Analysis of Acquisition and Merger Premiums," *Journal of Financial and Quantitative Analysis,* 8, March 1973, pp. 139–162.

Pontiff, Jeffrey, Andrei Shleifer, and Michael S. Weisbach, "Reversions of Excess Pension Assets after Takeovers," *RAND Journal of Economics,* 21, Winter 1990, pp. 600–613.

Prescott, E. C., and M. Visscher, "Organization Capital," *Journal of Political Economy,* 88, June 1980, pp. 446–461.

Roll, Richard, "The Hubris Hypothesis of Corporate Takeovers," *Journal of Business,* 59, April 1986, pp. 197–216.

———, "Empirical Evidence on Takeover Activity and Shareholder Wealth," Chapter 5 in Thomas E. Copeland, ed., *Modern Finance & Industrial Economics,* New York: Basil Blackwell, 1987, pp. 74–91.

Rosen, Sherwin, "Learning by Experience as Joint Production," *Quarterly Journal of Economics,* August 1972, pp. 366–382.

Shleifer, A., and L. W. Summers, "Breach of Trust in Hostile Takeovers," Chapter 2 in A. J. Auerbach, ed., *Corporate Takeovers: Causes and Consequences,* Chicago: University of Chicago Press, 1988.

Shleifer, Andrei, and Robert W. Vishny, "Large Shareholders and Corporate Control," *Journal of Political Economy,* 94, June 1986, pp. 461–488.

Smith, Clifford W., Jr., "Investment Banking and the Capital Acquisition Process," *Journal of Financial Economics,* 15, January/February 1986a, pp. 3–29.

———, "Raising Capital: Theory and Evidence," *Midland Corporate Finance Journal,* Spring 1986b, pp. 6–22.

Spatt, Chester S., "Strategic Analyses of Takeover Bids," Chapter 3 in S. Bhattacharya and G. Constantinides, eds., *Financial Markets and Incomplete Information,* Totowa, NJ: Rowman & Littlefield, 1989, pp. 106–121.

Spence, A. Michael, "Job Market Signalling," *Quarterly Journal of Economics,* 87, August 1973, pp. 355–379.

———, "Competitive and Optimal Responses to Signals: Analysis of Efficiency and Distribution," *Journal of Economic Theory,* 7, March 1974, pp. 296–332.

Warga, Arthur, and Ivo Welch, "Bondholder Losses in Leveraged Buyouts," *Review of Financial Studies,* 6, 1993, pp. 959–982.

Williamson, O. E., *Markets and Hierarchies: Analysis and Antitrust Implications,* New York: Free Press, 1975.

_____, "Comment," Chapter 2 in A. J. Auerbach, ed., *Corporate Takeovers: Causes and Consequences,* Chicago: University of Chicago Press, 1988, pp. 61–67.

# Measurement of Abnormal Returns

## STEPS IN CALCULATION OF RESIDUALS

The first step in measuring the effect on stock value of an "event" (announcement of a tender offer, share repurchase, and so on) is to define an event period. Usually this is centered on the announcement date, which is designated day 0 in event time. The purpose of the event period is to capture all the effects on stock price of the event. Longer periods will make sure all the effects are captured, but the estimate is subject to more noise in the data. Many studies choose a period like days $-40$ to $+40$, that is from 40 days before the announcement to 40 days after the announcement. Note, day 0 is the date the announcement is made for a particular firm and will be different calendar dates for different firms.

The next step is to calculate a predicted (or normal) return, $\hat{R}_{jt}$, for each day in the event period for each firm. The predicted return represents the return that would be expected if no event took place. There are basically three methods of calculating this predicted return. These are the mean adjusted return method, the market model method, and the market adjusted return method. For most cases the three methods yield similar results. Next the residual, $r_{jt}$, is calculated for each day for each firm. The residual is the actual return for that day for the firm minus the predicted return, $r_{jt} = R_{jt} - \hat{R}_{jt}$. The residual represents the abnormal return, that is, the part of the return that is not predicted and is therefore an estimate of the change in firm value on that day, which is caused by the event. For each day in event time the residuals are averaged across firms to produce the average residual for that day, $AR_t$, where $AR_t = \dfrac{\sum\limits_{j} r_{jt}}{N}$ and $N$ is the number of firms in the sample. The reason for averaging across firms is that stock returns are noisy, but the noise tends to cancel out when averaged across a large number of firms. Therefore, the more firms in the sample the better the ability to distinguish the effect of an event. The final step is to cumulate the average residual for each day over the entire event period to produce the cumulative average residual or return, $CAR$, where $CAR = \sum\limits_{t=-40}^{40} AR_t$. The cumulative average residual represents the average total effect of the event across all firms over a specified time interval.

### The Mean Adjusted Return Method

In the mean adjusted return method a "clean" period is chosen and the average daily return for the firm is estimated for this period. The clean period may be before the event period, after the event period, or both, but never includes the event period. The clean period includes days on which no information related to the event is released, for example days $-240$ to $-41$. The predicted return for a firm for each day in the event period, using the mean adjusted return method, is just the mean daily return for the clean period for the firm. That is:

$$\hat{R}_{jt} = \bar{R}_j = \frac{\sum\limits_{t=-240}^{-41} R_{jt}}{200}$$

This predicted return is then used to calculate the residuals, average residuals, and cumulative average residual as explained above.

### The Market Model Method

To use the market model a clean period is chosen and the market model is estimated by running a regression for the days in this period. The market model is:

$$R_{jt} = \alpha_j + \beta_j R_{mt} + \varepsilon_{jt}$$

where $R_{mt}$ is the return on a market index (for example, the S&P 500) for day $t$, $\beta_j$ measures the sensitivity of firm $j$ to the market—this is a measure of risk, $\alpha_j$ measures the mean return over the period not explained by the market, and $\varepsilon_{jt}$ is a statistical error term $\sum \varepsilon_{jt} = 0$. The regression produces estimates of $\alpha_j$ and $\beta_j$; call these $\hat{\alpha}_j$ and $\hat{\beta}_j$. The predicted return for a firm for a day in the event period is the return given by the market model on that day using these estimates. That is:

$$\hat{R}_{jt} = \hat{\alpha}_j + \hat{\beta}_j R_{mt}$$

where now $R_{mt}$ is the return on the market index for the actual day in the event period. Because the market model takes explicit account of both the risk associated with the market and mean returns, it is the most widely used method.

### The Market Adjusted Return Method

The market adjusted return method is the simplest of the methods. The predicted return for a firm for a day in the event period is just the return on the market index for that day. That is:

$$\hat{R}_{jt} = R_{mt}$$

The market adjusted return method can be thought of as an approximation to the market model where $\hat{\alpha}_j = 0$ and $\hat{\beta}_j = 1$ for all firms. Because $\hat{\alpha}_j$ is usually small and the average $\hat{\beta}_j$ over all firms is 1, this approximation usually produces acceptable results.

### Illustrations

The first step for any event study is to determine the date of the announcement. The actual date of the first release of the information to the public is not easily obtainable. The best one can do is to check a source such as the *Wall Street Journal Index (WSJI)* for the earliest date and use an event window sufficient to cover the period. In our example, the events of interest are three major mergers in the oil industry: Chevron–Gulf (March 5, 1984), Mobil–Superior Oil (March 9, 1984), and Imperial Oil–Texaco Canada (January 19, 1989). We chose 40 days prior and 40 days after the earliest announcement date found in the *WSJI*. We refer to $[-40, 40]$ as our event window.

To quantify the effects of the event on the stock returns, we need to calculate the residuals during the event window interval. The residuals are just the difference between the actual stock return and a benchmark of what would have been the expected return if the event had not happened. Three methods are used to calculate the expected returns. One is the **mean adjusted return method.** We use the mean return of the stock in a clean period prior to the event window as the expected return. In our example, we took 200 trading days prior to our event window to calculate a mean expected return for each firm. For illustration, let us consider the case of Chevron. The mean return from date $-240$ to $-41$ was found to be 0.00037 (see Table A5.1). Chevron's return on date $-40$ was 0.0036. Then $R1$, the mean adjusted residual on date $-40$ will be Chevron's return on date $-40$ minus the estimated mean return, or $0.0036 - 0.00037 = 0.00323 \approx 0.003$ (see first row $R1$ under Chevron columns in Table A5.2).

Two is the **market model method.** We use an expected return that takes into account the riskiness of the firm with respect to the market. The procedure involves a regression of the firm return series against a market index. The calculations must involve a period not included in the event window. We again used the 200 trading days returns prior to the event window and regressed them against a market index represented by the value-weighted CRSP index, which represents an aggregate of stocks including dividends traded in the major exchanges such as NYAM and AMSE. The regression of Chevron's returns against the returns of the CRSP index for the period $-240$ to $-41$ yielded an intercept, $\hat{\alpha}$, of $-0.0005$ and a slope, $\hat{\beta}$, of 1.2096 (see Table A5.1). On date $-40$, Chevron's return was 0.0036 and the CRSP market index return was 0.00431. $R2$, the market model adjusted residual, for date $-40$ will be $0.0036 - (-0.0005) - 1.2096(0.00431) = -0.0011 \approx -0.001$ (see first row $R2$ under Chevron column in Table A5.2).

Three is the **market adjusted return method.** The expected return for any stock is postulated to be just the market return for that particular day. Going back to our Chevron example, $R3$, the market adjusted residual, for date $-40$ will be $0.0036 - 0.00431 = -0.00071 \approx -0.001$ (see first row $R3$ under Chevron column in Table A5.2).

Table A5.2 shows the residuals for the three acquiring firms in our sample using the above three methods. Table A5.3 is a similar table corresponding to the target companies. The residuals are averaged across firms to obtain an average residual (AR) for each day in the event period. Three average residuals are presented corresponding to each of the above three methods. For example, $AR1$ for the acquiring companies is the average of the mean adjusted residuals: $R1$ Chevron, $R1$ Mobil, and $R1$ Imperial Oil. For date $-40$, $AR1 = \frac{1}{3}[0.003 + (-0.014) + 0.031] = 0.007$ (see first row $AR1$ under Average Residuals columns in Table A5.2). $AR2$ is for the market model. $AR3$ represents the average residuals using the market adjusted method.

---

**TABLE A5.1**   Parameters for Measuring Abnormal Returns

| | | | Targets | | | Acquirers | | |
| --- | --- | --- | --- | --- | --- | --- | --- | --- |
| | | | Gulf Corp. | Superior Oil | Texaco Canada | Chevron | Mobil | Imperial Oil |
| M1: Mean adjusted return model | $R1 = r_{jt}$ $= R_{jt} - \bar{R}_j$ | $\bar{R}_j$ | 0.0022 | 0.0012 | 0.0015 | 0.0004 | 0.0010 | -0.0007 |
| M2: Market model method | $R2 = r_{jt}$ $= R_{jt} - \hat{\alpha}_j - \hat{\beta}_j R_{mt}$ | $\hat{\alpha}_j$ $\hat{\beta}_j$ | 0.0015 | 0.0005 | 0.0012 | -0.0005 | 0.0001 | -0.0010 |
| | | | 0.9702 | 1.0807 | 0.6233 | 1.2096 | 1.3665 | 0.5136 |
| M3: Market adjusted return method | $R3 = r_{jt}$ $= R_{jt} - R_{mt}$ | | | | | | | |

**TABLE A5.2**    Event Study for Acquiring Companies

| | RESIDUALS | | | | | | | | | AVERAGE RESIDUALS | | | CAR | | |
| | Chevron Corp. | | | Mobil Corp. | | | Imperial Oil Ltd. | | | | | | | | |
| Event Date | R1 | R2 | R3 | R1 | R2 | R3 | R1 | R2 | R3 | AR1 | AR2 | AR3 | CAR1 | CAR2 | CAR3 |
|---|---|---|---|---|---|---|---|---|---|---|---|---|---|---|---|
| −40 | 0.003 | −0.001 | −0.001 | −0.014 | −0.013 | −0.013 | 0.031 | 0.032 | 0.032 | 0.007 | 0.006 | 0.006 | 0.007 | 0.006 | 0.006 |
| −39 | 0.000 | 0.003 | 0.002 | −0.005 | 0.000 | −0.001 | 0.027 | 0.026 | 0.023 | 0.007 | 0.010 | 0.008 | 0.014 | 0.016 | 0.014 |
| −38 | 0.007 | 0.012 | 0.011 | −0.005 | −0.004 | −0.004 | 0.007 | 0.004 | 0.000 | 0.003 | 0.004 | 0.002 | 0.017 | 0.020 | 0.017 |
| −37 | 0.000 | 0.001 | 0.001 | 0.008 | 0.004 | 0.006 | 0.032 | 0.035 | 0.036 | 0.013 | 0.014 | 0.014 | 0.030 | 0.033 | 0.031 |
| −36 | 0.007 | 0.008 | 0.007 | 0.003 | 0.006 | 0.006 | 0.004 | 0.002 | −0.001 | 0.005 | 0.005 | 0.004 | 0.035 | 0.039 | 0.035 |
| −35 | 0.007 | 0.012 | 0.010 | 0.025 | 0.029 | 0.028 | −0.005 | −0.009 | −0.014 | 0.009 | 0.011 | 0.008 | 0.043 | 0.049 | 0.043 |
| −34 | −0.011 | −0.010 | −0.011 | 0.003 | 0.012 | 0.010 | −0.005 | −0.010 | −0.015 | −0.004 | −0.003 | −0.005 | 0.039 | 0.046 | 0.038 |
| −33 | −0.007 | −0.010 | −0.010 | −0.013 | 0.000 | −0.004 | 0.001 | 0.002 | 0.001 | −0.007 | −0.003 | −0.004 | 0.032 | 0.043 | 0.034 |
| −32 | −0.018 | −0.016 | −0.016 | 0.024 | 0.020 | 0.022 | 0.001 | 0.002 | 0.002 | 0.002 | 0.002 | 0.002 | 0.034 | 0.046 | 0.036 |
| −31 | 0.025 | 0.029 | 0.028 | −0.005 | 0.004 | 0.002 | 0.001 | −0.003 | −0.009 | 0.007 | 0.010 | 0.007 | 0.041 | 0.055 | 0.043 |
| −30 | 0.017 | 0.025 | 0.023 | −0.001 | 0.006 | 0.004 | 0.007 | 0.003 | −0.002 | 0.008 | 0.011 | 0.009 | 0.049 | 0.067 | 0.052 |
| −29 | 0.000 | 0.011 | 0.009 | −0.001 | 0.003 | 0.002 | 0.001 | 0.000 | −0.001 | 0.000 | 0.005 | 0.003 | 0.049 | 0.071 | 0.055 |
| −28 | −0.014 | −0.018 | −0.017 | 0.011 | 0.024 | 0.021 | 0.001 | 0.003 | 0.004 | −0.001 | 0.003 | 0.003 | 0.048 | 0.074 | 0.057 |
| −27 | 0.010 | 0.018 | 0.016 | 0.009 | 0.008 | 0.008 | −0.005 | −0.006 | −0.008 | 0.004 | 0.007 | 0.006 | 0.053 | 0.081 | 0.063 |
| −26 | −0.004 | 0.002 | 0.001 | −0.013 | −0.007 | −0.008 | −0.006 | −0.004 | −0.005 | −0.008 | −0.003 | −0.004 | 0.045 | 0.078 | 0.059 |
| −25 | −0.004 | 0.000 | −0.001 | 0.007 | 0.004 | 0.005 | −0.009 | −0.008 | −0.008 | −0.002 | −0.001 | −0.001 | 0.043 | 0.077 | 0.057 |
| −24 | 0.017 | 0.028 | 0.026 | −0.005 | 0.014 | 0.009 | −0.002 | −0.001 | 0.000 | 0.003 | 0.014 | 0.012 | 0.046 | 0.090 | 0.069 |
| −23 | 0.013 | 0.013 | 0.012 | −0.022 | 0.001 | −0.004 | −0.002 | −0.001 | 0.000 | −0.004 | 0.004 | 0.003 | 0.043 | 0.095 | 0.072 |
| −22 | −0.007 | −0.001 | −0.003 | −0.005 | −0.007 | −0.006 | 0.010 | 0.007 | 0.003 | −0.001 | 0.000 | −0.002 | 0.042 | 0.095 | 0.070 |
| −21 | 0.020 | 0.017 | 0.018 | −0.018 | 0.005 | 0.000 | 0.017 | 0.013 | 0.009 | 0.006 | 0.012 | 0.009 | 0.049 | 0.107 | 0.078 |
| −20 | −0.017 | −0.001 | −0.004 | −0.005 | 0.002 | 0.000 | 0.016 | 0.018 | 0.018 | 0.002 | 0.006 | 0.005 | 0.046 | 0.113 | 0.083 |
| −19 | −0.025 | −0.005 | −0.008 | −0.001 | −0.007 | −0.005 | 0.004 | 0.004 | 0.003 | −0.007 | −0.003 | −0.003 | 0.039 | 0.110 | 0.080 |
| −18 | −0.008 | −0.009 | −0.009 | 0.003 | 0.017 | 0.014 | 0.001 | 0.001 | 0.001 | −0.001 | 0.003 | 0.002 | 0.038 | 0.114 | 0.082 |
| −17 | −0.022 | −0.001 | −0.005 | 0.003 | −0.009 | −0.005 | 0.010 | 0.008 | 0.005 | −0.003 | −0.001 | −0.002 | 0.035 | 0.113 | 0.080 |
| −16 | −0.008 | −0.001 | −0.003 | −0.005 | −0.003 | −0.003 | 0.007 | 0.008 | 0.009 | −0.002 | 0.001 | 0.001 | 0.033 | 0.114 | 0.081 |
| −15 | 0.003 | −0.002 | −0.002 | −0.001 | 0.002 | 0.001 | 0.004 | 0.003 | 0.002 | 0.002 | 0.001 | 0.001 | 0.035 | 0.115 | 0.082 |
| −14 | 0.003 | 0.016 | 0.013 | 0.029 | 0.033 | 0.032 | 0.007 | 0.004 | −0.001 | 0.013 | 0.017 | 0.015 | 0.048 | 0.133 | 0.096 |
| −13 | 0.007 | −0.004 | −0.002 | −0.022 | −0.012 | −0.014 | 0.001 | 0.002 | 0.002 | −0.005 | −0.004 | −0.005 | 0.043 | 0.128 | 0.092 |
| −12 | 0.003 | 0.005 | 0.005 | 0.012 | 0.016 | 0.015 | 0.004 | 0.008 | 0.011 | 0.006 | 0.010 | 0.010 | 0.049 | 0.138 | 0.102 |
| −11 | 0.011 | 0.013 | 0.012 | 0.007 | 0.011 | 0.010 | 0.010 | 0.003 | −0.004 | 0.009 | 0.009 | 0.006 | 0.059 | 0.147 | 0.108 |
| −10 | 0.032 | 0.036 | 0.035 | −0.001 | −0.027 | −0.020 | 0.030 | 0.029 | 0.027 | 0.020 | 0.013 | 0.014 | 0.079 | 0.160 | 0.122 |
| −9 | 0.007 | 0.016 | 0.014 | 0.036 | 0.021 | 0.025 | 0.024 | 0.022 | 0.020 | 0.022 | 0.020 | 0.020 | 0.101 | 0.179 | 0.142 |
| −8 | 0.000 | 0.003 | 0.002 | 0.007 | 0.026 | 0.021 | 0.029 | 0.028 | 0.026 | 0.012 | 0.019 | 0.017 | 0.113 | 0.198 | 0.158 |
| −7 | 0.010 | 0.013 | 0.012 | −0.001 | −0.004 | −0.003 | −0.013 | −0.012 | −0.012 | −0.001 | −0.001 | −0.001 | 0.112 | 0.198 | 0.157 |
| −6 | 0.003 | −0.020 | −0.016 | 0.011 | 0.003 | 0.005 | −0.002 | −0.004 | −0.007 | 0.004 | −0.007 | −0.006 | 0.116 | 0.190 | 0.151 |
| −5 | 0.037 | 0.024 | 0.026 | −0.005 | −0.014 | −0.011 | 0.009 | 0.007 | 0.004 | 0.014 | 0.006 | 0.006 | 0.130 | 0.196 | 0.158 |
| −4 | −0.014 | 0.003 | 0.000 | −0.025 | −0.014 | −0.016 | 0.001 | 0.000 | −0.002 | −0.013 | −0.003 | −0.006 | 0.117 | 0.193 | 0.152 |
| −3 | −0.014 | −0.016 | −0.016 | −0.021 | −0.007 | −0.011 | 0.001 | 0.000 | −0.002 | −0.011 | −0.008 | −0.009 | 0.106 | 0.185 | 0.142 |
| −2 | −0.027 | −0.035 | −0.034 | −0.005 | 0.010 | 0.007 | −0.002 | −0.001 | −0.001 | −0.012 | −0.008 | −0.009 | 0.094 | 0.177 | 0.133 |
| −1 | −0.007 | −0.015 | −0.014 | 0.007 | 0.004 | 0.005 | 0.001 | −0.004 | −0.009 | 0.000 | −0.005 | −0.006 | 0.094 | 0.172 | 0.127 |
| 0 | 0.000 | 0.009 | 0.007 | −0.005 | 0.002 | 0.000 | −0.002 | −0.003 | −0.005 | −0.003 | 0.003 | 0.001 | 0.092 | 0.175 | 0.128 |
| 1 | −0.046 | −0.033 | −0.036 | −0.018 | −0.031 | −0.027 | −0.021 | −0.021 | −0.022 | −0.028 | −0.028 | −0.028 | 0.064 | 0.146 | 0.100 |
| 2 | −0.008 | 0.006 | 0.003 | −0.005 | −0.010 | −0.008 | −0.028 | −0.024 | −0.023 | −0.013 | −0.009 | −0.009 | 0.050 | 0.137 | 0.090 |
| 3 | 0.011 | 0.008 | 0.008 | −0.005 | −0.004 | −0.004 | −0.020 | −0.025 | −0.030 | −0.005 | −0.007 | −0.009 | 0.045 | 0.130 | 0.081 |
| 4 | 0.007 | 0.013 | 0.012 | 0.007 | 0.002 | 0.004 | 0.004 | 0.003 | 0.000 | 0.006 | 0.006 | 0.005 | 0.051 | 0.136 | 0.087 |
| 5 | 0.000 | −0.012 | −0.010 | 0.012 | −0.002 | 0.002 | 0.007 | 0.003 | −0.002 | 0.006 | −0.004 | −0.003 | 0.057 | 0.132 | 0.083 |
| 6 | −0.004 | −0.008 | −0.008 | −0.013 | −0.001 | −0.004 | 0.001 | −0.002 | −0.006 | −0.006 | −0.004 | −0.006 | 0.052 | 0.128 | 0.077 |
| 7 | −0.011 | −0.010 | −0.011 | 0.007 | 0.001 | 0.003 | 0.001 | −0.001 | −0.003 | −0.001 | −0.003 | −0.004 | 0.051 | 0.125 | 0.074 |
| 8 | 0.014 | 0.010 | 0.010 | 0.028 | 0.030 | 0.030 | −0.005 | −0.009 | −0.013 | 0.012 | 0.010 | 0.009 | 0.063 | 0.135 | 0.083 |

**TABLE A5.2** *(cont.)*

| | | | | | | | | | | | | | | | |
|---|---|---|---|---|---|---|---|---|---|---|---|---|---|---|---|
| | | | | RESIDUALS | | | | | | AVERAGE RESIDUALS | | | CAR | | |
| | *Chevron Corp.* | | | *Mobil Corp.* | | | *Imperial Oil Ltd.* | | | | | | | | |
| *Event Date* | *R1* | *R2* | *R3* | *R1* | *R2* | *R3* | *R1* | *R2* | *R3* | *AR1* | *AR2* | *AR3* | *CAR1* | *CAR2* | *CAR3* |
| 9 | 0.000 | −0.012 | −0.011 | −0.021 | −0.007 | −0.010 | 0.004 | 0.004 | 0.003 | −0.006 | −0.005 | −0.006 | 0.057 | 0.130 | 0.077 |
| 10 | −0.018 | −0.007 | −0.009 | −0.005 | −0.004 | −0.004 | 0.004 | 0.004 | 0.003 | −0.007 | −0.002 | −0.003 | 0.051 | 0.128 | 0.073 |
| 11 | 0.014 | 0.009 | 0.009 | −0.005 | −0.004 | −0.004 | 0.001 | 0.000 | −0.001 | 0.003 | 0.002 | 0.001 | 0.054 | 0.130 | 0.074 |
| 12 | 0.000 | 0.002 | 0.001 | 0.007 | 0.004 | 0.005 | 0.001 | 0.002 | 0.001 | 0.003 | 0.003 | 0.003 | 0.057 | 0.132 | 0.077 |
| 13 | −0.019 | −0.006 | −0.008 | −0.005 | −0.023 | −0.018 | 0.001 | −0.004 | −0.010 | −0.008 | −0.011 | −0.012 | 0.049 | 0.121 | 0.065 |
| 14 | 0.003 | 0.005 | 0.004 | 0.003 | 0.005 | 0.005 | −0.002 | −0.001 | −0.001 | 0.001 | 0.003 | 0.003 | 0.050 | 0.124 | 0.068 |
| 15 | 0.018 | 0.019 | 0.019 | 0.007 | 0.010 | 0.009 | −0.008 | −0.004 | −0.002 | 0.006 | 0.008 | 0.009 | 0.056 | 0.132 | 0.076 |
| 16 | 0.014 | 0.011 | 0.012 | −0.013 | −0.004 | −0.006 | −0.002 | 0.004 | 0.009 | 0.000 | 0.004 | 0.005 | 0.056 | 0.136 | 0.081 |
| 17 | 0.025 | 0.009 | 0.011 | −0.001 | 0.004 | 0.003 | 0.001 | 0.001 | −0.001 | 0.008 | 0.005 | 0.005 | 0.064 | 0.141 | 0.086 |
| 18 | 0.014 | 0.015 | 0.015 | 0.003 | 0.005 | 0.005 | 0.007 | 0.007 | 0.007 | 0.008 | 0.009 | 0.009 | 0.071 | 0.150 | 0.094 |
| 19 | 0.027 | 0.029 | 0.029 | −0.001 | 0.020 | 0.015 | 0.013 | 0.009 | 0.005 | 0.013 | 0.019 | 0.016 | 0.084 | 0.170 | 0.110 |
| 20 | 0.000 | 0.008 | 0.006 | −0.009 | −0.009 | −0.009 | −0.005 | −0.006 | −0.008 | −0.005 | −0.002 | −0.003 | 0.079 | 0.167 | 0.107 |
| 21 | 0.003 | 0.007 | 0.006 | −0.001 | 0.000 | 0.000 | −0.002 | −0.005 | −0.008 | 0.000 | 0.001 | −0.001 | 0.079 | 0.168 | 0.106 |
| 22 | −0.014 | −0.012 | −0.013 | −0.001 | −0.003 | −0.002 | −0.011 | −0.010 | −0.010 | −0.009 | −0.008 | −0.008 | 0.071 | 0.160 | 0.098 |
| 23 | −0.014 | 0.005 | 0.001 | 0.003 | 0.011 | 0.010 | −0.011 | −0.004 | 0.002 | −0.007 | 0.004 | 0.004 | 0.063 | 0.164 | 0.102 |
| 24 | 0.003 | 0.004 | 0.003 | 0.024 | 0.006 | 0.011 | 0.001 | −0.001 | −0.003 | 0.009 | 0.003 | 0.004 | 0.073 | 0.167 | 0.106 |
| 25 | 0.010 | 0.011 | 0.011 | 0.011 | 0.013 | 0.013 | −0.002 | 0.005 | 0.010 | 0.006 | 0.009 | 0.011 | 0.079 | 0.177 | 0.117 |
| 26 | 0.010 | 0.008 | 0.008 | 0.007 | 0.001 | 0.003 | 0.010 | 0.010 | 0.008 | 0.009 | 0.006 | 0.006 | 0.088 | 0.183 | 0.124 |
| 27 | 0.000 | 0.007 | 0.005 | −0.005 | −0.011 | −0.009 | −0.002 | −0.004 | −0.006 | −0.003 | −0.002 | −0.003 | 0.085 | 0.180 | 0.120 |
| 28 | 0.036 | 0.020 | 0.023 | −0.013 | −0.005 | −0.007 | −0.005 | −0.003 | −0.003 | 0.006 | 0.004 | 0.004 | 0.091 | 0.184 | 0.125 |
| 29 | 0.006 | 0.007 | 0.007 | 0.015 | 0.016 | 0.016 | 0.025 | 0.021 | 0.016 | 0.015 | 0.015 | 0.013 | 0.107 | 0.199 | 0.138 |
| 30 | 0.016 | 0.011 | 0.011 | −0.001 | 0.009 | 0.006 | 0.013 | 0.011 | 0.008 | 0.009 | 0.010 | 0.009 | 0.116 | 0.209 | 0.146 |
| 31 | 0.009 | 0.004 | 0.005 | 0.003 | −0.004 | −0.002 | 0.004 | −0.001 | −0.007 | 0.005 | 0.000 | −0.001 | 0.121 | 0.209 | 0.145 |
| 32 | −0.016 | −0.009 | −0.010 | 0.003 | −0.001 | 0.001 | 0.004 | 0.005 | 0.004 | −0.003 | −0.002 | −0.002 | 0.118 | 0.207 | 0.143 |
| 33 | −0.013 | −0.013 | −0.013 | −0.005 | −0.018 | −0.014 | 0.013 | 0.012 | 0.011 | −0.002 | −0.006 | −0.005 | 0.116 | 0.201 | 0.138 |
| 34 | −0.023 | −0.014 | −0.016 | −0.001 | 0.001 | 0.001 | 0.015 | 0.016 | 0.015 | −0.003 | 0.001 | 0.000 | 0.113 | 0.202 | 0.138 |
| 35 | 0.019 | 0.013 | 0.014 | −0.009 | −0.009 | −0.009 | 0.001 | 0.002 | 0.002 | 0.004 | 0.002 | 0.003 | 0.117 | 0.204 | 0.140 |
| 36 | 0.000 | −0.004 | −0.003 | 0.001 | −0.012 | −0.008 | 0.024 | 0.021 | 0.017 | 0.008 | 0.002 | 0.002 | 0.125 | 0.206 | 0.142 |
| 37 | 0.013 | 0.001 | 0.003 | −0.005 | −0.010 | −0.008 | 0.012 | 0.012 | 0.012 | 0.006 | 0.001 | 0.002 | 0.131 | 0.207 | 0.144 |
| 38 | 0.000 | 0.001 | 0.001 | −0.013 | −0.009 | −0.010 | 0.017 | 0.016 | 0.013 | 0.001 | 0.003 | 0.001 | 0.133 | 0.210 | 0.145 |
| 39 | 0.009 | 0.009 | 0.009 | −0.009 | 0.005 | 0.002 | 0.006 | 0.002 | −0.002 | 0.002 | 0.006 | 0.003 | 0.135 | 0.215 | 0.148 |
| 40 | −0.010 | −0.021 | −0.019 | −0.001 | −0.002 | −0.002 | −0.007 | 0.003 | 0.012 | −0.006 | −0.007 | −0.003 | 0.129 | 0.209 | 0.144 |

*Source:* University of Chicago Center for Research on Security Prices (CRSP) tapes.

Finally, the average residuals are cumulated over the entire event period to obtain the cumulative average residual (CAR). For the acquiring firms in Table A5.2, the cumulative average residual based on the mean adjusted residual is defined as *CAR*1. On date −40, *CAR*1 is equal to 0.007, the *AR*1 on date −40. On date −39, *CAR*1 is equal to the sum of the *AR*1 from date −40 to −39 or 0.007 + 0.007 = 0.014. On date −38, the corresponding *CAR*1 would be 0.007 + 0.007 + 0.003 = 0.0017, and so on (see row *CAR*1 under *CAR* columns in Table A5.2). *CAR*2 and *CAR*3 are calculated in the same way.

The residuals, average residuals, and CARs for the target companies shown in Table A5.3 are calculated by the same procedures. The CARs in Table A5.2 for the acquiring firms are graphed in Figure A5.1. We see a picture of a sharp rise in the CARs from −40 to −5. A small decline is followed by a strong recovery. For this illustrative sample of three firms, the three methods give somewhat different results, but patterns

**TABLE A5.3**   Event Study for Target Companies

| Event Date | RESIDUALS | | | | | | | | | AVERAGE RESIDUALS | | | CAR | | |
| | Gulf Corp. | | | Superior Oil Co. | | | Texaco Canada Inc. | | | | | | | | |
| | R1 | R2 | R3 | R1 | R2 | R3 | R1 | R2 | R3 | AR1 | AR2 | AR3 | CAR1 | CAR2 | CAR3 |
| --- | --- | --- | --- | --- | --- | --- | --- | --- | --- | --- | --- | --- | --- | --- | --- |
| −40 | 0.054 | 0.051 | 0.052 | −0.008 | −0.007 | −0.006 | 0.019 | 0.020 | 0.022 | 0.022 | 0.021 | 0.022 | 0.022 | 0.021 | 0.022 |
| −39 | 0.006 | 0.009 | 0.010 | 0.015 | 0.020 | 0.020 | 0.022 | 0.021 | 0.021 | 0.014 | 0.016 | 0.017 | 0.036 | 0.038 | 0.039 |
| −38 | 0.035 | 0.039 | 0.041 | 0.002 | 0.003 | 0.003 | 0.010 | 0.006 | 0.005 | 0.016 | 0.016 | 0.017 | 0.052 | 0.054 | 0.056 |
| −37 | −0.025 | −0.024 | −0.022 | 0.012 | 0.009 | 0.010 | 0.006 | 0.009 | 0.012 | −0.002 | −0.002 | 0.000 | 0.049 | 0.052 | 0.056 |
| −36 | 0.019 | 0.020 | 0.021 | −0.014 | −0.012 | −0.011 | −0.009 | −0.011 | −0.011 | −0.001 | −0.001 | 0.000 | 0.048 | 0.051 | 0.055 |
| −35 | 0.011 | 0.015 | 0.016 | 0.044 | 0.048 | 0.048 | 0.018 | 0.013 | 0.011 | 0.024 | 0.025 | 0.025 | 0.072 | 0.076 | 0.081 |
| −34 | −0.012 | −0.012 | −0.010 | −0.004 | 0.002 | 0.002 | 0.017 | 0.012 | 0.010 | 0.000 | 0.001 | 0.001 | 0.072 | 0.077 | 0.081 |
| −33 | −0.007 | −0.010 | −0.008 | −0.017 | −0.006 | −0.007 | 0.002 | 0.003 | 0.005 | −0.007 | −0.004 | −0.003 | 0.065 | 0.073 | 0.078 |
| −32 | −0.007 | −0.005 | −0.004 | −0.001 | −0.004 | −0.004 | −0.013 | −0.011 | −0.009 | −0.007 | −0.007 | −0.006 | 0.058 | 0.066 | 0.072 |
| −31 | −0.028 | −0.025 | −0.023 | 0.024 | 0.031 | 0.031 | 0.006 | 0.001 | −0.001 | 0.001 | 0.002 | 0.002 | 0.059 | 0.068 | 0.075 |
| −30 | −0.002 | 0.004 | 0.006 | −0.035 | −0.030 | −0.030 | −0.002 | −0.006 | −0.008 | −0.013 | −0.011 | −0.011 | 0.046 | 0.057 | 0.064 |
| −29 | 0.011 | 0.020 | 0.022 | 0.046 | 0.049 | 0.050 | 0.032 | 0.031 | 0.032 | 0.030 | 0.034 | 0.035 | 0.075 | 0.091 | 0.099 |
| −28 | 0.053 | 0.050 | 0.052 | −0.025 | −0.016 | −0.016 | −0.002 | 0.001 | 0.004 | 0.009 | 0.012 | 0.013 | 0.084 | 0.103 | 0.112 |
| −27 | 0.010 | 0.016 | 0.018 | 0.039 | 0.038 | 0.039 | −0.002 | −0.002 | −0.001 | 0.016 | 0.018 | 0.019 | 0.100 | 0.120 | 0.130 |
| −26 | −0.010 | −0.005 | −0.003 | −0.016 | −0.011 | −0.011 | −0.002 | 0.000 | 0.002 | −0.009 | −0.005 | −0.004 | 0.091 | 0.115 | 0.126 |
| −25 | 0.050 | 0.053 | 0.054 | −0.004 | −0.007 | −0.006 | −0.005 | −0.004 | −0.002 | 0.013 | 0.014 | 0.015 | 0.104 | 0.129 | 0.142 |
| −24 | 0.007 | 0.016 | 0.018 | −0.010 | 0.004 | 0.004 | −0.009 | −0.007 | −0.004 | −0.004 | 0.005 | 0.006 | 0.100 | 0.134 | 0.147 |
| −23 | −0.009 | −0.010 | −0.008 | −0.020 | −0.001 | −0.002 | −0.002 | 0.001 | 0.003 | −0.010 | −0.004 | −0.003 | 0.090 | 0.130 | 0.145 |
| −22 | 0.036 | 0.041 | 0.042 | 0.011 | 0.010 | 0.011 | 0.006 | 0.002 | 0.001 | 0.018 | 0.018 | 0.018 | 0.108 | 0.148 | 0.163 |
| −21 | 0.048 | 0.046 | 0.047 | −0.023 | −0.004 | −0.005 | 0.016 | 0.012 | 0.011 | 0.014 | 0.018 | 0.018 | 0.122 | 0.166 | 0.180 |
| −20 | −0.033 | −0.020 | −0.018 | −0.011 | −0.005 | −0.005 | −0.002 | 0.001 | 0.003 | −0.015 | −0.008 | −0.007 | 0.107 | 0.158 | 0.174 |
| −19 | 0.007 | 0.023 | 0.025 | 0.005 | 0.000 | 0.001 | −0.002 | −0.001 | 0.000 | 0.003 | 0.007 | 0.009 | 0.110 | 0.165 | 0.183 |
| −18 | −0.020 | −0.021 | −0.020 | −0.014 | −0.003 | −0.003 | 0.006 | 0.006 | 0.008 | −0.009 | −0.006 | −0.005 | 0.101 | 0.159 | 0.178 |
| −17 | −0.009 | 0.008 | 0.010 | −0.001 | −0.011 | −0.010 | 0.005 | 0.003 | 0.003 | −0.002 | 0.000 | 0.001 | 0.099 | 0.159 | 0.179 |
| −16 | 0.037 | 0.042 | 0.044 | 0.040 | 0.042 | 0.043 | 0.005 | 0.007 | 0.010 | 0.028 | 0.031 | 0.032 | 0.127 | 0.190 | 0.211 |
| −15 | 0.002 | −0.002 | −0.001 | −0.007 | −0.005 | −0.005 | 0.012 | 0.012 | 0.012 | 0.002 | 0.001 | 0.002 | 0.129 | 0.191 | 0.213 |
| −14 | −0.057 | −0.047 | −0.045 | 0.005 | 0.008 | 0.009 | 0.016 | 0.012 | 0.010 | −0.012 | −0.009 | −0.009 | 0.117 | 0.182 | 0.204 |
| −13 | 0.065 | 0.057 | 0.058 | −0.023 | −0.015 | −0.015 | −0.008 | −0.007 | −0.005 | 0.011 | 0.012 | 0.013 | 0.128 | 0.194 | 0.217 |
| −12 | −0.035 | −0.033 | −0.031 | −0.004 | −0.001 | −0.001 | −0.002 | 0.004 | 0.008 | −0.014 | −0.010 | −0.008 | 0.115 | 0.183 | 0.209 |
| −11 | −0.031 | −0.029 | −0.028 | −0.026 | −0.024 | −0.023 | −0.002 | −0.009 | −0.013 | −0.020 | −0.021 | −0.021 | 0.095 | 0.163 | 0.187 |
| −10 | −0.002 | 0.001 | 0.002 | 0.018 | −0.003 | 0.000 | 0.022 | 0.021 | 0.021 | 0.013 | 0.006 | 0.008 | 0.108 | 0.169 | 0.195 |
| −9 | −0.028 | −0.020 | −0.019 | 0.024 | 0.012 | 0.013 | −0.002 | −0.003 | −0.003 | −0.002 | −0.004 | −0.003 | 0.106 | 0.165 | 0.192 |
| −8 | 0.107 | 0.110 | 0.111 | −0.009 | 0.006 | 0.005 | 0.005 | 0.004 | 0.005 | 0.034 | 0.040 | 0.041 | 0.140 | 0.205 | 0.233 |
| −7 | 0.094 | 0.097 | 0.098 | 0.008 | 0.006 | 0.007 | −0.008 | −0.007 | −0.005 | 0.031 | 0.032 | 0.033 | 0.172 | 0.237 | 0.266 |
| −6 | −0.024 | −0.042 | −0.041 | 0.030 | 0.023 | 0.024 | −0.002 | −0.004 | −0.005 | 0.002 | −0.008 | −0.007 | 0.173 | 0.229 | 0.259 |
| −5 | 0.092 | 0.081 | 0.082 | −0.019 | −0.026 | −0.025 | −0.011 | −0.014 | −0.014 | 0.020 | 0.014 | 0.014 | 0.193 | 0.243 | 0.273 |
| −4 | 0.007 | 0.021 | 0.022 | 0.002 | 0.010 | 0.010 | 0.039 | 0.038 | 0.039 | 0.016 | 0.023 | 0.024 | 0.209 | 0.266 | 0.297 |
| −3 | −0.004 | −0.006 | −0.004 | −0.016 | −0.005 | −0.006 | −0.009 | −0.010 | −0.009 | −0.010 | −0.007 | −0.006 | 0.199 | 0.259 | 0.291 |
| −2 | 0.005 | −0.001 | 0.000 | −0.035 | −0.023 | −0.023 | 0.006 | 0.008 | 0.009 | −0.008 | −0.005 | −0.005 | 0.191 | 0.254 | 0.286 |
| −1 | −0.002 | −0.008 | −0.007 | −0.043 | −0.046 | −0.045 | 0.002 | −0.003 | −0.005 | −0.014 | −0.019 | −0.019 | 0.177 | 0.235 | 0.267 |
| 0 | 0.016 | 0.024 | 0.025 | 0.049 | 0.054 | 0.055 | 0.002 | 0.001 | 0.002 | 0.022 | 0.026 | 0.027 | 0.199 | 0.261 | 0.294 |
| 1 | −0.023 | −0.013 | −0.012 | 0.008 | −0.002 | −0.001 | 0.029 | 0.029 | 0.030 | 0.005 | 0.005 | 0.006 | 0.204 | 0.265 | 0.300 |
| 2 | −0.067 | −0.056 | −0.054 | −0.042 | −0.046 | −0.045 | 0.002 | 0.006 | 0.009 | −0.036 | −0.032 | −0.030 | 0.168 | 0.233 | 0.270 |
| 3 | 0.033 | 0.030 | 0.031 | −0.001 | 0.000 | 0.000 | 0.002 | −0.004 | −0.006 | 0.011 | 0.009 | 0.008 | 0.179 | 0.242 | 0.279 |
| 4 | −0.030 | −0.025 | −0.024 | −0.011 | −0.015 | −0.014 | −0.002 | −0.003 | −0.003 | −0.014 | −0.015 | −0.014 | 0.165 | 0.227 | 0.265 |
| 5 | 0.015 | 0.006 | 0.007 | 0.049 | 0.038 | 0.039 | 0.002 | −0.003 | −0.004 | 0.022 | 0.014 | 0.014 | 0.187 | 0.241 | 0.279 |
| 6 | −0.034 | −0.038 | −0.036 | 0.011 | 0.022 | 0.021 | 0.000 | −0.003 | −0.004 | −0.008 | −0.006 | −0.006 | 0.179 | 0.235 | 0.272 |
| 7 | 0.019 | 0.020 | 0.022 | 0.018 | 0.012 | 0.013 | 0.000 | −0.002 | −0.002 | 0.012 | 0.010 | 0.011 | 0.192 | 0.245 | 0.284 |
| 8 | 0.011 | 0.007 | 0.009 | 0.017 | 0.019 | 0.019 | −0.002 | −0.006 | −0.008 | 0.009 | 0.007 | 0.007 | 0.201 | 0.252 | 0.290 |

**TABLE A5.3** *(cont.)*

| | RESIDUALS | | | | | | | | | AVERAGE RESIDUALS | | | CAR | | |
| | Gulf Corp. | | | Superior Oil Co. | | | Texaco Canada Inc. | | | | | | | | |
| Event Date | R1 | R2 | R3 | R1 | R2 | R3 | R1 | R2 | R3 | AR1 | AR2 | AR3 | CAR1 | CAR2 | CAR3 |
|---|---|---|---|---|---|---|---|---|---|---|---|---|---|---|---|
| 9 | 0.083 | 0.073 | 0.074 | −0.013 | −0.002 | −0.002 | −0.009 | −0.009 | −0.007 | 0.020 | 0.021 | 0.022 | 0.221 | 0.273 | 0.312 |
| 10 | 0.006 | 0.016 | 0.017 | −0.004 | −0.003 | −0.003 | −0.002 | −0.001 | 0.000 | 0.000 | 0.004 | 0.005 | 0.221 | 0.276 | 0.317 |
| 11 | 0.010 | 0.005 | 0.007 | 0.002 | 0.003 | 0.004 | −0.002 | −0.002 | −0.001 | 0.003 | 0.002 | 0.003 | 0.224 | 0.278 | 0.320 |
| 12 | 0.028 | 0.030 | 0.032 | −0.010 | −0.013 | −0.012 | 0.002 | 0.003 | 0.005 | 0.007 | 0.007 | 0.008 | 0.231 | 0.285 | 0.328 |
| 13 | −0.002 | 0.008 | 0.010 | 0.008 | −0.006 | −0.004 | −0.002 | −0.008 | −0.010 | 0.001 | −0.002 | −0.002 | 0.233 | 0.283 | 0.326 |
| 14 | −0.002 | −0.001 | 0.001 | 0.008 | 0.010 | 0.010 | −0.002 | 0.000 | 0.002 | 0.001 | 0.003 | 0.004 | 0.234 | 0.286 | 0.330 |
| 15 | 0.001 | 0.002 | 0.004 | 0.011 | 0.013 | 0.013 | 0.006 | 0.010 | 0.014 | 0.006 | 0.008 | 0.010 | 0.240 | 0.295 | 0.341 |
| 16 | 0.001 | −0.001 | 0.000 | −0.001 | 0.006 | 0.006 | −0.005 | 0.003 | 0.009 | −0.002 | 0.003 | 0.005 | 0.238 | 0.297 | 0.346 |
| 17 | 0.011 | −0.002 | −0.001 | −0.007 | −0.003 | −0.003 | −0.002 | −0.002 | −0.001 | 0.001 | −0.002 | −0.001 | 0.239 | 0.295 | 0.344 |
| 18 | 0.001 | 0.003 | 0.004 | −0.001 | 0.000 | 0.001 | −0.002 | −0.001 | 0.001 | −0.001 | 0.001 | 0.002 | 0.238 | 0.296 | 0.346 |
| 19 | −0.007 | −0.005 | −0.004 | −0.001 | 0.016 | 0.015 | 0.004 | 0.000 | −0.001 | −0.001 | 0.003 | 0.003 | 0.237 | 0.299 | 0.349 |
| 20 | 0.004 | 0.011 | 0.013 | −0.001 | −0.001 | 0.000 | −0.003 | −0.004 | −0.004 | 0.000 | 0.002 | 0.003 | 0.237 | 0.301 | 0.352 |
| 21 | 0.001 | 0.005 | 0.006 | 0.005 | 0.006 | 0.006 | 0.000 | −0.003 | −0.004 | 0.002 | 0.003 | 0.003 | 0.239 | 0.304 | 0.355 |
| 22 | −0.001 | 0.001 | 0.002 | −0.001 | −0.003 | −0.002 | −0.005 | −0.004 | −0.002 | −0.002 | −0.002 | −0.001 | 0.237 | 0.302 | 0.355 |
| 23 | −0.005 | 0.010 | 0.012 | −0.001 | 0.005 | 0.005 | 0.002 | 0.011 | 0.018 | −0.001 | 0.009 | 0.012 | 0.235 | 0.310 | 0.366 |
| 24 | −0.002 | −0.002 | 0.000 | −0.001 | −0.016 | −0.014 | −0.002 | −0.003 | −0.003 | −0.002 | −0.007 | −0.006 | 0.233 | 0.304 | 0.360 |
| 25 | −0.002 | −0.001 | 0.000 | −0.004 | −0.003 | −0.003 | 0.005 | 0.014 | 0.020 | 0.000 | 0.003 | 0.006 | 0.233 | 0.307 | 0.366 |
| 26 | 0.003 | 0.001 | 0.002 | −0.001 | −0.006 | −0.005 | 0.002 | 0.002 | 0.003 | 0.001 | −0.001 | 0.000 | 0.234 | 0.306 | 0.366 |
| 27 | −0.004 | 0.002 | 0.004 | −0.004 | 0.009 | −0.008 | −0.016 | −0.018 | −0.018 | −0.008 | −0.008 | −0.007 | 0.226 | 0.298 | 0.359 |
| 28 | 0.003 | −0.010 | −0.009 | −0.004 | 0.002 | 0.002 | −0.002 | 0.001 | 0.003 | −0.001 | −0.002 | −0.001 | 0.225 | 0.295 | 0.358 |
| 29 | 0.003 | 0.004 | 0.005 | −0.001 | −0.001 | 0.000 | −0.002 | −0.007 | −0.009 | 0.000 | −0.001 | −0.001 | 0.225 | 0.294 | 0.357 |
| 30 | −0.001 | −0.005 | −0.003 | −0.001 | 0.006 | 0.006 | 0.002 | 0.000 | 0.000 | 0.000 | 0.001 | 0.001 | 0.225 | 0.295 | 0.358 |
| 31 | 0.001 | −0.003 | −0.002 | −0.001 | −0.007 | −0.006 | 0.024 | 0.018 | 0.016 | 0.008 | 0.003 | 0.003 | 0.233 | 0.297 | 0.361 |
| 32 | −0.010 | −0.004 | −0.003 | 0.008 | 0.005 | 0.006 | −0.034 | −0.033 | −0.031 | −0.012 | −0.011 | −0.009 | 0.221 | 0.287 | 0.351 |
| 33 | 0.001 | 0.001 | 0.003 | 0.002 | −0.008 | −0.007 | −0.005 | −0.006 | −0.005 | −0.001 | −0.004 | −0.003 | 0.220 | 0.283 | 0.348 |
| 34 | 0.004 | 0.011 | 0.013 | −0.001 | 0.000 | 0.001 | −0.005 | −0.005 | −0.003 | −0.001 | 0.002 | 0.003 | 0.220 | 0.285 | 0.352 |
| 35 | 0.003 | −0.002 | −0.001 | −0.004 | −0.004 | −0.004 | 0.004 | 0.006 | 0.008 | 0.001 | 0.000 | 0.001 | 0.220 | 0.285 | 0.353 |
| 36 | −0.001 | −0.003 | −0.002 | 0.002 | −0.008 | −0.007 | −0.007 | −0.011 | −0.012 | −0.002 | −0.007 | −0.007 | 0.218 | 0.277 | 0.346 |
| 37 | 0.002 | −0.006 | −0.005 | 0.002 | −0.002 | −0.001 | 0.000 | 0.001 | 0.002 | 0.002 | −0.002 | −0.001 | 0.220 | 0.275 | 0.345 |
| 38 | −0.005 | −0.004 | −0.003 | 0.002 | 0.005 | 0.005 | −0.003 | −0.006 | −0.006 | −0.002 | −0.002 | −0.001 | 0.218 | 0.273 | 0.344 |
| 39 | 0.002 | 0.002 | 0.004 | −0.004 | 0.007 | 0.007 | 0.002 | −0.002 | −0.004 | 0.000 | 0.002 | 0.002 | 0.218 | 0.276 | 0.346 |
| 40 | −0.005 | −0.014 | −0.013 | −0.004 | −0.005 | −0.005 | −0.016 | −0.004 | 0.005 | −0.009 | −0.008 | −0.004 | 0.209 | 0.268 | 0.342 |

*Source:* CRSP tape.

are quite parallel. Figure A5.2 graphs the data from Table A5.3 for target firms. The patterns are again similar, but the CARs are much larger for the target companies.

## Absolute Gains and Losses

The residual returns are also known as the abnormal returns because they represent the return that was unexpected or different from the return that would have been expected if the event had not occurred. The absolute dollar gain or loss at time $t\,(\Delta W_t)$ due to the abnormal return during the event period is defined by,

$$\Delta W_t = CAR_t \times MKTVAL_o$$

where $MKTVAL_o$ is the market value of the firm at a date previous to the event window interval and $CAR_t$ is the cumulative residuals to date $t$ for the firm. The percent return times the market value of the firm is the total dollar gain or loss.

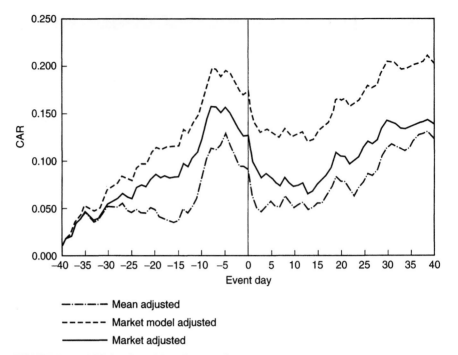

FIGURE A5.1  CAR for Acquiring Companies

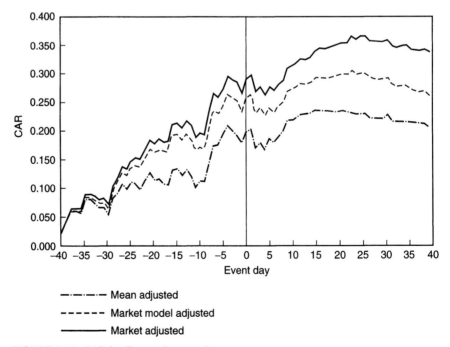

FIGURE A5.2  CAR for Target Companies

Table A5.4 presents the market adjusted residual returns ($R3$) that were previously displayed in Table A5.2 and A5.3. In Table A5.4, the $CAR3$s are the cumulative abnormal returns obtained by cumulating the daily abnormal returns $R3$ for each individual firm.

**TABLE A5.4**   Market Adjusted CAR for Individual Companies

| | TARGETS | | | | | | ACQUIRERS | | | | | |
|---|---|---|---|---|---|---|---|---|---|---|---|---|
| | Gulf Corp. | | Superior Oil | | Texaco Canada | | Chevron | | Mobil | | Imperial Oil | |
| Event Date | R3 | CAR3 | R3 | CAR3 | R3 | CAR3 | R3 | CAR3 | R3 | CAR3 | R3 | CAR3 |
| −40 | 0.052 | 0.052 | −0.006 | −0.006 | 0.022 | 0.022 | −0.001 | −0.001 | −0.013 | −0.013 | 0.032 | 0.032 |
| −39 | 0.010 | 0.063 | 0.020 | 0.013 | 0.021 | 0.043 | 0.002 | 0.001 | −0.001 | −0.013 | 0.023 | 0.055 |
| −38 | 0.041 | 0.104 | 0.003 | 0.017 | 0.005 | 0.048 | 0.011 | 0.012 | −0.004 | −0.018 | 0.000 | 0.055 |
| −37 | −0.022 | 0.081 | 0.010 | 0.026 | 0.012 | 0.060 | 0.001 | 0.013 | 0.006 | −0.012 | 0.036 | 0.091 |
| −36 | 0.021 | 0.102 | −0.011 | 0.015 | −0.011 | 0.049 | 0.007 | 0.020 | 0.006 | −0.007 | −0.001 | 0.091 |
| −35 | 0.016 | 0.119 | 0.048 | 0.063 | 0.011 | 0.060 | 0.010 | 0.031 | 0.028 | 0.022 | −0.014 | 0.077 |
| −34 | −0.010 | 0.108 | 0.002 | 0.066 | 0.010 | 0.070 | −0.011 | 0.020 | 0.010 | 0.032 | −0.015 | 0.061 |
| −33 | −0.008 | 0.100 | −0.007 | 0.059 | 0.005 | 0.075 | −0.010 | 0.010 | −0.004 | 0.028 | 0.001 | 0.063 |
| −32 | −0.004 | 0.096 | −0.004 | 0.055 | −0.009 | 0.066 | −0.016 | −0.006 | 0.022 | 0.050 | 0.002 | 0.064 |
| −31 | −0.023 | 0.073 | 0.031 | 0.086 | −0.001 | 0.064 | 0.028 | 0.022 | 0.002 | 0.051 | −0.009 | 0.056 |
| −30 | 0.006 | 0.079 | −0.030 | 0.057 | −0.008 | 0.056 | 0.023 | 0.045 | 0.004 | 0.055 | −0.002 | 0.054 |
| −29 | 0.022 | 0.101 | 0.050 | 0.106 | 0.032 | 0.088 | 0.009 | 0.054 | 0.002 | 0.057 | −0.001 | 0.053 |
| −28 | 0.052 | 0.153 | −0.016 | 0.091 | 0.004 | 0.092 | −0.017 | 0.037 | 0.021 | 0.078 | 0.004 | 0.057 |
| −27 | 0.018 | 0.171 | 0.039 | 0.130 | −0.001 | 0.091 | 0.016 | 0.053 | 0.008 | 0.087 | −0.008 | 0.049 |
| −26 | −0.003 | 0.168 | −0.011 | 0.119 | 0.002 | 0.092 | 0.001 | 0.054 | −0.008 | 0.078 | −0.005 | 0.045 |
| −25 | 0.054 | 0.222 | −0.006 | 0.113 | −0.002 | 0.090 | −0.001 | 0.052 | 0.005 | 0.084 | −0.008 | 0.037 |
| −24 | 0.018 | 0.240 | 0.004 | 0.117 | −0.004 | 0.086 | 0.026 | 0.078 | 0.009 | 0.093 | 0.000 | 0.036 |
| −23 | −0.008 | 0.231 | −0.002 | 0.114 | 0.003 | 0.089 | 0.012 | 0.091 | −0.004 | 0.088 | 0.000 | 0.036 |
| −22 | 0.042 | 0.273 | 0.011 | 0.125 | 0.001 | 0.090 | −0.003 | 0.088 | −0.006 | 0.082 | 0.003 | 0.039 |
| −21 | 0.047 | 0.321 | −0.005 | 0.120 | 0.011 | 0.101 | 0.018 | 0.106 | 0.000 | 0.082 | 0.009 | 0.048 |
| −20 | −0.018 | 0.303 | −0.005 | 0.115 | 0.003 | 0.103 | −0.004 | 0.102 | 0.000 | 0.082 | 0.018 | 0.066 |
| −19 | 0.025 | 0.328 | 0.001 | 0.116 | 0.000 | 0.104 | −0.008 | 0.093 | −0.005 | 0.077 | 0.003 | 0.070 |
| −18 | −0.020 | 0.309 | −0.003 | 0.113 | 0.008 | 0.111 | −0.009 | 0.085 | 0.014 | 0.091 | 0.001 | 0.070 |
| −17 | 0.010 | 0.319 | −0.010 | 0.104 | 0.003 | 0.114 | −0.005 | 0.079 | −0.005 | 0.085 | 0.005 | 0.075 |
| −16 | 0.044 | 0.362 | 0.043 | 0.146 | 0.010 | 0.124 | −0.003 | 0.077 | −0.003 | 0.082 | 0.009 | 0.084 |
| −15 | −0.001 | 0.361 | −0.005 | 0.142 | 0.012 | 0.136 | −0.002 | 0.075 | 0.001 | 0.084 | 0.002 | 0.086 |
| −14 | −0.045 | 0.316 | 0.009 | 0.150 | 0.010 | 0.147 | 0.013 | 0.088 | 0.032 | 0.116 | −0.001 | 0.085 |
| −13 | 0.058 | 0.374 | −0.015 | 0.136 | −0.005 | 0.142 | −0.002 | 0.086 | −0.014 | 0.102 | 0.002 | 0.087 |
| −12 | −0.031 | 0.342 | −0.001 | 0.135 | 0.008 | 0.149 | 0.005 | 0.091 | 0.015 | 0.117 | 0.011 | 0.097 |
| −11 | −0.028 | 0.314 | −0.023 | 0.111 | −0.013 | 0.136 | 0.012 | 0.103 | 0.010 | 0.127 | −0.004 | 0.093 |
| −10 | 0.002 | 0.317 | 0.000 | 0.111 | 0.021 | 0.157 | 0.035 | 0.138 | −0.020 | 0.108 | 0.027 | 0.120 |
| −9 | −0.019 | 0.298 | 0.013 | 0.124 | −0.003 | 0.154 | 0.014 | 0.152 | 0.025 | 0.133 | 0.020 | 0.140 |
| −8 | 0.111 | 0.410 | 0.005 | 0.129 | 0.005 | 0.159 | 0.002 | 0.154 | 0.021 | 0.154 | 0.026 | 0.166 |
| −7 | 0.098 | 0.508 | 0.007 | 0.136 | −0.005 | 0.154 | 0.012 | 0.166 | −0.003 | 0.152 | −0.012 | 0.155 |
| −6 | −0.041 | 0.466 | 0.024 | 0.160 | −0.005 | 0.150 | −0.016 | 0.150 | 0.005 | 0.157 | −0.007 | 0.147 |
| −5 | 0.082 | 0.548 | −0.025 | 0.135 | −0.014 | 0.136 | 0.026 | 0.175 | −0.011 | 0.146 | 0.004 | 0.151 |
| −4 | 0.022 | 0.571 | 0.010 | 0.146 | 0.039 | 0.174 | 0.000 | 0.175 | −0.016 | 0.130 | −0.002 | 0.150 |
| −3 | −0.004 | 0.566 | −0.006 | 0.140 | −0.009 | 0.165 | −0.016 | 0.159 | −0.011 | 0.119 | −0.002 | 0.148 |
| −2 | 0.000 | 0.567 | −0.023 | 0.117 | 0.009 | 0.175 | −0.034 | 0.126 | 0.007 | 0.125 | −0.001 | 0.147 |
| −1 | −0.007 | 0.560 | −0.045 | 0.072 | −0.005 | 0.170 | −0.014 | 0.112 | 0.005 | 0.131 | −0.009 | 0.138 |
| 0 | 0.025 | 0.585 | 0.055 | 0.126 | 0.002 | 0.171 | 0.007 | 0.119 | 0.000 | 0.131 | −0.005 | 0.134 |

**TABLE A5.4**  *(cont.)*

| | TARGETS | | | | | | ACQUIRERS | | | | | |
| | Gulf Corp. | | Superior Oil | | Texaco Canada | | Chevron | | Mobil | | Imperial Oil | |
| Event Date | R3 | CAR3 | R3 | CAR3 | R3 | CAR3 | R3 | CAR3 | R3 | CAR3 | R3 | CAR3 |
|---|---|---|---|---|---|---|---|---|---|---|---|---|
| 1 | −0.012 | 0.573 | −0.001 | 0.126 | 0.030 | 0.202 | −0.036 | 0.083 | −0.027 | 0.104 | −0.022 | 0.112 |
| 2 | −0.054 | 0.519 | −0.045 | 0.080 | 0.009 | 0.211 | 0.003 | 0.087 | −0.008 | 0.096 | −0.023 | 0.089 |
| 3 | 0.031 | 0.551 | 0.000 | 0.081 | −0.006 | 0.205 | 0.008 | 0.094 | −0.004 | 0.091 | −0.030 | 0.058 |
| 4 | −0.024 | 0.527 | −0.014 | 0.066 | −0.003 | 0.202 | 0.012 | 0.106 | 0.004 | 0.095 | 0.000 | 0.059 |
| 5 | 0.007 | 0.534 | 0.039 | 0.105 | −0.004 | 0.197 | −0.010 | 0.096 | 0.002 | 0.097 | −0.002 | 0.057 |
| 6 | −0.036 | 0.498 | 0.021 | 0.127 | −0.004 | 0.193 | −0.008 | 0.088 | −0.004 | 0.094 | −0.006 | 0.050 |
| 7 | 0.022 | 0.519 | 0.013 | 0.140 | −0.002 | 0.191 | −0.011 | 0.077 | 0.003 | 0.097 | −0.003 | 0.047 |
| 8 | 0.009 | 0.528 | 0.019 | 0.159 | −0.008 | 0.184 | 0.010 | 0.087 | 0.030 | 0.127 | −0.013 | 0.033 |
| 9 | 0.074 | 0.602 | −0.002 | 0.157 | −0.007 | 0.176 | −0.011 | 0.077 | −0.010 | 0.117 | 0.003 | 0.036 |
| 10 | 0.017 | 0.620 | −0.003 | 0.155 | 0.000 | 0.176 | −0.009 | 0.067 | −0.004 | 0.113 | 0.003 | 0.039 |
| 11 | 0.007 | 0.626 | 0.004 | 0.158 | −0.001 | 0.175 | 0.009 | 0.077 | −0.004 | 0.109 | −0.001 | 0.037 |
| 12 | 0.032 | 0.658 | −0.012 | 0.146 | 0.005 | 0.179 | 0.001 | 0.078 | 0.005 | 0.115 | 0.001 | 0.039 |
| 13 | 0.010 | 0.668 | −0.004 | 0.142 | −0.010 | 0.169 | −0.008 | 0.070 | −0.018 | 0.097 | −0.010 | 0.028 |
| 14 | 0.001 | 0.668 | 0.010 | 0.152 | 0.002 | 0.171 | 0.004 | 0.074 | 0.005 | 0.102 | −0.001 | 0.027 |
| 15 | 0.004 | 0.672 | 0.013 | 0.165 | 0.014 | 0.185 | 0.019 | 0.093 | 0.009 | 0.111 | −0.002 | 0.025 |
| 16 | 0.000 | 0.673 | 0.006 | 0.171 | 0.009 | 0.193 | 0.012 | 0.104 | −0.006 | 0.105 | 0.009 | 0.034 |
| 17 | −0.001 | 0.672 | −0.003 | 0.168 | −0.001 | 0.193 | 0.011 | 0.116 | 0.003 | 0.108 | −0.001 | 0.033 |
| 18 | 0.004 | 0.676 | 0.001 | 0.169 | 0.001 | 0.193 | 0.015 | 0.130 | 0.005 | 0.113 | 0.007 | 0.040 |
| 19 | −0.004 | 0.672 | 0.015 | 0.184 | −0.001 | 0.192 | 0.029 | 0.159 | 0.015 | 0.128 | 0.005 | 0.044 |
| 20 | 0.013 | 0.685 | 0.000 | 0.184 | −0.004 | 0.188 | 0.006 | 0.165 | −0.009 | 0.119 | −0.008 | 0.036 |
| 21 | 0.006 | 0.691 | 0.006 | 0.190 | −0.004 | 0.184 | 0.006 | 0.171 | 0.000 | 0.120 | −0.008 | 0.028 |
| 22 | 0.002 | 0.693 | −0.002 | 0.188 | −0.002 | 0.183 | −0.013 | 0.159 | −0.002 | 0.117 | −0.010 | 0.018 |
| 23 | 0.012 | 0.705 | 0.005 | 0.193 | 0.018 | 0.200 | 0.001 | 0.160 | 0.010 | 0.127 | 0.002 | 0.020 |
| 24 | 0.000 | 0.705 | −0.014 | 0.179 | −0.003 | 0.197 | 0.003 | 0.163 | 0.011 | 0.138 | −0.003 | 0.017 |
| 25 | 0.000 | 0.705 | −0.003 | 0.176 | 0.020 | 0.217 | 0.011 | 0.174 | 0.013 | 0.150 | 0.010 | 0.027 |
| 26 | 0.002 | 0.708 | −0.005 | 0.172 | 0.003 | 0.220 | 0.008 | 0.182 | 0.003 | 0.154 | 0.008 | 0.035 |
| 27 | 0.004 | 0.711 | −0.008 | 0.164 | −0.018 | 0.202 | 0.005 | 0.187 | −0.009 | 0.145 | −0.006 | 0.029 |
| 28 | −0.009 | 0.702 | 0.002 | 0.166 | 0.003 | 0.205 | 0.023 | 0.210 | −0.007 | 0.138 | −0.003 | 0.026 |
| 29 | 0.005 | 0.708 | 0.000 | 0.166 | −0.009 | 0.197 | 0.007 | 0.217 | 0.016 | 0.154 | 0.016 | 0.042 |
| 30 | −0.003 | 0.704 | 0.006 | 0.172 | 0.000 | 0.197 | 0.011 | 0.228 | 0.006 | 0.160 | 0.008 | 0.050 |
| 31 | −0.002 | 0.703 | −0.006 | 0.167 | 0.016 | 0.212 | 0.005 | 0.233 | −0.002 | 0.159 | −0.007 | 0.043 |
| 32 | −0.003 | 0.700 | 0.006 | 0.172 | −0.031 | 0.181 | −0.010 | 0.222 | 0.001 | 0.159 | 0.004 | 0.047 |
| 33 | 0.003 | 0.703 | −0.007 | 0.165 | −0.005 | 0.177 | −0.013 | 0.209 | −0.014 | 0.145 | 0.011 | 0.058 |
| 34 | 0.013 | 0.716 | 0.001 | 0.166 | −0.003 | 0.174 | −0.016 | 0.193 | 0.001 | 0.146 | 0.015 | 0.073 |
| 35 | −0.001 | 0.715 | −0.004 | 0.162 | 0.008 | −0.181 | 0.014 | 0.207 | −0.009 | 0.137 | 0.002 | 0.076 |
| 36 | −0.002 | 0.713 | −0.007 | 0.155 | −0.012 | 0.170 | −0.003 | 0.204 | −0.008 | 0.129 | 0.017 | 0.092 |
| 37 | −0.005 | 0.708 | −0.001 | 0.154 | 0.002 | 0.172 | 0.003 | 0.207 | −0.008 | 0.121 | 0.012 | 0.104 |
| 38 | −0.003 | 0.705 | 0.005 | 0.160 | −0.006 | 0.166 | 0.001 | 0.207 | −0.010 | 0.111 | 0.013 | 0.116 |
| 39 | 0.004 | 0.709 | 0.007 | 0.167 | −0.004 | 0.162 | 0.009 | 0.216 | 0.002 | 0.113 | −0.002 | 0.114 |
| 40 | −0.013 | 0.696 | −0.005 | 0.162 | 0.005 | 0.167 | −0.019 | 0.197 | −0.002 | 0.111 | 0.012 | 0.125 |

Table A5.5 illustrates the absolute dollar gain or loss at day $+1$ and at $+40$ for the six firms of interest. The reference $MKTVAL_o$ is obtained one day prior to the event window interval or at date $-41$. Thus, the absolute gain for Chevron on day $+1$ was $11,888 million times the CAR from day $-40$ to $+1$ of 0.083 or a gain of $987 million.

## Interpretation of Measurements

Residual analysis basically tests whether the return to the common stock of individual firms or groups of firms is greater or less than that predicted by general market relationships between return and risk. Most merger studies in recent years have made use of residual analysis. These studies have sought to test whether merger events provide positive or negative abnormal returns to the participants. The studies of abnormal returns provide a basis for examining the issue of whether or not value is enhanced by mergers.

The studies cover different time periods and different sample sizes. The studies are sometimes limited to conglomerate mergers. Other studies include horizontal and vertical mergers as well. Many studies deal with tender offers only. Some studies use monthly data; some use daily data; and some focus on individual mergers. At least one study analyzes firms engaged in programs of merger and tender offer activity over a period of years (Schipper and Thompson, 1983).

On average, the event studies predict the longer-term performance of merging companies. Healy, Palepu, and Ruback (1992) find a strong positive relationship between the abnormal stock returns related to the announcement of mergers and the subsequent postmerger changes in operating cash flows. Their findings support the view that the event returns, on average, represent accurate predictions of the subsequent performance of merging companies.

# STATISTICAL SIGNIFICANCE OF EVENT RETURNS

## One Day, One Firm

Once the measures of abnormal returns have been estimated, we must interpret these results. Can we infer with a certain level of confidence that the residuals are significantly

**TABLE A5.5**   Absolute Event Gains (Losses) ($ Million)

|  | Targets | | | Acquirers | | |
|---|---|---|---|---|---|---|
|  | Gulf Corp. | Superior Oil | Texaco Canada | Chevron | Mobil | Imperial Oil |
| Market value at $-41$* | $7,296 | $4,867 | $3,729 | $11,888 | $12,052 | $6,034 |
| On date $+1$ |  |  |  |  |  |  |
| CAR (market adjusted)** | 0.573 | 0.126 | 0.202 | 0.083 | 0.104 | 0.112 |
| Dollar gains (loss) | $4,183 | $612 | $752 | $989 | $1,254 | $673 |
| On date $+40$ |  |  |  |  |  |  |
| CAR (market adjusted)** | 0.696 | 0.162 | 0.167 | 0.197 | 0.111 | 0.125 |
| Dollar gains (loss) | $5,078 | $789 | $621 | $2,339 | $1,341 | $757 |

*Source: CRSP 1995 tape.

**Here the CARs represent the cumulative abnormal returns obtained by cumulating the daily abnormal returns in each of the individual company $R3$ columns in Table A5.2 and A5.3, which are repeated as the first of the two columns under each company name in Table A5.4.

different from zero? If we assume that the returns for each firm are independently and identically normally distributed, then $\dfrac{r_{jt}}{\hat{S}(r_j)}$ has a $t$-distribution. ($r_{jt}$ is the residual for firm $j$ on day $t$, $\hat{S}(r_{jt})$ is the estimated standard deviation of the residuals for firm $j$ using data from the estimation period, $\left[\dfrac{1}{199}\displaystyle\sum_{t=-240}^{-41}(r_{jt}-\bar{r}_j)^2\right]^{1/2}$, and the degrees of freedom are 199). For degrees of freedom above 30, the $t$-statistic has, approximately, a standard normal distribution. This statistic tests the null hypothesis that the one day residual for a single firm is equal to zero. Intuitively, we are comparing the value of the residual to its estimated sample standard deviation. Only if this ratio is greater than a specified critical value can we reject the null hypothesis with some degree of confidence. For instance, if this ratio is greater than 1.96 we can say that the one-day residual is significantly different from zero at the 5% level. If the ratio is greater than 2.58, we can reject the null hypothesis at a confidence level of 1%. Table A5.6 presents the statistical significance (the $t$-stat) of the individual firm's residual on the announcement day ($r_{jo}$). The positive abnormal returns for Superior Oil are the only ones significant at the 1% level. For the other firms, we cannot reject the null hypothesis of a zero residual.

## One Day, Average Over Firms

The corresponding test statistic for the hypothesis that the one-day residuals, averaged over three firms, $AR_t = \dfrac{1}{3}\displaystyle\sum_{j=1}^{3} r_{jt}$, is zero, is as follows:

$$\frac{AR_t}{\hat{S}(AR)} = \frac{AR_t}{\left[\dfrac{1}{199}\displaystyle\sum_{t=-240}^{-41}(AR_t-\overline{AR})^2\right]^{1/2}}$$

**TABLE A5.6**   One-Day Residuals (Announcement Day) Statistical Significance

| | | | Targets | | | | Acquirers | | | |
|---|---|---|---|---|---|---|---|---|---|---|
| | | | Gulf Corp. | Superior Oil | Texaco Canada | Average | Chevron | Mobil | Imperial Oil | Average |
| M1: Mean adjusted return model | $R1 = r_{jt}$ $= R_{jt} - \bar{R}_j$ | $r_{jo}$ | 0.0158 | 0.0489 | 0.0023 | *0.0223* | −0.0004 | −0.0051 | −0.0020 | *−0.0025* |
| | | $s_j$ | 0.0160 | 0.0236 | 0.0160 | *0.0104* | 0.0172 | 0.0171 | 0.0103 | *0.0083* |
| | | $t$-stat | 0.9890 | 2.0764 | 0.1430 | *2.1496* | −0.0215 | −0.2998 | −0.1947 | *−0.3021* |
| M2: Market model method | $R2 = r_{jt}$ $= R_{jt} - \hat{\alpha}_j - \hat{\beta}_j R_{mt}$ | $r_{jo}$ | 0.0236 | 0.0544 | 0.0014 | *0.0265* | 0.0094 | 0.0018 | −0.0028 | *0.0028* |
| | | $s_j$ | 0.0144 | 0.0223 | 0.0152 | *0.0103* | 0.0150 | 0.0142 | 0.0094 | *0.0074* |
| | | $t$-stat | 1.6385 | 2.4381 | 0.0906 | *2.5615* | 0.6264 | 0.1248 | −0.2911 | *0.3805* |
| M3: Market adjusted return method | $R3 = r_{jt}$ $= R_{jt} - R_{mt}$ | $r_{jo}$ | 0.0253 | 0.0546 | 0.0019 | *0.0273* | 0.0074 | 0.0003 | −0.0047 | *0.0010* |
| | | $s_j$ | 0.0144 | 0.0223 | 0.0155 | *0.0104* | 0.0151 | 0.0145 | 0.0102 | *0.0074* |
| | | $t$-stat | 1.7589 | 2.4450 | 0.1209 | *2.6126* | 0.4883 | 0.0194 | −0.4577 | *0.1326* |

where the sample standard deviation is $\hat{S}(AR) = \left[\frac{1}{199} \sum_{t=-240}^{-41} (AR_t - \overline{AR})^2\right]^{1/2}$ and $\overline{AR} = \frac{1}{200} \sum_{t=-240}^{-41} AR_t$. In Table A5.6, the positive average residuals for the target companies are statistically significant. For the acquirers, the small average residuals are not distinguishable from zero.

### Over 81 Days, Average Over Firms

The corresponding test statistic for the cumulative average residual (CAR), for the three firms and cumulating over 81 days [−40, + 40], is as follows:

$$\frac{CAR}{\hat{S}(CAR)} = \frac{\sum_{t=-40}^{+40} AR_t}{\sum_{t=-40}^{+40} \hat{S}(AR)} = \frac{\sum_{t=-40}^{+40} AR_t}{\sqrt{81}\hat{S}(AR)}$$

Note that the estimated standard deviation for each day in the event interval is the same because we are using the same estimation period for a sample drawn from independent and identically distributed excess returns. Table A5.7 presents the CAR for each individual firm and the average CAR for target and acquiring firms. Gulf Corp. is the only company that presents a significant abnormal return during the event interval. Both target and acquiring firms' average CAR are significant, except for the acquirers' average CAR using the mean adjusted return method.

The procedure we used to estimate the test statistics is the most simple to illustrate the calculations of statistical significance. There are several adjustment factors that must be recognized. For the mean adjusted return model and the market model, the estimation of $\hat{S}$ should be adjusted because the residuals involve prediction errors. These errors arrive from the estimation of the mean return for the mean

**TABLE A5.7**   Cumulative Average Residuals [−40, +40] Statistical Significance

|  |  |  | Targets | | | | Acquirers | | | |
|---|---|---|---|---|---|---|---|---|---|---|
|  |  |  | Gulf Corp. | Superior Oil | Texaco Canada | Average | Chevron | Mobil | Imperial Oil | Average |
| M1: Mean adjusted return model | $R1 = r_{jt}$ $= R_{jt} - \overline{R}_j$ | CAR | 0.4677 | 0.0079 | 0.1518 | *0.2091* | 0.1176 | −0.0249 | 0.2932 | *0.1287* |
|  |  | $s_j$ | 0.1436 | 0.2121 | 0.1436 | *0.0935* | 0.1552 | 0.1543 | 0.0926 | *0.0746* |
|  |  | $t$-stat | 3.2579 | 0.0370 | 1.0568 | *2.2371* | 0.7579 | −0.1613 | 3.1673 | *1.7241* |
| M2: Market model method | $R2 = r_{jt}$ $= R_{jt} - \hat{\alpha}_j - \hat{\beta}_j R_{mt}$ | CAR | 0.5715 | 0.1235 | 0.1084 | *0.2678* | 0.2470 | 0.1214 | 0.2575 | *0.2086* |
|  |  | $s_j$ | 0.1296 | 0.2008 | 0.1366 | *0.0930* | 0.1348 | 0.1280 | 0.0850 | *0.0663* |
|  |  | $t$-stat | 4.4081 | 0.6151 | 0.7934 | *2.8807* | 1.8319 | 0.9481 | 3.0277 | *3.1465* |
| M3: Market adjusted return method | $R3 = r_{jt}$ $= R_{jt} - R_{mt}$ | CAR | 0.6960 | 0.1620 | 0.1667 | *0.3416* | 0.1967 | 0.1113 | 0.1254 | *0.1445* |
|  |  | $s_j$ | 0.1297 | 0.2009 | 0.1392 | *0.0939* | 0.1355 | 0.1301 | 0.0918 | *0.0670* |
|  |  | $t$-stat | 5.3678 | 0.8066 | 1.1972 | *3.6372* | 1.4523 | 0.8555 | 1.3660 | *2.1575* |

adjusted model, and from the estimation of the regression coefficients for the market model. In addition, we did not take into account the possible changes in the variance outside the estimation period, nor did we consider time dependence or nonnormality in the returns. Finally, there is the possibility of cross-correlation in abnormal returns resulting, for example, from a government regulation that simultaneously impact a number of different securities. For a more complete exposition of the issues involved in event studies, see Brown and Warner (1980, 1985), and Boehmer et al. (1991).

---

## References

Boehmer, E., J. Musumeci, and A. Poulsen, "Event-Study Methodology Under Conditions of Event-Induced Variance," *Journal of Financial Economics,* 30, 1991, pp. 253–272.

Brown, S., and J. Warner, "Measuring Security Price Performance," *Journal of Financial Economics,* 8, 1980, pp. 205–258.

_____, "Using Daily Stock Returns: The Case of Event Studies." *Journal of Financial Economics,* 14, 1985, pp. 3–31.

Healy, Paul M., Krishna G. Palepu, and Richard S. Ruback, "Does Corporate Performance Improve After Mergers?" *Journal of Financial Economics,* 31, 1992, pp. 135–175.

Schipper, K., and R. Thompson, "Evidence on the Capitalized Value of Merger Activity for Acquiring Firms," *Journal of Financial Economics,* 11, 1983, pp. 85–119.

# 6

# The Timing
# of Merger Activity

In the previous chapter, we presented a number of alternative theories or explanations of why M&As take place. The present chapter starts the process of testing alternative explanations of M&A activity by examining the empirical evidence. We begin by reviewing the major merger movements that have taken place in the United States since the 1890s.

## EARLY MERGER MOVEMENTS

Several major merger movements have occurred in the United States (Golbe and White, 1988), and each was more or less dominated by a particular type of merger. All of the merger movements occurred when the economy experienced sustained high rates of growth and coincided with particular developments in business environments. Mergers represent resource allocation and reallocation processes in the economy, with firms responding to new investment and profit opportunities arising out of changes in economic conditions and technological innovations impacting industries. Mergers rather than internal growth may sometimes expedite the adjustment process and in some cases be more efficient in terms of resource utilization.

### The 1895–1904 Merger Movement

The combination movement at the turn of the century consisted mainly of horizontal mergers, which resulted in high concentration in many industries, including heavy manufacturing industries. The period was one of rapid economic expansion. The 1904 decision of the Supreme Court in the Northern Securities case [193 U.S. 197 (March 1904)] may have contributed to ending this merger wave. In the decision, the Court established that mergers could be successfully attacked by Section One of the Sherman Act, which prohibited "every combination in the form of trust or otherwise" in restraint of trade. It should be noted, however, that the merger activity began its downturn in 1901 as some combinations failed to realize their expectations and declined further by 1903 when the economy went into recession.

This merger movement of the turn of the century accompanied major changes in economic infrastructure and production technologies (Markham, 1955, p. 156; Salter and Weinhold, 1980, p. 7). It followed the completion of the transcontinental railroad system, the advent of electricity, and the increased use of coal. The completed rail system resulted in the development of a national economic market, and thus the merger activity represented to a certain extent the transformation of regional firms into national firms.

In addition to the goal of achieving economies of scale, two other motivational factors have been ascribed to this first major merger movement. Stigler (1950) characterized the merger movement as "merging for monopoly." Of 92 large mergers studied by Moody (1904), 78 controlled 50% or more of the market. However, in reviewing the early literature on mergers, Markham (1955) concludes that "out of every five mergers ostensibly monopolistic in character only one resulted in considerable monopoly control" (pp. 161–162) and that "it is certain that many mergers formed during the early merger movement did not have monopoly power as their principal objective and, accordingly, must be explained on other grounds" (p. 162). In reviewing the early literature, authors such as Markham (1955) and Salter and Weinhold (1979) concluded that professional promoters and underwriters or "producers" of mergers added to the magnitude of the merger wave.

Several studies attempted to measure the success of the early mergers in terms of profitability and to determine the reasons for their success or failure. Livermore (1935) attributed success to "astute business leadership" and, in particular, to rapid technological and managerial improvement, development of new products or entry into a new subdivision of the industry, promotion of quality brand names, and commercial exploitation of research. The causes for failure as given by Dewing (1953) included lack of efforts to realize economies of scale by modernizing inherited plant and equipment, increase in overhead costs and lack of flexibility due to large size, and inadequate supply of talent to manage a large group of plants.

### The 1922–1929 Merger Movement

As in the first merger movement, the second wave of mergers also began with an upturn in business activity, in 1922. It ended with the onset of a severe economic slowdown in 1929. Many combinations in this period occurred outside the previously consolidated heavy manufacturing industries. The public utilities and banking industries were among the most active. About 60% of the mergers occurred in the still fragmented food processing, chemicals, and mining sectors (Salter and Weinhold, 1980, p. 4). Accordingly, the question of monopoly was not applicable in most cases and the transformation of a near-monopoly to an oligopoly by "merging for oligopoly" was more frequent (Stigler, 1950). While oligopoly provided a motive for many mergers, it was limited to no more than a small fraction of the mergers (Markham, 1955, p. 169). A large portion of mergers in the 1920s represented product extension mergers, as in the cases of IBM, General Foods, and Allied Chemical; market extension mergers in food retailing, department stores, and motion picture theaters; and vertical mergers in the mining and metals industries.

As for the motivational factors of these mergers, both Markham (1955) and Stocking (1955) emphasized major developments in transportation, communication, and merchandising. A new transportation system utilizing motor vehicles broke down small local markets by enabling sellers to extend their sales areas and by making consumers more mobile. Mergers in such industries as food processing and chemicals accompanied the rise of automobile transportation, whereas mergers in heavy industries in the previous merger movement accompanied the rise of railroad transportation. The rise of home radio facilitated product differentiation through national-brand advertising. By the 1920s, mass distribution with low profit margins became a new method of merchandising. Both these developments caused an increase in the scale of operations and hence encouraged mergers. On the increase in vertical integration, Stocking noted that by the 1920s business had come to appreciate the advantages of integration. The advantages were related to technological economies such as shortening of processes or elimination of waste motions in a mechanical sense, or to reliability of input supply.

### The 1940–1947 Merger Movement

The Second World War and the early postwar years were accompanied by rapid growth of the economy and an upsurge in merger activity. Lacking any significant changes in technological and business environments, however, the merger movement was much smaller than earlier ones. Observers saw no pervasive motives for this merger movement other than "conventional" ones.

Government regulation and tax policies are pointed out by some economists as having motivated mergers in this period. According to Stigler (1951), a large number of firms merged vertically to circumvent price controls and allocations during the wartime and postwar periods. Butters, Lintner, and Cary (1951) showed that many owners were motivated to sell their firms because of high wartime and postwar income and estate taxes and the lower capital gains tax. Other sellers were motivated by such general business considerations as greater managerial organization and investment requirements for their firms, and buyers by the desire for a new product or production organization, or for greater vertical integration.

## THE CONGLOMERATE MERGER MOVEMENT OF THE 1960s

The Celler-Kefauver Act of 1950 amended Section 7 of the Clayton Act of 1914 to close the "asset-purchase" loophole and granted the federal government additional power to declare illegal those mergers that tended to increase concentration. (The Clayton Act had prohibited a corporation from acquiring the stock of another corporation if competition were to be substantially lessened. The act had referred only to acquisition of stock, but not of assets.) Thereafter, the relative importance of horizontal and vertical mergers declined in relation to conglomerate mergers. By 1967–1968 when the merger activity peaked, horizontal and vertical mergers declined to 17% of the total number of mergers. Among the conglomerate type of mergers, product extension mergers increased to 60% and market extension mergers became negligible in number. Other or pure conglomerates increased steadily to about 23% of all mergers (or 35% in terms of assets acquired). Merger activity reached its then historically highest level during the three-year period of 1967 through 1969. The period was also one of a booming economy. The number of mergers declined sharply as the general economic activity slowed down after 1969.

Most acquirers in the period that have subsequently been known as conglomerates were small or medium-sized firms that adopted a diversification strategy into business activities outside their traditional areas of interest. The acquired firms were also small or medium-sized and "operating in either fragmented industries or on the periphery of major industrial sectors" (Salter and Weinhold, 1980, p. 6). Based on an analysis of backgrounds and acquisition histories of the acquiring firms, Weston and Mansinghka (1971) suggested that the conglomerates were "diversifying defensively to avoid (1) sales and profit instability, (2) adverse growth developments, (3) adverse competitive shifts, (4) technological obsolescence, and (5) increased uncertainties associated with their industries" (Weston and Mansinghka, 1971, p. 928).

The largest single category of firms was from the aerospace industry. This industry was subject to wide fluctuations in total market demand as well as abrupt and major shifts in its product mix. Excess capacity developed, aggravated by entry of firms from other industries. The industrial machinery and auto parts companies were also subject to considerable instability in sales. Low growth prospects were associated with a major long-term decline in some markets. This was characteristic of the railway equipment industry, textiles, movie distribution (at an earlier period), and the tobacco industry.

Sometimes the conglomerate represented the personality of the chief executive such as Harold Geneen at ITT and Charles Bludhorn at Gulf & Western. Their successors sold off everything but a relatively focused core of activities. Some conglomerates were formed to imitate earlier conglomerates that appeared to have achieved high growth and high valuations. Many of the later conglomerates had no sound conceptual basis and were a substantial source of sell-offs in later years. Indeed, many writers view the merger activity of the 1980s as a correction to the unwise diversification of the 1960s (Shleifer and Vishny, 1990).

## MERGER TRENDS SINCE 1970

Following the recession in 1974–1975, the U.S. economy entered a long period of expansion, during which M&As trended upward. Table 6.1 expands the information presented in chapter 1 on recent trends in M&A activity. Column 1 shows the total dollar value paid where a purchase price was disclosed; this includes all of the large transactions. Column 2 shows that the net number of merger-acquisition announcements in 1985 was only about half the level of 1969. However, because the number of transactions valued at $100 million or more or $1 billion or more was much larger in later years, column 6 shows that the constant dollar consideration involved in mergers was higher in 1985 than in 1968 or 1969, the previous high years. In fact, it was not until 1984 that the constant dollar consideration in mergers exceeded the level that had been reached in 1968. A peak year was in 1988 when the constant dollar consideration in mergers-acquisitions was almost double that of 1968. A sharp decline in M&A activity took place in 1990–1992. This decline led one leading scholar (Jensen, 1993, p. 852) to observe, "The era of the control market came to an end, however, in late 1989 and 1990." This permanent decline was ascribed to adverse court decisions, state anti-takeover amendments, and other adverse regulatory restrictions. The resurgence of M&A activity in 1993-1995 suggests that the dominant influences were the nature of the economic and financial environments. New peaks were reached in 1995 and 1996.

Table 6.2 brings out the same point. During the decade of the 1970s, M&As averaged 1.3% of gross domestic product (GDP). The level of activity for the decade of the 1980s was at 3.6% of GDP. By 1994 M&A as a percentage of GDP had returned to approximately the levels of the 1980s. The argument may be made that M&As have come to be an alarming force in the economy. The counterargument here is that even in 1988 or 1995, peak years of M&A activity, M&As represented approximately 5% of GDP. Even this measure exaggerates the role of M&A activity, which involves the total **stock** of business assets while GDP is a measure of the **flow** of economic activity in a given year.

In Table 6.3, M&As are measured in relation to the total assets of all corporations. In this perspective, M&As have generally averaged below 1% of total assets outstanding. The average for the decade of the 1980s was less than 1%. Again, the data show a resurgence for 1994 through 1996.

**TABLE 6.1**   Merger Activity: The Mergerstat Series

| Year | (1) Total Dollar Value Paid ($ Billion) | (2) Number Total | (3) Number of Transactions Valued at $100 Million or More | (4) Number of Transactions Valued at $1,000 Million or More | (5) GDP Deflator (1992 = 100) | (6) 1992 Constant-Dollar Consideration |
|---|---|---|---|---|---|---|
| 1968 | 43.6 | 4,662 | 46 | — | 27.7 | 157.4 |
| 1969 | 23.7 | 6,107 | 24 | — | 29.0 | 81.7 |
| 1970 | 16.4 | 5,152 | 10 | 1 | 30.6 | 53.6 |
| 1971 | 12.6 | 4,608 | 7 | — | 32.1 | 39.3 |
| 1972 | 16.7 | 4,801 | 15 | — | 33.5 | 49.9 |
| 1973 | 16.7 | 4,040 | 28 | — | 35.4 | 47.2 |
| 1974 | 12.4 | 2,861 | 15 | — | 38.5 | 32.2 |
| 1975 | 11.8 | 2,297 | 14 | 1 | 42.2 | 28.0 |
| 1976 | 20.0 | 2,276 | 39 | 1 | 44.6 | 44.8 |
| 1977 | 21.9 | 2,224 | 41 | — | 47.5 | 46.1 |
| 1978 | 34.2 | 2,106 | 80 | 1 | 50.9 | 67.2 |
| 1979 | 43.5 | 2,128 | 83 | 3 | 55.3 | 78.7 |
| 1980 | 44.3 | 1,889 | 94 | 4 | 60.4 | 73.3 |
| 1981 | 82.6 | 2,395 | 113 | 12 | 66.1 | 125.0 |
| 1982 | 53.8 | 2,346 | 116 | 6 | 70.2 | 76.6 |
| 1983 | 73.1 | 2,533 | 138 | 11 | 73.2 | 99.9 |
| 1984 | 122.2 | 2,543 | 200 | 18 | 75.9 | 161.0 |
| 1985 | 179.6 | 3,001 | 270 | 36 | 78.6 | 228.5 |
| 1986 | 173.1 | 3,336 | 346 | 27 | 80.6 | 214.8 |
| 1987 | 163.7 | 2,032 | 301 | 36 | 83.1 | 197.0 |
| 1988 | 246.9 | 2,258 | 369 | 45 | 86.1 | 286.8 |
| 1989 | 221.1 | 2,366 | 328 | 35 | 89.7 | 246.5 |
| 1990 | 108.2 | 2,074 | 181 | 21 | 93.6 | 115.6 |
| 1991 | 71.2 | 1,877 | 150 | 13 | 97.3 | 73.2 |
| 1992 | 96.7 | 2,574 | 200 | 18 | 100.0 | 96.7 |
| 1993 | 176.4 | 2,663 | 242 | 27 | 102.6 | 171.9 |
| 1994 | 226.7 | 2,997 | 383 | 51 | 105.0 | 215.9 |
| 1995 | 356.0 | 3,510 | 462 | 74 | 107.6 | 330.9 |
| 1996 | 494.9 | 5,848 | 640 | 94 | 110.0 | 449.9 |
| *Annual Average:* | | | | | | |
| 1970–1980 | 22.8 | 3,126 | 39 | 1 | 42.8 | 50.9 |
| 1981–1989 | 146.2 | 2,534 | 242 | 25 | 78.2 | 181.8 |
| 1990–1992 | 92.0 | 2,175 | 177 | 17 | 97.0 | 95.2 |
| 1993–1996 | 313.5 | 3,755 | 432 | 62 | 106.3 | 292.1 |

*Sources:* Houlihan Lokey Howard & Zukin, *Mergerstat Review, 1997,* Los Angeles, CA; gross domestic product (GDP) deflator: *Economic Report of the President,* various issues.

**TABLE 6.2**   M&As in Relation to Size of the Economy

| Year | (1) Dollar Amount of M&As ($ Billion) | (2) GDP in Current Dollars ($ Billion) | (3) M&As as % of GDP |
|---|---|---|---|
| 1970 | 16.4 | 1,015.5 | 1.6 |
| 1971 | 12.6 | 1,102.7 | 1.1 |
| 1972 | 16.7 | 1,212.8 | 1.4 |
| 1973 | 16.7 | 1,359.3 | 1.2 |
| 1974 | 12.4 | 1,472.8 | 0.8 |
| 1975 | 11.8 | 1,598.4 | 0.7 |
| 1976 | 20.0 | 1,782.8 | 1.1 |
| 1977 | 21.9 | 1,990.5 | 1.1 |
| 1978 | 34.2 | 2,249.7 | 1.5 |
| 1979 | 43.5 | 2,508.2 | 1.7 |
| 1980 | 44.3 | 2,732.0 | 1.6 |
| 1981 | 82.6 | 3,052.6 | 2.7 |
| 1982 | 53.8 | 3,166.0 | 1.7 |
| 1983 | 73.1 | 3,405.7 | 2.1 |
| 1984 | 122.2 | 3,772.2 | 3.2 |
| 1985 | 179.6 | 4,014.9 | 4.5 |
| 1986 | 173.1 | 4,240.3 | 4.1 |
| 1987 | 163.7 | 4,526.7 | 3.6 |
| 1988 | 246.9 | 4,880.6 | 5.1 |
| 1989 | 221.1 | 5,200.8 | 4.3 |
| 1990 | 108.2 | 5,463.6 | 2.0 |
| 1991 | 71.2 | 5,632.5 | 1.3 |
| 1992 | 96.7 | 6,020.2 | 1.6 |
| 1993 | 176.4 | 6,343.3 | 2.8 |
| 1994 | 226.7 | 6,738.2 | 3.4 |
| 1995 | 356.0 | 7,245.8 | 4.9 |
| 1996 | 494.9 | 7,574.2 | 6.5 |
| *Annual Average:* | | | |
| 1970–1980 | 22.8 | 1,729.5 | 1.3 |
| 1981–1989 | 146.2 | 4,028.9 | 3.6 |
| 1990–1992 | 92.0 | 5,705.4 | 1.6 |
| 1993–1996 | 313.5 | 6,975.4 | 4.5 |

*Sources:* Column 1: Houlihan Lokey Howard & Zukin, *Mergerstat Review, 1997,* Los Angeles, CA; Column 2: *Economic Report of the President,* various issues; *Economic Indicators.*

Because M&A activity often involves equity values alone, the relevant base might also be total equities. In Table 6.4, this comparison is made. In 1981, for the first time, M&As exceeded 5% of all equities. But a decline took place in 1982 and 1983, before rising to the historical high of 6.9% in 1988. Both M&A data and total equity values have been pushed upward by the bull market in equities that began in the late summer of 1982, was interrupted on October 19, 1987, and then resumed its upward trend through the summer of 1996. Also, M&A activity has the effect of shrinking the denominator in this ratio. It has been estimated by Salomon Bros. and other financial research organizations that during the years 1984–1986, the aggregate amount of equity values that disappeared as a consequence of M&A activity was $110 billion per year.

| **TABLE 6.3**   M&As in Relation to the Corporate Universe | | | |
|---|---|---|---|
| Year | *(1)*<br>*Total Assets All*<br>*Corporations ($ Billion)* | *(2)*<br>*M&As Total Dollar*<br>*Value Paid ($ Billion)* | *(3)*<br>*M&As as %*<br>*of Total Assets* |
| 1970 | 3,115.9 | 16.4 | 0.53 |
| 1971 | 3,467.2 | 12.6 | 0.36 |
| 1972 | 3,948.3 | 16.7 | 0.42 |
| 1973 | 4,369.4 | 16.7 | 0.38 |
| 1974 | 4,671.5 | 12.4 | 0.27 |
| 1975 | 5,101.4 | 11.8 | 0.23 |
| 1976 | 5,646.2 | 20.0 | 0.35 |
| 1977 | 6,282.5 | 21.9 | 0.35 |
| 1978 | 7,182.6 | 34.2 | 0.48 |
| 1979 | 8,231.1 | 43.5 | 0.53 |
| 1980 | 9,276.5 | 44.3 | 0.48 |
| 1981 | 10,304.6 | 82.6 | 0.80 |
| 1982 | 11,184.5 | 53.8 | 0.48 |
| 1983 | 12,349.8 | 73.1 | 0.59 |
| 1984 | 13,678.3 | 122.2 | 0.89 |
| 1985 | 15,345.3 | 179.6 | 1.17 |
| 1986 | 17,144.8 | 173.1 | 1.01 |
| 1987 | 18,422.9 | 163.7 | 0.89 |
| 1988 | 19,903.6 | 246.9 | 1.24 |
| 1989 | 21,720.6 | 221.1 | 1.02 |
| 1990 | 22,321.8 | 108.2 | 0.48 |
| 1991 | 23,621.3 | 71.2 | 0.30 |
| 1992 | 24,785.5 | 96.7 | 0.39 |
| 1993 | 26,486.9 | 176.4 | 0.67 |
| 1994 | 27,672.2 | 226.7 | 0.82 |
| 1995 | 28,874.3 | 356.0 | 1.23 |
| *Annual Average:* | | | |
| 1970–1980 | 5,572.1 | 22.8 | 0.41 |
| 1981–1989 | 15,561.6 | 146.2 | 0.94 |
| 1990–1992 | 23,576.2 | 92.0 | 0.39 |
| 1993–1995 | 27,677.8 | 253.0 | 0.91 |

*Sources:* Column 1: Federal Reserve Statistical Release C.9, *Balance Sheets for the U.S. Economy, 1945-95*; Column 2: Houlihan Lokey Howard & Zukin, *Mergerstat Review, 1997.*

Table 6.5 shows that M&A activity over the years has been highly correlated with plant and equipment expenditures. A regression of M&As on total plant and equipment expenditures gives a slope coefficient of 32%. But in the peak years 1968, 1988, and 1995, M&A activity had risen to about 48 to 49% of plant and equipment expenditures. Some view the data as showing that M&As substitute for "real" economic investments. Others argue that while numerous factors influence M&As, the level of investment activity is a strong causal factor. They suggest that similar kinds of economic forces influence both forms of investment activity and that a similar economic rationale for both is operating.

**TABLE 6.4** M&As in Relation to the Market Value of All Equities

| Year | *(1)*<br>*Total Market Value of*<br>*All Equities ($ Billion)* | *(2)*<br>*M&As Total Dollar*<br>*Value Paid ($ Billion)* | *(3)*<br>*M&As as %*<br>*of All Equities* |
|---|---|---|---|
| 1970 | 906.2 | 16.4 | 1.8 |
| 1971 | 1,059.2 | 12.6 | 1.2 |
| 1972 | 1,197.1 | 16.7 | 1.4 |
| 1973 | 948.1 | 16.7 | 1.8 |
| 1974 | 676.9 | 12.4 | 1.8 |
| 1975 | 892.5 | 11.8 | 1.3 |
| 1976 | 1,052.0 | 20.0 | 1.9 |
| 1977 | 991.3 | 21.9 | 2.2 |
| 1978 | 1,034.2 | 34.2 | 3.3 |
| 1979 | 1,229.0 | 43.5 | 3.5 |
| 1980 | 1,596.5 | 44.3 | 2.8 |
| 1981 | 1,482.4 | 82.6 | 5.6 |
| 1982 | 1,688.1 | 53.8 | 3.2 |
| 1983 | 2,031.9 | 73.1 | 3.6 |
| 1984 | 1,987.6 | 122.2 | 6.1 |
| 1985 | 2,600.2 | 179.8 | 6.9 |
| 1986 | 3,176.9 | 173.1 | 5.4 |
| 1987 | 3,239.0 | 163.7 | 5.1 |
| 1988 | 3,577.2 | 246.9 | 6.9 |
| 1989 | 4,375.9 | 221.1 | 5.1 |
| 1990 | 4,132.3 | 108.2 | 2.6 |
| 1991 | 5,677.5 | 71.2 | 1.3 |
| 1992 | 6,505.0 | 96.7 | 1.5 |
| 1993 | 7,632.8 | 176.4 | 2.3 |
| 1994 | 7,612.7 | 226.7 | 3.0 |
| 1995 | 8,345.4 | 356.0 | 4.3 |
| *Annual Average:* | | | |
| 1970–1980 | 1,053.0 | 22.8 | 2.2 |
| 1981–1989 | 2,684.4 | 146.3 | 5.4 |
| 1990–1992 | 5,438.3 | 92.0 | 1.7 |
| 1993–1995 | 7,863.6 | 253.0 | 3.2 |

*Sources:* Column 1: Board of Governors of the Federal Reserve System, *Flow of Funds Accounts,* March 8, 1996; Column 2: Houlihan Lokey Howard & Zukin, *Mergerstat Review, 1997.*

## DIVESTITURES

Another characteristic of merger activity is that divestitures represent a substantial portion of acquisition activity. Table 6.6 shows that divestitures accelerated following the conglomerate merger movement of the late 1960s. Divestitures also increased following the 1981–1982 recession. Throughout the 1980s, they have represented over 35% of all mergers and acquisition transactions.

Many factors influence divestitures. In some cases, acquired firms were comprised of segments that were sought by the bidder and other segments that were

| | (1) | (2) Total Nonresidential | (3) |
|---|---|---|---|
| Year | Dollar Amount of M&As ($ Billion) | Gross Investment ($ Billion) | M&As as % of Total NRGI |

**TABLE 6.5** M&As in Relation to Total Private Nonresidential Gross Investment (NRGI)

| Year | Dollar Amount of M&As ($ Billion) | Total Nonresidential Gross Investment ($ Billion) | M&As as % of Total NRGI |
|---|---|---|---|
| 1970 | 16.4 | 106.7 | 15.4 |
| 1971 | 12.6 | 111.7 | 11.3 |
| 1972 | 16.7 | 126.1 | 13.2 |
| 1973 | 16.7 | 150.0 | 11.1 |
| 1974 | 12.5 | 165.6 | 7.5 |
| 1975 | 11.8 | 169.0 | 7.0 |
| 1976 | 20.0 | 187.2 | 10.7 |
| 1977 | 21.9 | 223.2 | 9.8 |
| 1978 | 34.2 | 272.0 | 12.6 |
| 1979 | 43.5 | 323.0 | 13.5 |
| 1980 | 44.3 | 350.3 | 12.6 |
| 1981 | 82.6 | 405.4 | 20.4 |
| 1982 | 53.8 | 409.9 | 13.1 |
| 1983 | 73.1 | 399.4 | 18.3 |
| 1984 | 122.2 | 468.3 | 26.1 |
| 1985 | 179.8 | 502.0 | 35.8 |
| 1986 | 173.1 | 494.8 | 35.0 |
| 1987 | 163.7 | 495.4 | 33.0 |
| 1988 | 246.9 | 530.6 | 46.5 |
| 1989 | 221.1 | 566.2 | 39.0 |
| 1990 | 108.2 | 575.9 | 18.8 |
| 1991 | 71.2 | 547.3 | 13.0 |
| 1992 | 96.7 | 557.9 | 17.3 |
| 1993 | 176.4 | 598.8 | 29.5 |
| 1994 | 226.7 | 667.2 | 34.0 |
| 1995 | 356.0 | 738.5 | 48.2 |
| *Annual Average:* | | | |
| 1970–1980 | 22.8 | 198.6 | 11.5 |
| 1981–1989 | 146.3 | 474.7 | 30.8 |
| 1990–1992 | 92.0 | 560.4 | 16.4 |
| 1993–1995 | 253.0 | 668.2 | 37.9 |

*Sources:* Column 1: Houlihan Lokey Howard & Zukin, *Mergerstat Review, 1997,* Los Angeles, CA; Column 2: *Economic Report of the President* (Table B-14) February 1996; *Economic Indicators.*

intended to be sold for lack of fit or to help pay for the parts retained. Divestitures were sometimes businesses having little relationship to the core activities of the company or having management and financial needs that were out of proportion with their performance. Some companies instituted divestiture programs that were as active as their acquisition programs. These companies have shifted operations to serve markets with promising investment opportunities or redeployed assets to support core businesses.

| | | **TABLE 6.6**    Divestitures, 1966–1995 | | | |
|---|---|---|---|---|---|
| Year | Number | *Percent of All Transactions* | Year | Number | *Percent of All Transactions* |
| 1966 | 264 | 11 | 1980 | 666 | 35 |
| 1967 | 328 | 11 | 1981 | 830 | 35 |
| 1968 | 557 | 12 | 1982 | 875 | 37 |
| 1969 | 801 | 13 | 1983 | 932 | 37 |
| 1970 | 1,401 | 27 | 1984 | 900 | 36 |
| 1971 | 1,920 | 42 | 1985 | 1,237 | 41 |
| 1972 | 1,770 | 37 | 1986 | 1,259 | 38 |
| 1973 | 1,557 | 39 | 1987 | 807 | 40 |
| 1974 | 1,331 | 47 | 1988 | 894 | 40 |
| 1975 | 1,236 | 54 | 1989 | 1,055 | 45 |
| 1976 | 1,204 | 53 | 1990 | 940 | 45 |
| 1977 | 1,002 | 45 | 1991 | 849 | 45 |
| 1978 | 820 | 39 | 1992 | 1,026 | 40 |
| 1979 | 752 | 35 | 1993 | 1,134 | 43 |
| | | | 1994 | 1,134 | 38 |
| | | | 1995 | 1,199 | 34 |

*Source:* Houlihan Lokey Howard & Zukin, *Mergerstat Review, 1997,* Los Angeles, CA.

## EFFECTS ON CONCENTRATION

### Impact on Macroconcentration

The high rate of divestitures is one of the reasons why merger activity in recent years has not greatly affected aggregate concentration in the economy. The share of assets of the largest 200 U.S. corporations to the assets of all nonfinancial corporations was about 38% in 1970. Their share declined to 36% by 1980 and to 34% by 1984 (Golbe and White, 1988, p. 277). Our studies show that this share has remained stable at about 35% through 1996. These data give a view that is biased upward in that the largest 200 firms in the numerator are the ones that rank highest in each year of measurement—the individual firms in the list change. If the same 200 group of firms is followed over a period such as 1970 to 1984, their share of assets or sales of all nonfinancial corporations would decline more substantially. The significance of the changing composition of the largest 200 firms from an economic point of view is that it reflects the vigor of competitive forces in the economy. Over time, some firms rise in relative size while others decline, depending on their relative success in the marketplace.

A *Business Week* article of April 29, 1996, raised concerns about "a dangerous concentration" (Mandel, 1996). The measure used is the market value of the top 50 companies in relation to the market value of the *Business Week* 1,000 companies based on first quarter data for each year. The measure rose from 35% in 1986 to almost 37% in 1987, dropping slightly in 1988. In 1991 the measure reached almost 41%, dropped to 36% in 1994, and rose to 39% in 1996. These results are all within a range surprisingly small given the volatility of equity prices. The peak year was 1991, the year of the lowest M&A activity for the time period covered by the article.

International competition also needs to be taken into account. If aggregate concentration were measured in global terms, the share of the top 200 would be smaller. These data have not been compiled because of the difficulty of obtaining data for the denominator on a world basis.

### Impact on Microconcentration

Concentration measures have also been calculated for individual industries. These are called measures of microconcentration. Historically, the most widely used measure has been the share of the four largest firms of industry sales, assets, employment, or the value added in manufacturing, with the last receiving most emphasis. When the four-firm concentration ratio exceeds 40%, one view holds that competition in the industry may be diminished to some degree. But this view has also been disputed both on theoretical and empirical grounds. The degree of concentration varies widely among individual industries. When measured by value added, the weighted average level of concentration in individual industries has stayed relatively constant at about 40% over the years during the decades of the 1960s and 1970s (Scherer, 1980).

However, the published microconcentration measures are based on U.S. domestic data, without taking international factors into account. This impact can be conveyed by measures of concentration for individual markets. In an earlier study, for example, we found that the share of the largest four U.S. firms in steel production in the United States was 52%. The share of the largest four steel companies (two were non-U.S.) of world steel production for the same year was 14% (Weston, 1982). More generally, we found that 75 manufacturing industries could be identified as having international markets. The four-firm concentration ratio (the sales or value added of the largest four firms to the industry total) for these 75 industries averaged 50%, somewhat higher than the 40% average concentration ratio for all manufacturing industries (about 450 in total). However, when adjustments are made for the international nature of the 75 markets, the average four-firm concentration ratio for these industries declines from 50 to 25% (Weston, 1982).

# INTERNATIONAL PERSPECTIVES

The data on M&A activities in other countries is not as complete as for the United States. But the evidence is clear that the increased M&A and restructuring activity is not unique to the United States. In all of the developed countries of the world, M&A activity in recent decades has paralleled the patterns in the United States (Gray and McDermott, 1989; Mueller, 1980). The underlying major force has been the internationalization of markets and the globalization of competition.

Industries and firms in countries throughout the world have experienced the pressures of the increased intensity of competitive forces. Some have argued that relaxed government policies in the early 1980s stimulated an M&A wave in the United States. But clearly antimerger laws and regulations were increased in the United Kingdom in the 1980s (Gray and McDermott, 1989). Also, the policies of the European Economic Community were to tighten antimerger regulations during the 1980s. Nevertheless, M&A activity increased in the United Kingdom and in all of Europe in the face of tighter legal restraints. This again suggests that M&A activity is determined primarily by underlying economic and financial forces.

# TIMING OF MERGER ACTIVITY

The foregoing summary of the major merger movements in U.S. history (paralleled by similar developments in other developed countries), suggests that somewhat different forces were operating in different historical economic and financial environments. The data show merger waves in the sense that in some groups of years merger activity increases sharply. But the evidence does not support merger waves in the sense of regular patterns of periodic rises and declines of merger activity. To the extent that merger activity during individual time segments reflects the special characteristics of the economic and financial environments, it might be difficult to identify statistically the pervasive factors that systematically explain higher or lower levels of M&A activity. Nevertheless, various attempts have been made to explain the timing of M&A activity. Serious statistical studies have been performed. Whether they completely succeeded or not in explaining levels of M&A activity, their efforts increased our understanding of the M&A processes.

## Mergers and the Macroeconomy

Merger activity appears closely associated with the business cycle. Nelson (1959) investigated the lead and lag relationships between merger activity and the general business cycle, industrial production, stock prices, stock trading, and business incorporations. Nelson showed that mergers were more positively correlated to stock price changes than to changes in industrial production in periods of high merger activity. Conversely, mergers were more positively (or less negatively) correlated to industrial production in periods of low merger activity.

These results are consistent with what Weston (1953) and Markham (1955) found earlier. Using regression analyses, Weston showed that merger activity was statistically significantly related to stock prices but not to industrial production. Markham calculated correlation coefficients that were statistically significant, but were larger between mergers and stock prices than between mergers and industrial production. One reason suggested by Nelson is that the phenomenon reflects the immediacy with which mergers start to produce revenues and profits. Internal investments may involve a protracted waiting period.

The relationship between merger activity and such macroeconomic variables as industrial activity, business failures, stock prices, and interest rates was analyzed by Melicher, Ledolter, and D'Antonio (1983) in a time-series analysis context:

1. An increase (decrease) in stock prices is followed in a quarter by an increase (decrease) in merger activity. Because merger negotiations begin on average about two quarters before consummation, merger negotiations may precede stock price movements by about one quarter.

2. Mergers respond inversely to prior changes in bond yields, although this relationship is weaker than the case of mergers and stock prices. Further, an increase in bond yields decreases stock prices in the same period, but an increase in stock prices leads to an increase in bond yields in the following period (due to an increase in business activity).

3. Changes in merger activity and changes in stock prices both lead changes in industrial production.

Melicher, Ledolter, and D'Antonio built a model that would explain future merger movements as a function of stock prices and bond yields. The results were consistent with the argument that capital market conditions (stock prices, interest rates) or their underlying causes could explain aggregate changes in merger activity. Because merger negotiations begin about two quarters before consummation, increased merger activity may reflect the expectation of rising stock prices and declining interest rates.

Linkages between mergers and the macroeconomy have also been studied by Becketti (1986). He related his series on mergers to a stock price index, the yield on three-month Treasury bills, the stock of money, the stock of domestic nonfinancial debt, the capacity utilization rate, and the GNP. His results showed that past values of the stock price index, capacity utilization rates, and the stock of debt were positively correlated with current merger activity, while past values of the T-bill rate and GNP were negatively correlated. These relationships are not always statistically significant; statistical significance varies depending on the measure of the merger series (number versus value of mergers) and the short-run versus long-run effects.

Golbe and White (1987) studied the determinants of merger activity. They tested (1) a bargains hypothesis, holding that mergers rise when a firm's asset price is low relative to the replacement value of assets; (2) a market change hypothesis, holding that relative price shifts signal changes in the efficient industry scale and lead to mergers; (3) a cost of capital hypothesis, maintaining that the real cost of capital influences the timing, financing costs, and expected profitability of mergers; (4) a tax regime dummy for tax law changes in 1954, 1963, and 1981; and (5) a divergence of opinion hypothesis, suggesting that merger activity rises with divergence of opinion as to future price movements. Their regressions found a strong relation between both nominal GNP and Tobin's $q$ (proxying for bargains hypothesis) and merger activity. $T$-statistics were not significant for any other variables. The positive coefficient on the Tobin's $q$ variable was inconsistent with the bargain theory, which predicted a negative relation between Tobin's $q$ and mergers.

Shughart and Tollison (ST) (1984) tested the hypothesis that historical merger activity could be represented as a white-noise process, that is, that the first differences in the merger series appeared to be random with positive drift. ST found that merger values for most previous years except for the last year would have no role to play in explaining current merger activity. An economic model generating mergers in a given year did not include as explanatory variables the levels of merger activity occurring more than one year earlier. However, the "results in no way detract from the idea of searching for the empirical determinants of merger activity" (Shughart and Tollison, 1984, p. 509).

The finding is in some ways to be expected. First, our earlier materials suggest that mergers occur in response to changes in economic and business conditions such as technological advances, developments in transportation and communication, changes in industry regulation, interest rates changes, and stock price changes. If these changes occur randomly, merger activity will also be characterized by randomness. Second, mergers occur to capture investment opportunities and more mergers will occur when favorable investment opportunities are expected. If expectations change randomly and quickly, then merger activity will also change similarly. Third, as Nelson (1959, pp. 116–117, 126) argued based on empirical observations, historical merger activity was characterized by large bursts of activity separated by long intervals of low activity. This discontinuous pattern and, in particular, the long intervals of low activity reflect the absence of continuously strong underlying forces. Also, the influence of external economic changes in periods of low merger activity is diffuse and erratic. Finally, the Shughart and Tollison analysis was conducted using annual time series of mergers. If the waves are of short duration extending over several quarters, then the use of quarterly data may yield a different result.

One hypothesis that can potentially provide consistent answers to many questions regarding the timing of merger activity is the investment opportunity synergy (IOS) hypothesis (Chung, 1982). This hypothesis argues that the acquiring firm seeks to internalize investment opportunities in the acquired firm's industry by realizing managerial and/or financial synergies. The IOS hypothesis predicts and the regression analyses show that both aggregate investment opportunities and financial market conditions determine aggregate merger activity for the period 1957–1977 when conglomerate mergers predominated.

Based on the IOS theory, we developed an econometric model explaining the timing of conglomerate merger activity. We restricted the analysis to conglomerates because most activity between 1950 and 1980 represented conglomerate mergers. We distinguished between product-extension conglomerate mergers (PEM) and pure conglomerate mergers (PCM). Two investment opportunity variables—the growth rate of real GNP, representing growth opportunities, and expected real long-term interest rates, representing the basic discount rate—successfully explained product-extension mergers. The pure conglomerate mergers required two additional explanatory macrofinancial variables. A risk premium was measured by the difference between AAA and BAA bond rates. The ease or tightness of monetary conditions was measured by the spread between short-term and long-term rates (the difference between the yields on four- to six-month prime commercial paper and the yields on longer-term AAA corporate bonds). We recognize that since 1980 more horizontal and vertical mergers have been permitted by the new federal government policies. Thus, another discontinuity in the nature of mergers has occurred.

--------------------------------------------------------------------------------

## Summary

To put the merger activity since 1980 in perspective, we have traced the major merger movements since the turn of the century. All of the merger movements coincided with sustained growth of the economy and with significant changes in business environments. The horizontal merger movement in the 1890s was associated with the completion of national transportation systems making the United States the first broad common market. Mergers in the 1920s were represented by both forward and backward vertical integration. They appeared to represent responses to radio, which made national advertising feasible, and to the automobile, which facilitated national distribution systems. The conglomerate merger movement of the 1960s appeared to reflect changes in management technology that had developed in the 1950s. These were associated with improved methods of financial planning and control, long-range planning, and the emergence of the methodology of strategic analysis.

Fluctuations in merger activity over the years have stimulated a number of attempts to explain the determinants of merger timing. These studies have demonstrated an association between merger activity and various macroeconomic characteristics. However, because they have not been founded in a general theory of merger activity, they have not demonstrated causation. Time-series data on merger activity have been recorded in one form or another since 1895. A number of separate series of data covering various periods compound the problem of analysis, because the series often do not use the same data sources, size criteria for inclusion, or date of recording (for example, as announced versus as consummated).

Studies based on these data have attempted to relate merger activity to the business cycle measured by industrial production, stock prices and trading, business incorporations, interest rates, and so on. The findings of these studies are that merger activity is cyclical and roughly coincident with stock price movements. The peak of M&A activity tends to precede the peak in the general business cycle, and increases in interest rates precede declines in M&As. Based on these associations, hypotheses of merger timing are formulated:

1. Mergers are used to increase capacity immediately to get into an expanding market.
2. Mergers are a less risky alternative to purchasing new plants and equipment.
3. Expectational differences between shareholders and outsiders increase during periods of rising stock prices, resulting in an assessment of undervaluation by outsiders.
4. Management optimism during economic upturns is expressed in increased merger activity.
5. Because acquiring firms rely heavily on borrowed funds, favorable conditions for public debt financing facilitate increased M&A activity.

For some periods, the data are consistent with one or more of the preceding hypotheses but none has general explanatory power. The economic rationale for and the relationship between the alternative theories of timing have not been adequately developed. Other studies have focused on whether or not merger waves exist; Golbe and White (1987) concluded that merger activity is not random, while Shughart and Tollison (1984) found that previous years' merger activity (except for the most recent) had no value in predicting merger activity for the current years.

Product-extension conglomerate mergers are highly correlated with investment opportunity conditions in the economy. According to the IOS hypothesis, this implies that these mergers are motivated by the possibility of transferring managerial resources, and the demand for such transfer is larger when greater investment opportunities exist in the economy. Pure conglomerate mergers cannot be explained by investment opportunity variables alone. The results indicate that macrofinancial variables measuring risk premiums and monetary conditions are required to account for cyclicality in PCMs. This is consistent with the hypothesis that these mergers occur to capture investment opportunities through the realization of financial economies arising from diversification effects and internal transfer of funds. The role of financial variables is weaker in effecting PEMs, although it seems that the money market condition also influences the occurrence of these mergers.

Different economic circumstances in each of the major merger movements since the 1890s have produced discontinuities that make it difficult to find one general model that successfully explains the timing of merger activity over the past 100 years.

This chapter provides a factual and analytical basis for a number of generalizations:

1. The merger movement in the United States since 1980 is not a new phenomenon, and not even the biggest.
2. Merger movements are not unique to the United States. They have been paralleled by merger movements in other developed countries and similar activities in developing countries.
3. Each merger movement has somewhat distinctive characteristics reflecting the dominant economic and technological factors operating during the period.
4. Merger activity in any year is relatively small when related to measures of the total economy.

5. While some previous merger movements may have been associated with changes in concentration in the economy, the merger activity since 1980 has had little effect on concentration measures for the economy as a whole or for individual industries.

6. While concentration measures have been little affected by M&A activity since the 1980s, major shifts in industry structures have been taking place. However, M&As are not the prime cause; fundamental technological and economic factors cause industries and firms to redefine and renew themselves. M&As are one of the ways restructuring activities are accomplished.

7. The significance of M&A activity cannot be fully conveyed by mere numbers. The effects on competition and efficiency are of greater significance for the functioning of the economy.

## Questions

6.1   Describe each of the major merger movements that have occurred in the United States, indicating the major forces involved.

6.2   Because of the financial excesses of the 1980s, M&A activity exceeded the level that was reached before or after. True or false.

6.3   On average, what percentage of gross domestic product is represented by M&A activity?

6.4   The total dollar of M&As is what percentage of total assets of all corporations in a particular year?

6.5   What is the level of M&As in relation to the market value of all equities?

6.6   In recent years, what percent of total plant and equipment expenditures has been represented by M&As?

6.7   In what percent of M&A transactions does the acquisition represent a divestiture from another company?

6.8   What are the reasons why M&A activity in recent years has not resulted in significant changes in either microconcentration or macroconcentration?

6.9   What information do studies of the timing of mergers provide when the focus is on the link between merger activity and stock prices, business cycles, and industrial activity?

6.10   Discuss the evidence in support of and refuting merger waves.

6.11   Discuss the effect of the following variables on merger activity:
   a. The growth rate of real GNP, $G$.
   b. The real interest rate, $r$.
   c. Tobin's $q$-ratio.
   d. The market risk premium, $PREM$.
   e. Monetary stringency, $SPD$.

6.12   To what extent are pure conglomerate mergers versus product-extension mergers explained by the preceding variables?

## References

Becketti, S., "Corporate Mergers and the Business Cycle," *Economic Review,* 71, Federal Reserve Bank of Kansas City, May 1986, pp. 13–26.

Butters, J. K., John Lintner, and W. L. Cary, *Effects of Taxation on Corporate Mergers,* Cambridge, MA: Harvard University Press, 1951.

Chung, Kwang S., "Investment Opportunities, Synergies and Conglomerate Mergers," unpublished doctoral dissertation, The Anderson School at UCLA, 1982.

Dewing, Arthur Stone, *The Financial Policy of Corporations,* Vol. 2, New York: The Ronald Press Company, 1953.

Golbe, Devra L., and Lawrence J. White, "A Time Series Analysis of Mergers and Acquisitions in the U.S. Economy," mimeo., Presented at National Bureau of Economic Research Conference on Mergers and Acquisitions, February 1987.

————, "A Time-Series Analysis of Mergers and Acquisitions in the U.S. Economy," Chapter 9 in Alan J. Auerbach, ed., *Corporate Takeovers: Causes and Consequences,* Chicago: The University of Chicago Press, 1988, pp. 265–309.

Gray, S. J., and M. C. McDermott, *Mega-Merger Mayhem,* London: Paul Chapman Publishing Ltd., 1989.

Houlihan Lokey Howard & Zukin, *Mergerstat Review, 1997,* and previous years.

Jensen, Michael C., "The Modern Industrial Revolution, Exit, and the Failure of Internal Control Systems," *Journal of Finance,* 48, July 1993, pp. 831–880.

Livermore, Shaw, "The Success of Industrial Mergers," *Quarterly Journal of Economics,* 50, November 1935, pp. 68–96.

Mandel, Michael J., "A Dangerous Concentration?" *Business Week,* April 29, 1996, pp. 96–97.

Markham, Jesse W., "Survey of Evidence and Findings on Mergers," *Business Concentration and Price Policy,* National Bureau of Economic Research, Princeton, NJ: Princeton University Press, 1955.

Melicher, R. W., J. Ledolter, and L. D'Antonio, "A Time Series Analysis of Aggregate Merger Activity," *The Review of Economics and Statistics,* 65, August 1983, pp. 423–430.

Moody, John, *The Truth About the Trusts,* New York: Moody Publishing Company, 1904.

Mueller, Dennis C., ed., *The Determinants and Effects of Mergers,* Cambridge, MA.: Oelgeschlager, Gunn & Hain, Publishers, Inc., 1980.

Nelson, R. L., *Merger Movements in American Industry, 1895–1956,* Princeton, NJ: Princeton University Press, 1959.

Salter, Malcolm S., and Wolf A. Weinhold, *Diversification Through Acquisition,* New York: The Free Press, 1979.

————, "Merger Trends and Prospects for the 1980s," U.S. Department of Commerce, Harvard University, December 1980.

Scherer, F. M., *Industrial Market Structure and Economic Performance,* Chicago: Rand McNally College Publishing Company, 1980.

Shleifer, Andrei, and Robert W. Vishny, "The Takeover Wave of the 1980s," *Science,* 249, August 1990, pp. 745–749.

Shughart, W. F., II, and R. O. Tollison, "The Random Character of Merger Activity," *Rand Journal of Economics,* 15, Winter 1984, pp. 500–509.

Stigler, George J., "Monopoly and Oligopoly by Merger," *American Economic Review,* 40, May 1950, pp. 23–34.

————, "The Division of Labor is Limited by the Extent of the Market," *Journal of Political Economy,* 59, June 1951, pp. 185–193.

Stocking, G. W., "Commentary on Markham, 'Survey of Evidence and Findings on Mergers,'" in *Business Concentration and Price Policy,* Princeton, NJ: Princeton University Press, 1955, pp. 191–212.

Weston, J. F., *The Role of Mergers in the Growth of Large Firms,* Berkeley and Los Angeles: University of California Press, 1953, Chapter 5.

————, "Domestic Concentration and International Markets," Chapter 7 in J. Fred Weston and Michael E. Granfield, eds., *Corporate Enterprise in a New Environment,* New York: KCG Productions, Inc., 1982, pp. 173–188.

————, and Surenda K. Mansinghka, "Tests of the Efficiency Performance of Conglomerate Firms," *Journal of Finance,* 26, September 1971, pp. 919–936.

# CHAPTER

# 7

# Empirical Tests
# of M&A Performance

Previous chapters have discussed alternative theories of why mergers and tender offers occur. This chapter reviews the relevant empirical tests. We begin with some central issues to have a brief reference framework for the tests.

## ISSUES IN EMPIRICAL STUDIES

There are a number of issues and questions that empirical studies may potentially elucidate. First and foremost, the goal is to provide tests of alternative theories. Another important objective from a public policy standpoint is to determine whether or not social value is enhanced by mergers. If, for example, the basic driving force for mergers is improved efficiency, the improvement represents a social gain regardless of the theory that explains how it is achieved.

Do value increases represent social gains or merely redistribution? The first issue then is: Is true social value increased?

If value is increased by mergers or tender offers, is it maintained? Is value maintained in the short term only for a period of six months or less? Or should the tests cover a subsequent period of five to ten years? A second basic issue is: Does the restructuring result in operating performance improvements that can be measured for subsequent years?

A third basic issue relates to industry effects. To what degree are restructuring activities related to fundamental technological, economic, regulatory, and other forces taking place in individual industries? Another important issue is to analyze the effects of restructuring by one firm on other firms in the same industry.

These three major issues are tested by a large number of studies. We organize them into the following topics: returns in successful mergers and takeovers, unsuccessful takeovers, methods of payment and managerial resistance, positive total returns versus negative total returns, effects of regulation, single bids versus multiple bids, runup versus markup returns, efficiency versus market power, postmerger performance, industry influences on M&A activity, and patterns of takeover activity.

## RETURNS IN SUCCESSFUL MERGERS AND TAKEOVERS

The *Journal of Financial Economics* published a compendium of studies of mergers and tender offers in 1983. In their comprehensive summary article, Jensen and Ruback

(1983) reviewed 13 studies with sample data ending mostly in the late 1970s. Six of the studies were on mergers and seven on tender offers.

## Returns to Targets

The summary table of Jensen and Ruback showed a 30% positive return to target shareholders in successful tender offers and a somewhat lower return of 20% to targets in successful mergers. (In mergers usually the larger firm is designated as the acquiring firm and the smaller firm as the acquired or target.)

Jarrell, Brickley, and Netter (1988) summarized results for 663 successful tender offers covering the period from 1962 through December 1985. They observed that premiums to targets in successful tender offers averaged 19% in the 1960s, 35% in the 1970s, and 30% for the period 1980–1985 (p. 51). Similar results were obtained by Bradley, Desai, and Kim (BDK) (1988). For the period July 1963 to June 1968, the returns to targets were 19%. For the subperiod July 1968 to December 1980, they were 35% and for the period January 1981 to December 1984, the returns were 35%. Their study covered 236 successful tender offer contests completed between 1963 and 1984.

The Schwert (1996) study covered the years 1975 through 1991, using a sample of 1,814 companies. For the entire period, the returns for tender offers was 35%. The unweighted average of the annual returns for all tender offers for the years 1985 to 1991 was 36.8%. For the years 1992 to 1996, covering 1,280 transactions, the average of the median premiums paid was 32%; the average of the average premiums was 41% (Houlihan et al., 1997, p. 23). These patterns were also confirmed by Howe and Wo (1994).

It is clear that targets in successful tender offers or mergers earn substantial premiums. It is clear also that the time trend of returns to targets has been upward. The reasons for the upward time trend may be summarized. In July 1968 the Williams Amendment gave the Securities and Exchange Commission (SEC) the power to regulate tender offers. In the same year the first state antitakeover law was passed by Virginia. The effect of government regulation was to require publication that a foothold position had been taken by the acquiring firm. In addition, government regulations provided for a delay before a tender offer could be completed. This enabled the targets to develop defenses and counterbids.

The period after the Reagan administration took office in early 1981 has its own distinctive characteristics. The regulatory agencies announced new standards toward mergers and takeovers that permitted horizontal and vertical mergers that would have been contested in earlier years. These developments were also accompanied by a rapid pace of innovations by financial intermediaries to finance mergers and tender offers. A counterdevelopment was the emergence of a wide array of defenses against takeovers. These included supermajority and fair-price amendments to corporate charters as well as the use of poison pills and various restructuring defenses. (These are all discussed in later chapters.)

Opposing forces are operating. However, it is clear that after the enactment of government regulations in the late 1960s, the returns to targets in successful tender offers increased from below 20% to somewhat over 30% on average.

While there is no question of large positive gains to target shareholders, Jarrell, Brickley, and Netter (1988, p. 52) observe that the evidence "probably understates the total gains to these shareholders." They observe that an active market for information develops about impending takeover bids. They point to a number of identifiable influences on prebid trading. These include articles in the financial press and information that develops on the bidder's foothold acquisition in the target. Also, in friendly bids there may be preliminary communications. They argue that factors such as these influence the earlier price runup and that these influences are distinct from illegal insider trading. Overall the shareholders of targets benefited by a substantial degree in successful tender offers and mergers. The evidence for bidders or acquiring firms, for unsuccessful events, and for total value increase requires a more careful assessment to which we now turn.

### Returns to Bidder Firms

There is no doubt that the returns to target shareholders are positive. The only issue is their magnitude. It is less clear whether or not the excess returns to the shareholders of bidder firms are positive. If the market for corporate control is perfectly competitive, we expect the excess returns to the shareholders of bidding firms to be zero. Bidders would earn only normal returns under competition. If this were the case, then overall M&A activity would be value increasing. The gains to the targets are positive and substantial. If the excess returns to bidder firms are zero, then overall the gains to the M&A activity would necessarily be positive. Only if the excess returns to bidder firms were negative would there be a possibility that the overall gains could be negative.

In their summary of the evidence, Jensen and Ruback (1983) concluded that the excess returns to bidder firms in successful tender offers was a positive 4%. They estimated zero returns to bidder firms in mergers. Jarrell, Brickley, and Netter (1988) examined the data on returns to shareholders of acquiring companies for a sequence of decades. For the 1960s, they obtained about the same result as Jensen and Ruback for tender offers. For a window of 10 days before the announcement date to five days after, the excess returns to successful bidders in tender offers were 4.4%. When the window was extended to 20 days after the event date, the cumulative excess returns rose to 4.95% and were highly significant from a statistical standpoint. The increase in excess returns during the subsequent 15-day period indicated that the postevent performance of the bidders improved somewhat with the longer postevent time period for analysis.

For the 1970s the excess returns to successful bidders dropped to about 2%, statistically significant. For the 1980s, the excess returns became negative at about 1% but were not statistically significant.

Bradley, Desai, and Kim (1988) found similar results for tender offers. For subperiods approximating the 1960s, the excess returns to acquiring firms were slightly over 4%. For a period roughly corresponding to the 1970s, the excess returns were 1.3%. For the 1980s, the excess returns became negative at slightly under 3%. The data for the 1960s and the 1980s were significant at the 1% level. The excess returns to acquiring firms for the total period 1960–1985 for Jarrell, Brickley, and Netter and 1963 through 1984 for Bradley, Desai, and Kim were positive and significant. Bradley, Desai, and Kim also calculated the dollar amount of wealth change. They found that the combined results for target and acquiring firms were positive for each of the subperiods, including the 1980s when the excess wealth return to acquirers was negative.

Schwert's (1996) data on bidder stock prices suggest that on average the abnormal returns to bidders for the period 1975 to 1991 were not significantly different from zero. The highly competitive nature of the takeover market has continued through 1996, suggesting that the abnormal returns to bidders continued at levels not significantly different from zero. If the abnormal returns to bidders were approximately zero from 1985 through 1996, the total wealth change continued to be positive through 1996, because the abnormal returns to targets were in the 35 to 40% range.

The preceding evidence suggests that the returns to target firms increased over the decades as government regulation increased and as sophisticated defensive tactics by targets were developed. The excess returns to bidding firms decreased over the decades for the same influences operating in the reverse direction. But even for the most recent period of the 1980s, it appears that the total wealth increase from M&A activity is positive.

These conclusions are also supported by the frequency distribution analysis of You, Caves, Smith, and Henry (1986). The mean return to target companies for 133 mergers during the period 1975 through June 1984 was about 20%. The excess returns to shareholders of bidder companies were a negative 1%. In addition to mean returns, You et al. presented frequency distributions. For target companies, 82% had positive excess returns. In fact, 20% of the companies had positive excess returns exceeding 40%. But 18% of the target companies had negative returns. For bidder companies, about 47% had positive returns while about 53% of the bidder companies had negative returns. However, most positive returns for bidder firms were modest in size. Twenty-five percent of the bidder companies had positive returns of from 0 to 5%. This is also true for the bidders that experienced negative returns—28% had excess returns of from 0 to −5%.

Thus, the mean returns cover up the wide diversity in experience both for target and bidder companies. Although bidder companies for some time period experienced negative returns, there is always a substantial fraction of the bidder companies who experience positive returns. This may provide motivation for bidder firms to continue to engage in M&A activity, although average results may be unfavorable. Each firm, based on the evidence, may formulate the judgment that its own results can be positive.

### The Effect of NASDAQ Trading

Most of the studies of M&A activity are for New York Stock Exchange (NYSE) and American Stock Exchange (ASE) targets. A study was made for NASDAQ targets for 1984 (Asquith, 1988). For the period −10 days to the announcement date, the excess return to targets was 19.0%. However, for day −1 to the announcement date the return was 10.7%. This is the order of magnitude of the data for NYSE and ASE companies. The results were not greatly different when broken down between successful and unsuccessful offers and between uncontested and contested offers.

# UNSUCCESSFUL TAKEOVERS

Jensen and Ruback (1983) found that for unsuccessful tender offers both target and bidder companies experienced negative excess returns of modest size, but not statistically significant. In mergers, target firms also experienced negative, but statistically insignificant returns. For bidder firms in mergers, the excess negative return was 5% and it was statistically significant.

### Returns to Targets

In discussing a sample of 112 unsuccessful takeovers, Bradley, Desai, and Kim (1983) divided the targets into three groups. The first group (58% of the sample) was subsequently taken over within 60 trading days after the announcement date (day zero). The cumulative abnormal return (CAR) was almost 50% during the two-day period

(−1 to 0) and rose to over 66% by the end of the 60 trading days. A second group (19% of the sample) was taken over more than 60 days after, but before five years. Their CAR for the two-day period (−1 to 0) was about 23%. By day +60, their CAR rose to over 55%. So they did almost as well as the first group, but the market did not react until later when the probability of a subsequent bid increased. For the third group (23% of the sample) which was not taken over within the five-year period, the CAR which was initially about the same as for the second group, became negative after two years and drifted between a range of a negative 5 to 10% during the subsequent three years.

### Returns to Unsuccessful Bidders

In discussing unsuccessful bidders, Bradley, Desai, and Kim (1983) divided their sample into two groups. Group 1 bidders lost out to a rival bidder by the end of 180 trading days after the announcement date. Their CAR was a negative 8% by the end of the 180 days. For group 2 bidders, no rival bidder had succeeded within the 180 days subsequent to the initial announcement. At the end of 180 days, these bidders experienced a small positive, but not significant CAR.

The results for the unsuccessful acquiring firms are of interest because of the impact on total value. As observed previously, if the returns to acquiring firms are sufficiently negative, this could cause the total activity to be a negative net present value activity rather than one that created positive values.

Bradley, Desai, and Kim (1983) found that for the period 1963–1980, the unsuccessful bidders in the multiple-bidder contests on average lost 8% of their preoffer value. They observed that the gains to successful bidders in multiple-bidder contests during the same period were not significantly different from zero. They concluded that it is better to win than to lose in a multiple-bidding contest. But this conclusion did not hold for the 1981–1984 period during which successful bidders in multiple-bidder contests lost 5.1% (highly significant) (Bradley, Desai, and Kim, 1988).

For a larger sample of tender offers, Opler (1988) found that for the period 1981–1986, unsuccessful bidders earned a positive 0.68%, marginally significant. The results for unsuccessful acquiring firms depended on a number of other variables, however. The cumulative average abnormal return was a positive 10% 18 months after termination during which a later takeover had occurred. When no later takeover occurred, the cumulative average abnormal return, however, was negative by about 5%.

The results differed also depending on whether the unsuccessful acquiring firms experienced positive CARs for the announcement period (the day before through the day after the announcement date). For the subsample of bidders that had positive announcement CARs and that made a later takeover during the subsequent 18 months, the cumulative abnormal returns by the end of the 18 months were 20%. For unsuccessful bidders with initial positive returns, but that made no later takeover, the cumulative average abnormal return was only slightly above zero.

For unsuccessful acquiring firms with negative initial event returns that made a later takeover within the 18 months after the announcement date, the cumulative return was positive for most of the 18-month period, but returned to approximately zero by the end of the 18 months. For those unsuccessful acquiring firms that made no subsequent takeover, the CARs declined sharply to about −18% by the twelfth month following the announcement date and then recovered to about a −10% CAR by the end of the 18 months.

These data and related patterns showed that the experiences of unsuccessful acquiring firms were quite different depending on the initial response in the announcement period and also whether or not the acquiring firm made a later takeover.

However, no inference on causality appeared possible because the better performance of unsuccessful bidders making later takeovers may not be the result of such a takeover, but simply be due to a selection bias (that is, better performance led to takeovers).

## METHODS OF PAYMENT AND MANAGERIAL RESISTANCE

Corporate finance theory implies that the method of payment used in a merger or tender offer may influence the returns to the stockholders of both the bidder and target firms. Of particular relevance is the theory of Myers and Majluf (1984) that holds that the method of financing an investment conveys information. They argue that when the firm sells common stock to finance a new project, it is because the managers judge the common stock to be overvalued. When the firm uses debt to finance a new investment, this implies that management judges its common stock to be undervalued. In addition, empirical studies suggest that there are negative returns to shareholders when new outside financing is used whether in the form of debt or equity.

The earlier studies by Gordon and Yagil (1981) and by Wansley, Lane, and Yang (1983) found higher abnormal returns for cash offers than for stock offers. The Gordon and Yagil study examined completed pure conglomerate mergers over the period 1948–1976. The Wansley, Lane, and Yang work covered mergers for the period 1970–1978. Wansley, Lane, and Yang found that the target firm cumulative average residual for the 41 days through the announcement date when the method of payment was cash was 33.54% as compared with 17.47% when securities were used. When the method of payment represented a combination of cash and securities, the CAR was 11.77%. They discussed the role of taxes in impacting these differential abnormal returns. They also observed that when stock is used, the bidding firm must go through Securities and Exchange Commission registration, which may take several months. Cash offers can be accomplished much more rapidly. The longer time to complete a takeover gives target management more possibilities for developing a defense to the takeover. They can stimulate additional bids resulting in high prices, which could be offset by higher preemptive cash bids.

A later study by Travlos (1987) analyzed the impact of methods of payment on both bidders and targets. For **target firms,** his results were similar to those of Wansley, Lane, and Yang. The two-day announcement period abnormal cumulative portfolio return when common stock was used was 12.04%. They found that significant positive abnormal returns started appearing a week before the announcement appeared in the *Wall Street Journal.* In cash transactions the two-day abnormal return was 17.06% and highly significant. Again some significant abnormal returns were observed in the pre-announcement period.

For the **bidding firms,** Travlos found that when stock was used as the method of payment, the two-day announcement period CAR was minus 1.47%, which was significant at the .01 level. Thus, the effect was small but still statistically significant. He observed that Gordon and Yagil found positive abnormal returns of 5.3% over the eight-month period prior to the completion date of the merger, but that the long period may confound the influence of other factors. The results of Travlos were more comparable to those of Eger (1983), who found in a sample of 37 pure common stock exchange mergers that bidding stockholders lost about 3% during the event period.

However, the results were different when the buying firms used cash to acquire target firms. The two-day announcement period cumulative abnormal return was 0.24%, which is insignificant. Travlos concluded that on average shareholders of bidding firms earned only normal rates of return when their firms paid cash in a takeover. Again his results differed from those of Gordon and Yagil, who found an abnormal cumulative (monthly) return of 7.9% over the eight-month period prior to the merger completion date.

The findings by Travlos on the results for bidder firms have great significance both for theory and practice. Studies that have found negative returns to bidding firms have argued that shareholders of bidding firms are penalized by takeover activities. They argue that an agency problem is involved. But if only normal returns are experienced when cash is used, this reflects the highly competitive nature of the takeover market. The negative returns when common stock exchanges are employed may simply reflect the negative information implications set out by Myers and Majluf (1984). When the studies do not distinguish between cash and common stock exchange takeovers, the average result may simply reflect the method of payment rather than a meaningful measure of the performance of bidding firms.

Harris, Franks, and Mayer (1987) compared the effects of means of payment in takeovers for the United Kingdom as well as for the United States. They found that acquired firm returns were higher for cash offers than for all equity offers both in the United States and in the United Kingdom. For the event month the effects were stronger in the United Kingdom. For the period encompassing four months prior and one month after the event month, the effects were about the same in both countries. For bidders during the event month, all cash offers yielded small positive abnormal returns that were statistically significant in the United States, but not significant in the United Kingdom. All equity offers had negative returns that were significant in the United States, but not in the United Kingdom. For the longer period of analysis covering months −4 to +1, cash offers yielded small positive abnormal returns both in the United States and the United Kingdom and had some statistical significance. Equity offers carried no statistical significance.

Queen (1989) also studied the effects of the form of payment. Queen brought in another variable, the extent to which the tender offer may have been anticipated prior to the announcement date. Her results can be summarized in the following matrix of returns:

|  | Preannouncement | Around Announcement | Total Periods |
|---|---|---|---|
| Target | noncash > cash | noncash < cash | noncash = cash |
| Bidder | noncash = cash | noncash = cash | noncash = cash |

It can be seen that her results when measured around the announcement date were similar to the results for the studies previously described. However, she extended the analysis into the preannouncement period. Here the target received more in a noncash tender than for a cash tender offer. For bidders, abnormal returns were the same whether the method of payment was cash or noncash. When she combined the two periods, Queen found that for the total periods, the abnormal returns to both the target and bidder were the same whether cash or noncash was employed. Queen, therefore, concluded that observed differences appeared because the extent to which the tender was anticipated was not adequately analyzed in the previous studies.

A study by Huang and Walkling (1987) combined the analysis of method of payment with acquisition form and managerial resistance. Whereas previous studies found higher abnormal returns (30 to 35%) for tender offers than for mergers (15 to 20%) for target shareholders, such studies did not consider the effect of payment method and target management resistance. Huang and Walkling found that when method of payment and degree of resistance were taken into account statistically, abnormal returns were no higher in tender offers than in mergers. Managerial resistance carried somewhat higher abnormal returns, but the results were not statistically significant. These results were not affected after controlling for form of payment and form of acquisition. The most powerful influence they found was the method of payment. After controlling for type of acquisition and for managerial resistance, cash offers had much higher abnormal returns than stock offers. The average CAR for cash offers was 29.3% compared with 14.4% for stock offers. For mixed payments, the average abnormal return was 23.3%, which fell between the values reported for stock and cash offers.

Huang and Walkling subjected the results to regression analysis. This enabled them to take the effects of form of payment, managerial resistance, and form of acquisition into account holding two of the influences constant while the third varied. The difference between the abnormal returns of tender offers and mergers disappeared when the influence of the form of payment and managerial resistance were taken into account. But the difference between cash and stock offers remained strong even after controlling for resistance and the form of acquisition, merger or tender offer.

For the years 1992 through 1996, cash was used in 27% of takeover transactions while stock was used in 39%. Rising stock prices encouraged the use of stock as a method of payment (Houlihan et al., 1997, p. 14). The median percent premium in cash transactions for the 1992 to 1996 period was about 31%. For stock transactions, the median percent premium was approximately the same. Thus, in the most recent years no difference was observed in the premium offered whether cash and stock was used as a method of payment. However, when a combination of cash and stock represented the method of payment, the average premium rose to 36% (Houlihan et al., 1997, p. 26).

## Interval Between Announcement and Completion

Wansley, Lane, and Yang (1983) studied 203 acquisitions between 1970 and 1978. They found that the average time interval between an acquisition's announcement and its completion date was 66 days. When segmented by method of payment, interval length differed substantially. Securities transactions took, on average, twice as long to complete as their cash counterparts. No significant differences in interval length were apparent when comparing companies that used all securities and those that used a combination of cash and securities. The empirical data that demonstrate longer intervals for securities transactions are not surprising. Securities transactions are required to receive approval from the Securities and Exchange Commission, a process that can take many months. Cash transactions are less restrictive and often only entail "cooling-off" periods.

A lengthy acquisition interval may involve disadvantages. Longer intervals allow the target company more time to prepare defenses. It also allows other suitors to evaluate the target and potentially enter the bidding. A competitive situation often leads to a higher price and lower returns for the eventual acquirer. When managers evaluate a potential acquisition, they need to predict reactions by the targets and potential competitor bids. If the acquisition is extremely time-critical, a cash transaction would have advantages. In addition, to forestall potential competitive bidders, the cash bid may be higher as a preemptive bid.

In summary, returns to targets in a merger transaction are in the 20 to 25% range as compared with a 30 to 40% range for tender offers. However, the method of payment in tender offers is usually cash while it is stock in mergers. So, it is the use of cash that may result in higher returns to targets rather than whether the transaction is a merger versus a tender offer. The possible reasons why the use of cash results in higher returns to target companies are:

1. Cash transactions are taxable to target shareholders and so the higher premiums paid compensate for taxes paid.

2. The information effect suggests that the bidder uses stock when it is overvalued, so more of it has to be used to compensate the target; this would be a countereffect.

3. The signaling effect may be that the use of cash by the bidder indicates that the bidder will be able to exploit the investment opportunities represented by the target; if so, the target is worth more and a higher premium may be paid.

4. The time interval to complete the transaction is shorter when cash is used because securities transactions may involve regulatory approval and much more documentation. A short interval reduces the time for targets to mount defenses including turning to additional bidders. However, preemptive cash bids could be even higher.

### Bad Bidders Become Good Targets

Mitchell and Lehn (ML) (1990) studied stock price reactions to acquisitions during 1982–1986. One sample was composed of firms that became targets of takeovers after they had made acquisitions. A control group consisted of acquiring firms that did not subsequently become targets of takeover bids. The stock prices of acquirers that became targets declined significantly when they announced acquisitions. The stock prices of acquiring firms that did not become subsequent targets increased significantly when they announced acquisitions.

Furthermore, ML found that for the entire sample of acquisitions, those that were subsequently divested had significantly negative event returns. Acquisitions that were not subsequently divested had significantly positive event returns. This suggests that when companies announce acquisitions, the event returns forecast the likelihood that the assets will ultimately be divested. Mitchell and Lehn pointed out that in the aggregate the returns to acquiring firms were approximately zero. But when acquiring firms experienced negative event returns, they were subsequently likely to become takeover targets. Bidders that experienced positive event returns were less likely to become targets. Event returns were able to discriminate between "bad" bidders and "good" bidders.

## POSITIVE TOTAL RETURNS
## VERSUS NEGATIVE TOTAL RETURNS

Of critical importance is whether the total event returns are positive or negative—whether value is created or destroyed. Berkovitch and Narayanan (1993) tested alternative theories of takeovers by grouping the results for positive total returns versus negative returns. Two hundred fifty-two transactions, 76% of their sample of 330, achieved positive total gains. The correlation between target returns and total returns is positive and highly significant. The correlation between target gains and bidder gains, however, is not statistically significant. Berkovitch and Narayanan suggested that hubris may be weakening the generally positive correlation in expected gains between bidders and targets.

For the sample of negative total gains, the correlation between target gains and total gains was negative and significant. This could result because target gains are always positive so that when total gains are negative, target gains would be negatively correlated with the nonpositive total gains. When target gains were related to bidder gains for the negative total gains sample, the correlation was again negative and highly significant. This implies that agency causes total gains to be negative and hubris still provides positive gains to targets, which implies that bidders will have negative returns.

Berkovitch and Narayanan also analyzed the influence of competition among bidders as reflected in multiple bid contests. For positive total gains, the correlation between target returns and total gains was strongly positive. It appeared that the synergy influence was reinforced. When total gains were negative, however, the correlation between target returns and total gains was negative. Multiple bidding appeared to aggravate the agency problem and to stimulate hubris as well.

Berkovitch and Narayanan conclude that total gains are mostly positive and that synergy appears to be the dominant driving force in mergers and takeovers. They suggest that the empirical data convey that agency and hubris play some role as well. They observe that in more than three-fourths of the cases in the sample they employ, total gains are positive. It is likely, therefore, that value is created by M&As. This reinforces the conclusions of other studies as well.

Houston and Ryngaert (1994) studied gains from large bank mergers using a sample of 131 completed mergers and 22 uncompleted for the period 1985–1991. They focused on the total return measured by the return to a value-weighted portfolio of the bidder and target. The average total return to a completed bank merger was slightly positive but not significantly different from zero. However, in the later years covered by their sample, the total merger returns were positive and significant.

Bidding banks were more profitable than target banks, but the differences in profitability did not explain the size of total abnormal returns. However, total abnormal returns were significantly higher when acquiring banks had been more profitable. Banks with good track records were considered more likely to engage in value-increasing acquisitions.

Houston and Ryngaert point out that most bank takeover bids are stock financed. When a bidding bank announced an acquisition, this may be interpreted as a signal that its stock is overvalued. This may partially account for the negative returns to bidder banks. They find that the market responds most favorably when acquisitions announcements are made by bidders that have a historical record of superior operating performance. Bank merger transactions in which there is a high degree of market overlap earn higher positive returns presumably because of a greater potential for cost savings.

## EFFECTS OF REGULATION

The Bradley, Desai, and Kim (BDK) (1988) study updated much of the earlier work. Their primary database is a sample of 921 tender offers during the period October 1958 to December 1984. The average duration between the announcement date and the execution of a tender offer was three to four weeks. The average percent of shares purchased was about 60%. In 66% of the tender offers, there had been no toeholds or previous purchases of target stock by the bidders.

They present two measures of premium. One is the standard cumulative abnormal return (CAR) using market model parameter estimates based on 300 to 60 trading days before the announcement date. They observe that studies using monthly data find a positive alpha or abnormal return for acquiring firms for periods preceding the announcement date. Their second measure is a blended premium (BP). The BP for their sample for the period 1981–1984 was 43%; the CAR for the corresponding period was 35%. Their regression of the CAR on the BP had a zero intercept and a .8 regression coefficient. They gave two reasons why the CAR is lower: One, the CAR is net of market movements. Two, the CAR is a simple arithmetic sum; the BP is a continuously compounded return. This would explain a difference, but generally a continuously compounded return is lower than an arithmetic average return.

Bradley, Desai, and Kim found that value was created in that the CAR was positive for the target and for the target and bidder combined for all subperiods and for the total period. Premiums to targets increased after 1968, the year of the adoption of the Williams Act, which provided for a 20-day waiting period. For acquirers, the CAR was positive and significant for 1963–1968; it was a small positive but insignificant for 1968–1980; it was negative and insignificant for the period 1981–1984. The combination of the Williams Act and increased competition as well as target defenses reduced the returns to bidders.

## SINGLE BIDS VERSUS MULTIPLE BIDS

The 1988 BDK study is also representative of the effects of multiple bidders. In multiple bidder contests, the CAR for targets rose to 26% on the announcement day (AD) and continued to rise to over 45% by 80 trading days after the AD. For their single-bidder subsample, the CAR was about the same on the announcement date but rose no further by 80 days after the AD. For single bidders, the CAR was a positive 2 to 3%. In multiple bids, the bidder CAR was essentially zero. Late bidder acquirers (white knights) lost 2.38%, statistically significant. The authors concluded that white knights on average "pay too much" (p. 30).

We have summarized the pattern of returns with single bidders versus multiple bidders for target firms in Figure 7.1 and for acquiring firms in Figure 7.2. These figures

**FIGURE 7.1  Cumulative Abnormal Returns of Target Firms**

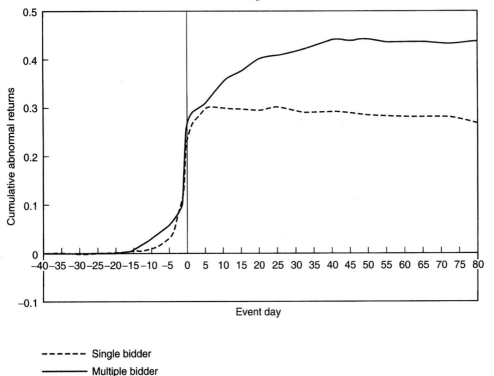

- - - - - -  Single bidder

————————  Multiple bidder

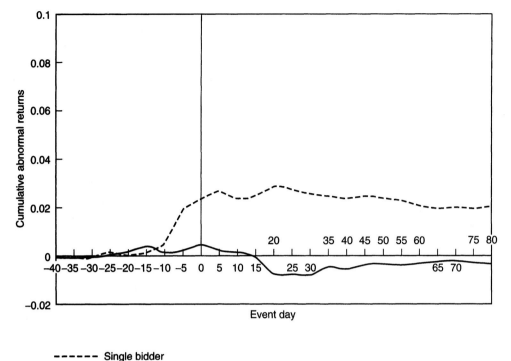

**FIGURE 7.2  Cumulative Abnormal Returns of Acquiring Firms**

seek to reflect patterns found in BDK (1988) and other studies of single-bidder versus multiple-bidder acquisitions. In Figure 7.1, the returns to target firms begin to rise about 20 days before the announcement date. On the announcement date, a further increase moves the abnormal returns of single-bidder target firms to about 30%. Shortly after the announcement date the returns to target firms drift down slightly. In multiple-bidder contests, the event returns to targets continue to rise after the announcement date. As subsequent bids take place, the event returns continue to rise. About 40 days after the announcement date for the first bidder, the event returns to the target firms level off at about 45%.

In Figure 7.2, we see that the event returns for acquiring firms that are single bidders rise to over 2% at the announcement date. Subsequently, the event returns drift down but only slightly. For acquiring firms that are competing in multiple-bidder contests, the event returns are slightly positive. But shortly after the announcement date as new bidders come onto the scene, the event returns drop to negative levels.

These relationships are confirmed by a detailed regression analysis in BDK (1988). The regression analysis found that the premium to targets was higher when the fraction of target shares purchased was higher. The authors observe that this finding is consistent with the positive supply curve for target shares.

## RUNUP VERSUS MARKUP RETURNS

An in-depth study has been made of the relationship between the CAR for the preannouncement period and for the postannouncement period (Schwert, 1996). The central finding is that the preannouncement CAR (the runup) and the postannouncement

CAR (the markup) are not correlated. The study concludes that because little substitution takes place between the runup and the markup, the runup is an added cost to the bidder. The role of private information versus public information, and the interpretation of the runup price increases, raise important issues not fully resolved. Schwert observed that his subsample that involved subsequent insider trading litigation resulted in higher runups. The gains to the insiders were only a fraction of the increased costs imposed on the bidders.

The Schwert study is of great value in updating empirical data on M&A activity. His empirical analysis uses the comprehensive database developed by Robert Comment covering all mergers and tender offers for NYSE and AMEX target firms from 1975 to 1991. A usable sample of 1,523 is the main basis for analysis. On average, for 1,174 successful deals, the runup and markup are about the same at 15% each. In the 564 tender offers, the runup is about 16% and the markup about 20%, approximating the 35% gain to targets in tender offers found in previous studies. In the 959 mergers, their runup is 12% with the markup 5%. The total premium of 17% is slightly below the average 20% found in earlier studies. In 173 MBOs, the runup and markup averages are approximately 10% each, totaling 20%.

In the 229 subsample of poison pills, the runup averages 12%, the markup about 18%. In the 312 subsample involving competitive bidding, the runup averages 13%, the markup 18%, a total premium only slightly above the 30% for successful single-bid transactions on average.

In the 135 transactions in which an insider trading case was brought, the runup was 18.3%, significantly higher than the 13.3% for the full sample. The markup was 21.2%, almost double the markup of 10.5% for the main sample. The Schwert study provides a valuable updating of the earlier empirical studies of target returns as well as extends the coverage of issues treated.

With regard to returns to acquirers, Schwert found, as did earlier studies, that in establishing parameters for measuring CARs, the market model had a positive slope during the preannouncement test period. Schwert calculated the market model regression for the trading days $-253$ to $-127$ in relation to the announcement date. Like earlier studies, Schwert found that bidder firms had unusual stock price increases prior to their decisions to make takeover bids (Asquith, 1983). Schwert sought to adjust for this by setting the intercepts of the market model regressions to zero. The consequence is that the negative CAR for bidders found in other studies that do not make such adjustments become zero. Our interpretation is that the abnormal returns to bidders on average are zero. This is consistent with a takeover market that is highly competitive so that bidders earn only normal returns on average.

At a number of places, Schwert argues that the pattern of returns in runup in relation to markup periods produces evidence inconsistent with the hubris hypothesis of Roll (1986). Schwert seems to use a different definition of hubris. The earlier discussion by Bradley, Desai, and Kim appeared to test hubris by whether the bidders experienced negative CARs over the runup plus markup periods combined. If so, "they paid too much," which seems to us faithful to Roll's definition. When the Schwert adjustments are made to the market model, the zero returns to bidders on average is consistent with no hubris on average. But this implies that bidders with returns below the average for the sample as a whole (negative CARs) exhibited behavior consistent with hubris. Our conclusion is similar to that of Berkovitch and Narayanan (1993) that hubris was exhibited in only a fraction of the sample they studied.

Schwert examined share trading volume related to announcements of M&A activity. He found that across the main sample of 1,506 firms for which delisting occurred within one year of the first bid (the transaction was completed), the average volume runup from −42 through +126 days in relation to the announcement date was 127.8%. The average volume runup was higher before tender offers and especially for transactions involving subsequent insider trading prosecutions.

## EFFICIENCY VERSUS MARKET POWER

The empirical studies find that total value is increased by mergers and takeovers. The evidence is also strong that the shareholders of acquired firms gain. However, whether the shareholders of acquiring firms gain depends on the presence of synergy or other motives. On balance, total value appears to be increased by M&As. The possibility remains that the value gains result from increases in market power, however, rather than from increases in efficiency. A number of studies are relevant to these issues.

Ellert (1975, 1976) studied these issues at great length. He analyzed the data for 205 defendants in antimerger complaints for the period 1950–1972. He found that for four years before the filing of the complaint, the residual performance was positive and statistically significant for the defendants. As expected, the residuals become negative upon the filing of a complaint. However, the negative residuals were relatively small. Ellert observed that the record of effective asset management in the years preceding merger activity by acquiring firms may result in complaints by their rivals to antitrust authorities. Ellert termed such legal actions a "harassment" hypothesis. He indicated that incentives exist for complaining rivals to follow this course. The government agencies bear the costs of prosecution; and if successful, the complaining firms' actions will handicap their rivals. The complaining parties may then file private treble damage suits. The harassment hypothesis is clearly the opposite of a monopoly explanation of merger activity. In addition, if a doubt exists about whether the acquiring firms obtain gains from the merger, this doubt itself is inconsistent with the monopoly theory. If the monopoly theory is valid, both parties should gain from the merger.

The monopoly theory has been pursued even further in studies by Stillman (1983) and Eckbo (1981), who looked at the residuals of the rivals of firms participating in mergers. The problem is complex because at the theoretical level a number of alternative hypotheses can be formulated as illustrated in Table 7.1.

Three studies appear to support the efficiency basis for mergers. Ellert emphasized that acquiring firms had positive residuals in prior years, and acquired firms had negative residuals in prior years. Stillman's evidence showed that rival firms did not benefit from the announcement of proposed mergers, which is inconsistent with the concentration-collusion hypothesis. Eckbo found positive residuals on the merger announcement but no negative effects on rivals when it appeared that the merger would be blocked by the antitrust authorities. He interpreted this pattern of relationships as indicating that the main effect of the merger is to signal the possibility of achieving economies for the merging firms and to provide information to rivals that such economies may also be available to them.

## POSTMERGER PERFORMANCE

The seminal study of postmerger performance was by Healy, Palepu, and Ruback (HPR) (1992). They studied the postacquisition performance of the 50 largest U.S. mergers between 1979 and 1984. They used accounting data primarily but tested their results using market valuation measures as well. They analyzed both operating

**TABLE 7.1** Alternative Hypotheses of Merger Effects

| | *Participating Firms* | *Rival Firms* |
|---|---|---|
| | **I. Announcement of Merger** | |
| Collusion Efficiency | + Higher profits from colluding<br>+ External investment with large positive NPV | + Are part of the collusion<br>+ Demonstrate how to achieve greater efficiency<br>− Tougher competition<br>0 Competition in marketplace unaffected by purchase of undervalued firm |
| | **II. Announcement of Challenge** | |
| Collusion Efficiency | − Collusion prevented<br>− Prevents a positive NPV investment, also litigations costs<br>0 Could do same thing internally | − Collusion prevented<br>+ Threat of more efficient rivals reduced<br>− Also prevented from mergers for efficiency<br>0 Can do internally |
| | **III. Announcement of Decision** | |
| Collusion | − Collusion definitely prevented<br><br>0 (1) Negative impact already, at challenge date<br>(2) Leakage of likely judicial decision during trial<br>(3) Underlying economics of the industry not affected | − Collusion prevented<br>+ Defendants prevented from being more efficient<br>0 (1) Negative impact already, at challenge date<br>(2) Leakage of likely judicial decision during trial<br>(3) Underlying economics of the industry not affected |
| Efficiency | + Increased efficiency | + Can now legally merge for efficiency<br>− Tougher competition<br>0 Could have accomplished the same thing internally |

*Note:* The +, −, 0 signs denote the predicted positive, negative, and zero impacts, respectively, on the firms' values.

characteristics and investment characteristics. The first two measures of operating characteristics are the cash-flow margin on sales and asset turnover. When these two measures are multiplied, they obtain the margin on the market value of assets.

Their third variable measures the effect of the merger on employment. They calculate the change in the number of employees during a given year as a percentage of the number of employees in the previous year. This is to test the hypotheses that gains in mergers are achieved by downsizing and reducing the number of employees.

Their fourth measure is pension expense per employee. Again, this is to test whether gains from mergers come at the expense of reducing pension protection for employees.

The authors next consider a number of effects on investment. Here they are testing whether gains may come from underinvesting for the future, from selling off assets, or by reducing research and development activities.

They look at the results for the firms themselves and then make a further adjustment. They make an industry adjustment to test whether the changes in the variables occurred because of industry effects as distinguished from the effects of the mergers on the individual firms. For example, the merged firms may have reduced employment. But if employment reduction in nonmerging firms in the same industry was even greater, industry-adjusted employment in the merged firms would have increased.

Their data show that industry-adjusted employment did decrease. This implies that the merging firms did more restructuring and reorganization than other firms in the industry. But the cash flow margin on sales did not significantly change. However, asset turnover significantly improved. The return on the market value of assets also improved significantly. However, because the cash flow margin on sales had not changed, this implies that the improvement in the return on assets did not come from the reduction of employment costs, which would have increased the cash flow margin on sales. It was better asset management that increased the return on assets. Pension expense per employee was reduced somewhat, but not by a statistically significant degree. None of the investment characteristics were significantly changed using industry-adjusted performance except asset sales measured at book value.

These results imply that industry-adjusted performance of the merging firms had improved. The improvement came not at the expense of labor income, but by improving the management of assets. The investments in capital equipment and investments in research and development were not significantly changed.

One of the important findings in the HPR study related to the event returns calculated as described in connection with the previous studies summarized in this chapter: the event returns for the firms are significantly correlated with the subsequent accounting returns during the postmerger period. This is evidence that, for their sample, event returns, on average, correctly forecast postmerger performance.

Agrawal, Jaffe, and Mandelker (AJM) (1992) also studied postmerger performance. They developed a larger sample of 937 mergers and 227 tender offers. Thus, their sample included firms smaller than the HPR study, which focused on the 50 largest mergers. They adjusted for size effect and for beta-weighted market returns. They found that shareholders of acquiring firms experienced a wealth loss of about 10% over the five years following the merger completion.

This finding has some interesting implications. First, it represents an anomaly in the sense that it provides an opportunity for a positive abnormal investment return. If acquiring firms always lose after a merger, this suggests that investors short the acquiring firm on a long-term basis at the time of a merger announcement. Of course, over time this anomaly should be wiped out.

Another implication may be explored. Healy, Palepu, and Ruback (1992) found that industry-adjusted postmerger performance was positive. Agrawal, Jaffe, and Mandelker (1992) found that market or economy-wide adjustments result in negative returns. These two results together imply that merger activity took place mainly in industries where performance was subpar compared to the market or the economy as a whole.

Franks, Harris, and Titman (FHT) (1991) found that postmerger share-price performance is sensitive to the benchmark employed. Using an equally-weighted index, their findings confirmed earlier studies that found negative postmerger performance. However, use of a value-weighted benchmark results in positive postmerger performance. When various multiportfolio benchmarks are employed, no statistically significant abnormal performance is found.

Langetieg (1978) found that when the adjustment is made by use of matched control firms in the same industry, postmerger abnormal performance is not significantly changed. In another pair of studies, Magenheim and Mueller (1988) found under-performance. But using the same sample with a different methodology, Bradley and Jarrell (1988) did not find significant underperformance in the three years following acquisitions.

When we consider these findings and counterfindings and the many variables discussed at the beginning of this chapter influencing event returns as well as postmerger performance, it is clear that results are sensitive to sample selection and measurement methodology. Some mergers perform well, others do not. Also it is probable that industry conditions also influence merger results. This leads to the final section of this chapter, which considers industry influences and their implications.

## INDUSTRY INFLUENCES ON M&A ACTIVITY

This chapter began with a review of some central issues in evaluating merger performance from the standpoint of the individual firm. In assessing broad economic forces explaining merger activity, the causal factors are formulated somewhat differently. One broad influence cited is the incentive to improve management. A second view is that mergers of the 1980s sought to reverse prior paid acquisitions and to focus a firm's activities on core industries. A third view states that merger activity facilitates an efficient adaptation of existing industry structure that has become suboptimal because of relatively broad changes in the economy. The hostile takeovers of the 1980s "affected industries in decline or sharp change" (Shleifer and Vishny, 1990). The leverage-increasing transactions of the 1980s were said to have been most numerous in industries with relatively poor investment opportunities and high capital costs (Blair and Schary, 1993).

An in-depth analysis has been made of industry effects. Mitchell and Mulherin (1996) studied industry-level patterns of takeover and restructuring activity during the 1982–1989 period. They found that in their sample of 1,064 firms, 57% were the object of a takeover attempt or experienced a major restructuring during the 1980s. Of the firms involved in takeovers or restructuring, 40% were hostile takeover targets. Somewhat more, 47% of the firms, were targets of friendly takeovers. The remaining 13% of the firms engaged in defensive asset restructuring or financial recapitalization.

Among their 51 sample industries, they found significant differences in the rate of M&A activity as well as in the timing of the activity. Most of the M&A activity occurred in relatively few industries due to identifiable major shocks defined as factors causing a marked change in overall industry structure and corporate control activity. One major force was deregulation, which had a major impact on the air transport, broadcasting, entertainment, natural gas, and trucking industries.

A second major factor was the oil price shocks occurring in 1973 and in 1979. These shocks affected not only the oil industry, but also the structure of industries in which energy represented 10% or more of input costs. The industries most directly affected were integrated petroleum, natural gas, air transport, coal, and trucking.

A third major factor was foreign competition. This is measured by changes in the import penetration ratio measured by the ratio of imports to total industry supply. The industries with the largest change in import penetration ratios were shoes, machine tools, apparel, construction equipment, office equipment and supplies, autos and auto parts, tire and rubber, and steel.

A fourth major influence was innovations. The ability to use public markets for leveraged financing increased both the rate of takeovers and the size of takeover targets.

Mitchell and Mulherin conclude that the interindustry patterns in takeovers and restructuring reflect the relative economic shocks to the industries. Their results support the view that a major influence on the takeover activity of the 1980s was broad underlying economic and financial forces.

## PATTERNS OF TAKEOVER ACTIVITY

Mergers and takeovers do not represent a simple phenomenon (Table 7.2). Mergers are mostly friendly and with a single bidder. The bidder typically is in a mature industry, has surplus cash, and is seeking a target with growth opportunities that require cash.

Tender offers may be friendly or hostile. Hostile bids typically are resisted, leading to multiple bidders. Management ownership of targets is low in hostile bids, but relatively higher in friendly bids. Target firms in hostile bids typically are below the industry average in performance, and the market values of their securities are well below the replacement costs of their assets. In a friendly merger, the target is above the industry average in performance, with a market value of securities greater than the replacement cost of assets.

The generalizations in Table 7.2 are complicated somewhat by the changes in the relationship between the bidder company and the target company during the period a tender offer is under consideration. Comment and Jarrell (CJ) (1987) developed some interesting material relevant to the characteristics of tender offers. The original orientation of their study was the issue of two-tier versus "any-or-all" tender offers. The issue here is whether a high premium on the front end and a low premium or other adverse treatment coerces targets to accept the tender offer. They studied a sample of 210 cash

**TABLE 7.2**    A Taxonomy of Types of Takeover Activity

| *Mergers* | *Tender Offers* | |
|---|---|---|
| *Friendly, Negotiated* | *Friendly* | *Hostile* |
| 1. Not resisted | 1. Not resisted | 1. Resisted |
| 2. Stock | 2. Cash or stock | 2. Cash |
| 3. Single bidder | 3. Single bidder | 3. Multiple bidders |
| 4. Announcement anticipated | 4. Anticipated to some degree | 4. Surprise |
| 5. Management ownership higher | 5. Management ownership high | 5. Management ownership low |
| 6. Bidder firm with surplus cash seeking a target with growth opportunities, needing cash | 6. Target above industry average in performance | 6. Target below industry average in performance |
| | 7. Target in growth industry | 7. Target in mature industry |
| | 8. Industry and firm q-ratio equal to average and higher than q for hostile targets | 8. Industry and firm q-ratios are low |
| | 9. Bidder likely to be another firm seeking new favorable investment opportunities | 9. Bidder likely to be a raider |

tender offers between 1981 and 1984. One-third were two-tier offers. They found that the percentage premium paid was about the same whether two-tier or not. For their sample, the average premium paid was 56%. Further they found that 75% of the two-tier offers had less than a 20% difference between the front-end and the back-end of tender prices. If the two-tier offers were intended to be coercive, the difference would be expected to be greater than 20%. Surprisingly, in two-tier offers, only 62% of outstanding shares are tendered compared with 75% in any-or-all offers.

What is particularly relevant in describing the nature of tender offers is that at the time of the initial tender offer about 50% were negotiated. By the time a tender offer is executed, in the sense that some share purchases have taken place, 82% of the tender offers have been negotiated, in the sense that a written agreement with the management of the target firm had been reached (CJ, p. 295). Written agreement implies some degree of negotiation and friendliness between bidder and target. However, it is also possible that the superior bargaining position of the bidder or credible threats strong-armed the target managements into a written agreement.

## Summary

The empirical literature appears to support the notion that value is created by M&A activities. The gains to acquiring firms around the announcement date are generally close to zero, which is the appropriate excess return in perfectly competitive markets for corporate control. The gains to target firms are more substantial. Returns to targets in merger transactions are in the 20 to 25% range while in tender offers the gains are in the 30 to 40% range, where the upper limit of return ranges involve multiple bidder contests. The difference in the returns between tender offers and mergers could be explained by the method of payment for the acquisition. Mergers usually involve stock transactions while tender offers are usually for cash. Securities transactions entail a longer period for the takeover to be completed because they require approval from the regulatory agencies. This allows target companies to prepare defenses and permit other bidders to enter the contest. In contrast, cash transactions have less restrictions. Higher cash bids involve information and signaling effects, and can preempt potential competitive bidders.

If the takeover is unsuccessful, cumulative abnormal returns for both bidder and target firms are generally negative but modest in size. This may indicate that the market slightly penalizes the firms for the foregone value-creating opportunity. For unsuccessful bidders with negative event return for their bids, the market seems to identify these as "bad bidders" subsequently likely to become takeover targets.

Target firms depict a general upward trend in the pattern of their cumulative abnormal returns. A more pronounced rise is observed in multiple bids contest, drifting upward as each subsequent bid takes place. There is little correlation between the runup returns (preannouncement period) and the markup returns (postannouncement period). The respective pattern for bidders is a slight positive announcement date rise with subsequent slight drift downward, trending to negative levels in the case of multiple bidders. Acquiring companies have unusual increases in their stock price prior to the announcement of a takeover bid.

The evidence for the total gains in M&A activity confirms that they are mainly positive and synergy appears to be the dominant driving force. In mergers with negative total gains, agency problems and hubris are involved. The total value increase by M&A activity could be attributable to increases in market power and not to increases in efficiency, but empirical studies do not support the monopoly theory.

The gains from M&A activity seem to persist in the period following the merger. The industry-adjusted postmerger performance of merging firms show improvement. The source of these improvements are mainly from better management of the assets and not from reductions in labor costs, capital investment, or research and development (R&D) expenditures. There is evidence that mergers are mainly concentrated in industries where performance was subpar compared with the economy as a whole. Factors that cause major adjustments in individual industries seem to drive the rate and timing of M&A activity.

## Questions

7.1  If residual analysis indicates positive abnormal returns to merging firms, what theory (or theories) of mergers is supported? If residual analysis indicates negative abnormal returns, what theory (or theories) is supported?

7.2  How do abnormal returns vary for acquiring and acquired firms during the period well before any merger announcement? What do these returns imply?

7.3  How do state and federal regulation affect returns to merging firms?

7.4  a.  What do the following merger theories predict about the correlation between abnormal returns of buyer and seller returns in mergers:
    Managerialism
    Inefficient management
    Synergy/efficiency
    b.  Discuss the empirical results of tests of the correlation between buyer and seller returns.

7.5  How should the returns to rivals of the merging firms be affected under the market power (monopoly) and efficiency theories?

## References

Agrawal, Anup, Jeffrey F. Jaffe, and Gershon N. Mandelker, "The Post-Merger Performance of Acquiring Firms: A Re-examination of an Anomaly," *Journal of Finance,* 47, September 1992, pp. 1605–1621.

Asquith, Daniel, "Evidence on Theories of Volume, Bid-Ask Spreads, and Return Premia Among NASDAQ Targets of Tender Offer Bids," Doctoral Research Paper, The Anderson School at UCLA, November 1, 1988.

Asquith, P., "Merger Bids, Uncertainty, and Stockholder Returns," *Journal of Financial Economics,* 11, April 1983, pp. 51–83.

Berkovitch, Elazar, and M. P. Narayanan, "Motives for Takeovers: An Empirical Investigation," *Journal of Financial and Quantitative Analysis,* 28, September 1993, pp. 347–362.

Blair, Margaret M., and Martha A. Schary, "Industry-Level Pressures to Restructure," in Margaret M. Blair, ed., *The Deal Decade,* Washington, D.C.: Brookings Institution, 1993, pp. 149–191.

Bradley, M., Anand Desai, and E. Han Kim, "The Rationale Behind Interfirm Tender Offers: Information or Synergy?" *Journal of Financial Economics,* 11, 1983, pp. 183–206.

————, "Synergistic Gains from Corporate Acquisitions and their Division Between the Stockholders of Target and Acquiring Firms," *Journal of Financial Economics,* 21, 1988, pp. 3–40.

Bradley, Michael, and Gregg Jarrell, "Comment," Chapter 15 in John Coffee, Jr., Louis Lowenstein, and Susan Rose-Ackerman, eds., *Knights, Raiders and Targets,* Oxford, England: Oxford University Press, 1988, pp. 253–259.

Comment, Robert, and Gregg A. Jarrell, "Two-Tier and Negotiated Tender Offers," *Journal of Financial Economics,* 19, 1987, pp. 283–310.

Eckbo, B. E., "Examining the Anti-Competitive Significance of Large Horizontal Mergers," unpublished Ph.D. dissertation, University of Rochester, 1981.

Eger, Carol Ellen, "An Empirical Test of the Redistribution Effect in Pure Exchange Mergers," *Journal of Financial and Quantitative Analysis,* 18, December 1983, pp. 547–572.

Ellert, J. C., "Antitrust Enforcement and the Behavior of Stock Prices," doctoral dissertation, University of Chicago, June 1975.

————, "Mergers, Antitrust Law Enforcement, and Stockholder Returns," *Journal of Finance,* 31, May 1976, pp. 715–732.

Franks, Julian R., Robert S. Harris, and Sheridan Titman, "The Postmerger Share-Price Performance of Acquiring Firms," *Journal of Financial Economics,* 29, 1991, pp. 81–96.

Gordon, Myron J., and Joseph Yagil, "Financial Gain from Conglomerate Mergers," *Research in Finance,* 3, 1981, pp. 103–142.

Harris, Robert S., Julian R. Franks, and Colin Mayer, "Means of Payment in Takeovers: Results for the U.K. and U.S.," Cambridge, MA: National Bureau of Economic Research, Working Paper No. 2456, 1987.

Healy, Paul M., Krishna G. Palepu, and Richard S. Ruback, "Does Corporate Performance Improve After Mergers?" *Journal of Financial Economics,* 31, 1992, pp. 135–175.

Houlihan Lokey Howard & Zukin, *Mergerstat Review,* Los Angeles, CA, 1997.

Houston, Joel F., and Michael D. Ryngaert, "The Overall Gains from Large Bank Mergers," *Journal of Banking & Finance,* 18, December 1994, pp. 1155–1176.

Howe, Jonathan, and C. Scott Wo, "Determinants of Target Abnormal Returns Associated with U.S. Acquisition Announcements, 1989–1992," ms., The Anderson School at UCLA, January 14, 1994.

Huang, Yen-Sheng, and Ralph A. Walkling, "Target Abnormal Returns Associated with Acquisition Announcements," *Journal of Financial Economics,* 19, 1987, pp. 329–349.

Jarrell, G. A., J. A. Brickley, and J. M. Netter, "The Market for Corporate Control: The Empirical Evidence Since 1980," *Journal of Economic Perspectives,* 2, Winter 1988, pp. 49–68.

Jensen, M. C., and R. S. Ruback, "The Market for Corporate Control: The Scientific Evidence," *Journal of Financial Economics,* 11, 1983, pp. 5–50.

Langetieg, T. C., "An Application of a Three-Factor Performance Index to Measure Stockholder Gains from Merger," *Journal of Financial Economics,* 6, December 1978, pp. 365–384.

Magenheim, Ellen B., and Dennis C. Mueller, "Are Acquiring Firm Shareholders Better Off After an Acquisition?" Chapter 11 in John Coffee, Jr., Louis Lowenstein, and Susan Rose-Ackerman, eds., *Knights, Raiders and Targets,* Oxford, England: Oxford University Press, 1988, pp. 171–193.

Mitchell, Mark L., and Kenneth Lehn, "Do Bad Bidders Become Good Targets?" *Journal of Political Economy,* 98, 1990, pp. 372–398.

Mitchell, Mark L., and J. Harold Mulherin, "The Impact of Industry Shocks on Takeover and Restructuring Activity," *Journal of Financial Economics,* 41, June 1996, pp. 193–229.

Myers, Stewart C., and Nicholas J. Majluf, "Corporate Financing and Investment Decisions When Firms Have Information That Investors Do Not Have," *Journal of Financial Economics,* 13, June 1984, pp. 187–221.

Opler, Tim C., "The Information Content of Corporate Takeover Announcements: Issues and Evidence," ms., The Anderson School at UCLA, October 1988.

Queen, Maggie, "Market Anticipation of Corporate Takeover and the Gain for the Bidders," unpublished doctoral dissertation, The Anderson School at UCLA, 1989.

Roll, Richard, "The Hubris Hypothesis of Corporate Takeovers," *Journal of Business,* 59 April 1986, pp. 197–216.

Schwert, G. William, "Markup Pricing in Mergers and Acquisitions," *Journal of Financial Economics,* 41, 1996, pp. 153–192.

Shleifer, Andrei, and Robert W. Vishny, "The Takeover Wave of the 1980s," *Science,* 249, August 1990, pp. 745–749.

Stillman, R. S., "Examining Antitrust Policy Towards Horizontal Mergers," *Journal of Financial Economics,* 11, April 1983, pp. 225–240.

Travlos, Nicholaos G., "Corporate Takeover Bids, Methods of Payment, and Bidding Firms' Stock Returns," *Journal of Finance,* 42, September 1987, pp. 943–963.

Wansley, James W., William R. Lane, and Ho C. Yang, "Abnormal Returns to Acquired Firms by Type of Acquisition and Method of Payment," *Financial Management,* 12, Autumn 1983, pp. 16–22.

You, Victor, Richard Caves, Michael Smith, and James Henry, "Mergers and Bidders' Wealth: Managerial and Strategic Factors," Chapter 9 in Lacy Glenn Thomas, III, ed., *The Economics of Strategic Planning,* Lexington, MA: Lexington Books, 1986, pp. 201–220.

C H A P T E R

# 8

# Strategy, Diversification, and Takeovers

The M&A activities of the 1990s have been widely described as "strategic" in their orientation. Company executives involved in mergers and takeovers in the 1990s emphasize that they were looking ahead 10 years. Some spoke of augmenting their capabilities. Others emphasize getting back to their core. Some companies state that they are adjusting to new legislation such as the Telecommunications Act of February 8, 1996. Some companies are reacting to new technological developments. The cable television industry may be threatened by a launching of wireless cable by Pacific Telesis in 1997 (Grover and Gross, 1996).

Mergers and takeovers often involve major strategic decisions. The Disney–Capital Cities ABC acquisition was said to be motivated by Disney's strategic aim to have a greater presence in the distribution of its movies for television. The Gerber baby food company judged it necessary to increase its international sales if it were to remain healthy. Sandoz, with strength in international marketing, wanted to broaden its product line into baby foods. Sandoz acquired Gerber in 1994. In 1993 Merck bought Medco, a drug distribution company, because of major changes in the health care industry; some drug companies later bought other distribution firms. The list of examples of strategic M&As could go on and on. A central proposition of this book is that M&As should take place within the broad strategic planning processes of firms. The subject of strategy is central to M&A analysis because it provides the framework required for making sound M&A decisions.

All organizations face strategic alternatives, choices, and decisions. Consider some of the fundamental strategic alternatives faced by business firms. Should the firm focus on one product or many? If many products, should they fall into a family of products that seek to cover all segments of the market? Or should the firm seek an individual niche in which it can be profitable? Should the firm focus on a core of products? Or should the firm have a family of products that are related? Are there advantages of managing a family of unrelated products? Should the firm choose product groups that provide hedges against major changes that can take place in the world? Should the firm choose its product family so that the firm has a hedge against uncertain inflation and/or uncertain deflation? Should the firm choose products to provide automatic hedges against fluctuations in the prices of key commodities such as gold, oil, or agricultural commodities? What role should M&As and/or joint ventures-alliances perform?

Should the firm seek to concentrate its activities in those segments of the value-chain or value-added activities that represent the largest percentage of a product's cost? Or should the firm concentrate on the critical functions in producing and selling a product that will give it a strong position in the industry? For example, should a firm emphasize hardware or software in the computer industry?

What degree of vertical integration should a firm seek? What activities should be performed in an integrated chain within the firm? For what activities will the firm gain learning and knowledge that will give it advantage over its competitors? What relationship should a firm have with its suppliers? Should it be arm's length or should it have cross-ownership holdings with its suppliers as is done in Japan?

When a firm seeks to add related product activities, at what level of operations should the firm seek to broaden its product lines? Should adding related products take place at the R&D level? At the production level? In distribution systems? Should the firm seek to add related technologies? Should the firm seek to become strong in technologies that will strengthen its position in the industry? Should the firm be integrated backward to assure the desired quality and quantity of supply? Should a firm integrate forward to control distribution channels to the ultimate consumer? Should such shifts be through M&As or by internal development?

The above listings represent only a sample of the strategic alternatives faced by business firms. It is within this broader framework that M&A decisions should be made. There is wide agreement that M&A activity should represent a strategic fit with the broader long-range plans of a business firm. It is, therefore, essential that we provide an overview summary of the strategy literature and concepts as a foundation for M&A decisions. If mergers and acquisitions are focused on strategic fit, we need to know what this really means. This chapter provides the material essential for sound decisions on achieving strategic fit in M&A decisions.

# STRATEGY

Many different theories and approaches to strategy formulation and implementation are presented in the literature. Some writers distinguish between strategy as a concept and strategy as a process. Others emphasize that strategy is a way of thinking. However defined, strategy is concerned with the most important decisions made in an enterprise. The central thrust of these decisions is the future of the organization. While the horizon is the long view, strategy to be implemented properly must also take account of mid-term and short-run decisions and actions.

Strategy is formulated in many different ways. The strategic planning process can be performed on the basis of a set of formal procedures and/or informally in the minds of managers. Strategy is not static. Individual strategies, plans, policies, or procedures are utilized, but they are not the whole story. Strategic planning is behavior and a way of thinking, requiring diverse inputs from all segments of the organization. Everyone must be involved in the strategic planning processes.

## Ultimate Responsibility

Because strategic planning is concerned with the future of the organization, it follows that ultimate responsibility resides in the top executive (group). While many others perform important roles and have responsibilities for strategic planning processes, the chief executive (group) must take ultimate responsibility for its success or failure. The chief executive officer (CEO or group) is responsible for the strategic planning process for the firm as a whole; the top manager of a division must be responsible for strategic planning for that division and for conforming it to the strategic planning for the organization as a whole.

### Basic Steps in Strategic Planning

While different approaches to strategic planning may be found, they include the steps set forth in Table 8.1, which lists the critical activities involved in strategic planning processes. These procedures are described at length in the vast literature on strategy. Whether these represent formal or informal procedures, they are elements to be covered. In each of the strategic planning activities, both staff and line personnel have important responsibilities in the strategic decision-making processes.

## DIVERSITY IN STRATEGIC PLANNING PROCESSES

Some general elements required for all strategic planning activity have been identified. In other aspects of strategic planning wide diversity is encountered. These involve a number of different activities and aspects involved in strategic planning.

### Monitoring Environments

A key to all approaches to strategic planning is continuous monitoring of the external environments. The environments should encompass both domestic and international dimensions and include analysis of economic, technological, political, social, and legal factors. Different organizations give different emphasis and weight to each of the categories.

### Stakeholders

The strategic planning processes must take into account the diverse stakeholders of organizations. These are the individuals and groups that have an interest in the organization and its actions. They include customers, stockholders, creditors, employees,

---

**TABLE 8.1    Essential Elements in Strategic Planning Processes**

1. Assessment of changes in the environments.
2. Evaluation of company capabilities and limitations.
3. Assessment of expectations of stakeholders.
4. Analysis of company, competitors, industry, domestic economy, and international economies.
5. Formulation of the missions, goals, and policies for the master strategy.
6. Development of sensitivity to critical external environmental changes.
7. Formulation of internal organization performance measurements.
8. Formulation of long-range strategy programs.
9. Formulation of mid-range programs and short-run plans.
10. Organization, funding, and other methods to implement all of the preceding elements.
11. Information flow and feedback system for continued repetition of preceding and for adjustments and changes at each stage.
12. Review and evaluation of preceding processes.

governments, communities, media, political groups, educational institutions, financial community, and international entities.

Writers disagree on the appropriateness of the stake of each of the groups listed. One view is that the firm need only maximize profit or shareholder stock values to maximize the long-run interests of every group. Another is that by balancing properly the interests of major stakeholders, the long-range interests of all will be maximized.

## Organization Cultures

How the organization carries out the strategic thinking and planning processes also varies with its cultures. Illustrative organization cultures include the following:

1. Strong top leadership versus team approach.
2. Management by formal paperwork versus management by wandering around.
3. Individual decision versus group consensus decisions.
4. Rapid evaluation based on performance versus long-term relationship based on loyalty.
5. Rapid feedback for change versus formal bureaucratic rules and procedures.
6. Narrow career paths versus movement through many areas.
7. Risk taking encouraged versus "one mistake and you're out."
8. Big-stakes (bet-your-company) decisions versus low-risk activities.
9. Narrow responsibility assignments versus "everyone in this company is a salesman (or cost controller, or product quality improver, and so on)."
10. Learn from the customer versus "we know what is best for the customer."

The above list conveys the wide differences in corporate cultures and how the strategic thinking and planning processes may be affected. Failure to mesh divergent cultures may be a major obstacle to the full realization of the potentials of a merger (*Economist,* 1997).

## Alternative Strategy Methodologies

We draw a distinction between different strategy methodologies and different analytical frameworks employed in developing strategy. First, some alternative approaches to methodologies used in strategy formulation are considered in Table 8.2.

The first 12 in the list will be described somewhat more fully. The remainder are well-known or self-explanatory and do not require elaboration.

### WOTS UP Analysis

Identifying strengths and weaknesses and opportunities and threats would appear to be easily accomplished. However, much subjectivity is involved. Different managers may have different judgments. While opportunities may exist, the differences in cost may require a careful balancing of considerations. On balance this approach may provide a useful starting point for developing a strategic planning process and for stimulating strategic thinking in an organization.

### Gap Analysis

In the assessment of goals versus forecasts or projections, goals may be first formulated. These may be expressed in quantitative terms, such as sales of $2 billion by 19XX or net income of $100 million by 19XX or a return on shareholder equity of 15%. But a reasonable assessment of the future based on the firm's existing capabilities may

---

**TABLE 8.2**    Alternative Strategy Methodologies

1. SWOT or WOTS UP—inventory and analysis of organizational strengths, weaknesses, environmental opportunities, and threats.
2. Gap analysis—assessment of goals versus forecasts or projections.
3. Top-down and/or bottom-up—company forecasts versus aggregation of segments.
4. Computer models—opportunity for detail and complexity.
5. Competitive analysis—assess customers, suppliers, new entrants, products, and product substitutability.
6. Synergy—look for complementarities.
7. Logical incrementalism—well-supported moves from current bases.
8. Muddling through—incremental changes selected from a small number of policy alternatives.
9. Comparative histories—learn from the experiences of others.
10. Delphi technique—iterated opinion reactions.
11. Discussion group technique—stimulating ideas by unstructured discussions aimed at consensus decisions.
12. Adaptive processes—periodic reassessment of environmental opportunities and organization capability adjustments required.
13. Environmental scanning—continuous analysis of all relevant environments.
14. Intuition—insights of brilliant managers.
15. Entrepreneurship—creative leadership.
16. Discontinuities—crafting strategy from recognition of trend shifts.
17. Brainstorming—free-form repeated exchange of ideas.
18. Game theory—logical assessments of competitor actions and reactions.
19. Game playing—assign roles and simulate alternative scenarios.

---

indicate that these goals cannot be achieved by the target dates. The divergence may stimulate an assessment of whether the goals should be revised or how the organization could augment its capabilities in order to close the gap between goals and projections.

### Top-Down Versus Bottom-Up Forecasts

In the history of strategic planning, a variety of approaches can be observed. In some companies overall projections are made with an assignment of requirements for individual segments so that the overall company results could be achieved. At the other extreme, the projections of individual segments could be added up with the result representing the outlook for the company as a whole. Good practice avoids both extremes.

There is evidence that successful companies begin with planning premises formulated at the overall corporate level. These planning premises begin with the outlook for the economy and the industry, translated into what appears plausible for the particular firm. The planning premises are supplied to the individual segments who use them as a basis for their own individual forecasts. The individual segment forecasts are aggregated to provide an outlook for the company as a whole. Meetings and discussions between the corporate level and the individual segments take place. A communication process is developed and iterations of meetings continue until a consensus is reached. The desired goal is a company plan that is understood and reasonable from the standpoint of the various segments and results in an overall company outlook that is satisfactory from the standpoint of top management.

### Computer Models

Computer models provide the opportunity for considerable detail and complexity. However, the models must reflect a theory or logic to guide their content. Otherwise, there is a great risk that the methodology will be overwhelmed by the resulting complexity.

### Competitive Analysis

A number of approaches to competitive analysis may be found (see, for example, Porter, 1979). Our approach is conveyed by Figure 8.1. A firm's competitive position is determined by important factors involved in demand conditions and in supply conditions. On the demand side, what is critical is the degree of feasible product substitutability. On the supply side, the nature and structure of costs are critical. Of particular importance is the ability to switch among suppliers of inputs. This may be critically affected by switching costs—the costs involved in shifting from one supplier to another. Supply competition from other firms including potentials for capacity expansion are also major influences on the competitive position of the firm.

### Synergy

Synergy represents the two plus two equals five effect. The concept of synergy was highly regarded at an earlier period, but then subsequently came into disrepute. What is critical is how the extra gains are to be achieved. One example of synergy is found in the history of the pharmaceutical industry when after World War II the major firms shifted from producing bulk chemicals for others to process, to an emphasis on basic research and packaging products that were ready for final sale. A sales organization was also required. After a number of years, synergistic mergers took place involving companies strong in research or marketing with companies that had complementary strengths and weaknesses. Synergy can be a valid concept if it has a basis in reality.

### Logical Incrementalism

After extensive field interviews, Quinn (1977, 1980) concluded that major changes in strategy are carried out most effectively when the changes involved are relatively small or on an incremental basis. In addition, he emphasized that a number of steps are required to involve the organization as broadly as possible. The process he emphasized also involved the exercise of effective leadership qualities.

**FIGURE 8.1  Competitive Analysis**

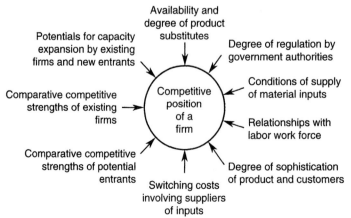

### Muddling Through

This represents another form of the incremental approach. Lindblom (1959, 1965) called the approach "muddling through." He also used the term *disjointed incrementalism* to describe the process. The basic idea is that instead of attempting an evaluation of a wide range of alternatives, decision makers focus only on those policy alternatives that differ incrementally from existing policies. An iterative process is then employed to formulate and implement decisions.

### Comparative Histories

This methodology is widely used by many firms in monitoring the behavior of their rivals. It was used in a fundamental research mode by Chandler (1962) in an analysis of the interrelationships among the economic environments of firms, their strategies, and their organization structures. Chandler compared the history of organizational changes among 50 large companies during a century beginning with the period after the Civil War in the United States. From his studies he developed theories about the relationship between a firm's strategy and its organization structure at various stages of development. Individual firms continuously monitor the policies, actions, and reactions of rivals.

### Delphi Technique

A questionnaire developed to obtain information on problems or issues is distributed by mail to informed individuals. The responses are summarized into a feedback report and returned with a second questionnaire designed to probe more deeply into the ideas generated by the first questionnaire. Several iterations can be performed.

### Discussion Group Technique

The group leader begins with a statement of the problem. An unstructured group discussion ensues for the purpose of generating ideas. Information and judgments are generated. The goal is to reach a consensus decision or to make a decision based on a majority voting procedure.

### Adaptive Processes

In some sense all approaches to strategy employ adaptive processes. The approach was first formalized by Ansoff (1965). The nature of the problem is structured on a tentative basis. Analysis is facilitated by a series of checklists or analysis of matrix relationships. Successive iterations take place until a basis for formulating policies and reaching decisions is achieved. The method emphasizes developing a strong information feedback system to achieve flexibility in organization capability adjustments to its environmental changes. This approach is especially important in merger analysis.

The remainder of the approaches in Table 8.2 do not require further elaboration. The list conveys the profusion of methodologies encountered in strategic planning. The particular approaches to strategy adopted by individual firms and consultants involves selection from alternative strategy methodologies as listed in Table 8.2 combined with different groups of alternative analytical frameworks of the kind discussed next.

## Alternative Analytical Frameworks

Many different alternative analytical frameworks are employed in the formulation of strategy. Their nature is indicated by the list in Table 8.3.

| **TABLE 8.3**   Alternative Analytical Frameworks |
|---|

1. Product life cycles—introduction, growth, maturity, decline stages with changing opportunities and threats.
2. Learning curve—costs decline with cumulative volume experience resulting in first mover competitive advantages.
3. Competitive analysis—industry structure, rivals' reactions, supplier and customer relations, product positioning.
4. Cost leadership—low-cost advantages.
5. Product differentiation—develop product configurations that achieve customer preference.
6. Value chain analysis—controlled cost outlays to add product characteristics valued by customers.
7. Niche opportunities—specialize to needs or interests of customer groups.
8. Product breadth—carryover of organizational capabilities.
9. Correlations with profitability—statistical studies of factors associated with high profitability measures.
10. Market share—high market share associated with competitive superiority.
11. Product quality—Customer allegiance and price differentials for higher quality.
12. Technological leadership—keep at frontiers of knowledge.
13. Relatedness matrix—unfamiliar markets and products involve greatest risk.
14. Focus matrix—narrow versus broad product families.
15. Growth/share matrix—aim for high market share in high growth markets.
16. Attractiveness matrix—aim to be strong in attractive industries.
17. Global matrix—aim for competitive strength in attractive countries.

Many of the items in Table 8.3 are self-explanatory. Others are described in the references provided. We would like to comment on the wide use of matrix patterns of strengths and weaknesses or alternative approaches to markets.

A simple approach is the product-market matrix shown in Figure 8.2. It is based on the relatedness concept that is widely used in formulating strategy. The thrust of Figure 8.2 is that in developing new product markets the lowest risk is to stay "close to home." The highest risk is to venture forth into unrelated products and unrelated markets. This analysis clearly depends on how risk is defined. It may be very risky to stay where you are if, for example, the prospects for growth of existing products and markets are unfavorable and the industry has excess capacity. This represents a strong motive for mergers to gain entry to markets with more favorable growth opportunities.

| Market \ Product | Present | Related | Unrelated |
|---|---|---|---|
| Present | Low risk | | High risk |
| Related | | | |
| Unrelated | High risk | | Highest risk |

**FIGURE 8.2 Product-Market Matrix**

Figure 8.3 portrays one formulation of a competitive-position matrix. It suggests a choice of emphasis between product differentiation versus cost leadership. In addition, the focus may be on a narrow market segment or niche or product representation to provide presence in a broad range of markets.

The matrix shown in Figure 8.4, the growth-share matrix, has been associated particularly with the Boston Consulting Group. Products for which the firm has a high market share in an industry with favorable growth rates are potential "stars" with high profitability. As an industry matures, its growth slows so that if a firm continues to have high market share, the attractive profits are available for investment in markets with more favorable growth rates so the products become "cash cows." Products and markets with low growth where the firm has a small market share are "dogs" and the firm should discontinue such products, according to the simple product portfolio approach.

A variant of the growth-share matrix is the strength-market attractiveness matrix shown in Figure 8.5. The greatest opportunities for investment and growth are where the outlook for an industry is attractive and the firm has high capabilities for performance in that industry. Where the industry outlook is unfavorable and the firm has weakness in such markets, the firm should divest or close down such businesses.

Figure 8.6 moves the analysis to an international basis. In the international setting the most attractive countries in terms of growth or political stability in which the firm has competitive strengths offer the most favorable growth opportunities. The opposite, of course, occurs in countries of low attractiveness where the firm's competitive strengths are low.

In our view the preceding examples of the matrix approach to strategy represent in spirit the checklist approach to formulating alternatives. They are useful devices for suggesting factors to take into account in formulating strategies.

The different analytical frameworks set forth in Table 8.3 are not mutually exclusive. In strategic planning a wide range of analytical approaches may usefully be

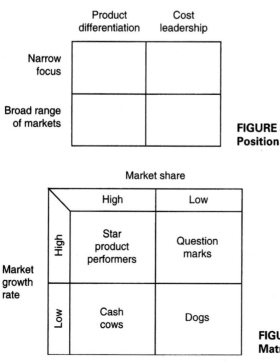

FIGURE 8.3  Competitive-Position Matrix

FIGURE 8.4  Growth-Share Matrix

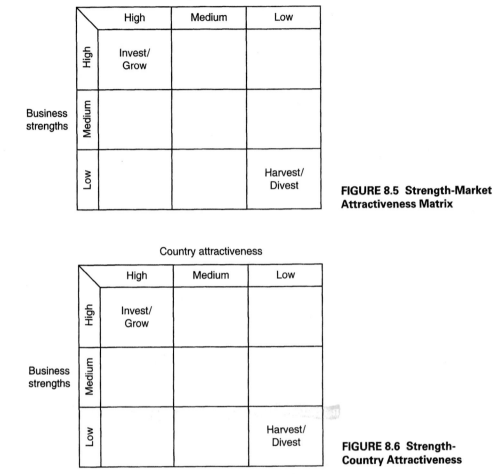

FIGURE 8.5  Strength-Market Attractiveness Matrix

FIGURE 8.6  Strength-Country Attractiveness

employed. Their use is facilitated by a checklist and adaptive approach to strategic planning. Practicing consultants as well as individual firms have employed a combination of methodologies and analytic approaches with considerable success. Three approaches that combine different methodologies and alternative analytic approaches are described next.

## APPROACHES TO FORMULATING STRATEGY

Many different schools of thought in the strategy field can be observed. Each represents some combination of the methodologies and/or analytical frameworks in the preceding lists. Three approaches are discussed more fully to illustrate how alternative methodologies and analytical frameworks are used in practice. They are (1) the Boston Consulting Group, (2) the Porter approach, and (3) adaptive processes.

### The Boston Consulting Group

The Boston Consulting Group (BCG) historically emphasized three concepts: the experience curve, the product life cycle, and portfolio balance (Boston Consulting Group, 1985; Henderson, 1984).

The experience curve represents a volume-cost relationship. It is argued that as the cumulative historical volume of output increases, unit costs will fall at a geometric rate. This is said to result from specialization, standardization, learning, and scale effects. The firm with the largest cumulative output will have lower costs, suggesting a strategy of early entry and price policies to develop volume.

The product life cycle holds that every product or line of business proceeds through four phases: development, growth, maturity, and decline. During the first two stages, sales growth is rapid and entry is easy. As individual firms gain experience and as growth slows in the last two stages, entry becomes difficult because of the cost advantages of incumbents. In the decline phase of the product line (as other product substitutes emerge) sales and prices decline; firms that have not achieved a favorable position on the experience curve become unprofitable and either merge or exit from the industry.

Related to the product life cycle is the concept of portfolio balance. In the early stages of the product life cycle, rapid growth may require substantial investments. Such business segments are likely to require more investment funds than are generated by current profitability levels. As the requirements for growth diminish, profits may generate more funds than required for current investment requirements. Portfolio balance seeks to combine attractive investment segments (stars) with cash-generating segments (cash cows), eliminating segments with unattractive prospects (dogs). Overall, total corporate cash inflows will roughly balance total corporate investments.

While the volume-cost relationships implied by the experience curve have been documented for some industries, particularly commodity-type products, their general applicability has not been substantiated. Microeconomics would suggest that the emphasis on cost advantage neglects opportunities provided by product quality, variety, and innovation. The emphasis on growth and/or portfolio balance may be inconsistent with maximization of shareholder value. The practical application of the BCG strategy to develop a dominant market share in an emerging industry may be difficult to implement; if many firms try to do the same thing their efforts may become self-canceling. Some argue also that substantial aspects of experience are a part of knowledge that rapidly diffuses across firms and industries (Thomas, 1986).

## The Porter Approach

Michael Porter's (1980, 1985, 1987) approach has three parts: (1) select an attractive industry, (2) develop competitive advantage through cost leadership and/or product differentiation, and (3) develop attractive value chains.

First, Porter (1987, p. 46) defines an attractive industry or strategic group as one in which

> entry barriers are high, suppliers and buyers have only modest bargaining power, substitute products or services are few, and the rivalry among competitors is stable. An unattractive industry like steel will have structural flaws, including a plethora of substitute materials, powerful and price-sensitive buyers, and excessive rivalry caused by high fixed costs and a large group of competitors, many of whom are state supported.

The difficulty of generalizing about industries is demonstrated by Porter's example. During the past decade minimills have flourished and by 1988 some major steel firms had returned to profitability. In addition, there appears to be an inconsistency in that high fixed costs are considered to be an entry barrier in Porter's theory.

Second, Porter formulates a matrix for developing generic strategies. Competitive advantage may be based on cost leadership or on product differentiation. Cost advantage is achieved by consideration of a wide range of checklist factors including BCG's learning curve theory. The focus of cost advantage or of product differentiation can be on narrow market segments, or niches (for autos, the luxury car market—Cadillac, Continental, BMW, Mercedes, and so on) or broader market groups (compact and standard cars) or across the board (GM).

Porter's third key concept is "the value chain." A matrix relates the support activities of infrastructure, human resource management, technology development, and procurement to the primary activities of inbound logistics, operations, outbound logistics, marketing-sales, and service. The aim is to minimize outlays in adding characteristics valued by customers.

Porter's prescriptions can be interpreted as finding an industry or industry sector in which a small number of firms can "cooperate" (collude) behind high entry barriers. While many insights are found in the related checklists developed, it is similar in spirit to the structural theory of industrial organization economics, which evidence in recent years has controverted (Weston, 1978, 1982, and references cited). If barriers to entry are high, the costs of entry or acquisition will permit only a normal rate of return. Moreover, the dimensions of products and prices are so numerous and subject to such rapid change that collusive efforts could not achieve sustained effectiveness. Furthermore, the benefits of competitive superiority far outweigh the dubious gains from attempts at collusion.

### Adaptive Processes

Other writers have been more eclectic than the preceding two approaches. These writers view strategy more as an adaptive process or way of thinking (see, for example, Ansoff, 1965; Bogue and Buffa, 1986; Quinn, Mintzberg, and James, 1988; Steiner, 1979; Steiner, Miner, and Gray, 1986). Some writers also emphasize the uniqueness of each firm. "In essence, the concept is that a firm's competitive position is defined by a bundle of unique resources and relationships and that the task of general management is to adjust and renew these resources and relationships as time, competition, and change erode their value" (Rumelt, 1984, p. 557). Mergers perform a role in these renewal efforts.

More generally the adaptive processes orientation involves matching resources to investment opportunities under environmental uncertainty compounded with uncertain competitors' actions and reactions. The methodology for dealing with these kinds of "ill-structured problems" requires an iterative solution process. Most managers in an organization have responsibilities for the inputs and studies required for the repeated "going around the loop" in the strategic planning processes outlined in Table 8.1.

In performing the iterated checklist procedures, difficult questions are encountered. For example, is the firm maximizing its potential in relation to its feasible environment? Is there a gap between the firm's goals and prospects based on its present capabilities? Should the firm attempt to alter its environment or capabilities or both? Should the firm change its missions? What will be the cost of each alternative? What are the risks and unknowns? What are the rewards of success and penalties of failure?

The methodology involves not closed-form mathematical solutions but **processes.** It involves ways of thinking that assess competitors' actions and reactions in relation to the changing environments. The process approach is especially applicable to merger analysis because it is difficult to find out all that is needed when combining with another entity.

## EVALUATION OF THE ALTERNATIVE APPROACHES

While some approaches emphasize generalizations, all make heavy use of checklists that have evolved into expert systems. Writers who have emphasized strategy implementation have recently shifted from a list of precepts to an emphasis on flexibility.

## Checklists and Iterations

The adaptive processes methodologies emphasize the use of checklists to stimulate insights, but the BCG and Porter approaches to strategy formulation also rely heavily on similar techniques. For example, in his earlier book, *Competitive Strategy* (1980), Michael Porter utilized 134 checklists and checklist-like diagrams—one about every three pages. In his later *Competitive Advantage* (1985), the number had expanded to 187 checklists and checklist-like diagrams—about one every 2.5 pages. Stryker (1986) (adaptive approach) had 174 checklists in 269 pages—one checklist per 1.5 pages. Thus, the process of strategic planning includes the art of making checklists, going around the loop iteratively, with the expectation that the thinking stimulated will lead to useful insights and sound strategies, policies, and decisions.

The BCG and Porter approaches emphasize prescriptions. But in their actual implementation, they employ checklists not limited to the generalizations each emphasizes. In practice all approaches to strategy become relatively eclectic.

With the greater use of computers in strategic planning, the different approaches appear to have more and more elements in common. Particularly in recent years, expert systems and other decision support systems have been developed. These represent a disciplined approach to strategic planning in which rules are used to guide implementation of the iterated checklist approach, making use of ideas from a wide range of philosophic perspectives (Chung and Davidson, 1987).

## Some Recent Developments

Publications by writers who have popularized strategy implementation exhibit a recent change in emphasis. In their earlier book, *In Search of Excellence,* Peters and Waterman (1982) asserted that the precepts for success could be reduced to a short checklist: (1) bias for action; (2) close to the customer; (3) autonomy and entrepreneurship; (4) productivity improvement; (5) hands-on, value driven; (6) stick to core businesses; (7) simple form, lean staff; and (8) loose-tight properties.

Peters and Waterman (1982) admonished their readers to learn how the best-run American companies use eight basic principles to stay "on top of the heap!" Although *In Search of Excellence* was a commercial success, it also received criticisms (Carroll, 1983; Johnson, Natarajan, and Rappaport, 1985; Ramanujam and Venkatraman, 1988). Of particular interest to business economists was the analysis in the cover story of the November 5, 1984 issue of *Business Week* entitled, "Who's Excellent Now? Some of the Best-Seller's Picks Haven't Been Doing So Well Lately." *Business Week* (p. 74) studied the 43 "excellent" companies and concluded that many had encountered difficulties. The article observed:

> Of the 14 excellent companies that had stumbled, 12 were inept in adapting to a fundamental change in their markets. Their experiences show that strict adherence to the eight commandments—which do not emphasize reacting to broad economic and business trends—may actually hurt a company.

Peters and Waterman appear to acknowledge the deficiencies in their earlier prescriptive approach by shifting their emphasis in later publications. In *The Renewal Factor,* Waterman (1987) emphasizes flexibility; he quotes with approval the executive who stated that he wanted his managers to be "Fred Astaires—intellectually quick, nimble, and ready to act" (p. 6.) Similarly, the coauthor of the earlier book, *In Search of Excellence,* in his 1987 publication, begins, "There are no excellent companies. The old saw 'If it ain't broke, don't fix it' needs revision. I propose: 'If it ain't broke, you just haven't looked hard enough.' Fix it anyway" (Peters, 1987, p. 1). Similarly, two executives associated with the Boston Consulting Group have proposed that to manage for increased competitiveness companies need to "make decisions like a fighter pilot" (Hout and Blaxill, 1987, p. 3).

But flexibility and rapid adjustments are more the stuff of tactics, not strategy! We believe that these recent developments in the literature on implementing strategy continue to suffer from the criticism conveyed by the *Business Week* article previously quoted. They make inadequate use of perspectives offered by economic analysis. Economics is forward looking, projecting market and supply conditions and patterns. Economic analysis can help identify prospective changes in such areas as demand, product differentiation, market growth segments, and behavior of rivals. Analysis of supply conditions can help identify areas of potential cost changes and thus targets for cost control. Economic analysis can delineate critical monitoring variables to indicate when changes in economic directions are likely to occur. Given this information, trade-off analysis (the bread and butter of economic marginal analysis) can identify and analyze alternative paths of action and their consequences. In short, economics aids in dealing with uncertainty and in anticipating change, rather than reacting to events after they have occurred.

Economics seeks an understanding of environmental developments to identify the trends and discontinuities important to strategy formulation and implementation, as well as for providing a framework within which flexibility and adjustments can be achieved efficiently. From the preceding analysis of alternative approaches to strategy, we can now develop guidelines for formulating a merger strategy.

## FORMULATING A MERGER STRATEGY

The literature on long-range strategic planning indicates that one of the most important elements in planning is continuing reassessment of the firm's environment. To determine what is happening in the environment, the firm should analyze its industry, competitors, and social and political factors.

Industry analysis allows the firm to recognize the key factors required for competitive success in the industry and the opportunities and threats present in the industry. From competitor analysis, the firm finds out the capabilities and limitations of existing and potential competitors, and their probable future moves. Through these analyses and with additional consideration of societal factors, the firm's strengths and weaknesses relative to present and future competitors can be ascertained.

The purpose of the environmental reassessment is to provide the firm with a choice among strategic alternatives. For this choice, the firm then considers whether its current goals and policies are appropriate to exploit industry opportunities and to deal with industry threats. At the same time, it is necessary for the firm to examine whether the goals and policies match the managerial, technological, and financial resources available to the firm, and whether the timing of the goals and policies appropriately reflects the ability of the organization to change.

The firm then works out feasible strategic alternatives given the results of the analyses. The current strategy (represented by its goals and policies) may or may not be included in the set of feasible alternatives. A strategic choice is made from this set such that the chosen strategy best relates the firm's situation to external opportunities and threats. Mergers represent one set of alternatives.

A brilliant exposition of how a company must be alert to important changes is set forth by Andrew S. Grove, President and CEO of Intel Corporation (1996). Grove describes how a firm must adjust to the six forces: existing competitors, potential competitors, complementors, customers, suppliers, and industry transformations. He presents illuminating case studies of the approach to strategy that we have called eclectic adaptive processes.

## Business Goals

General goals may be formulated with respect to size, growth, stability, flexibility, and technological breadth. Size objectives are established in order to use effectively the fixed factors the firm owns or buys. Size objectives have also been expressed in terms of critical mass. Critical mass refers to the size a firm must achieve to attain cost levels that enable the firm to operate profitably at market prices.

Growth objectives may be expressed in terms of sales, total assets, earnings per share, or the market price of the firm's stock. These are related to two valuation objectives. One is to attain a favorable price/earnings multiple for the firm's shares. A second is to increase the ratio of the market value of a firm's common stock to its book value.

Two major forms of instability can be distinguished. The first is exemplified by the defense market, which is subject to large, erratic fluctuations in its total size and abrupt shifts in individual programs. Another form of instability is the cyclical instability that characterizes producers of both industrial and consumer durable goods.

The goal of flexibility refers to the firm's ability to operate in a wide variety of product markets. Such flexibility may require a breadth of research, manufacturing, or marketing capabilities. Of increased interest in recent years is technological breadth. With the increased pace of technological change in the U.S. economy, a firm may consider it important to possess capabilities in the rapidly advancing technologies.

Goals may be stated in general or specific terms, but both are subject to quantification. For example, growth objectives may be expressed in relationship to the growth of the economy or the firm's industry. Specific objectives may be expressed in terms of percentage of sales in specified types of markets. The quantification of goals facilitates comparisons of goals with the potential for achieving them.

Efforts to achieve multiple goals suggest a broader range of variables in the decision processes of the firm. Decisions require judgments of the nature of future environments, the policies of other firms with respect to the dimensions described, and new needs of customers, technologies, and capabilities. In short, to the requirements of operating efficiency and optimal output adjustments has been added the increased importance of the planning processes.

## Aligning the Firm to Its Changing Environments

When it is necessary to take action to close a prospective gap between the firm's objectives and its potential based on its present capabilities, difficult choices must be made. For example, should the firm attempt to change its environment or capabilities? What will be the costs of such changes? What are the risks and unknowns? What are the rewards if successful? What are the penalties of failure? Because the stakes are large, an iterative process is employed. A tentative decision is made. The process is repeated, perhaps from a different management function orientation and at some point, the total-enterprise point of view is brought to bear on the problem. At some point, decisions are made and must involve entrepreneurial judgments. Mergers may help or hurt.

The emphasis is on the effective alignment of the firm with its environments and constituencies. Different approaches may be emphasized. One approach seeks to choose products related to the needs or wants of the customer that will provide large markets. A second approach focuses on technological bottlenecks or barriers, the solution of which may create new markets. A third strategy chooses to be at the frontiers of technological capabilities on the theory that some attractive product fallout will result from such competence. A fourth approach emphasizes economic criteria including attractive growth prospects and appropriate stability.

If it is necessary for the firm to alter its product-market mix or range of capabilities to reduce or close the strategic gap, a diversification strategy may be formulated. Thus, the key connection between planning and diversification or mergers lies in the evaluation of current managerial and technological capabilities relative to capabilities required to reach objectives.

## DIVERSIFICATION STRATEGY

Other things being equal, a preferred strategy is to move into a diversification program from a base or core of existing capabilities or organizational strengths. Guidance may be obtained by answers to the following questions: Is there strength in the general management functions? Can the company provide staff expertise in a wide range of areas? Can the firm's financial planning and control effectiveness have a broad application? Are there specific capabilities such as research, marketing, and manufacturing that the firm is seeking to spread over a wider arena?

The firm should be clear on both its strengths and its limitations. To remedy weaknesses, the firm should clearly define the specific new capabilities it is seeking to obtain. If the firm does not possess a sufficient breadth of capability to use as a basis for moving into other areas, an alternative strategy may be employed. This would be to establish a beachhead of capabilities in one or more selected areas. The firm is then in a position to develop concentrically from each of these nuclei.

To understand the potential carryover of capabilities even in pure conglomerate mergers, one needs to recognize that the nature of firms and the boundaries of industries have become much more dynamic and flexible in recent years. The emphasis of traditional economic theory, as reflected in the Census Bureau's Standard Industrial Classification, is on industry boundary delineation that is mainly product or process oriented. However, organization theory and the behavior of individual firms reflect an emphasis increasingly on missions and capabilities.

In a world of continuing change, managements must relate to **missions,** defined in terms of customer needs, wants, or problems to be solved. In addition to missions, another important dimension of the concept of industries is a **range of capabilities.** Technological capabilities embrace all processes from basic research, product design and development, and applications engineering through interrelated manufacturing methods and obtaining feedback from consumers. Managerial capabilities include competence in the **generic management functions** of planning, organizing, directing, and controlling, as well as in the **specific management functions** of research, production, personnel, marketing, and finance. Another important dimension of managerial capabilities is coordinating and achieving an effective organization system or entity.

The development of such a range of capabilities requires substantial investments in the training and experience of people. It includes investments in holding organizations together during periods of depressed sales. Market demand-and-supply forces place a high value on executive talent and staff expertise. Managerial technology and the effectiveness of management practices are key factors in the efficiency performances of firms.

Potential competition has been enlarged. Industry boundaries defined by products become less meaningful than industries defined by the ability to perform the critical functions for meeting customer needs. The ease of entry is increased because the critical factors for success in changing environments include a range of technologies, experience developed in international markets, and even the adoption of new managerial techniques.

## Internal Versus External Growth

Growth and diversification may be achieved both internally and externally. For some activities, internal development may be advantageous. For others, careful analysis may reveal sound business reasons for external diversification.

Factors favoring external growth and diversification through mergers and acquisitions include the following:

1. Some goals and objectives may be achieved more speedily through an external acquisition.
2. The cost of building an organization internally may exceed the cost of an acquisition.
3. There may be fewer risks, lower costs, or shorter time requirements involved in achieving an economically feasible market share by the external route.
4. The firm may be able to use securities in obtaining other companies, whereas it might not be able to finance the acquisition of equivalent assets and capabilities internally.
5. Other firms may not be utilizing their assets or managements as effectively as they could be utilized by the acquiring firm.
6. There may be tax advantages.
7. There may be opportunities to complement the capabilities of other firms.

In general, internal development is favored when the preceding advantages are minimal. Frequently the firms available for acquisition will not provide attractive opportunities for achieving the goals that have been set forth; as in make-or-buy decisions, internal development may be more feasible from an economic standpoint. Merger and acquisition activity involves very large stakes and high risks.

From a practical business standpoint, growth through mergers and diversification represents a sound alternative to be taken into account in business planning. We do not wish to imply that external growth and diversification should be the major form of growth, but experience suggests that at times external growth may contribute to opportunities for effective alignment to the firm's changing environments. Combining firms, however, does not provide an automatic basis for success. Even the combination of related activities presents formidable challenges to effective managerial planning and control performance. Concentric mergers that involve the carryover of specific capabilities provide more direct opportunities for cost reduction and scale economies. However, even with conglomerate mergers, important social and business gains are possible.

## Empirical Evidence

Berger and Ofek (1995) studied the effects of diversification by estimating the value of a diversified firm's segments by treating them as separate firms. Over the 1986–1991 sample period, they estimated that diversification reduces value by 13 to 15%. The value loss was smaller when the segments of the diversified firm were in the same two-digit standard industrial classification (SIC) code. They attribute the value loss to over-investment and cross-subsidization.

Comment and Jarrell's (1995) main measure of focus was a revenue-based Herfindahl Index (explained in chapter 2 of this book) of the degree of concentration. An index of one represents the highest degree of focus. They found that a change of a positive increase of 0.1 is associated with an improvement in stock return of about 4%.

They tested some earlier theories for diversification such as (1) managerial economies of scale, (2) economies of scope, and (3) financial synergies such as combining uncorrelated earnings streams and the efficiencies of an internal capital market. The opposing theory was that diversification reflects the unwise use of unused borrowing power and large free cash flows. They found that diversified firms did not (1) make greater use of debt, (2) substitute intersegment cash transfers for external financing, or (3) increase the likelihood of a takeover. Some evidence suggested that diversification caused firms to become takeover targets themselves.

### Diversification Planning, Mergers, and the Carryover of Managerial Capabilities

From an economic standpoint, does any justification exist for these long-range-planning efforts of firms to achieve the regeneration of their organization systems? Particularly, does any justification exist for the use of mergers to seek continuity of firms? One justification for the continuity of firms whose performance is falling short of their competitors is the reduction in the expected present value of the costs of bankruptcy or liquidation. Whether bankruptcy is due to, for example, financial causes, operating or managerial weakness, or inappropriate balance with the environment, one of the potential areas of loss is in investment in reputation and organization capital (which represents firm-specific information embodied in employees or used in forming efficient production and management teams in the organization).

Data compiled on conglomerate mergers by the Federal Trade Commission divide them into three groups: (1) product extension, (2) market extension, and (3) others that might be called pure conglomerate mergers. Product-extension and market-extension mergers usually provide opportunities for the carryover of industry-specific management capabilities such as research, applications engineering, production, marketing, and so on. Pure conglomerate mergers, then, would involve, at least initially, the potential carryover only of the general management functions of planning, organizing, directing, controlling, and so on. While finance is a specific management function, its role in the generic functions of planning and control and the broad generality of its applications suggest its treatment as a general management function as well.

The motivation on the part of the diversifying or acquiring firm is an expectation that it has or will have excess capacity of general managerial capabilities in relation to its existing product-market activities. Furthermore, there is an expectation that in the processes of interacting on the generic management activities, particularly overall planning and control and financial planning and control, the diversifying firm will develop industry-specific managerial experience and firm-specific organization capital over time.

However, even this formulation is somewhat restrictive. It applies to companies such as ITT in which under Harold Geneen a high level of capability had been achieved in financial planning and control systems. But other types of carryovers were also involved. For example, for Litton Industries the original conception was to apply advanced technologies from its defense business to industries for which such applications appeared to have a sound economic and business basis as well as to bring to organization interactions a systems approach to management (again developed out of prior experience of the top managers of Litton). A high percentage of conglomerates came out of the defense industry, not only with an objective to apply organizational capital and the desire to avoid the destruction of such organization capital, but also with a need to acquire additional critical managerial capabilities to be successful in the nondefense sector of the economy. Particularly critical for the defense firms was the establishment of a capability for performing industrial marketing. This suggests that where the desired capability requires an organizational learning and development process that involves time and uncertainties, merger enables the firm to obtain such critical capabilities at a determinate cost and to avoid the risks of extreme and uncertain outcomes.

Another capability that defense firms had was the ability to manage change, which represented an important contribution to a wide range of nondefense industries that had not developed this kind of organization knowledge. Again, even though there appeared to be no relationships between the merging firms, there was a complementarity when firms were viewed as groups of capabilities in the framework of an organization.

# INFLUENCES ON DIVERSIFICATION

Four factors have influenced diversification decisions by business firms: (1) the revolution that has taken place in management technology since World War II, (2) the increased pace of technological change in the U.S. economy, (3) the higher fixed costs for management-staff services, and (4) changes in the equity markets that have reinforced these other factors.

## Advances in Managerial Technology

Important changes in management technology include the following:

1. The developments in the theory and practice of planning.
2. The relating of long-range planning to management by financial objectives.
3. The changes in information science brought about by computers and the increased computerization of information analysis within a firm.
4. The development and use of formal decision models, which may be summarized in the term *management science.*
5. The increased use of a systems-analysis approach to the firm with emphasis on viewing all aspects of the firm's operations in a dynamic process (in contrast to the static microeconomic theory of the firm).
6. The increased role of management functions in the firm's operations.
7. The increased use of balanced centralized and decentralized decision making.
8. The increased recognition of the quality and continuity of the firm's management organization as an important economic variable.
9. The increased recognition of the value of investments in people, resulting in more extensive training programs throughout the worker and management organizations.

These nine developments in management technology have led to an emphasis on increased diversification by business firms. The increasing range of management capabilities has made it advantageous to spread these abilities over a greater number of activities. However, these management capabilities are not evenly distributed throughout industries. Consequently, opportunities have developed for firms to extend their capabilities to other firms and to new areas in order to increase the returns on investments in both management and physical assets. An offsetting factor is that unrelated areas may not be understood, managed poorly, and require divestiture.

## Increased Technological Change

The second trend stimulating greater business diversification has been the increased rate of technological change in the U.S. economy. The increased pace of product development shortens the life cycles of products. The growth rates in sales for individual industries and individual products begin to level off in less time, while opportunities for growth in new areas multiply at a faster pace. Thus, the opportunities for diversification have increased along with the pressures for change. Technological expertise is spread unequally among business firms and industries, and the prospect for economic profits from supplying advanced technological capabilities to industries and firms who need them provides an increased incentive to diversify.

It has been argued that diversification can be achieved as well through internal expansion as through external acquisition. This view fails to recognize the size and risks of the investments and costs involved in diversification activity. For a firm with advanced technological capability, but without the requisite industrial production or marketing facilities and experience, to attempt to apply these capabilities de novo in diverse areas represents a high-risk investment. The high cost of capital associated with such risks would be prohibitive for some firms and thus some of these investments would not be made. Other investments of this type would take place, but at a much slower pace than that which typifies external acquisition.

Thus, business firms hope to achieve synergistic or carry-over effects from the distinctive attributes or qualities which they bring to a merger. These gains to the individual firms are also social gains. They represent an increase in the pace at which efficiencies are spread throughout the economy. They contribute to the quality, level, and growth rate of output in the economy. However, unrelated areas may be so complex that value may be increased by focusing on core activities.

### Larger Fixed Costs for Staff Services

The advances in management technology and the increased pace of technological change, coupled with more dynamic economic and cultural environments, have increased the complexity of business operations. Furthermore, the expanding role and requirements of government bodies have necessitated a larger complement of staff services in modern business firms. Both the need and the costs for staff services have increased. The need to maintain an effectively competitive position in the world economy has also resulted in a larger management staff with a broader range of management capabilities and has thus increased the fixed costs of business operations. Scale economies have increasingly resulted from investment in managerial organizations rather than from investment in physical plants.

The economies derived from spreading the fixed costs for managerial staff and specialist functions over a wide range of activities have increased. Small firms have difficulty attracting management with a full range of abilities. Even if the small firms were able to bid successfully for such capabilities, their fixed costs would be substantially raised. Many staff and specialist functions are applicable in different types of industries. Thus, a further stimulus to diversification, both internal and external, has resulted. A proliferation of executive staff can lead to bloated administrative costs. Restructuring may require less diversification and a reduction in executive staff.

### Developments in the Equity Markets

Trends in the equity markets have reinforced the influence of the foregoing factors in encouraging diversification by external acquisition. One significant influence was the discovery of the concept of growth stocks by the financial press and academic writers in the late 1950s and early 1960s. Higher valuations were placed on stocks with recognized potential for growth in earnings and dividends than on stocks with little or no expected growth in earnings or dividends. Thus, higher price/earnings (P/E) ratios resulted for growth stocks. Because of the upward drift in price/earnings ratios from the 1950s through the early 1960s, the growth rate for stock prices increased more rapidly than the growth rate for earnings or dividends during that period.

The increased interest in growth stimulated mergers in various ways. It intensified management's search for product markets with growth opportunities. Along with improved methods of financial planning and control, management had incentives to seek methods for effectively controlling costs in order to increase both average earnings and the growth rate of earnings. A wide variety of financial methods were available to contribute to favorable performance and to the growth in earnings per share of the companies' securities. However, since the early 1980s the markets began to assign a penalty to diversified firms. Shedding unrelated activities became a method of improving market valuations.

Thus, in the 1960s, the markets valued diversification that achieved profitable growth. Beginning in the 1980s the markets have favored less diversified, more focused companies. It is difficult to generalize. The General Electric Company, for example, has continued to increase the diversity of its operations yet has achieved favorable multiples of market to book and price to earnings ratios.

## Summary

Evaluation of how strategy is performed by business firms depends on the particular conceptual approach to the subject. The BCG and Porter approaches argue that well-formulated principles can guide firms unerringly to the right decisions. The BCG approach emphasizes gaining market share in emerging industries to always be farther along the experience curve than your competitors. The Porter approach incorporates the tenets of the structural theory of industrial organization economics. This theory claims that firms can erect and protect monopoly advantages. The Porter approach to strategy reflects this basic ideology: find an attractive industry or industry segment, defined as an area in which large firms can collude behind entry barriers buttressed by credible deterrence. With this clear prescription, firms should not have a high rate of product-market adjustments and changes. In this framework divestiture represents a mistake. Hence, Porter's tests of effective strategy rely on a measure of the rate of divestitures to movements into new areas.

In the process approach to strategy each firm has a set of capabilities and opportunities. The firm must seek to exploit these effectively in relation to its changing environments. It must recognize that the dynamics of competition and economic change will require continuous reassessment of its position and realignment to its new challenges and opportunities. In this view the firm is required to make strategic decisions in the face of much uncertainty and considerable risk, especially with respect to mergers.

In this process view of strategy, divestitures represent a form of a strategic adjustment process. Divestitures are not necessarily management mistakes. Numerous case studies demonstrate that many divestitures were planned in advance in order to retain the desired parts of an acquisition. Or divestitures can represent a method of making acquisitions and paying them off in part or sometimes entirely by the segments sold off. At a minimum this may help make the diversification effort a low-cost one. Hence, it is erroneous to conclude that divestitures represent management mistakes.

Internal and external investment programs (mergers) may be successful or unsuccessful. Firms may try either or both approaches in their efforts to increase shareholder value. The generalizations of writers on strategic planning contain valuable insights for helping firms carry out strategies with a higher degree of efficiency than they otherwise would have been able to attain. The critical need is a rapid information feedback system in the firm to improve its capabilities for adapting to change, correcting errors, and seizing new opportunities. It is in this framework that merger and takeover decisions should be made.

---

## Questions

8.1 What is strategy?

8.2 The Boston Consulting Group approach identifies three main concepts. Discuss the implications and limitations of the following three concepts:
   a. The experience curve
   b. The product life cycle
   c. Product-market portfolio balance

8.3 What is an attractive industry according to Porter?

8.4 What does Porter mean by "competitive advantage" through cost leadership? Through product differentiation?

8.5 What are entry barriers and what is their significance?

8.6 What is the adaptive approach to strategy? (Include a discussion of the role of checklists and iterative processes.)

8.7 Discuss different types of business goals.

8.8 What is meant by aligning a firm to its environment(s)?

8.9 Why does a firm seek to continue to exist after its main products are either obsolete or out of favor for health or other reasons?

8.10 What factors resulted in the conglomerate merger movement of the late 1960s?

---

## C A S E  8-1

# Merck Acquisition of Medco

On July 28, 1993 Merck & Co., then the world's largest drug manufacturer, announced that it planned to acquire, for $6.6 billion, Medco Containment Services Inc., the largest prescription benefits management (PBM) company and marketer of mail order medicines in the United States. This merger reflected fundamental changes taking place in the pharmaceutical industry.

### GROWTH IN MANAGED CARE

Perhaps the most significant change involves the growth of managed care in the health care industry. Managed care plans typically provide members with medical insurance and basic health care services, using volume and long-term contracts to negotiate discounts from health care providers. In addition, managed care programs provide full coverage for prescription drugs more frequently than do traditional medical insurance plans. Industry experts estimate that by the turn of the century 90% of Americans will have drug costs included in some kind of managed health care plan and 60% of all outpatient pharmaceuticals will be purchased by managed care programs.

The responsibility for managing the provision of prescription drugs is often contracted out by the managed care organizations to PBMs. The activities of PBMs typically include managing insurance claims, negotiating volume discounts with drug manufacturers, and encouraging the use of less expensive generic substitutes. The management of prescription benefits are enhanced through the use of formularies and drug utilization reviews. Formularies are lists of drugs compiled by committees of pharmacists and physicians on behalf of a managed care organization. Member physicians of the managed care organization are then strongly encouraged to prescribe from this list whenever possible. Drug utilization reviews consist of analyzing physician prescribing patterns and patient usage. They can identify when a patient may be getting the wrong amount or kind of medicine, or when a member physician is not prescribing from a formulary. Essentially, this amounts to an additional opportunity for managed care or PBM administrators to monitor costs and consolidate decision-making authority.

The key aspect of the shift to managed care is that the responsibility for payment is linked more tightly to decision making about the provision of health care services than it is in traditional indemnity insurance plans. The implications for drug manufacturers are far-reaching. With prescription decision-making authority shifting away from doctors to managed care and PBM administrators, drug manufacturer's marketing strategies will similarly shift their focus from several hundred thousand doctors to a few thousand formulary and plan managers. This, in turn, will result in a dramatic reduction in the sales forces of pharmaceutical manufacturers.

Several other significant changes in industry structure are expected to occur. Many industry experts predict that managed care providers will rely on a single drug company to deliver all of its pharmaceutical products and services rather than negotiating with several drug companies. This will favor those firms with manufacturing, distribution, and prescription management capabilities. In addition, many experts believe only a handful of pharmaceutical companies will exist on the international scene in a few years. They point to intense competition, lower profits, and a decrease in the number of new drugs in the "research pipeline" as contributing factors.

## BENEFITS OF THE ACQUISITION

Merck & Co. and Medco Containment Services Inc. believe that a merger between the two firms will create a competitive advantage that will allow for their survival. Merck executives identify Medco's extensive database as the key factor motivating the merger.

Medco maintains a computer profile of each of its 33 million customers, amounting to 26% of all people covered by a pharmaceutical benefit plan. Medco clients include one hundred Fortune 500 companies, federal and state benefit plans, and 58 Blue Cross/Blue Shield groups and insurance companies.

Numerous opportunities exist for Merck to utilize the information contained in Medco's database. First, the database will allow Merck to identify prescriptions that may be switched from a competitor's drug to a Merck drug. Merck pharmacists will then suggest the switch to a patient's doctor. This prospect of increasing sales is enormous. Second, the database will allow Merck to identify patients who fail to refill prescriptions. The failure to refill needed prescriptions amounts to hundreds of millions of dollars in lost sales each year. Finally, Merck will be able to use Medco's computerized patient record system as a real-life laboratory with the goal of proving that some Merck drugs are worth the premium price charged. This will take place by identifying who takes what pill and combining that information with the patient's medical records. This may allow Merck to establish the supremacy of its products.

Additional benefits of the merger include $1 billion annual savings in redundant marketing operations and reducing Merck's sales force as a result of more precise marketing strategies brought about by Medco's database and the industry emphasis on marketing to plan managers instead of doctors. Merck & Co.'s acquisition of Medco Containment Services Inc. is essentially an attempt to increase market share in an industry with decreasing prices by capitalizing on the most valuable asset in the pharmaceutical industry—information. It is also intended to increase its competitive position in the growing managed care arena by aligning itself with a PBM.

Merck & Co.'s strategy was quickly emulated when British drug maker SmithKline Beecham announced plans to acquire Diversified Pharmaceutical Services Inc., one of the four largest drug wholesalers in the United States, from United Healthcare for $2.3 billion, and Roche Holdings Ltd. reported that it planned to acquire Syntex Corporation. Also, in the summer of 1994, Eli Lilly and Company announced its intention to acquire PCS Health Systems from McKesson Corp. for $4 billion. These mergers were not only a reaction to the changing industry structure, but caused the change to accelerate.

---

## Questions on Case Study C8.1

C8.1.1 What was the major force driving this acquisition?

C8.1.2 What is the role of prescription benefits management (PBM) companies?

C8.1.3 What role was envisaged for the use of Medco's database?

C8.1.4 What competitive reactions took place in response to Merck's acquisition of Medco?

---

--------------------------------- C A S E  8–2 ---------------------------------

# Acquisition of Lotus Development Corp. by IBM

Lotus Development Corp., the second largest PC software firm, was taken over via a hostile bid by IBM Corp. in 1995 for $3.52 billion.

## THE TAKEOVER PROCESS

### Previous Relations Between IBM and Lotus

According to executives familiar with the situation, Jim Manzi, the CEO of Lotus Development Corp., offered to sell the company's desktop software applications to IBM but did not want to sell the entire company. In August 1994 Manzi suggested to James Cannavino, IBM's top strategist at the time, a joint venture in desktop applications or the sale of that part to IBM. IBM declined the offer. In January 1995 Manzi repeated the offer to the new IBM senior vice president in charge of the software group, John M. Thompson. Thompson offered to acquire the entire company, to which Manzi responded that Lotus was not for sale. Manzi ruled out anything but a minority stake for IBM of Lotus's communications business. The two met for the last time in March when Manzi objected to the acquisition again.

### Announcement of the Bid

On June 5, 1995, IBM announced its first ever hostile bid in the form of a $60 cash per share tender offer. That day, Lotus's stock price soared $29 from $32.375 closing at $61.375 on the NASDAQ (a 90% premium), while IBM stock dropped $2.625 from $93.875 closing at $91.25 on the NYSE (a 2.8% decline).

The bid was the culmination of months of strategy. In April 1995 IBM analyzed the fit of Lotus products with IBM software and decided to pursue Lotus. IBM realized that Lotus Development Corp. wanted

to remain independent if they were to be acquired. With this in mind, Louis V. Gerstner Jr., the chairman of IBM, approved the hostile deal on May 12. On May 22 IBM incorporated White Acquisition Corp., a subsidiary specifically created to execute the acquisition of Lotus. On June 5, 1995, IBM sent a message promising Lotus employees that they would not be assimilated into IBM after the merger. IBM agreed to this stipulation because they did not want to lose key Lotus employees such as the software developer of Lotus Notes, Raymond Ozzie.

Shortly after 8 A.M. on the morning of the bid, IBM's Delaware law firm filed a lawsuit challenging Lotus's poison pill. The activated Lotus pill with a trigger set at 15% would have dramatically increased the number of Lotus shares and the cost of the acquisition to a potential acquirer. At 8:25 A.M., Gerstner informed Manzi of the bid. Manzi agreed to consider the offer knowing that he was not promised a position should Lotus be acquired. At 8:30 A.M., IBM informed the exchanges on which IBM and Lotus traded, the NYSE and NASDAQ, respectively. Gerstner also called the CEO of Hewlett Packard and chairman of AT&T, two partners of Lotus who were also potential white knights, to inform them of IBM's intent.

At a 1:30 P.M. press conference, Gerstner spoke of the three different ages of computing. The first age of computing, the mainframe, was dominated by IBM, while the second age of personal computers remained very competitive. The race is currently on for dominance of the third age, networked computing. Networked computing allows users of different software and hardware platforms to work together in a collaborative manner. The network would offer the user-friendliness and the applications of a desktop along with the security, dependability, and capacity of large-scale systems. IBM's acquisition of Lotus is an attempt to gain a significant share of the networked computing market.

In addition to the press conference on June 5, IBM took the first steps toward consent solicitation to put pressure on the Lotus board. Lotus bylaws permitted shareholders to vote at any time on whether to retain the board. With the threat of being ousted, the Lotus board would be forced to pay careful attention to the wishes of the shareholders. Shareholders were likely to want the premium given the recent poor performance of the company stock. Institutions held the bulk of Lotus's stock. Directors and officers only held 3.3% of Lotus's stock but 2.54% of that number, or 1.2 million shares, was held by Manzi, the largest individual holder of Lotus stock.

The announcement of the bid appeared to be anticipated given the 11% rise of Lotus stock on Friday, June 2, which triggered an SEC insider trader investigation. Rumors that IBM might acquire Lotus had existed for several months prior to the bid.

### Acceptance of the Offer

On Sunday, June 11, Lotus accepted a sweetened $64 a share, or $3.52 billion offer from IBM. The final price represented four times Lotus's 1994 revenues. IBM anticipated writing off approximately $1.8 billion in goodwill after a one-time charge. Also under the terms of the deal, Manzi would remain the CEO of Lotus and become senior vice president of IBM. He would be allowed to run Lotus with a high degree of independence in addition to receiving a $78 million windfall from his Lotus stock.

In Manzi's own words, he was staying on not in a "transitional role," but rather to help make Lotus Notes the industry standard for network software, to protect Lotus employees, and to protect the Lotus organization (Glenn Rifkin, "How Shock Turned to Deal for Lotus Chief," *The New York Times,* June 13, 1995, p. D6). Though analysts were surprised that Manzi would remain in charge of Lotus, they predicted that he would not stay with the company for long. Analysts spoke of the clash of egos they felt would occur between Gerstner and Manzi.

Manzi said that the previously announced restructuring of Lotus into four business units would still take place in spite of the merger. Some Lotus employees may have favored the merger because of the stability involved in joining IBM's team, the capital IBM could invest in the company, and the soaring

value of their Lotus stock options. Prior to the merger Lotus's future looked grim. Lotus was vulnerable due to its recent poor performance, lack of a white knight, and corporate bylaws that allowed a direct appeal to Lotus shareholders. Lotus shares traded at 66% below their 1994 high, and efforts to find a white knight may have been impeded by the fact that Lotus was a competitor of the powerful Microsoft, with which very few companies were able or willing to compete.

On July 5, 1995, the acquisition was finally completed.

## STRATEGIC ANALYSIS OF THE ACQUISITION

### Previous History of Lotus

Lotus was founded by a college dropout named Mitch Kapor in 1982. Eight months later the company successfully introduced Lotus 1-2-3, the first spreadsheet program to translate numbers into graphics. In 1983 a McKinsey and Company consultant by the name of Jim Manzi was assigned to help manage Lotus's rapid growth. Later that year Manzi joined the Lotus board as vice president of marketing and sales. In 1986 Kapor left the firm and made Manzi his successor.

In the early 1980s the Lotus 1-2-3 spreadsheet package was the most popular PC business application. But because Lotus was slow to develop a version of 1-2-3 for Windows, many users switched to Microsoft Excel or Borland's Quattro Pro for Windows.

The growing popularity of Windows created other problems for Lotus as well. Late in developing software suites, the company tried to rectify this through acquisitions. In 1990 Lotus acquired Samna Corp. and its Ami Pro word processing line for $65 million, and in March 1991 Lotus purchased cc:Mail. Also, in June 1994 Lotus acquired SoftSwitch Inc. for $70 million in stock, or 1.3 million shares. Unfortunately these acquisitions did little to help improve Lotus's weakened state.

The reduction in its desktop applications and continued reputation for being weak on marketing and updating programs contributed to Lotus's subsequent decline. Lotus's desktop software accounted for two-thirds of Lotus's revenues, so it was particularly troublesome when in 1994 these revenues declined 20% to $620 million. In the first quarter of 1995 Lotus lost another $17.5 million due in part to a 50% price cut on Notes announced in January 1995.

The price cut was intended to increase the market share of Notes before the release of MS Exchange.

The company's troubles prompted Manzi to announce a restructuring on April 19, 1995. Cost cuts and reorganization meant layoffs and low employee morale. In two weeks, Lotus eliminated 32 high level positions with lower level layoffs expected in the near future. This restructuring was directed by Richard S. Braddock, a powerful outside director and former president of Citicorp.

### Motivations Behind the Merger

The main motivation behind the acquisition was IBM's desire to own Lotus's network software program called Notes. Released in December 1989, Notes had propelled Lotus to a 65% market share in groupware, a market that was anticipated to grow from $500 million to $5 billion by the end of the decade. In 1994 sales of Notes nearly doubled to $350 million, with the majority coming from existing customers. By January 1995 one million people used Notes in 4,500 companies and third-party companies have created over 700 commercial applications that work with Notes. Moreover, the Notes customer base has increased because while it was originally only available on OS/2 servers it can now run on Windows NT and other operating systems. Notes is currently regarded as the best groupware software on the market and is considered to have little competition.

Primarily used by large corporations and large networks, groupware enables groups of workers to communicate with one another and to share or have access to the same data. It is often used as the central framework for managing entire corporate systems and can be customized by using it as a platform on which to build additional applications.

To understand the usefulness of Notes, one can examine some of its features. Replication allows each user to have the latest version of a document or database. In addition, Notes allows the user to send documents to subsets of people, store and retrieve images of contracts, send and receive faxes, and share letters, messages, memos, etc. This is a step above networked computers, which can only share information in the form of lists stored in the same format. With the release of the new version of Notes 4.0 in 1995, users can now send and receive information from the Internet.

Competition in this market is likely to increase rapidly. Microsoft plans to release a competing product called Microsoft Exchange in late 1996. Though not as powerful as Notes, MS Exchange will provide easier use and less expensive support and service requirements. Novell is also working on an entry into groupware.

With the IBM and Lotus Development Corp. merger, IBM also acquired Lotus's PC software suite product, SmartSuite, which is third in suite sales. SmartSuite includes the WordPro word processor, 1-2-3 spreadsheet, Freelance Graphics package, Organizer Personal information manager, and the Approach database.

Overall, IBM hoped the acquisition would allow them to increase their share of the worldwide PC software market. The shares had been Microsoft 18.7%, Novell 7.7%, IBM 3.7%, and Lotus 3.2%. Finally, by acquiring Lotus, IBM eliminated a major competitor in the E-mail market and created opportunities for synergy. For example, IBM believes that its strong marketing will help with the sale of software suite packages and cc:Mail, the leading E-mail product.

### The Fit of the Two Companies

IBM's strength lies in managing and integrating large computer systems, while Lotus has expertise in linking smaller networks. IBM has larger resources in the area of marketing, finance, information management, product support, and technology—resources especially helpful given the sophistication of Notes. IBM is no newcomer to groupware; it spent years trying to develop network software but discontinued the project known as OfficeVision/2 LAN in June 1992. The Lotus purchase will help IBM in this area and give it a quick entry into new markets. IBM also has a global sales force and plenty of consultants who can push the Notes product. In fact, under a licensing agreement, the IBM sales force has already been selling Notes since June 1991.

IBM would also like to see its OS/2 succeed in a network server-operating system and its minicomputers (a $13 billion business) as servers. The biggest problem for OS/2 is not technological inferiority, but a lack of software. Only a small percentage of software is supported by, or compatible with, the OS/2 server. Because Lotus was the only large software company writing applications for OS/2, losing Lotus to a rival, as IBM had feared, would have been a serious setback. Also, the problems facing OS/2 were likely to become more severe because OS/2 could run Windows applications, but not Windows 95 applications.

### Can IBM and Lotus Compete with Microsoft?

The importance of groupware to the future software market is agreed upon by most analysts. Gerstner believes that groupware will be the fastest growing segment of software in the 1990s (William J. Cook, "Software Struggle," *US News & World Report,* June 19, 1995, p. 46). The question is whether IBM can establish Notes as the industrywide standard before the introduction of Microsoft Exchange in 1996. Some suggestions to help Notes compete are to bundle it with IBM PCs and to widen its abilities by enabling it to serve hundreds and thousands of users on a network. In turn, Microsoft could bundle Exchange with its own operating systems, which could essentially lead to a price war between the two companies. According to Microsoft Chairman Bill Gates, "In general, our software position seems very strong. The one exception is in Lotus Notes. Everyday we delay our product in that category, our position weakens" (Steve Lohr, "IBM's Big Move: The Leaders," *The New York Times,* June 7, 1995, p. D4).

If Notes devises the ability to run with operating systems such as Microsoft Windows, Apple's Macintosh, and AT&T's UNIX, it may very well become an industrywide standard. This is the biggest concern for Microsoft because Windows is the operating system for 85% of the world's computers.

IBM can bring several strengths to Notes. First, IBM has experience with client/server systems from the standpoint of large-scale, centralized computing. This can be enhanced by the addition of Notes. IBM also has the financial strength to lower the price of Notes and take advantage of high volume and lower margins. The high cost of Notes had put it out of reach for smaller corporations.

In operating systems, Microsoft Windows is the industry leader. IBM's operating system, OS/2, has been on the market for seven years but only supports a few applications like 1-2-3, which is declining in popularity. Microsoft has also created Windows NT and Microsoft Network. MS Network is an on-line service like IBM and Sears's Prodigy.

## POSTACQUISITION DEVELOPMENTS

### Analysts Explain Manzi's Resignation

On October 11, 1995, former Lotus President and CEO Jim Manzi resigned from office only 99 days after the merger with IBM. Manzi's abrasive personality was not conducive to IBM's bureaucratic corporate culture, which led him to publicly criticize the company. Manzi leaves Lotus and IBM with over $78 million he received from the IBM acquisition.

Analysts were surprised when Manzi agreed to become a senior vice president after IBM acquired Lotus. Analysts believe that this resignation was a result of his inability to assume leadership over all of IBM's software development. Essentially, the software development group Manzi wanted to assume leadership over is an $11 billion business of which he lacked expertise. The software development group of IBM handles products such as corporate database applications and mainframe operating systems that cover a much broader range of knowledge than Manzi possessed. Analysts anticipated that the resignation would not harm the IBM/Lotus merger unless it caused Lotus software developers to resign. Although some other top executives from Lotus resigned, the key Lotus software programmers have remained with IBM.

The very next day IBM appointed Michael D. Zisman and Jeffrey Papows to head Lotus. Over the previous years they worked as partners in running Lotus's communications group. John M. Thompson, an IBM senior vice president and groups executive for software, has assured analysts and investors that Ray Ozzie, the key developer and creative genius behind Lotus Notes, will stay on to oversee the next release of Notes, Version 4.0.

### Notes's Competition

IBM's expensive acquisition of Lotus in July 1995 was made to give IBM access to Lotus's popular Notes workgroup software. IBM made the acquisition because it saw workgroup software as the next great opportunity in the computer software industry. IBM hopes to increase Notes usage more than six-fold over the next few years, from 1995's 3.5 million users. This strategy has, however, run into unexpected competition from the Internet. The existence of the new Intranets could destroy any hope that IBM will realize a profit from Notes. Intranets are private networks that operate via the Internet's World Wide Web. Intranets are less expensive to operate than Notes, and considerably easier to manage.

------------------------------------------------------------------------

## Questions on Case Study C8.2

C8.2.1 What were IBM's strategic strengths and weaknesses in the computer industry?
C8.2.2 What role was the acquisition of the Lotus acquisition expected to perform?
C8.2.3 What are the key remaining strategic challenges facing IBM?

------------------------------------------------------------------------

## References

Ansoff, H. Igor, *Corporate Strategy,* New York: McGraw-Hill, 1965.

Berger, Philip G., and Eli Ofek, "Diversification's Effect on Firm Value," *Journal of Financial Economics,* 37, January 1995, pp. 39–65.

Bogue, Marcus C., III, and Elwood S. Buffa, *Corporate Strategic Analysis,* New York: The Free Press, 1986.

Boston Consulting Group, *The Strategy Development Process,* Boston: The Boston Consulting Group, 1985.

Carroll, D. T., "A Disappointing Search for Excellence," *Harvard Business Review,* 61, November–December 1983, pp. 78–88.

Chandler, Alfred D., Jr., *Strategy and Structure: Chapters in the History of the American Industrial Enterprise,* Cambridge, MA: The M.I.T. Press, 1962.

Chung, Mary, and Alistair Davidson, "Business Experts," *PC AI,* 1, Summer 1987, pp. 16–21.

Comment, Robert, and Gregg A. Jarrell, "Corporate Focus and Stock Returns," *Journal of Financial Economics,* 37, January 1995, pp. 67–87.

*Economist,* "Why Too Many Mergers Miss the Mark," January 4, 1997, pp. 57–58.

Grove, Andrew S., *Only the Paranoid Survive: How to Exploit the Crisis Points That Challenge Every Company and Career,* New York: Currency Doubleday, 1996.

Grover, Ronald, and Neil Gross, "A Wireless Weapon in the Cable Wars," *Business Week,* October 14, 1996, p. 105.

Henderson, Bruce D., *The Logic of Business Strategy,* Cambridge, MA: Ballinger, 1984.

Hout, Thomas M., and Mark F. Blaxill, "Make Decisions Like a Fighter Pilot," *New York Times,* November 15, 1987, Sec. 3, p. 3.

Johnson, W. Bruce, Ashok Natarajan, and Alfred Rappaport, "Shareholder Returns and Corporate Excellence," *Journal of Business Strategy,* 6, Fall 1985, pp. 52–62.

Lindblom, Charles E., "The Science of 'Muddling Through'," *Public Administration Review,* 19, Spring 1959, pp. 79–88.

———, *The Intelligence of Democracy: Decision Making Through Mutual Adjustment,* New York: The Free Press, 1965.

Peters, Thomas J., *Thriving on Chaos,* New York: Alfred A. Knopf, Publishers, 1987.

———, and Robert H. Waterman, Jr., *In Search of Excellence,* New York: Harper & Row, 1982.

Porter, Michael E., "How Competitive Forces Shape Strategy," *Harvard Business Review,* 57, March–April 1979, pp. 137–145.

———, *Competitive Strategy,* New York: The Free Press, 1980.

———, *Competitive Advantage,* New York: The Free Press, 1985.

———, "From Competitive Advantage to Corporate Strategy," *Harvard Business Review,* May–June 1987, pp. 43–59.

Quinn, James Brian, "Strategic Goals: Process and Politics," *Sloan Management Review,* Fall 1977, pp. 21–37.

————, *Strategies for Change: Logical Incrementalism,* Homewood, IL: Irwin, 1980.

————, Henry Mintzberg, and Robert M. James, *The Strategy Process,* Englewood Cliffs, NJ: Prentice Hall, 1988.

Ramanujam, Vasudevan, and N. Venkatraman, "Excellence, Planning, and Performance," *Interfaces,* 18, May–June 1988, pp. 23–31.

Rumelt, Richard P., "Towards a Strategic Theory of the Firm" Chapter 26 in R. B. Lamb, ed., *Competitive Strategic Management,* Englewood Cliffs, NJ: Prentice Hall, 1984.

Steiner, George A., *Strategic Planning,* New York: The Free Press, 1979.

————, John B. Miner, and Edmund R. Gray, *Management Policy and Strategy,* 3rd ed., New York: Macmillan, 1986.

Stryker, Steven C., *Plan to Succeed: A Guide to Strategic Planning,* Princeton, NJ: Petrocelli Books, 1986.

Thomas, Lacy Glenn, III, ed., *The Economics of Strategic Planning,* Lexington, MA: Lexington Books, 1986.

Waterman, Robert H., Jr., *The Renewal Factor,* New York: Bantam Books, 1987.

Weston, J. Fred, *Concentration and Efficiency: The Other Side of the Monopoly Issue,* Special Issues in the Public Interest No. 4, New York: Hudson Institute, 1978.

————, "Section 7 Enforcement: Implementation of Outmoded Theories," *Antitrust Law Journal,* 49, 1982, pp. 1411–1450.

# 9

# Alternative
# Approaches
# to Valuation

This chapter discusses valuation in relation to merger and acquisition activity. This subject is critical for the study of M&As because a major cause of acquisition failures is that the bidder pays too much. Sometimes a bidder makes a tender offer, which may stimulate competing bidders. The securities laws provide for a 20-day waiting period to give shareholders the opportunity to evaluate the proposal. This also gives other potential bidders time to evaluate the situation, to determine whether a competitive bid will be made. In a bidding contest, the winner is the firm with the highest estimates of value for the target. A framework is essential to discipline valuation estimates.

The leading methods used in the valuation of a firm for merger analysis are the comparable companies or comparable transactions approaches, spreadsheet approach, and formula approach. In this chapter we explain and illustrate the logic or theory behind each of these three approaches. In chapter 10 we develop further the implementation of the leading valuation methods.

## COMPARABLE COMPANIES OR COMPARABLE
## TRANSACTIONS APPROACHES

In the comparable companies or comparable transactions approaches, key relationships are calculated for a group of similar companies or similar transactions as a basis for the valuation of companies involved in a merger or takeover. These approaches are widely used especially by investment bankers and in legal cases. The theory is not complicated. Marketplace transactions are used. They are commonsense approaches that say similar companies should sell for similar prices. These straightforward approaches appeal to businessmen, to their financial advisors, and to the judges in courts of law called upon to give decisions on the relative values of companies in litigation. For a full elaboration of these approaches, emanating from considerable application in court cases, see Cornell (1993).

First, a basic idea is illustrated in a simple setting, followed by applications to actual companies in an M&A setting. In Table 9.1, the comparable companies approach is illustrated. We are seeking to place a value on company W. We find three companies that are comparable. To test for comparability we would consider size, similarity of products, age of company, and recent trends, among other variables.

| TABLE 9.1 | Comparable Companies Ratios (Company W Is Compared with Companies A, B, and C) | | | |
|---|---|---|---|---|
| | *Company A* | *Company B* | *Company C* | *Average* |
| Market**/sales | 1.2X* | 1.0X | 0.8X | 1.0X |
| Market/book | 1.3X | 1.2X | 2.0X | 1.5X |
| Market/net income ≡ price/earnings ratio | 20X | 15X | 25X | 20X |

*X stands for "times."

**Market refers to the market value of equity.

*(handwritten: $MV = SH \, qs \times Price$)*

Assume that companies A, B, and C meet most of our comparability requirements. We then calculate the ratio of the market value of shareholders' equity to sales, the market value of equity in relation to the book value of equity, and the price-to-earnings ratio for the individual companies. The resulting ratios are found in the top part of Table 9.1. These ratios are then averaged. These average ratios will then be applied to the absolute data for company W. For the averages to be meaningful, it is important that the ratios we calculate for each company be relatively close in value. If they are greatly different, which implies that the dispersion around the average is substantial, the average (a measure of central tendency) would not be very meaningful. In the example given, the ratios for the three comparable companies do not vary widely. Hence, it makes some sense to apply the averages.

We next postulate that for a relevant recent time period, company W had sales of $100 million, a book value of $60 million, and a net income of $5 million as shown in Table 9.2. We next apply the average market ratios from Table 9.1 to obtain the indicated value of equity for company W. We have three estimates of the indicated equity value of W based on the ratio of market value to sales, to book, and to net income. The results are close enough to be meaningful. When we average them, we obtain $97 million for the indicated market value of equity for company W.

One of the advantages of the comparable companies approach is that it can be used to establish valuation relationships for a company that is not publicly traded. This is a method of predicting what its publicly traded price is likely to be. The methodology is applicable in testing for the soundness of valuations in mergers also. Both the buyer and the seller in a merger seek confirmation that the price is fair in relation to the values placed on other companies. For public companies, the courts will require such a demonstration if a suit is filed by an aggrieved shareholder.

| TABLE 9.2 | Application of Valuation Ratios to Company W | | |
|---|---|---|---|
| *Actual Recent Data for Company W* | | *Average Market Ratios* | *Indicated Value of Equity* |
| Sales                  = $100 | | 1.0X | $100 |
| Book value of equity   =   60 | | 1.5X | 90 |
| Net income             =    5 | | 20X | 100 |
| | | | Average = $ 97 |

The data in Table 9.1 can also be reinterpreted to illustrate the comparable transactions approach. The data would then represent companies involved in the same kind of merger transactions in which company W is involved. In connection with merger transactions, a clarification should be made. When the term *market* is used, it does not refer to the prevailing market price of the companies' common stock before the merger announcement. In this context, market refers to the transaction price in a deal recently completed. Typically, merger transactions involve a premium as high as 30 to 40% over the prevailing market price (before news of the merger transaction has leaked out). The relevant valuation for a subsequent merger transaction would be the transaction prices for comparable deals.

Now let us reinterpret Table 9.1 as shown in Table 9.3. We postulate that the premiums over market that were paid caused the multiples to be increased. This is illustrated in Table 9.3, which covers comparable transactions. We now view the companies as targets in acquisitions. The market values are now interpreted as the transaction market prices that were paid when these companies were acquired. Before a merger transaction, the prevailing market prices of companies include some probability that they might be acquired. But when they are actually acquired, the transaction price now reflects the actual takeover event. Because takeover bids typically involve a premium over prevailing market prices, we have accordingly illustrated this in the multiples reflected in Table 9.3. We now observe that the average transaction ratios for the comparable transactions have moved up. The indicated market value of company W is now $114 as compared with $97, reflecting a premium of 17.5% over general market valuation relationships.

The practical implication of this is that if company W was going to be purchased and no comparable transactions had taken place, we would take the comparable companies approach as illustrated in Tables 9.1 and 9.2. But this would be only a starting point. There would then be some merger negotiations and probably some premium paid over prevailing market prices for the comparable companies.

In Tables 9.1 through 9.4, we have illustrated the comparable companies and comparable transactions approaches using the ratio of the market value of equity to book value, market value to sales, and the ratio of market value to the net income of the company. In some situations, other ratios might be employed in the comparable companies or comparable transactions approach. Additional ratios could include sales or revenue per employee, net income per employee, assets needed to produce $1 of sales or revenue. Note that market values are not included in the ratios just listed. The additional ratios provide information on supplementary aspects of performance of the companies. This additional information could be used for interpreting or adjusting the average multiples obtained by using the comparable companies or comparable transactions approaches. Our experience has been that in actual merger or takeover transactions, investment

**TABLE 9.3** Comparable Transactions Ratios (Company W Is Compared with Companies TA, TB, and TC)

|  | Company TA | Company TB | Company TC | Average |
|---|---|---|---|---|
| Market**/sales | 1.4X* | 1.2X | 1.0X | 1.2X |
| Market/book | 1.5X | 1.4X | 2.2X | 1.7X |
| Market/net income ≡ price/earnings ratio | 25X | 20X | 27X | 24X |

*X stands for "times."

**Market refers to the market value of equity.

**TABLE 9.4**   Application of Valuation Ratios to Company W

| Actual Recent Data for Company W | | | Average Transaction Ratios | Indicated Value of Equity |
|---|---|---|---|---|
| Sales | = | $100 | 1.2X | $120 |
| Book value of equity | = | 60 | 1.7X | 102 |
| Net income | = | 5 | 24X | 120 |
| | | | | Average = $114 |

bankers employ both the comparable companies approach and the comparable transactions approach, and develop additional comparative performance measures as well.

In the end-of-chapter exercises, we shall apply the preceding methodology to actual companies. The reader will then have the opportunity to use the methodology illustrated in Tables 9.1 through 9.4 in addition to the spreadsheet and formula valuation approaches.

## THE SPREADSHEET APPROACH TO VALUATION AND MERGERS

The spreadsheet approach makes projections of the relevant cash flows. It begins with presentations of historical data for each element of the balance sheet, the income statement, and cash flow statement. This provides the basis for a detailed financial ratio analysis to discover the financial patterns of the company. This detailed financial analysis covers data for the previous 7 to 10 years. For detailed and comprehensive illustrations of this approach, see Copeland, Koller, and Murrin (1994); see also chapter 17 in Weston and Copeland (1992). In addition to a review of the historical financial data on the company involved in a merger or takeover, the analysts compile considerable material on the business economics of the industry in which the company operates, the company's competitive position historically and prospectively into the future, and an assessment of financial patterns, strategies, and actions of its competitors—comparable companies.

Whereas the spreadsheet approach in practice involves many items of the balance sheets, income statements, and cash flow statements, the basic underlying logic builds on a basic capital budgeting analysis.

### Capital Budgeting Decisions

Capital budgeting represents the process of planning expenditures whose returns extend over a period of time. Examples of capital outlays for tangible or physical items are expenditures for land, building, and equipment. Outlays for research and development, advertising, or promotion efforts may also be regarded as investment outlays when their benefits extend over a period of years. While capital budgeting criteria are generally discussed in relation to investment in fixed assets, the concepts are equally applicable to investment in cash, receivables, or inventory, as well as M&As and other restructuring activities.

Several methods for evaluating projects have been developed. The net present value methodology is widely agreed to be the superior method for evaluation and ranking of investment proposals. The net present value (NPV) method is the present value of all future cash flows discounted at the cost of capital, minus the cost of the investments made over time compounded at the opportunity cost of funds.

All of the formal models widely used in practice reflect the basic capital budgeting net present value analysis. We shall begin by illustrating the idea of the spreadsheet approach by relating it to a basic capital budgeting NPV approach. An acquiring firm (A) has the opportunity to buy a target (T) company. The target company can be purchased for $180 million. The relevant net cash flows that will be received from the investment in the target company will be $40 million for the next 10 years after which no cash flows will be forthcoming. The relevant cost of capital for analyzing the purchase of the target is 14%. Does this acquisition represent a positive NPV project? The applicable formula for calculating the NPV is:

$$NPV = \sum_{t=1}^{n} \frac{CF_t}{(1+k)^t} - I_0$$

$$NPV = \sum_{t=1}^{10} \frac{\$40}{(1.14)^t} - \$180$$

where:

$NPV$ = net present value

$PVIFA$ = present value interest factor for an annuity

$CF_t$ = net cash flows in year $t$ (after taxes) = $40 million

$k$ = marginal cost of capital = 14%

$n$ = number of years, investment horizon = 10

$I_0$ = investment outlay in year zero = $180

We can now calculate the NPV of the acquisition.

$$NPV = \$40[PVIFA(14\%, 10 \text{ yrs.})] - \$180$$
$$= \$40(5.2161) - \$180$$
$$= \$208.644 - \$180$$
$$NPV = GPV - I_0$$
$$= \$28.644 \text{ million}$$

The present value of the cash inflows is the gross present value of the acquisition ($GPV$). From the $GPV$, the present value of the investment outlays ($I_0$) is deducted to obtain the $NPV$ of the acquisition.

From this simple illustration of the analysis of an acquisition in the framework of capital budgeting principles, we can illustrate a very significant principle. Even acquisitions that achieve synergies will be unsound if the buyer (bidder, acquirer) pays too much. For example, if the bidder paid $250 million for the target company, the $NPV$ of the acquisition would then become a negative $41.4 million.

$$NPV = \$208.644 - \$250.000$$
$$= -\$41.356 \text{ million}$$

The underlying concept that an acquisition is fundamentally a capital budgeting problem should be kept in mind even when the transactions involve great complications. Some mergers among firms have been called "marriages made in heaven." They make considerable sense from the business standpoint. The two companies blend beautifully. But if the acquirer (A) pays too much, it is a negative $NPV$ investment and the value of the bidder will decline. The market recognizes this and the event return for

A will be negative. The financial press will report, "A acquired T and as a consequence the market value of A fell by $4 billion. A paid too much."

## Spreadsheet Projections

The basic idea of the spreadsheet approach can be conveyed in a somewhat more detailed capital budgeting analysis. Company A is considering the purchase of a target company T. A detailed spreadsheet analysis of the financial statements of the target has been made. On the basis of that analysis and of all aspects of the business economics of the target's industry, the acquiring firm has made the spreadsheet projections exhibited in Table 9.5. The first row of Table 9.5 is projected sales. They start at $1,000 and are expected to grow at a 20% rate. Row 2 of the table represents the total capital that is required to support the sales levels shown in row 1. Total capital requirements consist of net working capital plus net property, plant, and equipment. For the target company, a total capital investment of 50¢ is required for each dollar of sales. This represents a capital turnover of 2, so that row 2 is 50% of the figures in row 1. Company T represents an investment opportunity in which revenues will grow at 20% for four years after which sales will level off at $2,070 as shown in Table 9.5. Because the ratio of total capital to sales remains constant when sales level off, the total capital requirement also becomes constant.

In row 3, the annual investment requirements are shown. Investment is defined as the addition to total capital made in a given year to have the total capital required to support sales in the following year. Thus, the investment of $100 made in year 0 increases the total capital of line 2 from $500 in period 0 to $600 in period 1. This simple example illustrates the economic concept that the change in total capital in a given year over the previous year defines the investment outlay.

From the historical patterns and the economic outlook, the investment bankers make the spreadsheet projections that net operating income will be 40% of total capital. This is essentially equivalent to saying that the return on net total assets is 40%. The net operating income is projected in row 4. Corporate taxes of 40% are postulated and shown in row 5. Deducting taxes paid, we obtain net operating income after taxes shown in line 6.

The reader will recognize that the column values for each row in Table 9.5 grow at a 20% rate per annum. These assumptions were made for the convenience of simplicity.

**TABLE 9.5**   Spreadsheet Projections of Company T

| | *Years in the Future* | | | | | |
|---|---|---|---|---|---|---|
| | 0 | 1 | 2 | 3 | 4 | ..... ∞ |
| 1. Sales ($S_t$) | $1,000 | $1,200 | $1,440 | $1,728 | $2,074 | .....$2,074 |
| 2. Total capital ($A_t$) | 500 | 600 | 720 | 864 | 1,037 | ..... 1,037 |
| 3. Investment ($I_t$) | 100 | 120 | 144 | 173 | 0 | ..... 0 |
| 4. Net operating income | 200 | 240 | 288 | 346 | 415 | ..... 415 |
| 5. Taxes at 40% | 80 | 96 | 115 | 138 | 166 | ..... 166 |
| 6. Net operating income after taxes | 120 | 144 | 173 | 208 | 249 | ..... 249 |

*Total capital is measured as net working capital plus net property, plant, and equipment.

One of the advantages of the spreadsheet approach is that the growth rate for each of the items listed in the rows could be different from one another and from year to year. The spreadsheet approach provides great flexibility in the projections. However, it is equally important to recognize that when one is presented with a set of projections as is done in the spreadsheet approach, it is useful to raise the question of what underlying growth patterns are illustrated by these projections? Further questions should be pursued. Are the growth rates in the projections consistent with forecasts for the economy? For the industry? For market share in relation to competitors? And so on. Although the numbers shown in Table 9.5 are quite simplified, the basic principles that are illustrated would be equally valid however complicated the numbers turn out to be in real-life applications of the spreadsheet methodology.

Given the projections in the spreadsheets reflected in Table 9.5, we can next illustrate the calculation of a value for the target beyond which the acquiring firm cannot pay if it is to earn its 10% cost of capital. Alternatively, we could say that if an acquirer pays more than the value we calculate in Table 9.6 for the target, it will be making a negative net present value investment.

Table 9.6 is a worksheet that rearranges the data from Table 9.5 to explain how free cash flows are measured. Each row is expressed in symbols that will be used throughout the book. Row 1 is before-tax cash flows $(X_t)$ taken from row 4 of Table 9.5. In row 2, the 40% tax rate $(T)$ is applied. Row 3 is after-tax cash flows $[X_t(1 - T)]$. Annual investment outlays $(I_t)$ are shown in row 4. Row 5 represents the free cash flows. When we discount the free cash flows at the applicable cost of capital $(k)$, we obtain the NPV of the acquisition because the investment outlays have been deducted year by year.

We can now develop a spreadsheet valuation of the target company by discounting the free cash flows in Table 9.6 at the applicable cost of capital of 10%. The basic NPV expression is shown in equation (9.1).

$$NPV_0 = \frac{NCF_1}{(1 + k)} + \frac{NCF_2}{(1 + k)^2} + \dots \frac{NCF_n}{(1 + k)^n} + \frac{NCF_{n+1}}{k(1 + k)^n} \quad \textbf{(9.1)}$$

$$NPV_0 = \frac{24}{(1.10)} + \frac{29}{(1.10)^2} + \frac{35}{(1.10)^3} + \frac{249}{(.10)(1.10)^3}$$

$$NPV_0 = \frac{24}{1.10} + \frac{29}{1.21} + \frac{35}{1.331} + \left(\frac{249}{.10}\right)(1.331)^{-1}$$

$$= 21.82 + 23.97 + 26.30 + 1{,}870.77$$

$$= 72.09 + 1{,}870.77 = \$1{,}942.86$$

Note that for the NPV at period 0, we discount back the net cash flows from year 1 to infinity. So, the discount factor (in equation 9.1) is to the first power for the cash

**TABLE 9.6** Valuation of the Target

|  | 1 | 2 | 3 | 4 | 5 | 6 | ...∞ |
|---|---|---|---|---|---|---|---|
| 1. Before-tax cash flows $(X_t)$ | 240 | 288 | 346 | 415 | 415 | 415 | ...415 |
| 2. Taxes at 40% $(T)$ | 96 | 115.2 | 138.4 | 166 | 166 | 166 | ...166 |
| 3. After-tax cash flows $[X_t(1 - T)]$ | 144 | 172.8 | 207.6 | 249 | 249 | 249 | ...249 |
| 4. Investments $(I_t)$ | 120 | 144 | 172.8 | | | | |
| 5. Free cash flows $[X_t(1 - T) - I_t]$ | 24 | 29 | 35 | 249 | 249 | 249 | ...249 |

flows in year 1, to the second power for the cash flows in year 2, and to the third power in the cash flows in year 3. The discount factor for the cash flows of $249 beginning in year 4 involve some subtlety related to time indexing. At the end of year 3, we now observe constant cash flows beginning in the following year and continuing to infinity. The value of the constant cash flows is obtained by dividing by the discount factor of 10%. This gives us the so-called exit value of the target firm as of the end of the third year. This value of $2,490 is discounted back for three years under the general principle that we begin discounting with next year's cash flow. This timing of the discounting of the constant cash flows to infinity is followed in the widely used formulas employed by investment bankers and consulting firms in actual applications.

From the calculations based on equation (9.1), we determine the value of the target firm. We find that a value of the target firm that would enable the acquiring firm to earn its cost of capital would be $1,943. If the acquiring firm is able to obtain the target for something less than $1,943, and if the projections are fulfilled, this would be a positive net present value investment. If the acquiring firm pays more than $1,943, it will be making a negative net present value investment and its own market value will decline.

### Brief Evaluation of the Spreadsheet Approach

An advantage of the spreadsheet approach is that it is expressed in financial statements familiar to businessmen. A second major advantage is that the data are year by year with any desired detail of individual balance sheet or income statement accounts. Judgment and flexibility can be reflected in formulating the projections.

The spreadsheet approach also has some pitfalls. The specific numbers used in the projections may create the illusion that they are the actual or the correct numbers. This is misleading. Projections are subject to error. Sometimes the bases for the projections may be obscured. A clear link is not always established between the projected numbers and the economic or business logic by which they were determined. Another limitation is that the spreadsheet may become highly complex. The advantage of including many details is also subject to the risk that the detail obscures the forces that are really important in making the projections. This is the reason that in our initial explanation of the spreadsheet approach we employed a very simple numerical example. More complex applications are developed in chapter 10 when applications are made to actual companies.

## FORMULA APPROACH

In this section, we focus on the formula approach to valuation. There is no real distinction between the spreadsheet approach and the formula approach. Both use a discounted cash flow analysis. The spreadsheet approach is expressed in the form of financial statements over a period of years. The formula approach summarizes the same data in more compact expressions. Both give the same numerical results as we shall illustrate.

Valuation formulas appear in many different shapes, sizes, and expressions. The four basic formulas are shown in Table 9.7 (derivations in Appendix A). The concepts follow from basic finance materials. They will all be illustrated in the case examples we subsequently present on valuations in acquisitions. In Table 9.8, the widely used textbook constant dividend growth model is derived from equation (9.3). Tables 9.7 and 9.8 present the formulations most widely used in practice. The leading practitioners in valuation employ these basic expressions in various guises. Their use is described in books

**TABLE 9.7** Formulas for Free Cash Flow Valuation of a Firm

No growth:

$$V_0 = \frac{X_0(1 - T)}{k} \tag{9.2}$$

Constant growth:

$$V_0 = \frac{X_0(1 - T)(1 - b)(1 + g)}{k - g} \tag{9.3}$$

Temporary supernormal growth, then no growth:

$$V_0 = X_0(1 - T)(1 - b)\sum_{t=1}^{n} \frac{(1 + g)^t}{(1 + k)^t} + \frac{X_0(1 - T)(1 + g)^{n+1}}{k(1 + k)^n} \tag{9.4}$$

Temporary supernormal growth, then constant growth:

$$V_0 = X_0(1 - T)(1 - b_s)\sum_{t=1}^{n} \frac{(1 + g_s)^t}{(1 + k)^t} + \frac{X_0(1 - T)(1 - b_c)}{k - g_c} \times \frac{(1 + g_s)^{n+1}}{(1 + k)^n} \tag{9.5}*$$

where:
- $X_0$ = the initial earnings before interest and taxes (EBIT) or net operating income (NOI)
- $T$ = the actual tax rate
- $b$ = investment per period normalized by (divided by) the after-tax EBIT
- $r$ = marginal profitability rate measured by the change in after-tax profits divided by investments
- $g$ = the growth rate in after-tax cash flows
- $n$ = the number of periods of supernormal growth
- $k$ = the applicable marginal weighted cost of capital

*In equation (9.5), the subscript $s$ indicates that the $g$ or $b$ is for the supernormal growth period; the subscript $c$ indicates that the $g$ or $b$ is for the period of constant growth.

authored by executives of well-known consulting firms. These include McKinsey & Company's *Valuation* by Copeland, Koller, and Murrin (2nd edition, 1994) and an exposition of what the consulting firm ALCAR does, which is described in Alfred Rappaport's *Creating Shareholder Value* (1986). The ways in which Stern Stewart & Co. use the basic valuation formulas were first presented by Joel Stern (1974) and further elaborated by G. Bennett Stewart in his book *The Quest for Value* (1991).

As we shall demonstrate in Appendix B to this chapter, these different approaches define their symbols somewhat differently. Their valuation expressions look different but by specific examples we shall demonstrate that they all give the same numerical results.[1]

## The Basic Formula

In this section we set forth the formula for valuing free cash flows growing at a supernormal growth rate for a period of years followed by no growth. We use the data from Table 9.6, which illustrated the spreadsheet approach. We will evaluate the same data

[1]The different formulations all owe their intellectual basis to two academic articles: Miller and Modigliani (1961) and Malkiel (1963).

**TABLE 9.8**   Constant Dividend Growth Valuation Model

Start with equation (9.3):

$$V_0 = \frac{X_0(1-T)(1-b)(1+g)}{k-g} \qquad\qquad (9.3)$$

If no debt: $V_0 = S_0$, the market value of shareholders' equity, $k$ is the cost of equity $k_s$, so we have:

$$S_0 = \frac{X_0(1-T)(1-b)(1+g)}{k_s-g} \qquad \text{Substitute } NI_0 \text{ for } X_0(1-T)$$

$$S_0 = \frac{NI_0(1-\text{``}b\text{''})(1+g)}{k_s-g} \qquad NI_0 = \text{initial value of net income} \qquad (9.6)$$

where:

"$b$" = retention rate or ratio of investment to net income

$$\text{``}b\text{''} = \frac{NI - \text{Div}}{NI} \qquad\qquad \text{Divide through by } NI \text{ and subtract 1 from each side}$$

$$(1-\text{``}b\text{''}) = 1 - \left(1 - \frac{\text{Div}}{NI}\right) \qquad \text{Rearrange and remove parentheses}$$

$$(1-\text{``}b\text{''}) = \frac{\text{Div}}{NI} = \text{Payout ratio} \qquad \text{Multiply both sides by } NI$$

$$NI(1-\text{``}b\text{''}) = (NI)\left(\frac{\text{Div}}{NI}\right) \text{ Hence} \qquad \text{Substitute in (9.6)}$$

$$S_0 = \frac{\text{Div}_0(1+g)}{k_s-g} = \frac{D_1}{k_s-g} \qquad \text{Equation (9.6) in dividend form} \qquad (9.6a)$$

$$P_0 = \frac{d_1}{k_s-g} \qquad\qquad \text{Equation (9.6a) on a per share basis}$$

where:
$P_0 = $ price per share
$d_1 = $ next period dividend per share

using the equation (9.4) formula to demonstrate that we obtain exactly the same numerical result. The widely used equation (9.4) for free cash flows has a period of supernormal growth followed by no growth as repeated below.

$$V_0 = X_0(1-T)(1-b)\sum_{t=1}^{n}\left(\frac{1+g}{1+k}\right)^t + \frac{X_0(1-T)(1+g)}{k} \times \frac{(1+g)^n}{(1+k)^n} \qquad (9.4)$$

where the symbols are identified along with their Table 9.6 values.

$X_0 = $ the initial EBIT or NOI = \$200

$T = $ the actual tax rate = 0.4

$b = $ investment per period normalized by (divided by) the after-tax EBIT or NOI or
$b = I_t/[X_0(1-T)] = 120/144 = 0.833$

$r$ = marginal profitability rate measured by the change in after-tax profits divided by investments or $r = [X_{t+1}(1-T) - X_t(1-T)]/I_t = (172.8 - 144)/120 = 0.24$

$g$ = the growth rate in after-tax cash flows or $g = (X_{t+1} - X_t)/X_t = (172.8 - 144)/144 =$

0.20 or $g = br = (0.833)(0.24) = 0.20$, Note: $\dfrac{(X_{t+1} - X_t)(1-T)}{X_t(1-T)} \cdot \dfrac{I_t}{I_t} =$

$\dfrac{(X_{t+1} - X_t)(1-T)}{I_t} \cdot \dfrac{I_t}{X_t(1-T)} = rb = g$

$n$ = the number of periods of supernormal growth = 3

$k$ = the applicable marginal weighted cost of capital = 0.10

Using these data from Table 9.6, we obtain the values for each of the symbols that we included in the definition list. We insert these as shown in equation (9.4a).

$$V_0 = 200(0.6)(0.16667)(1.09091)\left[\frac{(1.09091)^3 - 1}{0.09091}\right] + \frac{120}{.1}(1.09091)^3(1.2)$$

**(9.4a)**

The resulting value is $1,942. Recall that when we performed a discounted cash flow (DCF) analysis on the spreadsheet data in Table 9.6, we had obtained a value of $1,942.86. This illustrates that we obtain the same result using the spreadsheet approach as we have just obtained using the formula set forth in equation (9.4). The two approaches are complementary. The spreadsheet approach allows flexibility in making projections on a year-by-year basis. The formula approach helps us focus on the underlying elements or drivers that determine value.

We can illustrate the power of the formula approach by considering a more complex case example. The Rowe Company is analyzing the purchase of the Colema Company. Rowe has calculated the following values for the key value drivers that determine the value of Colema. What is the maximum that Rowe could pay for Colema to earn at least its 15% cost of capital? Here are the value drivers that Rowe has calculated.

$X_0$ = $600,000 = NOI = EBIT
$T$ = 0.40     = actual tax rate
$b$ = 0.50     = ratio of net investment to after-tax EBIT
$g$ = 0.10     = rate of supernormal growth
$n$ = 5        = years of supernormal growth
$k$ = 0.15     = cost of capital

Note that we did not supply $r$, the marginal profitability rate. It is implied by the relationship $g = br$. Because we have $b$ and $g$, $r$ can be calculated as 0.20. Again, we use the model shown in equation (9.4). The calculations could be performed using the diskette provided with the text. To have a better understanding of the computer calculations, we will work through the valuation step by step. We will let the term $(1+g)/(1+k) = (1+h)$, which for the numbers of our example will be:

$$(1+g)/(1+k) = (1+h) = (1.10)/(1.15) = 0.9565$$

We can now put numbers in equation (9.4). The initial expression is equation (9.4b).

$$V_0 = \left[ \$600(0.6)(0.5)(0.9565)\left[ \frac{(0.9565)^5 - 1}{-0.0435} \right] + \frac{600(0.6)}{0.15}(0.800617)(1.1) \right]10^3$$

$$= [180(0.9565)(4.5835) + 2,400(0.800617)(1.1)]10^3 \qquad \textbf{(9.4b)}$$

$$= 789,141 + 2,113,629$$

$$= \$2,902,770$$

The reason for the extra $(1 + h)$ in the first term is that the sum of an annuity expression is based on growth for $(n - 1)$ periods. Because equation (9.1) is for $n$ periods of super-normal growth, we need an extra $(1 + h)$ where $(1 + h) = (1 + g)/(1 + k)$. The rest are straightforward calculations arriving at $2,902,770.

So, based on the initial inputs, the value of Colema is $2,902,770. One of the values of the formula method can now be demonstrated. The value drivers utilized by Rowe in placing a value on Colema were based on the best judgments or projections the senior vice president of acquisitions of the Rowe Company could make. But he is also interested in analyzing what the effects on the price that could be paid for Colema are if his best estimates of the key value drivers have to be altered. Accordingly, in Table 9.9, a sensitivity analysis is made of the results of varying the value drivers.

From Table 9.9, we can see that when $r$ exceeds $k$ an increase in investment requirements or opportunities will greatly increase value. Line 1 is the initial case. While the value of profitability, $r$, was not given, because $g = br$ the value of $r$ can be obtained by dividing $g$ by $b$. In the base case shown in line 1 of the solution, the valuation is $2.9 million. In line 2, we observe that the investment requirements or opportunities have doubled. Because profitability exceeds the cost of capital, this causes the valuation to increase and it moves up to $3.6 million. Note that in line 2 the $(1 - b)$ expression in

**TABLE 9.9**   Sensitivity Analysis of Varying the Value Drivers

| | $k$ | $b$ | $r$ | $g$ | $n$ | $T$ | Valuation | 2nd Term as % of Total |
|---|---|---|---|---|---|---|---|---|
| Initial Case | | | | | | | | |
| 1) | .15 | .50 | .20 | .10 | 5 | .40 | 2,902,770 | 73 |
| Change $b$, $g$, and $r$: | | | | | | | | |
| 2) | .15 | 1.0 | .20 | .20 | 5 | .40 | 3,562,948 | 100 |
| 3) | .15 | 1.0 | .30 | .30 | 5 | .40 | 5,759,465 | 100 |
| 4) | .15 | 1.5 | .20 | .30 | 5 | .40 | 4,439,733 | 130 |
| Back to initial case, but vary $k$: | | | | | | | | |
| 5) | .13 | .50 | .20 | .10 | 5 | .40 | 3,493,511 | 76 |
| 6) | .17 | .50 | .20 | .10 | 5 | .40 | 2,461,903 | 70 |
| Back to initial case, but vary $n$: | | | | | | | | |
| 7) | .15 | .50 | .20 | .10 | 4 | .40 | 2,855,023 | 77 |
| 8) | .15 | .50 | .20 | .10 | 6 | .40 | 2,949,019 | 69 |
| Back to initial case, but vary $T$: | | | | | | | | |
| 9) | .15 | .50 | .20 | .10 | 5 | .38 | 2,999,834 | 73 |
| 10) | .15 | .50 | .20 | .10 | 5 | .42 | 2,806,296 | 73 |

the first term of equation (9.4) becomes zero so that the entire first term becomes zero. Nevertheless, the valuation increases by a substantial amount. This is because the higher $b$ results in a higher $g$. Hence, the level of free cash flow at the beginning of the no-further-growth period is much higher than in the initial case. In line 3, profitability increases. This causes growth to increase as well. The valuation rises to $5.8 million. In line 4, profitability returns to its previous level but investment requirements increase further. Hence, growth in line 4 is greater than in line 2 and valuation increases from $3.6 million to $4.4 million. In lines 5 and 6, we return to the initial case but vary $k$, the cost of capital. When we reduce the cost of capital, valuation rises from $2.9 million to $3.5 million (line 5). When we increase the cost of capital, the valuation falls (line 6). Valuation is found to be very sensitive to variations in the cost of capital.

We then again return to the initial case but vary $n$, the number of periods of growth. We obtain the readily predictable results in lines 7 and 8. When the period of supernormal growth is reduced in line 7, valuation is reduced, compared to the initial case in line 1. When the period of supernormal growth is increased in line 8, valuation is increased.

In lines 9 and 10, we vary the tax rate. Again, the results are readily predictable. When the tax rate is reduced, valuation is increased compared to the initial case in line 1. When the tax rate is increased, the valuation is reduced.

## Temporary Growth Followed by Constant Growth

As another form of sensitivity analysis we also consider the effects of making alternative assumptions about what happens to free cash flows after the period of supernormal growth. Because we now have a period of supernormal growth and a period of constant growth, we need to subscript some of the symbols. The subscript $s$ refers to what is taking place during the period of supernormal growth. The subscript $c$ refers to the period of constant growth. Because this is another widely used formula by practitioners, we need not elaborate its explanation but apply it. The use of equation (9.5) is reflected in Table 9.10. In this table we perform a sensitivity analysis using equation (9.5).

Temporary supernormal growth, then constant growth:

$$V_0 = X_0(1-T)(1-b_s)\sum_{t=1}^{n}\frac{(1+g_s)^t}{(1+k)^t} + \frac{X_0(1-T)(1-b_c)(1+g_c)}{(k-g_c)} \times \frac{(1+g_s)^n}{(1+k)^n}$$

$$(9.5)$$

### TABLE 9.10 Temporary Supernormal Growth, Then Constant Growth

| | $b_c$ | $r_c$ | $g_c$ | Valuation | 2nd Term as % of Total |
|---|---|---|---|---|---|
| 1) | .20 | .17 | .034 | 2,975,957 | 73 |
| 2) | .10 | .16 | .016 | 2,918,840 | 73 |
| 3) | .30 | .17 | .051 | 3,031,179 | 74 |
| 4) | .40 | .18 | .072 | 3,228,276 | 76 |
| 5) | .50 | .17 | .085 | 3,228,276 | 76 |
| 6) | .60 | .17 | .102 | 3,431,533 | 77 |

All inputs same as initial case in Table 9.9, plus new inputs, $b_c$, $r_c$, and $g_c$.

We focus on the key value drivers *b*, *r*, and *g*. We have to make a distinction between their values during the period of supernormal growth by using the subscript *s* and their values during the period of constant growth by using the subscript *c*.

Lines 1 to 6 illustrate that combining different levels of investment requirements with different levels of profitability produces a resulting range of constant growth factors. It is clear from the results that the higher the constant rate of growth the higher the resulting valuation.

It will be noted that in both Tables 9.9 and 9.10, the second term in the valuation model represents the higher proportion of the valuation. This is true in many practical cases. This should alert those who are performing the valuation to be quite careful as to the assumptions made about the factors that affect so-called exit or terminal values.

# COST OF CAPITAL MEASUREMENT

In the valuation calculations to this point we have explained the measurement of all the value drivers except *k*, the cost of capital. This we will do in the present section. Several steps are involved: (1) estimate the cost of equity capital, (2) calculate the cost of debt, (3) formulate the applicable financial structure or financial proportions for the firm, (4) apply the applicable financial proportions to the cost of equity capital and to the cost of debt, (5) the result is the weighted cost of capital. The above procedure provides us with a weighted marginal cost of capital.

Four approaches could be employed in developing an estimate of the cost of equity:

1. Capital asset pricing model (CAPM)
2. Bond yield plus equity risk premium
3. Investor's average realized yield
4. Dividend growth model

To make the discussion more meaningful, we shall make a concrete application to one of the major food companies, ConAgra.

## Capital Asset Pricing Model (CAPM)

The basic CAPM equation is:

$$k_s = R_f + [\overline{R}_M - R_f]\beta_j \tag{9.7}$$

where:

$$R_f = \text{risk-free rate}$$
$$\overline{R}_M - R_f = \text{long-term average market price of risk}$$
$$\beta_j = \text{the systematic risk of the individual asset or firm}$$
$$k_s = \text{the cost of equity capital}$$

We need to obtain estimates for each term on the right-hand side of the equation.

Many alternative approaches can be used to estimate the risk-free rate. The general practice now is to use the yield to maturity on 10-year government securities. The advantage of this is that with government securities default risk is relatively low. Using the medium-term maturity avoids the sharp fluctuations in shorter-term government securities. In addition, 10 years is a reasonable time horizon for which to make estimates of the cost of equity capital. For this analysis, we used 7%.

The next parameter we need to estimate is $(\overline{R}_M - R_f)$. This difference between the return on the market and the risk-free rate represents the average market price of risk. A number of sources have estimated this parameter, on average, over a period of years to be in the range of 6.5 to 8.5 percentage points. For our analysis, it is reasonable to use 7.5%.

A number of financial services supply estimates of beta for individual companies. Most sources set a beta of something over 1 for ConAgra in the time period under analysis. We employ a beta of 1.10.

Utilizing the numerical values for each of the terms on the right-hand side of equation (9.7), we obtain a numerical value shown in equation (9.7a).

$$k_s = 7\% + 7.5\%(1.10) = 15.25\% \tag{9.7a}$$

This gives an estimate of the cost of equity for ConAgra of 15.25%.

The arbitrage pricing theory (APT) holds that security returns depend not directly on the market return, but on other fundamental factors. The APT has also been used to estimate the cost of capital. Four macroeconomic factors have been found to be correlated with returns on portfolios that mimic the underlying factors. They are (1) the growth rate of industrial production, (2) a default risk premium measured by the differences in promised yields on long-term government bonds versus Baa corporate bonds, (3) the slope of the yield curve as measured by differences in promised yields on long-term versus short-term government bonds, and (4) the rate of unanticipated inflation. These four factors represent plausible economic influences. Stock prices are the present values of expected future cash flows. The first variable is related to profitability; the other three are related to the discount rate.

Several consulting firms provide estimates of the cost of capital based on the APT rather than on the CAPM. This is an additional useful information input. But the cost of capital cannot usually be determined by quantitative procedures alone. An understanding of the underlying business economics of the industry and firm is required to develop an informed judgment of the applicable cost of capital for equity funds.

### Equity Risk Premium over Debt Yield

The logic of this estimate is that on average the cost of equity should exceed the cost of debt, because equity is junior in priority to debt. The procedure is to analyze the historical yield shareholders require for equity as compared with the average yield to maturity on the firm's bonds. Because ConAgra's long-term debt is rated Baa, we can use a yield to maturity, 8.2%, as an estimate of its cost of debt. Historical data suggest that the average equity risk premium over debt yield for ConAgra is about 350 basis points. These numerical values can be used to obtain an estimate of the cost of equity for ConAgra of 11.7%.

$$k_s = 8.2\% + 3.5\% = 11.7\%$$

### Investor's Average Realized Yield

Another approach is to use what investors historically have required as their return on investment in this company or in this industry. This yield can be calculated on a market basis or on accounting returns. Data for both these measures are shown for ConAgra in Table 9.11.

The accounting return has trended slightly downward with an unweighted average of 17.2%, a weighted average of about 16.1%. Market returns over the previous decade have averaged between these two averages at 16.7%. Of course, market measures are the most meaningful so this approach suggests that investors on average have expected about a 16.7% average annual return from holding the equity of ConAgra.

**TABLE 9.11**   Shareholder Realized Returns—ConAgra, Inc.

| | MARKET RETURNS | | | | | | ACCOUNTING RETURNS | | |
|---|---|---|---|---|---|---|---|---|---|
| | *(1)* | *(2)* | *(3)* | *(4)* | *(5)* | *(6)* | *(7)* | *(8)* | *(9)* |
| Year | *High Price* | *Low Price* | *Average Price* | *Price Change (%)* | *Dividend Yield (%)* | *Total Yield (%)* | *Net Income* | *SHE ($ Million)* | *Return (%)* |
| 1986 | 14.250 | 8.625 | 11.438 | | 2.1 | | 148.7 | 736 | 20.2 |
| 1987 | 16.875 | 9.333 | 13.104 | 14.6 | 2.0 | 16.6 | 154.7 | 824 | 18.8 |
| 1988 | 15.125 | 10.500 | 12.813 | −2.2 | 2.4 | 0.2 | 197.9 | 958 | 20.7 |
| 1989 | 20.125 | 12.875 | 16.500 | 28.8 | 2.2 | 31.0 | 231.7 | 1,098 | 21.1 |
| 1990 | 25.500 | 15.125 | 20.313 | 23.1 | 2.0 | 25.1 | 311.2 | 2,173 | 14.3 |
| 1991 | 36.250 | 22.250 | 29.250 | 44.0 | 1.6 | 45.6 | 372.4 | 2,588 | 14.4 |
| 1992 | 35.750 | 24.500 | 30.125 | 3.0 | 1.9 | 4.9 | 270.3 | 2,410 | 11.2 |
| 1993 | 33.625 | 22.750 | 28.188 | −6.4 | 2.3 | −4.1 | 437.1 | 2,583 | 16.9 |
| 1994 | 33.125 | 25.500 | 29.313 | 4.0 | 2.8 | 6.8 | 495.6 | 2,850 | 17.4 |
| 1995 | 41.750 | 29.750 | 35.750 | 22.0 | 2.4 | 24.4 | | | |
| *Unweighted Average:* | | | | | | 16.7 | | | 17.2 |
| *Weighted Average:* | | | | | | | | | 16.1 |

*Source: Moody's Handbook of Common Stocks,* Spring 1996.

## Dividend Growth Model

This approach estimates the cost of capital by using the constant-growth dividend valuation model derived in Table 9.8 as equation (9.6).

$$S_0 = \frac{D_1}{k_s - g} \tag{9.6}$$

A number of assumptions underlying the dividend valuation model should be noted to understand how it may be used to estimate the required return on equity for a firm. The growth rate, $g$, refers to the growth in dividends. The model requires constant growth that continues through infinity.

The logic of the model indicates that $g$ refers to the growth rate in dividends, but under the assumptions of the model everything else also grows at the same rate. If dividends grow at 10%, and the payout ratio (or equivalently the retention rate) and financial leverage ratio are constant, earnings and total assets of the firm must also be growing at a 10% rate. And over time, the value of the firm and the price of its common stock will be growing at a rate of 10% as well. There are interdependencies between $S_0$, the value of the equity, and the growth rate in earnings, dividends, and the total assets of the firm. Thus, the model does not provide an unambiguous basis for estimating $k_s$.

Nevertheless, the dividend valuation model is widely used in practice, both for valuing common stock and for estimating the cost of equity capital. In estimating the cost of equity capital, the valuation expression is solved for $k_s$ as shown in equation (9.8).

$$k_s = \frac{D_1}{S_0} + g \tag{9.8}$$

Equation (9.8) states that the required return on equity is the expected dividend yield plus the expected growth rate in dividends. The expected dividend is obtained by taking the current dividend, $D_0$, and applying the expected growth rate. It is difficult to arrive at a reliable figure for the expected growth rate. One approach is to begin with the growth over a previous period. But the position of the firm is likely to be affected by developments in the economy as a whole as well as in its own industry. One intractable problem is that the model calls for the growth rate to infinity. But no growth rate to infinity for an individual firm can exceed the growth rate of the economy as a whole or the firm would exceed the size of the economy at some point in the future. Thus, the most plausible valuation formula has a period of supernormal growth followed by no growth in excess of normal growth in the economy reflected in the discount rate.

Nevertheless, various financial services provide estimates of expected growth in earnings and dividends for individual firms. By a combination of these forecasts we arrive at an expected growth rate in dividends for ConAgra of 13%. We estimate the expected dividend yield at 2.6% to obtain a 15.6% estimate of the required return on equity.

Summarizing thus far, we have the following results for the four methods:

1. CAPM—15.25%
2. Bond yield plus equity risk premium—11.7%
3. Realized investor yield—16.7%
4. Dividend growth model—15.6%

Thus, three of the four measures of ConAgra's cost of equity capital are in the 15 to 16% range. We would also want to make comparisons of cost of equity estimates for other firms in the food processing industry. We shall begin with a cost of equity capital of ConAgra of 15%.

## Cost of Debt

The cost of debt should be on an after-tax basis because interest payments are tax deductible. Therefore, the cost of debt capital is calculated as follows:

$$k_b(1 - T) = \text{after-tax cost of debt}$$

Here $T$ is the corporate tax rate used previously. Thus, if the before-tax cost of debt were 10% and the firm's effective corporate tax rate were 40%, the after-tax cost of debt would be 6%.

We start with the firm's before-tax cost of debt and multiply it by the $(1 - T)$ factor to obtain the relevant after-tax cost. How do we obtain the before-tax cost of debt in practice for an actual firm? Two main procedures may be used: (1) We can look in any of the investment manuals to determine the rating of the firm's outstanding publicly held bonds. Various government agencies and investment banking firms periodically publish promised yields to maturity of debt issues by rating categories. (2) We can take a weighted average of the yield to maturity for all the firm's publicly traded bonds.

We shall use an estimate of 8.4% for the before-tax cost of debt for ConAgra based on the Baa rating of its long-term debt. Its after-tax cost of debt, using a tax rate of 40%, would be 5.04%.

## Cost of Preferred Stock

Preferred stock is a hybrid between debt and common stock. Like debt, preferred stock carries a fixed commitment on the part of the corporation to make periodic payments; in liquidation, the claims of the preferred stockholders take precedence over those of the common stockholders. However, failure to make the preferred dividend payments does not result in default as nonpayment of interest on bonds does. Thus, to the firm, preferred stock is somewhat less risky than common stock but riskier than bonds. To the investor, preferred stock is also less risky than common but riskier than bonds.

From the standpoint of the issuing firm, preferred stock has the disadvantage that its dividend is not deductible for tax purposes. On the other hand, the tax law provides that a high percent of all dividends received by one corporation from another is not taxable. This dividend exclusion makes preferred stock a potentially attractive investment to other corporations. This attractiveness on the demand side pushes the yields on preferred stock to slightly below yields on bonds of similar companies. Although preferred issues may be callable and may be retired, most are perpetuities. If the preferred issue is a perpetuity, then its yield is calculated as follows:

$$\text{Preferred yield} = \frac{\text{Preferred dividend}}{\text{Price of preferred stock}} = \frac{d_{ps}}{p_{ps}} \tag{9.9}$$

## The Marginal Cost of Capital

We now have estimates of all of the costs of the individual components in financing. We next consider how we can pull all of this information together to calculate the weighted average marginal cost of capital for ConAgra as a whole, an expression that is referred to as WACC or MCC.

The cost of capital, $k$, is a weighted average of the marginal costs of its equity, debt, and preferred stock. Because ConAgra has a negligible amount of preferred stock, we will consider only equity and debt. The relevant formula is shown in equation (9.10).

$$k = k_b(1 - T)(B/V) + k_s(S/V) \tag{9.10}$$

Recall that:

 $B$ = market value of debt

 $S$ = market value of shareholders' equity

 $V$ = total market value of the firm

We had calculated the cost of debt for ConAgra at 8.4%. Initially we shall use the cost of equity of 15%. At book values ConAgra has about equal proportions of debt and equity. We feel that market values are more relevant. At market values ConAgra's debt to total firm values is about 30%. But in our judgment target debt proportions higher than 30% should also be considered. Accordingly, we calculate the weighted cost of capital for ConAgra at debt and equity proportions of the total value of the firm over a range of debt to value factors from 50 to 30% as shown in Table 9.12. The weighted cost of capital in Table 9.12, shown for alternative capital structure proportions, ranges from about 10 to 12%. In illustrating alternative approaches to valuation in the

**TABLE 9.12** Alternative Cost of Capital Estimates, ConAgra, Inc.

| Proportion debt/value | After-Tax Cost | Weighted Cost | | |
|---|---|---|---|---|
| | | 50% | 40% | 30% |
| Debt | 5.04% | 2.52% | 2.02% | 1.51% |
| Equity | 15.00% | 7.50% | 9.00% | 10.50% |
| Weighted cost of capital | | 10.02% | 11.02% | 12.01% |

preceding sections, we used an estimate of the cost of capital of 11%, which falls between the range of values depicted in Table 9.12. However, in a sensitivity analysis of the valuation of a specific company, it is useful to consider the effects of using a range of estimates of the weighted cost of capital as we have demonstrated. In doing this, we should be guided by estimates of cost of capital for comparable companies and for comparable transactions (cf. Kaplan and Ruback, 1995).

## THE INFLUENCE OF INFLATION

In teaching these valuation materials to students and businessmen from developing or emerging countries, the subject of inflation invariably is addressed. They point out that they experience annual inflation rates of 10 to 20% or more per annum. The question is raised of how inflation affects the valuation of companies involved in mergers and takeovers.

We demonstrate this by using the valuation formula (9.4) for temporary supernormal growth followed by no growth, assuming no significant price increases. We arrange the terms somewhat differently to facilitate our demonstration of the impact of inflation.

This is an especially significant question for countries in which the inflation rate per annum is at the two-digit levels and above. We begin with the valuation formula for temporary supernormal growth followed by (equilibrium) no growth without appreciable price increases.

$$V_0 = X_0(1-T)(1-b)\sum_{t=1}^{n}\left(\frac{1+g}{1+k}\right)^t + \frac{X_0(1-T)(1+g)}{k} \times \frac{(1+g)^n}{(1+k)^n} \quad \textbf{(9.4)}$$

We can now write the corresponding formula including inflation in equation (9.11).

$$V_0 = X_0(1-T)(1-b)\sum_{t=1}^{n}\left(\frac{1+g^*}{1+k^*}\right)^t + \frac{X_0(1-T)(1+g^*)^{n+1}}{(k^*-p)(1+k^*)^n} \quad \textbf{(9.11)}$$

where:

$p$ is the inflation rate
$g^*$ is equal to $(1+g)(1+p)-1$
$k^*$ is equal to $(1+k)(1+p)-1$

To give meaning to these general expressions, we present a numerical example. In example (1), we will go from calculations in real terms to calculations in nominal terms. We postulate the following values for the value drivers.

**EXAMPLE 1. INITIAL CASE WITH NO INFLATION**

$X = \$1,000$
$T = 30\%$
$b = 50\%$
$N = 10$
$r = 40\%$
$k = 8.0000\%$
Growth $g = br = 20.00\%$
$(1+h) = (1+g)/(1+k) = 111.11\%$

Using formula (9.4), which is equivalent to equation (9.11) with $p$ equal to zero, the numerical results would be as shown in equation (9.11a).

| | 1st Term | 2nd Term | Total | |
|---|---|---|---|---|
| $V_0 =$ | \$6,538 | \$30,114 | \$36,652 | **(9.11a)** |

We now assume an inflation rate of 3% to demonstrate that the results work for even moderate amounts of inflation. The values of $g$ and $k$ become:

$$g^* \text{ (nominal growth)} = (1 + g)(1 + p) - 1 = 23.60\%$$

$$k^* \text{ (nominal COC)} = (1 + k)(1 + p) - 1 = 11.24\%$$

We now use equation (9.11) to obtain the results shown in equation (9.11b).

***Model Output***

| | 1st Term | 2nd Term | Total | |
|---|---|---|---|---|
| $V_0 =$ | \$6,538 | \$30,114 | \$36,652 | **(9.11b)** |

Alternatively, we could start from the nominal expression, convert to the real expression, and again obtain the same results.

It is not surprising that we get identical results. From an economic standpoint, the current price of a stock or the current value of a company already takes into account the expected rate of inflation. The market has already reflected the expected future rate of inflation in the pricing processes.

The intuition of the mathematics of the formula is also quite straightforward. Equation (9.11) has the average inflation rate ($p$) built into it. It is obtained by changing every $g$ and $k$ in equation (9.4) from real terms to nominal terms by multiplying each term in equation (9.4) containing $g$ or $k$ by $(1 + p)$. The $k$ in the denominator of the second term becomes $k(1 + p)$. By adding and subtracting 1 and $p$ to $k(1 + p)$ and rearranging terms, we obtain $(1 + k)(1 + p) - 1 - p$, which is equal to $(k^* - p)$.

Because we have established that equations (9.4) and (9.11) give the same results, we can drop the asterisks on $k^*$ and $g^*$ because all the value drivers will be in nominal terms. In addition, we will modify equation (9.11) to take account of the additional investments required under inflation. Equation (9.11) is based on the original Miller and Modigliani (1961) article, which was based on the assumption that investment requirements were equal to the amount of funds available from depreciation. In an inflationary environment, replacement investment must (in nominal dollars) be greater than the amount of depreciation as each of the elements in the balance sheet and income statement grow with inflation. As a consequence, we need to add another element in the second term of equation (9.11) so that it becomes equation (9.12).

$$V_0 = X_0(1 - T)(1 - b) \sum_{t=1}^{n} \frac{(1 + g)^t}{(1 + k)^t} + \frac{X_0(1 - T)(1 + g)(1 - z)}{(k - p)} \frac{(1 + g)^n}{(1 + k)^n}$$

**(9.12)**

In equation (9.12), $z$ is defined as the additional investment requirement caused by inflation. We have separated the second term in equation (9.12) into two parts. The first part now looks like the standard constant growth formula. The $p$ substitutes for $g$ where all growth results from inflation. The $z$ takes the place of the $b$ where investment requirements would be zero in real terms, but in nominal terms reflects the greater nominal investment per annum due to inflation. This is the most general form of the temporary supernormal growth followed by constant real growth equation. This general expression can be used for the valuation of companies in an inflationary economy. We have eliminated the asterisks because the analysis is in nominal terms and all expressions are understood to include the role of inflation, if it is present. For companies in the United States where inflation rates have been quite low in recent years, $p$ and $z$ would be so small they can be treated as zero. The $(k - p)$ term becomes $k$ and the $(1 - z)$ term becomes 1 so we would have equation (9.4) as a special case of equation (9.12).

The above results are dependent on the postulate that the structures of prices and costs under inflation do not change. This in turn implies that there is perfect indexing of all prices and costs by the expected inflation rate, which is known to all. But there are a number of real life practical problems. First, when a high rate of inflation is under way, it becomes very difficult to predict what the actual rates of inflation in prices and costs are going to be. Second, relative price and cost structures do change under inflation. This is one of the real costs of inflation. Third, different stakeholders are affected unequally. Fundamental questions of equity and social justice become very important. A high rate of inflation threatens political and social stability. Each type of stakeholder seeks to protect its position.

It is because the structure of prices and costs changes that inflation makes valuation difficult and uncertain. This is not the fault or defect of the formula approach. Similar difficulties would arise in using a spreadsheet or comparable companies approach. When the structure of prices and costs changes, valuation depends heavily on expectations of how changes in the structure of prices and costs will affect individual firms and individual types of stakeholders. But if the structure of prices and costs were to remain unchanged, as with perfect indexing, the valuation formulas with inflation can be developed as shown in equation (9.12).

## APPLICATIONS

We have now developed all the methodology required for valuation analysis. We illustrated their nature and use. In the following chapter, we show their applications in a number of different settings related to actual merger and acquisition case examples.

--------------------------------------------------------------------------------

## Questions

9.1  How are mergers and acquisitions related to capital budgeting?

9.2  List four methods of valuation and briefly set forth the advantages and limitations of each.

9.3  What is the difference between gross basis and net basis cash flows?

9.4  How are the following valuation parameters related to each other? How do they affect the general free cash flow valuation model?
Sales
Total capital
Investment
Net operating income
Profitability rate
Growth rate

9.5 The following are three expressions for calculating total firm value that you are likely to encounter:

1. $$V_0 = X_0(1+g)(1-T)\frac{(1-b)}{(1+k)}\sum_{t=1}^{n}\left[\frac{1+g}{1+k}\right]^{t-1} + \frac{X_0(1-T)(1+g)}{k}\left[\frac{1+g}{1+k}\right]^{n}$$

2. $$V_0 = \frac{NOI_1(1-T)}{WACC} + \frac{NOI_1(1-T)b(r-WACC)}{WACC(1+g)}\sum_{t=1}^{n}\left(\frac{1+g}{1+WACC}\right)^{t}$$

3. $$V_0 = \frac{X_0(1-T)(1+g)}{k}\left[1 + \frac{b(r-k)}{g-k}\left[\left[\frac{1+g}{1+k}\right]^{n} - 1\right]\right]$$

where:

$X_0 = EBIT_0 = NOI_0 = \$100{,}000{,}000$
$T$ = the relevant tax rate = 0.4
$b$ = the investment rate = 0.6
$r$ = the profitability rate on new investment = 0.48
$k = WACC$ = the relevant weighted average cost of capital = 0.12
$n$ = the number of years of supernormal growth (after which there is no growth) = 10

a. For the data given, calculate total firm values by each formula.
b. Are there differences in the amounts you obtain by the use of each formula?

## References


Copeland, Tom, Tim Koller, and Jack Murrin, *Valuation: Measuring and Managing the Value of Companies,* 2nd ed., New York: John Wiley & Sons, 1994.

Cornell, Bradford, *Corporate Valuation,* Homewood, IL: Business One Irwin, 1993.

Kaplan, Steven N., and Richard S. Ruback, "The Valuation of Cash Flow Forecasts: An Empirical Analysis," *Journal of Finance,* 50, September 1995, pp. 1059–1093.

Malkiel, Burton G., "Equity Yields, Growth, and the Structure of Share Prices," *American Economic Review,* 53, December 1963, pp. 1004–1031.

Miller, Merton H., and Franco Modigliani, "Dividend Policy, Growth, and the Valuation of Shares," *Journal of Business,* 34, October 1961, pp. 411–433.

*Moody's Handbook of Common Stocks,* Spring 1996.

Rappaport, Alfred, *Creating Shareholder Value,* New York: The Free Press, 1986.

Stern, Joel M., "Earnings Per Share Don't Count," *Financial Analysts Journal,* 30, July–August 1974, pp. 39–40, 42–43, 67–75.

Stewart, G. Bennett, *The Quest for Value,* New York: HarperBusiness, 1991.

Weston, J. Fred, and Thomas E. Copeland, *Managerial Finance,* 9th ed., Fort Worth, TX: The Dryden Press, 1992.

# Derivation
# of Valuation Formulas

We present a derivation of the free cash flow basis for valuation. It has its roots in a generalization of the basic capital budgeting equation. We develop four basic models, but we could easily derive many other variants reflecting any range of assumptions postulated for analysis. There are four basic models:

1. No growth
2. Constant growth
3. Supernormal growth followed by no growth
4. Supernormal growth followed by constant growth

We start with equation (A9.1).

$$V_0 = \frac{X_1(1-T) - I_1}{(1+k)} + \frac{X_2(1-T) - I_2}{(1+k)^2} + \cdots + \frac{X_n(1-T) - I_n}{(1+k)^n} \quad \textbf{(A9.1)}$$

Equation (A9.1) is a general capital budgeting expression. The symbols have all been defined in chapter 9. Because $b$ equals $I_t/X_t(1-T)$, we can write $I_t = bX_t(1-T)$. We substitute this expression into (A9.1) to obtain (A9.2):

$$V_0 = \frac{X_1(1-T) - bX_1(1-T)}{(1+k)} + \frac{X_2(1-T) - bX_2(1-T)}{(1+k)^2}$$
$$+ \cdots + \frac{X_n(1-T) - bX_n(1-T)}{(1+k)^n} \quad \textbf{(A9.2)}$$

The initial $X_0$ grows at some rate, $g$, which can be positive, negative, or zero. We replace the $X_t(1-T)$ values in (A9.2) by $X_0(1-T)(1+g)^t$ to obtain (A9.3):

$$V_0 = \frac{X_0(1-T)(1+g) - bX_0(1-T)(1+g)}{(1+k)}$$
$$+ \frac{X_0(1-T)(1+g)^2 - bX_0(1-T)(1+g)^2}{(1+k)^2}$$
$$+ \cdots + \frac{X_0(1-T)(1+g)^n - bX_0(1-T)(1+g)^n}{(1+k)^n} \quad \textbf{(A9.3)}$$

We factor the common expression $X_0(1-T)(1+g)^t$ from each term in the numerator to obtain a $(1-b)$ term.

$$V_0 = \frac{X_0(1-T)(1+g)(1-b)}{(1+k)} + \frac{X_0(1-T)(1+g)^2(1-b)}{(1+k)^2}$$
$$+ \cdots + \frac{X_0(1-T)(1+g)^n(1-b)}{(1+k)^n} \quad \textbf{(A9.4)}$$

We factor from each term in (A9.4) a common expression:

$$X_0(1 - T)(1 + g)(1 - b)/(1 + k)$$

This gives equation (A9.5)

$$V_0 = \frac{X_0(1 - T)(1 - b)(1 + g)}{(1 + k)}\left[1 + \frac{(1 + g)}{(1 + k)} + \frac{(1 + g)^2}{(1 + k)^2} + \cdots + \frac{(1 + g)^{n-1}}{(1 + k)^{n-1}}\right]$$

**(A9.5)**

From the expression in (A9.5), we can obtain all the valuation expressions by specifying how $g$, the growth rate, behaves.

## THE NO-GROWTH CASE

First assume that $g = 0$. If $g = 0$, the firm requires no investment, so $b = 0$ as well. Equation (A9.5) becomes (A9.6):

$$V_0 = \frac{X_0(1 - T)}{(1 + k)}\left[1 + \left(\frac{1}{1 + k}\right) + \left(\frac{1}{1 + k}\right)^2 + \cdots + \left(\frac{1}{1 + k}\right)^{n-1}\right] \quad \textbf{(A9.6)}$$

The term in front of the brackets has parameters that are all constants. The terms inside the brackets form a geometrical progression that starts with the constant term 1 and increases by the ratio $1/(1 + k)$. A geometric progression can be written as follows:

$$a + ar + ar^2 + ar^3 + \cdots + ar^{n-1} = a[1 + r + r^2 + r^3 + \cdots + r^{n-1}]$$

Note that the constant term, $a$, can be factored out and the form of the standard geometric progression is exactly as in equation (A9.6). When there is a finite number of terms, $n$, the sum of these terms is:

$$S^n = a(r^n - 1)/(r - 1)$$

When $n$ goes to infinity the sum of this geometric progression is equal to $S^\infty = \frac{a}{1 - r}$ when ($r < 1$). We use both of these summation formulas.

We can write (A9.6) (when $k > 0$, $r < 1$ and $n$ goes to infinity) as:

$$V_0 = \frac{X_0(1 - T)}{(1 + k)}\left[\frac{1}{1 - \frac{1}{1 + k}}\right] = \frac{X_0(1 - T)}{(1 + k)}\left[\frac{1}{\frac{1 + k - 1}{1 + k}}\right]$$

$$= \frac{X_0(1 - T)(1 + k)}{k(1 + k)}$$

Cancel the $(1 + k)$ in the numerator and denominator to obtain equation (9.2) in Table 9.7 of chapter 9.

$$V_0 = \frac{X_0(1 - T)}{k} \quad \text{for } k > 0 \qquad \textbf{(9.2)}$$

The result in equation (9.2) is the familiar formula for the valuation of a stream of receipts or cash flows that continues at a constant level to infinity. This is the standard valuation expression for a perpetuity or bond that has no maturity, often called a consol.

## CONSTANT GROWTH

For the second basic case, assume that $g$ is not zero but a constant. We return to equation (A9.5). The constant ratio is equal to $(1 + g)/(1 + k)$. Here we use the expression for the summation of a geometric progression that continues to infinity, which is $a/(1 - r)$ where $r = (1 + g)/(1 + k) < 1$. Equation (A9.5) can be written as:

$$V_0 = \frac{X_0(1 - T)(1 - b)(1 + g)}{(1 + k)} \left[ \frac{1}{1 - \frac{1 + g}{1 + k}} \right]$$

Simplifying, we obtain equation (9.3) in Table 9.7:

$$V_0 = \frac{X_0(1 - T)(1 + g)(1 - b)}{(k - g)} \quad \text{for } g < k \tag{9.3}$$

Equation (9.3) is the valuation expression (when $k$ is larger than $g$) for cash flows that grow at a constant rate, $g$, to perpetuity.

## SUPERNORMAL GROWTH FOLLOWED BY NO GROWTH

The third basic case is temporary supernormal growth followed by no growth. The fourth will be constant growth during the second phase. We develop an expression for the first term of temporary supernormal growth to which we add a second term, representing either no growth or constant growth. Equation (A9.5) becomes the first term set equal to $S^n$ in equation (A9.7),

$$S^n = \frac{X_0(1 - T)(1 - b)(1 + g)}{(1 + k)} \left[ 1 + \frac{(1 + g)}{(1 + k)} + \frac{(1 + g)^2}{(1 + k)^2} + \cdots + \frac{(1 + g)^{n-1}}{(1 + k)^{n-1}} \right]$$

$$\tag{A9.7}$$

The series inside the bracket of (A9.7) can be written as a summation expression in (A9.8)

$$S^n = \frac{X_0(1 - T)(1 - b)(1 + g)}{(1 + k)} \sum_{t=1}^{n} \frac{(1 + g)^{t-1}}{(1 + k)^{t-1}} \tag{A9.8}$$

We can move the first $(1 + g)/(1 + k)$ term into the summation expression to obtain equation (A9.8a)

$$S^n = X_0(1 - T)(1 - b) \sum_{t=1}^{n} \frac{(1 + g)^t}{(1 + k)^t} \tag{A9.8a}$$

The formula for our third case of temporary supernormal growth followed by zero growth combines equation (A9.8a) and equation (9.2) as shown in (9.4)

$$V_0 = X_0(1 - T)(1 - b) \sum_{t=1}^{n} \frac{(1 + g)^t}{(1 + k)^t} + \frac{X_0(1 - T)(1 + g)^{n+1}}{k(1 + k)^n} \tag{9.4}$$

In the second term of equation (9.4), we grow $X_0(1 - T)$ at $g$ for $(n + 1)$ periods and capitalize it at $k$ to obtain its value at the end of $n$ periods. We then discount it back to the present by $1/(1 + k)^n$ to obtain the present value of the second term, which is added to (A9.8a) to obtain the formula in (9.4).

## SUPERNORMAL GROWTH FOLLOWED BY CONSTANT GROWTH

By the same logic, we can develop the expression for the fourth case. The first term is equation (A9.8a) and the second term is based on equation (9.3).

$$V_0 = X_0(1 - T)(1 - b_s) \sum_{t=1}^{n} \frac{(1 + g_s)^t}{(1 + k)^t} + \frac{X_0(1 - T)(1 - b_c)}{(k - g_c)} \times \frac{(1 + g_s)^{n+1}}{(1 + k)^n}$$

$$(9.5)$$

In the second term, $X_0$ grows at the supernormal rate $g_s$ for $(n + 1)$ periods, after which it grows at a constant rate, $g_c$, to perpetuity. The investment rate for the constant growth period is $b_c$. The numerator of the second term is capitalized at $(k - g_c)$. This capitalized value is discounted back to the present by $1/(1 + k)^n$.

Thus, from a general capital budgeting equation, valuation expressions for four patterns of growth have been derived. The formulas for the four free cash flow patterns are summarized in Table 9.7 of chapter 9.

# Comparisons
# of Valuation Models

The purpose of background materials for the development of valuation models and formulas is to improve understanding of how they may be effectively utilized. In this section, further materials are presented with the same objective in mind.

## COMPARISON WITH THE MILLER-MODIGLIANI MODEL

The intellectual source of modern valuation models is the classic article by Miller and Modigliani (1961). They demonstrated that the same basic valuation model could be derived using four different approaches. The discounted cash flow approach is essentially a basic capital budgeting approach. The stream of dividends approach is a modified version of the dividend growth valuation model in equation (9.6). Their stream of earnings approach is equivalent to their current earnings plus future investment opportunities approach. These latter two methods are equivalent to the free cash flow models that are the emphasis of our presentation and summarized in Table 9.7.

In addition to representing the intellectual foundation of the best valuation models in use, the Miller-Modigliani approach contains some useful insights. To show this we employ a variant of their equation (22a) (page 352, footnote 15) developed by them "assuming that the special investment opportunities are available not in perpetuity but only over some finite interval. . . ." We present this as equation (B9.1).

$$V_0 = \frac{X(1-T)}{k} \left\{ 1 + \frac{b(r-k)}{g-k} \left[ \left( \frac{1+g}{1+k} \right)^n - 1 \right] \right\} (1+g) \qquad \textbf{(B9.1)}$$

We can illustrate the use of the Miller-Modigliani model using the following inputs:

$$T = 40\%$$
$$g = 9.0\%$$
$$k = 10\%$$
$$b = 60\%$$
$$n = 15$$
$$X(1-T) = \$100,000$$
$$r = 15\%$$

Using this information in equation (B9.1) we obtain:

$$V_0 = \$100,000 \times 1.09/0.1 \times [1 + (-3.000) \times (-0.128)]$$
$$V_0 = \$1,508,560$$

This result can be compared with the use of our free cash flow model, for temporary supernormal growth, followed by no growth, which is our equation (9.4).

$$V = X_0(1 - T)(1 - b_s)\sum_{t=1}^{n} \frac{(1 + g_s)^t}{(1 + k)^t} + \frac{X_0(1 - T)(1 + g_s)^{n+1}}{k(1 + k)^n} \qquad (9.4)$$

We then insert the numbers from the example.

$$V_0 = \$100{,}000 \times 0.40 \times \left(\frac{1.09}{1.10}\right) \times 14.08205 + \$100{,}000/0.10 \times 0.8719813 \times 1.09$$

$$= \$558{,}161 + \$950{,}460$$

$$= \$1{,}508{,}621$$

We see that we obtain approximately the same result. What is the value of the Miller-Modigliani formulation because it gives the same result? A number of insights can be derived from the Miller-Modigliani model. First, it highlights the critical relation between profitability, $r$, and the cost of capital, $k$. This relationship appears only one place. It is in the numerator of the expression in their formula that determines the degree to which value will be increased beyond that of a no-growth firm. If $r$ were exactly equal to $k$, the whole expression in brackets would simply become 1 and we would have a no-growth firm. If the firm can earn no more than its cost of capital, then it will not be a growth firm. This gives us the definition of a growth firm. The growth firm is one that is able to attain at least for a limited period of time a profitability rate that exceeds its cost of capital. Second, the Miller-Modigliani formulation emphasizes that each firm is indeed a no-growth firm unless it has favorable investment opportunities.

For these reasons the Miller-Modigliani (1961) article is not only the classic writing on the subject but continues to be as applicable and modern today as it was when first published. The Copeland, Koller, and Murrin (1994) treatment is a variation on the Miller-Modigliani equation shown in (B9.1).

## COMPARISON WITH STERN-STEWART APPROACH

Joel Stern (1974, 1977) and G. Bennett Stewart (1991) showed how the Miller-Modigliani article provided the foundations for analytic approaches to financial planning. They argue that their valuation approach provides the basic theme work for planning most types of fundamental financial policy decisions.

In Stern-Stewart's extended explanation of the correct procedures for valuation, they build on the original Miller-Modigliani (1961) article. However, in their numerical calculations, they set forth two tables that have multiplier or interest factors. While the verbal discussion is all Miller and Modigliani (and properly so), their numerical methods were based on our basic equation (9.4), the free cash flow model for temporary supernormal growth. The Stern-Stewart model can be summarized as follows:

$$V_0 = FCF_1 \text{ (Table 9.1 Interest Factor)} \qquad + NOPAT_1 \text{ (Table 9.2 Interest Factor)}$$

$$= \text{value of supernormal growth period} + \text{value at end of growth period discounted to present}$$

where:

$$FCF = X_1(1 - T)(1 - b)$$

$$NOPAT = X_1(1 - T)$$

Table 9.1 Interest Factor $= \dfrac{\text{FVIFA } (h\%,\, n \text{ yrs.})}{1 + k}$

Table 9.2 Interest Factor $= \dfrac{\text{FVIF } (h\%,\, n \text{ yrs.})}{k}$

The Stern-Stewart model gives exactly the same result for any set of facts as the MM model in equation (B9.1) or our free cash flow formulations in Table 9.7. One great value of the Stern-Stewart presentations is that they make clear the critical role that a sound valuation model has for all aspects of financial planning.

## COMPARISON WITH THE RAPPAPORT APPROACH

In a number of articles and in his book, *Creating Shareholder Value* (1986), Alfred Rappaport developed materials that he elaborated into a model for use on the personal computer for valuing a firm. Again one of the strengths of Rappaport's approach was that he demonstrated how the use of a financial model could be helpful in strategic planning and in improving returns for shareholders.

Profitability was measured by the profit margin on sales. But as indicated earlier, it is generally recognized that profit margin on sales is not a good index for comparing profitability among firms in different industries. Because of different degrees of capital intensity, the normal profit margin in a highly capital-intensive industry should be relatively high. But in an industry where turnover is relatively high as in wholesale and retail trade, the expected profit margin on sales should be relatively low. Thus, profit margin on sales does not facilitate good planning in terms of a target or standard for profitability.

Another limitation of the Rappaport approach is that it is unnecessarily cumbersome. Because the model is essentially verbal in nature, it requires a relatively complex computer program to work through to solutions. However, by recasting some of his variables in a modest way his model is seen to be readily simplified to the cash flow models we have employed.

To illustrate this point we can utilize the example that he presented in his 1986 book (p. 64). He presented a measurement of cash flow that embodied verbally all of the key input assumptions as follows.

[(Sales in prior year) (1 + Sales growth rate) (Operating profit margin) (1 −Cash income tax rate)] − [(Sales in prior year) (Sales growth rate) (Incremental fixed plus working capital investment rate)]

$$= [(100)(1 + .16)(.13)(1 - .50)] - [(100)(.16)(.21 + .15)]$$

$$= 7.54 - 5.76$$

$$= \$1.78 \text{ million.}$$

Defining the words used in the preceding expression in our symbols, we can write a number of relationships and derive the value for the expression that is called investment requirements, $b$, in the free cash flow formulation. This can be done as follows:

$$I_t = 0.36\Delta S = 0.36(S_t - S_{t-1}) = 0.36(1.16 S_{t-1} - S_{t-1})$$

$$= 0.36(0.16 S_{t-1})$$

$$I_t = 0.0576 S_{t-1} = (0.0576 S_t)/(1.16) = 0.04966 S_t$$

$$X_t(1 - T) = 0.065 S_t \quad S_t = 15.385 X_t(1 - T)$$

$$I_t = 0.04966(15.385) X_t(1 - T)$$

$$I_t = 0.764 X_t(1 - T)$$

$$\therefore b = 0.764$$

We can now put the Rappaport material into our basic free cash flow model for temporary supernormal growth followed by no growth. This is our equation (9.4).[1]

$$V_0 = X_0(1 - T)(1 - b_s)\sum_{t=1}^{n}\left(\frac{1 + g_s}{1 + k}\right)^t + \frac{X_0(1 - T)}{k}\left(\frac{1 + g_s}{1 + k}\right)^n \qquad \textbf{(9.4)}$$

We can then insert the Rappaport numbers for each of the terms. Rappaport defined the operating profit margin as 13% on sales of 100. Hence, initial net operating income would be $13. This is the first term in equation (9.4). He assumes the tax rate to be 50% so $(1 - T)$ would be .5. He has assumed an implicit $b$ of .764 so the $(1 - b)$ term would be .236. He assumes a growth rate of 16% for $n = 5$ years and a $k$ of 20%. We can, therefore, write his valuation expression as follows.

$$V_0 = 13(0.5)(0.236)\sum_{t=1}^{n}\left(\frac{1.16}{1.20}\right)^t + \frac{13(.5)}{.2}\left(\frac{1.16}{1.20}\right)^n$$

$$V_0 = 1.534\sum_{t=1}^{5}(0.967)^t + 32.5(0.844)$$

$$= 1.534(0.967)\left(\frac{0.844 - 1}{-0.033}\right) + 27.43$$

$$= 1.483\left(\frac{-0.156}{-0.033}\right) + 27.43$$

$$= 1.483(4.7) + 27.43$$

$$= \$6.97 + 27.43 = \$34.40$$

We can then proceed to evaluate our standard free cash flow model to obtain a result of $34.40 million. This is the same result that Rappaport obtained in his Table 3-1 on page 66 where he made the calculation on a yearly basis. The $34.40 million is equivalent to the $34.371 that he obtained before adding marketable securities and investments and deducting the market value of debt and other obligations.

No elaborate computer program is required to obtain Rappaport's results if the problem formulation is slightly modified to tighten its analytics. Making the calculations amenable to solution by the use of compact formulas greatly facilitates a sensitivity analysis and improves insights on related plans and strategies.

---

[1]Because of different time-indexing assumptions, the last exponent is $n$, not $(n + 1)$ as in our equation (9.4).

---

## References

Copeland, Tom, Tim Koller, and Jack Murrin, *Valuation: Measuring and Managing the Value of Companies,* 2nd ed., New York: John Wiley & Sons, 1994.

Miller, Merton H., and Franco Modigliani, "Dividend Policy, Growth, and the Valuation of Shares," *Journal of Business,* 34, October 1961, pp. 411–433.

Rappaport, Alfred, *Creating Shareholder Value,* New York: The Free Press, 1986.

Stern, Joel M., "Earnings Per Share Don't Count," *Financial Analysts Journal,* 30, July–August 1974, pp. 39–40, 42–43, 67–75.

_____, *Analytical Methods in Financial Planning,* The Chase Manhattan Bank, N.A., November 1977.

Stewart, G. Bennett, *The Quest for Value,* New York: HarperBusiness, 1991.

# CHAPTER

# 10

# Increasing the Value of the Organization

In the preceding chapter, we described and illustrated three approaches to valuation that would be useful in merger analysis: comparable companies or comparable transactions, the spreadsheet approach, and the formula methodology. We discussed their strengths and weaknesses, and we concluded that each approach has something to offer. We recommended that in an acquisition analysis all three be used for the guidance they could provide. In addition, other supplementary tests could be employed to judge the valuations in M&A transactions.

In this chapter we demonstrate how the three can be used in actual practice. Valuation must be related to the economic and strategic factors affecting business firms. To facilitate consideration of these broader influences that are involved in making valuations, it is necessary to focus on the industry in which the acquisition transaction takes place. We choose the oil industry because it is one of the three largest in the U.S. economy and has much economic as well as political and military importance. We focus on the acquisition in 1984 of Gulf Oil by the Chevron Corporation (at that time called the Standard Oil Company of California, SOCAL). This was a transaction of considerable importance for the oil industry as well as for the economy as a whole. It is also representative of the considerable amount of M&A activity and restructuring activities in the oil industry since the 1950s. (For an in-depth study of M&A and restructuring activities in the oil industry, see Siu and Weston, 1996.)

## EVENT ANALYSIS OF THE CHEVRON TAKEOVER OF GULF

In response to a takeover attempt by a group led by T. Boone Pickens, Gulf Oil held an auction. Chevron won the auction in March 1984 with an $80 per share bid. The market price of Gulf before share purchases by Pickens was $39 per share. The premium paid by Chevron was $41 or 105%. Gulf had 165.3 million shares of common stock outstanding; at the purchase price of $80 a share the total paid was $13.2 billion, representing a gain to Gulf shareholders of about $6.8 billion.

The event returns for Chevron are more difficult to measure because the Federal Trade Commission delayed the consummation of the merger until Chevron sold off some specified assets. The *Wall Street Journal* reported on March 1, 1983 that Gulf had been talking with several oil companies including Chevron as a possible buyer. But final completion of the merger was delayed until May 1984. During the four months from February 1984 through May 1984, Chevron experienced a positive event return of $2 billion. Gulf's shareholders gained the difference between the $13.2 billion paid by

Chevron and in its $6.45 billion value before it was put in play. The event return to Gulf shareholders was about $6.8 billion. So the combined event return was about $8.8 billion. Thus, the market judged the merger to be value increasing—that real synergistic gains would be achieved. The empirical studies discussed in chapter 7 demonstrate that the event returns are good predictors of the subsequent performance in M&A transactions. The subsequent analysis in this chapter confirms that Chevron's acquisition of Gulf was a positive net present value (NPV) investment.

We will analyze the price paid by Chevron from a number of other perspectives, including the approaches we described in the preceding chapter. We begin with the comparable transactions approach.

## COMPARABLE TRANSACTIONS ANALYSIS OF THE GULF PURCHASE

Table 10.1 presents the information needed for making a comparable transactions analysis of the $13.2 billion paid by Chevron for Gulf. The upper part of the table summarizes key information on five transactions similar to the Gulf transaction. The prices paid range from about $4 billion to $8 billion. While none is as large as the Gulf purchase, they are all multibillion-dollar transactions. After presenting data on the price

**TABLE 10.1**    Comparable Transactions Analysis of Gulf Purchase

| | | | | Acquired or Seller | | | |
|---|---|---|---|---|---|---|---|
| Year | Buyer | Seller | Price Offered | Revenues | EBITDA* | Book Equity | Market Equity |
| 1984 | Chevron Corp. | Gulf Corp. | 13,205.5 | 26,581 | 3,717 | 10,128 | 7,027 |
| 1981 | E.I. du Pont de Nemours & Co. | Conoco Inc. | 8,039.8 | 18,326 | 4,048 | 4,585 | 7,049 |
| 1981 | U.S. Steel Corp. | Marathon Oil Corp. | 6,618.5 | 8,754 | 3,162 | 1,923 | 4,257 |
| 1984 | Mobil Corp. | Superior Oil Co. | 5,725.8 | 1,793 | 849 | 2,468 | 4,628 |
| 1981 | Societe Nationale Elf Aquitaine-France | Texasgulf Inc. | 4,293.7 | 1,090 | 440 | 1,168 | 1,972 |
| 1982 | Occidental Petroleum Corp. | Cities Service Co. | 4,115.6 | 8,546 | 954 | 2,107 | 3,572 |

| | | | Multiple | | | |
|---|---|---|---|---|---|---|
| Year | Buyer | Seller | Revenues | EBITDA | Book Equity | Market Equity |
| 1981 | E.I. du Pont de Nemours & Co. | Conoco Inc. | 0.44 | 1.99 | 1.75 | 1.14 |
| 1981 | U.S. Steel Corp. | Marathon Oil Corp. | 0.76 | 2.09 | 3.44 | 1.55 |
| 1984 | Mobil Corp. | Superior Oil Co. | 3.19 | 6.74 | 2.32 | 1.24 |
| 1981 | Societe Nationale Elf Aquitaine-France | Texasgulf Inc. | 3.94 | 9.76 | 3.68 | 2.18 |
| 1982 | Occidental Petroleum Corp. | Cities Service Co. | 0.48 | 4.31 | 1.95 | 1.15 |
| | *Unweighted mean* | | 1.76 | 4.98 | 2.63 | 1.45 |
| | *Weighted average* | | 0.75 | 3.05 | 2.35 | 1.34 |
| | **Value of Gulf (using weighted average)** | | 19,875 | 11,322 | 23,803 | 9,420 |

*Earnings before interest, taxes, depreciation, and amortization.

paid, we present data for the acquired firm or seller for the latest period before the transaction took place. The four measures we use are widely employed by investment bankers: revenues, which represent the market position and profit potential; the earnings before interest, taxes, depreciation, and amortization (EBITDA); book equity, which represents shareholders' investment as shown on the balance sheet; and market equity, which is the market value of shareholders' equity.

In the bottom half of the table, for each of the five transactions comparable to the Chevron-Gulf purchase we present the multiple of the price paid to revenues, EBITDA, book equity, and to market equity. We calculate both an unweighted mean and a weighted average of each of the four multiples for the five comparable transactions. Because the unweighted mean gives undue weight to outliers or multiples, we apply the average weighted multiple to the Gulf figures for 1983 to obtain the indicated value of Gulf. Based on the ratio of the price paid to the preacquisition market value in the other five transactions, Chevron should have paid $9.4 billion for Gulf. Based on the ratio of price paid to EBITDA, the indicated price for Gulf would have been $11.3 billion. Based on revenues, the value of Gulf would have been $19.9 billion. Based on the multiple of price paid to book equity, the price could have been $23.8 billion. The price paid by Chevron falls between two high estimates and two somewhat lower indicated values. One should generally give greater weight to the multiples related to EBITDA and to the market equity.

However, the comparable transactions approach can only be a starting point. Presentations on valuation include a comparable transactions approach but consider other approaches as well. Of critical importance is whether there were particular characteristics of Gulf that provided the basis for a somewhat higher premium over the preexisting market and a higher multiple of EBITDA. Another possibility is that the market value of Gulf was temporarily depressed as well as its EBITDA for the year measured. Some sensitivity analysis could be made of the ratio of the price paid to EBITDA averaged over recent years as well as forecasts for the future.

Another sensitivity approach would be to consider some transactions that took place after the Chevron-Gulf purchase as shown in Table 10.2. Obviously, this information would not have been available to Chevron management at the time. In evaluating the price paid by Chevron, however, we can gain the benefit of hindsight for making a judgment. Two of the later transactions were in the following year and a third was five years later. Three of the multiples are higher, one is slightly lower. The multiple based on EBITDA is almost precisely what Chevron paid. Multiples based on revenues and book equity would suggest a higher price for Gulf. Multiples based on market equity would suggest a lower price.

This second use of the comparable transactions approach provides additional evidence for the judgment that the price Chevron paid for Gulf was similar to multiples paid in comparable transactions.

## SPREADSHEET AND FORMULA APPROACHES

In this analysis, we combine the spreadsheet and formula approaches because, as we demonstrated in the preceding chapter, they are simply somewhat different formats for doing the same thing. We begin with the historical spreadsheets of Chevron and Gulf as a basis for calculating the value drivers, which are the key determinants of the value of a firm.

**TABLE 10.2**   The Comparable Transactions Analysis of Gulf Including Later Deals

| | | | | Acquired or Seller | | | |
| Year | Buyer | Seller | Price Offered | Revenues | EBITDA | Book Equity | Market Equity |
|---|---|---|---|---|---|---|---|
| 1984 | Chevron Corp. | Gulf Corp. | 13,205.5 | 26,581 | 3,717 | 10,128 | 7,027 |
| 1981 | E.I. du Pont de Nemours & Co. | Conoco Inc. | 8,039.8 | 18,326 | 4,048 | 4,585 | 7,049 |
| 1981 | U.S. Steel Corp. | Marathon Oil Corp. | 6,618.5 | 8,754 | 3,162 | 1,923 | 4,257 |
| 1984 | Mobil Corp. | Superior Oil Co. | 5,725.8 | 1,793 | 849 | 2,468 | 4,628 |
| 1981 | Societe Nationale Elf Aquitaine-France | Texasgulf Inc. | 4,293.7 | 1,090 | 440 | 1,168 | 1,972 |
| 1989 | Exxon Corp. | Texaco Canada Inc. —Canada | 4,149.6 | 2,119 | 445 | 1,668 | 4,484 |
| 1982 | Occidental Petroleum Corp. | Cities Service Co. | 4,115.6 | 8,546 | 954 | 2,107 | 3,572 |
| 1985 | U.S. Steel Corp. | Texas Oil & Gas Corp. | 4,094.4 | 2,053 | 836 | 1,508 | 3,756 |
| 1985 | Occidental Petroleum Corp. | MidCon Corp. | 3,085.6 | 4,160 | 532 | 1,160 | 1,243 |

| | | | Multiple | | | |
| Year | Buyer | Seller | Revenues | EBITDA | Book Equity | Market Equity |
|---|---|---|---|---|---|---|
| 1981 | E.I. du Pont de Nemours & Co. | Conoco Inc. | 0.44 | 1.99 | 1.75 | 1.14 |
| 1981 | U.S. Steel Corp. | Marathon Oil Corp. | 0.76 | 2.09 | 3.44 | 1.55 |
| 1984 | Mobil Corp. | Superior Oil Co. | 3.19 | 6.74 | 2.32 | 1.24 |
| 1981 | Societe Nationale Elf Aquitaine-France | Texasgulf Inc. | 3.94 | 9.76 | 3.68 | 2.18 |
| 1989 | Exxon Corp. | Texaco Canada Inc. —Canada | 1.96 | 9.32 | 2.49 | 0.93 |
| 1982 | Occidental Petroleum Corp. | Cities Service Co. | 0.48 | 4.31 | 1.95 | 1.15 |
| 1985 | U.S. Steel Corp. | Texas Oil & Gas Corp. | 1.99 | 4.90 | 2.72 | 1.09 |
| 1985 | Occidental Petroleum Corp. | MidCon Corp. | 0.74 | 5.80 | 2.66 | 2.48 |
| | *Unweighted mean* | | *1.69* | *5.61* | *2.63* | *1.47* |
| | *Weighted average* | | *0.86* | *3.56* | *2.42* | *1.30* |
| | **Value of Gulf (using weighted average)** | | 22,769 | 13,238 | 24,498 | 9,106 |

### Historical Data Used in a First Estimate of the Value Drivers

In Table 10.3, we present spreadsheets of data required to calculate the value drivers for Chevron before the acquisition of Gulf. We begin with the calculation of the value drivers based on historical data for the previous nine years. These historical patterns suggest what is a plausible initial scenario for the next planning horizon. However, we should adjust the historical numbers to take into account judgments about prospective developments over the future planning horizon.

Table 10.3 illustrates one of the strong points of the formula approach. Only eight items of data are required to provide a basis for estimating the value drivers. The first four columns are used to develop estimates of net working capital requirements as a form of investment by the firm. From current assets in column 1, we deduct marketable securities to obtain current assets needed to support the operating activities of the firm. Interest-bearing debt in column 4 is deducted from total current liabilities in column 3

**TABLE 10.3**   Chevron Corp. Valuation at End of 1983 Without Gulf

| | (1) Current Assets Total | (2) Marketable Securities | (3) Current Liabilities Total | (4) Debt in Current Liabilities | (5) Pretax Income | (6) Income Taxes Total | (7) Interest Expense | (8) Property, Plant, and Equipment Total (Net) | (9) Net Working Capital $(1-2)-(3-4)$ | (10) Total Capital $(8+9)$ | (11) Investment (delta 10) | (12) EBIT $(5+7)$ |
|---|---|---|---|---|---|---|---|---|---|---|---|---|
| 1975 | $5,001 | $485 | $4,201 | $116 | $1,405 | $632 | $80 | $5,782 | $431 | $6,213 | | $1,485 |
| 1976 | 5,448 | 711 | 4,333 | 118 | 1,407 | 527 | 120 | 5,962 | 522 | 6,484 | 271 | 1,527 |
| 1977 | 6,216 | 1,104 | 4,645 | 84 | 1,772 | 756 | 116 | 6,199 | 552 | 6,751 | 267 | 1,889 |
| 1978 | 7,145 | 1,616 | 5,477 | 313 | 1,928 | 822 | 164 | 7,153 | 364 | 7,518 | 767 | 2,092 |
| 1979 | 8,286 | 1,464 | 5,879 | 95 | 2,935 | 1,150 | 156 | 7,309 | 1,038 | 8,348 | 830 | 3,091 |
| 1980 | 10,707 | 2,789 | 6,985 | 246 | 4,298 | 1,897 | 158 | 8,780 | 1,179 | 9,959 | 1,611 | 4,456 |
| 1981 | 8,902 | 1,328 | 6,261 | 100 | 3,996 | 1,616 | 197 | 11,738 | 1,413 | 13,151 | 3,192 | 4,193 |
| 1982 | 7,147 | 1,692 | 5,434 | 382 | 2,554 | 1,177 | 171 | 13,552 | 403 | 13,955 | 804 | 2,725 |
| 1983 | 7,098 | 2,370 | 5,117 | 102 | 2,932 | 1,342 | 174 | 14,232 | −287 | 13,945 | −10 | 3,106 |
| *Totals* | | | | | $23,227 | $9,919 | | | | | $7,732 | $24,564 |

$X_0 =$ $3,106

$T =$ 42.7%

$b =$ *Inv. oppot rate* 48.0%

$r =$ *marginal Profitab rate* 13.8%

$g =$ 6.6%

$n =$ 10

$k =$ 12.0%

$(1 + h) = (1 + g)/(1 + k)$ 0.95

$p =$ inflation rate = 0.0%

$z =$ reinvestment rate = 0.0%

Valuation:

1st term $= X_0(1 - T)(1 - b)\sum_{t=1}^{n}\left(\dfrac{1+g}{1+k}\right)^t =$     $7,123 (42.5%)

2nd term $= \dfrac{X_0(1 - T)(1 - z)}{k - p}\left(\dfrac{1+g}{1+k}\right)^n (1 + g) =$ $9,645 (57.5%)

Total value $=$     $16,769 (100.0%)

*Source: Compustat.* (Dollar amounts in thousands.)

*Note:* Additions may differ by small amounts because of computer rounding of input numbers.

to give a measure of spontaneous financing, which is netted against current asset invest-ment requirements. On the basis of the first four columns of Table 10.3, estimates of net working capital requirements from year to year are presented in column 9. Column 5 presents pretax income. Column 6 is income taxes actually paid. The reported income statements present taxes including deferred taxes. This is usually an overstatement of taxes paid and an understatement of net income. To correct for this, we use actual taxes. If the data are being compiled from annual reports, actual taxes are generally found in one of the footnotes to the financial statements. The source of our data in Table 10.3 is *Compustat,* which does provide information on actual taxes paid. Column 7 is interest expense. Column 8 is property, plant, and equipment after deducting the reserve for depreciation.

From the above eight items we can now proceed to calculate all the value drivers. Column 10 is total capital obtained by adding columns 8 and 9. Column 11 measures investment, which represents the year-to-year changes in total capital. Column 12 is earnings before interest and taxes (EBIT) obtained by adding column 5, pretax income, and column 7, interest expense. We use the symbol $X$ to stand for EBIT as discussed in the preceding chapter. Whether we use a formula approach or spreadsheet approach or both, EBIT is multiplied by one minus the tax rate to obtain after-tax cash flows. It is well established in corporate finance that $X(1 - T) =$ net income plus after-tax interest expense; so $X(1 - T) =$ cash flows from operations before accounting for investment requirements. As explained in the preceding chapter, $X(1 - T)$ minus investment requirements is net cash flows. We would get the same measure of net cash flows if we started with EBITDA (instead of EBIT) and deducted gross investment rather than investment net of depreciation charges as we are doing in the present analysis. We would get the same result whether we used the formula approach or a spreadsheet analysis for the measurement of net cash flows.

We now have all the information we need for calculating the value drivers. They are listed in the footnote of Table 10.3. $X_0$ is $3,106 found in the 1983 row of column 12. It is the starting point EBIT. $T$, the tax rate, is obtained by taking the ratio of total actual taxes paid in column 6 to total pretax income in column 5, which is ($9,919)/($23,227) or 42.7%.

The next value driver is $b$, the investment opportunities rate. The numerator of the ratio that defines $b$ is investment; the denominator normalizes the investment in terms of the after-tax EBIT or after-tax net operating income. For implementation, the numerator would be the change in total capital or the sum of all investments over the period of analysis shown in column 7 as $7,732. The denominator is the sum of EBIT after taxes, which is the column 12 sum of $24,564 multiplied by one minus the tax rate or 0.573. The result $14,075, divided into the numerator, gives a $b$ value of 55%. The expression for $b$ in formal terms is shown in equation (10.1).

$$b = \frac{A_n - A_0}{\sum_{t=1}^{n} [X_t(1 - T)]} = \frac{\sum_{t=1}^{n} I_t}{\sum_{t=1}^{n} [X_t(1 - T)]} = \frac{\$7,732}{\$14,075} = 55\% \qquad (10.1)$$

This equation says that $b$ is the ratio of the change in capital over some period (or the total amount of investments during the same period) to the total of after-tax cash flows for the same period. Because exploration was unprofitable, our forecast is a reduction to 48%.

We next consider $r$, the marginal profitability rate. This is defined as the change in after-tax cash flows over some period divided by the sum of investments over the corresponding period. The denominator for $r$ is the same as the numerator for calculating $b$. So we already have that figure of $7,732. The numerator is the incremental after-tax cash flows over the same period: the ending period cash flows less the beginning period cash flows. The result is 12.0% as shown in equation (10.2). With reduced exploration activity, we forecast a rise in $r$ to 13.8%.

$$r = \frac{X_n(1 - T) - X_1(1 - T)}{\sum_{t=2}^{n} I_t}$$

$$= \frac{\$3,106(0.573) - (\$1,485)(0.573)}{\$7,732} \qquad (10.2)$$

$$= \frac{\$929}{\$7,732} = 12.0\%$$

We can calculate growth for any of the time series in the first ten columns of Table 10.3. The multiple measures provide a basis for a judgment of a dependable measure of growth. We can check this with the product of $b \times r$ as shown in equation (10.3).

$$g = br$$
$$g = 0.48(0.138) = 0.066 \qquad (10.3)$$

The next value driver we need is *n,* which is defined as the period over which supernormal growth is expected to take place. The length of this period depends on the nature of the industry and the firm's competitive position in it. It is a judgment call. For the present example, we use 10 years. After our initial valuation calculation, we can do a sensitivity analysis by successively varying each of the value drivers. Because *n* is a judgment call, we would certainly do a sensitivity analysis for alternative estimates of *n.*

## The Applicable Cost of Capital

The next term we need is the applicable cost of capital. Determining the cost of capital is always difficult at best and some judgment must be exercised. This was especially true for the 1983–1984 years.

We begin with an estimation of the applicable cost of debt. Required yields on corporate high-grade bonds in 1983 were 12.04%. However, bond yields had reached a peak in 1981 at 14.17% and were moving downward year by year. The AAA bond yield had averaged about 4.3% in the first half of the 1960s, about 5% for the second half of the 1960s, about 8% for the first half of the 1970s, and at about 8.8% for the second half of the 1970s. Then, after the high yields in the first half of the 1980s, reported above, for the second half of the 1980s, bond yields had moved down to about 9.25%, and by 1995 AAA bond yields had moved down to 7.59%. Of course, in 1983, the future cost of long-term corporate debt capital could not be known with certainty. The term structure provides the market's estimate of the movement of future levels of interest rates. While the future could not be known with certainty, there was wide recognition in the financial press in 1983 and in 1984 that government policy was to move interest rates in a downward direction. At the higher levels of interest rates in the early 1980s, the emerging countries were having difficulty meeting interest payments on the large debts they had incurred. To protect the stability of the international financial system, under the leadership of the United States, monetary policy throughout the world had become expansionary. Therefore, it was plausible that interest rates would continue to move downward. With that expectation, stock prices began rising in mid-1982 as interest rates declined. We use a before-tax cost of debt for Chevron in 1983 of 10%. With Chevron's tax rate of 0.427, the after-tax cost of debt for Chevron was $[0.10(1 - 0.427)] = 5.73\%$.

Estimation of the cost of equity poses similar challenges. We begin with the capital asset pricing model (CAPM) presented as equation (9.7) earlier:

$$k_s = R_f + [\overline{R}_M - R_f]\beta_j$$

This states that the required yield on equity is equal to the risk-free rate plus the market price of risk multiplied by the firm's beta. The risk-free rate measured 10-year U.S. treasury securities in 1983 was 11.10%. The beta for major oil companies such as Chevron in recent years has been from about 0.6 to 0.7. Since the first oil price shock of 1973, the returns to major oil companies have been a function more of OPEC supply control and price policies than movements in gross national product or stock prices generally. Using a relatively high beta of 0.8 and a market price of risk of 7.5% gives 6%. The yield on 10-year treasuries in 1983 was about 11%. But this was near a cyclical peak. By the same reasoning as in our discussion of the cost of debt for Chevron, we use 8% for the risk-free rate. When added to the beta-weighted market price of risk of 6%, we obtain 14% as the estimate of the cost of equity for Chevron at the end of 1983. This 14% represents a differential over the pretax cost of its debt (10%) of 4 percentage points. This would have been about the normal spread between the cost of debt and cost of equity for a company like Chevron in the early 1980s.

## Capital Structure Proportions

We next consider the applicable capital structure proportions to estimate the weighted cost of capital for Chevron at the end of 1983. The market value of the equity of Chevron at the end of 1983 was approximately $12 billion. It had about $2 billion of interest-bearing debt outstanding. So the ratio of the $2 billion debt to the total value of Chevron was 2/14 or 14.3%. Because we are valuing Chevron in contemplation of its purchase of Gulf Oil, and Chevron planned to make the purchase by selling an additional $10 billion of debt, it is clear that Chevron had unused debt capacity. It would seem more appropriate, therefore, to consider a higher leverage ratio. Chevron had announced a target leverage ratio of 30%. Using this leverage ratio with the after-tax cost of debt of 5.73% and a cost of equity of 14% we have:

$$k = 0.3(5.73\%) + 0.7(14\%)$$
$$= 1.719\% + 9.8\%$$
$$= 11.519\%$$

The result is a weighted cost of capital for Chevron of somewhat over 11.5%. We rounded this up to 12% as the cost of capital used in the valuation presented in Table 10.3.

Table 10.3 shows an indicated total value for Chevron at the end of 1983 without Gulf of $16.8 billion. With about $2 billion interest-bearing debt outstanding, this would give an indicated market value of the equity for Chevron of $14.8 billion. The actual market value of Chevron at the end of 1983 was about $12 billion. Our calculations, therefore, would suggest that the full potentials of Chevron were not fully recognized by the market as of the end of 1983. However, our figures are not greatly different. The small difference between our computation of the market value of Chevron and its actual market value should give plausibility to the methodology and judgments we have employed.

## Spreadsheet Methodology

To this point we have employed the formula method for analyzing that portion of the value of the firm generated by the period of temporary supernormal growth. We could also use the spreadsheet method to analyze the period of super growth. We have done so in Table 10.3A.

A widely used practice is to develop a spreadsheet beginning with cash flows before taxes or EBIT. We next determine the amount of investment required to support the cash flows. Again, the prevailing methodology is to calculate the required increase in net property, plant, and equipment. To this we add the increases in working capital required to support the sales levels that ultimately generate the EBIT. Investment is subtracted from the after-tax cash flows to give the free cash flows for the year. These are discounted at the applicable cost of capital to give the present value or the capitalized value of the free cash flows during the period of supernormal growth. The result can be compared with the first term in the formula approach. They both yield $7.1 billion rounded.

This demonstrates that there is no difference conceptually in the formula approach and the spreadsheet approach. They are different ways of arranging the numbers. The formula approach focuses on the value drivers. The spreadsheet approach presents the material in the familiar financial statement formats. However, because they are both doing the same thing, they yield the same results. To this point we have used the formula approach and the spreadsheet approach to establish the value of Chevron in

**TABLE 10.3A**   Valuation of Chevron Corp. at End of 1983 Without Gulf (Assumption: EBIT, PPE, CA, STI, CL, DCL Growing at a Rate = g = 6.6%, k = 12%)

| | 0<br>1983 | 1<br>1984 | 2<br>1985 | 3<br>1986 | 4<br>1987 | 5<br>1988 | 6<br>1989 | 7<br>1990 | 8<br>1991 | 9<br>1992 | 10<br>1993 |
|---|---|---|---|---|---|---|---|---|---|---|---|
| EBIT | 3,106 | 3,310 | 3,526 | 3,757 | 4,004 | 4,266 | 4,545 | 4,843 | 5,161 | 5,499 | 5,859 |
| Actual taxes % ($T$) | 42.7% | 42.7% | 42.7% | 42.7% | 42.7% | 42.7% | 42.7% | 42.7% | 42.7% | 42.7% | 42.7% |
| EBIT ($1 - T$) | 1,780 | 1,896 | 2,021 | 2,153 | 2,294 | 2,444 | 2,605 | 2,775 | 2,957 | 3,151 | 3,357 |
| PPE total (net) | 14,232 | 15,164 | 16,158 | 17,217 | 18,345 | 19,547 | 20,827 | 22,192 | 23,646 | 25,195 | 26,846 |
| Current assets (CA) | 7,098 | 7,563 | 8,059 | 8,587 | 9,149 | 9,749 | 10,387 | 11,068 | 11,793 | 12,566 | 13,389 |
| Marketable securities | 2,370 | 2,525 | 2,691 | 2,867 | 3,055 | 3,255 | 3,468 | 3,696 | 3,938 | 4,196 | 4,471 |
| Current liabilities (CL) | 5,117 | 5,452 | 5,809 | 6,190 | 6,596 | 7,028 | 7,488 | 7,979 | 8,502 | 9,059 | 9,652 |
| Debt in current liabilities (DCL) | 102 | 109 | 116 | 123 | 131 | 140 | 149 | 159 | 169 | 181 | 192 |
| Net working capital | −287 | −306 | −326 | −347 | −370 | −394 | −420 | −448 | −477 | −508 | −541 |
| Total capital | 13,945 | 14,859 | 15,832 | 16,870 | 17,975 | 19,153 | 20,407 | 21,745 | 23,169 | 24,687 | 26,305 |
| Investment | −10 | 914 | 974 | 1,037 | 1,105 | 1,178 | 1,255 | 1,337 | 1,425 | 1,518 | 1,618 |
| FCF | 1,790 | 983 | 1,047 | 1,116 | 1,189 | 1,267 | 1,350 | 1,438 | 1,532 | 1,633 | 1,740 |
| PV of FCF | | 877 | 835 | 794 | 755 | 719 | 684 | 651 | 619 | 589 | 560 |
| Sum of PV of FCF = | 7,082 | | | | | | | | | | |

where:
EBIT = Earnings before interest and taxes
PPE  = Property, plant, and equipment
CA   = Current assets
STI  = Short-term investments
CL   = Current liabilities
DLC  = Interest-bearing debt in current liabilities
FCF  = Free cash flows

1983 before the acquisition of Gulf. Next we apply a similar methodology to place a value on Gulf. We will look at alternative measures of how Gulf was valued. We will then be able to evaluate whether the $13.2 billion that Chevron paid for Gulf was a positive NPV investment.

# THE VALUE OF GULF, 1983

We shall employ a number of methodologies to estimate the value of Gulf in 1983. Our main purpose is to test whether the price of $13.2 billion paid by Chevron was a reasonable one.

Table 10.4 presents the formula approach to the valuation of Gulf based on the nine-year period ending in 1983, the last year of Gulf's independent existence. The resulting value drivers are shown in the footnote of the table. The figures shown for each of the value drivers is developed from the vertically oriented spreadsheets presented in the table except $T$ and $k$. $T$ is set at 50%. The cost of capital of 13% for Gulf is developed as shown below:

$$k_s = 0.08 + 0.075(1.15)$$
$$= 0.08 + 0.08625$$
$$= 0.16625$$
$$k_b = 0.10(1 - 0.5)$$
$$= 0.05$$
$$k = 0.70(0.16625) + 0.30(0.05)$$
$$= 0.1164 + 0.015$$
$$= 0.1314$$

We use the CAPM to calculate the cost of equity for Gulf. We use the same market parameters that we used in the calculation of the cost of equity for Chevron. We use an estimate of beta of 1.15 for Gulf taken from a Harvard Business School case on the same subject (Case No. 285-053). In calculating the cost of debt, we use the same 10% estimate as the required yield to maturity on debt for an AA-rated company for the reasons we set forth in the discussion of our calculation of Chevron's cost of debt. For the weighted

## TABLE 10.4   Gulf Corp. Valuation at End of 1983 Without Chevron

|  | (1) Current Assets Total | (2) Marketable Securities | (3) Current Liabilities Total | (4) Debt in Current Liabilities | (5) Pretax Income | (6) Income Taxes Total | (7) Interest Expense | (8) Property, Plant, and Equipment Total (Net) | (9) Net Working Capital (1−2)−(3−4) | (10) Total Capital (8+9) | (11) Investment (delta 10) | (12) EBIT (5+7) |
|---|---|---|---|---|---|---|---|---|---|---|---|---|
| 1975 | $5,473 | $1,754 | $3,738 | $217 | $2,772 | $2,012 | $114 | $6,236 | $198 | $6,434 |  | $2,886 |
| 1976 | 6,179 | 1,935 | 4,191 | 139 | 2,270 | 1,392 | 109 | 6,632 | 192 | 6,824 | 390 | 2,379 |
| 1977 | 5,187 | 1,097 | 4,232 | 264 | 2,236 | 1,435 | 110 | 8,332 | 122 | 8,454 | 1,630 | 2,346 |
| 1978 | 5,162 | 963 | 4,240 | 205 | 1,976 | 1,135 | 127 | 9,063 | 164 | 9,227 | 773 | 2,103 |
| 1979 | 6,524 | 1,478 | 5,107 | 101 | 3,161 | 1,760 | 139 | 9,884 | 40 | 9,924 | 697 | 3,300 |
| 1980 | 6,863 | 1,563 | 5,154 | 132 | 4,179 | 2,651 | 134 | 10,886 | 278 | 11,164 | 1,240 | 4,313 |
| 1981 | 6,290 | 1,384 | 5,779 | 685 | 3,421 | 2,092 | 223 | 13,013 | −188 | 12,825 | 1,661 | 3,644 |
| 1982 | 5,378 | 1,225 | 4,989 | 624 | 2,548 | 1,597 | 324 | 13,876 | −212 | 13,664 | 839 | 2,872 |
| 1983 | 5,653 | 1,713 | 4,756 | 304 | 2,699 | 1,628 | 291 | 14,090 | −512 | 13,578 | −86 | 2,990 |
| Totals |  |  |  |  | $25,262 | $15,702 |  |  |  |  | $7,144 | $26,833 |

| | | Valuation: |
|---|---|---|
| $X_0 =$ | $2,990 | |
| $T =$ | 50.0% | |
| $b =$ | 53.2% | |
| $r =$ | 0.7% | 1st term $= X_0(1-T)(1-b)\sum_{t=1}^{n}\left(\dfrac{1+g}{1+k}\right)^t =$   $3,860 (52.2%) |
| $g =$ | 0.4% | |
| $n =$ | 10 | |
| $k =$ | 13.0% | 2nd term $= \dfrac{X_0(1-T)(1-z)}{k-p}\left(\dfrac{1+g}{1+k}\right)^n (1+g) = \$3,535$ (47.8%) |
| $(1+h)=(1+g)/(1+k)$ | 0.89 | |
| $p =$ inflation rate $=$ | 0.0% | |
| $z =$ reinvestment rate $=$ | 0.0% | Total value $=$   $7,395 (100.0%) |

cost of capital, we use a leverage ratio of 30% following the logic of the Chevron target capital structure. The resulting cost of capital for Gulf shown above is slightly above 13%. This is the source of the 13% figure used as the value driver in Table 10.4.

Using the standard temporary supergrowth followed by zero growth formula results in a valuation of Gulf of $7.4 billion. The actual value of Gulf at the time was an equity value of $6.4 billion plus interest-bearing debt of $2.6 billion for a total of $9 billion. Inspection of the value drivers shows that the marginal profitability rate of Gulf had been running at about 0.7%. Its cost of capital was at least 13%. Whenever the profitability rate is less than the cost of capital, a firm should not be investing. It should be disinvesting. This reveals the basic problem that made Gulf vulnerable to a takeover. Its investment rate as measured by $b$ was relatively high. But its profitability rate was very low.

If we value Gulf as a no-growth company using equation (9.2), we would obtain:

$$V_0 = \frac{X_0(1-T)}{k} = \frac{2{,}990(0.50)}{0.13} = \frac{1{,}495}{0.13} = \$11.5 \text{ billion}$$

The resulting $11.5 billion value is greater than the actual market value of $9 billion because the cash flows of Gulf had been declining since 1980. Thus, the use of a zero growth formula results in a greater value for Gulf than its actual market value.

But both the $11.5 billion and the $9 billion are below the $13.2 billion paid by Chevron. The synergies must be included in the valuation so let us consider some other alternative approaches to establishing the value of the Gulf acquisition to Chevron.

## Finding Cost Analysis

The approach taken in the Harvard Business School (HBS) case on the Gulf takeover (Case No. 285-053) calculates the negative returns from Gulf's exploration and development (E&D) programs. It then calculates the losses that could be avoided by curtailing or shutting down the unprofitable E&D activity of Gulf. A summary outline of the HBS analysis is shown in Table 10.5.

The time lag in reserve use is obtained by dividing reserves by annual production to obtain eight years. This is a critical number because it means that finding costs in a

---

**TABLE 10.5**   Returns from E&D Programs in the Oil Industry, Early 1980s

1. Time lag in reserve use = reserves/annual production = 2,313 bbl/290 bbl = 8 years
2. Finding costs (FC) = $(E\&D)_{t-1}$/(reserve additions)$_t$ = $2,671/336.5 = $7.94/bbl
   Expensed in 1 year (E1%) 26%; expensed in 8 years (E8%) 74%
3. Tax shelter = $(FC)(E1)(T)(1/cc) + (FC)(E8)(T)[1/cc^8]$   $T$ = tax rate   $cc = (1+k)$
   $(\$7.94)(0.26)(0.5)(1/1.17) + (\$7.94)(0.74)(0.5)[1/(1.17)^8] = \$.88 + \$.84 = \$1.72/bbl$
4. Operating profit = (Op. revs. $22.42 − direct operating costs $7.08) times $(1-T) =$
   $7.67/bbl
4a. Present value = Op. profit $(1+p)^8 [1/(1+cc)^8] = \$7.67(1.05)^8 [1/(1.17)^8] = \$3.25/bbl$
5. Net present value of company E&D programs
5a. P.V. of Op. profit $3.25 + P.V. of E&D tax shelters $1.72 − P.V. of finding costs
   $7.94 = $(2.97)/bbl
5b. Total = Amt./bbl ($2.97) times reserve additions 336.5 = ($999)
5c. Capitalized value of perpetuity: $(999)/(0.17 − 0.05) = $(8,325)
5d. $(8,325) ÷ # of Gulf shares = $(8,325 million) ÷ 165.3 million = $50.36/share

---

*Source:* Developed by the authors from information in Harvard Business School, "Gulf Oil Corporation—Takeover," Case No. 285-053, November 7, 1984; revised 1992.

given year are not recovered in the sale of crude (if the E&D efforts are successful) until some years later. As a consequence, accounting profit and loss statements that do not take the time value of money into account are likely to overstate returns because of the substantial time lag between outlays incurred and revenues received.

In line 2, finding costs per barrel are obtained by dividing the outlays by the reserve additions with which they are associated. Using the Gulf financial data, finding costs were $7.94 per barrel in the early 1980s; 26% expensed in year 1 and 74% in year 8. In line 3, the actual dollar amount of tax shelter is calculated from the above relationships. The present value of tax shelter is calculated as $1.72 per barrel. This analysis uses a projected inflation rate for oil prices ($p$) of 5%, for direct operating costs ($q$) of 5%, and a weighted average cost of capital ($k$) of 17%.

In line 4, the operating profit per barrel after taxes is calculated. Operating revenues less direct operating costs times $(1 - T)$ is found to be $7.67 per barrel. In line 4a, this operating profit is compounded at the inflation rate for oil prices for eight years and then discounted back for eight years at the applicable cost of capital. The result is $3.25 per barrel as the present value of after-tax operating profits per barrel.

We now have all of the results needed to calculate the net present value of Gulf's E&D programs as shown in lines 5a–5d. The present value of operating profit ($3.25) plus the present value of the E&D tax shelters ($1.72) less the present value of finding cost ($7.94) is a negative $2.97 per barrel, as shown in line 5a of the table. In line 5b, the amount per barrel is multiplied by the related reserve additions to obtain the total negative net present value of $999 million. The HBS case analysis postulated a continuation of this annual loss to perpetuity. It capitalizes the perpetuity at 12%, the applicable cost of capital (17%) less the inflation rate for oil prices (5%). The result is a total loss of $8.3 billion. Dividing by the number of Gulf shares (165.3 million) gives a loss of $50.36 per share. Thus, it was argued that a firm buying Gulf could avoid a destruction to shareholder value of $50.36 per share by simply shutting down Gulf's E&D programs. The HBS case concluded that adding this savings of $50.36 per share to the existing $39 price of Gulf would give a value of $89 per share, justifying the $80 per share actually paid by Chevron.

The Harvard Case analysis used a cost of capital of 17% for Gulf. This was based on the relatively high interest rate levels of 1983. We had calculated a lower estimate of 13% for the cost of capital for Gulf. Our lower estimate was based on a longer-term view of interest rate levels. Using the same pattern as in Table 10.5 with a cost of capital of 13% results in a loss per barrel of $42.10 from Gulf's E&D programs. When the existing $39 market price of Gulf is added, the result is $81 per share. The $80 purchase would still return SOCAL's cost of capital on the Gulf purchase.

The HBS case also quoted a *Wall Street Journal* article (March 7, 1984, p. 22), stating that Chevron had acquired Gulf's reserves for a price equivalent to about $4.40 per barrel. The article also stated that the $4.40 was less than half of Chevron's average finding cost over the prior five years. If this saving of finding costs were $5 per barrel and applied to Gulf's total reserves of 2.313 billion barrels equivalent, it would represent a savings of $11.6 billion. Thus, another approach to testing the value of Gulf to Chevron is to look at it as a bargain purchase of reserves already in place. This estimate is also close to the $13.2 billion actually paid for Gulf by Chevron.

### The Effect of the Gulf Purchase on the Value of Chevron

Another approach to evaluating an acquisition is to look at the impact on the acquiring company. This is a less precise measure of the direct impact because so many other things may be going on. Over a period of years, other restructuring efforts are taking place, cost reduction programs are under way, other acquisitions are made.

Nevertheless, as a part of a number of strategic moves, we can make some judgments about the effects of a major acquisition by looking at the subsequent performance of the acquiring company.

In Table 10.6, we perform a valuation of Chevron at the end of 1994. We develop the value drivers as shown in the footnote of the table. They are based on the historical data between 1986 and 1994, but modified taking into account the underlying trends in the industry and the position of Chevron in the industry. Chevron, like other oil companies, was benefiting from technological change that increased the average oil field recovery from 35% to as high as 75% (Finizza, 1996). For major oil fields in the United States, production costs per barrel declined from $7.20 in 1984–1986 to $4.10 per barrel in 1989–1992, a decline of 42% (Finizza, p. 10). Other estimates place the reduction in U.S. production costs since 1983 to be as high as 62%. The pattern of two key value drivers, investment and profitability, changed dramatically over three time segments for Chevron as shown below:

|  | 1975–1983 | 1986–1994 | Estimated 1994–2004 |
|---|---|---|---|
| Investment rate (b) | 55% | 4% | 40% |
| Marginal profitability rate (r) | 12.0% | 24% | 30% |

During the 1975–1983 period, Chevron had a high investment rate of 55% with modest profitability of 12.0%. After the acquisition of Gulf, during the period 1986–1994 Chevron's investment rate dropped to only 4% with an improvement of the

**TABLE 10.6**   Chevron Corp. Valuation at End of 1994 with Gulf

|  | (1) | (2) | (3) | (4) | (5) | (6) | (7) | (8) | (9) | (10) | (11) | (12) |
|---|---|---|---|---|---|---|---|---|---|---|---|---|
|  | Current Assets Total | Marketable Securities | Current Liabilities Total | Debt in Current Liabilities | Pretax Income | Income Taxes Total | Interest Expense | Property, Plant, and Equipment Total (Net) | Net Working Capital $(1-2)-(3-4)$ | Total Capital $(8+9)$ | Investment (delta 10) | EBIT $(5+7)$ |
| 1986 | $9,050 | $2,986 | $6,485 | $619 | $1,740 | $1,025 | $885 | $22,746 | $198 | $22,944 |  | $2,625 |
| 1987 | 9,828 | 850 | 7,494 | 915 | 2,876 | 1,869 | 786 | 21,736 | 2,399 | 24,135 | 1,191 | 3,662 |
| 1988 | 7,941 | 518 | 7,003 | 469 | 2,899 | 1,131 | 661 | 23,798 | 889 | 24,687 | 552 | 3,560 |
| 1989 | 8,620 | 476 | 7,583 | 126 | 1,306 | 1,055 | 680 | 23,040 | 687 | 23,727 | −960 | 1,986 |
| 1990 | 10,089 | 458 | 9,017 | 59 | 4,213 | 2,056 | 635 | 22,726 | 673 | 23,399 | −328 | 4,848 |
| 1991 | 9,031 | 445 | 9,480 | 1,706 | 2,252 | 959 | 546 | 22,850 | 812 | 23,662 | 263 | 2,798 |
| 1992 | 8,772 | 403 | 9,835 | 2,888 | 3,463 | 1,253 | 478 | 22,188 | 1,422 | 23,610 | −52 | 3,941 |
| 1993 | 8,682 | 372 | 10,606 | 3,456 | 2,426 | 1,161 | 371 | 21,865 | 1,160 | 23,025 | −585 | 2,797 |
| 1994 | 7,591 | 893 | 9,392 | 4,014 | 2,803 | 1,110 | 419 | 22,173 | 1,320 | 23,493 | 468 | 3,222 |
| Totals |  |  |  |  | $23,978 | $11,619 |  |  |  |  | $549 | $29,439 |

| | | Valuation: |
|---|---|---|
| $X_0 =$ | $3,222 | |
| $T =$ | 40.0% | |
| $b =$ | 40.0% | |
| $r =$ | 30.0% | |
| $g =$ | 12.0% | |
| $n =$ | 10 | |
| $k =$ | 10.0% | |

1st term $= X_0(1-T)(1-b)\sum_{t=1}^{n}\left(\dfrac{1+g}{1+k}\right)^t =$  $12,825 (33.1%)

$(1+h) = (1+g)/(1+k)$   1.02

2nd term $= \dfrac{X_0(1-T)(1-z)}{k-p}\left(\dfrac{1+g}{1+k}\right)^n (1+g) =$ $25,927 (66.9%)

$p =$ inflation rate $=$   0.0%

$z =$ reinvestment rate   0.0%

Total value $=$   $38,752 (100.0%)

marginal profitability rate to 24%. The improvement in the profit rate for the period 1986–1994 did not result from simply shutting down Gulf's E&D efforts. Chevron evaluated the full set of E&D efforts making no distinction between their own and those acquired with Gulf. The best were kept and the least favorable were closed down. Thus, the average level of Chevron's E&D efforts were improved by the acquisition. So Chevron's overall investment activity declined sharply in the 1986–1994 period. With the reductions of finding costs and production costs and new strategic alliances in attractive programs abroad, our judgment estimate of Chevron's investment rate for 1994–2004 is 40% and the marginal profitability rate up to 30%. *T* is set at 40%.

Thus, at the end of 1994 Chevron increased its investment rate by strategic joint alliances with producers abroad. In addition, Chevron had achieved substantial cost savings in both E&D efforts and in production operations. These improvements are reflected in Table 10.6. That results in an estimate of total value for Chevron at the end of 1994 of $38.8 billion. The actual value of Chevron at the end of 1994 was a market value of equity of $29.1 billion with interest-bearing debt outstanding of $8.1 billion for a total of $37.2 billion. This is not greatly different from the results in Table 10.6. Both indicate substantial value increases to Chevron after 1984, consistent with the judgment that the Gulf acquisition was a positive NPV investment.

We do not mean to imply that being close to the actual market validates our estimates. Our estimates were performed independently before looking at actual market values. The methodology employed would be valuable even if the estimation were far above or far below actual market values. If our estimates were below actual market values, we could investigate whether value drivers implied by the actual market values were consistent with reasonable measures of the value drivers; similarly, if our estimates were above actual market values. In one sense, the value drivers are a basis for arriving at intrinsic value. It is one method of finding overvalued or undervalued securities.

Several generalizations can be drawn from the foregoing analysis. In evaluating the price of $13.2 billion paid by Chevron for Gulf, we used a number of approaches. We used comparable transactions, spreadsheet methods, and formula approaches. In addition, we analyze the savings in finding costs—the costs of adding to reserves. It is useful to employ several approaches to valuation. First, valuations are forward looking so projections or forecasts are required. In a dynamic and turbulent world, such forecasts are subject to error. Second, by using a number of methodologies the margin of error can be reduced. Third, each methodology has strengths and limitations. This should sensitize decision makers to rapidly adjust to changes in future developments in the economy and to the strategies of competitors. Fourth, the data and forecasts for individual firms must forecast the important business, political, and cultural developments that will impact the underlying value drivers. Fifth, ultimately valuations must reflect historical patterns, financial statement data, and importantly the analytic judgments of the important developments of the environments in which the firm under analysis operates.

By employing these multiple methodologies, we were led to the conclusion that the purchase of Gulf by Chevron in 1984 was a positive net present value investment.

--------------------------------------------------------------------------------

## Summary

We have illustrated three fundamental approaches to valuation. The comparable transactions or comparable companies approach looks at information directly supplied from the marketplace. The formula approach is most useful when the firm has reached a relatively steady pattern of relationships that lend themselves to the value driver computations. The spreadsheet approach is a formula method in that the discounted cash flow methodology is applied. Its advantage is that the year-to-year projections can be related to portray the impact of new programs and lumpy events related to individual years. The formula and spreadsheet methods are different presentations of the *same* approach.

We also illustrated how in particular industries there might be key forces that are the main determinants of value. For the oil industry, it is the cost of finding new reserves. Alternatively, a company might be bought based on the proved reserves it already possesses. Cable firms are bought and sold on the basis of the number of or potential number of subscribers.

New approaches to valuation involve the use of options concepts. Additional insights can be obtained even in basic capital budgeting analysis by the recognition of options ideas (Brennan and Schwartz, 1985). The options to make a small investment and then make further investments subject to sequential information has value in the flexibility provided. Options to delay, options to shut down and restart, options to recombine, production input proportions, and technologies all can influence value. In addition, potential future growth options can greatly influence the value of the firm (Myers, 1977). Some of these approaches have been quantified effectively; others have not. But the insights provided by options analysis should also be a part of the analysis and used as aids to valuation judgments.

Because valuation inherently involves projections of the future, some judgment must be exercised to arrive at values. With the help of computer technology, it is relatively inexpensive to assemble data reflecting a multiple of approaches. Our emphasis is not that any one valuation method is best. Each valuation method provides information. Use each approach to obtain as much information as possible. Ultimately, the value of a company to be acquired or the value of a business segment to be divested involves the exercise of judgment.

----

## Questions

10.1 Discuss the four methods of calculating the cost of equity capital and how they are used in the valuation model.

10.2 The Smith Company has free cash flows ($X$) of $19 million, and is expected to grow at a rate of 26.5% for the next five years. Its ratio of investment to after-tax NOI ($b$) is 0.5. The applicable tax rate is 30%; Smith's cost of capital is 10%. After the period of supernormal growth, Smith Company is not expected to grow any further.
   a. What is the value of Smith Company?
   b. What is the implied profitability rate ($r$)?
   c. If Smith has $110 in interest-bearing debt, what is the value of Smith's equity?

10.3 The Jones Company has the same parameters as the Smith Company in question 2, except that its investment rate ($b$) is 1.0, and its profit rate is 26.5%.
   a. What is the value of Jones Company?
   b. If Jones Company has $68 million in interest-bearing debt, what is the value of Jones's equity?

10.4 Given the following information on the Paul Company and the Rick Company, as well as the Smith and Jones Companies, use the investment banker comparables method to value the equity of Smith and Jones. All four firms are roughly similar in size and have similar product-market mix characteristics. In performing the comparables analysis, use the following ratios:
   a. Market to book value
   b. Market to replacement cost

c. Market to sales
d. Price to earnings ($P/E$)
e. Market to after-tax EBIT [EBIT$(1 - T)$]

| | Paul Co. | Rick Co. | Smith Co. | Jones Co. |
|---|---|---|---|---|
| Revenues | $600 | $400 | $500 | $400 |
| EBDIT | 40 | 40 | 33 | 40 |
| Depreciation | 6 | 8 | 7 | 13 |
| EBIT | 34 | 32 | 26 | 27 |
| Interest expense | 10 | 10 | 8 | 8 |
| EBT | 24 | 22 | 18 | 19 |
| Current taxes | 7 | 6 | 5 | 6 |
| Net income | 17 | 16 | 13 | 13 |
| Current ratio | 2/1 | 2/1 | 2/1 | 2/1 |
| Interest-bearing debt to net worth | 50% | 50% | 55% | 45% |
| Fixed-charge coverage | 3X | 3X | 3X | 3X |
| Revenue growth | 25% | 30% | 24% | 31% |
| EBIT growth | 30% | 30% | 26.5% | 26.5% |
| Net income growth | 30% | 30% | 28% | 28% |
| Marginal free cash flow to total investment capital, net ($r$) | 50% | 25% | 53% | 26.5% |
| Marginal investment requirements to free cash flow, net ($b$) | 0.6 | 1.2 | 0.5 | 1.0 |
| Market value | $400 | $350 | _391_ | _226_ |
| Book value | 300 | 200 | 150 | 100 |
| Replacement cost | 500 | 400 | 300 | 300 |

10.5 This case-problem analyzes the sensitivity of prospective gains to the bidder as a function of the purchase price paid for the target. In the table below, the first two columns of data present the initial value drivers plus the market value of debt for a bidder and a target. It is postulated that the two combine. The remaining five columns of the table present the value drivers under alternative kinds of interactions between the bidder and target after the merger. The purpose of the exercise is to illustrate how various combinations of the value drivers cause differences in resulting valuation. Answer the questions listed below the table.

| | Bidder | Target | Combined | | | | |
|---|---|---|---|---|---|---|---|
| | | | Base | Case 1 | Case 2 | Case 3 | Case 4 |
| Market value of debt, $B_0$, (millions) | $50 | $20 | $70 | $70 | $70 | $70 | $70 |
| Net operating income, $X_0$, (millions) | $20 | $10 | $30 | $30 | $30 | $30 | $30 |
| Tax rate, $T$ | 40.0% | 40.0% | 40.0% | 40.0% | 40.0% | 40.0% | 40.0% |
| Investment rate, $b$ | 20.0% | 110.0% | 50.0% | 80.0% | 110.0% | 130.0% | 60.0% |
| Marginal profit rate, $r$ | 10.0% | 20.0% | 15.0% | 20.0% | 30.0% | 10.0% | 40.0% |
| Growth rate, $g = br$ | 2.0% | 22.0% | 7.5% | 16.0% | 33.0% | 13.0% | 24.0% |
| Weighted cost of capital, $k$ | 10.0% | 11.0% | 10.0% | 10.0% | 11.0% | 11.0% | 11.0% |
| Supernormal growth period, $n$ | 10 | 10 | 10 | 10 | 10 | 10 | 10 |
| Inflation rate after period of supernormal growth, $p$ | 3.0% | 3.0% | 3.0% | 3.0% | 3.0% | 3.0% | 5.0% |
| Reinvestment requirement, $z$ | 1.0% | 2.0% | 1.0% | 0.0% | 2.0% | 3.0% | 2.0% |

a. What is the initial value of each firm before the merger?
b. What is the value of equity of each firm before a merger?

c. What is the value of the combined firm under the five cases?

d. What is the value of equity of the combined firm under the five cases?

e. What is the gain in value to the bidder for the base case and the four variations on it, under different assumptions for the size of the premium paid over the intrinsic value of equity of the target before the merger ($200)? Calculate the gain in value to the bidder from the acquisition of the following alternative levels of premia paid: 0%, 10%, 20%, 40%, 50%, 100%.

Among other things, this case illustrates that even in a synergistic merger if the premium paid is excessive, it will be a negative NPV investment for the bidder and cause the market equity value of the bidder to decline.

10.6 This question seeks to focus on a basic technique to employ in applying valuation analysis to M&As. In practice, many alternative methodologies are employed. Typically a graph is developed that provides a sensitivity analysis of the effect on earnings per share or return on book investment based on alternative prices paid for the target or targets. These other techniques are useful in providing some perspectives but have defects as well. They are based on accounting data. They take a static approach based on the latest years' earnings data.

The advantage of the methodology here proposed is that basic valuation concepts are employed. The acquisition decision is based on whether and by how much the value of the bidder is increased. Our basic valuation approach is applied to the bidder and targets on a stand-alone basis and then after an acquisition takes place.

The following data are on three companies: a bidder and target 1 and target 2. The supernormal growth period is 10 years and zero growth thereafter; the applicable tax rate is 40%. The other relevant data are given in the following table.

| | (1) Bidder Alone | (2) Target 1 Alone | (3) Target 2 Alone | (4) Bidder Acquires Target 1 | (5) Bidder Acquires Target 2 |
|---|---|---|---|---|---|
| Net operating income (millions) | $20.0 | $10.0 | $10.0 | $30.0 | $30.0 |
| Market value of debt (millions) | 50.0 | 20.0 | 20.0 | 70.0 | 70.0 |
| Investment rate, $b$ | 1.00 | 1.10 | 1.50 | 1.10 | 1.00 |
| Growth rate, $g = br$ | 21.0% | 22.1% | 23.2% | 26.5% | 23.2% |
| Weighted cost of capital | 10.0% | 11.0% | 12.0% | 10.0% | 12.0% |

a. What is the value of the firm for each of the five cases?

b. What is the value of the equity of the firm under each of the five cases?

c. What is the gain in value to the bidder if target 1 is purchased at its preacquisition value? This also shows the size of the premium the bidder could pay to the target and still increase its own value.

d. What is the gain in value to the bidder if target 2 is purchased at its preacquisition value? This also shows the size of the premium the bidder could pay to the target and still increase its own value.

e. Should the bidder buy both targets, neither, or only one?

------------------------------------------------------------------------

# References

Brennan, M., and E. Schwartz, "Evaluating Natural Resource Investments," *Journal of Business,* 58, April 1985, pp. 135–157.

Finizza, Anthony J., "The Future of Oil," *Business Economics,* 31(4), October 1996, pp. 7–11.

Harvard Business School, "Gulf Oil Corporation—Takeover," Case No. 285-053, November 7, 1984; revised 1992.

Myers, S., "Determinants of Corporate Borrowing," *Journal of Financial Economics,* 19, November 1977, pp. 147–175.

Siu, J. A., and J. F. Weston, "Restructuring in the U.S. Oil Industry," *Journal of Energy Finance & Development,* 1, 1996, pp. 113–131.

# APPENDIX A
# TO CHAPTER 10

# Calculating Growth Rates

Growth rates play a crucial role in many areas of financial analysis. This appendix describes three ways to calculate the growth rate of a particular variable, such as net operating income (NOI) or stock price for example, over a series of time. The data in Table A10.1 represent net operating income (NOI) for a company that has grown at a steady annual rate of 20%.

The first method calculates a **discrete compound annual growth rate, $d$,** as discussed in the text. It is a geometric average based on the end points of the time series, and is found by dividing the final year by the initial year, then taking, for this example, the tenth root. This is done below:

$$(61.9/10.0)^{(1/10)} = 1.20 = 1 + d$$

Thus, the discrete growth rate is 20%. Note that these data plot as a curved line (concave from above) on arithmetic graph paper and as a straight line on semilog paper (Figures A10.1 and A10.2).

The second method calculates a **continuously compounded growth rate, $c$,** as shown in Table A10.2. It is found as the slope of the regression line where the natural logarithm of NOI (in this case) is the dependent variable, and the year (designated as 1, 2, 3 . . . rather than as the actual year number such as 1996) is the independent variable. This is easily accomplished on a personal computer using Excel or other software packages, and even on some handheld calculators. For our data, the slope of the regression equation tells us that the continuously compounded growth rate is 18.23%.

Because of the nature of the data, the only difference in the growth rates is caused by the compounding assumption in each case. The regression method results in a

| TABLE A10.1 | Data to Illustrate Growth at 20% |
|---|---|
| *Time Period* | *NOI* |
| 1 | $10.0 |
| 2 | 12.0 |
| 3 | 14.4 |
| 4 | 17.3 |
| 5 | 20.7 |
| 6 | 24.9 |
| 7 | 29.9 |
| 8 | 35.8 |
| 9 | 43.0 |
| 10 | 51.6 |
| 11 | 61.9 |

■ 225 ■

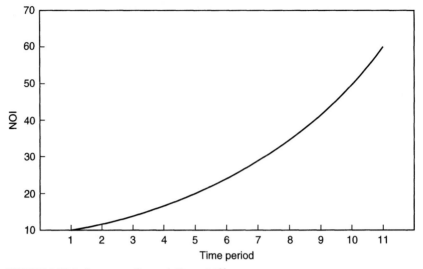

**FIGURE A10.1 Constant Growth Rate, 20%**

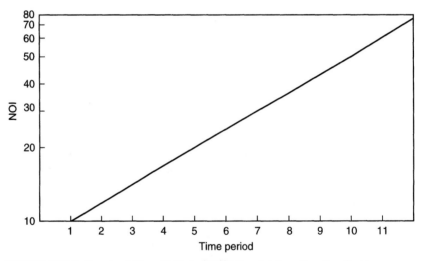

**FIGURE A10.2 Constant Growth Rate (20%) Graphed on Semilog Paper**

continuously compounded growth rate, while the end-points method implicitly assumes annual compounding. This is illustrated using the standard formula relating discrete and compound growth rates: $d = e^c - 1$. We first solve the equation for $d$, the discrete rate, using the continuously compounded growth rate we obtained in the regression.

$$d = e^{.182321} - 1 = 1.20 - 1 = 20\%$$

Alternatively, we can solve for $c$, using the $d$ we obtained in the end-point method:

$$0.20 = e^c - 1$$
$$1.20 = e^c$$

Taking the natural logarithm of both sides of the equation we have

$$\ln(1.20) = \ln(e^c)$$

**TABLE A10.2**   Regression Method of Calculating Growth Rate—Constant Growth

| Time Period | NOI | ln (NOI) | Regression Output | |
|---|---|---|---|---|
| 1 | 10.0 | 2.302585 | Constant | 2.120411 |
| 2 | 12.0 | 2.484906 | Std. err. of Y est. | 0.000909 |
| 3 | 14.4 | 2.667228 | R squared | 0.999997 |
| 4 | 17.3 | 2.850706 | No. of observations | 11 |
| 5 | 20.7 | 3.030133 | Degrees of freedom | 9 |
| 6 | 24.9 | 3.214867 | | |
| 7 | 29.9 | 3.397858 | X coefficient(s) | 0.182302 |
| 8 | 35.8 | 3.577947 | Std. err. of coef. | 0.000086 |
| 9 | 43.0 | 3.761200 | | |
| 10 | 51.6 | 3.943521 | | |
| 11 | 61.9 | 4.125520 | | |

Because the natural logarithm of $(e^x)$ is simply $x$, we have

$$\ln (1.20) = c = 0.1823$$

These results obtain only for the special case we have illustrated in which the discrete growth rate has no fluctuations. Now consider a case where the NOI does fluctuate, while still exhibiting overall growth, as depicted in Table A10.3.

Figure A10.3 portrays the greater variability. The discrete growth rate, $d$, using end points, is calculated as:

$$(3{,}700/1{,}000)^{(1/10)} = 1.1397 = 1 + d$$

Thus, $d = 14\%$.

Using the regression method, the continuously compounded growth rate, $c$, is 12.6% as shown in Table A10.4. As before, the continuously compounded growth rate is lower than the discrete rate. In this example, the difference is not due solely to the compounding method, but also because the regression method considers the fluctuations.

**TABLE A10.3**   Data to Illustrate Fluctuating Growth Rates

| Time Period | NOI ($) |
|---|---|
| 1 | 1,000 |
| 2 | 1,400 |
| 3 | 1,250 |
| 4 | 1,600 |
| 5 | 1,250 |
| 6 | 2,000 |
| 7 | 3,300 |
| 8 | 2,800 |
| 9 | 2,600 |
| 10 | 3,000 |
| 11 | 3,700 |

**FIGURE A10.3 Fluctuating Growth Rates**

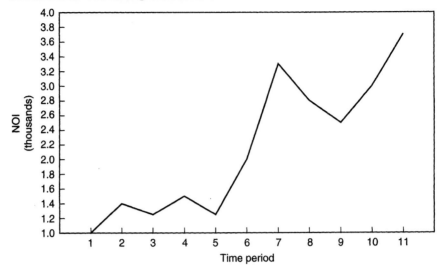

**TABLE A10.4** Regression Method of Calculating Growth Rate—Fluctuating Growth

| Time Period | NOI | ln (NOI) | Regression Output | |
|---|---|---|---|---|
| 1 | 1000 | 6.907755 | Constant | 6.835528 |
| 2 | 1400 | 7.244227 | Std. err. of Y est. | 0.189571 |
| 3 | 1250 | 7.130898 | R squared | 0.844064 |
| 4 | 1600 | 7.377758 | No. of observations | 11 |
| 5 | 1250 | 7.130898 | Degrees of freedom | 9 |
| 6 | 2000 | 7.600902 | | |
| 7 | 3300 | 8.101677 | X coefficient(s) | 0.126157 |
| 8 | 2800 | 7.937374 | Std. err. of coef. | 0.018074 |
| 9 | 2600 | 7.863266 | | |
| 10 | 3000 | 8.006367 | | |
| 11 | 3700 | 8.216088 | | |

If we again use the standard relationship between $d$ and $c$, we obtain the discrete rate. Solving for $d$, using $c$, we have

$$d = e^{.126157} - 1 = 1.13446 - 1 = 13.45\%,$$

which is below the end-point result of $d = 14\%$.

Alternatively, the annual compounding 14% result found by the end-points method can be converted into a continuously compounding rate:

$$0.14 = e^c - 1$$
$$1.14 = e^c$$
$$\ln (1.14) = c = .1310 = 13.1\%$$

This is above the 12.6% continuously compounded rate found using the regression method. The end-points method is a useful rough method of calculating growth rates. But the end-points method may be seriously flawed if the end values are not representative. The regression method takes into account all data points.

**C H A P T E R**

# 11

# Restructuring and Divestitures

This chapter discusses the broad strategies of corporate restructuring and reorganization. These take many forms.

## CORPORATE RESTRUCTURING STRATEGIES

To place the subject matter in perspective, Table 11.1 provides a general framework in four sections: asset management, ownership organizations, reorganizing financial claims including recontracting, and other strategies.

Table 11.1 suggests a broad framework within which to review the major strategic decisions of the firm. In previous chapters, we have shown that the firm operates in economic, social, and competitive environments with considerable turbulence. The future

| **TABLE 11.1** General Framework for Corporate Restructuring and Reorganization |
| --- |

1. Reorganization of assets (chapter 11)
   a. Acquisitions
   b. Sell-offs or divestitures
2. Creating new ownership relationships (chapter 12)
   a. Spin-offs
   b. Split-ups
   c. Equity carve-outs
3. Reorganizing financial claims (chapter 13)
   a. Exchange offers
   b. Dual-class recapitalizations
   c. Leveraged recapitalizations
   d. Financial reorganization (bankruptcy)
   e. Liquidation
4. Other strategies
   a. Joint ventures (chapter 14)
   b. ESOPs and MLPs (chapter 15)
   c. Going-private transactions (LBOs) (chapter 16)
   d. Using international markets (chapter 17)
   e. Share repurchase programs (chapter 18)

is difficult to assess. The firm must have a grand plan and a strategic framework. These are useful, broad guides for developing policies and decisions. But even broad strategic plans are subject to revision and augmentation both in anticipation of and in reaction to dynamic changes. Firms, like individuals, must continuously engage in sequential learning and in adjusting and improving. The product mix and scope of a firm's activities are continuously reviewed and modified on the basis of external changes and new knowledge and understanding.

Table 11.1 conveys the wide range of types of adjustments that the firm may employ in the effort to survive and grow to yield benefits in a balanced way in each class of its stakeholders. Section one topics in Table 11.1 are covered in the present chapter. The remaining topics are discussed in the next seven chapters.

## Some Basic Forces

The restructuring of business firms stems from a number of forces. Basic is the need to meet global competition. Other factors: One objective addresses the agency problem of the conflict of interest between managers and shareholders. A central purpose of restructuring is to align better the interests of managers and shareholders. A second function of restructuring is to move assets to owners who can utilize them more effectively. This helps the economic system move assets to their highest valued uses.

A third general reason given for the restructuring of the 1980s is to reverse the conglomerate merger movement of the 1960s. Some argue that it was unsound to combine many diverse activities into conglomerates as occurred in the 1960s. Conglomeration appeared to be the result of management theories that held that at the level of general management functions particularly, executives could effectively manage a wide range of business types. Another factor involved in conglomeration was that firms in industries with depleting resources such as forestry and a range of mining industries, or industries with narrow or specialized product lines or with uncertain outlooks such as defense industries, sought defensive diversification. In addition, horizontal and vertical mergers were effectively prohibited by the administration of the antitrust laws in the United States. Some ascribe the need to break up conglomerates as a consequence of the intensification of competition in the U.S. economy, particularly increased international competition. Others view the conglomeration as a result of a learning process and an emphasis on developing new core businesses with more favorable outlooks or better suited to the capabilities possessed by the managements of individual conglomerate firms. Voluntary liquidations and "bust-up" takeovers reflect the judgment that the sale of individual parts of some firms could realize greater values than the combination of the parts in one corporate enterprise. Thus, the subject matter of this chapter deals with a fundamental new force in the economy—the restructuring of corporate America.

## Definitions and Examples

Most studies have focused on divestitures and spin-offs as a means of eliminating or separating a product line, division, or subsidiary. Divestitures represent the sale of a segment of a company to a third party. Assets, product lines, subsidiaries, or divisions are sold for cash or securities or some combination thereof. The compensation received, net of capital gains taxation, may be used however the seller's management sees fit. The assets are revalued by the sale for purposes of future depreciation by the buyer. Dun and Bradstreet's 1983 sale of its television stations is an example of a divestiture. Divestitures are related to merger and acquisition (M&A) transactions in that in recent years about 40% of acquisition activities represented divestitures by other firms. This percentage has fluctuated in the 35 to 40% range during the 1980s, down from a peak of 53 to 54% during 1976 and 1975, respectively. Purchase prices are available on only about half of the transactions, with divestitures in recent years running at about 35% of the dollar value of transactions (Houlihan Lokey Howard & Zukin).

**Spin-offs** are more often associated with controlled subsidiaries. In a spin-off, a company distributes on a pro rata basis all the shares it owns in a subsidiary to its own shareholders. Two separate public corporations with (initially) the same proportional equity ownership now exist where only one existed before. No money changes hands, and the subsidiary's assets are not revalued. The transaction is treated as a stock dividend and a tax-free exchange. AT&T's court-ordered reorganization in 1984 represented a massive (albeit involuntary) spin-off of its operating subsidiaries.

In 1995 **split-ups** of very large corporations, such as ITT and AT&T, made the headlines. In a split-up, two or more new companies come into being in place of the original company. Split-ups are usually accomplished by spin-offs.

Spin-offs are distinguished from **equity carve-outs,** in which some of a subsidiary's shares are offered for sale to the general public, bringing an infusion of cash to the parent firm without loss of control. In 1983–1984, Trans World Corporation initially sold 15 to 20% of its stock in TWA (its airline subsidiary) to the general public in an equity carve-out. (This transaction was followed by a spin-off in which the remaining controlling interest in TWA was spun off, that is, distributed on a pro rata basis to Trans World Corporation's shareholders.)

Other types of sell-offs include **split-offs** in which some, but not all, parent company shareholders receive the subsidiary's shares in return for which they must relinquish their parent company shares. Dome Petroleum purchased an equity interest in Conoco, which they subsequently traded for ownership of Conoco's Hudson Bay oil and gas fields.

If all of the above is not confusing enough, these terms are often used in different ways by different writers. However, because of the potential for confusion, most writers are careful to describe exactly the type of transaction they mean by each term.

In this chapter, we discuss aspects of divestitures. In chapter 12, we discuss the rationale for spin-offs, split-ups, and equity carve-outs, and include case studies. In chapter 13, we discuss exchange offers, dual-class recapitalizations, leveraged recapitalizations, financial reorganization (bankruptcy), and liquidation.

# DIVESTITURES

We first discuss divestitures because of the major role they perform in M&A activity. Like M&A activity in general, the explanations for divestitures are multiple and diverse.

## Background Materials on Divestitures

Both acquisition and divestiture activity may represent efforts by business firms to adjust to their changing economic environments. After the post–World War II adjustments appeared to have been made, the war in Korea caused new shifts in the U.S. economy. Major post–Korean War adjustments took place in the latter half of the 1950s. These abrupt changes stimulated the development of the literature on long-range planning and corporate strategy. The 1960s included the involvement in the war in Vietnam. This was the period of the conglomerate merger movement in which about half the firms actively involved were from the defense industry or natural resource industries with depleting resources. The decade of the 1970s marked a change in international currency standards, floating exchange rates, oil shocks, and relatively high rates of inflation throughout the world. The 1980s were initiated by tight monetary policy in the United States followed by an easing in part to control the debt service costs of the huge indebtedness incurred by many of the less developed nations. It was a period of deregulation in a number of major industries in the United States.

M&A activity as well as divestitures represented one set among strategies by business firms in attempting to adjust to these successive changes in their economic and political environments. Some firms succeeded better than others in these efforts.

In the effort to deal with the changing economic environments discussed earlier, many firms used M&As as well as internal start-ups to probe opportunities in other product-market areas. Some firms sought to utilize the strengths in their existing product-market areas to combine with new capabilities in new environments. (The strategy literature urged them to attempt to do so; see the pioneering book by Ansoff, 1965.) A related strategy was to seek at least a toehold in new product-market areas. The hope was that initial entry could be a beachhead for further growth and development. Much M&A activity involved moving from industries with unfavorable outlooks to industries with more favorable opportunities. Sometimes firms did not have the capabilities to effectively exploit the possible opportunities. Divestitures enabled selling firms to salvage a portion of their investments by selling to other firms that could exploit the opportunities more effectively.

The pressures for overcoming a firm's strategic planning gap or aligning more effectively with the changing environments have varied from industry to industry and during different time periods. Like the circumstances besetting firms at different times in different industries, the motives for divestiture activity are many and diverse.

## Motives for Divestitures

1. *Dismantling conglomerates.* The 1960s marked the height of conglomerate merger activity. In part, it stemmed from "defensive" diversification out of the aerospace and natural resource industries. In part, it represented the philosophy that general managerial capabilities could be profitably transferred to diverse businesses. Many such conglomerates have proven to be inefficient combinations over time. Divestitures have been used to reduce the number and diversity of activities that had been assembled in firms such as Gulf & Western (Paramount) and ITT.

2. *Abandoning the core business.* The sale by a company of its original business cannot be attributed to a diversification mistake, but to changing opportunities or circumstances. In 1987 Greyhound sold its bus business. In 1988 DuPont divested its original commercial explosives business, Wurlitzer sold its basic piano and electric keyboard business (to Baldwin Piano), and B. F. Goodrich Co. sold its remaining stake in the tire business.

3. *Changing strategies or restructuring.* A change in strategic focus may reflect mistakes, learning, or realignment with the firm's changing environments. In 1983 Warner-Lambert sold its successful bakery unit, Entenmann's, to General Foods. In 1982 General Dynamics divested its telecommunications switching business to concentrate on defense business. In 1987 and 1988 Allegis Corp. sold its hotel and car rental units to become UAL Corp. and concentrate on operating United Air Lines, a reversal of a previous strategic plan. Alco Standard Corp. sold off distribution businesses and most manufacturing units after 1987 to focus on paper distribution, office products, and food service equipment. Between 1985 and 1988, TRW divested about $1 billion worth of lower-technology businesses in favor of the high-technology segments of aerospace and defense, automotive components, and information systems and services. Household International sold its manufacturing units to concentrate on financial services. IBM sold Rolm's manufacturing and development oper-

ations to Siemens AG, with whom a joint venture was formed for U.S. sales and service operations for Rolm's switchboard business.

4. ***Adding value by selling into a better fit.***   Dow Jones divested its textbook business to concentrate on business publishing and regional newspapers by selling its Richard D. Irwin unit to Times Mirror, a newspaper company that was seeking to expand in textbook and professional publishing. In 1986 IBM sold 81 IBM Products Centers, its U.S. retailing operations, to NYNEX, one of the regional telephone companies created in the AT&T court-directed divestiture. In 1988 IBM sold most of its U.S. copier business to Eastman Kodak. Such sales may reflect different capabilities, different strategic philosophies, or different expectations.

5. ***Large additional investment required.***   Sometimes remaining in a business requires additional investments that a firm is unable or unwilling to make. Thus, in 1988 Eaton sold its defense electronics business, including the B-1B electronics system, to focus on two other major business areas. For similar reasons, Gould sold its antisubmarine warfare business to Westinghouse Electric.

6. ***Harvesting past successes.***   Some divestitures represent the harvesting of successful investments, often stimulated by favorable market conditions. Here the purpose is to make financial and managerial resources available for developing other opportunities. Such divestitures represent successes rather than failures (or mistakes). Hanson PLC is said to make a business of this activity. Other examples are hotel sales by Hilton and Marriott.

7. ***Discarding unwanted businesses from prior acquisitions.***   Some divestitures of the type that involved selling to a value-increasing buyer were planned at the time of prior M&A activity. Such divestitures may have been preplanned because they represented a poor fit with the acquiring firm. Sometimes such divestitures could be turned at a profit, sometimes they involved a loss that was offset by the good segments retained. Examples are Pullman's sales of Bruning Hydraulics and Waterman Hydraulics to Parker Hannifin in 1988 following its acquisition of Clevite Industries in 1987.

8. ***Financing prior acquisitions.***   A number of divestitures also regularly follow major acquisitions or LBOs for financing reasons. Campeau Corp., which acquired Allied Stores in 1986, stated that it would sell 16 Allied divisions to pay down bank debt. Similarly, after its $6.5 billion acquisition of Federated Department Stores, Campeau engaged in a program of divestitures beginning in late 1988. Other similar patterns followed Beazer PLC's acquisition of Koppers Co. and Maxwell Communications' takeover of Macmillan Inc. Earlier, DuPont, which acquired Conoco in 1981, had sold off $2 billion of Conoco's assets by 1984.

9. ***Warding off takeovers.***   Divestitures have functioned as a takeover defense by removing the "crown jewel" that attracted the takeover threat. A clear example was the sale by Brunswick Corp. of its medical division in 1982 to American Home Products when facing a takeover threat from Whittaker. The proceeds to Brunswick from the sale of the division were $100 million more than Whittaker had offered for the entire company. Ironically, faced with a similar threat in 1989, Whittaker sold its chemical and technology operations.

10. ***Meeting government requirements.***   Divestments are a common requirement for obtaining government approval of a combination. Baker Hughes was required to divest its Reed Tool Co. subsidiary to comply with the Justice Department conditions for approval of its merger. Similarly, in 1988 Santa Fe Southern Pacific Corp. was required by the ICC to sell one of its railroads. In general, the government may require divestitures as a condition for approval when a combination includes segments with competing products. This holds for LBOs as well. KKR was required to sell off some RJR Nabisco product segments that overlapped with KKR's prior holdings.

11. ***Selling businesses to their managers.***   Corporate sales of divisions or business units to operating management are increasing both in number and size. LBOs and other going private transactions have averaged a consistent 11% of total corporate divestitures.

**12.** *Taking a position in another firm.* Divestitures may be used to finance an investment in another firm. An example is the sale in 1989 by Emerson Electric of five units for $149 million to BSR International PLC for a 45% stake in the U.K. firm.

**13.** *Reversing mistakes.* Exxon's acquisition of Reliance Electric and Mobil's purchase of Montgomery Ward are widely cited as failed attempts at diversification. Both sales were management buyouts.

**14.** *Learning.* Successful companies may divest businesses after learning more about them. Merck & Co., whose growth has been mainly internal, divested Baltimore Aircoil Co. and part of a Calgon Corp. acquisition after its experience and review process indicated that the businesses "no longer fit its basic long-range strategy" (Horan, 1987). ARA Services, which grew principally by acquisition, eventually divested a construction management business because of lack of fit. Also, it divested a management consulting firm because it found that the business depended on key individuals while ARA was built on systems and controls.

Porter (1987, p. 49) gives a number of examples of how divestment can perform a very valuable role in the strategic activities of a firm: "Once the results of the one-time improvement are clear, the diversified company no longer adds value to offset the inevitable costs imposed on the unit. It is best to sell the unit and free up corporate resources."

The preceding are examples of the useful functions that divestitures may perform in a company's evolving planning process.

Another general observation is that the use of acquisitions to achieve diversification was severely restricted during the period 1950 through 1980 by government antitrust policies. The 1950 Celler-Kefauver Amendment to the 1914 Clayton Act effectively gave the government the power to stop horizontal and vertical mergers or acquisitions, and the government vigorously exercised its expanded powers. The legal and regulatory environment caused most large mergers during 1950–1980 to be the conglomerate form.

However, Matsusaka (1996) observes that antitrust restrictions did not motivate or cause corporate diversification during the 1960s. In a sample of 549 acquisitions, diversification was equally common in large and small mergers. Antitrust barriers would have caused diversification to occur more frequently when large firms merged than when small firms merged. He also cites evidence that diversification movements were also taking place in other developed nations where antitrust enforcement was not tough.

With this background on the economic and political setting of acquisition-divestiture activity, the evidence on the results is now examined.

## FINANCIAL EFFECTS OF DIVESTITURES

Studies on divestitures have found significant positive abnormal two-day announcement-period returns of between 1% and 2% for selling firm shareholders. The announcement effects on returns to buyers did not appear to be statistically significant (Alexander, Benson, and Kampmeyer, 1984; Jain, 1985; Linn and Rozeff, 1984). A later study by Klein (1986) looked at divestitures in greater depth. Klein analyzed the announcement date effects by whether the selling firms initially announced the price of the sell-off or whether no price was initially announced. When no price was announced, there was no statistically significant effect on share price for the seller. When firms initially announced the price, the size of effects depended on the percentage of the firm being sold as measured by the announced price of the sell-off divided by the market value of the equity on the last day of the month prior to the announcement period.

There is no significant price effect when the percentage of the equity sold is less than 10%. When the percentage of equity sold is between 10 and 50%, the abnormal returns to the seller average a positive 2.53%. When the percentage of the equity sold is greater than 50%, the percentage abnormal return is 8.09%.

When the abnormal gains to sellers from divestitures are aggregated, the totals represent substantial dollar amounts. Black and Grundfest (1988) estimate that for the period 1981–1986, the abnormal value increases to sellers in corporate divestitures could be conservatively placed at $27.6 billion.

Lang, Poulsen, and Stulz (LPS) (1995) studied a sample of 93 significant asset sales during the period 1984–1989. The firms were divided into a payout sample (40 sales) and a reinvest sample (53 sales). The event return analysis showed that the payout firms have positive abnormal returns of about 2% from day −1 to day zero. The reinvest sample had negative event returns of about 0.5% than over the same window. The payout sample firms, on average, had poorer prior performance and higher leverage. Managerial ownership as a fraction of total equity was about 17% for the payout sample compared with 11% for the reinvest sample.

Lang, Poulsen, and Stulz concluded that the positive stock price reaction to asset sales was significantly positive only for firms that plan to pay out the proceeds. The reinvest firms did not have positive event returns because the market is concerned with the agency costs of managerial discretion in the use of the funds. One concern is that managers will use the retained funds to engage in ill-advised diversification. The authors judge their evidence to be inconsistent with the hypothesis that the positive returns associated with asset sales led to more efficient redeployment of assets and that the selling firm captures some of the gains from increased efficiency.

Kaplan and Weisbach (1992) provide an insightful analysis of divestiture results. Their study covers a sample of 271 acquisitions between 1971 and 1982 of at least 100 million 1982 dollars. By 1989, 119 had been divested after a median holding period of seven years.

Almost 60% of the acquisitions in which the acquirer and target are not highly related have been divested. Fewer than 20% of the highly related acquisitions have been divested over the same time period. Only 44% of the acquirers who report an accounting result for the divestiture report a loss on sale. The remaining 56% report a gain or no loss.

When they can compare sales prices to purchase prices for divested units, they find that most units are sold for more than they cost. Deflated by the S&P 500, the average sale price of these divested units is 90% of the purchase price; a small return, but not the failure suggested by previous work. The sale price (deflated by the S&P 500) averages 143% of the target's pretakeover market value. Targets appear to be worth less than the bidders pay, but more than the target is worth before the takeover occurs. Acquirer returns and total (acquirer and target) returns at the acquisition announcement are significantly lower for divestitures they classify as unsuccessful than the corresponding returns for divestitures they do not classify as unsuccessful and for acquisitions that are not divested. This last result has two implications. First, in a setting where the nature of the news being revealed is not initially obvious, results suggest that stock market prices do react to fundamentals. Second, it suggests that acquisitions that ultimately prove unsuccessful are considered poor investments by the market when they are made.

We can simplify their findings by setting the pretakeover value (PTV) of the acquisition subsequently divested as 100%. Their data show that the sales price was 171.6% in relation to the PTV of 100%. During the average seven-year holding period, the Standard & Poor's 500 stock index rose by 20%. When we divide the sales price by 1.2, we obtain a deflated sales price equal to 143% of PTV. They state that the deflated sales price was 0.9 of the purchase price. The purchase price, therefore, must have been 159.9% of PTV.

Thus, the story on this large-sample study is that the purchase price was about 60% higher than the pretakeover value. The sales price was about 72% higher.

Deflated, the sales price is only 43% higher than PTV. Thus, compared with the original pretakeover value, the predeflated sales price represented a very substantial increase in value. Even after deflation, the sales price represents a 43% gain over the pretakeover value. However, the purchase price was 60% higher than the pretakeover value. So while value was added, the acquirer paid too much in the sense that the deflated value of the sales price was only 90% of the purchase price. If the acquisition price had been roughly 10% lower, the acquirers would have earned the 20% rise in the S&P 500 over the average seven-year holding period. Because these data are on acquisitions that subsequently divested, we may infer that the acquisitions not subsequently divested performed even better.

The data on divestiture/acquisition rates portray a continued healthy dynamism among U.S. firms. Divestitures perform vital economic functions. Resources, on average, are being moved from less valued uses to higher valued uses. Whether or not sell-offs by one firm to another may sometimes represent efforts to correct previous mistakes, they are evidence that the market system is working. Irrespective of their implications for individual company strategies, divestitures contribute to the resource mobility essential to the effective operation of an enterprise economy.

## CASE STUDIES OF SPIN-OFFS AND DIVESTITURES

In addition to the positive average gains noted for samples of sell-offs, several individual cases of dramatic value increases have been documented. Hite and Owers (1984) describe the Dillingham case, which is a virtual textbook illustration of restructuring. Over the period 1978–1983, Dillingham was involved in divestitures, a spin-off, partial liquidations and suspended operations, proxy contests, antitakeover amendments, a tender offer buy-back from small shareholders, a premium buy-back with standstill agreement to thwart a takeover, and finally a leveraged buyout to take the company private. Although a few of these moves had immediate adverse effects, over a four-year period Dillingham's shareholders experienced abnormal positive returns of 185%, over 85% of which occurred before the LBO announcement. While these returns may not be typical, they do illustrate the potential for gains from restructuring in a dynamic setting.

Linn and Rozeff (1984) analyze the specific returns in two divestitures. In 1983, Warner-Lambert sold its Entenmann's bakery subsidiary to General Foods; the general rationale for gains was discussed earlier; here we look at the numbers involved. The sale price for Entenmann's was $315 million. Upon announcement of the sale, the value of Warner-Lambert stock increased by $101 million and the value of General Foods stock increased by about $44 million (both adjusted for market effects). Both parties benefited from the transaction. From the point of view of Warner-Lambert shareholders, we have:

| | |
|---|---|
| Sale price of Entenmann's received | $315 million |
| Less: Stock value increase | 101 million |
| Implied value of Entenmann's as part of Warner-Lambert | $214 million |

From the point of view of General Foods shareholders, we have:

| | |
|---|---|
| Purchase price of Entenmann's paid | $315 million |
| Plus: Stock value increase | 44 million |
| Implied value of Entenmann's as part of General Foods | $359 million |

Warner-Lambert's shareholders received a premium over what they perceived to be the value of Entenmann's to them; General Foods' shareholders could expect that they would receive benefits from Entenmann's in excess of costs. The total value increase as a result of the divestiture amounted to $145 million, distributed approximately 70/30 between seller and buyer. That the seller received the larger proportion of the gain is not inconsistent with merger studies.

Another case involved the sale of Hospital Affiliates International (HAI) by INA Corporation to Hospital Corporation of America (HCA) for $650 million in 1981. INA was primarily in the insurance business, and the economic rationale for the divestiture seemed to have been that while HAI was a "poor fit" with INA's other operations, HCA would be able to realize operating economies as a result of the acquisition. INA shareholders realized a $75 million abnormal gain upon announcement of the sale, and shareholders of HCA realized $126 million. In this case the total value increase was $201 million, divided approximately 40/60 between seller and buyer respectively.

## RATIONALE FOR DIVESTITURES

Linn and Rozeff (1984) analyze the various motives given for divestitures. Among the reasons given for selling assets are to raise working capital and to pay off debt. However, these are financing decisions and can potentially be accomplished by actions that do not include divestitures. Furthermore, financing as such should not be expected to significantly increase the seller's share price (Smith, 1986a,1986b).

Linn and Rozeff (1984) argue that there are only two valid reasons for divestitures:

1. The assets are worth more as part of the buyer's organization than as part of the seller's.
2. The assets are actively interfering with other profitable operations of the seller.

For example, it is sometimes said that the reason for a divestiture is that the subsidiary is losing money. However, the present value of the subsidiary's future cash flows is already reflected in the seller's stock price. Unless the subsidiary is sold for more than this present value (that is, it is worth more to the buyer), no gain will result from the divestiture. However, if the subsidiary is actually preventing other operations from realizing their potentials, the removal of this negative synergy could cause a positive price impact even if no more than the present value of the subsidiary were received.

The fact that gains to divestitures (1 to 2%) are on average smaller than for spin-offs (3 to 5%) may reflect poor performance prior to the divestiture. Information about worse-than-expected performance may be revealed to the market simultaneously with the divestiture announcement, offsetting to an extent any positive price effect that might otherwise occur. The seller may have to dispose of assets quickly to avert a liquidity crisis, and may not be able to wait for a "fair price" (Linn and Rozeff rejected this rationale).

The smaller gains from divestitures may reflect their smaller relative scale. On average, divestitures may be smaller in relative magnitude than spin-offs. The managerial incentive factor may also perform a role. Spun-off subsidiaries become free-standing independent firms with their own common stock. But divested operations may become segments of another company.

John and Ofek (1995) studied the motives and effects of divestitures. They found that value gains resulted from improved management of the assets remaining after divestiture. This, in turn, was attributed to increased focus measured by an increase in the Herfindahl Index and a decrease in the number of reported lines of business. Also they found that 75% of the divested divisions are unrelated to the core activities of the seller.

They observed that some of their findings supported the hypothesis that a better fit between the buyer and the divested division accounts for some of the value gains. For example, seller returns were higher when the buyer was an LBO group, which is likely to improve operating performance from the organizational changes and strengthening of incentive systems.

---

## Summary

Because divestitures are voluntary decisions by management, we would expect them to represent positive NPV strategies toward the goal of maximizing shareholder wealth. Several principles form the basis for the value increase observed in sell-offs. In some cases the underlying cause is clear; in others it may be impossible to distinguish between two or more possible sources.

### Tax and/or Regulatory Effects

These are clearly identifiable as the source of gains in many sell-offs. They are, however, just as clearly not available in all situations. Spin-offs can be tax exempt transactions.

### Poor Fit

There are at least two aspects involved. The parent firm's management may lack the expertise to manage dissimilar assets. The assets may be creating negative synergy, that is, actively interfering with other profitable operations of the parent. The high incidence of sell-offs after a period of acquisitions and rapid growth may reflect this motive.

### Information Effects

In sell-offs, the transaction is initiated by the seller who has discovered a higher-valued use for a subset of business assets elsewhere. However, gains that take place at the sell-off announcement dissipate if the sell-off is canceled. This may indicate that no new information has been uncovered. Alternatively, it is possible that the new information cannot be exploited in canceled sell-offs. It is possible that another organization is required to have the knowledge or capabilities to develop the potential of the business segment involved.

### Management Focus and Incentives

This theory holds that more homogeneous organizations may be managed more effectively and evaluated more accurately by financial analysts. In addition, managers may receive incentives and rewards more closely related to actual performance than when the quality of performance may be obscured in consolidated financial statements, or monitored by superiors unfamiliar with the unique problems of a disparate subsidiary. In spin-offs, the creation of a free-standing stock price, reflecting the market's assessment of management's performance on a continual basis, may help assure that management compensation plans based on stock options will more directly measure and reward performance.

Divestitures and sell-offs represent mistakes in a sense because previous investment decisions are altered. However, they may also represent the harvesting of sound investments made earlier. Some sell-offs were planned at the time of earlier acquisitions, sometimes to help finance the larger transactions. Sell-offs may also reflect organization learning or reorientation of business strategies. To some degree at least, divestitures represent the movement of business resources to higher-valued uses.

## Questions

11.1 What are the gains in divestitures and why?

11.2 What are pure-play securities and what is their role in the information and managerial efficiency hypothesis of divestitures?

11.3 According to Linn and Rozeff, what are the only two valid reasons for divestitures?

11.4 How do tax and/or regulatory factors affect returns to divestitures?

11.5 What is the magnitude of divestiture activity in relation to merger and acquisitions activity generally?

## References

Alexander, Gordon J., P. George Benson, and Joan M. Kampmeyer, "Investigating the Valuation Effects of Announcements of Voluntary Corporate Selloffs," *Journal of Finance,* 39, June 1984, pp. 503–517.

Ansoff, H. Igor, *Corporate Strategy,* New York: McGraw-Hill, 1965.

Black, Bernard S., and Joseph A. Grundfest, "Shareholder Gains from Takeovers and Restructurings Between 1981 and 1986: $162 Billion Is a Lot of Money," *Journal of Applied Corporate Finance,* 1, Spring 1988, pp. 5–15.

Hite, Gailen, and James E. Owers, "The Restructuring of Corporate America: An Overview," *Midland Corporate Finance Journal,* 2, Summer 1984, pp. 6–16.

Horan, John J., "Merck & Co.: Study in Internal Growth," chapter 8 in Milton L. Rock, ed., *The Mergers & Acquisitions Handbook,* New York: McGraw-Hill Book Company, 1987.

Houlihan Lokey Howard & Zukin, *Mergerstat Review,* various years.

Jain, Prem C., "The Effect of Voluntary Sell-Off Announcements on Shareholder Wealth," *Journal of Finance,* 40, March 1985, pp. 209–224.

John, Kose, and Eli Ofek, "Asset Sales and Increase in Focus," *Journal of Financial Economics,* 37(1), January 1995, pp. 105–126.

Kaplan, Steven N., and Michael S. Weisbach, "The Success of Acquisitions: Evidence from Divestitures," *Journal of Finance,* 47(1), March 1992, pp. 107–138.

Klein, A., "The Timing and Substance of Divestiture Announcements: Individual, Simultaneous and Cumulative Effects," *Journal of Finance,* 41, 1986, pp. 685–697.

Lang, Larry, Annette Poulsen, and René Stulz, "Asset Sales, Firm Performance, and the Agency Costs of Managerial Discretion," *Journal of Financial Economics,* 37(1), January 1995, pp. 3–37.

Linn, Scott C., and Michael S. Rozeff, "The Corporate Sell-off," *Midland Corporate Finance Journal,* 2, Summer 1984, pp. 17–26.

Matsusaka, John G., "Did Tough Antitrust Enforcement Cause the Diversification of American Corporations?" *Journal of Financial and Quantitative Analysis,* 31(2), June 1996, pp. 283–294.

Porter, Michael E., "From Competitive Advantage to Corporate Strategy," *Harvard Business Review,* 65, May–June 1987, pp. 43–59.

Smith, Clifford W., Jr., "Investment Banking and the Capital Acquisition Process," *Journal of Financial Economics,* 15, January/February 1986a, pp. 3–29.

———, "Raising Capital: Theory and Evidence," *Midland Corporate Finance Journal,* 4, Spring 1986b, pp. 6–22.

C H A P T E R

# 12

# Restructuring Ownership Relationships

In this chapter, we continue the analysis of several forms of restructuring. Here we focus on restructuring ownership relations: spin-offs, split-ups, equity carve-outs, and targeted stock.

## SPIN-OFFS

In a spin-off, a company owns or creates a subsidiary whose shares are distributed on a pro rata basis to the shareholders of the parent company. The subsidiary now becomes a publicly owned corporation. The dollar value of spin-off activity reached $26 billion in 1993. An article in *Barron's* in early 1994 presented a sample of leading spin-offs during 1993 (Bary, 1994). Large ones included the spin-off by Sears of the Dean Witter Discover operation, whose initial value was $530 million. The spin-off by Eastman Kodak of Eastman Chemical represented a $3.7 billion initial valuation. The Almanac issue of *Mergers & Acquisitions* (March/April 1996) commented on the increased volume of spin-offs "in recent years" (p. 27) and presented a list of 21 major spin-offs in 1995 (p. 29). These included spin-offs by well-known parent companies such as Dole Food, General Mills, Host Marriott, ITT, Kimberly Clark, Hanson PLC, and U S West.

Of the 25-company sample, the average gain from the date of issue to the end of 1993 was 27% compared with an average gain of only 7% for the S&P 500 during comparable periods of time. Some gains were spectacular. For example, the Pittston Company spun off its Pittston Minerals Group on July 6, 1993 with an initial value of $92 million. By year's end the shares had increased in value by 122%. But not all spin-offs are gainers. Ralston Purina created the Ralston Continental Baking Company on June 17, 1993 which by year's end had dropped in value by 30%. Similarly, Mediq Inc. did a spin-off on August 25, 1993 of Mental Health Management; by year's end the price had dropped by 19%.

### Event Return Studies of Spin-Offs

Schipper and Smith (1983) found a positive 2.84% abnormal return to the parent (statistically significant) on the spin-off announcement date. The size of the announcement effect is positively related to the size of the spin-off relative to parent size (the average size of the spin-off is about 20% of the original parent). Spin-offs motivated by avoid-

■ 240 ■

ance of regulation experienced an abnormal return of 5.07% as compared to 2.29% for the remainder of the sample. Examples of regulation avoidance include separating a regulated utility subsidiary from nonutility businesses and spinning off a foreign subsidiary to avoid restrictions by the U.S. Congress.

Hite and Owers (1983) find abnormal returns of 3.8%, somewhat higher than for the full sample of Schipper and Smith. They also find a positive relation between the relative size of the spin-off and the announcement effect. Neither study found an adverse effect on bondholders.

The Copeland, Lemgruber, and Mayers (1987) study extends the earlier studies in a number of dimensions. Particularly, they test for postselection bias. In their first sample, they do this by including announced spin-offs that are not completed (11% of the sample). This leads them to study the effects of successive announcements. A second expanded sample, subject to postselection bias, confirms the impact of successive announcements. They also study ex-date effects that they also find to have positive abnormal performance. They find that taxable spin-offs do not have positive abnormal returns, whereas nontaxable spin-offs do. However, when they control for the size of the spin-off, the difference between the two tax categories disappears.

For their small sample with no postselection bias, the two-day abnormal return from the first announcement is 2.49%; for the larger sample it is 3.03%. Both results are highly significant from a statistical standpoint. Thus, avoiding the postselection bias makes a difference; the return is lower for the sample which includes firms with announced spin-offs that were never consummated. For the eight firms with announced spin-offs that were never made, the two-day average return was a negative (but insignificant) 0.15%.

Copeland, Lemgruber, and Mayers (1987) also calculate the effects of announcements subsequent to the first (most firms had at least three or four announcements; one had 13). They find that, excluding the ex-date from the estimate, the abnormal return for a firm that actually completes the spin-off is 5.02%. They conclude that the first announcement return is not a good estimate of the effect of a completed spin-off because not all spin-offs are completed and that earlier studies had underestimated the wealth effect of a completed spin-off.

In terms of dollar value, overall company gains are roughly equal to the value of the subsidiary spun off. The parent's value is virtually unchanged by the restructuring, while the subsidiary has a new independent market value of its own. For example, if the original firm pre–spin-off value is 5, and the subsidiary's value becomes 1, the post–spin-off value of the parent remains at 5. Thus, the total value would be 6.

A later study by Cusatis, Miles, and Woolridge (CMW) (1993) covers returns for a sample of 146 spin-offs for the 1965–1988 period. They measure the market performance of spin-offs and their parent firms for periods of up to three years after the distribution. For the 146 spin-offs, unadjusted returns are significantly positive for each of the time segments subsequent to the distribution—one-half year, one year, two years, and three years. The mean return for the three-year period following the spin-off is 76%. They also calculate the adjusted returns net of the contemporaneous returns to firms matched on the basis of market value and industry classification. The returns remained significantly positive for the two- and three-year holding periods, but not significant for the shorter holding periods. These findings differ from the results for samples of initial public offerings (IPOs), which achieve high initial returns, but over the longer term, such as three years, underperform the market and matched firms. In contrast, CMW find positive long-term abnormal returns for spin-offs.

Similarly, the raw returns of the parent firms of 146 spin-offs achieve positive and significant abnormal returns for each of the four time segments. For example, the raw mean return over a three-year period is 67.2%. The matched firm adjusted returns remain positive for all of the time periods, but only marginally significant for the three-year holding period.

The authors also find that both the spin-offs and their parents are more frequently involved in takeovers than the comparable firms in their control groups. One-third of the spin-off–parent combinations become involved in takeover activity within three years of the spin-off. For parent firms, most of the takeovers take place within the first two years following the spin-off, the years during which the stock returns of the parent firms are highest. For the spin-offs, most of the takeovers occur in years two and three, which are the years of their strongest stock performance. Interestingly, when the firms involved in takeovers are removed from their sample, the adjusted returns remain positive but not significantly different from zero for most intervals. This implies that parent firms and their spin-offs that engage in no further restructuring activity earn only normal returns during the subsequent three-year period of time. It is the parent firms and their spin-offs that engage in further restructuring through takeovers that account for the positive abnormal returns during the subsequent three-year period of time.

## SPLIT-UPS

In recent years, dramatic examples of restructuring in which companies split themselves into two or more parts have taken place. This is usually accomplished by spin-offs of individual parts from one or more core activities. The rationale for split-ups is conveyed by three case studies.

### The ITT Corp.

The ITT Corp. has a long and interesting history. When Harold Geneen became head of ITT in 1959, it was drifting. It was heavily dependent on running telephone companies in countries outside the United States, often in less developed countries subject to a high degree of political and social risk. Geneen determined to reduce this vulnerability of ITT to political instability abroad. Under his direction, ITT embarked on a vast acquisition of a wide variety of products.

Subsequently, Geneen was succeeded by Rand V. Araskog as the head of ITT in 1979. In the 15-year period through 1994, Araskog sold off 250 of ITT's business units. A December 26, 1994 article in *Barron's* (Ward, 1994) observed that during the 15-year period the price of ITT shares had lagged the S&P 500 Index by 43% and the S&P conglomerate group by 11% with a stock price of $84 near year-end 1994. The article observed that accounting changes made at ITT in late 1994 effectively split the company into three parts: insurance, manufacturing, and leisure. The aim was to improve the share price performance of ITT. The article noted that if ITT sold in three parts, their combined stock market value could be as high as $130 per share, representing a 55% increase over the $84. In the restructuring, the umbrella company for the hotels, casinos, and entertainment companies would be ITT Holdings, which would be headed by Araskog. It was reported that Araskog was seeking to add a broadcast TV network to this group and had tried to buy CBS and General Electric's NBC network. The market was pleased that ITT failed to acquire a network. The view was that ITT did not have the experience or capability to successfully run a network.

In March 1994 ITT had completed the spin-off of its forest products business, ITT Rayonier. In late August 1994 ITT announced its intention of buying the famed Madison Square Garden along with its MSG Cable Network, the New York Knicks, and the New York Rangers. The purchase price was to be $1.1 billion in an equal partnership with Cablevision Systems, then the nation's fourth largest cable-TV firm. During the week in late August 1995 when the agreement to buy the Garden was announced, the ITT shares dropped from $86 to $79. The completion of the deal was delayed by the U.S. Department of Justice so that it could conduct a study of the deal's antitrust implications.

In the meantime, in mid-December 1994, ITT announced it would buy Caesar's World, which owned gambling operations in Las Vegas, Lake Tahoe, and Atlantic City, for approximately $2 billion. The market saw synergy with Sheraton's chain of hotels and casinos, including the Desert Inn in Nevada. The stock rose 3% to $84 on the Friday before Christmas 1994.

In addition to ITT Holdings, which would manage hotels, casinos, and entertainment companies, there would be two other major parts of ITT. The second would be ITT Insurance and Finance, which would represent 52% of ITT's 1993 revenues of $23 billion. This group included ITT Hartford, a life insurance as well as a property and casualty insurance company. Hartford was strong in the life segment as an underwriter in variable annuities.

The third area would be ITT Industries, which along with about 3% of miscellaneous activities, accounted for 30% of ITT revenues. This segment included the automotive business, where ITT has been a leader in antilock brake systems. ITT fluid technology would also be in this group with favorable prospects as the nation's largest pump maker and a major producer of valves, heat exchangers, and fluid-management systems.

There was talk that further divestment might occur in insurance and finance, accounting for over 50% of ITT revenues. ITT's emphasis appeared to be aimed at the leisure and entertainment segment, accounting for about 18% of 1993 revenues. This is the area where apparently ITT top management felt that stock market multiples would be most favorable. Nevertheless, the risks of concentrating on leisure and entertainment as compared with the other two segments appeared to be substantial. These risks included the usual one of overpaying for acquisitions in areas of intense competition, where future growth depended on the ability to successfully extrapolate future social trends and spending patterns.

## The AT&T Restructuring

At 9:11 A.M. (Eastern time) on September 20, 1995 Chairman Robert E. Allen announced that at a special meeting earlier in the morning, the board of AT&T (ticker symbol is T) had approved plans for a strategic restructuring that would split AT&T into three publicly traded global companies. Under the plan, T shareholders would receive shares in two other companies. A fourth business, AT&T Capital Corp., would be sold. Note that this restructuring in the form of a split-up is accomplished by means of spin-offs of two additional companies.

The AT&T name would continue for the Communications Services group with revenues of about $50 billion. This would include the long distance business, AT&T Wireless (formerly McCaw Cellular Communications), and Universal Card operations. About 15% of Bell Lab employees would also be retained. It would also include a newly established AT&T Solutions consulting and systems integration organization.

The second company would be an equipment company called Communications Systems (later renamed Lucent Technologies). Its production would encompass public network switches, transmission systems, wire and cable, and wireless equipment whose total revenue in 1994 was somewhat over $10 billion. Communications products include business phone systems and services, consumer phones and phone rentals totaling about $6.5 billion. Microelectronics consisting of chips and circuit boards represented another $1.5 billion of revenues. The equipment company would also include an AT&T Laboratories unit around the core (85%) of Bell Laboratories for research and development in communications services. The equipment company would have about 20,000 of the Bell Lab employees with about 6,000 remaining with the long distance company.

Splitting off the equipment business from long distance was motivated by the need to split AT&T's role as a supplier and a competitor. AT&T's biggest equipment customers continue to be the seven regional Bell companies. But the Bell companies and the long distance carriers are competitors, each seeking to invade the others' telephone services markets.

The third company would be the Global Information Solutions (GIS) (later renamed back to NCR). It was further announced that NCR would halt the manufacture of personal computers. It would continue to offer customers personal computers as a part of total solutions, but to use outside suppliers. NCR would continue to support and service all of its current hardware and software installations and would market its capabilities to all industries, particularly the three key segments where it has a strong market position—financial, retail, and communications. NCR, with 43,000 people in more than 120 countries, announced major cost-cutting initiatives that would eliminate 8,500 jobs.

NCR would be a remnant of AT&T's efforts to be an effective competitor in the computer business. AT&T long had a vision of a presence in the computer business because central stations switching equipment units are simply large-scale specialized computers. AT&T long felt that it could be a presence in the computer business, but for many years was prevented from doing so by a Consent Decree with the Department of Justice entered into in 1956. A part of the divestiture decree of 1984 gave AT&T increased freedom to compete in other businesses including computers. But AT&T had the disadvantage of starting far behind the established computer companies. The purchase of NCR in 1991 was an effort to catch up. However, the computer industry itself went through such major dynamic changes that even the former leader, IBM, was unable to keep up. The acquisition of NCR did not help AT&T realize its aspirations in the computer business.

The main reasons for the AT&T split-up can be briefly summarized. The equipment business was spun off in the effort to avoid conflicts with its main customers with which the phone service activities were in competition. Selling off the computer business it was hoped would improve the valuation multiples for the core AT&T long distance and other phone services. The taint of poor performance in the computer business would thereby be removed from the main AT&T operations.

### The Melville Corporation

The Melville Corporation is one of the 10 largest retailers in the United States. On October 25, 1995, it announced a major restructuring by selling two of its chains and packaging the other seven units into three separate publicly traded companies. Melville had started as a shoe retailer in 1892. It had diversified into drugstores, clothing, leather goods, and toys, but its stock price had lagged. Institutional shareholders such as the California Public Employees' Retirement System (CALPERS) and the Council of

Institutional Investors had been pushing the company to increase its returns to investors. It had sold its Marshalls clothing chain to the TJX Companies, taking a charge of $9.5 million against fourth quarter 1995 profits. This further restructuring would involve an additional charge of $585 million.

Melville would become three companies: a footwear company, a toy company, and a drugstore holding company. The core business of Melville had been shoe retailing. The footwear company would itself represent three major parts. It would include Thom McAn, which operates 310 shoe stores acquired by Melville over 50 years ago. In 1961 Meldisco was started by Melville. This is a lease shoe operation in 2,176 Kmart stores and in 389 Payless drugstores. Meldisco is a joint venture owned 51% by Melville and 49% by Kmart. The footwear company would also include Footaction, which sells athletic shoes and clothes at 439 stores. Footaction was acquired by Melville in 1991.

The second major part of Melville would be a toy company with the name Kay-Bee, acquired in 1981, operating in 1,012 stores nationwide.

The third company would be the drugstore holding company. The core of this company would be CVS, acquired by Melville in 1969, a drugstore chain with 1,356 stores mainly in the East. The drugstore holding company would also include Linens'n Things, a specialty retailer with 146 stores in 27 states, acquired in 1983. The third segment would be Bob's, a casual clothing and footwear chain with 34 stores, acquired in 1990. The company also announced plans to sell Wilson's, a leather goods retailer, and This End Up, a furniture chain.

A general implication of the Melville restructuring is that it is an example of the failures of retail conglomerates. It is recognition of the "more is too much" problem (Steinhauer, 1995). It is also an illustration of the philosophy that better stock performance can be achieved by separating losers from winners and enabling management to concentrate on a narrower range of businesses.

# EQUITY CARVE-OUTS

An equity carve-out is the IPO of some portion of the common stock of a wholly owned subsidiary. These are also referred to as "split-off IPOs." An IPO of the equity of a subsidiary resembles a seasoned equity offering of the parent in that cash is received from a public sale of equity securities. But there are also differences. The IPO of the common stock of the subsidiary initiates public trading in a new and distinct set of equity claims on the assets of the subsidiary.

Other changes often take place as well when the subsidiary equity is "carved out" from the consolidated entity of the parent. The management system for operating the assets is likely to be restructured in this new public entity. A public market value for the operations of the subsidiary becomes established. Financial reports are issued on the subsidiary operations and are studied by financial analysts as a separate entity. Ongoing public information on the value of the subsidiary may have a positive influence on performance in the subsidiary. In addition, as an entity now separate from the parent, evaluation of performance may be facilitated. Incentives may be strengthened by relating the compensation of the executives in the subsidiary to the performance of the publicly traded stock. If the parent should decide to sell the subsidiary, having established a public market for the stock may facilitate reaching an agreement with a buyer on a sales price.

An equity carve-out or split-off IPO is similar to a voluntary spin-off in that both result in subsidiary's equity claims that are traded separately from the equity claims on the parent entity. The equity carve-out differs from a spin-off in two respects. In a spin-off a distribution is made pro rata to the shareholders of the parent firm as a dividend—a form of noncash payment to the shareholders. In an equity carve-out, the stock of the subsidiary is sold in the public markets for cash that is received by the parent. A second distinction is that in a spin-off, the parent firm no longer has control over the subsidiary assets. In a carve-out, the parent generally sells only a minority interest in the subsidiary and maintains control over subsidiary assets and operations.

As compared with a divestiture, the split-off IPO is similar in that cash is received. But a divestiture is usually to another company. Hence, control over the assets sold is relinquished by the parent-seller and the trading of subsidiary stock is not initiated.

Spin-offs generally result in abnormal returns to the parent firm of 2 to 3% on average. Divestitures result in gains of 1 to 2% to selling firms on average. New seasoned equity issues are associated with announcement period negative residuals of about 2 to 3%. Because equity carve-outs have characteristics in common with each of the three types of transactions, it is not readily predictable what the announcement-period market reactions will be.

Schipper and Smith (1986) studied the performance of a usable sample of 81 equity carve-outs announced between 1965 and 1983. Underwritten offerings represented about 73% of the sample. This is lower than the 93% underwriting used in common stock issues of exchange-listed firms for the period 1971–1975 reported by Smith (1977). Less than 50% of the subsidiary shares were sold in 81% of the cases. The parent took a minority position in about 9% of the issues and data were not available on the other 10%. The dollar amount sold ranged widely from $300,000 to as high as $112 million. About 30% were below $10 million in size, but 26% were over $30 million. The proceeds represented a relatively small percentage of parent common equity value measured at the end of the month preceding the carve-out announcement. Data were not available on 20% of the sample. Of the 65 offerings for which data were available, 62% represented an amount less than 10% of the size of the parent common equity. Another 15% were in the 10% to under 15% range.

The initial percentage return on the stock of the new subsidiaries was calculated (Schipper and Smith, 1986) by relating the closing bid price on the first day of trading for which a price could be obtained (within 10 trading days of the offering) to the offering price. The average initial return was 4.9%, whereas the median was 2.1%. When an outlier is removed, the average initial return drops to 1.7%. These returns are much lower than those observed in studies of public offerings generally. Ibbotson (1975) found average initial returns of 11.4% for 120 IPOs for the period 1960–1969. For the period 1977–1982, Ritter (1984) observed average initial returns of 26.5% for 1,028 initial public offerings, but these results were greatly influenced by the high initial returns on natural resource stocks during 1980–1981, probably related to the oil price increases in 1979 by OPEC.

Although the large initial returns on IPOs generally were not matched by these split-off IPOs, substantial returns were observed in a small sample reported by *Corporate Restructuring* (1988) for the period between 1986 and the first half of 1988, which includes the major market decline of October 1987. The postoffering performance of the IPOs was related to the trends of the industries in which the firms were situated. The best performance was achieved by three split-off IPOs in the chemicals industry. During the period of the study, profits in this segment of the industry had risen because of increased demand for their output while raw materials prices remained stable. USX Corporation in late 1986 took public an entity named Aristech Chemical Corp. Its offering price of 17¾ on November 26, 1987 rose to 35¼ by July 6, 1988, a gain of almost 100%. Similar gains were achieved by Borden Chemicals & Plastics, which was taken public by its parent, Borden Inc., on November 20, 1987 and by IMC Fertilizer Group taken public by International Minerals & Chemicals on January 26, 1988. Five other companies achieved large positive gains that averaged 38%. The stock prices of two were unchanged. Three carve-outs by firms in financial services declined an average 32%. The latter firms were greatly affected by the decline in public trading following the market drop in October 1987. The other split-off IPOs provided excellent returns for the difficult time period involved.

Equity carve-outs on average are associated with positive abnormal returns of almost 2% over a five-day announcement period (Schipper and Smith, 1986). This is in contrast to findings of significant negative returns of about 2 to 3% when parent companies publicly offer additional shares of their own (as opposed to their subsidiary's) stock (Smith, 1986a, 1986b).

Michaely and Shaw (MS) (1995) compared the performance aspects of spin-offs with equity carve-outs. Unlike early studies, this one covered a special set of spin-offs and equity carve-outs in which the organization form is master limited partnerships (MLPs), which like other partnerships, do not pay tax on entity income. The tax is paid by each shareholder on the pro rata share of MLP income. Dividends received by partnership shareholders are not taxed, avoiding the double taxation borne by corporate shareholders. These tax benefits were augmented by the Tax Reform Act of 1986 under which the marginal and average tax rates paid by individuals were lower than for corporations.

Although the shares of MLP are publicly traded on major stock exchanges, the shares are nonvoting. The sponsoring corporation or one of its units functions as the general partner and has sole control over all of the decisions of the MLP. One of the reasons for the creation of an equity carve-out or spin-off is to formulate compensation schemes that will strengthen management incentives and motivation. But with control completely held by the general partner, the discretionary power of management may be circumscribed.

The special characteristics of MLPs may affect their empirical results. For example, MS found that for a two-year period, the parents of carve-outs experienced a 27.3% increase in stock prices compared with 23% for a control group; the parents of spin-offs had a 70% reduction in equity values compared with a 22% decline for their control group. The shares of both the carve-out and spin-off MLPs underperformed a similar group of existing firms. The authors acknowledge that their results for spin-off firms differed from those of Cusatis, Miles, and Woolridge (1993), who found that both the parents and the new entities experience positive abnormal stock price performance. The value increases are associated with the firms that subsequently engaged in takeover activity.

However, with regard to event returns, MS found a positive reaction to both spin-off and carve-out announcements. Over a four-day window, the event returns to spin-off parents was about 4.5%, but only 0.4% for the carve-out parents. The market appeared to respond more favorably to spin-offs than to equity carve-outs for their sample. They also found that the larger, less leveraged, and more profitable parent firms more often chose to use equity carve-outs. Only the spin-off parents decreased debt levels at the time of the transaction, probably transferring debt into the spin-off firm.

The authors note that over half the spin-off sample is from the oil and gas industry, which had very poor performance during the 1980s, the time period of their study. Because they used control matched samples, they feel that industry characteristics do not explain their results. However, it is our experience that MLPs are at least sometimes formed to give the control group, the general partner, protection while the firm works through some performance problems. MLPs may also involve adverse selection or timing the market. The Boston Celtics basketball team was converted from private ownership to publicly traded MLPs. The timing was just before the retirement of key players, resulting in the loss of the premier position of the Boston Celtics.

Slovin, Sushka, and Ferraro (SSF) (1995) extended the study of equity carve-outs, spin-offs, and asset sell-offs to the firms' rivals. Their motivation was to test the effects on the relevant subsidiary. However, because the subsidiary does not have stock price data at the time of the restructuring announcement, the rivals of the subsidiary are used as proxies. The authors found a negative valuation effect of −1% on rivals of carved-out subsidiaries. Because a carve-out is a form of an IPO of common stock, they measured the effects on rival firms of the announcements of conventional IPOs; they found similar negative returns.

However, for spin-offs, rivals of subsidiaries have positive share price effects. For asset sales, rivals experience normal returns. The authors confirmed that parent firms earn positive returns from carve-outs, spin-offs, and asset sales; the rivals of parent firms earn normal returns. They concluded that managers try to time equity carve-outs or conventional IPOs for when outside investors are likely to overvalue these new equity issues. They cite previous models of decisions on going public based on informational advantages of managers over outside investors.

The authors also found that the aggregate loss in shareholder wealth for industry rivals over a two-day window is $2.5 billion, representing 39% of the gross proceeds of the carve-out, spin-off, or asset sale. They contrast this to the finding by Hertzel (1991) that the rivals of firms announcing stock repurchases experience normal returns.

They also found that decisions by the parent to sell noncore assets result in positive returns for the parent. In addition, the event returns are significantly positive but small (0.55%) for rivals. This suggests that greater focus by one firm increases the likelihood that its rivals imitate this behavior.

Slovin, Sushka, and Ferraro cite the Healy and Palepu (1990) study that found that firms that make seasoned equity issues experience postissue increases in market risk. This is consistent with the hypothesis that managers raise additional equity funds to reduce financial leverage when they forecast an increase in business risk. Slovin et al. tested this by calculating the betas of rivals to firms engaged in equity increasing transactions. They found the equity betas for industry rivals to be stable for the relevant period. They concluded that the negative effects on rivals (of equity carve-outs and conventional IPOs) do not result from new information about changes in industry systematic risk.

## TARGETED STOCK

In a targeted stock transaction, a company's business operations are split into two or more common equity claims, but the businesses remain as wholly owned segments of a single parent (Logue, Seward, and Walsh (LSW), 1996). For example, in May 1991 USX distributed U.S. Steel stock to its existing shareholders and redesignated the USX common stock as USX-Marathon stock. In September 1992 USX created a third targeted stock when it sold shares of the USX-Delhi group stock in an initial public offering. Thus, the quarterly 10Q report for the period ending September 30, 1995, for the USX Corporation presents financial information (1) for the consolidated corporation, (2) for the Marathon group (oil), (3) for the U.S. Steel group (steel), and (4) for the Delhi group (natural gas). The 10Q shows common stock outstanding on September 30, 1995 of 287 million shares for the USX-Marathon group, 83 million shares for the USX-U.S. Steel group, and 9 million shares for the USX-Delhi group. Each targeted stock is regarded as common stock of the consolidated company and not of the subsidiary.

Other characteristics of targeted stock can be brought out by comparison with the alphabet stocks of General Motors. We summarize the comparison made by LSW:

| Rights | Targeted Steel Stock | GM Class H Stock (Hughes) |
|---|---|---|
| Voting rights | Based on relative values | Fixed at one-half vote per share |
| Liquidation rights | In proportion to relative market values | In proportion to voting rights |
| Dividends | Based on performance of each target stock segment | Based on performance of the segment |

Logue, Seward, and Walsh suggest a number of benefits of creating separate public equity securities in the form of targeted stock:

**1.** The financial markets can value different businesses based on their own performance.

**2.** Investors are provided with quasi-pure play opportunities.

**3.** Targeted stock increases flexibility in raising equity capital.

**4.** Targeted stock provides alternative types of acquisition currency.

**5.** Stock-based management incentive programs can be related to each targeted business unit.

They point out that targeted stock still preserves some of the advantages of a consolidated entity: (1) no change in management or board, (2) preservation of tax consolidation, (3) company operating synergies are maintained, (4) debt capacity is consolidated, and (5) later equity restructuring options are preserved.

The main potential disadvantage of targeted stock is the conflicts between different targeted business units over cost allocations or other internal transfer transactions.

For the nine targeted transactions announced between February 1, 1991, and February 1, 1995, the cumulative average two-day abnormal return was 2.9%. Four companies experienced positive abnormal returns of 4% or more. Logue et al. conclude that targeted stock provides a useful financial innovation with characteristics related to but different from corporate spin-offs, equity carve-outs, and dual-class recapitalizations.

# EXPLANATIONS AND RATIONALE FOR GAINS TO SELL-OFFS AND SPLIT-UPS

A number of hypotheses have been advanced to explain the positive returns found in spin-offs, split-ups, equity carve-outs, and targeted stock.

## Information

The information hypothesis holds that the true value of subsidiary assets is obscured by the complexity of the business structure in which they are embedded. The supposed stock market preference for "pure-play" or single-industry securities is cited in support of this hypothesis. Given the disclosure requirements of public corporations and the nature and extent of the securities analysis industry, it might seem unlikely that parts of a firm would be undervalued. But security analysts tend to specialize. An oil industry analyst may undervalue an oil company's chemical and real estate businesses because he or she does not follow these industries. Also, to the extent that spin-offs and equity carve-outs enhance the incentive to gather and analyze a greater amount of publicly available information through their creation of new publicly traded securities, the information effect may explain at least part of the gains.

### Managerial Efficiency

The managerial efficiency hypothesis suggests that the preference (if any) for pure-play securities stems not from lack of confidence in the market's ability to value complex organizations, but from the perceived inability of managers to manage them effectively. Even the best management team may reach a point of diminishing returns as the size and diversity of assets under their control increases. Part of the problem is that top management may be unaware of the unique problems and opportunities of a subsidiary in a different line of business. An announced motive in many sell-offs is to sharpen the corporate focus by spinning off (or divesting) units that are a poor fit (anergy) with the remainder of the parent company's operations. Writers on corporate strategy have long emphasized the principle of relatedness to guide business planning. Equity carve-outs are often preceded by asset regroupings in the effort to achieve greater efficiency (and are often followed by spin-offs or divestitures). Warner-Lambert's sale of its Entenmann's bakery subsidiary to General Foods is an example of the efficiency source of sell-off gains.

Both Entenmann's and Warner-Lambert stood to benefit from the transaction: Warner-Lambert management could now focus attention in their area of comparative advantage, pharmaceuticals; and Entenmann's would be controlled by managers more experienced with a food company's operations. The managerial efficiency hypothesis is supported by evidence of acquisition activity in the pre–spin-off period as well as dissimilarities between the business lines of the parent firms and spun-off subsidiaries.

### Management Incentives

The issues of management incentives and accountability are related to management efficiency. Bureaucratization of management and consolidation of financial statements can stifle entrepreneurial spirit and result in good (bad) performance going unrewarded (unpunished). The problem is compounded when the subsidiary's outlook and objectives are not the same as the parent's, for example, a high-growth subsidiary of a parent in a mature industry, or a regulated subsidiary of a nonregulated parent. Incentive compensation plans tied to parent company stock options may be meaningless or even counterproductive. A spun-off subsidiary has the advantage of an independent stock price directly reflecting the market's response to management actions, and more closely linking compensation to performance.

### Tax and/or Regulatory Factors

Another important source of gains available in some sell-offs is tax and/or regulatory advantages. Subsamples of spin-offs citing these motives exhibited higher abnormal returns than the more inclusive samples. Tax advantages can be achieved by the creation and spin-off into natural resource royalty trusts or real estate investment trusts; as long as these entities pay out 90% of their income to their shareholders, they pay no income tax. Thus, the parent company can shelter income from taxes and benefit the spun-off subsidiary's shareholders, who are the same (initially) as the parent's shareholders.

Regulated subsidiaries are sometimes penalized by their association with profitable parents if regulators look to parent company earnings when considering rate increases. The spun-off subsidiary might have a greater chance of being granted rate increases, and the nonregulated operations of the parent would be freed from regulatory scrutiny. Some parent firms have spun-off foreign subsidiaries so that they will not be subject to the laws and regulations of the home country of the parent.

## Bondholder Expropriation

Agency costs are involved in the hypothesis that the gains to shareholders are the result of bondholder expropriation. A spin-off reduces (and a divestiture changes the nature of) the collateral initially relied on by bondholders. However, this argument assumes that sell-offs are unanticipated (and unanticipatable) events. In fact, most, if not all, bond covenants contain dividend restrictions (limiting stock dividends, including spin-offs) and restrictions on asset disposition (limiting divestitures).

Furthermore, many subsidiaries already have their own debt, and many are assigned a pro rata share of parent debt when they are spun off. Bondholders may actually benefit if hitherto junior claims on the parent become senior claims on the spun-off subsidiary. Studies by Hite and Owers (1983) and Schipper and Smith (1983) have found little evidence of bond prices or ratings decline to support the bondholder expropriation hypothesis.

## Changing Economic Environment

Yet another rationale advanced for the positive price effects is that there has been a major shift in the economic environment affecting the firm. Thus, the opportunity sets of both parent and subsidiaries may be altered. While joint operations may have been optimal in the past, separate operations may have become more appropriate.

## Avoiding Conflicts with Customers

A strong motive in the AT&T split-up was to separate the equipment, manufacturing, and sales activity from the core phone business of AT&T. The regional Bell operating companies are the biggest customers for equipment that AT&T sells. Yet the "Baby Bells" are seeking to invade the long distance markets of AT&T. AT&T is considering a number of ways of competing with their offspring, operating companies in their local markets. It was hoped that by spinning off the equipment company it would not be subject to the irritation to the regional operating companies stemming from the competition from AT&T.

## Provide Investors with Pure Winners

When some segments of a firm are losing money or sell products that are in disrepute to some people, it may lower the valuation multiple on the overall company. Thus, there has been pressure to separate the tobacco and food businesses of RJR Nabisco. AT&T put its computer activities in a separate company so that its core long distance and related phone operations would command a better valuation multiple. The Melville case study provides similar examples.

## Option Creation

A more esoteric explanation of the value creation is based on options theory and the state preference model. The idea is that since incorporating limits the stockholders' liability, spin-offs multiply the protection. If common stock is viewed as an option on the underlying technologies of the firm, then a spin-off creates two options on the same assets. Two options will be more valuable than only one (Sarig, 1985).

## Increase Market Spanning

Another theoretical benefit of sell-offs is related to financial market spanning or whether financial markets are complete. (For further explanation see Copeland and Weston, 1988, chapter 5.) John Lintner (1971) had made a similar argument for conglomerate mergers. To the extent that financial markets may be incomplete, spin-offs increase the number of securities for a given number of possible states of the world. In addition, the opportunities for investment of the parent and its divisions will be expanded. Also, the parent and the spun-off subsidiaries may provide investors with a wider range of different investment policies and financial policies. The parent and the new entities may package dividends, retained earnings, and capital gains possibilities in different proportions to appeal to different investor clienteles.

### Enable More Focused Mergers

Spin-offs are also used to facilitate mergers when the bidder is interested in only a subset of the target's operations. That is, there may be some segments of the target that the bidder does not want to acquire. If for some reason the target/parent firm does not want to sell these segments outright before the merger (for instance, for tax reasons), a future spin-off may be included in the merger planning. At the time of the spin-off, the acquiring (bidder) firm is the parent of the subsidiary. Abnormal positive returns at the spin-off announcement may represent the market realization to the parent's (acquiring firm) shareholders of the increased value reflected in the premium paid earlier to the target shareholders.

Thus, a wide range of plausible reasons may account for the positive gains from sell-offs. Any one factor could contribute to the 3 to 5% abnormal positive gain to shareholders when a spin-off takes place.

---

## Summary

In a spin-off, a company creates a subsidiary whose shares are distributed on a pro rata basis to the shareholders of the parent company. A new publicly owned corporation results. In a split-up, a company engages in restructuring to create two or more separate entities. An equity carve-out is the initial public offering (IPO) of a portion of the common stock of a previously wholly owned subsidiary. The parent generally retains majority control. When a company creates targeted stock, it splits its business operations into two or more common equity claims. However, the businesses remain as wholly owned segments of a single parent.

The stock market response to these four types of restructuring is positive. The size of the positive response depends on individual circumstances. The factors that influence the size of the market event returns are related to the motives and effects of these restructuring activities, which include (1) tax effects, (2) regulatory effects, (3) separate market prices for the entities, (4) avoidance of a confusing mix of activities with favorable and unfavorable prospects, (5) security analysts are better able to understand and evaluate each separate entity, (6) a better match between the activities of the segments and the capabilities of managers, (7) more accurate evaluation of managerial performance, (8) more effective formulation of compensation contracts with managers, and (9) stronger managerial incentive systems.

---

## Questions

12.1  What is the nature and reasons for creating targeted stock?
12.2  Summarize the case study of the creation of targeted stock by USX.

12.3  What are the gains in spin-offs, split-ups, equity carve-outs, and targeted stock?

12.4  What role does the information hypothesis have in explaining gains resulting from spin-offs?

12.5  How do tax and/or regulatory factors affect returns to spin-offs, split-ups, equity carve-outs, and targeted stock?

12.6  Summarize the ITT split-up and evaluate its soundness.

12.7  Summarize the AT&T split-up and discuss its reasons.

12.8  Summarize the Melville split-up and discuss the reasons for the failures of retail conglomerates.

---------------------------------- C A S E    12–1 ----------------------------------

# Sears, Roebuck and Co. Restructuring[1]

On November 10, 1994, Sears, Roebuck and Co. announced that it intended to spin off its 80.1% stake in the Allstate Corporation, the nation's largest publicly held property and casualty insurance company. This divestiture will amount to Sears's final major step in its plan to return exclusively to its core retailing operations established in 1886.

The 1980s witnessed Sears's declining market share in retailing as discount stores such as Wal-Mart and Kmart, and specialty stores such as The Gap, Inc. and Limited Inc. captured a large portion of the retailing market from Sears. Many analysts contend that Sears's diversification into the real estate and financial services markets as well as its hefty investment in the insurance industry precipitated this decline.

Recognizing that Sears's future success depended on successful retail operations, management announced in September 1992 that it had developed a strategy to refocus its resources almost exclusively on Sears's retail operations. Over the next two years this included:

1. Spinning off securities broker Dean Witter Reynolds, Inc. and its associated Discover Credit Card operation, the largest issuer of general purpose credit cards.

2. Selling 19.9% interest in Allstate in the largest initial public offering in U.S. history up until that date.

3. Selling 100% of Coldwell Banker Residential Services, which had earned record profits in 1991 and which analysts considered one of Sears's most valuable assets.

These actions raised $4.2 billion in cash and eliminated $19 billion in debt.

Between the time of the September 1992 announcement and November 10, 1994, the day of the Allstate spin-off announcement, Sears dramatically improved its position in both the retail market and the stock market. Sears outpaced its major rivals in the first three quarters of 1994 as operating profit for its merchandise group increased 26% and revenues increased 9.4%. In addition, since September 1992 shareholder return amounted to 66% and the market value of the corporation increased by more than $8 billion as the price of Sears stock rose from $41.375 to $51.625 per share. According to one analyst, Sears's management had recognized and began to benefit from the theory that often "the sum of the parts is worth more than the whole."

The spin-off of Allstate, which occurred in mid-1995, was intended to continue the positive momentum. Under the agreement, Sears's 80.1% (approximately 360 million) shares were distributed to Sears shareholders in the form of a tax-free dividend at an expected rate of 0.95 Allstate shares per Sears share. The spin-off was expected to be valued at $9 billion, making it one of the largest spin-offs in U.S. history. Analysts believed that this action would increase the value of the retailing operations. They cited the fact that the improved retail results had not been fully reflected in the price of Sears stock primarily because of the way insurance stocks were valued. Analysts' expectations were reflected on Wall Street

[1]This case was prepared with Scott Miller, a Research Associate in the Research Program in Competition and Business Policy, The Anderson School at UCLA.

as the price of Sears stock rose $2.75 per share (5.6%) to $51.625 immediately following the announcement.

Edward A. Brennan, chief executive officer and chairman, who had previously resisted attempts to break up the Sears-Allstate relationship explained the rationale behind the divestiture: "It's the right time, Sears and Allstate are ready, and the economic environment is right." As independent concerns, Sears and Allstate "will have greater flexibility to pursue their own growth strategies." In addition, Sears's management cited eroding marketing synergies as a reason for the breakup. Whereas Allstate agents previously relied heavily on Sears by working directly out of their department stores, Allstate's sales force presently consists of a network of neighborhood sales offices. Also, the split will provide stronger incentives to employees of both corporations now that they know their actions will more directly affect the value of the stock they own. Finally, although Allstate will lose some tax advantages of being consolidated, Brennan expects the loss will amount only to a modest 5 to 10 cents per share loss on Allstate stock in 1995.

Upon completion of this divestiture and the anticipated sale of Homart Development Co., a leading regional mall and community center developer, Sears will be left with approximately 800 department stores, 1,200 specialty stores, 61% of Sears Canada, and 75% of Sears Mexico. This will leave Sears virtually debt-free and allow the new Sears to commit all of its debt to support a high-quality credit card receivables portfolio.

---

## Questions on Case Study C12.1

C12.1.1   Summarize the restructuring of Sears initiated in November 1994.

C12.1.2   Evaluate the reasons for the spin-offs.

C12.1.3   Compare the stock market performances of Sears and the spin-offs.

---

C A S E    12–2

# GM Spin-Off of EDS

The spin-off of EDS by GM announced on August 7, 1995, appeared to be a part of a pattern in which General Motors had been selling off its nonautomotive operations. In June 1995 GM sold its national car rental unit. After the spin-off of EDS, GM would have one nonautomotive unit, Hughes Electronics. GM has stated that it has no plans to dispose of Hughes because of the technological capabilities as a strategic asset.

EDS performs a wide range of information-processing activities for government agencies and other companies. It is regarded as the inventor of "outsourcing," representing the farming out of computer operations to third-party specialists companies. EDS sells a wide range of telecommunications, systems integration, and computer services. GM accounts for about 35% of its business. Some big customers include Xerox Corporation with which it has a 10-year, $3.2 billion contract. It also provides services to the Internal Revenue Department of Great Britain. The EDS-NET is the company's global digital network. It processes about 43 million transactions a day, linking 411,000 personal computers and has storage capacity 45 times the size of the Library of Congress. EDS also has capabilities in the emerging global health care information technology.

EDS has an interesting history:

- 1962: Company founded by Ross Perot with $1,000 of his wife's savings.
- 1966: EDS becomes active in Medicare and Medicaid transaction processing.
- 1968: EDS goes public priced at $16.50 per share.
- 1979: Ross Perot sends an EDS squad to free two company employees who had been held prisoners in Iran.
- October 1984: GM acquires EDS for $2.5 billion. Perot received approximately $1 billion in cash plus a substantial number of shares of GM preferred stock. GM held 100% of the capital stock of EDS, issuing a new class of GM stock called class E, 70% owned by the public and 30% by GM's Hourly Worker Pension Fund. The class E stock receives the EDS dividend stream as well as one-eighth of a liquidation right in GM's net assets relative to a holder of GM stock. Another provision specifies that if GM sells more than half of the capital stock of EDS, it must buy out class E shareholders at a 20% premium over the market, using GM common stock.
- Fall 1984: Ross Perot joins the GM board and begins public criticism of company management.
- Fall 1986: GM holds talks with AT&T to sell part or all of EDS, but no agreement is reached.
- December 1986: Les Alberthal, an executive of EDS, becomes president and chief executive of EDS as Perot and three other top officials depart. GM pays $743 million to Mr. Perot for his preferred stock plus a premium on his $12 million class E shares. Mr. Perot agrees to resign from the GM board.
- Spring 1993: EDS and British Telecommunications PLC hold talks about a sale of 25% of class E shares. No agreement is reached.
- June 1994: EDS seeks to separate from GM through a spin-off and subsequent merger with Sprint Corp. Sprint is unwilling to accept the EDS asking price.

- March 1995: GM contributes $173 million class E shares valued at $6.3 billion to a GM pension fund.
- June 1995: EDS buys the A.T. Kearney consulting firm for $300 million.
- August 7, 1995: GM announces that it will spin off EDS through an exchange of EDS stock for shares of GM class E stock with the market value of about $22 billion, almost 10 times the price GM paid for EDS in 1984. The spin-off is subject to an appropriate tax ruling from the Internal Revenue Service.

The announced reason for the spin-off was to enable EDS to adjust more flexibly to the rapidly changing competitive environment in which it operates. The news reports also suggested that EDS was seeking participation in multimedia and on-line services. An independent EDS would have greater flexibility for mergers with a telecommunications company as a part of the general trend toward vertical integration in the emerging information age.

It appeared also that the original reasons for the acquisition of EDS by GM were no longer considered valid. Roger B. Smith, the chairman of GM in 1984, viewed EDS as a strategy for achieving high-tech diversification to offset cyclical fluctuations in automotive sales. It was also hoped that EDS could revolutionize factory automation, but this was not achieved. It was also recognized that GM did not need to own EDS to buy its computer services.

Thus, the GM-EDS story represents a strategic move that did not achieve its original objectives. However, the rise in the market value of the company from $2.5 billion to $22 billion during a 10-year period represents a value gain as well as a learning experience for GM management. As a competitive environment changes, company strategies are adjusted and spin-offs represent one method of restructuring a company.

---

## Questions on Case Study C12.2

C12.2.1  Summarize the reasons for the original acquisition of EDS by GM.

C12.2.2  What were the reasons for the spin-off?

C12.2.3  Was the EDS acquisition and subsequent spin-off a success or failure for GM? For EDS?

------------------------------------------------------------------------------------

# References

Bary, Andrew, "Corporate Castaways," *Barron's,* January 10, 1994, pp. 19–20.

Copeland, Thomas E., E. F. Lemgruber, and D. Mayers, "Corporate Spinoffs: Multiple Announcement and Ex-Date Abnormal Performance," chapter 7 in T. E. Copeland, ed., *Modern Finance and Industrial Economics,* New York: Basil Blackwell, 1987.

Copeland, Thomas E., and J. Fred Weston, *Financial Theory and Corporate Policy,* 3rd ed., Reading, MA: Addison-Wesley Publishing Company, 1988.

*Corporate Restructuring, Mergers & Acquisitions,* August 1988.

Cusatis, Patrick J., James A. Miles, and J. Randall Woolridge, "Restructuring Through Spinoffs," *Journal of Financial Economics,* 33, 1993, pp. 293–311.

Healy, Paul, and Krishna Palepu, "Earnings and Risk Changes Surrounding Primary Stock Offers," *Journal of Accounting Research,* 28, 1990, pp. 25–48.

Hertzel, Michael, "The Effects of Stock Repurchases on Rival Firms," *Journal of Finance,* 46, 1991, pp. 707–716.

Hite, Gailen, and James E. Owers, "Security Price Reactions around Corporate Spin-off Announcements," *Journal of Financial Economics,* 12, 1983, pp. 409–436.

Ibbotson, R., "Price Performance of Common Stock New Issues," *Journal of Financial Economics,* 2, September 1975, pp. 235–272.

Lintner, John, "Expectations, Mergers and Equilibrium in Purely Competitive Securities Markets," *American Economic Review,* 61, May 1971, pp. 101–111.

Logue, Dennis E., James K. Seward, and James P. Walsh, "Rearranging Residual Claims: A Case for Targeted Stock," *Financial Management,* 25(1), Spring 1996, pp. 43–61.

*Mergers & Acquisitions,* 30, March/April 1996, pp. 27–29.

Michaely, Roni, and Wayne H. Shaw, "The Choice of Going Public: Spin-offs vs. Carve-outs," *Financial Management,* 24(3), Autumn 1995, pp. 5–21.

Ritter, J., "The 'Hot Issue Market' of 1980," *Journal of Business,* 57, 1984, pp. 215–240.

Sarig, Oded H., "On Mergers, Divestments, and Options: A Note," *Journal of Financial and Quantitative Analysis,* 20, September 1985, pp. 385–389.

Schipper, Katherine, and Abbie Smith, "Effects of Recontracting on Shareholder Wealth," *Journal of Financial Economics,* 12, 1983, pp. 437–467.

————, "A Comparison of Equity Carve-Outs and Equity Offerings: Share Price Effects and Corporate Restructuring," *Journal of Financial Economics,* 15, 1986, pp. 153–186.

Slovin, Myron B., Marie E. Sushka, and Steven R. Ferraro, "A Comparison of the Information Conveyed by Equity Carve-Outs, Spin-Offs, and Asset Sell-Offs," *Journal of Financial Economics,* 37(1), January 1995, pp. 89–104.

Smith, Clifford W., Jr., "Alternative Methods for Raising Capital: Rights Versus Underwritten Offerings," *Journal of Financial Economics,* 5, December 1977, pp. 273–307.

————, "Investment Banking and the Capital Acquisition Process," *Journal of Financial Economics,* 15, January/February 1986a, pp. 3–29.

————, "Raising Capital: Theory and Evidence," *Midland Corporate Finance Journal,* 4, Spring 1986b, pp. 6–22.

Steinhauer, Jennifer, "Melville Plans To Split Into 3 Companies," *New York Times,* October 25, 1995, pp. D1, D3.

Ward, Sandra, "Giving Gifts," *Barron's,* December 26, 1994, pp. 21–24.

# CHAPTER

# 13

# Financial
# Restructuring

We emphasize throughout this book that M&A policies should take place within the framework of the strategic planning processes of the firm. Equally important, M&A decisions are not separate compartments. It is impossible to separate internal programs for growth and the use of the external M&A markets. Financing and M&A decisions also interact. In this chapter, we illustrate the implementation of these generalizations, particularly in some of the areas of traditional financial management. We include the following topics: leverage and leveraged recapitalizations, dual-class stock recapitalizations, exchange offers, reorganization processes, financial engineering, and liquidations and takeover bust-ups.

## UNLOCKING THE VALUE IN THE FIRM

As an overview we utilize the relationships depicted in Figure 13.1, which presents some major factors affecting the value of the firm. First is the value of a firm when it is all equity financed. To this can be added the present value of tax shields. A third source of value growth is the present value of other benefits of leverage such as pressures for efficiency to meet debt obligations (Jensen, 1986; Wruck, 1990, pp. 430–433).

A fourth group of benefits involves top management changes and changing roles of other control groups such as banks, insurance companies, and pension funds. Fifth, M&As can perform a constructive role in augmenting the capabilities and product-market spans of firms.

Sixth, in taking positive actions for growth and improvement such as expansion, M&As, leverage changes, and dealing with financial distress, performance improvement is essential. The present value of benefits of changes in strategies, policies,

**FIGURE 13.1 Sources of Value Increases**

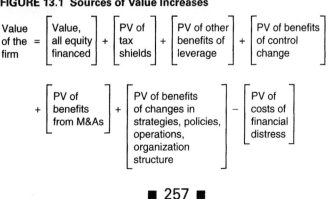

operations, as well as organization structure and processes, can be substantial (Wruck, 1990, pp. 434–435). A demonstration of a leveraged recap plus efficiency improvements is in a case study of the Sealed Air Corporation developed by Wruck (1994). Finally, the present value of the costs of financial distress would reduce the value of the firm. Figure 13.1, therefore, summarizes major factors that influence the success of the individual restructuring efforts we now describe.

## LEVERAGE AND LEVERAGED RECAPITALIZATIONS

Capital structure and leverage decisions are often involved in mergers and takeovers. A firm with zero leverage may be vulnerable to takeover by a firm seeking to capture the tax benefits of debt. Capital structure and leverage decisions represent potentials for value enhancement, for acquiring other firms, or to defend against being acquired by others. We start with a simple example that provides a foundation for more complex financial recapitalizations.

Table 13.1 presents the initial input values for the analysis. Table 13.2 presents a series of balance sheets to illustrate the effects of increasing leverage. Before the financial recapitalization, the firm has no debt. The next two columns illustrate taking on debt equal to 20% or 40% of the market value of the firm before adding leverage. Table 13.2 depicts $600 of debt or $1,200 of debt. Table 13.3 presents the effects of tax shields on share prices. The present value of tax shields is calculated by multiplying the amount of debt by the tax rate of the firm, which was given in Table 13.1 as 40%. This is a simplified version of the tax effects, but the qualifications would not change the central principles we are illustrating (DeAngelo and DeAngelo, 1996; Mitchell and Mitchell, 1996). Line 4 of Table 13.3 shows that the market value of the firm has been increased by the present value of the tax shields.

**TABLE 13.1**   Initial Input Values

| | |
|---|---|
| 1. Operating income (millions) | $300 |
| 2. Shares outstanding (millions) | 100 |
| 3. Management ownership | 20% |
| 4. Market value per share | $30 |
| 5. Market value of the firm (millions) | $3,000 |
| 6. Tax rate | 40% |

**TABLE 13.2**   Balance Sheets with Increasing Leverage

| | Before Recap | 20% Debt | 40% Debt |
|---|---|---|---|
| 1. Cash | $10 | $10 | $10 |
| 2. Other current assets | 100 | 100 | 100 |
| 3. Long-term assets, net | 90 | 90 | 90 |
| 4. Total assets | $200 | $200 | $200 |
| | | | |
| 5. Debt | $0 | $600 | $1,200 |
| 6. Equity at book | 200 | −400 | −1,000 |
| 7. Total claims | $200 | $200 | $200 |

**TABLE 13.3   Effect of Tax Shields on Share Prices**

|  | *Before Recap* | *20% Debt* | *40% Debt* |
|---|---|---|---|
| 1. Debt % original firm value | 0% | 20% | 40% |
| 2. Amount of debt | $0 | $600 | $1,200 |
| 3. Present value of tax shields | $0 | $240 | $480 |
| 4. Market value of the firm | $3,000 | $3,240 | $3,480 |

Table 13.4 illustrates other effects of increasing leverage. We start with the total market value of the firm from Table 13.3. In line 2, the amount of debt is deducted to obtain the market value of equity. The values shown in lines 3 to 5 are calculated simultaneously because the shares repurchased and the share price must be determined simultaneously. For example, with 20% debt, we would have the following expression for the new share price, $P$.

$$P = 2,640/[100 - 600/P] \qquad \qquad \textbf{(13.1)}$$

In words, the expression says:

New Share Price = Market Value of Equity/(Previous Shares
Outstanding − Shares Purchased)

Solving equation (13.1), we obtain $32.40 for the share price. The second term in the denominator of (13.1) represents shares repurchased with the debt proceeds and equals 18.52. When this number is subtracted from the previous shares outstanding of 100, we obtain the new shares outstanding with 20% debt of 81.48. The amounts for lines 3 to 5 with 40% debt are calculated in the same way.

In the remainder of the table, we calculate some ratios and coverages. Line 6 is developed by using the data in Table 13.2 on the balance sheets. For example, in Table 13.2, the total assets remain the same after incurring $600 of debt. This is because the proceeds of debt were used to retire equity shares outstanding. Because total assets and total claims remain at $200, equity at book that had been $200 must be a negative $400 for total claims to continue to equal assets of $200. Book equity becomes negative. This is what is observed in actual cases of leveraged recapitalizations. Whereas book equity

**TABLE 13.4   Leverage Ratios and Interest Coverage**

|  | *Before Recap* | *20% Debt* | *40% Debt* |
|---|---|---|---|
| 1. Market value of the firm | $3,000 | $3,240 | $3,480 |
| 2. Market equity | $3,000 | $2,640 | $2,280 |
| 3. Shares repurchased with debt proceeds | 0.00 | 18.52 | 34.48 |
| 4. Shares outstanding | 100.00 | 81.48 | 65.52 |
| 5. Share price | $30.00 | $32.40 | $34.80 |
| 6. Book equity | $200 | −$400 | −$1,000 |
| 7. Debt to market equity | 0.00 | 0.23 | 0.53 |
| 8. Pretax cost of debt | 8.0% | 9.5% | 11.5% |
| 9. Interest expense | $0.0 | $57.0 | $138.0 |
| 10. Operating income | $300 | $300 | $300 |
| 11. Interest coverage | — | 5.3 | 2.2 |

becomes negative, the debt to market equity ratio is positive because market equity is positive.

In lines 8 through 11 we calculate the interest coverage. Some plausible levels of the pretax cost of debt are shown in line 8. When these percentages are multiplied by the level of debt outstanding, we obtain the amount of interest expense. Operating income was given in Table 13.1 at $300. The ratio of operating income to interest expense gives the interest coverage shown in line 11.

In this base case example of increasing leverage, we can draw a number of generalizations. Using the original Modigliani-Miller measure of the tax shield benefits of debt, we have demonstrated that management has increased the value of the firm by adding leverage where there was none before. Other measures of tax benefits might produce different levels of value increases for the firm. However, adding leverage where there had been none before is likely to move the firm away from a suboptimal (zero) level of debt.

Table 13.5 illustrates the impact of a leveraged recapitalization on the percentage of control by the management of the firm. In the previous examples, the funds were used to repurchase shares. Table 13.5 illustrates the effects of using the funds from selling debt to pay a cash dividend to nonmanagement shareholders who are assumed to hold 80% of the outstanding shares. The funds raised from selling debt are divided by 80 to obtain dividends of $7.5 per share when the funds raised by debt are $600 and $15 per share for the $1,200 level of debt, as shown in line 3. Recall that before debt is sold, the value per share of stock was $30. Therefore, for management to receive the equivalent in shares of stock, they would receive 0.25 of a share of stock for each share held. When the dividend per share is $15, the share fraction due management is 0.50. Taking into account the original number of management shares, as shown in line 5, the new total number of management shares would be 25 and 30, as shown in line 7.

As shown in Table 13.5, it is straightforward to see that the share of ownership by management would rise as high as 27.3% when the amount of debt sold is $1,200. If higher levels of debt were incurred and paid out as a dividend, the patterns in Table 13.5 would become even more pronounced.

Table 13.6 goes through an analysis in which the interest-bearing debt becomes 77.5% of the pre-recap market value of equity. In this example, each shareholder receives not only all the funds raised by selling debt, but by drawing down $40 of available

**TABLE 13.5** Leveraged Recapitalization: Alternative #1

|  | 20% Debt | 40% Debt |
|---|---|---|
| 1. Amount of debt | $600 | $1,200 |
| 2. Shares held by nonmanagement shareholders | 80 | 80 |
| 3. Dividend per share | $7.5 | $15.0 |
| 4. Fraction of shares received by management | 0.25 | 0.50 |
| 5. Original number of management shares in total | 20 | 20 |
| 6. Additional number of management shares | 5 | 10 |
| 7. New total number of management shares | 25 | 30 |

| Ownership % | Before Recap | After Recap | | | |
|---|---|---|---|---|---|
| Shareholders | 80.0% | 80 | 76.2% | 80 | 72.7% |
| Managers | 20.0% | 25 | 23.8% | 30 | 27.3% |
|  |  | 105 |  | 110 |  |

**TABLE 13.6**   Recap to Increase Management Control

### A.  Basic Data Inputs

| | |
|---|---|
| Market value of equity per share | $24 |
| Net operating income (NOI), millions | $30 |
| Shares outstanding, millions | 10 |
| Shares owned by management, millions | 1 |

Each shareholder (SH) receives

| | | |
|---|---|---|
| Cash | | $24.00 |
| Stub | 1 @ $4 | $ 4.00 |
| | | $28.00 |

Each management share receives

| | | |
|---|---|---|
| Stub | 7 @ $4 | $28.00 |

### B.  Sources and Uses of Cash

| Sources of cash: | | Uses of cash: | |
|---|---|---|---|
| Cash on books | $40 | Cash offer per SH | $24.00 |
| Short-term interest-bearing debt | 0 | Number of stubs for SH | × 9 |
| Senior long-term debt | 100 | | $216 |
| Subordinated debt | 76 | | |
| | $216 | | |

### C.  Balance Sheets

| | | Before Recap | After Recap |
|---|---|---|---|
| Cash | | $50 | $10 |
| Other current assets | | 100 | 100 |
| Long-term assets, net | | 120 | 120 |
| Total assets | | $270 | $230 |
| Noninterest-bearing ST debt | | $60 | $60 |
| Short-term interest-bearing debt | @ 10% | 10 | 10 |
| Senior long-term debt | @ 12% | 0 | 100 |
| Subordinated debt | @ 15% | 0 | 76 |
| Equity | | 200 | −16 |
| Total liabilities and shareholders' equity (SHE) | | $270 | $230 |
| Difference | | 0 | 0 |

### D.  Ownership Proportions

| Total number of shares | Before Recap | After Recap |
|---|---|---|
| Owned by shareholders | 9  (90%) | 9  (56%) |
| Owned by managers | 1  (10%) | 7  (44%) |
| | 10 | 16 |

### E.  Interest Coverage

| | Before Recap | After Recap |
|---|---|---|
| Net operating income (NOI) | $30 | $30 |
| Interest expense: | | |
| Short-term interest-bearing debt (STIBD) | $1 | $1 |
| Senior long-term debt | 0.0 | 12.0 |
| Subordinated debt | 0.0 | 11.4 |
| | $1 | $24 |
| NOI/interest expense | 30.0 | 1.2 |

cash. The example illustrates the case where the shareholders receive in cash the full pre-recap market value of the equity. In addition, it is assumed that the market value of share per stock falls to $4 and that the nonmanagement shareholders receive in exchange for their old shares one share of the new equity stub. The common equity is referred to as a stub when a financial recap results in the decline of its market value to 25% or less of its previous market value. Management receives no cash, but seven equity stubs instead for each equity share to obtain the same value received by each nonmanagement share. As a result, as shown in section D of Table 13.6, the ownership proportion held by managers rises from 10 to 44%. Thus, the higher percentage of original equity raised in debt form and distributed to nonmanagement, the larger the increase in management's share of ownership.

## The Effects of the Use of Leveraged Recaps

In the preceding section, we presented models of leveraged recaps (LRs). In this section, we discuss the rationale for their use. From the preceding examples, we see that a leveraged recap involves (1) a relatively large issue of debt, (2) the payment of a relatively large cash dividend to nonmanagement shareholders, and (3) as an alternative to the cash dividend or combined with it, a repurchase of common shares.

A number of empirical studies show that book leverage measured by total debt to total capitalization increases from about 20% to about 70% (Gupta and Rosenthal, 1991; Handa and Radhakrishnan, 1991; Kleiman, 1988). The ownership share of management increases from 9 to 24% on average.

The market response to announcements of leveraged recaps depends on whether the action was defensive or proactive. In defensive LRs, the actions are taken in response to actual takeovers or indications of a likely takeover bid. Proactive LRs are a part of a longer-run program of improving the performance of the firm. Event returns in a proactive LR experience a cumulative abnormal return of about 30%, similar to the level in tender offers (Gupta and Rosenthal, 1991; Handa and Radhakrishnan, 1991; Kleiman, 1988). Surprisingly, in such LRs the event returns to bond shareholders have been a positive 5% even though leverage has been substantially increased.

For defensive LRs, the abnormal returns include negative as well as positive values. The range is so wide as to make generalization difficult (Kleiman, 1988). Gupta and Rosenthal (1991), however, show cumulative abnormal returns of 48% over a window beginning 30 days before the start of the takeover and ending 150 days after the completion of the leveraged recapitalization and a positive 5% to bondholders.

## Subsequent Performance

Critical to the performance of the firm following an LR (proactive or defensive) is whether other operating improvements are made. This has been demonstrated clearly in a number of case studies (Healy and Palepu, 1995; Mitchell and Mitchell, 1996; Stewart, 1991; Wruck, 1994). The evidence is also consistent with a positive disciplinary role of debt (Dann, 1993; Gupta and Rosenthal, 1991). The large overhang of debt stimulates management to improve operations to generate sufficient cash flows to pay down the debt.

One study (Denis and Denis, 1995) found that 31% of their 29-firm sample completing LRs between 1985 and 1988 encountered financial distress. The high rate of financial distress, however, resulted mainly from unexpected and adverse macroeconomic and regulatory developments. The main factors influencing subsequent performance appear to be (1) industry conditions, (2) whether defensive or proactive LRs, and (3) whether operating improvements were achieved.

### The Functions of Leveraged Recaps

A leveraged recapitalization is likely to achieve the best results if it is a part of a strategic plan to improve the performance of a firm in relation to its changing environments. In addition to the financial restructuring, the success of an LR depends heavily on programs to improve operating performance.

A defensive LR may succeed by returning cash to shareholders that is close to or more than the takeover offer. In addition, share owners continue to hold the equity stubs received. The substantial increases in leverage may also discourage the outside bidders. The high leverage ratios may represent a form of scorched-earth policy. Prospective bidders may be reluctant to face the task of returning the firm to leverage ratios closer to historical industry patterns. Although LRs are used as a takeover defense, a high percentage of firms that adopt them are subsequently acquired.

In summary, LRs may perform a useful role in strategic programs to improve a firm's performance. If such a program is successful, a firm's vulnerability to a takeover offer will be reduced. On the positive side, LRs can help the firm enhance long-run benefits for its stakeholders.

## DUAL-CLASS STOCK RECAPITALIZATIONS

In dual-class recapitalizations (DCRs), firms have created a second class of common stock that has limited voting rights and usually a preferential claim to the firm's cash flows. Most firms create the new class by distributing limited voting shares pro rata to current shareholders. A typical DCR creates a class A type of shares with one vote per share but with a higher dividend rate than the other class. The class B shares can cast multiple votes such as 3, 5, or 10 per share; their dividend rate is lower than for the class A shares. As a result of a DCR, officers and directors as a group will usually have from 55 to 65% of common stock voting rights (DeAngelo and DeAngelo, 1985; Partch, 1987). However, the officers and directors have a claim on about 25% of the total cash flows from common stock. In a substantial proportion of companies with dual classes of common stock, the control group represents founding families or their descendants (DeAngelo and DeAngelo, 1985). In one-third of a sample of firms, two or more of the top executives are related either by blood or marriage.

### Reasons for Dual-Class Recapitalizations

A positive reason for DCRs is for top management to solidify their control so that long-run programs can be carried out. This avoids pressure for showing good results every quarter. This motive would be particularly applicable if the operations of the firm are relatively complex so that it is difficult for acquirers to evaluate managerial performance.

A related rationale is that managers may develop firm-specific abilities that are fully compensated when long-range plans come to fruition. Before the longer-term results are in, these managers would suffer the risk that their prospective rewards would be appropriated when outside shareholders respond favorably to an acquisition offer. Alternatively, it is also possible that managers who are not performing well may have the motive of entrenching their positions against a takeover so that they are not replaced.

### Market Response to Dual-Class Recaps

One way to test the alternative motives for DCRs is to measure the market response. In such studies the 90-day period preceding the announcement of a DCR represents a period of positive abnormal returns of over 6% (Lease, McConnell, and Mikkelson,

1984; Partch, 1987). When the event return is measured over a narrow window of two or three days related to the announcement of plans to create limited voting common stock, the market response is about a 1% significantly positive gain. When the average stock price reaction is cumulated over the time period from the announcement of the plan to the shareholder meeting at which it is approved, the response is negative but not significantly different from zero. The conclusion is that shareholder wealth is not adversely affected by the adoption of a DCR.

However, it was found that when a firm was taken over, the holders of superior voting right shares received a differentially higher payment than the holders of inferior voting shares (DeAngelo and DeAngelo, 1985). But other studies find that few firms with dual-class stock have experienced takeover bids. A virtual laboratory test of this issue was provided when the Ontario Securities Commission, on March 2, 1984, adopted a policy that it would not approve a prospectus offering for inferior voting shares unless they were given coattails that would permit them to participate equally in any takeover bid for the superior shares. After some experience, the commission reversed this policy on October 12, 1984. It was found that the premium to superior shares was increased again (Maynes, 1996). The consensus view appears to be that superior shares sell at a premium and mainly for the reason that they receive more in a takeover (Lease, McConnell, and Mikkelson, 1983).

### Paradox of the Entrenchment

Shareholder approval is required for the adoption of a DCR. Why do DCRs continue to be approved if their purpose is management entrenchment? In some cases, the voting power of insiders will be sufficient in achieving shareholder approval, but this cannot explain all approvals. Ruback (1988) developed a model that explains shareholders' behavior in exchange offers in which shareholders are given the opportunity to exchange common stock for shares with limited voting rights but higher dividends. These offers induce shareholders to exchange their shares for limited voting rights shares carrying higher dividends, even though such shareholders are harmed by the exchange as a result of the decline in the share price. In these offers, the wealth of shareholders who retain the superior-vote shares is transferred to shareholders who elect the inferior-vote shares with higher dividends. Thus, all outside shareholders rationally choose the higher dividend. This leads to the approval of the exchange plan and in turn to the decline in their wealth. If collective action were possible, outside shareholders would collude to defeat the exchange offer in order to avoid the reduced probability of receiving a takeover bid caused by the recapitalization.

Lehn, Netter, and Poulsen (LNP) (1990) compared DCRs with leveraged buyouts on the reasoning that both are forms of increasing ownership by managements. They found that DCRs experienced significantly higher growth rates in sales and number of employees than LBO firms. This is predictable because during the period of their study, 1977 through 1987, LBOs were mainly in relatively mature industries with stable cash flows. The ratios of research and development expenditures to sales and advertising expenditures to sales were higher for the DCR firms. The recap firm also had lower pretransaction tax liabilities.

With respect to performance after the transaction, LNP found that the dual-class firms use a higher percentage of their cash flows for capital expenditures than the LBO firms. A large proportion of the dual-class firms issue equity following the recapitalization. For the period studied, the LBOs were in more mature industries, whereas the dual-class firms were in industries with higher growth prospects. Significant increases in industry-adjusted operating income to sales ratios are achieved by dual-class firms. The LBO firms outperform dual-class firms in terms of size of improvement and performance, reflecting the turnarounds associated with managers with substantially increased equity stakes in LBOs. Insiders of dual-class firms already held 43.1% of the common equity before the transaction. In a contrast to LBOs, which were often used as antitakeover transactions, LNP found that takeover rumors or bids preceded recaps in only three of the 97 firms. Dual-class firms have relatively lower leverage policies and do not alter them as a consequence of the transaction.

All of the above findings on DCRs are consistent with the other studies. Insiders in DCR firms seek to consolidate their control so as to carry through their long-run plans. They are willing to sacrifice some current dividend income for the prospect of larger long-term capital gains.

Moyer, Rao, and Sisneros (MRS) (1992) examined the hypothesis of whether DCRs are accompanied by ways to decrease managerial control of the corporation—specifically by increasing leverage, dividends, and monitoring by security analysts and institutional investors. Their sample consisted of 114 firms that announced in the *Wall Street Journal* or in some SEC document (on a date that could be identified) DCRs during the 1979–1987 period. The average asset size per firm was $517.1 million. The authors show that the mean proportion of outside directors on the board changed from 53.7 to 59.1% over the two years preceding the announcement. Only the change in debt ratio and the mean number of analysts following the firm showed significant change. Changes in dividend payout and changes in the number of institutions holding the stock after the recapitalization were statistically insignificant. For prior ownership levels of up to 7.5%, the change in debt ratio is significantly greater in the low prior ownership groups than in the high prior ownership groups. The mean number of analysts following the sample firms is 5.72 prior to announcement and 7.47 after the announcement. A moderate increase in external control took place.

# EXCHANGE OFFERS

An exchange offer provides one or more classes of securities the right or option to exchange part or all of their holdings for a different class of securities of the firm. Like a tender offer repurchase, an exchange offer is usually open for about one month. However, the offer is frequently extended. To induce the security holders to make the exchange, the terms of exchange offered necessarily involve new securities of greater market value than the pre-exchange offer announcement market value. Exchange offers usually specify the maximum number of securities that may be exchanged. Also, many exchange offers are contingent upon acceptance by a minimum number of securities to be exchanged. Masulis (1980) reports that initial announcement dates precede the beginning of the exchange offer by, on average, nine weeks. He states that the average life of the offer is about seven weeks.

## Tax Aspects of Exchange Offers

When a company sells bonds at a discount, this generally implies that the coupon interest rate is below the market rate of interest. If the amount of the discount is material, the discount for tax purposes must be amortized over the life of the debt instrument. The amount of the amortized discount is treated as an additional interest payment to make up for the low coupon. It is, therefore, a tax expense to the corporation. When a corporation sells a bond at a premium, this means that the coupon payment is higher than the market rate. The amortization of the premium is a reduction in the interest tax expense to the corporation.

When a firm redeems debt at a price below the issue price, the difference is treated as ordinary income. If debt is redeemed at a price above the issue price, the difference is treated as an ordinary loss. It is generally the case that any change in the corporation's taxable income has an opposite effect on the taxable income of investors acquiring or tendering the debt (Masulis, 1980). When stock is tendered for debt, stockholders incur a capital gains tax liability just as if they had sold their stock for cash. Masulis (1980), therefore, observes that a debt for common stock exchange is likely to occur when stocks are selling at relatively low prices when most shareholders would incur little or no capital gains liability as a consequence.

### Empirical Evidence on Exchange Offers

With some of the characteristics of exchange offers as a background, we next turn to the empirical data. Table 13.7 shows that an exchange of debt for common stock involves the largest positive returns to shareholders. It is 14%, about the order of magnitude of wealth effects observed in stock repurchase tender offers. The exchange of preferred stock for common also carries a large gain of over 8%. The exchange of debt or the exchange of income bonds for preferred stock carries small but significant positive returns.

Table 13.8 summarizes the results of exchange offers with negative returns. Why do some types of exchange offer result in negative returns, while others achieve positive returns? A number of theories or explanations are possible. The effects appear to depend on whether the exchanges have one or more of the following consequences:

1. Leverage increasing or decreasing
2. Implied increases or decreases in future cash flows
3. Implied undervaluation or overvaluation of common stock
4. Management share ownership is increased or decreased
5. Control of management use of cash is increased or decreased
6. Positive or negative signaling effects

**TABLE 13.7** Exchange Offers with Positive Returns

| | |
|---|---|
| P1. Debt for common stock (Masulis, 1983) | +14.0% |
| P2. Preferred for common stock (Masulis, 1983; Pinegar and Lease, 1986) | + 8.2 |
| P3. Debt for preferred stock (Masulis, 1983) | + 2.2 |
| P4. Income bonds for preferred stock (McConnell and Schlarbaum, 1981) | + 2.2 |

**TABLE 13.8** Exchange Offers with Negative Returns

| | |
|---|---|
| N1. Common stock for debt (Masulis, 1983) | −9.9% |
| N2. Private swaps of common for debt (Finnerty, 1985; Peavy and Scott, 1985) | −0.9 |
| N3. Preferred stock for debt (Masulis, 1983) | −7.7 |
| N4. Common for preferred stock (Masulis, 1983; Pinegar and Lease, 1986) | −2.6 |
| N5. Calls forcing debt conversion (Mikkelson, 1981) | −2.1 |

The exchange offers in Table 13.7 have positive returns. They appear to have in common a number of characteristics: they are leverage increasing, they imply an increase in future cash flows, and they imply undervaluation of common stock. In two of the four cases, management share ownership is increased, and in three of the four cases, the control over management's use of cash is decreased. It is difficult to judge whether the leverage effect is also a signaling effect or whether it is purely a tax effect. It could be argued that the exchange of preferred for common stock does not carry tax implications for the corporation. On the other hand, because 80% of the dividends (85% before 1986) on preferred stock (for the period of these studies) could be excluded as income for a corporate investor, the incidence of this tax advantage accrued at least partially to the issuing corporation. Copeland and Lee (1991) judge the signaling effects to be most consistent with theory and empirical evidence.

Another curiosity in connection with the leverage-increasing exchange offers is noted by Vermaelen (1981). He points out that 30.1% of the leverage-increasing exchange offers in the sample developed by Masulis were announced during the period of dividend controls, roughly from mid-1971 through mid-1974. This suggests that they were by relatively smaller firms that were seeking to avoid the requirement that dividend increases could be no more than 4% per year. Of course, another strong external effect came about on the swaps that were stimulated by a tax law change in 1984 documented by Finnerty (1985). Because multiple explanations could account for the positive returns shown by Table 13.7, it is difficult to assign weights to each explanation.

Similarly, in Table 13.8, for exchange offers causing negative returns, it appears that the five explanations will run in the opposite direction. Swaps of common stock or preferred stock for debt carry about the same relatively large negative returns. However, private swaps of common stock for debt carry a small but significant return. Much more detailed studies would be required to attempt to assess the relative weight of each of the potential explanations for the pattern of abnormal returns observed.

One study introduces the q-ratio as an additional variable (Born and McWilliams, 1993). In a study of 127 equity-for-debt exchange offers, firms with q-ratios less than 1 experience significantly negative abnormal returns on announcement. This confirms the studies reported above. However, firms with q-ratios greater than 1 do not experience a significant event response. These findings suggest that the equity-for-debt exchanges with low q values may be used to rescue the firm from pressures resulting from the inability to service debt obligations.

Distressed exchanges have been widely used in recent years by firms that issued high-yield "junk" bonds and tried to work out what they felt was a short-term problem owing to overleveraging a basically sound operating company. Exchanges usually involve either a total exchange of preferred and/or common equity for the old debt or a combination of some equity and some new, but extended, debt for the old debt.

The classic distressed exchange involves a firm whose operating and financial condition has deteriorated due to both chronic and cyclical problems. It attempts to restructure both its assets and its liabilities. For example, International Harvester Corporation, a large farm equipment, truck, and bus manufacturer, was on the verge of total collapse in 1980–1982. The firm first exchanged preferred stock for its interest payment obligations to banks and extended both its interest payments to creditors and payables to suppliers. Next, it converted its short-term bank debt (1 to 3 years) to longer-term "junk" bonds (10 to 12 years). Finally, it exchanged common equity in its newly named entity, Navistar International, for the "old" junk bonds. These distressed restructuring strategies helped the firm improve its operations; it eventually paid its short- and long-term creditors in full (Chen, Weston, and Altman, 1995).

# REORGANIZATION PROCESSES

Several forms of financial restructuring may take place when a firm experiences financial distress. Financial distress is defined here as the condition in which the liquidation value of the firm's assets is less than the total face value of creditor claims.

## Out-of-Court Procedures

Figure 13.2 provides an overview of alternative adjustments that a firm may make to financial distress. The three main alternatives are informal procedures, merger, and legal proceedings. In out-of-court procedures, the firm can either continue or be liquidated. If the firm continues, a residual or equity claim can be substituted for a debt priority claim. Or the maturity of the debt can be postponed. A third alternative is to scale down the obligation. All three procedures are based on the idea that if the creditor firm is given some breathing room to improve operations, the creditors will ultimately receive more than they would otherwise.

## Merger into Another Firm

Mergers may also be used to rescue a floundering or failing firm. A study of 38 takeovers of distressed firms between 1981 and 1988 (Clark and Ofek, 1994) found that such combinations were more likely to involve firms in the same industry and less likely to be hostile takeovers than general patterns. In the sample of 38 restructuring efforts by the use of mergers, Clark and Ofek classified 20 as failures, nine as marginally successful, and nine as clearly successful. These evaluations were based on the use of five different measures to evaluate the postmerger performance of the combined and target firms: (1) ratio of earnings before interest, taxes, and depreciation (EBITD) to sales, (2) return to the bidder on its investment in the target, (3) beta excess return during the two years after completion of the merger, (4) the bidder's excess equity return over its industry three-

**FIGURE 13.2  Alternative Adjustments to Financial Distress**

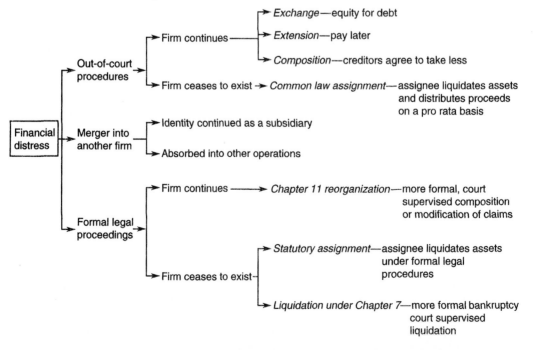

digit SIC code median during the two years after merger completion, and (5) a qualitative variable that equals +1 if successful, 0 if it was marginal, and −1 if a failure.

Clark and Ofek also study the relation between the announcement period cumulative abnormal return (CAR) and each of their five performance variables. The bidder CAR is positively related to each of the five performance measures. This is another study that demonstrates the ability of market event returns to forecast postmerger results.

They found also that bidders overpay for the distressed targets. Much of the postmerger performance results appear to be dominated by industry factors. Takeovers of target firms that are financially distressed are more likely to be successfully restructured than target firms whose operating performance is poor. Distressed targets that are smaller relative to the bidder yield positive returns to the bidder. Clark and Ofek conclude that, in the majority of cases, takeovers do not successfully restructure a distressed target. But they observe that the effort to do so may appear to be the best alternative available at the time.

## Formal Legal Proceedings

When informal extensions or scaling down the obligations as well as the merger alternative do not appear to solve the problems of a distressed firm, more formal legal proceedings are utilized. The formal court proceedings follow the bankruptcy law adopted in 1978. Its five major provisions are (1) an automatic stay, (2) debtor in possession (DIP), (3) increased power of managers in the recontracting process, (4) new voting rules for creditors, and (5) some flexibility in applying absolute priority rules.

An automatic stay permits the firm to stop all principal and interest payments, preventing secured creditors from taking possession of their collateral. This makes it easier for the firm to obtain additional financing. Debtor-in-possession financing makes it possible to issue new debt claims with priority over existing debt.

Managers retain considerable power after a firm has filed for bankruptcy. Managers are able to continue to make operating decisions, and, for 120 days after the Chapter 11 filing, managers have the exclusive right to propose a reorganization plan. The court often grants one or more extensions of this deadline. Management has 180 days from the filing date to obtain creditor and shareholder approval. If management fails to propose a plan or its plan is rejected, creditors can propose their own plan. To do so, they must provide proof of values for claims to be issued and assets to be retained or sold. This requires costly appraisals and hearings, as compared with a management plan that requires the bankruptcy judge to evaluate it as "fair and reasonable."

The 1978 Bankruptcy Code introduced new voting rules for approval by creditors of a reorganization plan. It specifies majority (in number) requirements for approval of the plan and provides that dissenters must accept the same terms as approved by the majority.[1] In this sense, each class of creditors behaves as one part in which minority creditors cannot hold out. The new voting rules facilitate renegotiation of the debt so that the potential for investment efficiency is improved by reducing bargaining costs.

---

[1]If the reorganization is proposed in an out-of-court distressed restructuring, i.e., not under Chapter 11, then a virtually unanimous acceptance by those creditors who are impaired must be received. This explains the relatively recent phenomenon known as a "prepackaged Chapter 11," whereby the required (but not necessarily unanimous) proportion of accepting creditor votes is assembled for a plan *prior to* the filing of the petition for relief (which initiates the bankruptcy process). In most cases, the formal Chapter 11 reorganization that follows the prepack agreement is a relatively simple procedure. The actual time spent in the bankruptcy process has been as little as one month, and it generally averages only a few months. The money spent in a prepackaged bankruptcy is also typically less. See Altman (1993), Betker (1995), McConnell and Servantes (1991), and Salerno and Hansen (1991) for discussions of prepackaged plans and their recent experience. Betker analyzes 49 cases and concludes that while direct costs of prepacks are comparable to those of traditional Chapter 11's, gains come from the binding of holdouts and from favorable tax treatment on tax loss carryforwards.

The code also provides for absolute priority rules in establishing the order of claims under reorganization. Frequent, but small (2.3 to 7.6%) deviations from absolute priority occur. Here are two possible explanations: (a) one or more classes of claimants may provide new or future financing as a basis for improving their position over what it would have been under absolute priority; (b) estimated market values are used as a basis for establishing priority positions. But market values depend on the success of the restructuring and the future performance of the firm. The value estimates are subject to negotiation among the claimants. Thus, deviations from absolute priority may facilitate approval of a plan earlier than otherwise would be possible.

The basic goal for the legal, bankruptcy-restructuring process is to preserve organization value. By recontracting with claimants, the aim is to restore the firm to operating and financial health. Thus, there is a positive side to the procedures for restructuring financially distressed firms.

## FINANCIAL ENGINEERING

Financial engineering involves the use of calls, puts, swaps, and forward and futures contracts to influence the payoffs from taking various types of financial exposures. These instruments have helped in limiting the financial exposures of business firms as well as other types of investors. This is a rich literature. We limit our discussion to one example of how financial engineering can facilitate a merger transaction (Mason et al., 1995; Tufano, 1996).

In 1991 in its strategic planning processes, AMOCO, a major oil company, made a decision to dispose of its marginal oil and gas properties. It created a new organization, MW Petroleum Corporation, as an entity with interest in 9,500 wells in more than 300 producing fields. The Apache Corporation, a smaller independent oil and gas company, was interested in purchasing AMOCO's unit. Apache's strategy was to acquire properties that others regarded as marginal and use its lower cost operations to achieve higher returns. The negotiations were taking place during the spring of 1991, just after Iraq's invasion of Kuwait had pushed up oil prices. Future oil prices were highly uncertain. Financial engineering provided a solution.

AMOCO was willing to write Apache a guarantee that if oil prices fell below a specified level during the first two years after the sale, AMOCO would make compensating payments to Apache. Apache, in turn, agreed to pay AMOCO if oil prices exceeded a specified level over a 5- to 8-year period. Thus, the commodity risk of the transaction was shared. In financial engineering terms, AMOCO and Apache had created a "collar"—a combination of a call option and a put option. Option pricing theory can price a collar.

After the merger was completed, each company was approached with an offer to purchase their option position. Thus the financial markets gave them the opportunity of monetizing (selling) their options and thereby closing their risk exposures if they so desired. The literature of financial engineering is rich with creative transactions. Their implications for facilitating M&As is illustrated by the above example.

## LIQUIDATIONS AND TAKEOVER BUST-UPS

Corporate liquidations can be either involuntary or voluntary. Creditors force a firm to liquidate if it is worth more "dead than alive." In other words, attempting to operate an unsuccessful firm may cause values to deteriorate even further. Voluntary liquidations have a much more positive orientation. When a firm can be sold in parts or as a whole for an amount that exceeds the market values of the firm's securities, liquidation will realize more for the security holders. Managers may be stimulated to take such actions because of the threat that an acquirer will mount a proxy contest for control or launch a tender offer to buy the firm and then liquidate it. Even the threat of such "bust-up" takeovers is enough to stimulate voluntary liquidations.

Corporate liquidations are often associated with bankruptcy proceedings, but these are generally involuntary. The general rule is that a liquidation in bankruptcy will preserve values to a greater degree than continuing to attempt to operate an unsuccessful firm. But voluntary liquidations have a much more positive motivation. When a firm can be sold for an amount that exceeds the existing market value of the firm's outstanding securities, liquidation is in the best interests of the security holders. One factor stimulating managers to take such actions is the threat that outsiders will mount a proxy contest for control and conduct the liquidation themselves.

An important tax advantage of liquidations was removed by the Tax Reform Act of 1986. Under the General Utilities Doctrine, the corporate capital gains to the selling firm were not taxable if it adopted a plan of complete liquidation and all liquidating dividends were paid to shareholders within 12 months after the plan was adopted. One effect of the repeal of the General Utilities Doctrine by the 1986 act was to eliminate the tax incentive for firms to liquidate voluntarily after partial sell-offs. The 1986 act also eliminated the preferential personal capital gains tax rate, which makes the deferral of realization in nontaxable mergers more attractive. It appears that the Tax Reform Act of 1986 reduced the tax advantages of liquidations as compared with nontaxable mergers.

## Empirical Studies

Skantz and Marchesini (1987) studied a sample of 37 firms announcing liquidation between 1970 and 1982. They found that the announcement-month average excess return is +21.4%. Interestingly, they found that their sample firms were "not highly dissimilar to their industry members" (p. 71) in profitability prior to the liquidation decision.

Of the possible reasons for the positive abnormal return, Skantz and Marchesini found only one to be applicable. While divestitures had been generally subject to capital gains taxes, voluntary liquidations could be structured to qualify for preferential tax treatment on a major portion of the gains. This does not explain the much higher positive gains to liquidations (21.4% for the announcement with a cumulative average excess return of 41.3%) than for spin-offs, which are also treated as tax-free exchanges. The reason may be that spin-offs average only 20% of the original parent; if the abnormal returns found by Copeland, Lemgruber, and Mayers (1987) of 5.02% are multiplied by 5 for comparable sizing of investment, the gains are similar.

Hite, Owers, and Rogers (1987) included an analysis of total liquidations in their study of the market for interfirm asset sales. They analyzed 49 voluntary liquidations during the period 1963–1983. The median market value of equity was $41 million. The median book value of total assets was about $72 million. Although mergers were eliminated, they found that 21 of the 49 firms had been targets in earlier merger, tender offer, or leveraged buyout bids in the 24 months preceding the liquidation proposal. An additional three firms had been involved in proxy solicitation control contests.

The authors observed a two-day announcement period average abnormal return of 12.24% for total liquidations, and more than 80% of the sample observations were positive. They estimated that for the seven liquidating firms that had senior securities, an equally weighted portfolio yielded a two-day holding period average return of 8.57%. Their analysis of the source of the positive returns to both the shareholders and senior claimants is that assets are being moved to higher-valued uses.

The study of voluntary liquidations by Kim and Schatzberg (1987, 1988) covered a sample of 73 liquidating firms over the period 1963–1981. They observed that their sample is composed of relatively small firms. The median market value of equity was $23 million. The median ratio of the market value of equity of the liquidating firm to the market value of equity of the acquiring firm was 0.28. Kim and Schatzberg found that the liquidation announcement was associated with an average three-day market adjusted return of 14% to the shareholders of liquidating firms. An additional 3% abnormal return took place at shareholder confirmation. Acquiring shareholders experienced a small positive return at a liquidation announcement and a small negative return at confirmation, but these returns were not statistically significant.

As in the Hite, Owers, and Rogers (1987) study, the liquidation announcements were often associated with prior news relating to mergers, tender offers, or partial sell-offs. At the time of the prior announcements, an abnormal return of 9% was realized. When Kim and Schatzberg took into consideration all public announcements, they obtained even higher returns. They measured the abnormal returns for shareholders from two days before the earliest announcement date until two days after the last announcement date, obtaining total gains of 30% for firms without prior announcements and 34% for firms with prior announcements. The average gain to the shareholders of acquiring firms is not statistically significant.

The Kim and Schatzberg (KS) (1987, 1988) papers confirm the beneficial effect on senior claimants found by Hite, Owers, and Rogers (1987). The majority of the firms in the KS sample retired debt that had a market value less than the face value. Kim and Schatzberg also analyzed the question of why liquidations increase market values. They observe that one advantage of liquidations is that there may be several purchasers, whereas in a merger there is likely to be only one. This enables the selling firm to move its assets to the individual purchasers from whom the greatest value can be realized.

Kim and Schatzberg also compared the tax effects of liquidations with those of nontaxable mergers, and they discuss the impact of the Tax Reform Act of 1986. In general, a nontaxable merger had the advantage of deferring the recognition of a gain to the stockholders of the selling firm until a subsequent sale of the securities involved. First, in a liquidation, the selling stockholders must recognize the gain immediately. Second, unused tax credits and losses belonging to either of the premerger firms are carried over in a nontaxable merger, but those of the selling firm are lost at liquidation. Third, a liquidation permits the acquiring firm to step up the tax basis of the assets acquired, but this cannot be done in a nontaxable merger.

Berger and Ofek (1996) found that between 1986 and 1991 the average diversified firm destroyed about 15% of the value its individual segments would have had if they had been operating as independent business units. For a sample of 100 large aquisitions, they found that half of the large diversified targets were broken up. The negative value of diversification that was recovered by the bust-up ranged from 21 to 37%. The large targets not broken up after they were taken over had a mean value effect of diversification of only 5%, implying that they were not broken up after the aquisition because not much could be gained by doing so. They studied the buyers of the divested divisions in the bust-up group and found that 75% of the buyers were LBO associations (financial groups taking segments private in a leveraged buyout) or focused, related firms. This indicates that the bust-up was performed to move the segments to firms with experience in related businesses.

## Summary

The firm's internal growth program is closely tied to the external market for corporate control. Capital structure and leverage decisions represent potentials for value enhancement, for acquiring other firms, or to defend against being acquired by others. These are illustrated in the financial restructuring transactions currently in use.

Leveraged recapitalizations involve a relatively large issue of debt that is used for the payment of a relatively large cash dividend to nonmanagement shareholders or for the repurchase of common shares, or a combination of both. The end result is an increase in the ownership share of management. Leveraged recaps should be proactive as part of a long-run program to improve the performance of the firm rather than defensive in response to actual or possible takeovers.

In dual-class stock recapitalizations (DCRs), firms create a second class of common stock that has limited voting rights but usually with a preferential claim to the firm's cash flows. Top management may use DCRs as a way to solidify their control to pursue long-run improvement programs or, alternatively, to entrench their positions against takeovers or being replaced. As a result of a DCR, officers and directors will have, on average, from 55 to 65% of the common stock voting rights, but a claim on only about 25% of the total cash flows.

An exchange offer provides one or more classes of securities the right or option to exchange part or all of their holdings for a different class of securities of the firm. Positive returns are associated with exchange offers that increase leverage, imply an increase in future cash flows, suggest undervaluation of common stock, increase management share ownership, and/or decrease management control over cash. These are illustrated by debt-for-common and preferred-for-common exchanges. In recent years, distressed exchanges have been widely used by firms in attempts to restructure both assets and liabilities.

Financial distress becomes a driving force for financial restructuring to take place. There are many alternative adjustments that a distressed firm can take. Out-of-court procedures allow the firm's obligations to be restructured to give it some breathing room. Mergers may be used to rescue a floundering or failing firm. However, takeovers do not, in the majority of cases, successfully restructure a distressed target firm. Takeovers are more likely to be successful for financially distressed target firms than for target firms whose operating performance is poor. As a last resort, formal legal proceedings such as filing for a Chapter 11 reorganization or for bankruptcy may be utilized.

Firms have used financial engineering to limit their financial exposure. Financial engineering has also been used to facilitate merger transactions. If the acquiring firm and the prospective target firm are able to share the risk exposures of their mutual transaction, it is more likely that the deal will be completed.

If the firm is worth more "dead than alive," creditors will force the firm to liquidate. The firm can be sold in parts or as a whole for an amount that exceeds the preliquidation market values of the firm's securities. Liquidation can also be voluntary when there is the threat of a "bust-up" takeover. Managers may prefer to liquidate if outsiders are likely to mount a proxy contest for control or launch a tender offer to buy the firm and conduct the liquidation themselves.

## Questions

13.1   What are the goals for leveraged recapitalizations?

13.2   What are the pros and cons of dual-class recapitalizations?

13.3 What types of exchange offers have positive event returns and what types have negative event returns?

13.4 Discuss the relationship between financial reorganizations of various types including a Chapter 11 reorganization.

13.5 How can financial engineering be used to facilitate M&As?

13.6 How do bust-up takeovers and subsequent liquidation of the parts increase the total value realized over the market price of the firm prior to its sale by parts?

------------------------------------ C A S E   13–1 ------------------------------------

# Management Assistance, Inc.

Liquidating for profit is discussed from the standpoint of case studies plus the analysis of what is going on. When a firm "liquidates," its economic resources have not necessarily been destroyed. Indeed, even though an individual firm may cease to exist, it typically sells some or most of its assets to other ongoing firms. In the hands of the buying companies, the assets may be put to a higher economic use than when they were held by the seller.

The case study of Management Assistance, Inc. (MAI) illustrates a number of the concepts involved in liquidating a company (Rosenberg, 1985). MAI had started as a company leasing punch card equipment and then later became a computer leasing company in the late 1950s. It was somewhat unique as a leasing company in that it emphasized having strong marketing and customer engineering organizations. Particularly, it emphasized customer engineering as a method of assuring customers that the products it leased would receive prompt and effective attention to maintain their serviceability.

In the 1970s MAI was a leader in the development of personal computers with its Basic Four Information Systems. This enabled MAI to record a $19 million profit in 1979. With increased competition in personal computers, the company recorded a $17 million loss in fiscal 1984. The reported losses caused the price of its stock to decline substantially. MAI caught the attention of Asher Adelman early in his career in corporate takeovers. "But where others saw only red ink, Adelman discerned hidden value" (Rosenberg, 1985, p. 9). The customer engineering and service activity of MAI had been placed in a corporate subsidiary named Sorbus Service. Adelman says that he judged that this activity alone would sell for more than two times the then current market price of the common stock of MAI as a whole. The personal computer business of MAI had been placed in a corporate subsidiary with the name Basic Four Information Systems. The division was experiencing losses but Adelman saw potential in the strong marketing organization as a distribution operation, selling not only the products of MAI but the products of other companies as well. By January 1985 Adelman had won control of the board of directors and sold off Sorbus and Basic Four. In February 1985 MAI began to distribute liquidating dividends of about $26 a share to stockholders. It is said that Adelman made a profit of $11 million on his investment of $15 million, a gain of 73%.

--------------------------------------------------------------

--------------------------------------------------------------

## Questions on Case Study C13.1

C13.1.1 Were the main assets of MAI destroyed?

C13.1.2 What happened to Sorbus and Basic Four?

C13.1.3 Why didn't the previous control group at MAI liquidate MAI?

# References

Altman, E. I., *Corporate Financial Distress and Bankruptcy,* 2nd ed., New York: John Wiley & Sons, 1993.

Berger, Philip G., and Eli Ofek, "Bustup Takeovers of Value-Destroying Diversified Firms," *Journal of Finance,* 51, September 1996, pp. 1175–1200.

Betker, B., "An Empirical Examination of Prepackaged Bankruptcy," *Financial Management,* Spring 1995, pp. 3–18.

Born, Jeffery A., and Victoria B. McWilliams, "Shareholder Responses to Equity-for-Debt Exchange Offers: A Free-Cash-Flow Interpretation," *Financial Management,* 22, Winter 1993, pp. 19–20.

Chen, Yehning, J. Fred Weston, and Edward I. Altman, "Financial Distress and Restructuring Models," *Financial Management,* 24, Summer 1995, pp. 57–75.

Clark, Kent, and Eli Ofek, "Mergers as a Means of Restructuring Distressed Firms: An Empirical Investigation," *Journal of Financial and Quantitative Analysis,* 29, December 1994, pp. 541–565.

Copeland, Thomas E., and Won Heum Lee, "Exchange Offers and Stock Swaps—New Evidence," *Financial Management,* 20, Autumn 1991, pp. 34–48.

Copeland, Thomas E., E. F. Lemgruber, and D. Mayers, "Corporate Spinoffs: Multiple Announcement and Ex-Date Abnormal Performance," chapter 7 in T. E. Copeland, ed., *Modern Finance and Industrial Economics,* New York: Basil Blackwell, 1987.

Dann, Larry Y., "Highly Leveraged Transactions and Managerial Discretion Over Investment Policy: An Overview," *Journal of Accounting & Economics,* 16, January–April–July 1993, pp. 237–240.

DeAngelo, Harry, and Linda DeAngelo, "Managerial Ownership of Voting Rights: A Study of Public Corporations with Dual Classes of Common Stock," *Journal of Financial Economics,* 14, 1985, pp. 33–69.

———, "Ancient Redwoods, Junk Bonds, and the Politics of Finance: A Study of the Hostile Takeover of the Pacific Lumber Company," ms., University of Southern California, 1996.

Denis, David J., and Diane K. Denis, "Causes of Financial Distress Following Leveraged Recapitalizations," *Journal of Financial Economics,* 37, February 1995, pp. 129–157.

Finnerty, John D., "Stock-for-Debt Swaps and Shareholder Returns," *Financial Management,* 14, Autumn 1985, pp. 5–17.

Gupta, Atul, and Leonard Rosenthal, "Ownership Structure, Leverage, and Firm Value: The Case of Leveraged Recapitalizations," *Financial Management,* 20, Autumn 1991, pp. 69–83.

Handa, Puneet, and A. R. Radhakrishnan, "An Empirical Investigation of Leveraged Recapitalizations With Cash Payout as Takeover Defense," *Financial Management,* 20, Autumn 1991, pp. 58–68.

Healy, Paul M., and Krishna G. Palepu, "The Challenges of Investor Communication: The Case of CUC International, Inc.," *Journal of Financial Economics,* 38, 1995, pp. 111–140.

Hite, Gailen, James E. Owers, and R. C. Rogers, "The Market for Interfirm Asset Sales: Partial Sell-offs and Total Liquidations," *Journal of Financial Economics,* 18, 1987, pp. 229–252.

Jensen, Michael C., "Agency Costs of Free Cash Flow, Corporate Finance and Takeovers," *American Economic Review,* 76, May 1986, pp. 323–329.

Kim, E. H., and J. D. Schatzberg, "Voluntary Corporate Liquidations," *Journal of Financial Economics,* 19, 1987, pp. 311–328.

———, "Voluntary Liquidations: Causes and Consequences," *Midland Corporate Finance Journal,* 5, Winter 1988, pp. 30–35.

Kleiman, R. T., "The Shareholder Gains from Leveraged Cashouts: Some Preliminary Evidence," *Journal of Applied Corporate Finance,* 1, Spring 1988, pp. 46–53.

Lease, R., J. McConnell, and W. Mikkelson, "The Market Value of Control in Publicly Traded Corporations," *Journal of Financial Economics,* 11, 1983, pp. 439–472.

————, "The Market Value of Differential Voting Rights in Closely Held Corporations," *Journal of Business,* 75, 1984, pp. 443–467.

Lehn, Kenneth, Jeffry Netter, and Annette Poulsen, "Consolidating Corporate Control: Dual-Class Recapitalizations versus Leveraged Buyouts," *Journal of Financial Economics,* 27, October 1990, pp. 557–580.

Mason, Scott P., Robert C. Merton, André F. Perold, and Peter Tufano, *Cases in Financial Engineering: Applied Studies of Financial Innovation,* Upper Saddle River, NJ: Prentice Hall, 1995.

Masulis, Ronald W., "Stock Repurchase by Tender Offer: An Analysis of the Causes of Common Stock Price Changes," *Journal of Finance,* 35, 1980, pp. 305–319.

————, "The Impact of Capital Structure Change on Firm Value: Some Estimates," *Journal of Finance,* 38, March 1983, pp. 107–126.

Maynes, Elizabeth, "Takeover Rights and the Value of Restricted Shares," *The Journal of Financial Research,* 19, Summer 1996, pp. 157–173.

McConnell, John J., and Gary G. Schlarbaum, "Evidence on the Impact of Exchange Offers on Security Prices: The Case of Income Bonds," *Journal of Business,* 54, 1981, pp. 65–85.

McConnell, J., and H. Servantes, "The Economics of Prepackaged Bankruptcy," *Journal of Applied Corporate Finance,* 4, Summer 1991, pp. 93–97.

Mikkelson, W. H., "Convertible Security Calls and Security Returns," *Journal of Financial Economics,* 9, 1981, pp. 237–264.

Mitchell, Mark, and Janet Mitchell, "UST, Inc.," CaseNet, Boston, MA: South-Western College Publishing, 1996.

Moyer, R. C., Ramesh Rao, and P. M. Sisneros, "Substitutes for Voting Rights: Evidence From Dual Class Recapitalizations," *Financial Management,* 21, Autumn 1992, pp. 35–47.

Partch, M. Megan, "The Creation of a Class of Limited Voting Common Stock and Shareholder Wealth," *Journal of Financial Economics,* 18, 1987, pp. 313–339.

Peavy, J. W., and J. A. Scott, "A Closer Look at Stock-for-Debt Swaps," *Financial Analysts Journal,* May/June 1985, pp. 44–50.

Pinegar, J. Michael, and Ronald C. Lease, "The Impact of Preferred-for-Common Exchange Offers on Firm Value," *Journal of Finance,* 41, September 1986, pp. 795–814.

Rosenberg, Hilary, "Newest Kid on the Takeover Block," *Barron's,* March 11, 1985, pp. 8–9, 11.

Ruback, R. S., "Coercive Dual-Class Exchange Offers," *Journal of Financial Economics,* 20, Jan/Mar 1988, pp. 153–173.

Salerno, T., and C. Hansen, "A Prepackaged Bankruptcy Strategy," *Journal of Business Strategy,* 12, January/February 1991, pp. 36–41.

Sikora, Martin, ed., *Capturing the Untapped Value in Your Company,* Philadelphia, PA: MRL Publishing Company, 1990.

Skantz, Terrance R., and Roberto Marchesini, "The Effect of Voluntary Corporate Liquidation on Shareholder Wealth," *The Journal of Financial Research,* 10, Spring 1987, pp. 65–75.

Stewart, G. Bennett, *The Quest for Value,* New York: HarperBusiness, 1991.

Tufano, Peter, "How Financial Engineering Can Advance Corporate Strategy," *Harvard Business Review,* 74, January/February 1996, pp. 136–146.

Vermaelen, Theo, "Common Stock Repurchases and Market Signalling: An Empirical Study," *Journal of Financial Economics,* 9, 1981, pp. 139–183.

Wruck, Karen Hopper, "Financial Distress, Reorganization, and Organizational Efficiency," *Journal of Financial Economics,* 27, October 1990, pp. 419–444.

————, "Financial Policy, Internal Control, and Performance: Sealed Air Corporation's Leveraged Special Dividend," *Journal of Financial Economics,* 36, 1994, pp. 157–192.

C H A P T E R

# 14

# Joint Ventures

Mergers and tender offers involve a complete fusion of two independent firms or other entities into a single decision-making unit. Many other forms of relationships between firms can include licensing or cross-licensing of particular technologies, joint bidding on an individual contract, and franchising or other forms of short-term or long-term contracts. Joint ventures represent another form of relationship between two or more business entities and are widely and increasingly used by business firms. A *Wall Street Journal* article of November 1, 1995 describes joint ventures among competing firms (Templin, 1995). Texas Instruments and Hitachi have engaged in joint efforts since 1988 to develop new memory chips. In 1995 they jointly founded a $500 million plant near Dallas to produce memory chips. Another example is joint activity between Compaq Computer Corp. and Intel Corp., a major supplier of microprocessors. The two companies have worked together to develop new products. Compaq also has a joint venture with Digital Equipment Corp. to handle service and support for Compaq customers.

The value of combining different skills is demonstrated by the relationship between USX Corp., a large integrated steel producer and Nucor Corp., the leading mini-mill steel producer. USX researchers developed a theory for a new process of making steel from iron carbide, eliminating blast furnaces and supporting coke batteries. If successful, the new process would cut steel producing costs by as much as one-fourth. The two companies entered into agreement to study the feasibility of the process. Nucor possessed considerable experience and expertise on constructing the types of plants that would be required. They would interact with the physicists at USX, who had formulated the new concepts.

Additional examples encompass several different industries. Since 1984 Hewlett-Packard has sold more than 15 million laser printers that use a motor made by Canon. These machines compete with Canon's own laser printers. In telecommunications, we find examples of companies competing in the United States but participating in international joint ventures. U S West Inc. competes with Tele-Communications Inc. (TCI), a leader in cable in the U.S. market. The two have formed a joint venture in Great Britain to sell phone and cable services on one network. But in the U.S. market, U S West has a relationship with Time Warner to offer local service in the New York market of NYNEX Corp. U S West and NYNEX are participants in a four-company enterprise to sell wireless personal communications—cellular phones. TCI is also joint venturing with Sprint Corp., a competitor to U S West and other telephone operating companies that were spun off from AT&T in 1984. Chrysler Corp. had a joint venture with Mitsubishi Motors Corp. for the purchase of as many as 200,000 vehicles a year. As Chrysler has introduced successful new products, it has announced plans to discontinue purchases from Mitsubishi by the year 2000.

Joint ventures have been used for many years—decades before the highly publicized activities of the 1980s. In an early study Bachman (1965) described the entry of oil and gas companies into chemicals, using joint ventures to a considerable degree. For the early 1960s, some illustrative joint ventures and the products they produced included:

Alamo Polymer (Phillips Petroleum and National Distillers)—polypropylene

American Chemical (Richfield Oil and Stauffer)—vinyl chloride, ethylene

Ancon Chemical (Continental Oil and Ansul)—methyl chloride

Avisun (Sun Oil and American Viscose)—polypropylene resins

Goodrich-Gulf (Gulf Oil and Goodrich Rubber)—S-type rubber

Hawkeye Chemical (Skelly Oil and Swift)—ammonia

Jefferson Chemical (Texas Co. and American Cyanamid)—ethylene, propylene, and others

National Plastics Products (Enjay and J. P. Stevens)—polypropylene fiber

Sun Olin (Sun Oil and Olin)—urea, ethylene, and others

Witfield Chemical (Richfield Oil and Witco Chemical)—detergent alkylate

Joint venture participants continue to exist as separate firms with a joint venture representing a newly created business enterprise. The joint venture may be organized as a partnership, a corporation, or any other form of business organization the participating firms might choose to select.

In contract law, joint ventures are usually described as having the following characteristics:

1. Contribution by partners of money, property, effort, knowledge, skill, or other asset to a common undertaking

2. Joint property interest in the subject matter of the venture

3. Right of mutual control or management of the enterprise

4. Expectation of profit, or presence of "adventure"

5. Right to share in the profit

6. Usual limitation of the objective to a single undertaking or ad hoc enterprise

Thus, joint ventures are of limited scope and duration. Typically they involve only a small fraction of each participant's total activities. Each partner must have something unique and important to offer the venture and simultaneously provide a source of gain to the other participants. However, the sharing of information and/or assets required to achieve the objective need not extend beyond the joint venture. Hence the participants' competitive relationship need not be affected by the joint venture arrangement. Sometimes the joint arrangement is relatively informal, involving only an exchange of ideas and information while working on similar challenges. The term strategic alliances has been used to describe relationships among companies that are something short of establishing a joint venture entity.

It has been found that joint ventures and mergers display similar timing characteristics. The correlation between completed mergers and joint venture start-ups is over .95, highly significant from a statistical standpoint. Chapter 6 documented that merger activity is highly correlated with plant and equipment outlays. Both joint ventures and mergers are likely to be stimulated by factors that affect total investment activity generally.

# JOINT VENTURES IN BUSINESS STRATEGY

A number of motives have stimulated joint ventures:

1. Share investment expenses or combine a large company that has cash to invest with a smaller company with a product or production idea but with insufficient funds to pursue the opportunity. While outside investors may be reluctant to take high risks even on an equity basis, a business firm may be interested because it has more information on the project or has other projects that may benefit from the learning experience that may be gained from the joint venture.

2. A greater learning experience may be achieved.

3. Even for a large company, a joint venture is a method of reducing the investment outlay required and of sharing the risk.

4. Antitrust authorities may be more willing to permit joint ventures than to permit mergers (*Los Angeles Times*, 1984). While mergers result in a reduction in the number of firms, joint ventures increase the number of firms. The parents continue in operation and another firm is created. Particularly, joint ventures in research and development areas are likely to receive endorsement from government agencies.

Joint ventures may be used to acquire complementary technological or management resources at lower cost, or to benefit from economies of scale, critical mass, and the learning curve effect—all elements of strategic alliances. The "go together-split" strategy achieves these ends in the usual 50–50 or 60–40 joint venture of limited scope and duration, whereas the successive integration strategy uses joint venturing as a way of learning about prospective merger partners to full merger or acquisition.

Firms may also use joint venturing as an element of long-run strategic planning. The spider's web strategy is used to provide countervailing power among rivals in a product market and among rivals for a scarce resource. Thus, a small firm in a highly concentrated industry can negotiate joint ventures with several of the industry's dominant firms to form a self-protective network of counterbalancing forces. Indeed, it is reported that large companies such as General Electric are involved in over 100 joint ventures and that IBM, GM, AT&T, and Xerox participate in more than a dozen joint ventures. Companies of the type listed have both financial resources plus managerial and technical competence to bring to a joint venture (*Business Week*, 1986). This strategy presupposes, of course, that the small firm has something unique to offer the industry leaders.

## Joint Ventures and Complex Learning

The expressed purpose of 50% of all joint ventures is knowledge acquisition (Berg, Duncan, and Friedman, 1982). The complexity of the knowledge to be transferred is a key factor in determining the contractual relationship between the partners.

Where the knowledge to be transferred is complex or embedded in a complicated set of technological and organizational circumstances, learning-by-doing and teaching-by-doing (L/TBD) may be the most appropriate means of transfer. Successive adaptations to changing internal and environmental events may be necessary to achieve efficiency in the process being taught. It may be very costly or even impossible to give training in complex production tasks in a classroom situation—the atmosphere (operations, machines, work group) may be essential. In addition, job incumbents, no matter how skilled, may be unable to describe job skills to trainees except in an operational context. The demands of the task may make joint venture the most appropriate vehicle for the knowledge transfer; L/TBD may not be possible outside the joint venture setting.

## Tax Aspects of Joint Ventures

Tax advantages may be a significant factor in many joint ventures. If a corporation contributes a patent or licensable technology to a joint venture, the tax consequences may be less than on royalties earned through a licensing arrangement. For example, one partner contributes the technology, while another contributes depreciable facilities. The depreciation offsets the revenues accruing to the technology; the joint venture may be taxed at a lower rate than any of its partners; and the partners pay a later capital gains tax on the returns realized by the joint venture if and when it is sold. If the joint venture is organized as a corporation, only its assets are at risk; the partners are liable only to the extent of their investment. This is particularly important in hazardous industries where the risk of worker, product, or environmental liability is high.

A number of other more technical tax advantages may tip the scale toward the use of joint ventures in many circumstances. These include the limitation on operating loss carryover, the partnership status of unincorporated commercial joint ventures, the use of the equity method of incorporating the joint venture into the partners' financial statements, and the benefits of multiple surtax exemptions.

## Joint Ventures and Restructuring

Joint ventures have begun to perform a useful role in assisting companies in the process of restructuring. A number of case studies have been described (Nanda and Williamson (NW), 1995). In the late 1980s Philips, a large Dutch electronics company, decided to divest its appliances division, whose revenues had been running at $1.55 billion. It had a history of poor performance because of a number of problems. The division was trying to sell nine different brands with lack of coordination in marketing efforts. Production was spread across 10 plants in five countries and needed large investments for modernization. Nevertheless, the division had strong capabilities in design and manufacturing skills.

Whirlpool was seeking to expand beyond its U.S. base and saw a potential for developing the appliance business of Philips into a global, coordinated production and sales activity. But there were many uncertainties about the investment required, the future relationship with dealers, and the ability to turn around the operations. In 1989 Philips proposed a joint venture in which Whirlpool would own 53% of the appliance operation for $381 million and would have an option to buy the remaining 47% within three years. For Whirlpool, the joint venture enabled it to gain knowledge about the appliance division before committing further funds. Whirlpool also benefited from Philips' continued participation in a number of ways. For a period of time, the products were double branded as Philips-Whirlpool appliances. The incentive for Philips to help was that it would receive more for the remaining 47%, which it sold to Whirlpool in 1991 for $610 million. It was estimated that by the use of the temporary joint venture, Philips received about $270 million more than if it had tried to complete the transaction before the start of the joint venture two years earlier.

This example illustrates how the buyer can use the joint venture experience better to determine the value of brands, distribution systems, and personnel. Through direct involvement with the business, the risk of making mistakes is reduced.

How costly mistakes can be made is illustrated by the method used by the Maytag Corporation seeking to enter the European appliances market in 1989. It bought the Hoover appliances line from the Chicago Pacific Corporation. In seeking to penetrate the British market, the Hoover executives on behalf of Maytag sought to build on Hoover's historically strong relationships with small retailers in fragmented markets. But in Britain, six major retailers accounted for most of the market. Because of the difficulties of penetrating this market, the Hoover executives mounted a special promotional campaign offering free airplane tickets with the purchase of a major appliance in Great Britain and Ireland. In the United States, discounted airline tickets are widely available, but in Europe airfares are regulated and higher. About one of every 300 people in Britain and Ireland bought an appliance to receive the free flights. The people who bought the appliances for the free tickets soon put the appliances into an active market in second-hand Hoover appliances. In honoring the commitments of its promotion, Hoover incurred a $50 million charge. Maytag became discouraged by this unfortunate experience and disposed of the European portion of the Hoover appliances line in June 1995, booking a $130 million loss.

Nanda and Williamson (1995) described how the Corning Company in 1985 used a joint venture to exit the U.S. medical diagnostics business. In that year, Ciba-Geigy was studying how to enter the U.S. pharmaceuticals market. The two companies formed a 50–50 joint venture called Ciba Corning with a payment of $75 million from Ciba-Geigy to Corning. The activity was operated as a joint venture until 1989. During the intervening years, Ciba-Geigy demonstrated its commitment to the new-product market area by making long-term investments. The business was integrated into the global operations of Ciba-Geigy. Customers, vendors, and employees remained loyal to the joint venture enterprise. Corning was able to demonstrate the value of the unit it was seeking to sell. In 1989 Ciba-Geigy purchased the remaining 50% portion of the joint venture at a price double the $75 million paid to establish Ciba Corning. This example illustrates the value of continuity, which retains the loyalty of stakeholders.

The time-phased aspect of the joint venture is also illustrated by the disposal of the Rolm Systems Division by IBM to Siemens of Germany. IBM had purchased Rolm with a view to exploiting some computer applications to PBX Systems. These potentials were not realized and IBM found it had no particular advantages in the thin-margin PBX market. Siemens was interested in broadening its position in the U.S. telecommunications market. The transaction illustrates the different treatment of tangible assets from intangible assets. The manufacturing activities of the Rolm business were sold outright to Siemens, but a 50–50 joint venture was formed between IBM and Siemens to handle marketing distribution and service for the Rolm products. This provided continuity for customer relationships and gave Siemens a basis for judging the value of Rolm's brand franchise. After three years, the joint venture moved entirely to Siemens, which during the course of the joint venture had paid $1.1 billion. This was a good price from IBM's standpoint. For Siemens, it provided a controlled cost for wider penetration of the U.S. telecommunications market.

The above examples from NW illustrate how, in a broad restructuring process, joint ventures can be used as a transitional mechanism. Several advantages have been illustrated by the examples: (1) The customers are moved to the buyer over a period of time in which both the seller and buyer continue to be involved. (2) The buyer builds experience with the new line of business. (3) The buyer receives managerial and technical advice and assistance from the seller during the transition period. (4) The experience and knowledge developed during the life of the joint venture enable the buyer to obtain a better understanding of the value of the acquisition. (5) Consequently, the seller is able to realize a larger value from the sale than it could have under an immediate, outright sale when the buyer must necessarily discount the purchase price because of lack of knowledge about the asset being purchased.

## INTERNATIONAL JOINT VENTURES

Joint ventures can be used to reduce the risk of expanding into a foreign environment. In fact, there may even be a legal requirement of a local joint venturer in some foreign countries. The contribution of the local partner is likely to be in the form of specialized knowledge about local conditions, which may be essential to the success of the venture. This topic is developed more fully in chapter 17, which discusses the international aspects of M&As.

## RATIONALE FOR JOINT VENTURES

The previous section indicated typical reasons given by firms for engaging in joint ventures. A survey of the literature indicates a number of general reasons, which can be summarized as follows:

1. To augment insufficient financial or technical ability to enter a particular line of business
2. To share technology and/or generic management skills in organization, planning, and control
3. To diversify risk
4. To obtain distribution channels or raw materials supply
5. To achieve economies of scale
6. To extend activities with smaller investment than if done independently
7. To take advantage of favorable tax treatment or political incentives (particularly in foreign ventures)

In view of alternative forms of business relationships, a basic issue is why the use of joint ventures versus other forms of contractual arrangements is justified. The literature suggests that the underlying theoretical justification for joint ventures lies in the transaction cost theory of the firm.

Every exchange between productive agents involves transaction costs. The benefits of interaction arise from using resources efficiently, but resources are used up by the organizing activity itself through obtaining information on exchange opportunities, negotiating and enforcing contracts, and so on. The exchange and organizational patterns viewed in the marketplace are responses to varying levels of transaction costs, which affect the allocation of resources in society. According to the theory, resource misallocation cannot exist in the absence of transaction costs.

Complementary production refers to the joint use of assets or inputs to create products that cannot be unambiguously attributed to any single input. Nor can the inputs simply be summed to yield the total output of the process, that is, synergy. A complementary asset is one whose value in a production process depends on its combination with other assets or a specifically chosen technology. Difficulty arises when these inputs are owned by different firms.

In general, an asset's productivity increases with its specialization to other inputs used in the production process. However, specialization also increases the risk of loss to the owner of the complementary asset if the other inputs are withdrawn. Complementary or composite quasi-rent is the economic term for the investment cost of the complementary asset that is nonrecoverable if the other inputs with which it is used are withdrawn. Thus, the owners of the other inputs, by threatening to remove their inputs, can expropriate the owner of the complementary asset by taking a larger share of the return from the process (which, by definition, cannot be unambiguously attributed to any single input).

Input owners will choose the organizational form that minimizes transaction costs. Long-term explicit contracts and common ownership of the complementary assets are possible solutions to the problem. However, a flexible contract may result in litigation for interpretation. A comprehensive contract is costly both to write and to enforce. These costs may outweigh the benefits of the contract. Business complexity increases the number of contingencies that might arise, thus increasing the cost of enumerating contingencies, the risk of omitting to specify contingencies, and costs of monitoring in a contractual relationship.

Finally, the greater the frequency of exchange of inputs, the greater the likelihood of joint ownership. The prospect of recovering the investment cost of specialized assets increases with the frequency of the transaction. In a contractual relationship, repetitive activity would mean repetitive contracting and thus higher contracting costs. The specialized organizations required in common ownership are easier to justify for recurring transactions than for identical transactions occurring only occasionally.

In some cases, common ownership might extend to complete merger, but in general, joint venture is appropriate where:

**1.** Complementary production activity involves only a limited subset of the firms' assets.
**2.** Complementary assets have limited service life.
**3.** Complementary production has limited life.

### Reasons for Failure

Joint ventures are a form of a long-term contract. Like all contracts they are subject to difficulties. As circumstances change in the future, the contract may be too inflexible to permit the required adjustments to be made. There is also evidence that in many joint ventures, the participants early become enamored of the idea of the joint activity, but do not spend sufficient time and effort to lay out a program for implementing the joint venture. *Business Week* (1986) refers to independent studies by McKinsey & Co. and Coopers & Lybrand that found that about 70% of joint ventures fell short of expectations or were disbanded. Other studies suggest that on average joint ventures do not last as long as one-half the term of years stated in the joint venture agreement (Berg, Duncan, and Friedman, 1982). An independent survey by the present authors uncovered many examples of joint ventures that came apart either before they started or early into the venture. Some of the reasons for the abortive lives of joint ventures are:

**1.** The hoped-for technology never developed.
**2.** Preplanning for the joint venture was inadequate.
**3.** Agreements could not be reached on alternative approaches to solving the basic objectives of the joint venture.
**4.** Managers with expertise in one company refused to share knowledge with their counterparts in the joint venture.
**5.** Management difficulties may be compounded because of inability of parent companies to share control or compromise on difficult issues.

Some joint ventures raise critical issues of public policy and long-term strategies of individual business firms. The announcement of a joint venture between Boeing Co. and a group of Japanese companies touched off much controversy (Harris and Wysocki,

1986). Boeing is the world's largest airplane builder accounting for the production of 60% of the world production of jetliners. In early 1986 it was announced that Boeing had entered into an agreement to form a joint venture with three Japanese companies—Kawasaki Heavy Industries Ltd., Mitsubishi Heavy Industries Ltd., and Fuji Heavy Industries Ltd. The joint venture would build a new 150-passenger airplane that would be ready in the early 1990s. The Japanese would contribute $1 billion of the $4 billion or more expected development cost. In return they would receive a share of the profits and learn about the manufacturing, marketing, and servicing of jetliners through their association with Boeing.

Great concern was expressed by a number of Americans that the Japanese would learn the secrets of aircraft manufacturing from Boeing. Because some of the key Boeing civilian aircraft had developed from military versions, concern was also expressed that this would help Japan build up a military aircraft production capability. But the major concern was that the Japanese would become leaders in commercial aviation as they had in autos, electronics, steel, and construction by copying and improving on American methods.

Boeing officials said that they were aware and concerned about such possibilities. But they pointed out that the Japanese companies had solicited joint venture proposals from other Western companies including Airbus, McDonnell Douglas, and Fokker of the Netherlands. Hence, in part, the Boeing action to agree to form the joint venture was a defensive strategy. As the then president of Boeing, Frank Shrontz, stated: "We'd rather work with them [the Japanese] than have somebody else work with them and against us" (Harris and Wysocki, 1986, p. 1).

Early in the negotiations, the usual problems with joint ventures began to crop up. The Japanese complained that Boeing assigned to the project too many young, inexperienced executives who did not understand Japanese business practices. Americans complained that the Japanese negotiators lacked technical knowledge.

## JOINT VENTURES AND ANTITRUST POLICY

Legal challenges may be faced by joint ventures. Although we have distinguished joint ventures from mergers, they are often subject to the same regulatory scrutiny and challenge by rivals. For example, Chrysler raised an antitrust challenge to the Federal Trade Commission approval of the General Motors–Toyota joint venture. (The challenge was dropped before the case went to the courts.) Court actions have been brought under the Clayton Act (for real or potential anticompetitive effects) and under the Sherman Act (for cartel behavior, boycotts, and exclusion of competitors). Three landmark cases illustrate legal actions against joint ventures in the past. The main objections raised are the threat of industrywide collusion, loss of potential competition, and restraints on distribution.

A number of factors led to the antitrust decision in the 1950 *U.S. v. Minnesota Mining and Manufacturing Co. et al.* These included the implied market dominance of the joint venture partners, the existence of a joint sales agency, and concern of spillover of joint venture cooperation into collusion. The venture was formed in 1929 to export coated abrasives for its nine partners. The partners could not export except through the joint venture; however, they could, and did, set up foreign manufacturing subsidiaries to supply foreign buyers. The courts ruled that this joint venture represented an illegal conspiracy and further suggested that the joint venturers would compete less vigorously in the American market as well.

In 1964 the main issue in *U.S. v. Penn-Olin* was the loss of potential competition. An Oregon firm, Pennsalt, wanted to penetrate the southeastern U.S. market for sodium chlorate, a bleaching agent used in paper pulp processing. The southeastern region accounted for 50% of all U.S. sales of sodium chlorate; however, two firms already dominated this area with a combined market share of 91.3% in 1960. Pennsalt's first step was to form a sales arrangement with Olin-Mathieson, a firm that did not manufacture sodium chlorate but that had a marketing presence in the Southeast. The success of this arrangement and projections of future capacity shortages in the area led to the formation of a 50–50 joint venture in 1960. A local manufacturing plant was operated by Pennsalt, while Olin continued to market the output.

The court's decision focused on whether the firms would have entered the market independently in the absence of the joint venture. That is, say Pennsalt entered the market independently; would Pennsalt and the other firms in the market view Olin as a threatening potential entrant? Would Olin view itself as a potential entrant, or would it drop out of the race, abandoning the idea of entering the market? If both firms could have seriously considered entering independently, then the joint venture has decreased potential competition (by adding only one new productive entity to the market instead of potentially two). The final decision permitted the joint venture. Independent entry by both firms was judged to be improbable due to the low expected rate of return (as a result of the high cost to a single firm of building an optimum-size plant) and due to possible excess capacity if two optimum-size plants were constructed.

The decision against the joint venture in *Yamaha v. FTC* (1981) was based on many factors (loss of potential competition, high industry concentration, spillover collusion, potential permanence of the joint venture). However, the distinguishing feature in terms of this discussion involves the collateral agreements between the venture partners. In 1972 Brunswick and Yamaha formed a joint venture to produce and sell outboard motors; the joint venture was to have a ten-year life with automatic three-year extensions. The same motor produced by the venture would be sold through Yamaha dealers as a Yamaha and through Brunswick dealers as a Mariner. (Brunswick had been selling motors worldwide since 1961, and Mariner was to be its second line.) Collateral agreements restricted distribution by assigning exclusive rights to sell the joint venture motor in certain parts of the world. Brunswick had North America, Australia, and New Zealand; Yamaha had exclusivity in Japan, and the rest of the world was open to competition. Other collateral agreements restricted competition beyond the joint venture. Yamaha could not make or distribute any motor similar to the joint venture's, and Brunswick was prohibited from making any products then produced by Yamaha (except snowmobiles).

The court determined that the joint venture eliminated Yamaha as a potential entrant (prior to the joint venture Yamaha had twice attempted unsuccessfully to penetrate the U.S. market) and that such independent entry would have reduced concentration in an industry becoming increasingly highly concentrated due to firm exits. It was felt that Brunswick would not allow the joint venture motor to compete with its other line, and therefore the joint venture could not be treated as a new entrant. The court found no efficiencies inherent in the collateral agreements restricting distribution and production. They were judged to be anticompetitive and thus potentially collusive.

Some industry conditions make collusion more likely. Other industry conditions make collusion difficult and probably impossible. These characteristics are summarized in Table 14.1. Any one condition in the second column of conditions that make collusion difficult is enough to deny the validity of the structural approach. Contemplation of the characteristics of most actual industries in the United States would indicate characteristics

| TABLE 14.1 | Industry Characteristics and Possibility of Collusion | |
|---|---|---|
| | *Collusion Possible* | *Collusion Difficult* |
| | Product homogeneity | Heterogeneous products |
| | Equality of costs across firms | Inequality of costs |
| | Stability of demand, supply, and technology | Rapid and unstable changes in demand, supply, and technology |
| | Difficulty of entry and expansion | Ease of entry and expansion |
| | Similarity in firm strategies and policies | Dissimilarity in firm strategies and policies |
| | Few firms | Many firms |
| | Low costs of enforcing collusive agreement and of being detected relative to benefits | Difficulties in enforcing collusion; high risk and cost of being detected |
| | Low price elasticity of demand | High price elasticity of demand |

that make collusion difficult. These would include heterogeneous products; inequality of costs; rapid and unstable changes in demand, supply, and technology; dissimilarity in firm strategies and policies; substitutability among products on the demand side; and the likelihood of additions to the supply of products by other firms if one firm restricted supply.

## OUTSOURCING

Outsourcing falls within the broader framework of the make or buy decision. Outsourcing involves the use of a subcontractor or supplier or outside firm to perform some percentage of the total production of a product. Outsourcing can be used to produce only a small fraction of the total production process for a product such as an individual part or component or a very high percentage. An example of the latter is the TopsyTail Company (*Economist,* 1995). Between 1991 and 1995, its cumulative volume of sales was approximately $100 million of hair-styling devices. It has virtually no permanent employees. The major functions of design, manufacturing, marketing, distribution, and packaging are performed by subcontractors. This heavy reliance on outsourcing was chosen as a strategy to facilitate rapid growth by the use of outside organizations, avoiding the need to build the required competencies within the company itself. Outsourcing has been identified as a modern version of the use of division of labor to increase efficiency. It is estimated that in 1996 American firms will spend $100 billion on outsourcing, thereby reducing costs by 10 to 15%. In Japan, outsourcing accounts for more than one-third of total manufacturing costs, achieving cost reductions by over 20%.

Although outsourcing has advantages, it also has limitations. This is especially true when the outside supplier is in a foreign country. Companies have found it necessary to develop executive personnel to monitor outsourcing activities in the companies that perform the outside functions.

Another limitation of outsourcing is that as firms become more experienced and more successful in improving their manufacturing operations, they may be able to produce components at a cost lower than outside suppliers. Restructuring and other methods by which costs have been reduced may cause a company to switch from outsourcing to production in-house as the low-cost method of production.

With experience, some companies have also changed their strategy in how they conduct outsourcing. To improve communication and still retain the benefits of competition among suppliers, some companies limit the number of outsourcing firms used. They still retain competition but also emphasize close monitoring by a management group.

One limitation of outsourcing relates to product quality. Some companies require daily quality data and product-integrity audits and reviews. Even though some final product defects may be due to the work of individual outsourcing suppliers, the firm that sells the final product must take responsibility for the quality and performance of the products.

Trade unions often resist outsourcing because they view it as reducing employment, particularly for the workers in an affected union. In recent years, consumers have increasingly demanded variety and custom designs. Some companies have found that only by producing totally within the company can it achieve the flexibility and speed needed for building to order. In the evolution of manufacturing activities, the advantages of outsourcing may be more than matched by efficient use of resources owned by the firm that produces the final products.

Overall, outsourcing has grown substantially during the first half of the 1990s. Outsourcing represents a different form of arm's-length alliances similar to joint ventures. As industries and firms evolve, however, the benefits versus the costs of this activity may shift. The make or buy decision may need to change as the relative efficiency of in-house operations versus outside suppliers changes over time.

## EMPIRICAL TESTS OF THE ROLE OF JOINT VENTURES

Two major types of studies of joint ventures have been made. One type is a business and economic analysis. The other is the use of event returns.

### Business and Economic Patterns

One of the most comprehensive and methodologically robust studies of joint venture activity is that of Berg, Duncan, and Friedman, reported in their 1982 book, *Joint Venture Strategies and Corporate Innovation*. They identify three primary incentives for joint venture participation: (1) risk avoidance; (2) knowledge acquisition; and (3) market power. Using cross-firm and cross-industry analysis on a large sample of joint ventures from the period 1964–1973, they used multiple regression to evaluate the relationships between joint ventures and concentration, research and development (R&D), financial variables, and firm size.

They found that industry joint venture participation also rose with average firm size, average capital expenditure, and average profitability. Technologically oriented joint venture participation also rose with average R&D intensity. Within each industry, they attempted to distinguish the characteristics of those large firms engaging in joint ventures from those that did not, and found firm size to be the *only* pervasive influence across industries.

Cross-firm patterns indicated that joint ventures substitute for research and development in the chemicals and engineering industries, but not in resource-based industries, and the authors found that the long-term R&D substitution effect was stronger than the short-term substitution effect. Joint ventures were also found to have a significant negative impact on large firms' rates of return in chemicals and engineering in the short run, although the long-run effect on rate of return was not significant.

At the industry level, technologically oriented and nonhorizontal joint ventures showed strong positive effects on R&D intensity, indicating that joint ventures and R&D are complements at the industry level. These same types of joint ventures also have a significant negative impact on industry average rates of return, consistent with the reduced risk or reduced time lag that may result from technological or commercial knowledge-acquisition joint ventures. The result is also consistent with using joint ventures as a vehicle for new market entry.

## Event Returns

The most thorough study of the performance of joint ventures was conducted by McConnell and Nantell (MN) (1985) using residual analysis. Their study covered a selection from all joint ventures reported in *Mergers and Acquisitions* for the period 1972–1979. Their sample consisted of 210 firms engaged in 136 joint ventures. The average size of the joint ventures was about $5 million. The two-day announcement period abnormal return was 0.73% which was significant at the .01 level. The cumulative average residual (abnormal return) over the 62-day period ending on the event day (announcement day) was 2.15%, significant at the .10 level. The cumulative average residual remains at 2.15% after 60 days subsequent to the joint venture announcement, indicating no further valuation effect following the initial announcement.

McConnell and Nantell compare the size of the abnormal return with the results for companies involved in mergers using a representative study of mergers by Asquith (1983). Asquith found excess returns for the two days ending in the announcement to be 6.5% for the target firm and 0.3% for the bidding firm. Because joint ventures do not identify an acquiring and acquired firm, their results should fall between the two, which they do. Asquith found that over a 60-day period prior to the merger announcement the CAR increases by 11% for acquired firms and is unchanged for the acquiring companies. Again the CAR for joint ventures lies between.

Because real estate and entertainment joint ventures constitute 23% of their sample, MN also test for overrepresentation by calculating results without this group. Their results are similar. They also eliminate firms for which other information was released near the joint venture announcement date. Again the results are not changed.

McConnell and Nantell also study the relative size effect. They note that in mergers, the dollar value of gains appears to be evenly divided between the two companies. But if the acquiring company is 20 times as large as the target that gains 10% in market value, the acquiring company will gain only 0.5% in stock value. Accordingly, the firms in their joint venture sample are divided into large and small groups based on the total market value of their common stock 61 trading days before the announcement of the joint venture. Information was available to do this for 65 joint ventures, but not for 80 other companies that were placed into a third, "all other," category. The statistical tests were repeated for the three groups. The small firms gained 1.10%, the large firms gained 0.63%, and all others gained 0.57%—all of these statistically significant. The dollar gain to the small-firm sample was $4.538 million, and to the large-firm sample $6.651 million. Thus, as in mergers, the dollar gain is about evenly divided, but the percentage gains are much higher for the smaller firms.

When the dollar gains are scaled by the amounts invested in the joint venture, the average premium is 23% (after removing one outlier). This result lies in the range of premiums observed in mergers and tender offers. McConnell and Nantell observe that the gains in mergers and tender offers could be from either synergy or displacement of less effective management. Because joint ventures do not change the managements of the parents, McConnell and Nantell (1985, p. 535) conclude that "we are inclined to interpret our results as supportive of the synergy hypothesis as the source of gains in other types of corporate combinations."

-------------------------------------------------------------------------------

## Summary

Joint ventures are new enterprises owned by two or more participants. They are typically formed for special purposes for a limited duration. This brings the participants into what is essentially a medium- to long-term contract that is both specific and flexible. It is a contract to work together for a period of time. Each participant expects to gain from the activity but also must make a contribution.

To some degree the joint venture represents a relatively new thrust by each participant, so it is often called a strategic alliance. Probably, the main motive for joint ventures is to share risks. This explains why joint ventures are frequently found in bidding on oil contracts and in drilling oil wells, in large real estate ventures, and in movies, plays, and television productions. The second most frequently cited aim in joint ventures is knowledge acquisition. One or more participants is seeking to learn more about a relatively new product-market activity. This may be in all aspects of the activity, or in a limited segment such as R&D, production, marketing, or servicing products.

International joint ventures magnify the potential advantages and weaknesses of joint venture activity. The GM–Toyota joint venture illustrates the kind of potentials that may be achieved in a joint venture. GM hoped to gain new experience in the management techniques of the Japanese in building high-quality, low-cost compact and subcompact cars. Toyota was seeking to learn from the management traditions that had made GM the number one auto producer in the world and in addition to learn how to operate an auto company in the environment of the United States, dealing with contractors, suppliers, and workers. It appears that differences in cultures and management styles provide a valuable learning experience for both parties in this joint venture.

Other reasons for joint ventures are numerous. One frequently encountered is the small firm with a new product idea that involves high risk and requires relatively large amounts of investment capital. A larger firm may be able to carry the financial risk and be interested in becoming involved in a new business activity that promises growth and profitability. By investing in a large number of such ventures, the larger firm has limited risk in any one and the possibility of very high financial payoffs. In addition, the larger firm may thereby gain experience in a new area of activity that may represent the opportunity for a major new business thrust in the future. Case studies illustrate how joint ventures can facilitate different types of restructuring activities by either or both participant firms in the joint venture.

A basic tension is often found in joint ventures. Each participant hopes to gain as much as possible from the interaction, but would like to limit the gains to the other participants. This is particularly true when the firms are competitors in other areas of their activities.

Antitrust authorities often view joint ventures with suspicion. One concern is that each of the participants might have entered the new area independently. Hence, they reason that absent the joint venture, multiple new competitors might have emerged. But it is also possible that the risk to reward outlook is so uncertain that absent the joint venture, no additional competitors would have emerged. In areas of research and development activities, the antitrust authorities are more favorably disposed. For one reason, R&D activity is recognized to be inherently risky. For another, if the R&D joint venture effort turns out to be successful, it may contribute to the economic and competitive strength of the nation as a whole in the world economy.

On balance, the most thorough study of the value effects of joint ventures finds that positive returns are achieved. By the standard abnormal returns or residual analysis, joint ventures result in positive gains for the participants. When scaled to the size of investments, joint ventures appear to achieve about a 23% return higher than predicted by general capital market return-risk relationships. This may be biased somewhat upward, because only joint ventures that have actually been formed and been in operation for some time are included in the sample. The many joint ventures that never even reached the launching pad and those aborted shortly after takeoff could not be included in the sample.

---

## Questions

14.1   How do joint ventures differ from merger activity? In what ways are they similar?

14.2   What are the advantages and disadvantages of joint ventures?

14.3   How does the concept of complex learning relate to joint ventures?

14.4   What is the primary difference between a joint venture and a strategic alliance?

14.5   How can joint ventures be affected by public policy on antitrust?

14.6   How do joint venture returns compare with returns in mergers and tender offers?

---

## C A S E   14–1

# GM–Toyota Joint Venture

This case study brings together a number of the theoretical arguments and legal issues involved in connection with evaluating joint ventures. The GM–Toyota joint venture provided for production of a subcompact car in a GM plant in Fremont, California that previously had been closed down. The plan was approved by a 3–2 majority of the Federal Trade Commission (FTC) in December 1983. After approval by the FTC, Chrysler brought suit to stop the joint venture. After a series of legal skirmishes, Chrysler withdrew its suit. The following discussion is from an extended analysis of the joint venture (Weston, 1984).

The business reasons underlying the GM–Toyota joint venture are straightforward. GM hopes to obtain hands-on experience in the advanced management technology of building small cars, and to add this experience to other efforts under way to become more cost-efficient in producing a family of small cars.

For its part, Toyota aims to test its production methods in a new setting with different labor and supplier relationships. Each firm is seeking to become more efficient to meet the tough competition in the automobile industry. Because the cars will be produced at an unused plant in Fremont, California, the new investment costs are reduced. Hence, the risk/return prospects of the venture are improved compared with alternative methods of achieving their objectives.

In contrast to previous joint ventures that have been found illegal, this agreement expresses the intention of both parties to compete vigorously in all their markets for every product. This joint venture, as codified by the conditions of the FTC consent order, is quite circumscribed. It limits the annual volume of the one model the joint venture can produce for GM to 250,000. It limits the duration of the venture to a maximum of 12 years. It restricts the exchange of information that can pass between the parties. The order also requires that records be kept of certain contacts between the parties, and that both companies file annual compliance reports with the FTC.

The FTC majority weighed efficiency benefits against anticompetitive costs: "To the extent the Fremont venture can demonstrate successfully that the Japanese system can work in America, the Commission finds that this will lead to the development of a more efficient, more competitive U.S. automobile industry." The FTC determined that the GM–Toyota joint venture will achieve an important management technology transfer to the United States; it reinforced GM's strong commitment to the small-car market and provided incentives for other U.S. firms to do likewise.

------------------------------------------------------------

## Questions on Case Study C14.1

C14.1.1   What did GM hope to gain from the joint venture?
C14.1.2   What did Toyota seek to gain?
C14.1.3   In your judgment, was the joint venture procompetitive or anticompetitive?
C14.1.4   Do you think that the Fremont joint venture influenced Toyota's subsequent decision to establish its own manufacturing operations in the United States while continuing the Fremont activity?

## References

Asquith, Paul, "Merger Bids, Uncertainty, and Stockholder Returns," *Journal of Financial Economics,* 11, 1983, pp. 51–83.

Bachman, Jules, "Joint Ventures in the Light of Recent Antitrust Developments," *Antitrust Bulletin,* 10, 1965, pp. 7–23.

Berg, Sanford V., Jerome Duncan, and Philip Friedman, *Joint Venture Strategies and Corporate Innovation,* Cambridge, MA: Oelgeschlager, Gunn & Hain, 1982.

*Business Week,* "Corporate Odd Couples," July 21, 1986, pp. 100–105.

Department of Justice, *Merger Guidelines,* 1982, 1984, 1992, 1996.

*The Economist,* "The Outing of Outsourcing," November 25, 1995, pp. 57–58.

Harris, Roy J., Jr., and Bernard Wysocki, Jr., "Ready for Takeoff?: Venture With Boeing Is Likely to Give Japan Big Boost in Aerospace," *The Wall Street Journal,* January 14, 1986, pp. 1, 22.

*Los Angeles Times,* "Antitrust Chief Urges Ventures Over Mergers," November 3, 1984, part IV, p. 1.

McConnell, John J., and Timothy J. Nantell, "Corporate Combinations and Common Stock Returns: The Case of Joint Ventures," *Journal of Finance,* 40, June 1985, pp. 519–536.

Nanda, Ashish, and Peter J. Williamson, "Use Joint Ventures to Ease the Pain of Restructuring," *Harvard Business Review,* 73, November–December 1995, pp. 119–128.

Templin, Neal, "More and More Firms Enter Joint Ventures With Big Competitors," *The Wall Street Journal,* November 1, 1995, pp. A1, A9.

Weston, J. Fred, "The GM–Toyota Vows: A Reply to the Critics," *Across the Board,* The Conference Board Magazine, 21, March 1984, pp. 3–6.

*Yamaha v. FTC,* 657 F 2d. 971, 1981.

CHAPTER

# 15

# ESOPs and MLPs

An employee stock ownership plan (ESOP) is a type of stock bonus plan that invests primarily in the securities of the sponsoring employer firm. In a master limited partnership (MLP), the limited partnership interests are divided into units that trade as shares of common stock. Both ESOPs and MLPs have tax advantages, and both have been involved in takeover and takeover defense activities.

## NATURE AND HISTORY OF ESOPs

To analyze the role that ESOPs perform it is necessary to understand their fundamental nature as an employee benefit plan and their relationship to other employee benefit plans. The employee benefit plans involved are pension plans. A pension plan is established by an organization to provide for payments to plan participants after retirement. Such plans are subject to federal government regulation established by the Employee Retirement Income Security Act (ERISA) of 1974.

### Types of Pension Plans

ERISA divides employee pension plans into two major types: (1) defined benefit plans, and (2) defined contribution plans. The **defined benefit plans** are what people usually have in mind when they think about a pension plan. It is the type used by most large corporations. According to a formula set in advance, these plans specify the amounts that participants will receive in retirement. A flat benefit formula is a fixed amount per year of service, such as $10 for each year of service. An employee with 30 years of service would receive a pension of $300 per month, subject to a maximum percentage (for example, 60%) of (average) final salary. Under a unit benefit formula, the participant receives a fixed percentage of earnings per year of service, such as 2% of the average of the last five years. An employee with 30 years of service would receive a monthly pension based on 60% of the average final salary. Plans must meet federal fiduciary standards to qualify for favorable tax treatment. They are subject to minimum funding standards and are guaranteed by the Pension Benefit Guarantee Corporation (PBGC).

    **Defined contribution plans** make no fixed commitment to a pension level. Only the contributions into the plan are specified and participants receive over the period of their retirement what is in their accounts when they retire. Defined contribution plans can be of three kinds: stock bonus plans, profit-sharing plans, and money purchase plans. In a **stock bonus plan,** the firm contributes a specified number of shares of its common stock into the plan annually. The value of the contribution is based on the price of the stock at a recent date if it is traded; otherwise, an appraisal is required. The other two forms of defined contribution plans provide for the payment of cash into the plan. Contributions to qualified **profit-sharing plans** are related to profitability rates, so they can vary in dollar amounts from year to year. Defined contribution plans are required by law to make "prudent" investments. They are not subject to minimum funding standards, and are not covered by the PBGC.

ESOPs are defined contribution employee benefit pension plans that invest at least 50% of their assets in the common shares of the sponsoring corporation. Under ERISA, ESOPs are stock bonus plans or combined stock bonus plans and money purchase plans designed to invest primarily in qualifying employer securities. The plans may receive stock or cash, used by the plan managers to buy stock. A stock bonus plan can determine each year the amount to invest. A money purchase plan has a specific contribution schedule, such as 4% of ESOP salaries per year. ESOPs may also provide for employee contributions.

Since 1977, Treasury Department regulations have permitted ESOP contributions to represent a portion of a profit-sharing plan. But an ESOP is different from an employee stock purchase plan. Stock purchase plans are programs under which a firm enables employees to buy company stock at a discount. The Internal Revenue Code specifies that all or most employees participate and that the shares be sold at 85% or more of the prevailing market price of the shares.

ESOPs should also be differentiated from executive incentive programs. These are provided mainly to top management and other key employees. The programs are part of executive compensation packages aimed to align the interests of managers with those of the stockholders. While many forms can be used, the tax laws since 1981 govern two types of plans: incentive stock options (ISOs) and stock appreciation rights (SARs). The exercise price of ISOs must be equal to or greater than the stock price at time of issue. The SARs can have an exercise price as low as 50% of the stock price. Both can have a maximum life of 10 years from date of issue.

## Types of ESOPs

In its reports on ESOPs, the General Accounting Office (GAO) identified four main kinds: leveraged, leveragable, nonleveraged, and tax credit. Each of these is briefly described (United States General Accounting Office, 1986). Leveraged ESOPs were recognized under ERISA in 1974. In a **leveraged ESOP,** the plan borrows funds to purchase securities of the employer firm. The employer firm makes contributions to the ESOP trust in an amount to meet the annual interest payments on the loan as well as repayments of the principal. It is well known that corporations can deduct interest as a tax expense, but not principal. However, contributions by the corporations to ESOPs to cover both interest and principal (subject to some limitations) are fully deductible. Leveragable and nonleveraged ESOPs, also recognized under ERISA, are plans that have not used leveraging. In a **leveragable ESOP,** the plan is authorized, but is not required to borrow funds. The plan documents for nonleveraged ESOPs do not provide for borrowing. **Nonleveraged ESOPs** are essentially stock bonus plans that are required to invest primarily in the securities of the employer firm.

The Tax Reduction Act of 1975 provided for tax credit ESOPs. In addition to the regular investment credit in existence at that time, an additional investment credit of 1% of a qualified investment in plant and equipment could be earned by a contribution of that amount to an ESOP. The plans were called Tax Reduction Act ESOPs or TRASOPs. An additional 0.5% credit was added in 1976 for companies that matched contributions of their employees of the same amount to the TRASOP. In 1983 the basis for the credit was changed from plant and equipment investments to 0.5% of covered payroll. These types of plans were called payroll-based ESOPs or PAYSOPs. TRASOPs and PAYSOPs have been called tax credit ESOPs. The other three types of ESOPs are referred to as ERISA-type ESOPs.

## THE USES OF ESOPs

During the period, 1982–1987, the number of employees at companies with ESOPs increased by 66% to 9 million. During the following period, 1988–1993, the number increased by only 11% to 10 million (Bernstein, 1996). We estimate that about 11 to 12 million employees are covered by ESOP plans in 1997.

Employee stock ownership plans have been used in a wide variety of corporate restructuring activities (Bruner, 1988; GAO, 1986). Fifty-nine percent of leveraged ESOPs were vehicles used to buy private companies from their owners. This enabled the owners to make their gains tax free by investing the funds received into a portfolio of U.S. securities. ESOPs have also been used in buyouts of large private companies as well.

Thirty-seven percent of leveraged ESOPs were employed in divestitures. In a very substantial ESOP transaction the Hospital Corporation of America sold over 100 of its 180 hospitals to HealthTrust, a new corporation created and owned by an employee leveraged ESOP.

Leveraged ESOPs have also been used as rescue operations. An ESOP was formed in 1983 to avoid the liquidation of Weirton Steel, which subsequently became a profitable company. ESOPs used in the attempt to prevent the failure of Rath Packing, McLean Trucking, and Hyatt Clark Industries were followed by subsequent bankruptcies.

A number of leveraged ESOPs were formed as a takeover defense to hostile tender offers. Early examples of ESOPs established as takeover defenses were by Dan River in 1983, by Phillips Petroleum in 1985, and by Harcourt Brace Jovanovich in 1987.

Especially noteworthy was the use of an ESOP by Polaroid to defeat a takeover attempt in 1988 by Shamrock Holdings, the investment vehicle of Roy E. Disney. Shamrock Holdings had purchased a 6.9% stake in Polaroid with the expectation of making a tender offer for control. Polaroid created an ESOP that purchased 14% of its common stock. Polaroid was chartered in Delaware whose antitakeover statute prevents a hostile acquirer from merging with the target for at least three years unless 85% of the target's voting shares are tendered. (This is generally referred to as the Delaware "freeze-out" law.) By creating its ESOP, Polaroid made it virtually impossible for Shamrock to obtain the necessary 85% in a tender offer. Shamrock fought this ESOP defense by Polaroid in the courts but ultimately lost. After Polaroid, ESOPs became a widely used antitakeover weapon.

The Tax Reform Act of 1986 also permits excess pension assets to be shifted tax free if they are placed into an ESOP. Ashland Oil reverted $200 million and Transco Energy Co. $120 million into new ESOPs.

Employee stock ownership plans represent one among a number of restructuring activities. They may be used as a substitute for or in connection with buying private companies, divestiture activities, efforts to save failing companies, as a method of raising new capital, and as a takeover defense.

### ESOPs as Pension Plans

It is helpful in understanding how ESOPs are used to continue to view them in the setting of a form of employee benefits, particularly as a pension plan. The basic relationships involved in a pension plan are shown in Figure 15.1. An individual corporation is respon-

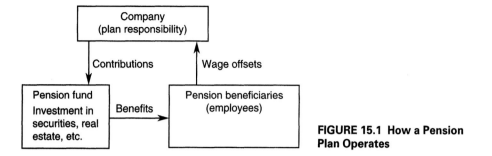

FIGURE 15.1  How a Pension Plan Operates

sible for setting up the pension fund. It makes dollar contributions either in the form of a defined benefit plan or defined contribution plan, as discussed earlier. The pension fund uses the dollar contributions to make investments in a wide range of securities, real estate, and so on. The implication of ERISA is that prudence generally requires diversification of the pension fund investments. The benefits of the pension fund accrue to and are finally paid to the pension beneficiaries who are the employees of the company. It is presumed that at least to some degree wages are lower than they otherwise would be because of contributions by the company to the pension fund on behalf of its employees.

Contributions by a company to a qualified pension fund are tax-deductible expenses at the time of payment by the company. However, these dollar flows are not taxable to the recipient at the time that the pension fund is set up. They are taxable to the recipient only when the benefits are actually received. Because the income of the employees would be expected to be lower after retirement, the employee has the benefit of a lower tax rate on the value of the contributions into the pension fund. In addition, of course, the pension fund earns income that augments the amount of benefits payable to the employees in the future. Both the original payments by the employer into the pension fund and earnings thereon receive the benefit of tax deferral until received by employees.

## Concept of a Leveraged ESOP

In an ESOP, the logic of the arrangement is the same as in Figure 15.1. The pension fund would be called an ESOP fund or trust. In a basic ESOP, the contribution by the company could be either cash or securities of the sponsoring company as described earlier. Like ordinary pension funds, ESOPs may also provide for employee contributions. Unlike the general pension fund, which is expected to diversify its investments widely for financial prudence, an ESOP is set up to invest in the securities of the sponsoring company. In practice, ESOPs are likely to utilize leverage to increase the tax benefits to the sponsoring company. The nature of a leveraged ESOP is shown in Figure 15.2.

We now have an additional element in the arrangement. This is the financial institution, which is the source of the borrowing by the ESOP. As shown in Figure 15.2, the lender transfers cash to the ESOP trust in return for a written obligation. The sponsoring firm generally guarantees the loan. The ESOP trust (ESOT) purchases securities from the sponsoring firm. Because the sponsoring firm has a contingent liability, it does not actually transfer the stock to the name of the ESOP trust until payments are made reducing the principal that the firm has guaranteed. As portions of the principal are repaid, the firm then transfers stock to the name of the ESOP trust. The source of payment of both interest and principal to the financial institution is the cash contributed to the ESOP trust by the company. Both the interest and principal amount transferred by the company are deductible expenses for tax purposes.

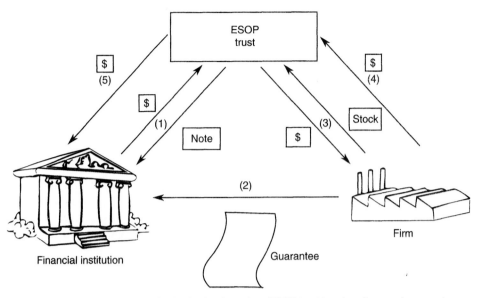

1. Financial institution lends cash to ESOP trust in return for promissory note.
2. Sponsoring firm guarantees note.
3. ESOP trust purchases stock from sponsoring firm.
4. Firm contributes cash to ESOP trust.
5. ESOP trust uses cash to make principal and interest payments on loan.

**FIGURE 15.2  Illustration of a Leveraged ESOP**

*Source:* United States General Accounting Office, *Employee Stock Ownership Plans: Benefits and Costs of ESOP Tax Incentives for Broadening Stock Ownership,* Washington, DC, December 1986, p. 49.

### Examples of the Use of ESOPs

An example with numbers can illustrate the nature of a leveraged ESOP. John Jones was the president and 100% owner of Ace Company. His entire estate was represented by the value of Ace. His children were grown and had no interest in running the business. His attorney recommended the sale of Ace because Jones did not have other investments. In the case of his death his estate would be unable to pay the required estate taxes and would be forced to sell the company under unfavorable conditions.

Jones had received an offer from Universal Company. It was to be a share-for-share stock exchange for each of the 300,000 Ace shares outstanding. Universal was trading at around $15 per share. Investment bankers had placed a value on Ace at around $20 per share. Because Jones was only 54 years old, he was reluctant to relinquish ownership and control of his company. Jones recognized the need to increase his liquidity, but did not want to sell the company at this time.

We can now illustrate how an ESOP could be helpful. An ESOP is established with all of the employees of Ace Company as beneficiaries. The ESOP borrows $2 million from a bank. These funds are used to purchase 100,000 shares of Ace Company stock from Jones. The loan from the bank to the ESOP is guaranteed by Ace Company and is secured by the 100,000 shares held in trust. Ace Company agrees to make ESOP contributions to cover both interest and repayment of principal. These are tax-deductible expenses for Ace Company. Note that at this point Jones has received $2 million in cash; presumably he will place this in a diversified portfolio with a relatively high degree of liquidity and/or marketability. So long as these funds are invested in other

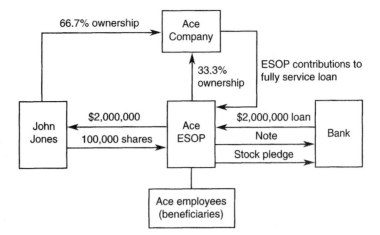

**FIGURE 15.3 Leveraged ESOP Example**

U.S. corporations within 12 months, the proceeds are not taxable to Jones at this time (see below for more detail).

As the ESOP repays the loan, the stock held in trust will be allocated to each individual employee's account. When the loan is completely paid off, the ESOP would have received and owned the 100,000 shares of stock representing 33.3% of the outstanding stock of Ace Company. These relationships are illustrated in Figure 15.3.

Another example will sharpen the advantages of the use of an ESOP as compared with a merger. It is similar to the previous illustration, which was streamlined to bring out the essential nature of a leveraged ESOP. In the present case study, more variables are considered in the analysis. Consider John Doe, the aging owner of 100% of the stock of Doeskin Textiles. Most of his personal wealth is tied to the firm's fortunes; he is thinking about retirement and worries about his relatively illiquid position as well as having all his eggs in one basket. In addition, declining health has caused him to consider the effect of substantial estate taxes, which might necessitate a hasty sale of the firm by his heirs in the event of his death. All these factors led him to seriously consider a recent overture from Polyestech Corporation to acquire Doeskin in a tax-free exchange of securities for $8,000,000. The offer is acceptable in terms of price, although Doe is somewhat concerned that the value received would deteriorate if Polyestech's stock price declined. Also, Polyestech has a rather unsavory reputation in terms of labor relations and social responsibility. Doeskin has been the mainstay of the Minnesota community where it is located, and Doe feels quite paternalistic toward his employees and managers. He is uneasy about turning the firm over to outsiders and would like to find another solution. ESOPs offer such a solution.

Suppose Doe would like to withdraw $2,500,000 of Doeskin's $8,000,000 value to invest in a diversified portfolio of publicly traded corporate securities to provide both diversification and liquidity. He should take the following steps:

1. Doeskin should establish an ESOP.
2. The ESOP should borrow $2,500,000 from a bank, insurance company, or other lender. (Recall that one-half the interest income commercial lenders receive on ESOP loans is exempt from taxation—this enhances their borrowing ability.) Doeskin would most likely be required to guarantee the ESOP loan.
3. Doe sells 31.25% of his stock to the ESOP for $2,500,000.

As long as Doe invests the $2,500,000 in securities of other U.S. corporations within 12 months, he can defer any federal tax on the transaction. This tax-free rollover is allowable under the 1984 Deficit Reduction Act so long as the ESOP owns at least 30% of the firm's stock following the sale and neither the owner nor his family participate in the ESOP once formed. (If Doe had sold less than 30%, he would have had to pay capital gains tax on the sale, but he would have been able to participate in the ESOP, reducing over time the extent of his ownership dilution.) Doeskin would make tax-deductible contributions to the ESOP sufficient to repay the loan principal and to pay interest. As the loan was repaid, the Doeskin shares belonging to the ESOP would be allocated to Doeskin employees participating in the plan. Thus, the owner of a privately held firm can achieve tax-free liquidity without selling his firm to outsiders and even maintaining control, depending on his need for cash and thus the proportion of stock sold to the ESOP.

Among the advantages and disadvantages of the ESOP versus the Polyestech offer are the following:

**ESOP:**
1. Increased employee loyalty as a result of stock ownership through ESOP.
2. Increased liquidity and diversification for Doe.
3. Dilution of ownership is not critical here because Doe maintains control.
4. The tax-free rollover is actually only a tax deferral until the replacement securities are sold.
5. Establishes a market value for Doeskin stock that may help in estate valuation. This may be a positive or negative effect.
6. Provides a market for Doeskin shares if heirs must sell shares to pay estate taxes—avoids "fire sale," and furthermore, 50% of the proceeds from the sale of stock to an ESOP may be excluded from the estate's value.

**SALE TO POLYESTECH:**
1. No liquidity enhancement until Polyestech shares are sold.
2. Potential deterioration of value received.
3. Complete loss of control over firm.
4. Tax advantage in tax-free exchange of securities is one of timing only. Tax must be paid when securities are sold to achieve liquidity.
5. No diversification effect because all eggs would still be in one basket, albeit a different and perhaps more marketable basket.

## ESOPs in Lieu of Subsidiary Divestiture

Large corporations often have subsidiaries or plants that they wish to divest for one reason or another. The usual alternatives are to sell the subsidiary to another corporation (although it may be difficult to find a buyer at an acceptable price), or to liquidate the subsidiary's assets, which is disruptive for the subsidiary's employees and often for others as well. An ESOP can function well in this type of situation. The subsidiary's employees are likely to be willing purchasers (through an ESOP), because they have a great deal at stake and the alternatives are highly uncertain.

First, a shell corporation is established. The shell establishes an ESOP; the debt capacity of the shell and the ESOP (with the guarantees of the parent corporation) is utilized to arrange financing to purchase the subsidiary from the parent. The shell corporation (now no longer a shell) operates the former subsidiary while the ESOP holds the stock. If successful, enough income will be generated to make the most of allowable tax-deductible contributions to the ESOP, which will enable it to service its debt. As the debt is reduced, the ESOP will allocate shares to the employees' accounts, and over time the former subsidiary will come to be owned by its employees.

This entire transaction is, of course, predicated upon the subsidiary's viability as an independent entity, and its ability to generate sufficient income to cover its financing. In many cases, the original motivation for divestiture is that the subsidiary is in a dying industry or requires extensive modernization of inefficient facilities. If so, selling the subsidiary to the employees benefits neither them nor the economy as a whole in the long run even though short-term disruption might be kept to a minimum. In such cases, liquidation might be the preferred solution.

# THE PERFORMANCE OF ESOPs

Six dimensions of the performance of ESOPs have been studied: (1) tax benefits, (2) corporate control or antitakeover defense, (3) a method of financing, (4) comparison with profit sharing, (5) effects on productivity, and (6) economic consequences.

## Tax Benefits

Scholes and Wolfson (1992) caution that many of the claimed tax advantages of ESOPs may be illusory. Expenses incurred by business firms to create pension benefits for its employees are generally tax deductible. The full deductibility of payments to an ESOP for the amortization debt is claimed to have tax advantages because repayments of principal as well as interest payments are involved. However, Scholes and Wolfson point out viewing such payments as pension benefits demonstrates that providing pension benefits directly would yield substantially the same tax benefits.

The Scholes and Wolfson argument may be illustrated by an example. Suppose a firm spends $100,000 in year X to add to its pension fund for employees. The total $100,000 would be a tax deductible expense for that year. If, instead, the firm had borrowed an amount in an earlier year to set up an ESOP and that the tax deductible amount paid in year X to amortize the debt was $100,000. The amount of tax deduction for the firm with an ESOP is no different than if the same amount had been paid in to its pension fund.

Beatty (1995) describes tax provisions that appear to apply exclusively to leveraged ESOPs, making their tax treatment different from other retirement plans. A bank, insurance company, or investment company can exclude from taxable income 50% of the interest income earned on loans to ESOPs that own more than 50% of the employer's equity. Although the 50% interest exclusion is accorded to the lender, competitive markets would result in lower interest rates on ESOP loans than on non-ESOP loans.

Another tax benefit is that the employer can deduct the dividends paid on ESOP shares if such dividends are used to repay ESOP debt. When dividends are used to repay ESOP debt, the value of the ESOP shares declines by the amount of the dividend. But the employer can deduct the entire market value of the shares at the time they are placed in the ESOP. Beatty presents an example. On May 9, 1988, the Barry Wright Corporation (BWC) loaned $24 million to its new ESOP, which purchased 1.525 million BWC newly issued common shares at $15.75 each. On the same day, a dividend of $8 per share was announced with a record date of May 31, 1988. The ESOP shares received $12.2 million of dividends used to repay about one-half the ESOP loan. The BWC shares dropped by exactly $8 a share on the ex-dividend date. Because the ESOP was not able to keep the dividend, it bought shares worth $7.75. The ESOP contribution, therefore, was worth $11.8 million, representing the balance of the ESOP loan that was repaid during 1988 by BWC. The corporation was permitted to deduct $24 million, but made only an $11.8 million contribution to the ESOP. Beatty observes that this example illustrates the Chaplinsky and Niehaus (1990, 1994) position that dividends used to repay ESOP debt provide a distinctive tax benefit.

But in the opposite direction, the method of allocating ESOP assets to the accounts of employees results in a smaller expected present value tax deduction for leveraged ESOPs compared with other retirement plans. Shares purchased by a leveraged ESOP are initially placed in a suspense account. The shares are allocated to employees on a percentage basis related to the repayment of principal and interest in each year of the loan. Other retirement plans provide for immediate allocation of assets to the employees. The value of the ESOP tax deduction is based on the market value of the shares when placed in the ESOP; but the deduction cannot be taken until the debt is repaid and the assets are allocated some years in the future. The present value factor is applied into the future value of the shares but on the generally lower value at the time they are placed into the suspense account.

Beatty (1995, p. 229) estimates that for ESOPs established in 1987 and later, the average net tax benefit was 0.3% of equity value. The General Accounting Office (1986) estimated that for the period 1977–1983 the federal revenue losses from ESOPs were about $13 billion, a per year average of $1.9 billion. These net tax benefits would cause event returns from the announcement of ESOPs to be positive.

### ESOPs as a Takeover Defense

Many individual case studies document how ESOPs have been used as a takeover defense. Beatty (1995) documents this evidence systematically from her sample of 145 ESOP announcements. Seventy-five percent of the transactions occur in 1987 or later when both the interest exclusion for lenders and the dividend deduction used to repay ESOP debt became effective. This is consistent with her data for tax benefits discussed above. She notes also that 57% of the transactions took place in 1988 and 1989 after the Polaroid decision and the related Delaware "freeze-out" law that increased the effectiveness of ESOPs as a takeover defense.

Empirical studies generally find that when a firm is subject to a takeover attempt, the announcement of an ESOP has a negative effect on equity values (Beatty, 1995, and references there cited). If the firm is not subject to a takeover attempt, the announcement of an ESOP is not associated with a change in equity values if the company was subject to the Delaware freeze-out law and the size of the ESOPs results in the establishment of an effective blocking-percentage ownership.

### ESOPs Versus Alternative Methods of Raising Funds

Bruner (1988) analyzes ESOPs as an alternative to other methods of raising funds. In one example, the outlays in a leveraged ESOP represented by interest expense and principal repayment represent a substitute for pension payments that otherwise would have been made. Another plausible assumption is that the interest rate charged by the lender will reflect all or some of the tax advantage that permits the financial institution to exclude from taxable income 50% of the income on loans to ESOPs. This would make the debt interest expense under a leveraged ESOP arrangement lower than under straight debt financing.

Another issue is control of the stock that is placed in the ESOP. Some people argue that management continues to control the ESOP, so that the stock remains in friendly hands. On the other hand, technically the stock belongs to the individual employees, and with a strong union speaking on behalf of the employees, there is always the risk that the employees and/or their union might vote the stock in a way that conflicts with the interests of management. The point was made in connection with Polaroid's establishment of an ESOP that the employees who wished to maintain the status quo and who did not want an outside firm to take over the company would be even more strongly opposed to the takeover than management. Typically after a takeover, employment is reduced, and to protect their positions, the employees are likely to be supporters of management when ESOPs are used as a takeover defense.

The view has been set forth that ESOP transactions represent economic dilution. Potentially they transfer shareholders' wealth to employees (Bruner, 1988). As we observed at the beginning of this chapter, ESOPs represent a form of an employee's pension program. If the ESOP contribution is not offset by a reduction to some degree in other benefit plans, or in the direct wages of workers, employees gain at the expense of shareholders. The argument has also been made that any borrowing by the ESOP uses some of the debt capacity of the firm (Bruner, 1988). It could also be argued that such borrowing substitutes for other forms of borrowing that the firm would otherwise use. To the extent that there is a valid belief that ESOP transactions represent economic dilution to the original shareholders, the price charged to the ESOP for the company stock transferred to it may be at a premium price to compensate for economic dilution. The Department of Labor's reviews of such transactions may be a source of its disagreements about the fairness of the price charged by management to the ESOP.

The impact of moving equity shares into the ownership of the employees is apparently an important disadvantage of ESOPs despite their considerable tax advantage. Kaplan (1988, note 12) has expressed this view in the following terms: "The infrequent use of ESOP loans in the sample analyzed in this paper (5 of 76 companies) suggests that the non-tax costs of using an ESOP are high. One such cost is the large equity stake that eventually goes to all contributing employees and significantly reduces the equity stake that can be given to managers and the buyout promoter." A potential advantage is that shares can be sold at higher prices over the years as the ESOP contributes to higher earnings through tax advantages and through the increased incentives and improved motivations of employees as a result of their stock ownership through the ESOP.

### Comparison with Profit Sharing

A study by Professor Daniel Mitchell (1995) compares profit sharing with ESOPs. He notes that deferred profit-sharing plans are found in about 16% of all medium-sized and large establishments as compared with only 3% for ESOPs. So, despite the tax subsidies to ESOPs, their coverage of workers is relatively small. Mitchell states that noninsured private pensions held $1.2 trillion in equity in 1991. Insured pensions account indirectly for additional equity holdings. Equity holdings by ESOPs for 1991 are estimated at only $47 billion. Thus, the worker coverage of ESOPs is relatively small compared with other pension plans in terms of its impact on helping workers achieve equity holdings.

Mitchell argues that profit sharing from an economic standpoint has advantages over ESOPs. Profit sharing introduces flexibility in worker compensation so it may improve the stability of employment desirable from the macroeconomic aspects of stabilizing the economy. ESOPs do not have the same macroeconomic benefits. An ESOP involves a form of bonus to employment in the form of equity shares in their own firm. An ESOP does not add to pay flexibility.

Mitchell considers the ability of the firm to deduct the repayment of both interest and principal in payments to retire the debt of an ESOP as a tax subsidy. He reasons that in publicly held companies, the principal repayment reflects the value of stock given to employees. If the valuation of the stock is accurate, the value of the stock represents a true cost to the employer and should be deductible just as wages are. But owners of closely held companies have the incentive to overvalue the stock assigned to employees, which according to Mitchell would represent a form of tax evasion. Mitchell accordingly argues that if tax subsidies are to be employed, they should be made to profit-sharing schemes that have macroeconomic benefits. He concludes that ESOPs are less worthy of favorable tax treatment.

### Effects on Company Productivity

Because one of the objectives expressed in the writings in support of the ESOP idea was to achieve "people's capitalism," it is of interest to consider the stock ownership and control of ESOPs. However, most studies indicate that ownership percentages have been relatively small—10% or less. Even when stock carries voting rights, the voting rights associated with the stock of ESOP accounts may be exercised by the plan trustees (usually the company management) without input by participants. This has given rise to the charge that ESOPs can be used by management to obtain tax benefits without sharing control with employees. This has been justified in the following terms (Hiltzik, 1984, p. 2).

> "Our programs are the antithesis of workplace democracy," says Joseph Schuchert, managing partner of Kelso & Co., the firm founded by Louis Kelso, which has installed about 800 ESOPs for companies since 1956 and has arranged 80 buy-outs with ESOP participation since 1970. "We've been criticized for not giving workers more participation, but we believe workers are natural shareholders, not natural managers."

There are interesting issues raised in connection with the preceding quote. Apparently the aim of ESOPs is to enable workers to participate in ownership for the purpose of augmenting their income from both dividends and capital gains. But ownership carries the ultimate control power in a corporation. If workers are not to participate in the decision-making process or to exercise ultimate control in their role as shareholders, some unresolved issues are posed.

With regard to productivity performance, the most exhaustive study was performed by the General Accounting Office (1987), which reviewed a number of prior studies on ESOPs and corporate performance. Few of these earlier studies found significant gains in either profitability or productivity. Only one of the studies reported a significant improvement in the growth rate of sales. No study reported a significant improvement in the growth rate of employment.

Later studies report mixed evidence. For example, Park and Song (1995) find that, on average, firms sponsoring ESOPs experience a permanent improvement in performance. But when they partition their sample between firms with large outside blockholders (block firms) and firms without them (nonblock firms), important differences are observed. The improvement in performance is limited to block firms. Their regression analysis finds a negative relation between the fraction of ownership held by the ESOPs and changes in performance for nonblock firms. But no systematic relationship is observed for block firms.

Conte, Blasi, Kruse, and Jampani (CBKJ) (1996) find that the financial returns of public companies with ESOPs are significantly higher than those of comparable non-ESOP companies. Paradoxically, after companies adopt an ESOP, their financial returns decline, indicating a negative incentive effect. CBKJ observe that these patterns are consistent with the proposition that most ESOPs in large publicly traded companies are adopted as takeover defenses. So the adoption of ESOPs in large companies lowers financial returns but has no significant effect in smaller companies. But the presence of an ESOP is a signal of superior financial returns.

Most systematic studies of the effects of ESOPs in the United States do not document performance improvements. Considerable anecdotal evidence can be found that suggests that ESOPs have had positive effects on individual companies. Some positive effects of an ESOP adopted in July 1994 by United Airlines have been reported (Bernstein, 1996). Following the 1994 ESOP operating revenue per employee increased, the number of employee grievances fell, the market share of United inched up, and pretax operating margins reached about 7½%. Between June 30, 1994, and March 5, 1996, the stock price of United Airlines increased by almost 150% as compared with an increase of only about 50% over the same period for four other major airlines. The establishment of the United ESOP was associated with concessions representing an average of 15% in pay cuts for 55% of the employees and reduced wage costs overall by 7% in 1995. In part, at least, the improvements in reported profitability and stock prices reflect a reduction in costs resulting from the wage concessions. Thus, the employees who accepted wage cuts became equity holders in the company. The effects on profitability and stock prices are similar to that which took place at TWA earlier when Carl Icahn obtained control. The positive results were only temporary, and three years later TWA faced severe financial problems again. TWA has gone through Chapter 11 bankruptcy twice. While in its second bankruptcy in 1995, employees agreed to forgo wage increases and to reduce their equity ownership share from 45 to 30%.

The use of an ESOP at United has not been an unqualified success (Chandler, 1996). Flight attendants were unwilling to participate because they felt the pay cuts were too large. With regard to individual measures of performance, United appears to still have problems. During 1995 United ranked fifth in comparison with 10 major carriers in late arrivals, sixth in mishandled baggage, and seventh in customer complaints.

ESOPs in other individual companies have also encountered some problems and conflicts. Avis set up a 100% ESOP in 1987, but management has not granted employees board seats or voting rights. The stock price of the company dropped from $22 in 1992 to $12.50 in 1996.

Weirton Steel Corporation was formed in 1984 when workers bought 100% of the company to avoid a shutdown. Since then they have had to accept successive wage and job reductions and sold 30% of their stock to pay for plant improvements and to reduce debt. In 1994 top management spent $550 million on plant modernization. To help finance this, the ESOP sold more stock, reducing its voting share to 49%. In the meantime, the company has filed a lawsuit against the workers for an illegal work stoppage. The union argues that safety concerns were the basis for the work stoppage.

Similar management versus worker conflicts are taking place at the Northwestern Steel & Wire Co. In a 1987 ESOP, employees accepted pay cuts to obtain 59% of the company and half the board seats. Financial difficulties in 1992 required the sale of stock to new investors, which reduced the employees' ownership share to 16%. Management has been in conflict with the employee union over a number of issues (Bernstein, 1996).

One problem illustrated by these examples is that management has been unwilling to grant employees full shareholder rights when ESOPs are formed. Employees own an average of 13% of their companies at 562 public corporations, according to a *Business Week* article citing Professor Joseph R. Blasi of Rutgers University (Bernstein, 1996). Most of the 562 companies are unionized, and in less than a dozen do employees hold board seats.

In contrast to the uneven experience with ESOPs in the United States, in a study of Japanese manufacturing companies for the period 1973–1988, Professors Derek C. Jones of Hamilton College and Takao Kato of Colgate University found positive results for ESOPs in Japan. They found that since 1973 the portion of publicly traded Japanese firms that have ESOPs jumped from 61% to more than 90%. By 1989 the average holdings per employee had reached about $14,000. Jones and Kato also found that in three to four years after setting up an ESOP, companies averaged a 4 to 5% increase in productivity. A 10% increase in employee bonuses relative to the bonuses of competitors resulted in a 1% increase in productivity in the next year (*Business Week,* 1995, p. 24).

These mixed results for ESOPs suggest that they have strong potentials but are not a panacea. It depends on how the ESOPs are utilized.

## Economic Consequences

Of great concern are the charges that ESOPs have been used by managements not only as instruments for increasing their control, but also to conduct financial transactions in their own interests and to the detriment of the ESOPs and the workers they represent. Some of the court cases in which these issues are at least raised include the following. In Hall-Mark Electronics, employees owned one-third of the company stock through their retirement plan. The issue in the court case is the allegation that three Hall-Mark executives arranged to have the ESOP sell its shares back to the company at $4 per share shortly before they participated in the sale of the company for $100 per share (Hiltzik, 1986, p. 1).

Another example is the Chicago Pneumatic Tool Company, which established an ESOP in 1985. The controlling trustee was the chief executive of the company. In March 1986 the company became the target of a hostile takeover. To defeat the bid, it is alleged that the chief executive transferred one million shares from the company's treasury to the ESOP under his own voting control. The U.S. Labor Department (which has responsibility for implementing the provisions of ERISA and of employee pension plans generally) stated that the cost of the transaction to the ESOP was $32.4 million for the shares, which were trading at about 30% over their historical average because of takeover speculation (Hiltzik, 1986, pp. 1, 6).

In 1985 the Labor Department blocked an ESOP-financed $500 million leveraged buyout of Scott & Fetzer, the publisher of *The World Book Encyclopedia.* The Labor Department objected to the arrangement, which provided that the Scott & Fetzer ESOP would invest $182 million in borrowed funds to receive 41% of the company in the leveraged buyout. A group consisting of Scott & Fetzer's top management plus Kelso & Co., were to invest $15 million, for which they would receive 29% of the company. The General Electric Credit Corporation, which financed the $182 million ESOP loan and provided other financing, would receive the remaining 30%. The Labor Department alleged that the ESOP was putting up more than 92% of the equity investment for only 41% of the company. The rebuttal view was that the ESOP investment represented a purchase of shares at market value (or takeover value), not an initial equity contribution. Another issue raised by this case is whether it was appropriate for Kelso & Co., a leading investment banking firm specializing in setting up ESOPs and formulating the terms of the deal, to have a substantial equity participation. There would appear to be the possibility of a conflict of interest.

The broader economic consequences of ESOPs have also been analyzed (Chen and Kensinger, 1988). If managements also control the ESOPs that are created, no increase in employee influence on the company takes place. While employees may receive stock that may be sold, the additions to their wealth may be relatively small. The amounts received may be insufficient to provide motivation for increased efforts by workers or to achieve harmonious relations between workers and management. On the other hand, if workers did receive substantial increases in control over the company through ESOPs, other harmful results might follow. Workers might use their increased ownership powers to redistribute wealth away from the original shareholders and other shareholders in the firm. The view has also been expressed that reliance can be placed upon market forces to bring about employee ownership where it is appropriate, without the necessity of tax subsidies. The tax subsidies may cause a misallocation of resources. Chen and Kensinger (1988, p. 75) see two risks:

> The tax preferences can keep a dying enterprise limping along, creating an imbalance in its industry which holds back the stronger competitors and so creates economic inefficiency. Perhaps even more damaging in the long run, these preferences may discourage valuable investment in new technologies and other growth opportunities by fostering an overly cautious attitude brought on by inefficient diversification of employees' capital.

They also observe that the greatest potential gains from employee ownership are in smaller high-growth companies in which human capital plays an important role in productivity performance. But in such companies, typically growth and profitability provide ample incentives. From a public policy standpoint, the tax preferences granted may cause distortions and departures from what would occur under the unrestricted operation of market forces. Some writers have concluded that "mature, diversified corporations with strong labor unions and few growth opportunities, on balance, are likely to be the best candidates for ESOP financing" (Chen and Kensinger, 1988, p. 75). In these situations, however, the advantages and disadvantages of ESOPs should be compared to alternatives such as takeovers, MBOs, and LBOs. It has been argued that, on balance, these alternatives to ESOPs do not involve tax subsidies of the same kind or to the same degree.

## EVALUATION OF ESOPs

The event return effects of establishing an ESOP depend on the circumstances. Chang (1990) calculated the two-day abnormal portfolio returns for 165 announcements of employee stock ownership plans. The announcement produces small positive event returns if the ESOP is used as a leveraged buyout (LBO) or as a form of wage concession. However, if the ESOP is established as a defense against a takeover, the event returns will be negative. Managers of such firms, on average, hold smaller ownership interest in their firms than do managers of comparable firms.

Sellers et al. (1994) sharpen the analysis of event returns to ESOPs. They eliminate from the sample those ESOPs that provide tax incentives. A positive market two-day return of 1.5% is consistent with other favorable effects of ESOPs, such as improvements in employee productivity. Similarly, Chang and Mayers (1992) find non-tax influences on event returns from the establishment of ESOPs. The largest positive event returns are observed when officers and directors initially control between 10 and 20% of share ownership. The positive effects on shareholder wealth are smaller when the initial control is less than 10% or more than 20%. When officers and directors control 40% or more of total shares, a negative association is found between event returns and the fraction of shares added to the ESOP.

Event return studies of ESOPs have obtained different results reflecting the multiple motives for ESOPs. Anne Beatty has published two empirical studies of ESOPs

(1994, 1995). In the first study she examines three motivations for leveraged ESOPs: (1) as a takeover defense, (2) incentives to employees, (3) tax savings. Her empirical study suggests that companies that adopt ESOPs are likely to have adopted other types of other takeover defenses as well. But companies that adopt ESOPs are likely to have characteristics consistent also with tax and incentive effects.

In her 1995 study, Beatty analyzed a sample of 122 ESOP transaction announcements during the 1976–1989 period. She finds an average 1% two-day cumulative positive return over the minus one to zero days. This increase in equity value reflects primarily tax effects. She also finds some relation between a positive share price reaction and the size of ESOP benefits. She also finds that equity values decline for firms that are subject to takeovers. This also supports the view that ESOPs are used as a takeover defense.

ESOPs are not panaceas for productivity improvement. The effects on the performance of the firm depend heavily on how they are employed. Some of the notable examples of the use of ESOPs have occurred in industries such as steel and the airlines. These are industries where changed economic circumstances forced employees to give up a portion of their wages for a partial equity position in the firm. Even in these circumstances management continued to exercise major control over decision processes in the firm. Thus, even where ESOPs have been used in a major way, employees have not received full shareholder rights and ownership incentives have been severely diminished.

Many ESOPs were established as takeover defenses. However, the proliferation of a broad arsenal of other takeover defenses has reduced the role of ESOPs in this area.

Finally, often the supposed tax advantages have been confused with the tax deductibility of employee benefits. A major tax advantage for closely held corporations is the tax shelter for the owners, but there are no clear effects on employee incentives. Arguments have also been made that the tax subsidies involved with ESOPs might have perversely negative effects. Any positive effects might also be achieved through alternative compensation arrangements.

## MASTER LIMITED PARTNERSHIPS

The corporation has been the dominant form of business organization in the United States when measured by total assets. When measured by numbers, proprietorships and partnerships are the most numerous, applying mostly to relatively small businesses. A corporation has four major advantages in raising large sums of money. (1) It provides for limited liability of stockholders. Stockholders are not personally liable if the firm is unable to pay its debts. (2) The corporation has an unlimited life. Managers can come and go and owners may change, but this does not affect the continuity of the corporation. (3) The ownership shares carry the residual risk, but they are divided into many units. Hence, investors can limit their risk exposure in any one firm, and this facilitates diversification by investors across many firms. (4) The shares of common stock are freely bought and sold. This facilitates tradability and transferability of ownership interest in the firm.

### The Nature of MLPs

In recent years the master limited partnership (MLP) has taken its place as a new form of business organization. The MLP is a type of limited partnership whose shares are publicly traded. The limited partnership interests are divided into units that trade as shares of common stock. In addition to tradability it has the advantages of limited liability for the limited partners. The tradability also provides for continuity of life. While the MLP retains many of the advantages of a corporation, it has a superiority over the corporation in that it eliminates the double taxation of corporate earnings. The MLP is not taxed as an entity; it is treated as any other partnership for which income is allocated pro rata to the partners. Unit holders reflect all income deductions and credits attributable to the partnership's operation in determining the unit holder's taxable income. The Tax Reform Act of 1986 enhanced the advantage to MLPs by lowering the top personal income tax rate (28%) to below the top corporate tax rate (34%).

The Internal Revenue Service has focused on four characteristics in distinguishing between a corporation and a master limited partnership (MLP): unlimited life, limited liability, centralized management, and transferability. To avoid being taxed as a corporation, an MLP may have only two, and no more, of the four corporate characteristics, which are usually centralized management and transferability. Master limited partnerships typically specify a limited life of 100 years more or less. The general partner or manager of the partnership has unlimited liability, even though the limited partners do not.

Probably in part because the general partner has unlimited liability, it also has virtually autocratic powers. Once a general partner and the formation of an MLP have been approved by the courts and been reviewed at least by the Securities and Exchange Commission, it is very difficult to change the general partner in the absence of readily provable fraud or the equivalent. The probability of success of an MLP is increased if it is structured to achieve an alignment of interests between the general partner and the public unit holders. One way to do this is by using management incentive fees such as providing the general partner with a sharing rule of 4 to 6% of the distributable cash flows from the MLP. Alignment of incentives is also achieved because the management of the general partnership usually owns a significant number of the limited partnership units.

Different types of MLPs have been identified. Mentz (1987, p. 19) has described four categories of MLPs based on their method of formation:

> (i) "roll-up MLPs," formed by the combination of two or more partnerships into one publicly traded partnership; (ii) "liquidation MLPs," formed by a complete liquidation of a corporation into an MLP; (iii) "acquisition MLPs," formed by an offering of MLP interests to the public with the proceeds used to purchase assets; or (iv) "roll-out MLPs," formed by a corporation's contribution of operating assets in exchange for general and limited partnership interests in the MLP, followed by a public offering of limited partnership interests by the corporation of the MLP, or both. A fifth category of MLP, that may well predominate in the future, is the "start-up MLP," formed by a partnership that is initially privately held but later offers its interests to the public in order to finance internal growth.

It will be noted that some of the distinctions are based on whether the MLP is formed out of a partnership or out of a corporation. Some writers would include the liquidation MLP as a special case of roll-out MLPs. Some writers would also combine acquisition MLPs with start-up MLPs. Our discussion considers three main categories of MLPs: (1) roll-up MLPs, (2) roll-out MLPs, and (3) start-up MLPs.

Roll-ups were the first type of MLPs organized. The roll-ups began with combining limited partnerships formed to invest in programs in the oil industry. The Apache Petroleum Company in 1981 formed the first MLP by rolling up a number of partnership syndications. Before that, the typical practice was to form oil and gas corporations by exchanges of common stock in the newly formed corporation for the previously existing private partnership interests.

Interestingly, computer technology contributed to the timing of the emergence of MLPs. By 1981 Apache had developed the complex computer programs required to report the annual gain, loss, and tax basis of individual partners in a publicly traded partnership with a relatively large number of investor/participants. Also, Apache was granted a ruling by the IRS that a master limited partnership would be treated as a partnership and not a corporation for tax purposes even though its shares were publicly traded. Later Apache became a corporation again.

The nature of a roll-up MLP is shown in Figure 15.4. The figure depicts three stages. Before the roll-up transaction, there are a number of limited partnerships in existence. The figure shows one general partner in common for all of the partnerships; this was the case with Apache Petroleum, which combined a number of limited partnerships that it had previously sponsored. One of the authors was involved in a roll-up transaction in which several different general partners were involved (Pan Petroleum MLP, 1989). They simply entered into an agreement similar to that depicted in the second stage (transaction column) of Figure 15.4. Basically, in return for their shares in the old limited partnerships, units in the new MLP are issued to the old limited partners. The resulting pattern is depicted in the third column, indicating the structure after the roll-up. After the MLP has been formed, there is a general partner for a master limited partnership. It has units that are owned by the limited partners. The units may trade on the stock exchange or they may trade over the counter; we depict the use of a stock exchange in Figure 15.4.

The second major type of master limited partnership is a roll-out, which is sometimes called a spin-off. Roll-outs represent a method by which corporations can transfer assets to avoid the double taxation of corporate dividends or to establish a value on assets that may be undervalued. Roll-out or spin-off MLPs are likely to be used increasingly because corporate tax rates under the Tax Reform Act of 1986 are higher than the top rate for personal taxes. Roll-out or spin-off MLPs are likely to be sold on a yield comparison basis. Transco Corporation, an interstate natural gas pipeline company, in

**FIGURE 15.4  Roll-Up Master Limited Partnership**

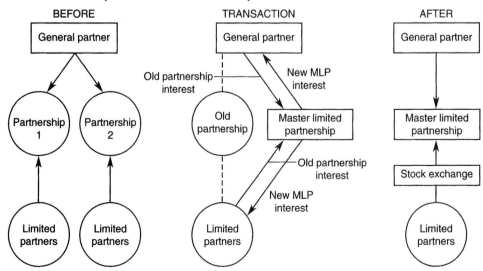

1983 apparently was the first corporation to spin off a portion of its assets into an MLP. It transferred its oil and gas reserves into a newly formed partnership and sold about 5% of the MLP units to the public. In March 1985 International Paper placed its timberlands into an MLP selling 15% of the units to the public. In December 1986 Penn Central Corporation sold its pipeline business, Buckeye Partners, to an MLP raising $240 million.

What takes place in these roll-out or spin-off MLPs is illustrated in Figure 15.5. Before the transaction, the corporation holds a number of business segments. In the transaction, the corporation places the assets of one or more of its business segments into a master limited partnership. The MLP transfers MLP units to the corporation, which in turn distributes them to its shareholders. The shareholders continue to own common stock in the corporation, but also own units in the MLP that was formed. In a variation on this pattern, the corporation could have sold a portion or all of the units to the outside public. It is likely that in a roll-out or spin-off, the corporation would designate some of its top officers to constitute the general partner for the MLP. At the completion of the transaction, there will continue to be shareholders in the corporation. It is likely that some of the units would be sold to the outside public so there would be a different set of shareholders who owned units in the MLP as well as some of the original shareholders in the corporation conducting the spin-off.

The third major type of MLP is the new issue, start-up, or acquisition MLP, illustrated in Figure 15.6. The existing entity transfers assets to the MLP. A management company may be involved that provides services to the MLP and probably will be its general partner. In return, it receives a certain percentage of the cash flow of the MLP. It is probably the key managers of the management company who would serve as the general partners. The general partner does not have to hold units in order to receive income. The partnership agreement provides that a fixed percentage of the income of the MLP is received by the general partners. Notable examples of the start-up MLP include the conversion of the Boston Celtics and Denver Nuggets basketball teams into MLPs. The Boston Celtics transaction in October 1986 raised $48 million. A hoped-for offering price of $20 per unit had to be reduced to $18 for the public offering. One can find a listing of this limited partnership unit in the New York Stock Exchange

**FIGURE 15.5  Roll-Out or Spin-Off Master Limited Partnership**

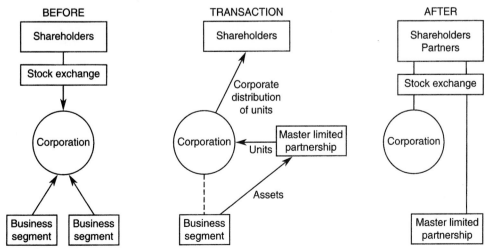

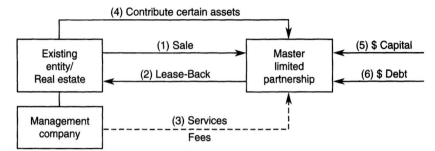

**FIGURE 15.6 New Issue, Start-Up, or Acquisition Master Limited Partnership**

Composite quotations. As of March 26, 1997, the quotation showed that the 52-week range in price for the units was a high of 25⅛ and a low of 20⅛. Based on dividend payments of $2.50 during the previous 52 weeks, the units were yielding 11.05%.

Various types of MLPs were described by Schultz (1988). He discussed the business aspects of each of the MLPs. It showed that their prices have fluctuated like common stocks. Although they typically sell on a yield basis (compete with bonds and preferred stock), the value of the MLP units fluctuates with the outlook for the performance of the MLP just as it would for a publicly traded corporation.

## Advantages of MLPs

A strong motivation for the formation of an MLP is the tax advantage, the idea that the MLP is taxed as a partnership and therefore avoids the double taxation to which corporate dividends are subject. The nature of the advantage to the use of an MLP is shown by Table 15.1. Under the old tax law, the marginal corporate rate of 46% was below the marginal personal rate of 50%. It is assumed that for the same $100 of income, the same $20 is required under either form for reinvestment in the operating activity. The investor would receive $30 under the MLP as compared with $17 under the corporation. This is 76% more income.

Under the new tax law, the top marginal corporate rate of 34% is now higher than the top marginal personal rate of 28%. Under the same assumptions as before, the after-

| | Pre-TRA 86 | | Post-TRA 86 | |
|---|---|---|---|---|
| | *Corp.* | *MLP* | *Corp.* | *MLP* |
| **TABLE 15.1** A Comparison of the Tax Benefits of MLPs Before and After the Tax Reform Act of 1986 | | | | |
| Company income | $100 | $100 | $100 | $100 |
| Company tax | 46 | 0 | 34 | 0 |
| After-tax income | 54 | 100 | 66 | 100 |
| Retained income | 20 | 20 | 20 | 20 |
| Payout | 34 | 80 | 46 | 80 |
| Personal tax | 17 | 50 | 13 | 28 |
| Investor after-tax income | $ 17 | $ 30 | $ 33 | $ 52 |

tax income to the investor is $33 under the corporation and $52 under the MLP. The investor receives 58% more income under the MLP than under the corporation. The differential under the old tax law was $13; the differential under the new tax law is $19. Thus, the absolute dollar value of benefit is greater under the new tax law. The percentage depends on the patterns of numbers assumed. Also, the comparison depends critically on the amount of retained income, because the partners pay tax whether the income is retained or not. The degree to which there is double taxation depends on the payout; the higher the payout, the more double taxation, so it is difficult to generalize. The MLP is likely to be most attractive in industries where reinvestment rates are relatively low. This implies high payout rates, and when payout rates are high, the advantage of avoiding double taxation is greater.

### Initial Pricing of MLPs

Muscarella (1988) has analyzed the price performance of MLP units. His sample consists of all initial public offerings of MLP units from January 1983 to July 1987. He analyzes the price performance of the MLPs for the 20 days following the initial public offerings. He found no significant underpricing or overpricing for his total sample or any subsample except for a slight overpricing of oil and gas and hotel/motel limited partnerships. This contrasts with substantial underpricing of initial public offerings (IPOs) of corporate securities. Ritter (1984), for example, had reported initial average returns of 26.5% for 1,028 IPOs from 1977 to 1982. Chalk and Peavy (1987) reported 22% initial returns for 649 firms from 1975 to 1982. Muscarella and Vetsuypens (1988) had found for the period 1983 to June 1987 an initial return of 7.61% for 1,184 firms. All of these studies represent substantial underpricing. Theoretical models of IPO underpricing argue that the size of IPO underpricing is related to the degree of uncertainty about the market value of the common stock of the issuing firm. The study of initial price performance of MLP units implies much less uncertainty in the valuation of MLP units. Muscarella is unable to provide an explanation why there should be relatively little uncertainty about the valuation of MLP units.

Moore, Christensen, and Roenfeldt (1989) found a two-day return (−1,0) of 4.61% (significant) and some evidence of anticipation of the MLP announcement. The reasons they give for the positive market reaction include (1) tax advantages, (2) reduced information asymmetry, (3) improved asset management, and (4) information signaling.

## Summary

Employee stock ownership plans were designed ostensibly to promote employee stock ownership and to facilitate the raising of capital by employers. They have a number of shortcomings in the performance of both functions. Nevertheless, ESOPs may be quite valuable in a number of circumstances, particularly for privately held companies engaged in ownership transfer or for firms near the limit of their debt capacity.

The argument for employee stock ownership holds that employees who own stock in their employer are more productive, because as part owners they have a greater stake in the firm's profitability. However, ESOPs provide a good deal less than direct stock ownership. Participants typically do not receive any distribution of securities from the plan until they separate from service. Dividends and voting rights are passed through only with respect to shares actually allocated to participants' accounts. But most participants are not allowed to sell even those shares that have been allocated to them and thus cannot achieve a level of diversification in their benefit plans. (ERISA excludes ESOPs from the requirement to diversify.) A 1987 report by the General Accounting Office (GAO) concluded that although ESOPs do broaden stock ownership within participating firms, given the limited number of ESOPs within the economy as a whole the effect is modest overall. Perhaps more important, it found little evidence of improved performance in terms of either profitability or productivity.

As a financing tool, ESOPs provide benefits midway between debt and equity financing. They can bring additional debt capacity to highly leveraged firms or provide a market for equity financing for closely held firms. They are very useful devices for transferring ownership. The same 1987 GAO report indicated that the use of ESOPs in corporate finance has not lived up to its potential—most leveraged ESOP funds are used to buy back stock from existing shareholders (for instance, retiring major shareholders) and not for capital expansion by the sponsoring firms. Thus ESOPs' contributions to corporate finance have been limited.

The MLP is a new organizational form that offers investors the structure and tax attributes of more traditional partnerships, but differs in one key respect. MLPs offer investors liquidity via an organized secondary market for the trading of partnership interests.

Tax advantages were an important motivating factor in the early development of MLPs. However, some of these advantages have been eroded. The Tax Reform Act of 1986 (TRA 86) eliminated an important tax benefit of corporate-MLP conversions with its repeal of the General Utilities doctrine. Before TRA 86, in a liquidation MLP the corporate sponsor would contribute assets to the MLP in exchange for units in a roll-out transaction. The units would then be distributed to the corporate sponsor's shareholders in a complete liquidation of the corporation. This transaction would be completely tax free. However, this is no longer the case with the repeal of the General Utilities doctrine. The general rule was that corporate gains from the sale of appreciated assets were taxed at the corporate level at the time of the sale and at the shareholder level when this income was distributed as dividends. Under the General Utilities doctrine, a significant portion of the assets involved in a corporate MLP conversion would escape corporate taxation at the time of conversion. But TRA 86 eliminated this exception and taxed at the corporate level the entire difference between the adjusted basis of the assets and their fair market value. In addition, the shareholders at time of conversion after TRA 86 continue to be taxed on the difference between their basis in the common stock and the market value of the MLP units at conversion.

The main tax advantages of MLPs following TRA 86 are the result of the differential between personal and corporate income tax rates, and the status of MLPs as nontaxable entities. All profits and losses of an MLP flow through to individual investors, to be taxed at lower personal rates, while avoiding the double taxation at both the corporate and personal levels of corporate dividend distributions to shareholders. However, these tax advantages are highly sensitive to an MLP's need to retain earnings, because MLP earnings are taxable to investors whether they are distributed or not.

Thus, the liquidity advantages of MLPs assume even greater importance. Siciliano (1987, p. 1) suggests that this aspect of MLPs has led to "a distinctly different investment and marketing thesis," appealing to investors to view MLP units as simply another component of their equity securities portfolio, rather than "as a long-term method of sheltering income from taxes."

## Questions

15.1  What are the advantages and limitations of ESOPs?

15.2  How successful have ESOPs been in achieving their goals of increasing employee stock ownership and facilitating capital raising by employers?

15.3  How do MLPs differ from ordinary limited partnerships?

15.4  What are the advantages and limitations of MLPs?

15.5  Explain the differences between leveraged and nonleveraged ESOPs. Compare the EPS and control dilution under equity financing versus financing through an ESOP.

15.6  How are MLPs similar to corporations? How do they differ?

------------------------------------ C A S E    15–1 ------------------------------------

# Pan Petroleum MLP

Most of the literature on MLPs has emphasized tax aspects. This case study of the Pan Petroleum MLP, whose formation was reviewed by the courts on April 26, 1989, illustrates the underlying business and economic rationales as well. The 1989 transaction involved a consolidation of a group of 45 oil and gas limited partnerships with Pan Petroleum MLP, a publicly traded master limited partnership. The consolidated partnership had approximately 4,300 limited partners. It was predicted that as a result of the consolidation, general and administrative expenses would be reduced by as much as $300,000 per year. These savings result from several types of economies of scale resulting from the consolidation. The savings in general and administrative expenses became possible because of the need for only one set of financial records rather than 46, one annual appraisal of mineral properties, one legal entity maintained, and one partnership tax return. Many of the limited partners in the constituent partnerships consolidating with Pan Petroleum MLP were limited partners in more than one partnership. This makes possible further cost savings with respect to record keeping and participant reporting. Many of the constituent partnerships owned interests in the same mineral properties. Duplicate accounting and record keeping could be eliminated as a result of the consolidation. The constituent partnerships participated mainly in wells drilled by two different major exploration companies. The consolidation provided Pan Petroleum MLP

with a majority of the working interest in many of the properties. This enables the MLP to conduct negotiations with the two large exploration companies on a more effective basis.

The basis for the consolidation appeared to be efficient and equitable. Engineering surveys established the proved reserves in developed producing properties as well as the nonproducing or undeveloped properties. From the estimates of proved reserves of oil and gas, the amounts of cash flows and their duration were projected. The same was done for the nonproducing or undeveloped properties. The cash flows for this latter group were reduced by 30% as an uncertainty factor. The resulting cash flows for both the developed producing properties and for the nonproducing or undeveloped properties were discounted at a 10% rate over the expected future economical producing lives of each of the properties. The MLP into which the other constituent partnerships were consolidated had its future cash flows discounted into a value figure on the same basis. For each constituent limited partnership and the Pan Petroleum MLP, the value of other assets and liabilities were also taken into account to arrive at a total "formula value." These were summed to arrive at a total figure of approximately $23 million. Of this amount something over $11 million represented the "formula value" of Pan Petroleum MLP, 49.2% of the total. Pan Petroleum MLP had 2,571,670 limited partnership units already outstanding. Using these as the reference factor, a total of 5,226,191 MLP units were issued of which Pan Petroleum accounted for 49.21%. The other constituent partnerships received MLP units representing the same percentage of the total MLP units issued that their formula value represented in relation to the total formula value. Inherently forecasts and projections were required, but the methodology appears to have represented a rational and equitable basis for making the apportionment of ownership and income rights.

Clearly one of the major advantages to the owners of the constituent limited partnerships is that they would now have ownership rights that could be freely traded, bought, and sold. A number of the constituent limited partnerships would have had to be liquidated and would have ceased to exist except for the consolidation with Pan Petroleum MLP. In addition, by exchanging their limited partnership units for units in the Pan Petroleum MLP, the limited partners now have pro rata ownership rights in an efficient business operation. Even with depressed prices for oil and natural gas, the Pan Petroleum MLP continues to be a viable entity. With improvements in future oil and natural gas markets, the investors in the MLP units have a potential for favorable future returns.

## Questions on Case Study C15.1

C15.1.1  What were the economics in grouping 45 oil and gas limited partnerships into one MLP?

C15.1.2  What were some advantages to the owners of the constituent limited partnerships of the formation of the MLP?

## References

Beatty, Anne, "An Empirical Analysis of the Corporate Control, Tax and Incentive Motivations for Adopting Leveraged Employee Stock Ownership Plans," *Managerial and Decision Economics,* 15, 1994, pp. 299–315.

———, "The Cash Flow and Informational Effects of Employee Stock Ownership Plans," *Journal of Financial Economics,* 38, June 1995, pp. 211–240.

Bernstein, Aaron, "Why ESOP Deals Have Slowed to a Crawl," *Business Week,* March 18, 1996, pp. 101–102.

Bruner, Robert F., "Leveraged ESOPs and Corporate Restructuring," *Journal of Applied Corporate Finance,* 1, Spring 1988, pp. 54–66.

*Business Week,* "How Japan Perks Up Productivity," August 28, 1995, p. 24.

Chalk, A. J., and J. W. Peavy, III, "Initial Public Offerings: Daily Returns, Offering Types, and the Price Effect," *Financial Analysts Journal,* 43, September/October 1987, pp. 65–69.

Chandler, Susan, "United We Own," *Business Week,* March 18, 1996, pp. 96–100.

Chang, Saeyoung, "Employee Stock Ownership Plans and Shareholder Wealth: An Empirical Investigation," *Financial Management,* 19, Spring 1990, pp. 48–58.

———, and David Mayers, "Managerial Vote Ownership and Shareholder Wealth," *Journal of Financial Economics,* 32, August 1992, pp. 103–131.

Chaplinsky, Susan, and Greg Niehaus, "The Tax and Distributional Effects of Leveraged ESOPs," *Financial Management,* 19(1), 1990, pp. 29–38.

———, "The Role of ESOPs in Takeover Contests," *Journal of Finance,* 49, September 1994, pp. 1451–1470.

Chen, A. H., and J. W. Kensinger, "Beyond the Tax Effects of ESOP Financing," *Journal of Applied Corporate Finance,* 1, Spring 1988, pp. 67–75.

Conte, Michael A., Joseph Blasi, Douglas Kruse, and Rama Jampani, "Financial Returns of Public ESOP Companies: Investor Effects vs. Manager Effects," *Financial Analysts Journal,* 52, July/August 1996, pp. 51–61.

Hiltzik, Michael A., "ESOPs Now a Boon for Management," *The Wall Street Journal,* December 30, 1984, pp. 1–2.

———, "Do ESOPs Aid Workers or Managers?" *Los Angeles Times,* May 25, 1986, Part IV, pp. 1, 6.

Kaplan, Steven, "A Summary of Sources of Value in Management Buyouts," Presentation at the Conference on Management Buyouts, Graduate School of Business Administration, New York University, Salomon Brothers Center for the Study of Financial Institutions, May 20, 1988.

Mentz, J. Roger, Department of the Treasury, Statement on June 30, 1987 in *Master Limited Partnerships,* Hearings before the Subcommittee on Select Revenue Measures of the Committee on Ways and Means, House of Representatives, 100th Congress, First Session, Serial 100-39.

Mitchell, Daniel J. B., "Profit Sharing and Employee Ownership: Policy Implications," *Contemporary Economic Policy,* 13, April 1995, pp. 16–25.

Moore, W. T., D. G. Christensen, and R. L. Roenfeldt, "Equity Valuation Effects of Forming Master Limited Partnerships," *Journal of Financial Economics,* 24, 1989, pp. 107–124.

Muscarella, C. J., "Price Performance of Initial Public Offerings of Master Limited Partnership Units," *The Financial Review,* 23, November 1988, pp. 513–521.

———, and M. R. Vetsuypens, "Initial Public Offerings and Information Asymmetry," Working Paper, Southern Methodist University, 1988.

Pan Petroleum MLP, Proposal, March 8, 1989.

Park, Sangsoo, and Moon H. Song, "Employee Stock Ownership Plans, Firm Performance, and Monitoring by Outside Blockholders," *Financial Management,* 24, Winter 1995, pp. 52–65.

Ritter, J. R., "The 'Hot' Issue Market of 1980," *Journal of Business,* 57, April 1984, pp. 215–240.

Scholes, Myron S., and Mark A. Wolfson, *Taxes and Business Strategy: A Planning Approach,* Englewood Cliffs, NJ: Prentice Hall, 1992.

Schultz, Ellen, "All That Payout and Capital Gains Too," *Fortune,* 118, October 10, 1988, p. 28.

Sellers, Keith F., Joseph M. Hagan, and Philip H. Siegel, "Employee Stock Ownership Plans and Shareholder Wealth: An Examination of The Market Perceptions of The Non-Tax Effects," *Journal of Applied Business Research,* 10, Summer 1994, pp. 45–52.

Siciliano, John M., "Investment Banking Considerations," in Lionel M. Allan, *Master Limited Partnerships for Real Property Investments,* Berkeley, CA: California Continuing Education of the Bar, 1987, pp. 1–13.

United States General Accounting Office, *Employee Stock Ownership Plans: Benefits and Costs of ESOP Tax Incentives for Broadening Stock Ownership,* Washington, DC, December 1986.

———, *Employee Stock Ownership Plans: Little Evidence of Effects on Corporate Performance,* Washington, DC, October 1987.

# 16

# Going Private and Leveraged Buyouts

"Going private" refers to the transformation of a public corporation into a privately held firm. There are a number of variations on this theme. In some cases, controlling shareholders seek to eliminate minority interests—called a "squeeze-out." A critical element in these going-private transactions is fairness to minority/outside shareholders to avoid accusations of security fraud against controlling shareholders. When structured properly, going private can result in gains to both parties—this is the gains-sharing hypothesis.

## CHARACTERISTICS OF LEVERAGED BUYOUTS

A leveraged buyout (LBO) is a general form of corporate restructuring. The traditional LBO represented the acquisition, financed largely by borrowing, of all of the stock or assets of a public company by a small group of investors. The buying group may be associated with buyout specialists (for example, Kohlberg Kravis Roberts & Co.). The buying group may also be associated with investment bankers or commercial bankers.

Leveraged buyout activity reached its peak during the years 1986–1988. The largest was RJR Nabisco (in 1988) with a purchase price of $24.6 billion. The next largest LBOs were the Beatrice Companies (in 1985) at $5.4 billion, the Safeway Stores (in 1986) at $4.2 billion, and the Borg Warner Corporation (in 1987) at $3.8 billion. The total purchase price of the 20 largest LBOs formed between 1983 and 1995 was $76.5 billion (Houlihan Lokey Howard & Zukin, 1996, p. 43).

Incumbent management is usually included in the buying group. Sometimes an entire company is acquired. Sometimes only a segment, a division, or a subsidiary of a public corporation is acquired from the parent company. These are usually of relatively smaller size and key executives perform such an important role that these going-private transactions are called unit management buyouts (MBOs). Notable examples of unit management buyouts announced in 1995 include the Merck & Co. sale to a management group of its Medco Behavioral Care Corporation at a purchase price of $340 million. Another example is the sale by Torchmark Corporation of a unit involved in energy asset management named the Torch Energy Advisors Inc. involving a purchase price of $115 million (*Mergerstat Review,* 1996, p. 34).

Especially when financial groups such as venture capital companies or other types of buyout specialists are involved, the LBO transaction is expected to be reversed with a public offering. The aim is to increase the profitability of the company taken private and thereby increase market value. The buyout firm seeks to harvest its gains within a three- to five-year period of time.

## THREE MAJOR STAGES OF LEVERAGED BUYOUTS

Leveraged buyout activity may be placed into three distinct time periods: the 1980s, the early 1990s, and post-1992. Leveraged buyouts did not begin with the 1980s. They actually have a long history. Before 1980 they were often referred to as bootstrap transactions characterized by highly leveraged deals. During the 1980s the economic and financial environments that stimulated M&A activity were also fertile environments for LBOs.

Economic and legislative changes as well as some unsound patterns in LBO transactions of the late 1980s resulted in a correction period. From a peak of a total of $88 billion LBO transactions in 1988, the volume declined to $7.5 billion in 1991 (Allen, 1996). New developments in the nature of LBO transactions and market participants led to a revival in LBO transactions to a level of $20.6 billion in 1995. As discussed in earlier chapters, the M&A market also reached a new peak in 1995.

The differences between these three periods are illustrated by some data on the characteristics of LBOs and MBOs. Table 16.1 shows that the mean and median price of LBOs was much larger in the 1986–1990 period than in the subsequent two periods. The size of LBOs dropped sharply in the 1991–1992 period. Surprisingly, the mean price of LBOs during the 1991–1992 period was lower than the mean price of MBOs (data were not available to compute the median price of MBOs). In the 1993–1995 period, the size of both LBOs and MBOs once again increased, but not to the levels of 1986–1990.

Table 16.2 sets forth the relative premiums paid during the three different time periods. For all acquisitions, the mean or median premium did not change greatly. However, the mean and median premium was substantially lower for LBOs in all three periods. The decline in the premiums paid in LBOs was relatively sharp during the 1991–1992 period, but for the 1993–1995 period, the premiums paid in LBOs were at about their 1986–1990 period levels.

**TABLE 16.1**    Relative Size of LBOs and MBOs (in $ Millions)

| Period | MBOs Mean Price | LBOs Mean Price | LBOs Median Price |
|--------|-----------------|-----------------|-------------------|
| 1986–1990 | 135.0 | 329.2 | 75.5 |
| 1991–1992 | 90.6 | 77.3 | 27.1 |
| 1993–1995 | 83.3 | 111.4 | 33.7 |

*Source:* Calculated from *Mergerstat Review,* 1997.

**TABLE 16.2**    Relative Premium Offered

| | All Acquisitions | | LBOs | |
|--------|--------------|----------------|--------------|----------------|
| Period | Mean Premium | Median Premium | Mean Premium | Median Premium |
| 1986–1990 | 40.3% | 30.5% | 34.0% | 27.5% |
| 1991–1992 | 38.1% | 32.1% | 24.3% | 14.1% |
| 1993–1995 | 41.8% | 32.4% | 35.5% | 24.7% |

*Source:* Same as Table 16.1.

| **TABLE 16.3** | Relative P/E Ratios | | |
|---|---|---|---|
| *Period* | *S&P 500 Mean P/E* | *LBOs Mean P/E* | *LBOs Median P/E* |
| 1986–1990 | 14.9 | 19.5 | 16.9 |
| 1991–1992 | 22.2 | 14.2 | 11.7 |
| 1993–1995 | 18.1 | 23.4 | 17.4 |

*Source:* Same as Table 16.1 plus *Economic Report of the President,* 1996.

In Table 16.3, it is clear that both the mean and median price earnings ratio reflected in the purchase price of the LBOs established, dropped sharply in the 1991–1992 period compared with the 1986–1990 period. Price earnings ratios (P/Es) paid in the 1986–1990 period appeared to be higher for the LBO transactions than for the benchmark S&P 500 period. The P/Es in the LBO transactions in the 1991–1992 period, however, were much lower than the benchmark S&P 500 period.

It is clear from the above data that distinct differences in LBOs between the three periods can be discerned. Accordingly, we first describe the basic pattern of LBO and MBO activity during the 1980s. We next describe the factors that caused LBO activity to drop sharply in the early 1990s. The final section of the chapter describes the new developments associated with the revival of leveraged buyouts after 1992.

## LBOs IN THE 1980s

In the traditional LBO of the 1980s, debt financing typically represented more than 50% of the purchase price. Debt was secured by the assets of the acquired firm or based on the expected future cash flows. The cash flows were typically measured by earnings before depreciation and amortization, before interest and taxes (EBITDA, also called EBDIT). Debt was scheduled to be paid off either from the sale of assets or from future cash flows generated by operations. Following completion of the buyout, the acquired company became a privately held corporation. It was expected that the firm would go public again after a period of three to five years at a gain. Before developing in some detail the financial patterns in an illustrative LBO, we first discuss the general economic and financial factors that stimulated the LBOs in the 1980s.

### General Economic and Financial Factors

In substantial measure the increase in the number and dollar volume of merger and restructuring activity in the 1980s reflected underlying forces in the economic and financial environments. The same general forces that produced mergers and restructuring appear also to have stimulated increased use of leveraged buyouts and management buyouts. Indeed, sometimes an LBO or MBO is a defensive measure against an unwanted takeover. On the other hand, sometimes the announcement of a going-private plan, an LBO, or an MBO will stimulate competing bids by outsiders. Thus, there are interactions between takeover activity and LBO activity. We briefly summarize here materials on the factors that have stimulated M&A and LBO activity in the 1980s.

One fundamental influence was the period of sustained economic growth between 1982 and 1990. A new peak in all categories of M&A activity had been reached in this period of sustained business expansion, as all previous major merger waves were also observed in periods of expansionary environments. Total M&A transactions, divestitures, and leveraged buyouts of public companies and divisions all followed similar patterns in the recent period; total M&A transactions and divestitures peaked in 1986 in terms of the number of transactions while leveraged buyouts peaked in 1988 (*Mergerstat Review,* 1996).

Another pervasive influence was (somewhat unanticipated) persistent inflation, which began to accelerate in the late 1960s and continued through 1982. The gross national product implicit price deflator during the period 1968–1982 increased by no less than 5%. Measured by the Consumer Price Index on all items, double-digit inflation or very close to that level was experienced in six out of the 14 years. The persistence of a relatively high level of inflation had a number of consequences. One was to cause the q-ratio to decline sharply. The q-ratio is the ratio of the market value of a firm to the replacement cost of its assets. When this ratio is less than 1 it is cheaper to buy capacity in the financial markets than in the real asset markets. The q-ratio moved from a peak of 1.3 in 1965 to a low of 0.52 in 1981. It began to rise in 1982 with the rise in stock prices after mid-1982. When the q-ratio was as low as 0.52 in 1981 this meant that a firm could be purchased in the financial markets at almost half of what it would cost to replace the firm's assets in brick-and-mortar and inventories. This undoubtedly motivated some takeovers, although takeovers may also be stimulated by the value creation reflected in high q-ratios.

In addition, the persistent inflation provided opportunities to realize tax savings through recapitalization. Because coupon payments on existing debt were not adjusted for inflation, real debt obligations declined with rising price levels. Thus the real levels of debt/equity ratios declined over the period of persistent but largely unanticipated inflation. Thus, opportunities existed for greater interest tax shields by releveraging business firms. On the other hand, increased free cash flows reflecting inflation and fixed interest payments (on old debt) may have allowed managers to increase self-aggrandizing but unprofitable expenditures, as suggested by Jensen (1986) when the situation called for increased leverage. For these reasons, firms that lagged in increasing leverage became inviting targets to outsiders who were ready, willing, and able to bring about the restructuring (Shleifer and Vishny, 1988). This in turn stimulated new forms of debt financing such as the use of high-yield bonds in the innovative financial markets. Developments in the financial markets were further stimulated by a succession of laws that deregulated financial institutions.

Other legislative factors also played a role. New tax laws stimulated restructuring and takeover activity. Particularly, the Economic Recovery Tax Act (ERTA) enacted in 1981 permitted old assets to be stepped up on purchase. These newly established high values could then be depreciated on an accelerated basis. In the period of high inflation, the nominal value of corporate assets was increased above their historical cost, enabling a large step-up in basis. Depreciation recapture was relatively small. Also under the General Utilities doctrine, the sales of assets in the liquidation process (actual or under technical legal terms) were not subject to capital gains taxes at the corporate level. (The General Utilities doctrine was repealed in the 1986 tax reform.)

Another legislative change that encouraged MBOs involved employee stock ownership plans (ESOPs). While these have been around for some years, the 1981 ERTA increased the ability of ESOPs to borrow from a bank to invest the funds in the firm's shares. The firm is able to treat as a deductible expense for tax purposes contributions to the ESOP sufficient to cover both the interest and the principal payments on the loan. In addition, in 1984 a further tax law change permitted banks to deduct half of their interest income on loans to ESOPs. This enabled the banks to make loans to ESOPs on relatively more favorable terms.

A new antitrust climate began in 1980. New appointees to the Federal Trade Commission and to the Department of Justice made it clear through public speeches and agency actions that the stringent prohibitions against horizontal and vertical mergers would no longer be supported. Efficiency considerations and a "new economic realism" were substituted for the older structural view that held that the effects on competition could be judged by market concentration ratios. At least three competing explanations for the change in the antitrust regulatory environment have been proffered. First, the new administration had different political views. Second, the culmination of more than a decade of new empirical research from the academic community provided support for a dynamic competition view of the interactions among large firms. Third, most significant U.S. industries had become subject to intense competition from foreign firms. Thus, competitive pressures provided the stimulus for restructuring and the recognition of these pressures was the basis for changed public opinion and regulatory policy toward mergers, takeovers, and restructuring.

It was these forces that increased merger activity and restructuring in a wide range of forms. LBOs and MBOs were part of this general pattern. Sometimes LBOs and MBOs were responses to the increased threat of takeover and their announcement often stimulated rival offers by outsiders.

## Illustration of an LBO

A simplified example illustrates the nature of a leveraged buyout transaction during the 1980s. Wavell Corporation, a successful, publicly traded manufacturer of glassware, was purchased in the 1970s by Eastern Pacific (EP), a large conglomerate, that during this period seemed bent on buying everything in sight. Eventually, however, Eastern Pacific began to focus its interests predominantly in the transportation, communications, and real estate industries. Wavell did not fit into the EP mold, and languished for a number of years. In 1983, when a small group of disgruntled Wavell executives began to consider the possibility of a leveraged buyout, EP was more than willing to consider divestiture; Wavell's growth rates did not meet EP's objectives, and EP had never been comfortable with Wavell's product line. Although the glassware industry was not growing rapidly, there was a constant steady demand for Wavell's product. The company had very stable production costs and good contribution margins, which consistently resulted in a strong steady cash flow. The production equipment was old, but in good condition, and its replacement cost far exceeded its book value. Up until the EP acquisition, Wavell had always been managed well, if conservatively, and had little debt.

Wavell's current sales were $7,000,000 with EBIT of $650,000 and net income of $400,000. Negotiations between Wavell management and EP settled on a purchase price of $2,000,000 (representing a price to EBITDA ratio of 5). Because of the high replacement cost of Wavell's assets, its strong cash flow, and its relatively unencumbered balance sheet, Wavell was able to take on a large amount of debt. Banks supplied $1,200,000 of senior debt at an interest rate of 13%; this debt was secured by the finished goods inventory, and by net property, plant, and equipment, and was to be amortized over a five-year period. An insurance company loan of $600,000 was also arranged in the form of subordinated debt, likewise to be amortized over a five-year period. The insurance company also took an equity position worth $100,000; Wavell was expected to repurchase this equity interest after five years for an amount that would provide the insurance company with a 40% annual yield. Finally, the Wavell management team put up $100,000 as their own equity position.

The following calculations illustrate the cash flow patterns that might be expected following the LBO. First, amortization tables are provided for the bank and insurance company loans:

### Bank Loan[a]

| Year | Interest | Principal | Balance |
|------|----------|-----------|---------|
| 1 | 156,000 | 185,177 | 1,014,823 |
| 2 | 131,927 | 209,250 | 805,573 |
| 3 | 104,724 | 236,453 | 569,120 |
| 4 | 73,986 | 267,191 | 301,929 |
| 5 | 39,248 | 301,929 | — |

[a]$1,200,000 at 13%; annual payment = $341,177.

### Insurance Company Loan[a]

| Year | Interest | Principal | Balance |
|------|----------|-----------|---------|
| 1 | 96,000 | 87,245 | 512,755 |
| 2 | 82,041 | 101,204 | 411,551 |
| 3 | 65,848 | 117,397 | 294,154 |
| 4 | 47,065 | 136,180 | 157,974 |
| 5 | 25,271 | 157,974 | — |

[a]$600,000 at 16%; annual payment = $183,245.

The following pro forma cash flow calculations are made on the basis of a number of conservative assumptions. First, no growth is assumed. The tax rate is assumed to be 40%. Depreciation is calculated on a straight-line basis over a period of 16.67 years (or 6%); accelerated depreciation would clearly enhance cash flows. Furthermore, it is unlikely that debt levels would decline to zero. As the original debt was repaid, it is likely that Wavell would take on additional debt, perhaps long term, to augment the declining interest tax shelter.

### Pro Forma Cash Flows

| | Year 0 | Year 1 | Year 2 | Year 3 | Year 4 | Year 5 |
|---|--------|--------|--------|--------|--------|--------|
| EBIT | 650,000 | 650,000 | 650,000 | 650,000 | 650,000 | 650,000 |
| − Interest | | 252,000 | 213,968 | 170,572 | 121,051 | 64,519 |
| EBT | | 398,000 | 436,032 | 479,428 | 528,949 | 585,481 |
| − Taxes | | 159,200 | 174,413 | 191,771 | 211,580 | 234,192 |
| NI | | 238,800 | 261,619 | 287,657 | 317,369 | 351,289 |
| + Depreciation | | 120,000 | 120,000 | 120,000 | 120,000 | 120,000 |
| CFBDR* | | 358,800 | 381,619 | 407,657 | 437,369 | 471,289 |
| − Principal repaid | | 272,422 | 310,454 | 353,850 | 403,371 | 459,903 |
| Cash flow cushion | | 86,378 | 71,165 | 53,807 | 33,998 | 11,386 |
| Equity | 200,000 | 438,800 | 700,419 | 988,076 | 1,305,445 | 1,656,734 |
| Debt | 1,800,000 | 1,527,578 | 1,217,124 | 863,274 | 459,903 | — |
| Total assets | 2,000,000 | 1,966,378 | 1,917,543 | 1,851,350 | 1,765,348 | 1,656,734 |
| % Debt | 90% | 78% | 63% | 47% | 26% | 0% |

*CFBDR: Cash flow before debt repayment.

If we now assume Wavell is sold at the end of year 5 for book value (again a very conservative assumption given the track record in the pro forma cash flows), we can calculate the annual compounded rate of return on equity as follows:

$$\text{ROE} = \left(\frac{1,656,734}{200,000}\right)^{1/5} - 1 = 53\% \text{ annual compounded rate of return}$$

Since Wavell is required to pay only 40% annually on the insurance company's equity interest, a payment of $537,824 would be sufficient to repurchase this equity. This would leave $1,118,910 for the management group, or an annual return of over 62% on their investment.

## Elements of a Typical LBO Operation

The preceding analysis has been a simplified example of an LBO operation. If we abstract from this example and many more real-world LBOs, the following picture emerges. The first stage of the operation consists of raising the cash required for the buyout and devising a management incentive system. Typically, about 10% of the cash is put up by the investor group headed by the company's top managers and/or buyout specialists. This becomes the equity base of the new firm. Outside investors provide the remainder of the equity. The managers also receive stock price-based incentive compensation in the form of stock options or warrants. Thus, the equity share of management (not including directors) will grow to a higher percentage, possibly to more than 30%. Frequently, managers are also provided with incentive compensation plans based on measures such as increases in share price values.

About 50 to 60% of the required cash is raised by borrowing against the company's assets in secured bank acquisition loans. The bank loan may be syndicated with several commercial banks. This portion of the debt can also be provided by an insurance company or limited partnership specializing in venture capital investments and leveraged buyouts. The rest of the cash is obtained by issuing senior and junior subordinated debt in a private placement (with pension funds, insurance companies, venture capital firms, and so on) or public offering as "high-yield" notes or bonds (that is, junk bonds). Subordinated debt is often referred to as "mezzanine money" and may carry payment-in-kind provisions. If adverse surprises result in the inability to meet interest obligations on portions of mezzanine financing, the debt holders receive more of the same paper in lieu of cash interest payments.

In the second stage of the operation, the organizing sponsor group buys all the outstanding shares of the company and takes it private (in the stock-purchase format) or purchases all the assets of the company (in the asset-purchase format). In the latter case, the buying group forms a new, privately held corporation. To reduce the debt by paying off a part of the bank loan, the new owners sell off some parts of the acquired firm.

In the third stage, the management strives to increase profits and cash flows by cutting operating costs and changing marketing strategies. It will consolidate or reorganize production facilities, improve inventory control and accounts receivables management, improve product quality, product mix, customer service, and pricing, trim employment, and try to extract better terms from suppliers. It may even lay off employees and cut spending on research and new plants and equipment as long as these are necessary to meet payment on the swollen debt. (However, in reviewing business plans, lenders would require that provisions for capital expenditures be adequate.)

In the fourth stage, the investor group may take the company public again if the "leaner and meaner" company emerges stronger and the goals of the group are achieved. This reverse LBO is effected through a public equity offering, referred to as a secondary initial public offering (SIPO). One purpose of this reconversion to public ownership is to create liquidity for existing stockholders. Aside from this, a study of 72 firms engaging in reverse LBOs over the period 1976–1987 reveals that 86% of the firms intended to use the SIPO proceeds to lower the company's leverage (Muscarella and Vetsuypens, 1990). Only eight out of 72 firms raised the funds for capital expenditures. The reverse LBOs are undertaken mostly by ex post successful LBO companies, and indeed the equity participants at the time of the LBO realized a median return of 1,965.6% on their equity investment, or a median annualized rate of return of 268.4% by the time of the SIPO. (The median length of time between the LBO and the SIPO was 29 months.)

## Conditions and Circumstances of Going-Private Buyouts in the 1980s

For LBOs of the 1980s, typical targets included manufacturing firms in basic, nonregulated industries with at least predictable and/or low financing (capital expenditure) requirements. Stability and predictability of earnings were essential in the face of substantial interest payments and loan amortization. The financing needs of very high-growth firms might put a strain on debt service capability. High-tech firms were considered less appropriate because they generally have a shorter history of demonstrated profitability, as well as greater business risk; they generally have fewer leveragable assets. Furthermore they command high P/E multiples well above book value because of future growth opportunities.

These generalizations are supported by the empirical data developed by Lehn and Poulsen (1988). They studied a sample of 108 leveraged buyouts during the period 1980–1984. Almost half of the firms were in five industries: retailing, textiles, food processing, apparel, and bottled and canned soft drinks. Note that these are all consumer nondurable goods industries for which the income elasticity of demand would be relatively low. Hence, these industries would be least subject to fluctuations in sales as the level of gross national product fluctuated. Note also that all of these are mature industries, with limited growth opportunities.

The success of an LBO in the 1980s was enhanced by a track record of capable management. The company should have a strong market position in its industry to enable it to withstand economic fluctuations and competitors' assaults. The balance sheet should be highly liquid; it should show a large, relatively unencumbered asset base for use as collateral, particularly a high proportion of tangible assets whose fair market value exceeds net book value.

The transaction required sufficient leverage to maximize return on equity, but not so much as to drain funds needed to sustain growth. Lenders were attracted by interest rates 3 to 5 percentage points above the prime rate and by the characteristics of the company and its collateral. Borrowing capacity was favorably affected by large amounts of cash or cash equivalents, and undervalued assets (hidden equity) whose market value exceeded depreciated book value. Lenders may also look to subsidiaries of the LBO candidate whose liquidation would not impact ongoing operations. In addition, lenders such as venture capital and insurance companies, which also take an equity interest in the LBO, look to the high rate of return they expect on their equity participation. Last, but by no means least, lenders must have confidence in the management group spearheading the LBO, whether incumbent or external. The managers involved typically have a proven record as highly capable executives. They are betting their reputations on the success of the venture, and are highly motivated by the potential for large personal wealth gains that might not be achievable in larger public corporations.

Among the sources of MBO targets are divestitures of unwanted divisions by public companies, privately owned businesses whose current growth rate is insufficient to provide opportunities for capable management or to attract corporate acquirers, and public companies whose shares are selling at low earnings multiples representing a substantial discount from book value.

## Empirical Results on Going Private in the 1980s

The earliest comprehensive study of going-private transactions was by DeAngelo, DeAngelo, and Rice (1984). Their sample consisted of 72 firms that made 72 initial and nine subsequent (revived) going-private proposals during the period 1973–1980. The median market value of total equity was about $6 million for the sample of 45 pure going-private proposals (that is, without third-party equity participation in the private firm) and somewhat over $15 million for 23 leveraged buyout proposals. Thus, the firms were relatively small. In addition, management held a relatively large ownership position. In 72 going-private proposals management's mean preoffer ownership fraction was 45% with a median measure of 51%. For the 23 LBOs with third-party participation, the mean and median were 32% and 33%, respectively.

DeAngelo, DeAngelo, and Rice found that the average change in stockholder wealth at announcement was a plus 22%, which was highly significant from a statistical standpoint. The cumulative increase in stockholder wealth over the 40 days including the announcement date was over 30%. They note that public stockholder gains measured as the average premium above market (two months before the proposal) were over 56% in 57 sample proposals involving all payment in cash.

DeAngelo, DeAngelo, and Rice also tested for the effects of the announcement of a going-private withdrawal. Their sample was 18 firms for the period 1973–1980. The announcement effect was a negative change in stockholder wealth of almost 9%. However, since the cumulative prediction error for the 40 days up to the announcement date was almost 13%, the cumulative prediction error for the 40 days through the announcement date was a plus 4%. During the subsequent 40 days the cumulative prediction error rises to about 8%. They note three potential explanations for the positive returns net of both proposal and withdrawal announcement effects. One is an information effect that causes a permanent upward revaluation of the firm's prospects. Second, a positive probability may remain that managers will revive the going-private proposal at a future date. Third, the positive return may reflect the possibility that another party will offer to acquire the firm.

The Lehn and Poulsen study (1989) covered 284 going-private transactions for the period 1980–1987. The mean equity value for the Lehn and Poulsen sample was $191 million. The size of going-private transactions increased significantly during the period covered. In a separate study, Lehn and Poulsen (1988) reported that the average pre-LBO debt/equity ratio for a sample of 58 firms was about 46%. For the post-LBO period the average debt/equity ratio rose to over 552%. Thus, substantial increases in leverage took place.

Lehn and Poulsen (1988) found that the average net-of-market stock price reaction to the announcement for 92 leveraged buyouts was slightly over 20%, measured over a period of 20 days before the announcement to 20 days after the announcement. The result was highly significant from a statistical standpoint. The average value of the premium paid in the LBO offer compared to the market price of the firm's common stock 20 trading days prior to the announcement was 41%, calculated for the 72 leveraged buyouts in the sample that were all cash offers. These results are somewhat lower than those found by DeAngelo, DeAngelo, and Rice. The Lehn and Poulsen sample represented larger firms for a later period. Also the Lehn and Poulsen study covered LBOs during the 1980–1984 period when the takeover and restructuring market was much more active. In addition, they measured the premium from a reference point 20 days prior to the announcement whereas DeAngelo, DeAngelo, and Rice measured the premium from a reference point two months before the announcement.

Another empirical study was performed by Lowenstein (1985). His sample was 28 management buyout proposals made from 1979 to 1984; each valued at least $100 million to the shareholders at the winning bid price. The percentage of shares owned by management for the Lowenstein sample was much smaller than for the DeAngelo, DeAngelo, and Rice sample. It was only 3.8% when measured by the median and 6.5% measured by the mean. In 15 new companies formed as the result of going private, management shares increased to 10.4% measured by the median and to 24.3% measured by the mean.

Lowenstein also measured the premium of the winning bid over the market price 30 days before the first significant announcement. He found that on all bids the premium was 58% measured by the median and 56% when measured by the mean. However, the size of the premium was higher the more bids that were involved in the going-private transactions. When three or more bids were received, the premium rose to 76% when measured by the median and 69% when measured by the mean. The premium of 11 successful third-party bids over the management bid was 8% (median) and 14% (mean). Lowenstein argued strongly for the creation of an auction that would ensure that multiple bids would be received. He acknowledged difficulties in implementing such a proposal. In addition, we would observe that the relatively small percentage of increase in third-party bids over the management bids casts doubt on the need for such a proposal. Furthermore, the Lowenstein findings corroborate those of DeAngelo, DeAngelo, and Rice in observing premiums for public stockholders of 50% or more over their market price a month or two before the announcement. This would appear to be a very substantial reward to public shareholders. If they left nothing "on the table" for the entrepreneurs involved in the LBO activity, it would leave little incentive for the transactions to take place. The subsequent losses to the public shareholders would be much greater than the relatively small kicking up of the bid when third-party offers are involved. Besides, market competition assures that if the entrepreneurs are taking too much, this will stimulate other nonmanagement outside offers. But in any event it is difficult to feel that a great injustice is done to the public shareholders or the subsequent minority shareholders because they have received premiums exceeding 50%.

Later studies also found large premiums and abnormal announcement returns to prebuyout shareholders (Kaplan, 1989a; Muscarella and Vetsuypens 1990; Travlos and Cornett, 1993).

For divisional management buyouts, Hite and Vetsuypens (1989) found small but statistically significant wealth gains to parent company shareholders. The mean abnormal return during the two-day period surrounding the buyout announcement was 0.55% for their sample of 151 unit MBOs. Because the mean sale price of the divisions represented only 16.6% of the market value of equity of an average seller, the abnormal return would translate into 3.3% for a full LBO, which is much lower than the gains found for LBOs above. The authors suggest that divisional buyouts reallocate ownership of corporate assets to higher-valued uses and that parent company shareholders share in the expected benefits of this change in ownership structure. For a sample of 45 divisional buyouts that subsequently went public (after an average period of 34 months), Muscarella and Vetsuypens (1990) reported a mean abnormal return of 1.98% to the seller in the two days around the announcement.

Harlow and Howe (1993) found that there was little insider trading before third-party LBOs. However, they found evidence that insider trading prior to management LBOs was associated with private managerial information. But the net buying by insiders resulted from decreased levels of insider sales of stock rather than from increased levels of purchases. In the MBO subsample, they found a positive correlation between the offer premium and the amount of abnormal net buying by insiders.

## Sources of Gains

The empirical evidence is consistent among studies in finding that the premiums paid are 40% or more of the market price of the stock a month or two before the announcement of the buyout. The standard residual analysis shows that these gains are substantially sustained in stock price performance after the completion of the change in ownership control. What are the sources of these large gains? A number of explanations have been offered: (1) taxes, (2) management incentives, (3) wealth transfer effects, (4) asymmetric information and underpricing, and (5) efficiency considerations. Each is considered in turn.

### Tax Benefits

The tax benefits are clearly there. The question is whether they are the only factor, the major factor, or simply a facilitating factor added to more fundamental business and economic forces. It is difficult to quantify the degree. Some students of the subject ascribe a major role to taxes. Lowenstein (1985), for example, argued that most of the premium paid is financed from tax savings. He stated that the new company can expect to operate tax free for as long as five to six years. Of course, an LBO is often sold after about this period of time when its debt/equity ratio has been pulled down from about 10 to 1 or under.

The sources of the tax gain are standard and have been detailed in previous pages. They include the following. The high leverage provides the benefits of interest savings. Asset step-ups can provide higher asset values for depreciation expenses. This tax advantage became much more difficult under the Tax Reform Act of 1986. The accelerated depreciation provisions of the 1981 ERTA had enhanced this benefit. Lowenstein (1985, p. 760) pointed out that the extent of write-up of assets depended in part on the ability to assign large value to items for which there is little recapture (inventory, film libraries, mineral resources, or real estate) than to items for which recapture may be substantial (equipment).

Tax benefits were further augmented by the Tax Reform Act of 1984, which broadened the benefits of the use of ESOPs. The ESOP purchases the shares using borrowed funds. The borrowings are secured by the employer's schedule of contributions to the fund. Both the interest and principal on the ESOP are deductible and the lender can exclude one-half of the interest income from taxable income. These are substantial benefits indeed. These changes increased the use of ESOPs in management buyouts, representing tangible evidence that this particular tax factor was of importance. However, Kaplan (1989a) suggested that ESOP loans are infrequently used due to non-tax costs. One such cost pointed out by Kaplan is that all contributing employees share in the equity and this will not leave an adequate equity stake to the managers and the buyout promoter.

Kaplan (1989b) also provided empirical evidence on the potential value of tax benefits. While it is not difficult to estimate current tax savings on new buyout debt, valuation of these savings flows is dependent on, among other factors, whether the debt is permanent and the appropriate marginal tax rate applied to the interest deduction.

Further, there is the argument that the interest rate on corporate debt is higher to compensate for higher personal taxation on interest income than equity income, and thus the use of debt to obtain tax savings may have no value. Assuming a marginal tax rate of 46% and permanent new debt yielded interest deductions worth a median 1.297 times the premium. A 30% tax rate and a maturity of eight years for new debt implied a median value equal to 0.262 times the premium. In Kaplan's sample of 76 companies, 33 were known to have elected to step up the basis of their assets, and the median value was estimated at 0.304 times the premium.

These tax benefits appear large but Kaplan argued that they are predictable and thus appropriable by the prebuyout shareholders. However, Kaplan found that only a portion of the tax benefits could be attributed to unused debt capacity or the inefficient use of tax benefits prior to buyout. This implies that a large portion of the tax benefits were the result of buyout and the buyout structure may be necessary to realize those benefits. It turns out that the buyout companies eliminated their federal taxes in the first two years after the buyout.

In regression analyses, the excess return to prebuyout shareholders is significantly related to the potential tax benefits generated by the buyout, but the excess return to postbuyout shareholders is not. Kaplan interpreted this result as indicating that prebuyout shareholders capture most of the tax benefits. The premium paid to prebuyout shareholders is also found to be positively related to the pre-LBO tax liability to equity ratio by Lehn and Poulsen (1988). This is interpreted as evidence that tax benefits play a significant role in LBOs.

The preceding findings on strong tax benefits are at odds with the regression result of Travlos and Cornett (1993) that capital structure change-induced effects fail to explain the abnormal returns experienced at the announcement of buyouts. One reason for this result might be that both the dependent and the independent variables only partly capture the full effects that they are supposed to measure. Travlos and Cornett (1993) defend their results by stating that increased leverage serves no long-term purpose but rather "functions primarily as a part of the mechanism to take the company private." The temporary nature of at least some portion of the new debt was also shown by Muscarella and Vetsuypens (1990). Their sample of 72 reverse LBO firms had an average debt to total value ratio of over 0.90 at the time of the LBO, an average debt to total asset ratio of 0.78 prior to the SIPO and the same ratio of 0.60 after the SIPO.

The preceding results indicate that tax factors can improve a deal, but come into play if some underlying business factors are also operating. This is where other factors come into consideration.

## Management Incentives and Agency Cost Effects

It is argued that management's ownership stake is enhanced by the LBO or MBO so that their incentives are stronger for improved performance. Some profitable investment proposals call for disproportionate effort of managers so that they will be undertaken only if managers are given a correspondingly disproportionate share of the proposal's income (Easterbrook and Fischel, 1982). However, such managerial compensation contracts might be viewed as "overly generous" by outside shareholders. In this case, going-private buyouts facilitate compensation arrangements that induce managers to undertake those proposals (DeAngelo, DeAngelo, and Rice, 1984; Travlos and Cornett, 1993). This reasoning is similar to the argument that the threat of a hostile takeover decreases incentives for managers and employees to invest in firm-specific human capital (DeAngelo and DeAngelo, 1987, p. 107). Going-private buyouts can guarantee compensation for those investments.

When information on managerial performance is costly, incumbent management can be mistakenly replaced. Managers waste resources to defend their position to potential proxy contestants and to outside shareholders. They may undertake projects that are less profitable but have payoffs more easily observable by outsiders (DeAngelo and DeAngelo, 1985). Going private may eliminate these costs. In many buyouts, the promoters retain a large equity stake and serve on the board. The equity stake and their desire to protect their reputation as efficient promoters give them the incentive to closely monitor postbuyout management. This will decrease the information asymmetry between the managers and shareholders. In this view, the concentrated ownership resulting from an LBO represents reunification of ownership and control, which must reduce agency costs.

Finally, free cash flows motivate managers to use them in self-aggrandizing expenditures rather than to pay them out as dividends. Increasing debt through leveraged buyouts commits the cash flows to debt payment, which is an effective substitute for dividend payment. Managers have less discretion over debt payments than over dividends. Thus, the increased debt reduces managerial discretion in the allocation of free cash flows; the agency costs of free cash flows will be decreased in LBOs (Jensen, 1986). If managers are risk averse, the increased debt will also put pressure on managers and give them an incentive to improve the firm's performance to prevent bankruptcy (because bankruptcy will cause a decline in their compensation and value of human capital). The LBO thus represents a debt-bonding activity; it bonds (precommits) managers to meet newly set targets.

These agency-cost arguments contrast with the notion that the internal controls of the firm already align managers' interests to those of the stockholders. The internal controls are compensation arrangements and settling up, stock options, bonuses based on performance, and surveillance by the board of directors. If internal controls do not take hold sufficiently, the market for corporate control and the threat of takeovers will ensure that managers operate to their full potential. However, a study by Baker, Jensen, and Murphy (1988) found that actual executive compensation contracts are insufficient to provide optimal incentives for managers; and that most CEOs hold trivial fractions of their firms' stock, although stock ownership generally swamps incentives generated by compensation. The median fractional ownership of CEOs in their sample of 73 large manufacturing firms was only 0.16%, while the average is 1.2%. The CEO salary plus bonus changes only two cents for every $1,000 change in equity value. They ascribe the low relation between pay and performance to pressures from other stakeholders and the public including the media.

Roden and Lewellen (1995) analyzed capital structures of LBOs to test traditional theories of capital structure. Their sample covered 107 LBOs formed during the period 1981–1990 accounting for about two-thirds of the total dollar volume of LBO activity during that period. The postbuyout capital structure of their LBO sample resembled what they call "an inverted pyramid." At the top was senior secured debt financing by banks representing just over 60% of total funds raised. The next layer was mezzanine financing consisting of unsecured subordinated long-term debt securities (junk bonds) of about 25%. Preferred stock was 4% and common equity about 7%. These patterns were consistent with prior studies. Within these averages, cross-sectional variations were observed. Their econometric analysis suggested that the prospective cash flow profile of the firm greatly influenced the capital structure. They presented a balancing model of the capital structure decision process. Leveraged-related benefits included the motivating and disciplining effects of debt on management and the tax shields provided by debt. They saw agency costs of high levels of debt and potential financial distress associated with excessive debt service obligations.

Empirical evidence consistent with the management incentive rationale is reported in other studies. First, ownership shares of management are increased substantially after MBOs. For a sample of 76 MBOs in 1980–1986, Kaplan (1989a) reported prebuyout and postbuyout equity ownership of management. The median prebuyout ownerships of the CEO, all managers, and all managers and directors were 1.4%, 5.88%, and 19.3%, respectively. (The corresponding mean values were 7.13%, 12.20%, and 22.89%.) The median postbuyout ownership fractions of the CEO and all managers were 6.40% and 22.63%, respectively. Thus, in terms of median values, the management ownership increased by about three times the prebuyout value. For a reverse LBO sample, Muscarella and Vetsuypens (1990) reported the before-SIPO (postbuyout) and after-SIPO management equity ownership fractions. The median before-SIPO fractions for the most highly paid officer, three most highly paid officers, and all officers and directors were 9.2%, 26.1%, and 61.6%, respectively. The management ownership remained high even after the firm went public through a SIPO. The median after-SIPO fractions were 6.5%, 18.8%, and 44.2%. Evidence on the concentration of ownership is provided by Smith (1990). The median post-MBO ownership share of all officers, outside directors, and other major holders was 95.26%. The corresponding pre-MBO ownership share was 75.45%.

The second set of evidence on management incentives was provided by Muscarella and Vetsuypens. They documented various management incentive plans in LBO firms. Almost all firms in their sample (69 out of 72) had implemented at least one type of incentive plan under private ownership and about 75% of the sample firms had at least two separate incentive plans. Among the different types of incentive plans, stock option plans and stock appreciation rights were the most popular. The importance of incentive plans was also vividly described in most anecdotes on individual LBOs. For example, see Anders (1988).

The third and most important evidence on the present hypothesis is the operating performance of LBO firms. However, it should be pointed out in advance that the following results on operating performance may be subject to a selection bias because the reverse LBO firms or firms with postbuyout data available might be only the more successful ones. Muscarella and Vetsuypens described the multiple restructuring activities under private ownership. Based on examination of the SIPO prospecti of the firms that went public again after the LBO, they found more than two-thirds of all firms (54 out of 72) disclosed at least one restructuring activity undertaken since the LBO. Among the activities were asset redeployment (reorganization of production facilities, divestitures, and so on), initiation of cost reduction programs, changes in marketing strategies involving product mix, product quality, pricing, and customer service. Judging from the tone of the offering prospecti, the authors suggested that these activities "represent a significant departure from pre-LBO strategies which would not have been implemented by the predecessor company" (p. 1390). As a result of these restructuring activities, the firms under private ownership realized substantial improvement in operating performance. In 35 cases for which data were available, total sales increased by 9.4% in real terms for the median firm between the LBO and SIPO (a median period of 29 months) and gross profits and operating profits increased 27.0 and 45.4%, respectively.

Kaplan (1989a) also provided evidence of improved operating performance following an LBO. The level of operating income in LBO firms increased more than in other firms in the same industry during the first two years after the LBO, but sales growth rates were lower. The results on operating income and sales suggested that the operating margins of LBO firms would improve relative to their industries. Statistical tests by Kaplan confirmed this proposition. One potential source of operating improvement was found to be in the area of working-capital management as the inventory/sales ratio declined in the postbuyout years.

Similar results were obtained by Smith (1990). She found that both the profit or before-tax operating margin and the ratio of sales to operating assets or employees increased significantly relative to other firms in the same industry. Improvement in working-capital management was evidenced by both a reduction in the inventory holding period and receivables collection period. There was little evidence that cutbacks in research and development, advertising, and maintenance were responsible for the increase in operating cash flows. Although the ratio of capital expenditures to sales was reduced after the MBO, this should not affect the short-run operating gains. Smith also provided regression results that suggested a positive relation between the change in operating returns and the changes in financial leverage and percentage stockholdings by officers, outside directors, and other major stockholders. These results were consistent with the debt-bonding effect, managerial-incentive effect, and the improved monitoring (concentrated ownership) effect. Smith conducted various empirical analyses to provide evidence that the improved post-MBO performance was not attributable to the sample selection procedures in her study. Overall, the results did not tend to indicate selection bias. Smith also considered whether favorable inside information on future cash flows explained the observed increase in operating returns associated with MBOs and provided indirect evidence that the improved performance did not reflect the realization of gains privately anticipated by the buyout group.

Travlos and Cornett found a statistically significant negative correlation between the abnormal return to prebuyout shareholders and the P/E ratio of the firm relative to its industry. They interpreted this result as being consistent with the joint hypothesis that the more severe the agency problems of the going private firms, the lower their P/E ratios; and that the lower this ratio, the larger the room for improvement, and thus the greater the efficiency gains to be obtained by taking the firm private. But this interpretation may not be correct because a low P/E ratio may simply mean lower growth opportunities. The Jensen hypothesis predicted that the LBO firms were mature firms with limited growth opportunities.

The theory of agency costs involving free cash flow also has empirical support. Lehn and Poulsen (1989) posit that a direct relationship between measures of cash flows and premiums paid to prebuyout shareholders was consistent with Jensen's hypothesis. Their data for 149 LBOs in the 1984–1987 period showed highly significant direct relationships between the undistributed cash flow to equity value ratio and the premium paid even after controlling for the effects of tax savings (by using the tax to equity variable). The likelihood of going private was also directly related to the cash flow to equity value ratio in their data for LBOs and matched control firms. Further evidence that appeared consistent with the free cash flow argument of Jensen included the results that most LBOs took place in mature industries and that the growth rates and capital expenditures of LBO firms (without controlling for divestitures after the buyout) were lower than their industry control sample in both the pre- and postbuyout periods (Kaplan, 1989a; Lehn and Poulsen, 1989).

However, one potential difficulty of the free cash flow argument is that it does not directly predict the strengthened incentive compensation schemes after the buyout, which are evidenced in the study by Muscarella and Vetsuypens. They also found an elasticity of compensation (defined as salary plus bonus) to sales of 0.46 for the most highly paid officer in their sample, whereas Murphy (1985) reported that the typical elasticity appeared to be about 0.3. But it may be the case that going private enabled the firm to institute more incentive compensation plans, which may not be possible for public firms due to the political process (Baker, Jensen, and Murphy, 1988). Holthausen and

Larcker (1996) argued that the performance and equity ownership incentive effects have not been fully demonstrated.

### Wealth Transfer Effects

Critics of leveraged buyouts argue that the payment of premiums in these transactions may represent wealth transfers to shareholders from other stakeholders including bondholders, preferred stockholders, employees, and the government. Increased efficiency cannot automatically be inferred from the rise in the equity value. Because debt is increased in LBOs, at least part of the increased value can be offset by a reduction in the value of the firm's outstanding bonds and preferred stock. Many bond covenants do protect existing bondholders in the event of changes of control, debt issues, and so forth, but some do not. The newly issued debt may not be subordinated to the outstanding bonds and/or may have shorter duration than the outstanding bonds. Further, the "absolute priority rule" for a senior security may not be strictly adhered to in bankruptcy court decisions.

Empirical evidence on the change in the value of outstanding debt at the time of LBO announcement is mixed. While Lehn and Poulsen (1988) found no evidence that (nonconvertible) bondholders and preferred stockholders lose value, Travlos and Cornett reported statistically significant losses at the announcement of going-private proposals. However, the losses were small relative to the gains to the prebuyout shareholders, which implies that wealth transfer cannot be an economically significant factor in explaining the shareholder gain. Such anecdotes as the lawsuit filed against RJR Nabisco by large bondholders do suggest that bondholders can lose substantially in certain cases (Quigley, 1988, pp. 1, 5). In the Nabisco case, it was charged that its $5 billion in highly rated bonds had lost nearly 20% ($1 billion) in market value since the announcement of a management-led buyout proposal involving new borrowing of $16 billion (Greenwald, 1988, p. 69).

Warga and Welch (1993) demonstrated that the source of bond price data greatly influences the empirical results. Previous studies used exchange-based data such as the Standard & Poor's Bond Guide data. Warga and Welch used trader-quoted data from a major investment bank. They give an illustration of the role of the data source. In an earlier study, Asquith and Wizman (1990) found LBO risk-adjusted announcement bondholder returns of −3.2%. Warga and Welch found negative returns of about 7% in a set of overlapping bonds for which the Asquith and Wizman data show a −3.8% return. They note that when they "either properly aggregate returns among correlated bonds or if we exclude RJR Nabisco" the S&P data source suggests no significant loss of bondholder wealth. When they use their trader-quoted data, however, they find a risk-adjusted bondholder loss of about 6%. However, these losses in the value of debt were only 7% of the size of shareholder gains. Their conclusion is that while bondholders do suffer negative returns, their losses account for only a very small percentage of shareholder gains.

Wealth may also be transferred from current employees to the new investors in hostile takeovers (Shleifer and Summers, 1988). The hostile bidder can break implicit contracts between the firm and employees by reducing employment and lowering wages to expropriate quasi-rents accruing to their past firm-specific investments. Whether this argument can be extended to leveraged buyouts is an empirical question, although the supposed hostility against existing employees does not appear to be present in most LBOs. Management turnover in buyout firms is lower than in an average firm, although sometimes a new management team is brought in after the LBO (Muscarella and Vetsuypens, 1990). The number of employees grows more slowly in an LBO firm than in others in the same industry and sometimes even decreases, but this appears to be the result of postbuyout divestitures and more efficient use of labor (Kaplan, 1989a; Muscarella and Vetsuypens, 1990).

There is also the argument that the tax benefits in an LBO constitute a subsidy from the public and cause a loss in tax revenues of the government (Lowenstein, 1985). Indeed, as discussed earlier, there is evidence that the premia paid in LBOs are positively related to potential tax benefits at the corporate level. However, the net effect of an LBO on government tax revenues may be positive (Morrow, 1988). Shareholders pay ordinary income taxes on the capital gains realized on the sale of their stock in the LBO tender offer. Of course, these gains might be realized even without the LBO, but the shareholders could postpone the capital gains taxes to a later date or even eliminate them by bequeathing stocks in an estate. If the firm becomes stronger and goes public at a later date, which is suggested by the empirical evidence reviewed earlier, then the LBO investor group will pay capital gains taxes and the firm will pay more corporate taxes. Amihud also pointed out that many of the tax benefits could be realized without LBOs and some advantages such as the stepped-up tax basis of assets are almost totally eliminated now.

### Asymmetric Information and Underpricing

Large premiums paid by the buyout investors are also consistent with the argument that managers or the investors have more information on the value of the firm than the public shareholders. In this theory, a buyout proposal signals to the market that future operating income will be larger than previously expected or that the firm is less risky than perceived by the public.

A variant of this theory is that the investor group believes the new company is worth more than the purchase price and thus the prebuyout shareholders are receiving less than adequately informed shareholders would receive. This theory amounts to the claim that the MBO proposal cannot reveal much of the information and establish a competitive price for the target firm (despite the fact that a special committee of the board of directors who do not participate in the new company has to approve the proposal).

Kaplan (1989a) provided evidence that runs counter to these arguments. He found that informed persons (managers and directors) often do not participate in the buyout even though these nonparticipants typically hold large equity stakes in the buyout firm (a median share of 10% compared to 4.67% held by the management participants). Also, as indicated earlier, Smith (1990) provided indirect evidence that asymmetric information cannot explain the improved performance of bought-out firms. For instance, MBO proposals that fail due to board/stockholder rejection, withdrawal, or a higher outside bid are not followed by any increase in operating returns among the involved firms.

### Efficiency Considerations

The other arguments are related to efficiency considerations. The decision process can be more efficient under private ownership. Major new programs do not have to be justified by detailed studies and reports to the board of directors. Action can be taken more speedily, and sometimes getting a new investment program under way early is critical for its success. In addition, a public firm must publish information that may disclose vital and competitively sensitive information to rival firms. These arguments are difficult to evaluate and empirical evidence on these has yet to come. Stockholders' servicing costs and other related expenses do not appear to be a major factor in going private (Travlos and Cornett, 1993).

### Evidence on Postbuyout Equity Value

We now turn to statistical evidence on how the investment in an LBO has fared and what has determined the rate of return. Muscarella and Vetsuypens (1990) first compared the total value of the firm at the time of the LBO (the purchase price paid plus the book value of debt assumed) to the value of the firm at the time of its SIPO (the book value of outstanding debt plus the market value of equity minus any proceeds from the SIPO used to retire existing debt). The median rate of change in firm value for the 41 companies that went public again was 89.0% for the entire period between an LBO and the subsequent SIPO. The mean rate was 169.7%. The median annualized rate of change was 36.6%.

The total shareholder wealth change was positively and statistically significantly correlated with the fraction of shares owned by officers and directors. Thus, larger shareholder gains under private ownership are associated with greater managerial stock ownership. Also, the correlation between the size-adjusted measure of salary and shareholder wealth was positive and statistically significant. This finding is consistent with the notion that well-compensated managers work harder to increase shareholder wealth. But the causality might be the reverse. The change in equity values was also associated with the improvements in accounting measures of performance. Thus, it is possible that the improved corporate performance led both to increased managerial compensation and higher equity value. Further, the improved corporate performance does not disprove that exploiting inside information alone can explain postbuyout shareholder gains.

Other interesting results were also obtained by Kaplan (1991). He first noted that returns on *leveraged* equity in a period of rising stock prices should be very large because interest payments are fixed. Thus, the really interesting comparison should be between the total return to all capital (debt and equity) invested in the buyout and the return on a stock index like the S&P 500. He found for his sample of 21 buyouts that the median excess return to postbuyout investors (both debt and equity) was 26.1% in excess of the return on the S&P 500 (the length of time is not stated). He suggested that this excess return is close to the premium earned by prebuyout shareholders. This implied that the prebuyout shareholders actually share handsomely in the gains to the buyout. Because the 21 companies in the sample had publicly available valuation of their securities, the result may be subject to selection bias; that is, they may represent the more successful LBOs.

Finally, Kaplan's regression analysis showed that the excess return to postbuyout investors was significantly related to the change in operating income, but not to the potential tax benefits. It is shown that the prebuyout shareholders capture most of the tax benefits that become publicly available information at the time of the LBO.

Degeorge and Zeckhauser (1993) analyzed a particular aspect of reverse LBO decisions. They found that on average reverse LBOs experienced an industry-adjusted rise in operating performance of 6.90% during the year before an initial public offering (IPO). In the year following an IPO, these same firms saw an industry-adjusted decline in operating performance of 2.59%.

Degeorge and Zeckhauser attributed the rise and fall of operating performance to information asymmetries and pure selection. More specifically, if management, and not the market, knew the expected profitability of the company, management would use this asymmetry and take the firm public only during exceptional years. Managers also had an incentive to quietly improve current performance at the expense of future profitability. The complementary theory of pure selection relied on the behavior, or perceived behavior, of IPO purchasers. Degeorge and Zeckhauser hypothesized that purchasers look at the strength of current performance and future growth. Subsequently, only strong companies had the ability to go public and experience normal mean reversion following the IPO.

Trends in operating performance do not translate into market inefficiencies. The market apparently understands the manager's incentive for performance manipulation and pure selection. Stock returns do not penalize the company for expected poor performance following the reverse LBO. In fact, reverse LBOs tend to outperform their peer group, although not significantly.

Mian and Rosenfeld (1993) also studied the long-run performance of reverse LBOs. They observed that their results were consistent with Muscarella and Vetsuypens (1990). They studied 85 firms that had reverse LBO during the period 1983–1989. They measured stock price performance for a three-year period beginning one day after the firm went public. They found evidence of significant positive cumulative abnormal returns. They observed that this performance differed from the performance of IPOs as reported by Ritter (1991).

Their deeper analysis found that about 39% of their sample firms were taken over within three years after going public. The CARs using the Comparable Firm Index for the first three years were 4.65%, 21.96%, and 21.05%. Most of the takeovers took place during the second year when the CARs were the highest. Firms that were taken over outperformed comparable investments by over 100%. For the sample of firms that were not taken over, the CAR was essentially zero. This suggests that the firms taken over had qualities attractive to the bidding firm. Mian and Rosenfeld also found that 79% of the acquired firms had gone private with an active investor. This suggests that the firm's interest in being taken over reflects the desire of the main investor to liquidate their ownership.

Holthausen and Larcker (1996) also studied the financial performance of reversed leveraged buyouts. They analyzed a sample of 90 LBOs that returned to public ownership between 1983 and 1988. They related changes in accounting performance to incentive variables. The firms outperformed their industries for the four years following the reverse LBO, with some weak evidence of a decline in accounting performance over the period. The firms increased capital expenditure subsequent to the public offering; working capital levels also increased. The authors observed that firm performance decreased with declines in levels of equity ownership by management and other insiders. They found no evidence that performance after the IPO was related to changes in leverage. The fact that capital expenditures increased after the LBO was consistent with these firms being cash constrained while they were LBOs. This would suggest that the high leverage during an LBO constrained investments, but that the reduced leverage after the IPO facilitated efficient investments.

Holthausen and Larcker also found that for the firms that were still public three years after the IPO, a median decline in ownership by management insiders was 15% and by nonmanagement insiders 20%. They also found that board structure moves toward the standard patterns of non-LBO firms.

## THE CORRECTION PERIOD 1991–1992

We have seen from the previous materials on LBOs that the investors in the companies that were bought out received substantial premiums. The mean premiums were on the order of magnitude of 35%, similar to the premiums found in cash takeovers. The groups that formed the LBOs and MBOs, on average, made returns in excess of the S&P 500 over the holding period as private companies. Returns to shareholders in the LBOs that again went public (the SIPOs) outperformed comparable companies over a four-year period following the reverse LBO. These performance results had at least two forms of selection bias. LBOs that were able to return to the public markets were the relatively more successful ones. In addition, most published empirical studies to date cover LBOs formed mostly during the early part of the 1980s. LBOs formed in the latter half of the 1980s did not perform as well (Kaplan and Stein, 1993).

Opler (1992) found that LBOs in the 1985–1989 period were associated by operating improvements comparable to those in earlier transactions. Kaplan and Stein (1993) found similar results for the later LBOs. However, despite improvements in operating performance, many of the later buyouts experienced financial distress. The defects in the later LBO deals were due to the relatively high prices paid and weakened financial structures for the LBOs formed. In addition, management, investment bankers, and other deal promoters, were able to take more cash up front, which also weakened the structure and incentives in the later deals (Kaplan and Stein, 1993).

Both some general economic principles and factors more specific to LBO activity explained the deterioration in the quality of LBOs in the second half of the 1980s. In an enterprise system, high return segments of the economy attracted more financial resources. Investments flowed to areas of high prospective returns (Weston and Chen, 1994). This occurred with the LBOs. Many specialized LBO funds were formed. More banks and other financial intermediaries participated. The dollar volume of funds seeking to organize LBO deals began to exceed the number of good prospects available. The successful LBOs of the early 1980s were able to make purchases on very favorable terms; purchase prices were as low as three to four times prospective cash flows (EBITDA). However, in the late 1980s the quantity of funds exceeded the availability of good prospects. As a consequence, the price to expected cash flow multiples rose sharply. The difference between the winning price and the next highest bid was often very substantial. Winner's curse operated in the extreme.

Public high-yield debt substituted for both private subordinated debt and "strip" financing in which subordinated debt holders also received equity stakes. This raised the cost of reorganizing companies that encountered financial difficulties.

Commercial banks took smaller positions. They sought to reduce their commitments, shorten maturities, and required an accelerated program for required principal repayments. As a consequence, the coverage of debt service declined. In some cases, coverage ratios were less than 1. Sometimes the first interest payment in the buyout could be achieved only if asset sales were accomplished and substantial cost reductions were achieved. Some deals utilized high-yield bonds with either zero coupons or interest payments consisting of more of the same securities, payment in kind (PIK). Cash requirements for debt service were postponed for several years after the formation of the LBO.

Consistent with the general economic principles about the flow of resources to high return areas, the leveraged buyout market began making some "corrections." Allen (1996, p. 22) observed that movement toward lower transactions prices, larger equity commitments, lower debt ratios, and lower up-front fees were under way. Despite the corrections under way, the rules of the game and the general economic environment were altered. Legislative and regulatory rule changes interacting with the economic downturn devastated the LBO market. The main legislative change was the S&L legislation in 1989, the Financial Institutions Reform, Recovery and Enforcement Act (FIRREA). Its major effect was to push masses of high-yield debt from S&L portfolios onto the marketplace. The downward impact on the prices of high-yield debt was predictable. Bank regulators put pressures on banks to reduce their exposures in highly leveraged transactions (HLTs). The recession of 1990–1991 brought to an end the rising levels of economic activity that supported the revenue growth and profitability of individual companies. Leveraged buyout activity in 1991 dropped to $7.5 billion, less than 9% of the $88 billion in 1988.

## THE ROLE OF JUNK BONDS

Junk bonds are high-yield bonds either rated below investment grade or unrated. Using Standard & Poor's ratings, junk bonds are defined at below BBB; using Moody's the level is below Baa3. Allegations have been made that junk bonds have contributed to excessive takeover activity and LBOs, and resulted in unsound levels of business leverage.

There have always been high-yield bonds. But prior to 1977 high-yield bonds were "fallen angels," bonds initially rated investment grade but whose ratings had been subsequently lowered. The first issuer of bonds rated below investment grade from the start is said to be Lehman Brothers in 1977. Drexel Burnham Lambert (Michael Milken) soon became the industry leader. Competition followed, but Drexel still had 45% of the market in 1986 and 43.2% of the market through mid-November 1987 (Frantz, 1987). However, as a result of its legal problems, Drexel's share of public underwritings of junk debt fell to only 16% in the first quarter of 1989 (Laing, 1989). Subsequently, Drexel declared bankruptcy and dropped from the market. By the early 1990s the volume of high-yield bond financing had exceeded the peak levels of the 1980s. Other investment banks took over the market share previously held by Drexel.

Between 1970 and 1977 junk bonds represented on average about 3 to 4% of total public straight debt bonds. By 1985 this share had risen to 14.4%. These are shares of the totals of public straight bonds outstanding. As a percentage of yearly flows of new public bond issues by U.S. corporations, the straight junk bond shares had risen from 1.1% in 1977 to almost 20% by 1985. Clearly, junk bonds began to play a significant role.

The use of high-yield bonds represented a financial innovation in opening public financing to less than investment grade credit firms. It was used to finance growing firms such as MCI. Junk bonds were also used in takeovers, making even the largest firms vulnerable to changes in ownership. Default rates for high-yield bonds by 10 years after issuance had run as high as 20 to 30%. The average recovery rate for junk bonds after default had been about 40% of their original par value. Taking default rates and average recovery rates into account, the realized return spreads between high-yield bonds and other investments had been calculated. Over most segments of the period 1978–1994, the promised yield spread between high-yield bonds and 10-year Treasury bonds had been about 4.5%. The realized return spread had been somewhat over 2 percentage points (Altman, 1989, 1996).

A study by Professor Glenn Yago (1991) covered all public firms issuing junk bonds during the period 1980–1986. About one-fourth of the proceeds were used for acquisition financing, whereas about three-fourths of the proceeds were used to finance internal corporate growth. Although high-yield bonds facilitated takeover activity, their significance was much broader. Junk bonds made financing available to high-risk growth firms and helped them realize their potentials. A high percentage of employment growth in the economy had been accounted for by the growth of firms using high-yield financing. These high-yield firms had higher than average rates of sales growth, capital expenditures, and productivity improvements.

High-yield financing was not the fundamental cause of the problems of the savings and loan industry during the 1980s. Their basic problem was that the changing nature of financial markets removed the economic basis for the existence of the industry. By 1980, before the era of takeovers and high-yield financing had started, the S&L industry had a negative net worth on a market-value basis of over $100 billion. Ninety percent of the firms in the S&L industry were suffering losses in 1980 and 1981.

Investments in junk bonds in total represented 1% or less of their total assets. Some individual S&Ls had high ratios of junk bonds in their portfolios. Legislation enacted by Congress in 1989 essentially required S&Ls to liquidate the high-yield bonds they currently held and prohibited them from further investing in high-yield bonds. This artificial interference with normal supply and demand conditions in the high-yield bond market caused temporary losses. However, by 1993 the junk bond market was achieving record high returns for investors and the size of the high-yield bond market reached new highs, suggesting a sound fundamental economic basis for this financial innovation.

Much has been written on the role of Michael Milken with opposing views reflected in two contrasting studies. The first was written by Ralph S. Saul, who served as a court appointed member of the oversight committee to monitor the liquidation of Drexel; he later served as the chairman of its board in reorganization (Saul, 1993). From his close and long association in overseeing the liquidation of Drexel, Saul also reviewed closely the activities of Michael Milken. His detailed review of Milken and his activities can be summarized into three charges: (1) securities parking, (2) market stabilization, and (3) market monopolization.

Securities parking entails having an associate or cooperating firm or firms hold securities in their account names. Historically, this was a common practice by investment banking firms to avoid technical violations of net equity or capital requirements in relation to assets held or obligations outstanding. The need to add to an investment banking firm's equity or net worth on a permanent basis was avoided by having other nominees hold temporary surges in asset holdings and related debt obligations incurred. But parking became a more serious violation when the Williams Acts, initially enacted in 1968 and subsequently amended, made it illegal to engage in parking to avoid triggering the Rule 13(d) requirement of filing a report with the SEC when 5% ownership of the equity securities of a firm had been reached. The main evidence of the charge against Milken for parking was from the testimony of Ivan Boesky.

Saul placed heaviest emphasis on the market stabilization activities of Milken. He stated that Milken was able to develop underwriting and investment participation by other institutions by guaranteeing them against losses on their high-yield bond investments during the time required for the markets to absorb them. In addition, Saul (1993, p. 44) states that Milken did not make "public disclosure in high-yield bond offering documents of the hundreds of millions in equities or warrants that he took as underwriting compensation." Furthermore, Saul pointed out, "In the most egregious cases, he made side payoffs, awarding interests in his investment partnerships to portfolio managers in return for investing institutional funds in his issues" (p. 43). Saul further stated that "such reprehensible conduct" helped Milken achieve his third crime of becoming the dominant firm or monopolist of the high-yield bond market. He then described the advantages that Milken achieved as the innovator or first mover in developing the high-yield bond market.

Saul then posed the question, "Why—in the fiercely competitive world of Wall Street, where a new financial product rarely has an edge for more than a few years at most—was no competitor able to challenge Milken?" (p. 42). The answer Saul gave was in three parts. First, they did not have Milken's network to be "highly confident" that it could successfully "place" or sell a high-yield offering. "Second, and most important, no other firm on Wall Street was prepared to commit so much of its capital to inventory high-yield bonds in secondary market trading" (p. 42). Third, Milken over time developed close relationships with client issuers, institutional customers, and his employees.

A positive case for Milken was developed by Professor Daniel Fischel (1995), who was a consultant on the Milken case and other lawsuits in the 1980s. Fischel has also served as an expert witness on behalf of several government agencies. Fischel addressed the question, "Was Milken guilty?" His summary view is as follows. "Milken was a tough and formidable competitor. . . . His success made him the envy of many. . . . After the most thorough investigation, the government came up with nothing" (p. 158).

Fischel described the action against Milken as a part of the hysteria against the "excesses of the 1980s," and the ability of the government to invoke the Racketeer Influenced and Corrupt Organizations Act (RICO), which would have enabled the government to seize all of Milken's assets at the start of a trial. At the time of his decision to avoid the application of RICO by his guilty plea, so many other defendants had lost their court cases that it appeared that Milken simply could not win. But in 1991 the Second Circuit court reversed numerous convictions that the U.S. attorney's office had previously achieved in the lower courts (Fischel, p. 183). Fischel argued that these reversals supported his position that Milken was not, in fact, guilty of breaking any security law violations.

## LBOs IN THE 1992–1995 PERIOD

Between 1992 and 1995 the economy experienced sustained economic growth, stock prices reached new highs, the size of the total market for high-yield debt reached new highs, and the size of aggregate LBO transactions moved to $20.6 billion, almost 300% of the volume in 1991. This more favorable economic environment was a major factor in the resurgence of LBOs. In addition, the financial structure of the deals changed. Innovative approaches were developed by LBO sponsor companies, LBO sponsor specialists, investment banks, and commercial banks. Because of innovative approaches, LBOs were applied increasingly beyond mature slow-growing industries to high-growth technology-driven industries.

The changed financial structure of the transactions after 1992 are first described. The price to EBITDA ratios paid moved down toward 5 to 6 times from the 7–8–10 multiples of the late 1980s. The percentage of equity in the initial capital structure moved up to 20 to 30% compared with equity ratios as low as 5 to 10% in the late 1980s. Interest coverage ratios moved up. The ratio of EBITDA to interest and other financial requirements moved to a standard of two times. This contrasts with the deals in the late 1980s when asset sales and immediate improvements in profitability margins were required to cover interest and other financial outlays in the first year of the LBO.

A major restructuring of the intermediaries has also been taking place. Milken-Drexel were no longer present to dominate LBO activity as in the 1980s. But the LBO has resumed its growth through other investment banking houses, the larger commercial banks, the traditional LBO sponsors such as Kohlberg Kravis Roberts (KKR), and innovative approaches by investment banking-sponsoring firms. For example, Forstmann Little & Company has emphasized using its own funds and participation in management over a period of time (Antilla, 1992, 1993). A general partner of Forstmann Little in a *New York Times* interview of December 27, 1992 stated, "We're looking more and more to finance our deals without any bank debt—substituting what was once bank debt with more of our own capital." This represents a strategy of substituting sponsor equity for bank debt. Sometimes deals are structured so that principal repayments are not required until 10 years after the deal. This reduces the pressure for immediate performance improvement or asset sales.

Clayton, Dubilier & Rice Inc. (CD&R) has emphasized a partnership structure with members who had considerable previous managerial experience. It structures the transaction, owns the majority of the equity, controls the company it acquires, and establishes management incentives by linking compensation to performance. Detailed examples of CD&R activities are provided in a *Business Week* story of November 15, 1993, pp. 70, 74. CD&R has emphasized buying undermanaged segments of larger companies to achieve a turnaround. Financial buyers may also develop joint deals with corporate strategic buyers to purchase companies on a leveraged basis.

The financial press provides numerous examples of innovative approaches by LBO sponsors. The increased participation by commercial banks is described in detail in a comprehensive survey by Allen (1996). He described the increased use of syndication of HLT transactions to other banks and the development of a highly liquid secondary loan trading market. He emphasized a continued close client-focused relationship by the commercial bank. This embraced not only LBO and M&A activity but the broad gamut of financial services the client company may require. He also described a range of capital structure strategies tailored to the characteristics of the transaction. Similar innovative approaches have been developed by investment banking firms and other financial intermediaries.

Financial buyers (LBO sponsors, investment banks, commercial banks) have faced increased competition from corporate buyers. All have adopted new strategies. One is the leveraged buildup. The leveraged buildup identifies a fragmented industry characterized by relatively small firms. Buyout firms based on partners with industry expertise purchase a firm as a platform for further leveraged acquisitions in the same industry (Allen, 1996, p. 27). They seek to build firms with strong management, developing revenue growth while reducing costs, with the objectives of improved margins, increased cash flow, and increased valuations.

---

## Summary

The 1980s were characterized by LBOs focused on mature industries with stable cash flows. High leverage was used to provide owners and LBO sponsors with a high percentage of the equity. The cash flows were used to pay off the debt. In the standard case, debt was 90%, equity was 10% of total capital. When the debt was paid off, the equity holders became owners of 100% of the company. It could then be sold with strong management incentives. A turnaround could achieve substantial operating improvements. The value of the company when sold represented good returns to the equity holders.

In the late 1980s buyers paid too much, and leverage was excessive for realistic future cash flows. The deals were unsound from a strategic and financial structure standpoint. In 1990–1991 the LBO market had almost dried up.

The LBO market since 1992 has revived. The volume of high-yield debt outstanding in 1995 was greater than it ever had been before. In addition, investments in the LBO market by sponsors' investment banks and commercial banks have also increased. Innovative approaches have augmented more traditional financial strategies. Financial structures have been related to the characteristics of the companies involved. Leveraged transactions have moved from mature industries to growth oriented technologically driven industries. There is often greater equity participation by financial buyers. In addition, financial buyers increasingly offer management expertise and close interaction with or control of operating management. In short, LBO activity appears to have moved to an age of renewal.

## Questions

16.1  Discuss the typical types of financing involved in LBOs and MBOs.

16.2  What were the characteristics of industries and firms in which LBOs and MBOs have taken place in the 1980s?

16.3  What have been the advantages and disadvantages of LBOs and MBOs?

16.4  What were the magnitudes of abnormal returns for LBOs and MBOs during the early 1980s?

16.5  What were the sources of these gains?

16.6  What were the reasons for the increase in LBO activity during the early 1980s?

16.7  Why were LBO/MBOs able to use such high leverage ratios compared with other forms of business organizations?

16.8  What were some of the unsound developments in the LBO market that began to take place in the late 1980s?

16.9  How were these developments corrected during the resurgence of the LBO market in 1992–1995?

------------------------------------ C A S E   16–1 ------------------------------------

# Sources of Value in LBOs

In the text, we use spreadsheets to convey how an LBO is set up and how cash flows can be used to pay down debt in a successful LBO. We can convey the same concepts more succinctly by use of the valuation formulas developed in chapter 9.

Consider the following set of value drivers:

| | |
|---|---|
| $X_0 =$ | $1,000 |
| $T =$ | 40.0% |
| $b =$ | 20.0% |
| $r =$ | 30.0% |
| $g =$ | 6.0% |
| $n =$ | 10 |
| $k =$ | 11.0% |
| $(1 + h) = (1 + g)/(1 + k)$ | 0.95 |
| $p =$ inflation rate $=$ | 0.0% |
| $z =$ reinvestment rate $=$ | 0.0% |

The above value drivers reflect a firm with the characteristics of the usual LBO candidate in the 1980s. The investment opportunities rate, $b$, is a modest 20%. The marginal profitability rate, $r$, is 30%. The growth rate is only 6%. The initial EBIT is set at $1,000 so that the results can be expressed in general terms. We postulate a cost of capital of 11%. Here is the resulting valuation:

$$\text{1st term} = X_0(1 - T)(1 - b)\sum_{t=1}^{n}\left(\frac{1+g}{1+k}\right)^t = \quad \$3,758$$

50.7%

$$\text{2nd term} = \frac{X_0(1 - T)(1 - z)}{k - p}\left(\frac{1+g}{1+k}\right)^n(1 + g) = \quad \$3,647$$

49.3%

Total value = $\overline{\$7,405}$

100.0%

In an LBO, the high use of debt could reduce the tax rate to 30%. Because a turnaround situation is usually involved, the profitability rate rises to 40%. With the higher use of debt in the capital structure, the cost of capital drops to 10%.

-------------------------------------------------------

## Questions on Case Study C16.1

C16.1.1  With the new value drivers, what will be the new value of the LBO?

C16.1.2  What other types of sensitivity analysis could be performed?

------------------------------- C A S E   16–2 -------------------------------

# RJR Nabisco LBO

Many studies set forth materials on the 1988 RJR Nabisco LBO. Two examples are: Allen Michel and Israel Shaked, "RJR Nabisco: A Case Study of a Complex Leveraged Buyout," *Financial Analysts Journal,* September–October 1991, pp. 15–27; and Harvard Business School Case of RJR Nabisco. Both articles project the cash flows from 1989 through 1998. In competition with other bidders, KKR won with a bid of $109 per share.

From the spreadsheets in the two sources cited above, the following value drivers could be estimated.

| | |
|---|---|
| $X_0 =$ | $2,848 |
| $T =$ | 40.0% |

| | |
|---|---|
| $b =$ | 30.0% |
| $r =$ | 46.7% |
| $g =$ | 14.0% |
| $n =$ | 10 |
| $k =$ | 12.0% |
| $(1 + h) = (1 + g)/(1 + k)$ | 1.02 |
| $p =$ inflation rate $=$ | 0.0% |
| $z =$ reinvestment rate $=$ | 0.0% |

Using the above data, the total value of RJR Nabisco could be calculated. From the total value, the debt outstanding of $5.4 billion would be deducted to obtain the equity value. The number of shares outstanding was 223.5 million.

------------------------------------------------------------

## Question on Case Study C16.2

C16.2.1  Compare the indicated value per share of RJR Nabisco using the value drivers above with the $109 per share paid by KKR.

------------------------------------------------------------

## References

Allen, Jay R., "LBOs—The Evolution of Financial Structures and Strategies," *Journal of Applied Corporate Finance,* 8, Winter 1996, pp. 18–29.

Altman, Edward I., "Measuring Corporate Bond Mortality and Performance," *Journal of Finance,* 44, September 1989, pp. 909–922.

———, "The Investment Performance of Defaulted Bonds for 1987–1995 and Market Outlook," ms. with Anthony C. Morris, New York University Salomon Center, January 1996, pp. 1–23.

Anders, George, "Leaner and Meaner: Leveraged Buy-Outs Make Some Companies Tougher Competitors," *The Wall Street Journal,* September 15, 1988, pp. 1, 14.

Antilla, Susan, "A Different Face on the L.B.O. Front," *New York Times,* December 27, 1992, Section 3, p. 13.

———, "Forstmann Turns Toward the Future," *New York Times,* November 14, 1993, Section 3, p. 13.

Asquith, P., and T. A. Wizman, "Event Risk, Covenants, and Bondholder Returns in Leveraged Buyouts," *Journal of Financial Economics,* 27, 1990, pp. 195–214.

Baker, G. P., M. C. Jensen, and K. J. Murphy, "Compensation and Incentives: Practice vs. Theory," *Journal of Finance,* 43, 1988, pp. 593–616.

DeAngelo, Harry, and Linda DeAngelo, "Managerial Ownership of Voting Rights: A Study of Public Corporations with Dual Classes of Common Stock," *Journal of Financial Economics,* 1985, pp. 33–69.

———, "Management Buyouts of Publicly Traded Corporations," chapter 6 in Thomas E. Copeland, ed., *Modern Finance & Industrial Economics,* New York: Basil Blackwell Inc., 1987, pp. 92–113.

———, and Edward Rice, "Going Private: Minority Freezeouts and Stockholder Wealth," *Journal of Law and Economics,* 27, October 1984, pp. 367–401.

Degeorge, Francois, and Richard Zeckhauser, "The Reverse LBO Decision and Firm Performance: Theory and Evidence," *Journal of Finance,* 48, September 1993, pp. 1323–1348.

Easterbrook, F. H., and D. R. Fischel, "Corporate Control Transactions," *Yale Law Journal,* 92, 1982, pp. 698–711.

Fischel, Daniel, *Payback,* New York: HarperCollins Publishers, 1995.

Frantz, Douglas, "Crash Hasn't Shaken Drexel's Faith in the Value of 'Junk Bonds,'" *Los Angeles Times,* November 19, 1987, Part IV, p. 1.

Greenwald, J., "Where's the Limit?" *Time,* December 5, 1988, pp. 66–70.

Harlow, W. V., and J. S. Howe, "Leverage Buyouts and Insider Nontrading," *Financial Management,* 22, Spring 1993, pp. 109–118.

Hite, G. L., and M. R. Vetsuypens, "Management Buyouts of Divisions and Shareholder Wealth," *Journal of Finance,* 44, 1989, pp. 953–970.

Holthausen, Robert W., and David F. Larcker, "The Financial Performance of Reverse Leveraged Buyouts," *Journal of Financial Economics,* 42, 1996, pp. 293–332.

Houlihan Lokey Howard & Zukin, *Mergerstat Review,* Los Angeles, CA, 90067, 1996, 1997.

Jensen, M. C., "Agency Costs of Free Cash Flow, Corporate Finance, and Takeovers," AEA Papers and Proceedings, May 1986, pp. 323–329.

Kaplan, Steven, "The Effects of Management Buyouts on Operating Performance and Value," *Journal of Financial Economics,* 24, 1989a, pp. 217–254.

———, "Management Buyouts: Evidence on Taxes as a Source of Value," *Journal of Finance,* 44, July 1989b, pp. 611–632.

———, "The Staying Power of Leveraged Buyouts," *Journal of Financial Economics,* 29, 1991, pp. 287–313.

———, and Jeremy C. Stein, "The Evolution of Buyout Pricing and Financial Structure (Or, What Went Wrong) in the 1980s," *Journal of Applied Corporate Finance,* 6, 1993, pp. 72–88.

Laing, J. R., "Up and Down Wall Street," *Barron's,* April 10, 1989, pp. 1, 49–50.

Lehn, Ken, and Annette Poulsen, "Leveraged Buyouts: Wealth Created or Wealth Redistributed?" chapter 4 in M. Weidenbaum and K. Chilton, eds., *Public Policy Towards Corporate Takeovers,* New Brunswick, NJ: Transaction Publishers, 1988.

———, "Free Cash Flow and Stockholder Gains in Going Private Transactions," *Journal of Finance,* 44, 1989, pp. 771–788.

Lowenstein, Louis, "Management Buyouts," *Columbia Law Review,* 85, 1985, pp. 730–784.

Mian, Shehzad, and James Rosenfeld, "Takeover Activity and the Long-Run Performance of Reverse Leveraged Buyouts," *Financial Management,* 22, Winter 1993, pp. 46–57.

Morrow, D. J., "Why the IRS Might Love Those LBOs," *Fortune,* December 5, 1988, pp. 145–146.

Murphy, K. J., "Corporate Performance and Managerial Remuneration: An Empirical Analysis," *Journal of Accounting and Economics,* 7, 1985, pp. 11–42.

Muscarella, C. J., and M. R. Vetsuypens, "Efficiency and Organizational Structure: A Study of Reverse LBOs," *Journal of Finance,* 45, December 1990, pp. 1389–1413.

Opler, Tim, "Operating Performance in Leveraged Buyouts: Evidence from 1985–1989," *Financial Management,* 21, Spring 1992, pp. 27–34.

Quigley, E. V., "Big Bondholders Launch Revolt Against Nabisco," *Los Angeles Times,* November 18, 1988, Part IV, pp. 1, 5.

Ritter, Jay R., "The Long-Run Performance of Initial Public Offerings," *Journal of Finance,* 46, March 1991, pp. 3–27.

Roden, Dianne M., and Wilbur G. Lewellen, "Corporate Capital Structure Decisions: Evidence from Leveraged Buyouts," *Financial Management,* 24, Summer 1995, pp. 76–87.

Saul, Ralph S., "DREXEL," *The Brookings Review,* 11, Spring 1993, pp. 41–45.

Shleifer, A., and C. H. Summers, "Breach of Trust in Hostile Takeovers," chapter 2 in A. J. Auerbach, ed., *Corporate Takeovers: Causes and Consequences,* Chicago: University of Chicago Press, 1988, pp. 33–56.

Shleifer, A., and R. W. Vishny, "Management Buyouts as a Response to Market Pressure," chapter 5 in A. J. Auerbach, ed., *Mergers and Acquisitions,* Chicago: University of Chicago Press, 1988.

Smith, Abbie, "Corporate Ownership Structure and Performance: The Case of Management Buyouts," *Journal of Financial Economics,* 27, September 1990, pp. 143–164.

Travlos, N. G., and M. M. Cornett, "Going Private Buyouts and Determinants of Shareholders' Returns," *Journal of Accounting, Auditing and Finance,* 8, 1993, pp. 1–25.

United States Government Printing Office, *Economic Report of the President,* Washington, DC, 1996.

Warga, Arthur, and Ivo Welch, "Bondholder Losses in Leveraged Buyouts," *Review of Financial Studies,* 6, 1993, pp. 959–982.

Weston, J. Fred, and Yehning Chen, "A Tale of Two Eras," *Business Economics,* 29, January 1994, pp. 27–33.

Yago, Glenn, *Junk Bonds: How High Yield Securities Restructured Corporate America,* New York: Oxford University Press, 1991.

## CHAPTER

# 17

---

# International Takeovers and Restructuring

The annual reports of individual business firms make increasing reference to international markets as sources of future growth. The world has truly become a global marketplace. A significant proportion of total takeover activity has an international dimension. United States firms are buying foreign firms, and foreign firms are buying U.S. entities.

In the first quarter of 1996, five of the 10 largest announced transactions involved foreign companies (Houlihan Lokey Howard & Zukin, 1997). Ranked 3 was the purchase by Fresenius AG, a German company, of the National Medical Care Unit from W. R. Grace & Company for $4 billion. Number 4 was the purchase by Thomson Corporation of Canada, a printing and publishing company of West Publishing Company of the United States, for $3.4 billion. Number 7 was the purchase by Farnell Electronics PLC of the United Kingdom of the Premier Industrial Corporation (both companies in wholesale and distribution) for $2.8 billion. Number 9 was the purchase by Royal Ahold NV of the Netherlands of Stop & Shop Companies, Inc. of the United States, both in retail distribution, at $1.8 billion. Number 10 was the acquisition of Hemlo Gold Mines Inc. of Canada by Battle Mountain Gold Company, a U.S. company, in a stock exchange valued at $1.5 billion. Tied for number 10 was the purchase by Robert Bosch GmbH of Germany of the Braking Business of AlliedSignal Inc. for $1.5 billion. In addition, on March 6, 1996, Ciba-Giegy and Sandoz, both Swiss pharmaceutical firms, announced a $29.6 billion merger that would represent the largest transaction, surpassing the RJR Nabisco transaction of $24.6 billion in 1988.

## HISTORICAL AND EMPIRICAL DATA

International takeover activity has substantially increased in recent decades (Table 17.1). United States acquisitions of foreign businesses were already large by the 1970s. After declining somewhat during the 1980s, U.S. acquisitions of foreign businesses have represented more than 10% of M&As during the 1990s, as shown in Table 17.1.

Foreign acquisitions of U.S. companies became very large in the late 1980s, measured both by number of transactions (Table 17.1) and by dollar values (Table 17.2). Foreign acquisitions of U.S. companies in dollar amounts represented over 30% of total M&A activity in 1990. This was also the peak year for U.S. acquisitions of foreign busi-

■ 344 ■

**TABLE 17.1** Number of Foreign and U.S. Acquisitions

| | | NUMBER OF TRANSACTIONS | | | |
|---|---|---|---|---|---|
| | | *Foreign Acquisitions of U.S. Companies* | | *U.S. Acquisitions of Foreign Businesses* | |
| *Year* | *Total M&As* | *Amount* | *% Total M&As* | *Amount* | *% Total M&As* |
| 1972 | 4,801 | 88 | 1.8 | 531 | 11.1 |
| 1973 | 4,040 | 143 | 3.5 | 323 | 8.0 |
| 1974 | 2,861 | 173 | 6.0 | 257 | 9.0 |
| 1975 | 2,297 | 184 | 8.0 | 178 | 7.7 |
| 1976 | 2,276 | 178 | 7.8 | 126 | 5.5 |
| 1977 | 2,224 | 162 | 7.3 | 112 | 5.0 |
| 1978 | 2,106 | 199 | 9.4 | 98 | 4.7 |
| 1979 | 2,128 | 236 | 11.1 | 119 | 5.6 |
| 1980 | 1,889 | 187 | 9.9 | 102 | 5.4 |
| 1981 | 2,395 | 234 | 9.8 | 101 | 4.2 |
| 1982 | 2,346 | 154 | 6.6 | 121 | 5.2 |
| 1983 | 2,533 | 125 | 4.9 | 146 | 5.8 |
| 1984 | 2,543 | 151 | 5.9 | 147 | 5.8 |
| 1985 | 3,001 | 197 | 6.6 | 175 | 5.8 |
| 1986 | 3,336 | 264 | 7.9 | 180 | 5.4 |
| 1987 | 2,032 | 220 | 10.8 | 142 | 7.0 |
| 1988 | 2,258 | 307 | 13.6 | 151 | 6.7 |
| 1989 | 2,366 | 285 | 12.0 | 220 | 9.3 |
| 1990 | 2,074 | 266 | 12.8 | 266 | 12.8 |
| 1991 | 1,877 | 188 | 10.0 | 244 | 13.0 |
| 1992 | 2,574 | 167 | 6.5 | 403 | 15.7 |
| 1993 | 2,663 | 190 | 7.1 | 400 | 15.0 |
| 1994 | 2,997 | 219 | 7.3 | 399 | 13.3 |
| 1995 | 3,510 | 218 | 6.2 | 483 | 13.8 |

*Source: Mergerstat Review,* annual issues through 1996.

nesses representing 16.7% of total M&A activity in 1990. It has been estimated that 80% of all foreign direct investment that takes place in the United States is by acquisitions.

Table 17.3 shows that 20 of the 100 largest mergers in history involving U.S. firms represented foreign transactions. All of these 20 transactions took place since 1984. In a previous compilation, 11 additional large foreign transactions were listed. These dropped out as the size of the top 100 increased. Table 17.4 lists the 11 additional large international transactions.

# THE THEORY OF THE MNE

To understand international mergers, acquisitions, and tender offers, we must begin with the theory of the multinational enterprise (MNE), because a firm that makes an acquisition in another nation thereby becomes a multinational firm. What are the

**TABLE 17.2**   Values of Foreign and U.S. Acquisitions

| | | DOLLAR VALUE ($ BILLION) | | | |
| | | Foreign Acquisitions of U.S. Companies | | U.S. Acquisitions of Foreign Businesses | |
| Year | Total M&As | Amount | % Total M&As | Amount | % Total M&As |
|---|---|---|---|---|---|
| 1972 | 16.7 | NA[a] | | NA | |
| 1973 | 16.7 | NA | | NA | |
| 1974 | 12.5 | NA | | NA | |
| 1975 | 11.8 | 1.6 | 13.6 | 0.4 | 3.4 |
| 1976 | 20.0 | 2.4 | 12.0 | 0.9 | 4.5 |
| 1977 | 21.9 | 3.1 | 14.2 | 1.0 | 4.6 |
| 1978 | 34.2 | 6.3 | 18.4 | 0.7 | 2.1 |
| 1979 | 43.5 | 5.8 | 13.3 | 1.5 | 3.5 |
| 1980 | 44.3 | 7.1 | 16.0 | 3.8 | 8.6 |
| 1981 | 82.6 | 18.8 | 22.8 | 1.1 | 1.3 |
| 1982 | 53.8 | 5.1 | 9.5 | 0.8 | 1.5 |
| 1983 | 73.1 | 5.9 | 8.1 | 2.5 | 3.4 |
| 1984 | 122.2 | 15.1 | 12.4 | 2.6 | 2.1 |
| 1985 | 179.8 | 10.9 | 6.1 | 1.4 | 0.8 |
| 1986 | 173.1 | 24.5 | 14.2 | 5.2 | 3.0 |
| 1987 | 163.7 | 40.4 | 24.7 | 11.0 | 6.7 |
| 1988 | 246.9 | 55.5 | 22.5 | 14.5 | 5.9 |
| 1989 | 221.1 | 40.0 | 18.1 | 22.2 | 10.0 |
| 1990 | 108.2 | 33.1 | 30.6 | 18.0 | 16.7 |
| 1991 | 71.2 | 12.3 | 17.3 | 5.7 | 8.0 |
| 1992 | 96.7 | 9.3 | 9.6 | 14.0 | 14.5 |
| 1993 | 176.4 | 12.4 | 7.0 | 12.7 | 7.2 |
| 1994 | 226.7 | 35.8 | 15.8 | 17.6 | 7.8 |
| 1995 | 356.0 | 39.5 | 11.1 | 49.8 | 14.0 |

[a]The information is not available.

Source: Mergerstat Review, annual issues through 1996.

business or economic reasons for being a multinational firm? Why should a firm be a multiplant firm and this particular form of a multiplant firm—the multinational, multiplant firm?

The basic issue in the theory of the firm is what determines whether a firm will use external markets to transact in resources or use managerial coordination within the firm. For international activities, the issues for the firm are why not export and import, or license, or use joint ventures rather than have a plant or plants abroad? The theory of the firm holds that a firm uses internal managerial coordination rather than the external market when the costs are lower or net revenue productivity higher. It is the cost and revenue comparison that is relevant. The basic challenge to the MNE is that when it operates a plant in a foreign country, its costs are likely to be higher and its revenue productivity lower than the indigenous firms with which it competes. The MNE does not know the foreign labor markets, foreign suppliers, local laws, nor culture and customs in the foreign locations. It is costly to learn these things. Why not produce in your familiar home territory and sell abroad, perhaps through a foreign sales agent?

| TABLE 17.3 | Foreign Transactions Included in the 100 Largest Mergers in History Involving U.S. Firms | | | |
|---|---|---|---|---|
| *Ranking* | *Year* | *Buyer* | *Seller* | *$ Billion* |
| 3 | 1989 | Beecham Group PLC–U.K. | SmithKline Beckman Corp. | 16.1 |
| 18 | 1987 | British Petroleum U.K. | Standard Oil Co. | 7.8 |
| 21 | 1995 | Hoechst A.G.–Germany | Marion Merrell Dow Inc./Dow Chemical Co. | 7.1 |
| 22 | 1995 | Upjohn Co. | Pharmacia A.B.–Sweden | 7.0 |
| 25 | 1990 | Matsushita Electric Industrial Co. | MCA Inc. | 6.6 |
| 26 | 1988 | Campeau Corp.–Canada | Federated Department Stores Inc. | 6.6 |
| 32 | 1988 | Grand Metropolitan PLC–U.K. | Pillsbury Company | 5.6 |
| 34 | 1984 | Royal Dutch/Shell Group Netherlands | Shell Oil Co. | 5.5 |
| 39 | 1988 | B.A.T. Ind PLC–U.K. | Farmers Group Inc. | 5.2 |
| 50 | 1993 | British Telecommunications PLC–U.K. | MCI (20.0%) | 4.3 |
| 51 | 1981 | Societe Nationale Elf Aquitaine–France | Texasgulf Inc. | 4.3 |
| 73 | 1994 | Sandoz A.G.–Switzerland | Gerber Products Co. Inc. | 3.7 |
| 77 | 1992 | Alcatel Alsthom–France | Alcatel N.V./ ITT Corp. | 3.6 |
| 80 | 1989 | Private Group/KLM Royal Dutch Airlines | NWA Inc. | 3.5 |
| 89 | 1995 | Fleet Financial Group Inc. | Nat West Bank N.A. | 3.3 |
| 90 | 1987 | Campeau Corp.–Canada | Allied Stores Corp. | 3.3 |
| 94 | 1986 | Unilever N.V.–Netherlands | Chesebrough–Pond's Inc. | 3.1 |
| 96 | 1988 | News Corp. Ltd.–Australia | Triangle Publications Inc. | 3.0 |
| 98 | 1989 | Sony Corp.–Japan | Columbia Pictures Entertainment Inc. | 3.0 |
| 100 | 1994 | SmithKline Beecham PLC–U.K. | Sterling Winthrop Inc./Eastman Kodak Co. | 2.9 |

*Source: Mergerstat Review,* 1996, pp. 178–185.

Other contractual arrangements such as licensing and or joint ventures may also be considered.

The theory of the MNE is that the use of foreign plants and other operations implies that costs are lower or revenue productivity higher than if alternative contractual arrangements were used. But what is the source of the net revenue advantage to the horizontal MNE—a multiplant firm with plants in different countries? A leading researcher on multinational enterprise asserts that, "The concept that has proved most fruitful for explaining the nonproduction bases for the MNE is that of intangible assets belonging to the firm" (Caves, 1982, p. 3). Production advantages may also exist, but Caves assembles evidence to show that the most important factors are the intangible assets.

Examples of intangible assets are: (1) Managerial know-how and experience. (2) Superior technological capabilities. (3) The firm may be a leader in repeated innovations. (4) It may hold patents, trademarks, or branded products. (5) The firm may

**TABLE 17.4**    Foreign Transactions Included in the 100 Largest Mergers Listing in 1988

| Ranking | Year | Buyer | Seller | $ Billion |
|---|---|---|---|---|
| 41 | 1984 | Nestlé Switzerland | Carnation | 2.9 |
| 42 | 1986 | Hoechst West Germany | Celanese | 2.9 |
| 43 | 1988 | Bridgestone Japan | Firestone Tire | 2.8 |
| 47 | 1981 | Seagram Co. Canada | Conoco | 2.6 |
| 51 | 1981 | Kuwait Petroleum Corporation | Santa Fe International | 2.5 |
| 58 | 1983 | Broken Hill Prop. Australia | G.E. (Utah International) | 2.4 |
| 61 | 1988 | Maxwell Communications United Kingdom | MacMillan | 2.3 |
| 65 | 1980 | Sun Co. Inc. | Seagram Ltd. Canada | 2.3 |
| 69 | 1985 | Olympia & York Dev. Canada | Chevron | 2.0 |
| 70 | 1987 | Sony Japan | CBS (CBS Records) | 2.0 |
| 89 | 1988 | Private group United Kingdom | Koppers | 1.7 |

*Source: Mergerstat Review,* 1988, pp. 41–46.

possess a special competence in styling, continued product quality improvement, or in product differentiation. But granting that a firm may have superior technology or managerial knowledge, why not sell it rather than use it in multilocation activities?

The answer provided by the literature of the MNE is illustrated by the special characteristics of the market for knowledge listed by Casson (1987, p. 12):

1. Uncertainty about the quality of the product.
2. The product is indivisible, but the supply capacity of one unit is infinite.
3. The supply of the product is irreversible and cannot be inspected.
4. Property rights to the product are ill defined and costly to enforce.
5. The product may have multiple uses.
6. The marginal cost of supply is low; each customer becomes a potential competitor.

Because of these "public good" characteristics of knowledge, the use of external markets will involve substantial transactions costs required to define property rights and to negotiate, monitor, and enforce contracts. An example based on Caves (1982) illustrates the idea. Assume six producers of widgets each independently owned and located in six different countries. Firm 1 achieves an innovation either in product quality or in the production process, which gives it a price or cost advantage. Firm 1 could expand its output and export to the other five countries, but would incur excessive transportation costs if (by assumption) the plants were all efficiently located to begin with. It could license its knowledge but will be unable to achieve revenues to recover its long-run supply price of innovation because of the "public good" nature of knowledge creation. The most profitable solution is for the six plants to combine into one MNE (Caves, 1982, pp. 5–6).

Caves further suggests that an empirical implication of the theory is that MNEs will be found to a higher degree in industries in which intangible assets are important. He also suggests further extensions of the theory. When the MNE utilizes an intangible asset in a foreign subsidiary, this may be viewed as making use of some excess capacity in such assets. An example is the top management capacity in a successful firm. Availability of internal cash flows may also motivate foreign investment, according to Caves (1982, p. 7). He calls a third extension the "going concern" value of a firm. We have referred to this aspect of intangible assets as organization learning. High reputation or high organization capital firms (in the sense of Cornell and Shapiro, 1987) will expand worldwide by direct investment rather than by licensing. The reason is that reputation is not separable from the operations of the firm. Thus, in this case, the intangible asset that is applied to a foreign subsidiary is not a transferable technology, but rather the general reputation of the firm.

Thus far we have been summarizing the literature on the theory of the horizontal MNE. The theories for vertically integrated MNEs or diversified MNEs are somewhat different. The relationships are summarized well by Caves (1982, p. 16): "The vertically integrated firm internalizes a market for an intermediate product, just as the horizontal MNE internalizes markets for intangible assets." Particular conditions encourage vertical integration and these apply to MNEs as well. The use of impersonal external market transactions may involve higher transactions costs under the following conditions: (1) when it is expensive to shift buyer-seller relationships (high switching costs), (2) when durable, relatively specialized assets are involved, (3) when costs of negotiating and monitoring arm's-length contracts are high, and (4) when relevant information is difficult to obtain (information impactedness) and some transactors behave deceptively or opportunistically.

The portfolio explanation for the MNE to achieve diversification is less persuasive. The empirical evidence suggests that the higher the ratio of foreign operations to total sales, the lower the variability of a firm's rate of return on equity capital. Other studies of MNEs provide weak support to benefits from international diversification. But the main influences are the systematic forces described earlier and a variety of special factors, such as the inability to repatriate funds from investments made in less developed countries.

Another special influence may be tariffs. When the European Community (EC) was established (called the Economic Union after 1994), it provided for reduction or elimination of tariffs within the community, but tariffs against outsiders. This provided increased incentives for U.S. firms (for example) to establish operations within the tariff walls of the EC. It also gave them the opportunity to utilize their long experience of operating within a large common market as they had been doing for decades in the United States.

Caves (1982, pp. 42–43) notes that exchange-rate relationships may have effects similar to those of tariffs. He observes that many writers have pointed to the positive relation between a strong dollar and increased foreign direct investments by U.S. firms. Similarly, a weak dollar is associated with increased direct investments by foreigners in the United States.

Finally, in this overview of the general theory of the MNE, the factors of experience and risk should also be noted. Researchers have found that the development of foreign operations proceeds on an incremental basis. A firm does well in its domestic operations. As it increases market share at home, the reactions of rivals are likely to intensify. In part, it may represent good strategy to move abroad to utilize its knowledge, experience, and advantages in foreign countries. But conditions are different in foreign countries and different kinds of risk are involved. So the firm may wish to begin by "dipping its toes in the foreign waters" and expanding abroad as it gains experience.

This also provides a stimulus to foreign acquisitions. A foreign firm has a stock of valuable knowledge about its local market conditions. A U.S. firm that acquires a foreign firm may be willing to pay the full going-concern value because it can utilize the knowledge and experience in other or expanded operations—because important synergies may be present. Firms that already have a substantial presence abroad are more likely to establish new foreign subsidiaries by new ventures, rather than by buying existing firms.

## REASONS FOR INTERNATIONAL M&As

Many of the motives for international mergers and acquisitions are similar to those for purely domestic transactions, while others are unique to the international arena. The motives include the following:

**I.** Growth
   A. To achieve long-run strategic goals.
   B. For growth beyond the capacity of saturated domestic markets.
   C. Market extension abroad and protection of market share at home.
   D. Size and economies of scale required for effective global competition.

**II.** Technology
   A. To exploit technological knowledge advantage.
   B. To acquire technology where it is lacking.

**III.** Extend advantages in differentiated products
   A. Strong correlation between multinationalization and product differentiation (Caves, 1982). This may indicate an application of the parent's (acquirer's) good reputation.

**IV.** Government policy
   A. To circumvent protective tariffs, quotas, etc.
   B. To reduce dependence on exports.

**V.** Exchange rates
   A. Impact on relative costs of foreign versus domestic acquisitions.
   B. Impact on value of repatriated profits.

**VI.** Political and economic stability
   A. To invest in a safe, predictable environment.

**VII.** Differential labor costs, productivity of labor

**VIII.** To follow clients (especially for banks)

**IX.** Diversification
   A. By product line.
   B. Geographically.
   C. To reduce systematic risk.

**X.** Resource-poor domestic economy
   A. To obtain assured sources of supply.

These motives, with examples of each, are now discussed.

### Growth

Growth is probably the most important motive for international mergers. Growth is vital to the well-being of any firm. Mergers provide instant growth, and merging internationally adds a whole new dimension to this instant growth. A 1973 study in the *Survey of Current Business* found the size of the target market to be the only significant determinant of foreign direct investment (including mergers and acquisitions) in the United States. The fact that the growth rate of the target market was not found to be meaningful may indicate an emphasis on immediate rather than potential future growth. Factors that may encourage a firm to merge internationally for growth follow.

A profitable firm in a slow-growing economy may be throwing off cash flow beyond its internal investment needs. It makes sense, all else being equal, to invest this surplus cash in a faster-growing economy than in the slow-growth domestic economy.

The company's domestic markets may be saturated, or the domestic economy may simply be too small to accommodate the growth of its corporate giants. Consider, for example, Royal Dutch Shell and Unilever of the Netherlands; the bulk of these firms' sales and growth must come from outside the Dutch economy.

Leading firms in the domestic market may have lower costs because of economies of scale. Overseas expansion may enable medium-sized firms to attain the size necessary to improve their ability to compete. This factor is one explanation for some recent mergers between medium-sized Japanese companies and U.S. firms, notwithstanding the traditional Japanese reluctance to merge with foreign firms. Medium-sized Japanese firms view these transactions as a means of enhancing their own competitive positions in relation to their larger Japanese rivals.

Finally, even with the most efficient management and technology, the globalization of world markets requires an absolute level of size simply to be able to carry out worldwide operations. Size enables firms to achieve the economies of scale necessary for effective global competition.

## Technology

Technological considerations impact international mergers in two ways: (1) a technologically superior firm may make acquisitions abroad to exploit its technological advantage, or (2) a technologically inferior firm may acquire a foreign target with superior technology to enhance its competitive position both at home and abroad. It is generally accepted that for an investment project (in this case, the acquisition of a foreign firm) to be acceptable, the present value of benefits must exceed the present value of costs. If an asset (the target firm) is correctly priced, the present value of benefits should equal the present value of costs. For positive net present values to occur, an acquiring firm must either be able to buy the target for less than the present value of its benefits (the target must be underpriced), or to increase the present value of future benefits. It is unlikely that target firms are systematically underpriced (even if they were, underpricing would be more difficult to detect in foreign firms in an unfamiliar market than in domestic firms). Hence, the acquiring firm must bring something to the target that will increase the present value of benefits; or the target firm brings something to the acquirer that enables the combined benefits of the merged firm to be greater than the sum of what the individual firms could have achieved separately—synergy.

In domestic mergers, the increased benefits often result when the superior management efficiency of the acquiring firm is applied to the target firm's assets. In international mergers, the acquiring firm may have an advantage in generic management functions such as planning and control or research and development. But capabilities in specific management functions such as marketing or labor relations, for example, tend to be quite environment specific, and are not readily transferable to different surroundings. Such factors may help to explain the predominance of the United Kingdom and Canada as international merger partners of the United States; that is, the common language and heritage, and similar business practices minimize the drawbacks, making such skills more transferable.

Technological superiority, on the other hand, is a far more portable advantage which may be exploited more easily without a lot of cultural baggage. The acquirer may deliberately select a technologically inferior target that, because of this inferiority, is losing market share and thus market value. By injecting technology into the acquired firm, the acquirer can improve its competitive position and profitability both at home and abroad.

Alternatively, one might find acquisitions by cash-rich but technologically backward companies attempting to obtain the technology necessary to remain viable as competitors on the worldwide scene.

In terms of technology transfer, Khoury (1980, p. 241) concluded that, in general, the net flow of technology transfer was into rather than out of the United States. The foreign firms investing in the United States are characterized by a substantial technology base (in addition to financial strength, managerial depth, and powerful marketing organizations).

Examples of international acquisitions to exploit a technological advantage (in this case, specifically in research and development) include Swiss purchases of U.S. drug companies for the production of such drugs as Valium and Librium. (These transactions also illustrate the appropriation of the knowledge advantage via patents.) Another example was the acquisition of the Budd Co., a user of steel in producing rail cars and wheels by Thyssen, a technologically superior diversified German steel firm. The 1986 Boeing Corporation purchase of de Havilland Aircraft of Canada (from the Canadian government as a result of its denationalization policy—see government policy following) for $113.9 million is another example of this type of merger. Federal Express's purchase of Lex-Wilkinson, Ltd. of the United Kingdom was also expected to result in an injection of the superior technology and efficiencies that have made the U.S. firm so successful, into the British firm.

Acquisitions to acquire technology would include a number of acquisitions by companies from oil-rich but technologically relatively backward nations, although technological backwardness is not an essential ingredient; the American-based Emhart Corporation cited technology acquisition as one motive for its expansion into Asia. Their Tokyo operations had identified potential technological contributions in glass container machinery manufacturing and door hardware (*Mergers and Acquisitions*, March–April 1986, p. 86).

### Product Advantages and Product Differentiation

A firm that has developed a reputation for superior products in the domestic market may find acceptance for the products in foreign markets as well. In the 1920s, the early days of the U.S. automobile industry, cars were exported to Europe in large numbers. This was before the auto industry was developed in European countries. The advantage of the United States in this mass-production industry made the U.S. cars cheaper despite the high foreign tariffs and motivated foreign direct investments. The tables then were turned. First Volkswagens came from Germany to the United States. Later cars from Japan came to have a strong acceptance in the United States. Further, manufacturing operations by foreign makers were established in the United States.

Indeed, the entry of foreign products and makers is likely to intensify competition in the markets in which it takes place. Most major American industries are now subject to international competition.

### Government Policy

Government policy, regulation, tariffs, and quotas can affect international mergers and acquisitions in a number of ways. Exports are particularly vulnerable to tariffs and quotas erected to protect domestic industries. Even the threat of such restrictions can encourage international mergers, especially when the market to be protected is large. Japan's huge export surplus, which led to voluntary export restrictions coupled with threats of more binding restrictions, was a major factor in increased direct investment by Japan in the United States.

Environmental and other government regulations (such as zoning, for example) can greatly increase the time and cost required to build facilities abroad for de novo entry. The added cost of compliance with regulation amplifies other effects that may be operating. Thus, the rationale for acquiring a company with existing facilities in place is reinforced by regulation.

Changes in government policy can make acquisitions in various countries more or less attractive. A good example of this was the policy instituted by the Canadian government in 1981 to reduce foreign ownership of Canada's energy resources. To implement the policy, the government gave Canadian-owned energy companies advantageous treatment, including subsidizing exploration and development costs, relative to foreign-owned energy companies operating in Canada. The resulting competitive disadvantage suffered by American-owned and other foreign-owned firms reduced their profitability relative to their Canadian-owned counterparts, and accordingly, reduced their market values. This made them attractive acquisition targets for Canadian energy companies. Thus, the government policy was directly responsible for a large number of divestitures of foreign-owned Canadian energy subsidiaries. In terms of U.S. merger and acquisition activity, these transactions show up as foreign acquisitions of (from) U.S. firms. In 1981 and 1982, 62 and 36 such transactions, respectively, represented 25% of all transactions for that period, and accounted for 40% of reported dollar volume. The 1982 purchase by Aberford Resources Ltd. of Canada of two subsidiaries of Marathon Oil Company for $225 million is typical.

The South African previous policy of apartheid, while not intended as an economic policy as such, has had a similar effect of causing the divestiture of local subsidiaries by U.S. firms in the face of mounting social and economic pressures against investment in that country. For the most part, these subsidiaries are purchased by South African interests, often the management group that had been in charge of the firm.

More recently, the Canadian government has begun to encourage investment in Canada, or at least not to discourage it. Prior to July 1985 virtually all foreign investment in Canada was subject to scrutiny by the Foreign Investment Review Board (FIRA). FIRA has now been replaced with an agency called Investment Canada. (Even the more upbeat name reflects the change in attitude.) The new policy exempts from review altogether most of those transactions that would have required FIRA review, streamlines the review process when it is required, and more clearly defines (and relaxes) the criteria by which transactions are judged. Merger and acquisition opportunities for both Canadian and foreign investors have also been expanded by the Canadian government's decision to privatize many of the companies it currently owns. (The Boeing–de Havilland transaction mentioned earlier in the technology section came about as a result of this decision.)

## Exchange Rates

Foreign exchange rates impact international mergers in a number of ways. The relative strength or weakness of the domestic versus foreign currency can impact the effective price paid for an acquisition, its financing, production costs of running the acquired firm, and the value of repatriated profits to the parent. Accounting conventions can give rise to currency translation profits and losses. Managing exchange rate risk is an additional cost of doing business for a multinational firm.

Dramatic examples can be cited. For example, the *Wall Street Journal* of January 21, 1988 reported that Japanese acquisitions in the United States during 1987 were almost $6 billion. The article referred to the increased strength of the yen in relation to the dollar (Sesit, 1988).

At about the same time an article in the *Los Angeles Times* referred to the "selling of America." It pointed out that lower stock prices and the weakness of the dollar in relation to many other major currencies made U.S. properties relatively inexpensive to foreigners (Moskowitz, 1988).

## Political/Economic Stability

The relative political and economic stability of the United States have been important factors in attracting foreign buyers. Political and/or economic instability can greatly increase the risk of what is already a riskier situation than purely domestic investments or acquisitions. Political stability considerations run the gamut from outright war (during which one does not observe many international acquisitions, though presumably there are bargains to be had) to the opposite extreme, with all the variations between. Acquiring firms must consider the frequency with which the government changes, how orderly is the transfer of power, and how much government policies differ from one administration to the next, including the degree of difference between the dominant political parties. They must assess the likelihood of government intervention on both the upside and the downside (for example, subsidies, tax breaks, loan guarantees, and so forth, on the one hand, all the way to outright expropriation on the other hand). Desirable economic factors include low, or at least predictable, inflation. Labor relations are another important consideration in economic stability. American unions are neither as strong nor as socialistic and militaristic as labor unions in many other parts of the world. Western European labor unions appear to have a far greater voice in the management of companies than do American unions. The stability of exchange rates is yet another factor in economic stability.

The United States excels in virtually every measure of economic and political stability (except exchange rate stability in recent years). It is also a superior target because of the size and homogeneity of the market and the sophistication of its infrastructure. Transportation and communications networks are among the best in the world; the depth and breadth of U.S. financial markets are attractive; there is little risk of expropriation. Indeed, most states offer inducements to investment, and the labor force is relatively skilled and tractable.

## Differential Labor Costs, Productivity

We previously raised the issue of labor relations and its effect on the attractiveness of the economic environment. The labor climate clearly impacts the costs of production, but here we are concerned more directly with labor costs and productivity. High labor costs and the declining productivity of the American worker have historically been cited as a barrier to entry in the United States. However, during the 1975–1980 period, declining dollar strength actually caused relative U.S. labor costs to fall, encouraging foreign acquisitions of U.S. firms (*Mergerstat Review*, 1984, foreign buyers section). Labor costs were presumably not equalized by exchange rates for this motive to have an impact. In terms of productivity, although American workers have come in for much criticism, a survey of foreign managers conducted by the U.S. Department of Commerce in 1975 indicated that American workers were considered to be at least the equal of foreign workers in both adaptability and motivation (Khoury, 1980, p. 53). Management systems impact labor productivity. When the closed GM Fremont, California plant was reopened under Toyota management, absenteeism dropped and productivity greatly increased.

### To Follow Clients (Especially by Banks)

The importance of long-term banking relationships is a major factor in international mergers in the banking industry. If enough of a bank's clients move abroad, it makes economic sense for the bank to expand abroad as well. Foreign firms abroad may wish to remain loyal to their longstanding, home-country banks. However, if the foreign bank does not have offices available for servicing its clients, it runs the risk of losing business to more convenient local banks.

For some time, foreign banks operating in the United States actually had an advantage over U.S. banks, especially in interstate banking, in that they were allowed to have branches in more than one state (with restrictions), while this was denied to U.S. banks. Over the years the playing field has become more equal.

### Diversification

International mergers can provide diversification both geographically and by product line. International conglomerate mergers are relatively rare; firms appear to be reluctant to add the risk of operating in a new product market to the risks of operating in a new geographic environment. Product diversification in the form of vertical integration, both backward and forward, is more common.

To the extent that various economies are not perfectly correlated, then merging internationally reduces the earnings risk inherent in being dependent on the health of a single domestic economy. Thus, international mergers can reduce systematic as well as nonsystematic risk.

### To Assure a Source of Raw Materials

This is an important motivating factor in vertical mergers, especially for acquiring firms from resource-poor domestic economies. Mergers are used as a means to forestall the erection of barriers against the import/export of raw materials. In the case of strategic raw materials, this approach may not be applicable, because many countries, including the United States, have restrictions on foreign ownership of such assets.

## PREMIUMS PAID

The *Mergerstat* data as well as academic studies find that foreign bidders pay higher premiums to acquire U.S. companies than premiums paid in all acquisitions. The data for recent years are presented in Table 17.5, which shows that the average premium offered by foreign buyers was higher than the overall average in seven of the past 10 years.

The data are subject to some limitations. The figures in parentheses in Table 17.5 are the small sample number of transactions on which the arithmetic means are calculated. However, these data are supported by academic studies of event returns. For example, in the Harris and Ravenscraft (1991) study for a sample of companies between 1970 and 1987, foreign bidders pay higher premia by 10 percentage points. They found also that high foreign currency values led to increased premia. Their data show that when foreign firms buy U.S. firms, they concentrate on research and development (R&D)-intensive industries. They find that the R&D intensity of foreign acquisitions is 50% higher than in purely domestic transactions. The Harris and Ravenscraft study finds also that U.S. bidders earn only normal returns in both domestic and cross-border acquisitions. These results are consistent with other studies of bidder and target returns.

| TABLE 17.5 | Average Premium Offered over Market Comparison of Foreign and Total Net Announcements, 1986–1995 | | | |
| --- | --- | --- | --- | --- |
| | Foreign Acquisitions (Base) | | All Acquisitions (Base) | |
| 1986 | 33.0% | (46) | 38.2% | (333) |
| 1987 | 39.4% | (37) | 38.3% | (237) |
| 1988 | 56.2% | (54) | 41.9% | (410) |
| 1989 | 38.9% | (59) | 41.0% | (303) |
| 1990 | 48.1% | (37) | 42.0% | (175) |
| 1991 | 39.8% | (16) | 35.1% | (137) |
| 1992 | 54.1% | (8) | 41.0% | (142) |
| 1993 | 41.8% | (17) | 38.7% | (173) |
| 1994 | 46.2% | (33) | 41.9% | (260) |
| 1995 | 41.9% | (34) | 44.7% | (324) |

*Source: Mergerstat Review, 1996, p. 27.*

# EVENT RETURNS

An early study (Doukas and Travlos, 1988) found that the announcement of international acquisitions was associated with positive abnormal returns for U.S. multinational enterprises that previously had not been operating in the target firm's country. When American firms expand internationally for the first time, the event returns are positive but not significant. When the American firm has already been operating in the target firm's home country, the event returns are negative but not significant. Shareholders of multinational enterprises gain the greatest benefits from foreign acquisitions when there is simultaneous diversification across industry and geographically.

Harris and Ravenscraft (1991) investigated shareholder returns for 1,273 U.S. firms acquired during the period 1970–1987. They found that in 75% of cross-border transactions, the buyer and seller are not in related industries, and that the takeovers are more frequent in R&D-intensive industries than are domestic transactions. The percentage gain to the U.S. targets of foreign buyers is significantly higher than the targets of U.S. buyers. The cross-border effects are positively related to the weakness of the U.S. dollar, indicating an important role for exchange movements in foreign direct investment.

A study of Japanese takeovers of U.S. firms (Kang, 1993) found that significant wealth gains are created for both Japanese bidders and U.S. targets. Returns to Japanese bidders and to a portfolio of Japanese bidders and U.S. targets increase with the leverage of the bidder, bidder's ties to financial institutions, and the depreciation of the dollar in relation to the Japanese yen. But a study that controls for relative corporate wealth and levels of investment in different countries finds no statistically significant relationship between exchange rate levels and foreign investment relative to domestic investment (Dewenter, 1995).

# INTERNATIONAL JOINT VENTURES

International joint ventures magnify both the potentials and the weaknesses of joint ventures. In general, joint ventures should involve complementary capabilities. The risks of different cultural systems among firms from different countries may increase the tensions normally found in joint ventures.

Despite the increased challenges of international joint ventures, the advantages of joint ventures may be expanded. Some of the particular benefits of international joint ventures may be noted (Zahra and Elhagrasey, 1994): (1) The joint venture may be the only feasible method of obtaining access to raw materials and of overcoming government barriers to exporting key raw materials. (2) Different historical backgrounds and different managerial and technological skills may be associated with firms in different countries. International joint ventures, therefore, may involve different capabilities and link together complementary skills. (3) Having local partners may reduce the risks involved in operating in a foreign country. (4) The joint ventures may be necessary to overcome trade barriers. In addition, some of the advantages of domestic joint ventures may be enhanced. These include the achievement of economies of scale in providing a basis for a faster rate of corporate growth.

Management styles may be different for companies from different countries. However, it appears that over time there has been increasing convergence of Western and Asian management styles (Swierczek and Hirsch, 1994). In the past, the basic values of Western management emphasized the individual, legal rules, and confrontation. In contrast, the Asian approach emphasized the group, trust, and compromise. With regard to management style, the Western approach was emphasized by rationality and structured relationships. The Asian approach involved relationships, flexibility, and adaptive behavior. Over time, however, a convergence of the different management styles has been taking place.

Because of the complexity of relationships of international joint ventures, some principles have been suggested for the management of successful collaborations (Shaughnessy, 1995). Because joint ventures are a temporary alliance for combining complementary capabilities, joint venture contracts should make it easy to terminate the relationship. The initial contract should take into account which firm will become the outright owner of the joint venture activity and formulate the terms under which one company can buy out the other. The control and ultimate decision makers should be specified in advance. The activities and information flows in the joint venture should be tied into normal communications structures.

Criteria for evaluation of performance should be a part of the contractual relationship. Because of the inherent uncertainties of the future alternative outcomes, scenarios should be visualized as a basis for allocation of rewards and responsibilities under different types of outcomes. Finally, it is in the international area particularly that the knowledge acquisition potentials of joint ventures can be substantial. However, contractual differences may also put these potentials at considerable risk or failure of realization.

A study of 88 international joint venture announcements finds statistically significant positive portfolio excess returns (Chen, Hu, and Shieh, 1991) when U.S. firms invest relatively small amounts in the joint ventures that gain significantly positive excess returns. When firms make relatively large investments in the joint ventures, the positive excess returns are no longer significant.

An in-depth book-length study of joint ventures in the steel industry documents the diverse motives and effects (Mangum, Kim, and Tallman (MKT), 1996). The authors place the steel industry in the setting of an industrial staircase that moves from the agrarian age to an industrial age and finally to the present information age. The steel industry is put in the setting of a basic intermediate product with a capital resource emphasis. Summary data are provided on the investments by 17 foreign steel makers in U.S. joint ventures. The foreign partners are mainly from Japan. In-depth case studies of seven joint ventures in steel are presented. The initial motive was the availability of foreign capital for modernizing the U.S. steel industry. Another important objective was to transfer the superior process technologies of the Asian partners to American plants. Cross-cultural differences added to the tensions usually found in joint ventures. Nevertheless, MKT judge the joint ventures to be generally successful. The only joint venture that experienced great difficulties was the combination between NKK of Japan and the National Steel Corporation of the U.S. NKK was Japan's second largest steel producer but accounted for only 15% of Japan's total output of finished steel as compared with 72% for number one Nippon Steel. National Steel had been formed in 1929 and was number seven in the United States. In the fall of 1983, it reorganized itself as National Intergroup Inc. (NII), announcing that it would withdraw from the steel business and diversify into pharmaceuticals, aluminum, financial services, and computer services. Early in 1984 NII sold its Weirton works to its employees under an ESOP. It offered the remainder of its steel making facilities to USX. But the Department of Justice blocked the sale on antitrust grounds.

Among the alternatives, the joint venture with NKK seemed the least unpalatable. NKK considered itself to be a world leader in steel technology but was unable to exploit its capabilities fully because of domestic overcapacity and rising obstacles to international trade. The joint venture with NII was viewed as the first step in its broader globalization plans. Despite considerable progress, the economic downturn in the United States in 1989–1990 caused losses. National Steel made a public offering of common stock as a device for NII to sell its ownership to the public. NKK's ownership share moved from 50 to 75%. NII "bailed out" of the joint venture. NKK took over ownership seeking to restore its profitability. For 1994 a net income of a positive $168.5 million was achieved. Mangum et al. conclude that while the joint venture came asunder, National Steel survived under a new management team.

## COST OF EQUITY FOR AN MNE

We calculate the cost of equity capital for an MNE by the use of the capital asset pricing model (CAPM). First, we discuss some privately circulated memoranda prepared by a number of investment banking companies and consulting firms. We then review a set of academic studies. We begin with the familiar CAPM equation reproduced as (17.1).

$$k_s = R_f + [\bar{R}_M - R_f]\beta_j \qquad (17.1)$$

where:

$R_f$ = risk-free rate

$(\bar{R}_M - R_f)$ = market price of risk

$\beta_j$ = the systematic risk of the individual asset or firm

$k_s$ = the cost of equity capital

The order of magnitude of the numerical counterparts to the capital asset pricing equation shown in equation (17.1) can be estimated. The risk-free rate is the required return on medium-term government bonds. At periods of relatively high interest rates this could be as much as 8% or more. For periods of relatively low interest rates, the risk-free rate could be as low as 6%. We shall use 7% in our example.

The market price of risk, which is the difference between the return on the market and the risk-free rate, is generally acknowledged to be in the range of about 6.5 to 8.5%. Using a risk-free rate of about 7% and the market price of risk of 7.5%, the average cost of equity (when beta equals 1) would be in the range of about 14.5%.

We next consider how the basic 14.5% rate might be higher for an emerging country with greater risk. The first thing we consider is how the risk-free rate might be adjusted for country risk ($C_s$). It is possible to separate currency translation risks from other forms of country risks. Often an emerging country will issue bonds denominated in the currency of the investor country such as dollars, marks, or yen. We could write equation (17.1a) on how we would adjust the U.S. risk-free rate for the individual country risk, $C_s$.

$$R_{fmex} = R_{fus} + C_s \qquad (17.1a)$$

For Mexico, the spread between 30-year U.S. Treasury bonds and Mexican 30-year dollar denominated bonds has averaged between 240 and 300 basis points. We will add 3 percentage points to the risk-free rate of the United States to obtain a risk-free rate for Mexico of about 10%. The higher required basic government bond rate in Mexico would reflect country risk. Some indicators of country risk are:

1. government deficit/GDP
2. current account deficit/GDP
3. gross external debt/exports
4. inflation and unemployment rates
5. exchange rate controls
6. inflows of foreign direct and portfolio investments
7. GDP growth rates
8. political stability

We next consider the equity risk premium. If the equity returns in the developing country are fully integrated with the returns in the United States, the capital asset pricing model could be written as in equation (17.2).

$$R_{mex} = R_{fus} + C_s + \beta_{mex} R_{us} \qquad (17.2)$$

In this equation, $R_{mex}$ is equal to the required equity return in the developing country, and $\beta_{mex}$ is the beta of equity returns in the developing country. Recall that beta can be written as in equation (17.3).

$$\beta_{mex} = \frac{Cov(R_{mex}, R_{us})}{\sigma_{us}^2} \qquad (17.3)$$

The numerator of this expression can be rewritten as the definition of covariance as shown in equation (17.3a),

$$\beta_{mex} = \frac{\rho_{mexus}\sigma_{mex}\sigma_{us}}{\sigma_{us}^2} \qquad (17.3a)$$

where rho ($\rho$) is the correlation coefficient between the equity returns in the developing country and the equity returns in the United States. In completely integrated markets, the correlation coefficient between the returns would be 1. Hence, beta would become simply the ratio of the standard deviation of returns in the two countries. On the other hand, if the two markets are not fully integrated, then the relationship would simply be whatever the measured beta turned out to be for equation (17.2).

Studies of Mexico indicate that by either measure, the beta or the ratio of standard deviations, the last term in equation (17.2) would be about 5½ percentage points higher than for the United States. Thus, the numerical value for the required return for a beta equal to 1 in the developing country would be as shown in equation (17.4).

$$R_{mex} = 7\% + 3\% + (7.5\% + 5.5\%) = 23\% \qquad \textbf{(17.4)}$$

The 7% represents the U.S. risk-free rate; the 3% represents the country risk; the 7.5% represents the U.S. market price of risk; the 5.5% is the equity risk premium for the developing country. Equation (17.4) suggests that the basic cost of equity securities in developing countries such as Mexico would be on the order of magnitude of about 23%.

We acknowledge that the CAPM may not apply perfectly in developing countries subject to political and social instabilities. If anything, our 23% estimate might be on the low side. However, we have observed estimates from investment banking firms whose studies assign a required return on equity for countries such as Mexico of about 14.5%. Surely this is too low. We have also checked with major investor participants in the Mexican market as to the equity returns they have required in practice. Responses from a number of sources support our estimate of about a 21 to 23% cost of equity capital on average for a company in Mexico. For individual companies, individual company betas would adjust these percentages upward or downward.

To generalize the above, we might have patterns such as shown in Table 17.6, which suggests that a U.S. company with a beta of about 1 would have a total cost of equity of about 14.5%. This contrasts with a large company in Mexico of the type we have just discussed. We would add elements for sovereign country risk and a stock market volatility or extra equity risk premium. This comes to a total of 23%.

The big question is a large multinational company in Japan, Germany, or Switzerland, relatively hard-currency countries. We would argue that their cost of equity would not be greatly different from that of a large U.S. MNE. The practical reasons are that in recent years Japanese, German, and Swiss companies finance in the U.S. We observe also that U.S., German, and Japanese companies may finance in instruments denominated in dollars, mark, or yen. Our judgment is that in recent years, the financial markets of the world have become essentially integrated for the developed countries of the world. We recognize that this is an area where disagreements may exist (Chan, Karolyi, and Stulz, 1992; Stulz, 1995a, 1995b; Stulz and Wasserfallen, 1995). An approach very close to ours is found in Godfrey and Espinosa (1996). Their estimate of the cost of capital for a company in Mexico is 22.3%—very close to our 23%. For a company in Brazil their estimate is 28.4%.

**TABLE 17.6**    Components of the Cost of Equity in an International Context

|  | Risk-Free Rate | Sovereign Risk | U.S. Market Price of Risk | Equity Risk Premium for Non-U.S. Company | Cost of Equity |
|---|---|---|---|---|---|
| United States | 7% | 0 | 7.5% | 0 | 14.5% |
| Mexico | 7% | 3% | 7.5% | 5.5% | 23.0% |
| Japan Germany Switzerland | 7% | 0 | 7.5% | 0 | 14.5% |

## THE COST OF DEBT

The interest rate parity theorem is used to explain the cost of debt in an international setting. The formal statement of the interest rate parity theorem can be expressed in equation (17.5).

$$\frac{X_f}{X_0} = \frac{1 + R_{f0}}{1 + R_{d0}} = \frac{E_0}{E_f} \tag{17.5}$$

where:

$X_f$ = current forward exchange rate expressed as foreign currency (FC) units per \$1

$E_f$ = current forward exchange rate expressed as dollars per FC

$X_0$ = current spot exchange rate expressed as FC units per \$1

$E_0$ = current spot exchange rate expressed as dollars per FC

$R_{f0}$ = current nominal foreign interest rate

$R_{d0}$ = current nominal domestic interest rate

Thus, if the foreign interest rate is 15% while the domestic interest rate is 10% and the spot exchange rate is $X_0 = 10$, the current forward exchange rate will be:

| Annual Basis | Quarterly Basis |
|---|---|
| $X_f = \dfrac{1 + R_{f0}}{1 + R_{d0}}(X_0)$ | $X_f = \dfrac{1 + R_{f0}/4}{1 + R_{d0}/4}(X_0)$ |
| $= \dfrac{1.15}{1.10}(10)$ | $= \dfrac{1.0375}{1.025}(10)$ |
| $= 10.45$ | $= 10.122$ |

Thus, the indicated foreign forward rate is 10.45 units of foreign currency per \$1, and the foreign forward rate is at a discount of 4.5% on an annual basis. If the time period of a transaction is 90 days, we have to rework the problem, first changing the interest rates to a quarterly basis. The discount on the 90-day forward rate would now be 1.22% on the quarterly basis, because the 90-day forward rate would be 10.122.

Alternatively, the example could be formulated for the effect on interest rates of expected changes in future foreign exchange rates.

The approximation for the interest rate parity theorem (IRPT) is:

$$R_{fi} - R_{di} \cong \frac{X_f - X_0}{X_0}$$

The data for the annual example are used to illustrate the approximation:

$$0.15 - 0.10 \cong \frac{10.45 - 10}{10}$$

$$0.05 \cong 0.045$$

The interest rate parity theorem has considerable practical relevance. It is essential for understanding the relative costs of obtaining debt funds domestically or abroad.

For example, the VP-finance of a Mexican company can borrow $1 million in the U.S. at 8% when $X_0 = 5.0$ and $X_f = 6.8 = X_1$. The equivalent borrowing cost in Mexico is:

**INTEREST RATE IN DOLLARS:**

| | |
|---|---|
| Loan | $1,000,000 |
| Interest | 80,000 |
| Total | $1,080,000 |

**INTEREST RATE BASED ON PESOS:**

$$\text{Paid } \$1,080,000 \ (6.8) = 7,344,000 \text{ pesos}$$
$$\text{Received } \$1,000,000 \ (5.0) = 5,000,000 \text{ pesos}$$
$$\text{Interest cost in pesos} = 2,344,000 \text{ pesos}$$
$$\text{Effective interest rate} = \frac{2,344,000}{5,000,000} \frac{\text{Interest paid}}{\text{Principal}}$$
$$= .4688$$

**CHECK WITH IRPT:**

$$\frac{1 + R_{f0}}{1 + R_{d0}} = \frac{X_f}{X_0}$$

$$\frac{1 + R_{f0}}{1.08} = \left(\frac{6.8}{5.0}\right)$$

$$1.36 \times 1.08 = 1.4688 = R_{f0}$$

Thus, given the data for the spot rate of 5 pesos per dollar, and the current forward rate of 6.8 pesos per dollar, borrowing at 8% in U.S. dollars is equivalent to borrowing at 46.88% in Mexican pesos. Thus, under the relationships specified, borrowing in Mexico at 40% would be cheaper than borrowing in the U.S. at 8%. As indicated, borrowing in Mexico at less than 46.88% would be cheaper than borrowing in the U.S. at 8%. This example demonstrates how foreign exchange rate movements can influence interest rate levels in an international context.

## Summary

International mergers are subject to many of the same influences and motivations as domestic mergers. However, they also present unique threats and opportunities. The issue of merger versus other means of achieving international business goals (such as import/export, licensing, joint ventures) builds on the fundamental issue in the theory of the firm—whether to transact across markets or to internalize transactions using managerial coordination within the firm.

When firms choose to merge internationally, it implies they have concluded this will result in lower costs or higher productivity than alternative contractual means of achieving international goals. In horizontal mergers, intangible assets play an important role in both domestic and international combinations. To exploit an intangible asset, such as knowledge, may require merger because of the public good nature of the asset. Attempts to exploit intangibles short of merger requires complex contracting, which is not only expensive, but likely to be incomplete (especially when compounded by the problems of dealing with a foreign environment) possibly leading to dissipation of the owner's proprietary interest in the asset. Similarly, vertically integrated firms exist to internalize markets for intermediate products on both the domestic and international levels.

Among the special factors impacting international mergers more than domestic are tariff barriers and exchange rate relationships. Operating within a tariff barrier may be the only means of obtaining competitive access to a large market, for example, the European Common Market. Exchange rates are also an important influence. A strong dollar makes U.S. products more expensive abroad, but reduces the cost of acquiring foreign firms. The reverse holds when the dollar is weak, encouraging U.S. exports and foreign acquisitions of U.S. companies.

Although the risks of operating in a foreign environment are greater, they can be reduced through careful planning, or by an incremental approach to entering the foreign market. Further, to the extent that the foreign economy is imperfectly correlated with the domestic economy, the systematic risk of the company as a whole may be reduced by international diversification.

The increasing globalization of competition in product markets is extending rapidly into internationalization of the takeover market. The best target to achieve a firm's expansion goals may no longer be a domestic firm but a foreign one. International M&A activity has experienced substantial growth over the past 20 years, and this is likely to continue into the future.

-----

## Questions

17.1. Why acquire a foreign firm rather than license, export, or joint venture the product?

17.2. a. What is the role of intangible assets in horizontal multinational enterprises?
   b. What factors are more important in vertical MNEs?

17.3. How will a product-specialized firm choose to enter a large foreign market as compared to a firm offering diverse products in diverse countries?

17.4. How should a firm react if its domestic market is under attack by a foreign firm that uses high profit margins at home to sell at low margins abroad?

17.5. How should a firm react if a domestic competitor expands into a large and growing overseas market that only provides normal returns?

----- C A S E    17–1 -----

# The Saga of Gerber Products

The case study of Gerber Products is a more detailed analysis of the role of international markets in the growth of food companies. For years, Gerber saw the necessity of expanding abroad. But somehow Gerber was unable to implement its goals of expanding internationally. The M&A market accomplished what Gerber was unable to do on its own.

## GERBER REBUFFS ANDERSON CLAYTON

In 1977 Gerber Products was approached by Anderson Clayton Company. Anderson Clayton was seeking to continue to expand its diversified operations, which had already included processing soy beans, coffee, and a life insurance company. Anderson

Clayton's overtures were rebuffed by Gerber Products. Nevertheless, Anderson Clayton made a tender offer for Gerber Products at $40 a share.

Gerber management mounted a strong defense. Gerber Products filed suit against Anderson Clayton in a federal court in Grand Rapids, Michigan, relatively near the Gerber headquarters in Fremont, Michigan. Gerber charged that the acquisition by Anderson Clayton would represent a serious antitrust conflict. It charged that potential competition between the companies in the future would be stifled by the merger. Gerber argued that Anderson Clayton could develop a baby products business in the future. Gerber also stated that it had been considering entrance into the salad oil market in which Anderson Clayton was already doing business. Gerber's lawsuit also charged that in its tender offer Anderson Clayton did not make adequate disclosure of $2.1 million in questionable payments it had made overseas. This charge obviously sought to embarrass Anderson Clayton by the adverse publicity that would be generated by raising this issue. Gerber also complained that Anderson Clayton had not made adequate disclosure of its financing arrangements in its tender offer filing. Under Michigan's antitakeover law, there is a requirement for a 60-day waiting period after a tender offer. Gerber Products used this time to seek out an acceptable white knight. Gerber began discussions with Unilever as a possible alternative purchaser. Anderson Clayton continued its friendly approaches to Gerber. In addition, Anderson Clayton secured a financing agreement from several New York banks to establish compliance with this requirement under Michigan's antitakeover law.

At its July 1977 annual meeting, Gerber reported that second-quarter earnings had dropped by one-third. Anderson Clayton indicated that Gerber was deliberately understating its earnings and lowered its offer from $40 to $37.

In the meantime, the Michigan courts issued a series of rulings, all favorable to Gerber. A trial on the securities charges was scheduled for September 1977. After this trial, there would be another in which the antitrust charges would be litigated. Faced with uncertain and expensive litigation and the possibility that over the extended period of time other bidders might force higher bids, Anderson Clayton withdrew its offer. In response to this announcement, the stock price of Gerber fell from $34.375 to $28.25.

## GERBER'S STRATEGIC PROBLEMS

In the intervening years, Gerber sought to reduce its vulnerability to a takeover. Gerber attempted to diversify into other areas such as children's apparel, furniture, farming, day-care centers, trucking, humidifiers, and life insurance. None of these appeared to have any real synergy with Gerber's baby-food business.

Although Gerber held 70% of the U.S. baby-food market, it was relatively weak abroad. Higher growth for Gerber would have meant increasing its sales outside the U.S. where 98% of the world's annual new births take place. Over the years, Gerber made some efforts to expand its overseas operations but hesitated to commit the funds that would have had a near-term negative impact on its profitability rates. Because it was an inexpensive way to go, Gerber often would license overseas manufacturers to make and distribute its baby food. Licensing has at least two drawbacks. First, the fees that can be charged for licensing are relatively small. Second, the licensee develops the critical capability and can always play one product off against another. Sometimes the licensing arrangements came to an end because the foreign manufacturer decided to shift to other products. As a consequence, increasingly Gerber was supplying Asia and the Middle East from its U.S. plants.

## THE AUCTION OF GERBER

As a consequence of its weak performance abroad, Gerber's revenues stayed flat at about $1.2 billion from 1990 through 1994 (Gibson, 1994). Its net income for the years 1990 through 1994 averaged less than $100 million. Gerber had stock splits in 1982, 1984, 1989, and 1992. But adjusted for all splits, the Gerber stock had stayed relatively flat in the range of $30 per share. Gerber realized it needed to go abroad but was reluctant to commit the resources that would have a negative impact on earnings. In early 1994 Gerber requested Goldman Sachs to explore a possible friendly buyout that would help Gerber become stronger in the overseas markets. Essentially, an auction was conducted. The winner was Sandoz AG, a Swiss company that bid $53 a share on May 23, 1994. When takeover speculation started, the price of Gerber's shares moved up by 33% between early February 1994 and the period just before the Sandoz offer. After the Sandoz offer, Gerber shares increased another $15.50 to $50.125. The $53 price was high because it represented 30 times current earnings, 20 times after-tax cash flow, and three times sales.

For Sandoz, the acquisition would expand its position in the food business and in nutritional product sales. Sandoz already had a strong position in food sales in Europe and Asia but only 14% of its food sales came from North America.

It was pointed out that the Sandoz bid would not include any form of stock option lockup. This followed from the court decision in the QVC takeover of Paramount. Paramount had granted Viacom, its preferred buyer, the right to buy 24 million Paramount shares for $69.14. When Paramount went to $80 a share, the option was worth $500 million to Viacom. Nevertheless, the Sandoz agreement involved a breakup fee. In a breakup fee arrangement, the original bidder receives a fee if it does not succeed in the takeover. Gerber agreed to pay $70 million to Sandoz if the Sandoz bid did not succeed.

Some writers argue that differences in tax laws made the acquisition more attractive to Sandoz than to a U.S. buyer (Sloan, 1994). The tangible net worth of Gerber was about $300 million. For a U.S. buyer, the difference between the $3.7 billion paid and the $300 million tangible net worth of Gerber would have represented goodwill. A U.S. company would have had to charge its after-tax profits, $85 million a year for 40 years, which was 75% of the $114 million net income of Gerber in its 1994 fiscal year. Sandoz, on the other hand, could charge the goodwill against its own net worth without affecting annual earnings. It was stated that the $114 million net income would represent a 38% return on the $300 million tangible assets Sandoz would add to its balance sheet (Sloan, 1994). In addition, there was also a possibility of a tax write-off by Sandoz in connection with the goodwill purchase and write-off.

## Questions on Case Study C17.1

C17.1.1  Why was Gerber interested in expanding in international markets?
C17.1.2  Why was Gerber unable to succeed on its own in developing international markets?
C17.1.3  Why did Gerber reject the earlier efforts by Anderson Clayton to acquire it?
C17.1.4  Why did Gerber request its investment banker to find a buyer who could develop Gerber's potential in international markets?
C17.1.5  Why was Sandoz interested in Gerber?

## C A S E   17–2
# Ciba-Geigy Merger with Sandoz*

In Basel, Switzerland on March 7, 1996, Ciba-Geigy and Sandoz issued a joint statement by the chairmen of both companies that they will merge into one company with the new name, Novartis (Olmos, 1996). The company will focus on its core businesses, which are pharmaceuticals, agribusiness, and nutrition. Each company will divest its divisions that do not relate to the core life-science focus of the new company Novartis. This includes for Ciba its division of specialty chemicals (Tanouye et al., 1996).

Ciba is well known for its New Vues disposable contact lens, Habitrol nicotine patches, Ritalin for hyperactive children, Sunkist vitamins, Maalox, Zantac, and Efidac, an over-the-counter cold medicine.

*Written by Erica Clark and J. F. Weston.

Sandoz is known for its nutrition division, which includes Gerber baby foods, Ovaltine, and Wasa crispbreads.

The new name Novartis is partly due to the strategy that the merger is between two equals who wish to become an innovator for the next century (Guyon, 1996). The new name was developed by London's Siegal & Gale consultants who were hired to create a powerful new marketing strategy for the company. The word derives from the Latin *novo,* which means new, and *artis,* which means skill. The new name had to be tested in 180 counties to make sure that it did not have any negative connotations.

Ciba-Geigy is the world's ninth largest drugmaker, while Sandoz is the 14th. The new merger will create a new company that will be the world's number one supplier in agricultural chemicals, a world leader in biotechnology, and a large presence in the nutrition products field. The new firm will still have only 4.4% of the global market. The new company would have the third largest pharmaceutical revenue with drug sales at $10.94 billion (1995 revenue).

On April 24, 1996, in Basel, Switzerland, the merger was put to a vote at the final Ciba annual general meeting. The meeting counted 6,896 people in attendance with 70% of share capital with voting privileges. The CEO of Ciba, Dr. Alex Krauer, told shareholders that the merger "will not only improve shareholder value, but also open a promising future for the majority of our employees." The merger was approved by 98.7% of the members present and 69.4% of the share capital. The Sandoz shareholders approved the merger on April 24, 1996. The next phase of merger approval will be regulatory agencies of the European Union and to a lesser extent that of the United States.

Shareholders of Ciba stock will receive 1.067 shares of Novartis, and shareholders of Sandoz stock will receive exactly one share of Novartis for each share they currently hold. Sandoz shareholders will receive 55% of the new company, whereas Ciba shareholders will receive 45% of Novartis.

The merger took many analysts by surprise, but most agree that it is an excellent strategic move because it is a proactive reaction to the general consolidation of the industry. The bankers who negotiated the deal were also praised because it was structured as a share swap instead of an outright purchase. This will cause the deal to be virtually tax free, and there will also be no write-down of "goodwill."

Goodwill compensates for the difference between sale price and the book value of assets, but can be a negative force because it reduces reported profits.

The news of the merger sent stock prices of the large pharmaceutical companies soaring. It also affected smaller companies that are seen as possible takeover targets for the large companies looking to compete with the new Novartis. Both companies are traded on the Swiss stock market and reaction to the news was positive for both companies, Sandoz's shares rising 20% and Ciba's rising 30%. This can also be attributed to the intended cut of 10% of the work force of the newly created company. The new company will have an estimated total market value of $60 billion.

## STRATEGIC REASONS FOR THE CIBA-SANDOZ MERGER

The consolidation of these two large companies reflects a growing trend in the fiercely competitive pharmaceuticals industry (Kraul, 1996). This is partly attributable to the high cost of research and development that is specific to the industry. There have been an estimated $80 billion in mergers since 1993 in the pharmaceutical industry. However, the top 20 companies still only make up 50% of total sales worldwide (*Economist,* 1994).

Both companies are facing the fundamental challenges that most drug companies are encountering in the current highly competitive market. The challenge is to develop a continuing supply of significant new drugs. This constant push for innovation based on the research and development of new products causes the pharmaceutical business to be inherently risky, because research and development is extremely costly but does not guarantee a constant stream of new products. In addition, the creation of new products is also heavily dependent on the approval of regulatory agencies such as the U.S. Food and Drug Administration (FDA). Of every 10 drugs that pass the initial investigation stage, only one will ultimately receive approval of the FDA. Of the few products that ultimately do gain regulatory approval, only a fraction generate sufficient sales to earn the cost of capital for a drug company, even a modest 10 to 12%.

Another major challenge facing these companies is that the pharmaceutical industry seems to produce important scientific breakthroughs in cycles.

Doukas, John, and Nickolaos G. Travlos, "The Effect of Corporate Multinationalism on Shareholders' Wealth: Evidence from International Acquisitions," *Journal of Finance*, 43, December 1988, pp. 1161–1175.

*The Economist*, "Drug Mergers: Understanding the Pill Poppers," August 6, 1994, p. 53.

Gibson, Richard, "Gerber Missed the Boat in Quest to Go Global, So It Turned to Sandoz," *The Wall Street Journal*, May 24, 1994, pp. A1, A4.

Godfrey, Stephen, and Ramon Espinosa, "A Practical Approach to Calculating Costs of Equity for Investments in Emerging Markets," *Journal of Applied Corporate Finance*, 9, Fall 1996, pp. 80–89.

Guyon, Janet, "What Is Novartis?" *The Wall Street Journal*, March 11, 1996, p. B1.

Harris, Robert S., and David Ravenscraft, "The Role of Acquisitions in Foreign Direct Investment: Evidence from the U.S. Stock Market," *Journal of Finance*, 46, 1991, pp. 825–844.

Houlihan Lokey Howard & Zukin, *Mergerstat Review*, Los Angeles, CA, 1997, and previous years.

Kang, Jun-Koo, "The International Market for Corporate Control: Mergers and Acquisitions of U.S. Firms by Japanese Firms," *Journal of Financial Economics*, 34, December 1993, pp. 345–371.

Khoury, Sarkis J., *Transnational Mergers and Acquisitions in the United States*, Lexington, MA: Lexington Books, 1980.

Kraul, Chris, "Pain-Relieving Compound: Ciba-Sandoz Plan Is Part of the Bigger Survival Picture," *Los Angeles Times*, March 8, 1996, p. D1.

Mangum, Garth L., Sae-Young Kim, and Stephen B. Tallman, *Transnational Marriages in the Steel Industry*, Westport, CT: Quorum Books, 1996.

*Mergers & Acquisitions*, March–April 1986.

Moskowitz, Milton, "Viewpoints," *Los Angeles Times*, January 24, 1988, Part IV, pp. 3, 17.

Olmos, David, "Two Swiss Drug Firms Agree to Merge in $27-Billion Deal," *Los Angeles Times*, March 8, 1996, p. A1.

Sesit, Michael R., "Japanese Acquisitions in U.S. Jumped To $5.9 Billion in '87; Strong Yen Cited," *The Wall Street Journal*, January 21, 1988, p. 18.

Shaughnessy, Haydn, "International Joint Ventures: Managing Successful Collaborations," *Long Range Planning*, 28(3), June 1995, pp. 10–17.

Sloan, Allan, "As Swiss Sandoz Scoops Up the Gerber Baby, Blame U.S. Accounting Law," *Los Angeles Times*, June 5, 1994, p. D1.

Stulz, René M., "The Cost of Capital in Internationally Integrated Markets: The Case of Nestlé," *European Financial Management*, 1, March 1995a, pp. 11-22.

———, "Globalization of Capital Markets and the Cost of Capital: The Case of Nestlé," *Journal of Applied Corporate Finance*, 8, Fall 1995b, pp. 30–38.

———, and Walter Wasserfallen, "Foreign Equity Investment Restrictions, Capital Flight, and Shareholder Wealth Maximization: Theory and Evidence," *The Review of Financial Studies*, 8, Winter 1995, pp. 1019–1057.

Swierczek, Frederic, and Georges Hirsch, "Joint Ventures in Asia and Multicultural Management," *European Management Journal*, 12(2), June 1994, pp. 197–209.

Taber, George, "Remaking an Industry," *Time*, September 4, 1996.

Tanouye, Elise, Steve Lipin, and Stephen D. Moore, "In Big Drug Merger Sandoz and Ciba-Geigy Plan to Join Forces," *The Wall Street Journal*, March 7, 1996, p. A1.

Zahra, Shaker, and Galal Elhagrasey, "Strategic Management of International Joint Ventures," *European Management Journal*, 12(1), March 1994, pp. 83–93.

# C H A P T E R

# 18

# Share Repurchase*

The topics covered in this chapter represent areas of considerable practical significance to corporate managements. The authors often receive phone calls from high-level executives asking questions related to the subject of this chapter, such as, "We are contemplating repurchase of up to 20% of the outstanding shares of our common stock. What will be the effects on share price and will our shareholders be happy or unhappy with this activity?"

Share repurchase generally deals with cash offers for outstanding shares of common stock. This repurchase has the effect of changing the capital structure for the firm if nothing else occurs because even if the amount of debt is not changed, the amount of common stock is reduced so the debt/equity ratio or leverage ratio is increased.

Some authors reason that the amount of cash and marketable securities in excess of the transaction needs for a company should be deducted from debt in determining a firm's leverage ratio, which would result in a reduction in the leverage ratio. The use of cash to extinguish common stock would magnify the leverage ratio because no longer would debt be reduced by the excess cash and equity would be smaller. Thus, the share repurchase is almost equivalent to a debt for common stock exchange. However, the two transactions have somewhat different characteristics.

## MAJOR TYPES OF SHARE REPURCHASE

We first briefly describe four major types of share repurchase. After this overview, we analyze in greater depth the nature and implications of each. The four major types are:

1. Fixed price tender offers (FPTs)
2. Dutch auctions (DAs)
3. Transferable put rights (TPRs)
4. Open market repurchases (OMRs)

### Fixed Price Tender Offers (FPTs)

A firm offers to buy a specified fraction of shares within a given time period. The fixed tender price offered is usually higher than the prevailing market price of the stock at the time of the offer. Most fixed price tender offers are at least fully subscribed. If the offer is oversubscribed—more shares are offered than sought—the firm can buy the shares back on a pro rata basis. Alternatively, the firm may elect to buy back all shares (more than the original target number or fraction) at the tender offer price. If the

---

*This chapter was substantially revised with the assistance of Piotr Jawien.

tender offer is undersubscribed, the firm may extend the offer hoping to have more shares tendered over time, or the firm may cancel the offer if it includes a minimum acceptance clause, or the firm may simply buy back whatever number or percentage of shares actually tendered. In a fixed price tender offer, the firm usually pays any transfer taxes involved and the shareholder pays no brokerage fees.

## Dutch Auctions (DAs)

In a Dutch auction, the firm announces the number of shares it would buy in a specified time period and the price range at which shareholders may offer to tender. For example, the current price of the stock may be $14. The company may offer to buy 4 million shares at a price range of $15 to $19 a share. Typically, the price offers will be at intervals such as 10¢ or 25¢. At the offer price that results in 4 million shares being offered, all shares offered at or below that price will be purchased at that price. Thus, even though some shareholders may have offered to sell at $16, if $17 is the price at which the 4 million shares are offered, all shareholders will receive the $17 per share. Oversubscription is possible in a Dutch auction if the reservation prices of the shareholders are lower than the lower-range price terms. Oversubscription may also occur from the lumpiness of bidding schedules. For example, if at $16.70 less than 4 million shares were offered but at $16.80, 4,100,000 shares were offered, the company might accept only a fraction of shares (4.0/4.1) of the amount tendered by each shareholder, or the firm might take the full 4.1 million shares at the $16.80.

## Transferable Put Rights (TPRs)

A firm seeks to purchase 5% of its outstanding common shares. Each shareholder would receive one TPR for every 20 shares held. Thus, if a firm had 100 million shares outstanding and is seeking to repurchase 5 million shares or 5%, then 5 million TPRs would be issued, and for every 100 shares a shareholder would receive five TPRs. A secondary market develops in which TPRs are bought and sold. If the prevailing market price of the stock were $14 and the TPR gives the shareholder the right to put the stock to the company at $15.50, trading may take place in the TPRs. For shareholders who feel the stock is worth less than $15.50, such shareholders would be glad for the opportunity to put the stock to the company at $15.50. These shareholders or other investors would be buyers of the TPRs. On the other hand, shareholders who feel the stock is worth more than $15.50, for example $16 or even $18, would want to continue to hold their stock and sell their TPRs.

## Open Market Repurchases (OMRs)

A firm announces that it will repurchase some dollar amount (e.g., $5 billion or $10 billion) of its common stock from time to time in the open market. This is the most frequent type of share repurchase, outnumbering the other three methods by a factor of 10 to 1. However, open market repurchases generally involve a smaller percentage of total shares outstanding than the other methods. OMRs probably average about 5% of shares outstanding versus around 16% for fixed price tender offers.

The foregoing provides an overview of each of the four major types of share repurchases. Each one will be examined at greater depth in the attempt to understand the theory and practical decision making involved in choosing the form and terms of a share repurchase. We will start the analysis with the fixed price tender offers because they represent a convenient vehicle for developing the basic logic of share repurchases.

# FIXED PRICE TENDER OFFERS (FPTs)

In a cash tender offer the company usually sets forth the number of shares it is offering to purchase and the price at which it will repurchase shares, as well as the period of time during which the offer will be extended. The tender offer price is generally higher than the market price at the time of offer (by approximately 20% on average). The tender offer price is usually the net price received by the shareholders who tender their shares, because the tendering shareholders pay no brokerage fees and the company generally pays any transfer taxes that are levied.

The number of shares set forth in the tender offer typically represents a maximum number of shares that the company seeks to repurchase. If the number of shares tendered exceeds this limit, the company may purchase all or a fraction of shares tendered in excess of the amount initially set forth. The company also may reserve the right to extend the time period of the offer. If a company purchases less than all shares tendered, the purchases must be made on a pro rata basis from each of the tendering shareholders. The adoption of SEC Rule 13e-4 in September 1979 made mandatory the pro rata repurchase of shares when the number tendered exceeds the number the company purchases.

If fewer shares are tendered during the initial offer period than targeted by management, the company may decide to extend the length of the offer period. If the offer period is lengthened, the company is likely to purchase all shares tendered before the first expiration date, and then purchase shares offered during the extension period either pro rata or on the basis of the order in which the shares are offered. The tender offer usually does not permit officers and directors of the repurchasing company to tender their shares. (This has an important implication from the standpoint of the managerial control and signaling that may be involved in a tender offer.)

## Empirical Evidence on Cash Tender Offers

Most empirical studies of stock repurchase have focused on cash tender offers. Tender offer repurchases are generally of larger magnitude and over a more accurately measured time period than open market repurchases. For tender offer repurchases one can obtain the announcement date, the actual dates of repurchase activity, and the repurchase price. The market impacts of the repurchase activity, therefore, will be more clearly defined and measurable.

Some interesting materials are provided in the summary by Vermaelen (1981) on undersubscribed versus oversubscribed stock repurchase offers, as shown in Table 18.1.

The cumulative abnormal returns (CARs) are about the same, around 13%. The average premium is much higher for oversubscribed issues than for undersubscribed issues, a differential of about 4 percentage points. The average target fraction was only about 13% for oversubscribed issues but over 18% for undersubscribed issues. The fraction actually purchased was over 16% for oversubscribed issues and under 12% for undersubscribed issues.

Another interesting set of relationships is provided by Vermaelen (1981) in comparing debt-financed with cash-financed stock repurchase tenders. These are shown in Table 18.2. The debt-financed offers have a much higher wealth effect than the cash-financed offers, 24% versus 18%. The premium in debt-financed offers is somewhat higher. The target fraction is over 20% for debt-financed offers but only about 15% for cash-financed offers. The two categories identified as debt financed or cash financed constitute only 62 observations of his total 131 observations. The information effect for

**TABLE 18.1** Summary Statistics on Undersubscribed and Oversubscribed Stock Repurchase Offers Occurring in the Time Interval 1962–1977

| | Number Before Extension (1) | Number After Extension (2) | Average Premium[a] (3) | Average $F*$[b] (4) | Average $F_p^c$ (5) | CAR[d] (6) | TOTAL $R^e$ (7) |
|---|---|---|---|---|---|---|---|
| Oversubscribed | 80 | 86 | 0.2395 | 0.1327 | 0.1619 | 0.1283 | 0.1463 |
| Undersubscribed | 51 | 45 | 0.2047 | 0.1842 | 0.1211 | 0.1377 | 0.1457 |
| Total | 131 | 131 | 0.2276 | 0.1504 | 0.1479 | 0.1319 | 0.1461 |

[a]Premium is computed as the tender price divided by the price five days before the announcement minus one.

[b]Target fraction.

[c]Fraction purchased.

[d]Cumulative average excess return to remaining shareholders from −5 until day +60.

[e]Average abnormal return to tendering and nontendering shareholders = $(3) \times (5) + (6) \times [1 - (5)]$.

*Source:* Theo Vermaelen, "Common Stock Repurchases and Market Signalling: An Empirical Study," *Journal of Financial Economics,* 9, 1981, p. 152.

**TABLE 18.2** Characteristics of the Total Sample, the Sample Financed by Debt, and the Sample Financed with Cash (Average Values with Standard Deviations in Parentheses)

| | Total Sample | Debt Financed | Cash Financed |
|---|---|---|---|
| Observations | 131 | 13 | 49 |
| INFO[a] | 0.157 | 0.236 | 0.178 |
| | (0.154) | (0.122) | (0.163) |
| Premium[b] | 0.227 | 0.283 | 0.268 |
| | (0.179) | (0.139) | (0.214) |
| $F*$[c] | 0.151 | 0.202 | 0.146 |
| | (0.108) | (0.134) | (0.098) |

[a]Total abnormal return to nontendering and tendering shareholders.

[b]Tender price ÷ the price five days before the announcement − 1.

[c]Target fraction.

*Source:* Theo Vermaelen, "Common Stock Repurchases and Market Signalling: An Empirical Study," *Journal of Financial Economics,* 9, 1981, p. 158.

his total sample is much lower than for either of the two subcategories. The same is true of the premium.

With this background on the nature of cash repurchases of stock by tender offer, we next turn to some of the basic analysis.

## BASIC STOCK REPURCHASE MODEL

To understand the implications of stock repurchasing and exchange offers, let us first set out some of the quantitative relationships involved. As is customary, it is necessary to set forth the assumptions of the model employed. The literature on the subject suggests a number of basic conditions involved in the equilibrium pricing of securities (Vermaelen, 1981):

1. The market is efficient in that at any time market prices reflect all publicly available information that influences the prices of securities.
2. This also implies that markets are informationally efficient, which specifies that information is costless and is received simultaneously by all individuals. In the economic literature these conditions are generally referred to as the condition of pure competition.
3. There is perfect competition in securities markets. This implies that individual investors are price takers and cannot influence the outcome of a stock repurchase offer.
4. Investors seek to maximize the value of their wealth, after taking into account taxes and transactions costs.
5. After the announcement date, investors have homogeneous expectations with respect to the change in value that will be caused by the share repurchase and with respect to the fraction of shares that will be tendered as well as the fraction of shares that will be purchased by the company.
6. Offers are maximum-limit offers. This means that if the offer is undersubscribed, the firm will buy all shares tendered. But if the offer is oversubscribed, the company will buy all shares tendered or will allocate shares pro rata—the company buys back the same fraction of the shares from every tendering shareholder.
7. The price changes analyzed in connection with share repurchase are after adjusting for marketwide price changes.

In the analysis that follows we employ a number of symbols:

$P_0$ = the preannouncement share price
$P_T$ = the tender price
$P_E$ = the postexpiration share price
$N_0$ = the preannouncement number of shares outstanding
$N_E$ = the number of shares outstanding after repurchase
$W$ = the shareholder wealth effect caused by the share repurchase
$F_P$ = the fraction of shares repurchased = $(N_0 - N_E)/N_0$
$1 - F_P$ = the fraction of untendered shares = $N_E/N_0$.

The basic condition that must be met is set forth in equation (18.1).

$$P_E N_E = P_0 N_0 - P_T(N_0 - N_E) + W \qquad (18.1)$$

Equation (18.1) states that the value of the shares outstanding after expiration of the repurchase offer equals the value of the shares existing before the announcement of the repurchase offer less the value of the shares repurchased plus the change in shareholder wealth associated with the repurchase offer. The source of $W$, the shareholder wealth effect, will be analyzed subsequently. If we then divide equation (18.1) by $N_0$ and substitute for the definition of fraction of shares repurchased and fraction of shares not repurchased, we obtain equation (18.2).

$$P_E(1 - F_P) = P_0 - P_T F_P + W/N_0 \qquad (18.2)$$

We next divide by $P_0$ and solve for the rate of increase in value or the rate of return created by the repurchase offer. This is shown in equation (18.3).

$$W/N_0 P_0 = (F_P)\frac{P_T - P_0}{P_0} + (1 - F_P)\frac{P_E - P_0}{P_0} \qquad (18.3)$$

Equation (18.3) reveals the two components of rate of return associated with the repurchase offer. The first component is the rate of return received by the tendering shareholders weighted by the percent of shares purchased. The second component is the rate of return received by nontendering shareholders weighted by the percent of nontendered shares.

Dann (1981) found for his sample of open-market share repurchases totaling 143 observations over the period 1962–1976 that the fraction of shares repurchased averaged 20%. The shareholder wealth effect was 15%. The initial premium represented by the tender offer was 23%. From this information we can solve for the relationship between the price of the stock at expiration of the repurchase offer and the initial price, $P_0$. This is done in equation (18.4).

$$15\% = 20\%(23\%) + 80\%X \tag{18.4}$$

The premium of the expiration price after the share repurchase is therefore 13% over the initial share price. Thus, as shown in equation (18.4a), of the 15% wealth effect associated with the share repurchase offer, 4.6% goes to the tendering shareholders and 10.4% goes to the nontendering shareholders.

$$
\begin{aligned}
15\% &= 0.2(23\%) + 0.8(13\%) \\
15\% &= 4.6\% + 10.4\%
\end{aligned}
\tag{18.4a}
$$

The relationship is quite similar for the Vermaelen (1981) study covering 131 open-market share repurchases over the period 1962–1977. The initial premium was the same, 23%, but the fraction repurchased was 15%. The wealth effect was 16%. The relationships are shown in equation (18.5).

$$
\begin{aligned}
16\% &= 15\%(23\%) + 85\%X \\
0.16 &= 0.0345 + 0.85X \\
X &= 0.1476 = 14.76\% \\
16\% &= 0.15(23\%) + 0.85(14.76\%)
\end{aligned}
\tag{18.5}
$$

The indicated postexpiration price is 14.76% over the initial price. Thus, using Vermaelen's data, the 16% wealth effect is composed of 3.45% to the tendering shareholders and 12.55% to the nontendering shareholders. Other studies of open-market share repurchases find similar results; these include Bradley and Wakeman (1983), Brickley (1983), Masulis (1980), and Vermaelen (1984).

Studies for the 1980s suggest that in recent years the pattern for fixed price tender offers represents a premium of about 20% over the pretender offer price. The percentage repurchased appears to be in the region of about 16%. The percent not repurchased, therefore, is 84%. The postexpiration premium appears to average about 10.5%. In a sense, this postexpiration premium is similar to the cumulative abnormal returns observed in takeover studies discussed in previous chapters. The 20% premium times the 16% repurchased represents 3.2%. The 84% not repurchased times the postexpiration premium of 10.5% gives approximately 8.8%. Thus, the total wealth effect of the fixed price tender offer is 12%.

We next consider the source of the postexpiration premia and the wealth effect observed in fixed price tender offers. The earlier literature analyzed alternative explanations in considerable detail. We first summarize this literature. Then we consider in greater depth the other three main types of share repurchases (DAs, TPRs, and OMRs) for further insights into the theory and practice of share repurchases.

# THE THEORIES BEHIND FIXED PRICE TENDER OFFERS

The empirical studies on fixed price tender offers show that the size of the premium offered to shareholders to tender their holdings is about 20% over the stock price then prevailing. At the expiration of the tender offer period, the price of the stock still remains 10 to 11% above the pretender offer announcement price. There appears to be a permanent increase in the market price of the firm's common stock as a consequence of the share repurchase program. How is this permanent increase in value to be explained? Six hypotheses have been offered.

1. Dividend or personal taxation hypothesis
2. Leverage hypothesis
3. Information or signaling hypothesis
4. Bondholder expropriation hypothesis
5. Wealth transfers among shareholders
6. Defense against outside takeovers

Each of these is analyzed in turn.

## Dividend or Personal Taxation Hypothesis

Cash dividends are taxable at ordinary income tax rates. Prior to the Tax Reform Act of 1986, which provides for a reduction in the preferential capital gains tax rate, capital gains were taxed at a substantially lower rate. The period covered by most of the empirical studies was from the early 1960s to the late 1970s. During this period of time the preferential capital gains tax treatment applied. Cash received by a shareholder as a result of a stock repurchase was taxable during that period only if the repurchase price exceeded the shareholder's acquisition price and at the preferential lower capital gains tax rate. Section 302 of the U.S. Internal Revenue Code provided that the redemption be "substantially disproportionate to the extent that after the repurchase the percentage ownership of the shareholder must be less than 80% of the percentage he held before the repurchase." The empirical studies show that this condition is rarely violated.

The personal taxation argument for explaining the value increase, therefore, suggests that share repurchase enables the stockholder to substitute a lower capital gains tax for a higher ordinary personal income tax rate on the cash received. But both Dann (1981) and Vermaelen (1981) express doubt about the validity of this personal tax savings hypothesis. Both review extensive theoretical literature and empirical studies on the central theoretical proposition involved here. This is the argument from the dividend policy literature that a higher tax rate on dividends versus capital gains implies that a corporation's dividend policy can affect the value of its common stock. The most compelling arguments in this area were made by Miller and Scholes (1978). They describe and illustrate a number of ways that investors can offset personal tax liabilities on dividends. All of these methods, however, involve transactions costs. The argument could then be that share repurchase reduces the transactions costs involved in helping stockholders offset personal tax liabilities on dividends. But share repurchases as a substitute for dividends also involve transactions costs. The question is whether transactions costs are reduced and whether the size of the reduction in transactions costs is sufficient to explain the relatively substantial gain of 10 to 11% of share price that persists after the expiration date for a tender offer repurchase episode.

There is a very interesting historical and empirical set of observations involved here. Vermaelen (1981) assembled evidence to show that during the period August 1971 to June 1974 a "voluntary" 4% limit on dividend increases was imposed as a part of the wage and price controls of the period. During the preceding ten years from 1962 until July 1971, only 32 repurchase offers were observed. During the period August 1971 to June 1974, somewhat less than three years, the number of share repurchases increased to 52, which averages over 17 per year. This increase of over 500% Vermaelen (1981, p. 171) refers to as a "dramatic increase in repurchasing activity."

Vermaelen (1981) breaks his data into three subperiods: before, during, and after the controls on dividend increases. We refer to these as periods 1, 2, and 3. During period 1 the abnormal return was 5.6%. The premium was 11.6% and the target fraction of shares for repurchase was 13.5%. The median market value of the firm involved was $59 million. During period 2 the abnormal return jumped to 19.3%, and the premium rose to 26.4%. The target fraction was 14%, while the median market value firm dropped substantially to approximately $22 million. It appears that during period 2, the period of controls on dividend increases, small firms used share repurchase to avoid the controls on dividend increases. In the third period all the variables were similar to those of the second period except that the target fraction rose from 14 to 17.2%. These data on the nature of the three subperiods are very significant from our standpoint. They shed light on how share repurchases came into being, or at least increased in their frequency. They also indicate the importance of firm size in participating in share repurchase for this period.

The fact that share repurchase was stimulated by controls on dividend increases clearly indicates an association between dividend activity and share repurchase activity. However, the aim appeared to be not so much to obtain the tax advantage of reducing personal taxes on dividends, but rather to achieve dividend increases. But again this suggests that to the owners of small firms dividends do indeed matter. However, the reasons why dividends may matter in these circumstances are not clear.

### Leverage Hypothesis

Stock repurchases increase the debt/equity ratio. If the repurchase is financed by excess cash and marketable securities, the extent of the increase depends on the method used to calculate the leverage ratio. If the share repurchase is financed explicitly by an issue of debt, the increase in the leverage ratio is even greater regardless of calculation method. Along with the leverage increase, financing the repurchase with debt also increases the amount of tax-deductible interest payments.

If there is a tax subsidy associated with the deductibility of interest payments on debt, and if this subsidy is passed through to shareholders, the price of the stock would increase. Just as the issue of reduction in personal taxes under the previous point involves the issue of dividend policy, the issue of a tax subsidy to debt involves the issue of debt policy. These issues are still unsettled. Modigliani and Miller (1958, 1963) developed a model in which there was a tax subsidy to debt. However, Miller (1977) later argues that debt is issued to the point where the corporate tax rate equals the personal income tax rate of the marginal bondholder. Under these conditions there exists no optimal debt/equity ratio for the individual firm. Others argue that there is a tax subsidy for debt or for debt substitutes that move the firm toward increased leverage. However, the existence of bankruptcy costs is an offsetting disadvantage so that there is an optimal amount of debt for the individual firm. The issue remains unsettled.

Masulis (1980) gives the greatest weight to the corporate tax shield hypothesis. He divided his sample of 138 share repurchase offers into those with more than 50% debt financing and those with less than 50% debt financing. The announcement period return for the 45 offers with greater leverage was 21.9%, whereas the 93 offers with a lower percentage of debt financing had announcement period returns of 17.1%. Masulis (1980) terms these results as consistent with a corporate tax shield hypothesis.

Vermaelen (1981), however, takes issue with the Masulis (1980) position on the leverage hypothesis as an explanation for the shareholder wealth increase. Vermaelen (1981) develops some regression relationships. He finds that the difference in the size of premiums explains 60% of the difference in what he calls information or wealth effect. He observes that the average premium was 27% for the more than 50% debt-financing group and 23% for the less than 50% debt-financing group of Masulis (1980). Thus, we have a difference of 4 percentage points in the premium associated with a difference of 4.8 percentage points in the wealth effect between the high-debt and low-debt groups. Employing the 60% regression coefficient on the premium explains 2.4 percentage points of the 4.8% difference in wealth effect. Vermaelen (1981) also finds positive explanatory power in the fraction of insider holdings, the target fraction of shares in the repurchase offer, and the fraction purchased in relation to the target fraction. Hence, he argues that the significance of the financing effect must be less than the remaining 2.4 percentage points of difference in the wealth effect.

Vermaelen (1981) argues that while the leverage hypothesis may play a role, it is not the predominant explanation for the observed abnormal returns following the share repurchase offer. He argues that the more plausible explanation is the signaling or information effect, which we take up next. We may note also that if leverage is regarded as a signal, then it is not possible to separate the leverage signaling effect from the leverage tax effect. We, therefore, turn to the information or signaling hypothesis.

## Signaling Hypothesis

The announcement by a company that it is going to engage in a share repurchase program provides a signal to investors. On first analysis the direction of the signal appears to be ambiguous. On the one hand it may be that the announcement of the use of cash to repurchase its own shares is an acknowledgment by management that it has no profitable investments in which the funds can be employed. But another interpretation is possible. When a company announces that it is willing to buy its shares at a substantial premium above the market price, and as is usually the case insiders cannot or do not participate, this may be taken as a signal that management believes that the common stock of the company is undervalued by the market. In many newspaper accounts of stock repurchase announcements, management states that it feels that investing in its own stock is the best bargain around.

Vermaelen (1981) makes a vigorous case for the signaling hypothesis. He runs regressions seeking to explain the size of the wealth effect. He successively uses as independent variables the premium in the repurchase announcement, the target fraction the company seeks to repurchase, the fraction of insider holdings in the company, and the fraction of the shares purchased in relation to the target fraction. From this he estimates that the size of the regression coefficient for the premium is 0.6. The signs on the other variables are always positive and significant in at least one of the nine regressions that he runs with alternative combinations of explanatory variables.

Vermaelen (1981) also reports that tender offers for share repurchase are associated with per share earnings of tendering firms that subsequently are above what would have been predicted by a time series model using preannouncement data. While such prediction methods are subject to limitations, the evidence is still supportive.

Vermaelen (1981) concludes, however, that it is possible that leverage or the financing effect does have some explanatory power. He feels that the signaling hypothesis carries greater weight in explaining the wealth effect but that the leverage effect may still play a role. Of course, if increased leverage also carries a signaling effect, then it is difficult to separate the role of the two alternative hypotheses.

### Bondholder Expropriation Hypothesis

Evidence on the effects on bondholders is obtained by analyzing bond price changes around the announcement dates of the equity repurchases via tender offers. Dann (1981) studied 41 issues of straight debt, 34 issues of convertible debt, 9 issues of straight preferred stock, and 38 issues of convertible preferred stock. He analyzed abnormal returns to each of these categories around the announcement date. Significant positive rates of return were observed for the convertible securities, which may be regarded as delayed issues of common stock. The abnormal rates of return were insignificantly different from zero for straight debt and for preferred stock. In addition he found that the correlations between common stock returns and the returns on straight debt as well as preferred stock were positive. This evidence seems inconsistent with the explanation of bondholder expropriation as an important motive for equity repurchases by tender offers.

### Wealth Transfers Among Shareholders

Wealth transfers may take place between those stockholders who tender their shares and those who do not. A variety of reasons may exist for these differences in behavior. There may be different constraints and costs among different groups of shareholders. Nevertheless, as the data presented earlier show, the largest portion of the wealth effect goes to the nontendering shareholders; they experience significant gains because the expiration price still remains from 10 to 11% above the price of the stock before the announcement of the repurchase tender offer. In addition, as a matter of practice, insiders with large shareholdings do not participate in the repurchase tender offer. Hence it would appear that they expect that the stock price at a longer distance into the future will be even more favorable than at the end of the expiration period, which is consistent with and further supports the information or signaling explanation for the favorable wealth effect.

### Defense Against Outside Takeovers

If insiders judge the firm to be undervalued, they may have concerns that the firm is subject to a takeover bid at a relatively small premium. Vermaelen (1984) reports a high correlation for the period 1962–1977 for takeover bid announcements and the number of repurchase tender offers. He suggests that this might protect shareholder interests in that noninsiders may be better off without a takeover bid than with a takeover bid at a low offer premium. The large premium involved in the repurchase tender offer may convey a signal to the noninsiders that the value of the shares is at least as high as conveyed by the premium and may be perhaps even higher in the future. This could put the market on notice that if a takeover bid is to succeed, it may have to be even higher than the repurchase tender offer premium, which, as we have seen, averages 20% or more.

Thus, the personal taxation, leverage, signaling, and takeover defense explanations for the wealth effect in tender offer share repurchases, appear to have explanatory power. Bondholder expropriation and wealth transfers among shareholders appear to be inconsistent with both analysis and empirical evidence. Further understanding of share repurchases may be gained by an analysis of other forms of share repurchase.

## DUTCH AUCTION REPURCHASES

A fundamental difference between fixed price tender offers and Dutch auction repurchases (DARs) is brought out by the description of the first firm to utilize the Dutch auction (Bagwell, 1992). In 1981 Todd Shipyards was planning a fixed price tender offer at $28 for about 10% of its 5.5 million shares outstanding. Bear Stearns, the investment banker for Todd, suggested instead a Dutch auction repurchase at a range of prices not to exceed $28. The fee paid to Bear Stearns would be 30% of the savings if the clearing price was less than $28. Todd employed the Dutch auction. The clearing purchase price was $26.50.

This example illustrates one of the basic differences between the FPT and the DAR. In the FPT, the tender offer is made for one price. In the DAR, a range of prices is made available within which investors can choose a price at which their shares will be tendered. In the Bagwell (1992) study, data for 32 firms employing Dutch auctions between 1981 and 1988 were obtained. These firms supplied schedules of the quantity of shares offered at each price within the specified range. Bagwell analyzed these data setting the preannouncement price equal to $100 and expressed the price range as a percentage of the preannouncement price. She also calculated the percent of total shares sought in the Dutch auction repurchase offer. Schedules are developed in which quantity is normalized to measure the cumulative percentage of outstanding shares tendered at or below each price within the price range. Bagwell presents supply curves for 17 firms that did not require confidentiality. We have directly contacted other firms conducting Dutch auctions requesting supply schedules. These supply schedules are consistent with the data presented in Appendix II in the Bagwell study.

An important finding from the Dutch auction supply curves is evidence of shareholder heterogeneity (Bagwell, 1992). Consistently upward sloping supply curves are obtained from shareholder tendering responses in the Dutch auctions. An upward sloping supply or valuation schedule is illustrated by equation (18.6).

$$V(r) = 80 + 0.04r \qquad \textbf{(18.6)}$$

The meaning of equation (18.6) and the definition of the terms in it can be further clarified with the help of Figure 18.1. The horizontal axis shows the number of shareholders ($r$) and each point up through 1,000 is for an individual shareholder, each holding one share of stock. The total number of shares outstanding ($N$) is also equal to 1,000. Each $r$th shareholder has a reservation price $V(r)$. The reservation price $V(r)$ is the price at which each $r$th shareholder would be willing to sell the share of stock held. $V(r)$ means that the reservation price (or value) depends on which $r$th shareholder we are talking about. For example, the 1st shareholder has a reservation price of $80 + $.04(1) or $80.04. The 100th shareholder has a reservation price of $80 + $.04(100) = $84 and so on. Equation (18.6) and its graph in Figure 18.1 show the relationship between the $r$th shareholder and his/her associated reservation price $V(r)$. The vertical axis in Figure 18.1 depicts these reservation prices, $V(r)$, for each $r$th shareholder. The intercept term 80 represents the prevailing market price of the stock. Shareholders with reservation prices at or below the prevailing market price of $80 would have already sold their shares.

We show what happens when the firm seeks to repurchase 200 shares ($R$) representing 20% of the shares outstanding. It offers to repurchase the shares at a range of prices between $84 and $90. If the reservation prices of the shareholders are depicted by the illustrative equation, $V(r) = 80 + 0.04r$, we would have the following result. The

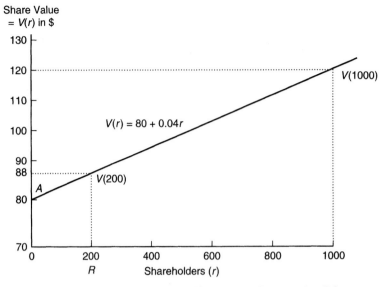

Share Value
= V(r) in $

V(r) = 80 + 0.04r

V(1000)

V(200)

A

R

Shareholders (r)

**FIGURE 18.1  Valuation Schedule for Shareholder Reservation Prices**

price that would elicit 200 shares in the Dutch auction would be $88. We can check this using equation (18.6).

$$V(r) = \$80 + 0.04(200) = \$88 \qquad\qquad \textbf{(18.6a)}$$

The gain to the tendering shareholders can be measured by triangle A:

$$0.5(88 - 80)200 = \$800$$

Because the prevailing market price of the stock before the tender offer was $80, the 200 shares had a market value of $16,000. The gain of $800, therefore, represents 5% of the pre-tender market value of the 200 shares ($80 times 200 = $16,000).

Let us next consider the situation of the nontendering shareholders (this analysis is based on Gay, Kale, and Noe, 1991). The nontendering shareholders now have a claim on the valuation curve less what was paid out to the tendering shareholders. The new upward sloping supply curve for the nontendering shareholders is given in equation (18.7) for $V'(r)$.

$$V'(r) = (0.04r + 80)/0.8 - 88(200)/800 = 0.05r + 78 \qquad\qquad \textbf{(18.7)}$$

Thus, the new valuation schedule will have a lower implied intercept but a steeper slope.

The practical significance of the more steeply sloped valuation schedule is that the reservation prices of the remaining shareholders are higher than the reservation prices of the original valuation schedule. The role of share repurchase as a takeover defense is highlighted. The reservation price of the marginal shareholder after the share repurchase is something over $88 versus the original $80. In addition, the reservation price of the 1,000th shareholder is now $50 + $78 = $128. Therefore, to compete with the share repurchase alternative, a bidder would have to pay a higher premium than would have been required under the original supply schedule. In a fixed price tender offer, the tender offer price probably would have been in excess of $88 to obtain 20% of the shares.

The premium paid in the Dutch auction share repurchase is somewhat lower (Kamma, Kanatas, and Raymar, 1992).

Comment and Jarrell (1991) pushed the analysis still further. They investigated the influence of pro rata transactions and the role of the risk exposure of officers and directors. The logic of the necessity of prorationing is straightforward. If the reservation prices of the shareholders are so low that the tender offer stimulates a flood of tenders by shareholders, it is not likely that wealth effects will be high.

Comment and Jarrell (1991) also investigated the impact of whether officers and directors are exposed to a personal wealth loss if their signaling is not credible. Comment and Jarrell consider that officers and directors (OD) are at risk if two conditions hold. First, their collective proportionate ownership interest in their company's stock must increase as a result of the tender offer. Second, the premium in the tender offer is more than 2% above the market price of the stock four days before the offer is announced.

We have summarized the empirical data for wealth effects that take into account the pro rata influence and the risk of officers and directors in Table 18.3. Average wealth effects in fixed price tender offers are in the range of 12 to 13% as discussed previously. For Dutch auctions, the wealth effect is smaller at about 8%. This is plausible because the average premium paid in Dutch auctions is lower, as shareholder heterogeneity results in an upward-sloping supply schedule. If prorationing is involved, then shareholder reservation prices are low. Signaling of future value increases is less likely to be credible. With prorationing, the wealth effects are virtually zero for both fixed price tender offers and for Dutch auctions. Where there is no prorationing, then the reservation prices of shareholders are relatively high. They are more likely to view the premia offered in the share repurchases as credible signals of future value increases. The wealth effects are relatively large.

Similarly, if officers and directors are at risk, the signaling will be credible and the wealth effects large. If officers and directors are not at risk, the wealth effects will be small or negligible.

After considering the kinds of evidence presented in Table 18.3, Comment and Jarrell (1991, pp. 1258–1259) conclude that Dutch auctions are favored by relatively large firms that are widely followed by security analysts and other informed investors. These are companies in which managements own relatively low percentages of stock. Because their stock is widely followed and management stakes are relatively low, these firms are "ill-suited" to send strongly credible signals in premium repurchase offers. For such firms, Comment and Jarrell conclude that Dutch auctions are likely to be substitutes for open market repurchases. They argue that the firms are not substituting Dutch auctions for fixed price tender offers, but rather would have switched to open market programs.

**TABLE 18.3** Wealth Effects

|  | Average | Pro Rata | | OD at Risk | |
| --- | --- | --- | --- | --- | --- |
|  |  | Yes | No | Yes | No |
| FPT | 12–13% | 0–5% | 15% | 16% | 4% |
| DA | 8% | 0 | 8% | 8% | 0 |

## TRANSFERABLE PUT RIGHTS (TPRs)

As summarized earlier, transferable put rights (TPRs) represent options granted to shareholders in proportion of the number of shares owned. In our previous example, we noted that if a company sought to repurchase 20% of its shares using TPRs, it would issue 20 TPRs for every 100 shares held by stockholders. If the put price represents a substantial premium over the prevailing market price, the TPRs will have value and trading in them will take place. Because all shares put to the firm are repurchased, the possibility of prorationing that occurs in a fixed price tender offer is avoided. This point is illustrated by the first company to use TPRs, which was Millicom, a small cellular telephone and electronic paging company (Kale, Noe, and Gay, 1989, p. 141). In April 1987 Millicom issued TPRs to its shareholders as a method of share repurchase. Millicom explained its choice of TPRs with reference to the prorationing problem. Under a fixed price tender offer (FPT), because of the possibility of prorationing, shareholders cannot be sure what percentage of their tendered shares will actually be repurchased. Shareholders can avoid this risk by selling to arbitragers who thereby achieve a strong bargaining position, particularly if a takeover or a control contest develops.

In their study, Kale, Noe, and Gay (1989) report the announcement by Vista Chemical Company in May 1989 of a plan to repurchase one-third of its 15 million shares outstanding at $70 a share through the issuance of TPRs. They also describe in some detail the use of TPRs by Gillette, the second company to initiate a share repurchase program with the use of TPRs. Gillette, the well-known maker of razor blades, pens, and other personal products, was subject to a series of hostile takeover attempts for various reasons. In 1986 Revlon's Ronald O. Perelman made a series of takeover bids that were fought off by a targeted share repurchase (greenmail) plus a standstill agreement.

In February 1988 Coniston Partners announced that it owned 6.8% of Gillette stock and was seeking four seats on Gillette's board. Gillette accelerated its open market share repurchase program. In the proxy fight for control, Gillette defeated Coniston by obtaining 52% of shareholder votes. Coniston filed a lawsuit claiming that Gillette had made false and misleading claims during the proxy contest. With the court contest under way, Gillette and Coniston reached a settlement announced August 1, 1988, associated with the initiation of a stock repurchase through TPRs. Gillette, with 112 million shares outstanding, issued one put per seven shares, which would result in the repurchase of 16 million shares. Each TPR enabled the holder to sell back one share to the company at $45 (the prevailing market was about $39) by September 19, 1988. The TPRs were issued to shareholders of record as of August 12, 1988. Trading in the TPRs started on August 16, 1988 and took place through September 19, 1988. Over that period of time, the stock price of Gillette averaged about $35 with the TPR price fluctuating slightly above and below $10. Thus, one TPR plus one share of stock approximated the put price of $45. The average daily volume of trading during the period August 16 to September 19 was about 359,000 TPRs.

The logic of the TPR trading documented for Gillette can be conveyed by the numerical example we developed in connection with our discussion of Dutch auction repurchases (DARs). Recall that we postulated a reservation supply price schedule for shareholders.

$$V(r) = 80 + 0.04r \qquad \textbf{(18.6)}$$

In our example for the DAR, if a firm had announced that it would repurchase 20% of its 1,000 shares at a schedule of prices from $80 to $88, the market would have cleared at a price of $88. Using the Kale et al. notation of LR for a low reservation price shareholder and HR for a high reservation price shareholder, we can see that the LR share-holders would have tendered and the HR shareholders would not have tendered. At the end of the DAR the new marginal shareholder would have a reservation price of $88.

But in practice, the firm knows that the supply schedule is positively sloped but does not know the price and quantity that would just clear the market with neither pro-rationing nor an undersubscription to the tender offer. We can illustrate how the use of TPRs solves this problem. Assume that a firm facing the shareholder valuation sched-ule depicted by Figure 18.1 offered to buy 20% of its shares at a price of $96. Based on the valuation schedule the number of shares and shareholders who would be interested in selling at $96 would be determined by the following equation:

$$\$96 = \$80 + 0.04r$$

Solving for $r$, 400 shares would be offered. But only 200 TPRs were issued. Hence, trading in the TPRs would take place. Shareholders with a reservation price below $88 (the LRs) would place the greatest value on the TPRs and would end up buying TPRs from the shareholders with the higher reservation prices (the HRs). By the end of the trading period when the TPRs would be exercised, the LRs would own the 200 TPRs and the HRs would have been net sellers. Two hundred shares, along with the 200 TPRs, would be put to the company. The result would be that the TPR trading discovered the market clearing price for the 20% of the shares that the company is seeking to repurchase.

Another use of the TPRs is in consolidating the control position of a group. We can identify three types of shareholders: the control group, dissidents fighting for con-trol, and others. Before the issuance of TPRs, the ownership position of each group is given in column 1 of Table 18.4. If one TPR is issued for each three shares held, and assuming that the number of shares is identical to the percentages indicated in column 1, 33.3 TPRs would be issued. Column 2 suggests that the control group would sell their TPRs but not their stock. Postulating that the put price represents a substantial pre-mium over the prevailing market price of the stock, the dissidents would be happy to accept the substantial premium. The third group would use the 14 TPRs received plus the 11.3 TPRs purchased from the control group to sell 25.3 of their shares. Column 3 shows the number of shares each group owns after the TPRs plus stock are put to the company. The company now has only 66.7 shares outstanding. Column 4 expresses each group's ownership as a percent of the total number of shares outstanding. The control group has moved from 34 to 51%. The share of the dissidents is unchanged at 24%. The percentage ownership of the other shareholders has dropped from 42 to 25%.

From the illustrative examples, from the real-life cases, and from the theoretical framework, we can understand the advantages of the use of TPRs. The trading in TPRs

**TABLE 18.4   TPRs and Control**

|  | (1) Before % | (2) Sell | (3) After | (4) After % |
|---|---|---|---|---|
| 1. Control group | 34 | 0.0 | 34.0 | 51 |
| 2. Dissidents | 24 | 8.0 | 16.0 | 24 |
| 3. Others | 42 | 25.3* | 16.7 | 25 |
| Total | 100 | 33.3 | 66.7 | 100 |

*25.3 = 14.0 + 11.3

results in the low reservation price shareholders putting their shares for repurchase. The remaining shareholders will be high reservation price shareholders. Thus, the TPRs are useful as a takeover defense. In addition, the TPRs may rearrange control positions as well.

We conclude this section with a consideration of why the reservation price schedule is upward sloping. The empirical data presented by Bagwell (1992) is solid evidence of upward sloping reservation price schedules. We have checked her findings by directly corresponding with a sample of companies using Dutch auctions in recent years. Although we have not received permission to publish these data, we can confirm that they are consistent with the data published in Bagwell (1992). So there is no question of the evidence of upward sloping reservation price schedules. However, in our idealized example, we have used a slope that seems to be higher than that exhibited in the Bagwell data and in the data that we have developed. So one question is, How strong is the upward sloping effect?

A second question is, Why does the upward sloping schedule exist? Most authors refer to the possibility of a different tax basis for LRs and HRs. Beyond that, shareholder heterogeneity and differing expectations and valuations are possible explanations. This is an area that requires much more investigation.

## OPEN MARKET SHARE REPURCHASES (OMRs)

Studies suggest that open market share repurchases outnumber the other three methods by a factor of perhaps 10 to 1. Detailed studies of open market share repurchases have been reported by Ikenberry, Lakonishok, and Vermaelen (ILV) (1995) and Ikenberry and Vermaelen (IV) (1996). They begin by observing that the aggregate value of stock repurchases for the period 1980–1990 was about one-third the dollar amount of cash dividends. In the later years of the 1980s, repurchases moved up to about one-half the amount paid as cash dividends. The ILV study covered 1,239 open market share repurchases announced between 1980 and 1990 by firms traded on the NYSE, ASE, or NASDAQ. Over the 11-year period, sample companies announced repurchases for 6.6% of their outstanding shares on average. The percentage was rising over the sample time period. The average market response to the announcement of an OMR was 3.5%. But this average was influenced by a number of factors.

For a window of −2 to +2 around the announcement date, the market response for the period 1980–1986 averaged about 4.2%. For the period 1987–1990, the market response was about 2.3%. The mean announcement period abnormal return for repurchase programs for more than 10% of the outstanding shares is 4.51%. For smaller repurchase programs (less than 2.5% of shares), the average market reaction is 2.58%. Ikenberry et al. (1995) interpret the stronger market reaction to larger share repurchase programs as consistent with the traditional signaling hypothesis (TSH). Firms ranked in the two smallest size deciles show the highest abnormal returns of 8.19%. Firms in the largest size deciles show an abnormal return of 2.09%. Viewing firm size as a proxy of information asymmetries, the inverse relationship between size and abnormal returns is consistent with TSH.

A result that ILV emphasize is that, on average, the market underreacts to OMR announcements. Using a buy and hold strategy, the four-year abnormal year performance following the announcement is more than 12%. Combined with the announcement effect, the total undervaluation is about 15%. They find further that firms ranked in the top book-to-market quintile achieve four-year abnormal performance of 45.3% following the OMR announcement. This measure is net of a benchmark that explicitly controls for size and book-to-market effects in stock returns. Firms in the bottom two quintiles by book-to-market exhibit a long-run performance close to zero. They conclude that the market reaction to new information is not always completed over short time periods. They observe that if the market underreacts to the first announcement of an OMR, managers who judge their shares to be undervalued may make a series of OMRs to gain the benefit of multiple announcement reactions.

So the initial announcement effect of a modest positive 3½% to an OMR does not fully capture the impact. Subsequent three-year abnormal performance represents an additional 12%. Ikenberry et al. (1995) argue that companies with high ratios of book to market that engaged in share repurchases are truly out of favor; their shares will show higher returns in the future compared with high book-to-market ratio stocks in general. Thus, added to our earlier discussion of the other methods of share repurchase, the in-depth analysis of OMRs over time yields further insights into the significant impact that share repurchases can make on shareholder returns.

Ikenberry et al. (1995, p. 207) draw another conclusion: "This evidence is consistent with other studies which find that managers have market timing ability." Furthermore, announcements of open market share repurchases are somewhat ambiguous. The company announces that it will buy up to $X$ shares over the following $Y$ number of months. If a major reason for buybacks is that companies believe their shares are underpriced, as share prices rise with the announcement and initiation of a repurchase program the incentives for managers to complete the total OMR are reduced.

A *Wall Street Journal* article on March 7, 1995 ("Heard on the Street," pp. C1, C2) cited a study of how the data on announcements are easier to track than data on actual buyback activity. The article cited a study by Eric T. Miller, chief investment officer at Donaldson, Lufkin & Jenrette, that as of March 7, 1995, only 15% of announced 1993 OMRs had been completed. OMRs of $65 billion had been announced for 1994, but by March 1995 it appeared that only $2–3 billion of the buyback programs had taken place. The article also quoted Ikenberry: "Once a stock price rises it may not make business sense to keep on buying stock."

Another aspect of management manipulation may be noted in connection with share repurchases. If the companies have a high ratio of market to book (a low ratio of book to market), the reduction in the book value of shareholders' equity as a result of share repurchases may be very substantial. The original accounting credit was at book; the debit to record the share repurchase can be made at market. For a given level of net income, the reported return on equity (ROE) would be expected to increase substantially. In pure finance theory, increased levels of ROE should not influence stock prices.

## Summary

We have described four methods of share repurchase:

1. Fixed price tender offers (FPTs)
2. Dutch auctions (DAs)
3. Transferable put rights (TPRs)
4. Open market repurchases (OMRs)

We have explained the mechanisms and logic behind each of the four types. Each has a different signaling effect and wealth effect. All result in significant positive abnormal returns to shareholders.

A number of hypotheses have been advanced to explain these gains. Tax effects appear to play a small role; gains to shareholders on repurchase are taxed as capital gains rather than as ordinary income in the case of dividends. This benefit is greatly reduced by the elimination of the lower rate on capital gains by the Tax Reform Act of 1986. Share repurchase represents an alternative means of making payouts to shareholders, which becomes even more important during periods of restrictions on dividends. Increased leverage may also be responsible for some of the shareholder wealth increase, especially in debt-financed repurchases, to the extent that there is a tax subsidy on debt interest payments, or that the firm has been operating at a suboptimal leverage level. Increased leverage is also related to the information or signaling hypothesis, which is another explanation for the source of gains. By increasing leverage, management signals that it believes cash flows will be sufficiently higher in the future to cover higher interest payments. Also, by repurchasing the shares at a premium over the current market price, management is signaling its belief based on inside information that the shares are undervalued by the market. And, because corporate insiders typically do not participate in the repurchase, they are increasing their percentage ownership in the firm, another signal that they are optimistic about the firm's prospects. The share repurchase premium also serves as a takeover defense; it may be higher than the premium offered by a raider. Thus, it alerts shareholders that it is not only the raider who sees the potential for increased value in the firm, but also the firm's own management. The bondholder expropriation theory suggests that the gains to shareholders come at the expense of the bondholders, but there is no evidence to support this hypothesis.

---

## Questions

18.1 What are four ways to carry out a share repurchase?

18.2 In a tender offer for share repurchase, how is the wealth increase distributed among tendering and nontendering shareholders?

18.3 What theory most plausibly explains the positive shareholder wealth effect observed in share repurchases?

18.4 A company has 8 million shares outstanding. It offers to repurchase 2 million shares at $30 per share; the current market price of the stock is $25. Management controls 500,000 shares and does not participate in the repurchase. What is the signaling cost of the repurchase if the true value of the stock is $20? If the true value of the stock is $29?

18.5 What is the influence of prorationing or not and OD at risk or not on wealth effects in share repurchases?

--------------------------------- C A S E 18–1 ---------------------------------

# FPL

A Harvard case published on March 15, 1995 (Esty and Schreiber) and an article published in spring 1996 (Soter, Brigham, and Evanson) highlight some aspects of share repurchase. The FPL group is a holding company whose principal operating subsidiary is Florida Power and Light Company (FPL), which serves most of the east coast and lower west coast of Florida, with a population of about 6.5 million. Its energy mix consists of purchased power (17%), oil (31%), nuclear (26%), gas (20%), and coal (6%).

Deregulation had been increasing competition in the public utility industry since 1978. The Public Utilities Regulatory Policies Act (PURPA) in 1978 encouraged the creation of power plants using renewable or nontraditional fuels. If specified efficiency and size standards were met, PURPA required local utilities to buy all of their electrical output. In 1992 the National Energy Policy Act (NEPA) was enacted by Congress. It required utilities to permit use of their transmission systems at the same level of quality and at fair cost. In early 1994 some states permitted retail wheeling, under which customers could buy power from utilities other than the local franchise supplier. The local utility would be required to permit competitors' use of its transmission and distribution network. Major utilities in states that proposed to phase in retail wheeling experienced substantial declines in market values. Electrical utility companies faced increased competition.

Florida Power and Light embarked on a diversification program into life insurance, cable television, information services, and citrus production between 1985 and 1988. In 1989 the new president emphasized a return to the core utility business. An aggressive capital expenditure program was launched to meet projected demand increases. Quality and efficiency programs increased plant availability above industry averages and lowered operating expenses.

The improved outlook for growth and profitability caused FPL to reassess the relationship between its long-term business strategies and its financial strategies. Increased growth opportunities were associated with increased competitive risks. Increased financial flexibility was required. With increased business risk, financial leverage was reduced.

A major reassessment of dividend policy was also made. With prospects for increased investment requirements and possible acquisition opportunities, a lower dividend payout policy made sense. The traditional utility company policy of consistent annual dividend increases was breached. A share repurchase program was announced. The initial stock price reaction to the dividend cut was negative. The share repurchase program signaled a favorable outlook for FPL and conveyed assurances that management would return cash to shareholders, if not required by its basic business strategy. In addition, a tax advantage resulted from the maximum personal rate on long-term capital gains at 28% versus a rate on dividend income as high as 39%.

The earnings of FPL continued to improve and its share price sharply increased above previous high levels. The stock price range in 1994 was $27 to $37; for 1995 it was $34 to $46.50. This case illustrates a number of the elements of share repurchase programs developed in the chapter.

---

## Questions on Case Study C18.1

C18.1.1   What was the major force that stimulated the diversification program by FPL?

C18.1.2   How successful were the diversification efforts of FPL?

C18.1.3   What was the impact of increased competitive risks and increased growth and profitability opportunities on the financial policies of FPL?

C18.1.4   What caused FPL to reduce its dividend payout?

C18.1.5   What kinds of signals were conveyed by the announcement of a share repurchase program?

---

## References

Bagwell, Laurie Simon, "Dutch Auction Repurchases: An Analysis of Shareholder Heterogeneity," *Journal of Finance,* 47, March 1992, pp. 71–105.

Bradley, Michael, and Lee M. Wakeman, "The Wealth Effects of Targeted Share Repurchases," *Journal of Financial Economics,* 11, 1983, pp. 301–328.

Brickley, James, "Shareholder Wealth, Information Signalling and the Specially Designated Dividend: An Empirical Study," *Journal of Financial Economics*, 12, 1983, pp. 103–114.

Comment, Robert, and Gregg A. Jarrell, "The Relative Signalling Power of Dutch-Auction and Fixed-Price Self-Tender Offers and Open-Market Share Repurchases," *Journal of Finance*, 46, September 1991, pp. 1243–1271.

Dann, Larry, "Common Stock Repurchases: An Analysis of Returns to Bondholders and Stockholders," *Journal of Financial Economics*, 9, 1981, pp. 113–138.

Esty, Benjamin C., and Craig F. Schreiber, "Dividend Policy at FPL Group, Inc.," HBS Case N9-295-059, March 15, 1995.

Gay, Gerald D., Jayant R. Kale, and Thomas H. Noe, "Share Repurchase Mechanisms: A Comparative Analysis of Efficacy, Shareholder Wealth, and Corporate Control Effects," *Financial Management*, 20, Spring 1991, pp. 44–59.

Ikenberry, David, Josef Lakonishok, and Theo Vermaelen, "Market Underreaction to Open Market Share Repurchases," *Journal of Financial Economics*, 39, October–November 1995, pp. 181–208.

Ikenberry, David L., and Theo Vermaelen, "The Option to Repurchase Stock," *Financial Management*, 25, Winter 1996, pp. 9–24.

Kale, Jayant R., Thomas H. Noe, and Gerald D. Gay, "Share Repurchase Through Transferable Put Rights," *Journal of Financial Economics*, 25, 1989, pp. 141–160.

Kamma, Sreenivas, George Kanatas, and Steven Raymar, "Dutch Auction Versus Fixed-Price Self-Tender Offers for Common Stock," *Journal of Financial Intermediation*, 2, 1992, pp. 277–307.

Masulis, Ronald W., "Stock Repurchase by Tender Offer: An Analysis of the Causes of Common Stock Price Changes," *Journal of Finance*, 35, 1980, pp. 305–319.

Miller, Merton H., "Debt and Taxes," *Journal of Finance*, 32, 1977, pp. 261–276.

———, and Myron S. Scholes, "Dividends and Taxes," *Journal of Financial Economics*, 6, December 1978, pp. 333–364.

Modigliani, Franco, and Merton H. Miller, "The Cost of Capital, Corporation Finance and the Theory of Investment," *American Economic Review*, 48, June 1958, pp. 261–297.

———, "Corporate Income Taxes and the Cost of Capital," *American Economic Review*, June 1963, pp. 433–443.

Soter, Dennis, Eugene Brigham, and Paul Evanson, "The Dividend Cut 'Heard 'Round the World': The Case of FPL," *Journal of Applied Corporate Finance*, 9, Spring 1996, pp. 4–15.

Vermaelen, Theo, "Common Stock Repurchases and Market Signalling: An Empirical Study," *Journal of Financial Economics*, 9, 1981, pp. 139–183.

———, "Repurchase Tender Offers, Signaling and Managerial Incentives," *Journal of Financial and Quantitative Analysis*, 19, 1984, pp. 163–181.

# 19

# Corporate Governance and Performance

A rich and growing literature on corporate governance has been developing within the framework of M&A issues. Because this literature is so vast and seemingly unconnected, it is useful to start with an outline that conveys a logical framework for the analysis of corporate governance, as shown in Table 19.1.

Pathbreaking work on these topics was developed in two symposia issues of the *Journal of Financial Economics*. The first appeared in the January/March 1988 issue

---

**TABLE 19.1**  Outline—Corporate Governance and Performance

    I.  Corporate governance systems in the United States
        A. Diffuse stock ownership
        B. Contractual theory of the firm
        C. Divergent interests of stakeholders
   II.  Internal control mechanisms
 III.  Role of the board of directors
        A. Composition of the board
        B. Compensation of board members
        C. Evaluating a board of directors
  IV.  Ownership concentration
        A. Ownership concentration and bond returns
        B. Financial policy and ownership concentration
   V.  Executive compensation
  VI.  Outside control mechanisms
        A. Stock prices and top management changes
        B. Public pension funds
 VII.  Multiple control mechanisms
VIII.  Proxy contests
        A. Wealth effects of proxy contests
        B. Proxy contests and value of control
        C. Proxy contests and takeover activity
        D. Efficiency aspects of proxy contests
  IX.  The M&A market for control
   X.  Alternative governance systems

---

entitled, "The Distribution of Power Among Corporate Managers, Shareholders, and Directors" (Jensen and Warner, 1988). The second appeared in two parts in 1990 entitled, "The Structure and Governance of Enterprise" (Jensen and Ruback, 1990). A rich abundance of follow-up articles appeared. Comprehensive book-length studies of corporate governance have been published (Chew, 1997; Monks and Minow, 1995). We shall seek to convey the central themes of this vast literature following the road map provided by Table 19.1.

# CORPORATE GOVERNANCE SYSTEMS IN THE UNITED STATES

In the United States, the system of corporate enterprise that emerged was the limited liability public corporation whose ownership in theory was widely dispersed among individual shareholders. After legislation in 1933, commercial banks were not permitted to make equity investments and insurance companies had long been circumscribed in the percentage of their funds they could invest in equities. In contrast, the system that grew up in Germany and Japan was characterized by large equity and loan investments by banks and insurance companies. In addition, substantial cross-holdings of ownership shares among corporations developed. We begin with an analysis of the U.S. model of corporate governance.

## Diffuse Stock Ownership

In the United States, for many years the dominant form of corporate ownership was diffuse limited liability ownership of the voting equity shares by a large number of individual investors. The growth of this form of ownership reflected some distinct advantages. Under limited liability, the investor could lose no more than was paid for the equity stock of the corporation. Relatively small investments could be made in a number of corporations so that the individual investor could achieve the benefits of diversification. Asset pricing models hold that diversification enables the investor to ignore the idiosyncratic risks of individual companies to earn the risk-free rate plus a market risk premium weighted by systematic risk, which implies that relatively little direct monitoring of the operations of individual business firms is required by investors.

In addition, the equity ownership shares of the corporation are readily bought and sold in active and relatively liquid markets. In the United States, by tradition and by legislation enacted in the 1930s, commercial banks and insurance companies are limited in their ability to hold large equity positions in individual corporations. Under this idealized scenario, issues of corporate governance and control are muted. But over time, the effectiveness of this governance system has been questioned. To understand the issues we begin with a brief summary of the theory of the firm.

## Contractual Theory of the Firm

The **contractual theory** of the nature of the firm has now become widely held (Alchian, 1982; Alchian and Woodward, 1988; Fama and Jensen, 1983a, 1983b). It views the firm as a network of contracts, actual and implicit, that specify the roles of the various participants or stakeholders (workers, managers, owners, lenders) and defines their rights, obligations, and payoffs under various conditions. The contractual nature of the firm implies multiple stakeholders. Their interests must be harmonized to achieve efficiency and value maximization.

Although contracts define the rights and responsibilities of each class of stakeholders in a firm, potential conflicts may occur. Contracts are unable to envisage the many changes in conditions that develop over the passage of time. Also, participants may have personal goals as well.

Most participants contract for fixed payoffs. Workers receive wages. Creditors receive interest payments and, at the maturity of debt contracts, are promised the repayment of principal. The shareholders hold residual claims on cash flows. In recent years, wage earners have been paid in part in the common stock of the firm in ESOPs or in return for wage concessions. Warrants and convertibles add equity options to debt contracts.

In this framework, the literature has expressed concern about the separation of ownership and control (Berle and Means, 1932). In general, the operations of the firm are conducted and controlled by its managers without major stock ownership positions. In theory, the managers are agents of the owners but in practice may control the firm in their own interests. Thus, conflicts of interest arise between the owners and managers.

Jensen and Meckling (1976) developed a number of aspects of the divergence of interest between owners (the principal) and management (their agent). They described how the agency problem results whenever a manager owns less than the total common stock of the firm. This fractional ownership can lead managers to work less strenuously and to acquire more perquisites (luxurious offices, furniture and rugs, company cars) than if they had to bear all of the costs.

To deal with agency problems, additional monitoring expenditures (agency costs) are required. Agency costs include (1) auditing systems to limit this kind of management behavior, (2) various kinds of bonding assurances by the managers that such abuses will not be practiced, and (3) changes in organization systems to limit the ability of managers to engage in the undesirable practices.

### Divergent Interests of Stakeholders

Traditionally, corporate governance has focused on the problem of the separation of ownership by shareholders and control by management. But increasingly we have come to recognize a broader framework. Firms must respond to the expectations of more categories of stakeholders. These include employees, consumers, large investors such as pension funds, government, and society as a whole. These diverse interests need to be harmonized. Firms must respond to the expectations of diverse stakeholders to achieve long-run value maximization (Cornell and Shapiro, 1987).

In recent years, externalities such as product safety, job safety, and environmental impacts have increased in importance. A business firm must be responsive to new and powerful constituencies for long-run viability. This point of view argues that business firms must recognize a wide range of stakeholders and external influences.

## INTERNAL CONTROL MECHANISMS

We first consider the internal control mechanisms available to balance the interests of the multiple stakeholders. In theory, under widely dispersed ownership, shareholders elect the board of directors to represent their interests. This poses issues of how other stakeholders obtain representation of their views and interests. These problems have not been fully resolved. Increasingly, public expectations look to the board of directors to balance the interests of all stakeholders. Some criticize such a view as soft-headed, unrealistic "do-goodism." An alternative view is that if the needs and goals of the multiple stakeholders—shareholders, creditors, consumers, workers, government, the general public—are not addressed, the political-economic system will not function effectively in the long run. These are matters of great importance on which the board of directors has considerable responsibilities.

# ROLE OF THE BOARD OF DIRECTORS

Monitoring by boards of directors can, in theory, deal with at least some problems of corporate governance. But there is the alternative view that boards have been ineffective in recognizing the problems of the firm and standing up to top officers, especially when tough decisions are necessary to solve the problems (Jensen, 1986). External control devices such as hostile takeovers have multiplied because of the failure of the board, according to this view.

The work by Morck, Shleifer, and Vishny (1989) was motivated by these opposing views and provided evidence on when the board could effectively deal with the problems of the firm and when the external control market comes into play. It is the view of Morck, Shleifer, and Vishny that when the company underperforms its relatively healthy industry, it is easier for the board to evaluate top management. But the board's problem is much harder when the whole industry is suffering. When the industry is having problems, it is difficult to judge whether the management is making mistakes. The boards of directors of firms in problem industries may be reluctant to force the CEO to take painful measures (for example, divest divisions, lay off workers, or cut wages) often required in slow growth, mature, or declining industries. Under these circumstances, an external challenge (M&As) to shake up the management and the board may be necessary to enforce shareholder wealth maximization.

## Composition of the Board

It is widely believed that outside directors play a larger role in monitoring management than inside directors. Fama (1980), for instance, argued that the inclusion of outside directors as professional referees enhanced the viability of the board in achieving low-cost internal transfer of control. This also lowered the probability of top management colluding and expropriating shareholders. Outside directors are usually respected leaders from the business and academic communities and have incentives to protect and develop their reputation as experts in decision control (Fama and Jensen, 1983a).

A study by Weisbach (1988) formally tested the hypothesis that inside and outside directors behave differently in monitoring top management and found that firms with outsider-dominated boards were significantly more likely than firms with insider-dominated boards to remove the chief executive officer (CEO). In Weisbach's study, firms were grouped according to the percentage of outsiders (directors who neither work for the corporation nor have extensive dealings with the company) on the board. In his sample of 367 New York Stock Exchange (NYSE) firms, the proportion of outside directors on the board centered around 50% with few firms in the tails of the distribution. In the study, outsider-dominated firms (128 firms) were those in which at least 60% of the board were outsiders. Insider-dominated firms (93 firms) had outsiders making up no more than 40% of the directors. Firms with between 41 and 59% outsiders were considered mixed (146 firms). For all the firms in the sample, there were 286 CEO resignations in the period 1974–1983. In the actual analysis, CEO resignations for reasons that are clearly unrelated to performance were eliminated from the sample.

When stock returns are used as predictors of CEO removal, the results show a statistically significant inverse relation between a firm's market-adjusted share performance in a year and the likelihood of a subsequent change in its CEO. The responsiveness of the removal decision to stock performance is three times larger for the outsider-dominated boards than for the other board types. Resignations are not sensitive to returns from periods preceding the event by more than a year, which suggests that the board's decision to replace the CEO takes place relatively quickly following poor share return performance. Using accounting earnings changes (net of industry effects) as the performance measure gives similar results. Also, there is an indication that the board of directors looks at accounting numbers (earnings before interest and taxes) to evaluate a CEO's performance, possibly more than at stock returns.

Weisbach (1988) provided evidence that the larger the shareholdings by both the top two officers of the firm and the rest of the board, the smaller the number of outsiders on the board. As expected, increased shareholdings of the CEO reduced the probability that he or she resigned. However, share ownership by noncontrolling directors (that is, directors excluding two top officers) does not appear to have any explanatory power, in addition to board composition. Thus, Weisbach suggested that the composition of the board rather than its equity ownership was what drove the level of monitoring. He also measured price responses to the announcement of CEO resignations. His results showed that the excess returns from a market model are significantly positive and thus imply that new information is revealed by these resignations.

Corporate governance reformers believe that outside directors are better monitors and therefore recommend that nominating committees should be composed of all independent outside directors. Outside directors are not officers of the firm and do not have a direct business relationship with the firm. It was GM's outside board members who played the pivotal role in ousting chairman, Robert C. Stempel in November 1992.

Using the *Wall Street Journal*'s "Who's News" section, Rosenstein and Wyatt (1990) examined the impact of the announcement that a company is appointing an outside director. The cumulative average prediction error (CAPE) for the total sample was significantly positive, which provided support for the argument that the appointment of outside directors adds to shareholder wealth.

Borokhovich, Parrino, and Trapani (1996) discussed the role of outside directors and CEO selection. They found a positive monotonic relation between the proportion of outside directors and the likelihood that an outsider is appointed CEO. This relation holds after controlling for firm size, firm performance, CEO stock ownership, and regulatory effects. Evidence from the stock returns around the succession announcements suggests that the market views the appointment of an outsider to the CEO position more favorably than the appointment of an insider, especially when the incumbent CEO is forced to resign. A new CEO from outside the firm appears to be perceived as more likely to alter firm policies in a way that benefits shareholders. On average, a significant positive abnormal return is observed when a CEO is replaced by an outsider following either voluntary or forced turnover. In contrast, while inside appointments following voluntary successions are associated with small positive abnormal returns, large negative abnormal returns are observed when insiders replace fired CEOs.

## Compensation of Board Members

Part of the solution might be a well-structured compensation system. While director compensation is a relatively recent phenomenon, it goes hand in hand with the increased director responsibility. In the past, directors did little monitoring and their own performance was not evaluated. They received a token fee for their services. Board members today take a greater leadership role by overseeing the appointment and assessment of officers, helping implement strategy, representing shareholders, and see-ing that the company fulfills its public responsibilities. Critics of the compensation as a motivating factor model point out that in some fields, particularly nonprofit, many directors volunteer their services without financial compensation.

If compensation is a significant motivating factor for directors, director stock ownership better aligns director interests more closely with those of shareholders. Some companies have adopted stock ownership requirements for directors and/or pay part or all of the directors' annual retainer in stock and stock options. Some finance their directors' retirements with stock. Studies find that directors of top-performing companies hold more stock than do their counterparts at poor performers, suggesting a positive link between director stock ownership and company performance.

### Evaluating a Board of Directors

*Business Week* (Byrne, 1996) carried a cover story entitled, "The Best & Worst Boards." Boards were rated by how close they came to meeting recommendations, which we summarize into nine items: (1) Evaluate CEO performance annually. (2) Link CEO pay to clear performance criteria. (3) Review and evaluate strategic and operating plans. (4) Require significant stock ownership and compensate directors in stock. (5) No more than three insiders. (6) Require election each year and mandatory retirement at 70. (7) Key committees should be composed of outside directors. (8) Limits on number of boards and ban on interlocking directorships. (9) Disqualify anyone receiving fees from the company.

The article listed the "best" and "worst" 25 companies based on the above crite-ria. Such listings throw the glare of publicity on the performance of boards of directors. The article also noted that some pension funds and mutual funds judge boards by the stock market performance of their companies. This is called a "blinkered view." It is argued that sound governance will improve the odds of good performance.

## OWNERSHIP CONCENTRATION

Equity ownership by managers must balance convergence or alignment of interests ver-sus entrenchment considerations. When managers' share ownership increases, their interests are better aligned with shareholder interests and thus deviation from value maximization will decline (convergence). But managerial ownership and control of vot-ing rights may give a manager enough power to guarantee his or her employment with the firm and pursue self-interest at the expense of shareholder wealth (entrenchment).

Stulz (1988) formulated a model in which at low levels of management ownership, increased equity holdings improved convergence of interests with shareholders, enhancing firm value. At higher levels of insider ownership, managerial entrenchment blocks takeovers or makes them more costly. This decreases the probability of a takeover, which is likely to decrease the value of the firm.

In Morck, Shleifer, and Vishny (MSV) (1988), performance (measured by the q-ratio) was related to management or insider ownership percentages. As ownership con-centration increased from 0 to 5%, performance improved. In the ownership range of from over 5 to 25%, performance deteriorated. As ownership concentration rose above 25%, performance improved but slowly. A simple explanation of this pattern is that in the 0 to 5% range the alignment-of-interest effect improved performance. In the above 5 to 25% range, management entrenchment influence may have a dampening effect on performance. In the over 25% range, incremental entrenchment effects were attenuated. But MSV questioned this simple interpretation. In the 0 to 5% range, they observed that the direction of causality may be reversed. (See also Jensen and Warner, 1988.) High-performance firms were more likely to give managers stock bonuses or make it profitable for them to exercise their stock options, resulting in large ownership percentages for management. They also referred to the point made by Demsetz and Lehn (1985) that firms with high performance may have substantial intangible assets that require greater ownership concentration to induce proper management of these assets. Morck et al. agreed that it appeared plausible that above the 25% ownership concentration additional entrenchment effects would be small.

Holderness and Sheehan (1988) analyzed 114 listed firms with ownership concentration more than 50% but less than 100%. Among the 114 firms, 27 became majority-shareholder firms during the period 1978–1984, but only 13 ceased to be such firms during the same period. Thus, there is little net outflow from majority ownership. This result is also confirmed for a much larger base of publicly traded firms. It appears that majority ownership is surviving as a viable organizational form. In the sample, the majority shareholders are approximately equally divided between individuals and corporations. Firms with individual majority shareholders are typically smaller than, and firms with corporate majority shareholders are slightly larger than, the typical NYSE or AMEX firms.

The average majority holding is 64% (median 60%) for all firms in the sample, which is substantially more than the minimum 50% that assures voting control. This evidence appears inconsistent with the proposition that majority blocks are held to expropriate minority shareholders. Expropriation-oriented majority shareholders might want to hold above 66% because of supermajority voting provisions in the firm's bylaws or articles of incorporation. However, only 36% of the sample firms involve blocks above 66%, the typical supermajority requirement, and for these firms the authors find no cases in which the requirement is mentioned in proxy statements.

Holderness and Sheehan (1988) also analyzed stock-price reaction to 31 announcements of majority-block trades to study the effect on firm value of changing shareholders. On average, stock prices increased over the day before announcement and the announcement day (a two-day window) by an abnormal 7.3%, and over the 30-day period around the announcement by an abnormal 12.8%. The results also indicated that on average firm value increases more when both the buyer and the seller are individuals rather than corporations. The abnormal return is higher for announcements involving simultaneous tender offers to minority shareholders (10 out of 31 cases) than announcements with no such tender offers (21 cases). In most of the consummated cases, new directors and officers were appointed after the trades.

When majority-shareholder firms are compared to firms with relatively diffuse stock ownership, Holderness and Sheehan (1988) found no statistical difference in investment expenditures, frequency of control changes, accounting rates of return, and Tobin's q. However, there was evidence that *individual* majority-shareholder firms underperformed their comparison firms in terms of q-ratios and accounting rates of return, whereas *corporate* majority-shareholder firms did not (see also Barclay and Holderness, 1991).

Slovin and Sushka (1993) analyzed the influence of ownership concentration on firm value by studying the effects of deaths of inside blockholders. They found that the abnormal returns for the two-day event interval from day $-1$ to the report of the executive death was a positive 3.01%, statistically significant. They found also that ownership concentration fell, and increased corporate control activity followed. A majority of the firms in which an inside blockholder dies subsequently become the target of a takeover bid. Two-thirds of the bids were friendly and three-fourths of them succeeded.

The preceding empirical studies yielded several implications. First, the positive stock price reactions were inconsistent with the proposition that the majority shareholders' primary objective was to expropriate or consume corporate wealth. If the expropriation hypotheses were valid, majority shareholders would not offer to buy out minority shareholders at substantial premiums. Yet such offers were made in one-third of the majority-block trading announcements. Second, majority shareholders or their representatives did not merely monitor management teams but actively participated in management. That the majority shareholder played a central role in management was consistent with the management and board turnover following majority-block trading. Third, the apparent premise for the antagonism toward large block shareholders (reflected in state regulations limiting their voting rights, antitakeover laws, poison pill charter amendments, and other "shareholder rights" initiatives) was not consistent with the empirical evidence.

### Managerial Ownership and Bond Returns

The relationships between concentration of managerial ownership and bond returns were tested by Bagnani, Milonas, Saunders, and Travlos (BMST) (1994). They employed the three-stage analysis of Morck, Shleifer, and Vishny (1988), discussed above. Their empirical analysis found no relation between bond returns and managerial ownership of 0 to 5%, a positive relation between above 5 to 25%, and a weak negative relation for ownership above 25%.

Bagnani et al. suggested some reasoning for these findings. The above 5 to 25% range represented a concentration of stock ownership that resulted in increased incentives for managers to act in shareholders' interests, taking risks that were potentially harmful to bondholders. In this range, rational bondholders required higher returns on their bonds.

At ownership above 25%, managers became more risk averse. As their stake increased, their wealth was less diversified with firm-specific, nondiversifiable human capital and/or they had greater incentives to protect their private benefits and objectives. Thus, their interests were more aligned with bondholders, implying lower bond return premia.

### Financial Policy and Ownership Concentration

In share repurchases financed by debt, the amount of equity is reduced. Because the insider group does not tender its shares in the repurchase, its percentage of equity shares is increased. This may increase the convergence of interest effect. We have seen in chapter 16 that LBOs and MBOs increase management ownership shares. Incentive effects of high management ownership percentages have performed a positive role in LBOs and MBOs.

Other effects have been noted. The Amihud, Lev, and Travlos (ALT) (1990) study measured whether the likelihood of an acquisition being financed by cash was an increasing function of the managerial ownership in the acquiring firm. Increasing debt, while increasing the probability of bankruptcy, can be used to increase management's equity stake if the debt is used to retire equity held by the public. The sample consisted of firms that appeared on the 1980 list of Fortune 500 companies and made cash acquisitions of over $10 million of other firms during the period 1981–1983. The results showed that cash acquisitions are associated with significantly larger insider ownership levels than stock financed acquisitions.

## EXECUTIVE COMPENSATION

We have presented materials on the relationship between managerial concentration of ownership and the convergence of interests of managers with owners. Executive compensation plans have also been proposed to achieve alignment of interests.

One view is that the conflict of interest between owners and managers would be substantially reduced if executive compensation plans more tightly related pay to performance. The view is widely held that executive compensation is not closely linked to performance measured by changes in the value of the firm. Jensen and Murphy (1990) found that executive pay changes only $3 for a $1,000 change in the wealth of a firm, an elasticity of 0.003 or 0.3%. This is argued to demonstrate that executive pay is not linked to performance. But this relationship may be at least partially explained by the large value of the firm in relation to executive compensation.

For example, the Disney Company at the end of 1995 had 524 million shares outstanding. At a price of $60 per share, this represented $31.44 billion. If its top executive received compensation of $10 million, this was 0.000318 of total firm value.

In one recent year its president, Michael Eisner, realized $200 million mainly from the exercise of stock options. From a low of $7 in 1986, the price of Disney stock, adjusted for splits, increased to a high of $64.25 in 1995. Based on the 524 million shares outstanding at the end of 1995, this represented an increase in value to Disney shareholders of approximately $30 billion. Thus, Eisner's salary change in the one unusual year represented about $6.7 for each $1,000 change in the wealth of Disney shareholders, an elasticity of 0.0067 or 0.67%. The result was not greatly different from the Jensen and Murphy relationship. This example suggested that while the elasticity of executive pay in relation to changes in firm value was small, the impact on the wealth position of executives could be very large.

A large impact on executive wealth position could have strong motivational influences. Haubrich (1994), using some reasonable parameter assumptions, derived the Jensen and Murphy results from some leading models of principal-agent theory. Haubrich's analysis led Shleifer and Vishny (1995) to observe that the Jensen-Murphy relationship would generate large swings in executive wealth and require considerable risk tolerance for executives.

Another criticism of past patterns in executive compensation was that bonuses and stock options had been based on accounting measures rather than on stock market–based performance measures. Rappaport (1986) provided some perspective on the choice of performance measure. He observed that early executive compensation performance plans *were* market based. However, during the 1970s, stock price movements were essentially flat. The average of daily closing prices for the Dow Jones Industrial Average was 911 for 1965 and was still only 884 for 1982. The broader S&P 500 Index also remained essentially flat over the same time period. As a consequence, performance measures for granting options shifted from market-based to accounting-based measures over this period (Rappaport, 1986, p. 177).

However, in recent years, performance is again moving to market-based measures. The data in chapter 16 on leveraged buyouts demonstrated that in going-private transactions top management increased its percentage ownership of equity shares in the company by substantial percentages. This was an important element in the strong motivational influences that led to the well-documented performance improvement in the LBOs during the first part of the 1980s.

Other proposals for improved pay-performance policies have been made in recent years:

1. Limit the base salaries of top executives.
2. Bonus and stock option plans should be based on stock appreciation.
3. Stock appreciation benchmarks should consider
   a. close competitors
   b. a wider peer group
   c. broader stock market indexes such as the Dow or the S&P 500.
4. Stock options should be based on a premium of 10 to 20% over the current market and should not be repriced if the shares of the firm fall below the original exercise prices.
5. Company loan programs should enable top executives to buy substantial amounts of the firm's stock so that subsequent stock price fluctuations substantially impact the wealth position of the top executives.
6. Directors should be paid mainly in stock of the corporation with minimum specified holding periods to heighten their sensitivity to firm performance.

These changes in corporate practice are consistent with the recognition of the need to align the interests of managers with the interests of owners. Recent developments in executive compensation are seeking to achieve a closer link between executive pay and company performance. To the degree that these efforts are successful, the interests of managers will, to a greater degree, be aligned with those of owners. Other aspects of designing optional executive compensation plans are discussed in Copeland and Weston (1988, pp. 665–672).

## OUTSIDE CONTROL MECHANISMS

To this point we have discussed internal control mechanisms for effective corporate governance. We have discussed the role of the board of directors, ownership concentration, and executive compensation. We now turn to outside control mechanisms, which include stock price performance, institutional investors, and proxy contests.

### Stock Prices and Top Management Changes

Warner, Watts, and Wruck (WWW) (1988) investigated the relation between a firm's stock price performance and subsequent changes in its top management including the CEO, president, and chairman of the board. They also provided new evidence on mechanisms for replacing inefficient managers and encouraging managers to maximize shareholder wealth. The data set used by WWW included top management changes for 269 NYSE and AMEX firms in the period 1963–1978.

Consistent with studies of CEO changes (Coughlan and Schmidt, 1985; Weisbach, 1988), WWW found that poor stock price performance was likely to result in an increased rate of management turnover. They also documented evidence of several internal control mechanisms such as monitoring by large blockholders, competition from other managers, as well as discipline by the board.

A number of earlier studies found significant positive price effects of changes in top management. Some found insignificant price reactions. In their later (1995) study,

Denis and Denis also found insignificant announcement period abnormal returns for all management changes. However, forced resignations are associated with a positive 1.5% significant period abnormal returns. Normal retirements have insignificant effects. Interestingly, for the preannouncement period of $-251$ to $-2$ days, the forced resignations were associated with a $-24\%$ CAR. Normal retirements were associated with a $-4\%$ CAR but not statistically significant.

Denis and Denis also found that forced top management changes were preceded by significantly large operating performance declines and followed by significant improvements. Forced management changes were associated with significant downsizing measured by declines in employment, capital expenditures, and total assets. Denis and Denis observed that improvements did not result from effective board monitoring. Only 13% of their large 853 sample were forced changes. Over two-thirds of the forced resignations were associated with blockholder pressure, financial distress, shareholder lawsuits, and takeover attempts. They found that 56% of the firms with a forced top executive change became the target of some corporate control activity, generally in the form of a block investment or some form of takeover. They concluded that internal control mechanisms were inadequate to do the job alone and required the pressure of external corporate control markets.

## Public Pension Funds

Public pension funds have the ability and size to become significant factors in corporate governance, yet only a small fraction have involved themselves in these issues. One of the more active pension funds is the California Public Employees' Retirement System (CALPERS), which invests $68 billion in pension funds for nearly 1 million public employees in California. In March 1992 CALPERS publicly announced the names of 12 companies with which it had failed to negotiate the adoption of corporate reforms. CALPERS accused these poorly performing companies of excessive executive pay or failing to maintain independent boards of directors.

In October 1993 the world's largest pension plan with $125 billion in assets, TIAA–CREF (formerly known as the Teachers Insurance and Annuity Association–College Retirement Equities Fund), announced a "corporate governance" policy. Although Chairman John Biggs said he was unwilling to sacrifice more than 0.1 percentage point in the annual return to fight for better corporate governance practices, TIAA encouraged companies to have independent, diverse boards, with a majority of independent directors, and to have directors held more accountable to shareholders (Scism, 1994, p. C1).

Wahal (1996) studied the activities of nine activist pension funds, from 1987 to 1993, with assets totaling $424 billion at the end of 1994. He noted that these funds averaged about 1% of the market value of equity of 146 targeted firms. In dollar terms, the ownership ranged from $8 million to $86 million. Inactive institutions as a group own approximately 51% ($3 billion) of the firms targeted by activist pension funds. The average inactive institution owns 0.3% ($14 million) of targeted firms. Takeover-related proxy proposals covered poison pills, greenmail, and antitakeover provisions. Governance-related targeting involved golden parachutes, board composition, and compensation. The activist proposals shifted from takeover-related proxy proposals in the late 1980s to governance-related proposals in the 1990s.

Wahal's results showed approximately a zero average abnormal return for shareholder proposals and small positive abnormal returns for attempts to influence target firms in using shareholder proposals (nonproxy targeting). But no evidence of significant long-term improvement was found in either stock price movements or accounting measures of performance in the post-targeting period.

Strickland, Wiles, and Zenner (SWZ) (1996) studied the United Shareholders Association (USA) from 1986 to 1993. The USA was founded in August 1986 by T. Boone Pickens as a not-for-profit organization for shareholder rights. It was disbanded on October 25, 1993, by a vote of the USA's board of directors. The USA developed a Target 50 list of firms on the basis of poor financial performance, executive compensation plans not tied to firm performance, and policies that limited shareholder input on governance issues. If the targeted firms did not respond, the USA, through its some 65,000 members, sought to sponsor proxy proposals changing the governance structure.

Strickland et al. recognized that proxy proposals do not bind the firm's board of directors. To judge whether the USA was effective, SWZ documented that USA successfully negotiated corporate governance changes covering 53 proposals before inclusion in proxy statements. At the announcement of such negotiated agreements, target firms' shareholders receive a 0.9% abnormal return, representing a wealth increase of $1.3 billion ($30 million per firm). The USA was most effective when the target firm was a poor performer with high institutional ownership.

## MULTIPLE CONTROL MECHANISMS

Most of the previous studies reviewed consider the influence of individual control mechanisms. The study by Agrawal and Knoeber (1996) considered seven mechanisms: insider shareholdings, outside representation on the board, debt policy, activity in the corporate control market, institutional shareholdings, shareholdings of large blockholders, and the managerial labor market. Their sample was composed of the 400 largest firms for which they could obtain required data to measure the seven mechanisms. Firm performance is measured by Tobin's q. Measuring the influence of each separately, the first four control mechanisms are statistically related to firm performance. Considering all of the mechanisms together, but not within a simultaneous equation system, the influence of insider shareholdings drops out. Finally, when the interdependence among the mechanisms is accounted for in a simultaneous system estimation, only the negative effect on firm performance of outsiders on the board remains. Agrawal and Knoeber concluded that the control mechanisms are chosen optimally except for the use of outsiders on boards. Most other studies find a positive benefit from the use of outside directors.

## PROXY CONTESTS

Proxy contests represent another corporate control mechanism. Proxy contests are attempts by dissident groups of shareholders to obtain board representation. Even though technically most contests are unsuccessful to the extent that the dissident group fails to win a majority on the board of directors, proxy contests can and do have significant effects on target firm shareholder wealth regardless of outcome. Some have argued that a better measure of success is whether the dissident group gains at least two members on the board of directors. "We want one person to propose a motion and a second person to second it. Then discussion of the motion will be in the minutes of the board meeting. In this way, we can monitor the majority group and record our views on important policy issues." This quote summarizes the view the authors have encountered in their experience with proxy contests.

A major change occurred in October 1992, when the SEC adopted proxy reform rules. Under the old rules, any shareholder who wanted to communicate with more than ten other shareholders was required to submit their comments for SEC approval prior to circulation. The new rules ease requirements for shareholders not seeking control of the company to communicate with one another.

Studies of proxy contests explain the shareholder wealth effects that take place in terms of the disciplinary value of proxy contests in the managerial labor market, the relationship between proxy contests and other forms of takeover activity, and the value of the vote, which takes on greater importance during a proxy contest. The study by Pound (1988) empirically identified the sources of inefficiency of the present system of proxy contests.

## Wealth Effects—Early Studies

Dodd and Warner (DW) (1983) examined 96 proxy contests for board seats on NYSE- or AMEX-listed firms over the period 1962–1978. They considered several hypotheses to explain why target shareholder returns were positive and significant on average (6.2% over the period from 39 days before the contest announcement through the contest outcome) in spite of the fact that dissidents won a majority on the board in only one-fifth of the cases studied.

First, even minority board representation allows the dissident group to have a positive impact on corporate policy leading to a permanent share price revaluation.

In cases where no board seats change hands, the fact of the challenge itself may cause incumbent management to implement changes in policy that benefit shareholders (Bradley, Desai, and Kim, 1983, "kick-in-the-pants" hypothesis). Scenarios that hypothesize stock price declines when proxy contests fail were not supported. These hypotheses emphasize the direct costs (in terms of corporate resources) of defending against the dissident group and ignore the possibilities for increased efficiency that may be exposed during the course of the contest. Abnormal returns at the contest outcome announcement were in fact negative for contests in which the dissidents failed to win any seats at all; however, the negative return was only −1.4%, not large enough to offset earlier gains and not significant.

The mechanics of waging a proxy contest almost guarantee that there will be leakage of information about dissident activity well before the proxy contest announcement in the *Wall Street Journal*. This is confirmed by significant abnormal returns of 11.9% over the period starting 60 days before the announcement through the announcement itself. These returns are not attributable to merger activity because the results are similar whether the dissident group included another firm or not; the sample did not exhibit unexpectedly higher earnings in the preannouncement period. Thus, the positive returns seem attributable to the changes that may be stimulated by the proxy contest itself.

A later study by DeAngelo and DeAngelo (1989) of 60 proxy contests from 1978 to 1985 corroborated many of DW's (1983) results. They found significant positive abnormal returns from 40 days before the contest through the outcome announcement of 6.02%, significant returns of 18.76% in the 40 days preceding any public indication of dissident activity. As in the earlier study, the gains (particularly those in the precontest period) were not dependent on contest outcome. Like DW they found negative returns at the contest outcome when the dissidents failed to win any seats on the board. These negative returns were larger than in the DW study: −5.45% over the two-day outcome announcement period. However, most of these negative returns were shown to result from the means by which the dissidents were defeated. Where the incumbents prevailed in a shareholder vote, the negative return was only −1.73% and not significant.

However, where the dissidents were defeated by other means, the return was a −7.19% (significant). These other means included the expenditure of corporate assets to buy off the dissidents, a white knight acquisition of the target, or court approval of the validity of the incumbent's defense in the face of which the dissidents withdrew. This result appeared to imply that when the incumbent management was securely entrenched or the probability of future control contests was reduced, the value of vote and/or the expected takeover premium capitalized in the share price declined.

As in the prior study, the dissidents were successful in only about one-third of the proxy contests. However, DeAngelo and DeAngelo (1989) go on to examine events in the target firm for three years after the contest. It was found that by the end of three years less than 20% of the target firms remained as independent publicly held corporations under the same management as before the contest. For example, in 20 of the 39 firms in which dissidents failed to win a majority, there were 38 resignations of the CEO, president, or chairman of the board over the next three years. These resignations were clearly linked to the proxy contest either explicitly in the financial press, or by the fact that the vacancy was filled by a member of the dissident group. The 60-firm sample included 15 cases where sale or liquidation of the firm in the three-year period following the contest was directly linked to the dissident activity.

In fact, DeAngelo and DeAngelo (1989) concluded that most of the gains to proxy contest activity are closely related to merger and acquisitions activity. The initial gains in the precontest period (approximately 20%) are attributed to the increased likelihood that the firm will eventually be sold at a premium at some time following the proxy contest. To support this conclusion, they divided their sample into two groups: those that were eventually sold/liquidated and those that were not. For the "sold" subsample, abnormal returns over the full period of dissident activity were a significant 15.16%; while for the "unsold" group, the gain was a less significant 2.90%. The fact that the initial runup was similar for both groups simply indicates that the market revises its opinion of the likelihood of a sale as more information becomes available. To the extent that proxy contests are indeed linked to takeover activity, the goal seems to be to get some representation on the board to persuade the rest of the board to sell or liquidate.

Sridharan and Reinganum (1995) sought to explain why tender offers occur in some cases and proxy contests take place in others. Their sample was composed of 79 hostile tender offers and 38 proxy contests. A proxy fight is more likely to take place when target firm performance is relatively poor, measured by return on assets and stock market returns. Managerial inefficiency leads to a proxy contest; failure to pursue new and profitable investment opportunities leads to a tender offer.

When shareholdings of management are high, they are more likely to be able to block a tender offer so dissidents will engage in a proxy contest. They find that tender offer targets tend to be less leveraged than firms experiencing proxy fights. The reason they give is that the lower the leverage the greater is the supply of shares available for purchase in a tender offer.

### Wealth Effects—Later Studies

Borstadt and Zwirlein (1992) sampled 142 NYSE or AMEX firms, taken from the SEC Directorate of Economics and Policy Analysis and the *Wall Street Journal* articles, that were involved in proxy contests waged from July 1, 1962 to January 31, 1986. The sample was further divided into a full-control and partial-control sample. The dissident success rate was 42% for the full-control sample, and 60% for the partial-control sample. The turnover rate of top management after the proxy contest was higher than average. On average, shareholders realize a positive abnormal return of 11.4% (significant) during the proxy contest period, defined as 60 days prior to the announcement of the contest through the contest resolution announcement.

Ikenberry and Lakonishok (IL) (1993) tested the hypothesis that the proxy contest, in challenging the management's slate for the board of directors, represented a referendum on management's ability to operate the firm and can act as a disciplinary mechanism. The sample of 97 election contests during the period 1968–1987 came from the *Weekly Bulletin* for NYSE and AMEX firms. Firms not followed by Compustat or cases where there was an earlier election contest within the 60 months prior were eliminated. For the period from month −60 to month −5 relative to the announcement of the contest, the CAR of proxy contest targets is −34.4% (significant). When compared with growth in operating income before depreciation, contest targets underperform control firms by 39.3% (significant) over the five-year period prior to the announcement of election contests. Thus, proxy contests appear to be stimulated by poor performance.

When the incumbent board members retain all their seats, the CAR is not significantly different from zero for the five-year period following the contest. In cases where dissidents gain at least one board seat, CAR from month +3 to +24 is −32.4% (significant). The negative returns over the same time period are more severe in cases where the dissidents gain control of the board, −48% (significant). When dissidents gain control of the board, IL speculate that the negative stock price behavior might be explained by either overoptimistic expectations of improved performance or the dissidents' discovery that the company faced more serious problems than anticipated.

The predominant findings of abnormal negative returns are different from the earlier studies, which found predominantly positive returns associated with proxy contests. We attempt some possible reasons for the difference in findings. The sample composition of the IL study is more heavily weighted with proxy contests that occurred after the mid-1980s when the M&A market was highly active and when shareholder activism, particularly by large pension funds, increased. In some sense, the IL sample reflects firms for which other control mechanisms were not utilized. For example, perhaps these firms were not acquired because the prospects were too poor to attract a bidder. Within the IL sample, the proxy contests in which incumbent board members retain all their seats, abnormal returns are not different from zero for the five-year period following the contest. These would be proxy contests in which dissidents could not mount a persuasive case for obtaining board membership. These possibilities require further research.

## THE M&A MARKET FOR CONTROL

In one sense, proxy contests, discussed in the preceding section, represent a form of external control if the dissidents are from outside the company, which is usually the case. The most widely recognized form of external pressures is the market for corporate control. Several empirical measures demonstrate that M&As do indeed impact business firms. One good metric is provided by Mitchell and Mulherin (1996). They analyzed the 1,064 firms listed in the Value Line Investment Survey at year-end 1981. By 1989, 57% of these firms had been either a takeover target or had engaged in substantial defensive asset restructuring. The more than half of the universe of firms with a relatively wide investment following that were subjected to the pressures of the M&A market is a measure only of the direct impacts. Surely a high percentage of the remaining 43% had to be aware that poor performance would subject them to a possible takeover. Also, superior performance might enable such firms to augment their resources by taking over firms whose performance could be improved.

Furthermore, the proprietary database of Robert Comment with information about all M&As for NYSE- and AMEX-listed target firms from 1975 to 1991 totaled 1,814 companies, a substantial number (Schwert, 1996). The total number of M&A announcements tracked by the annual *Mergerstat Review* has been running more than 3,000 in recent years and was 3,510 in 1995, jumping to 5,848 in 1996. Another metric is MBO activity, which represented 11.4% of the main sample of 1,523 firms in the Schwert study.

Thus, the M&A market is clearly a major source of external control mechanisms on business firms. However, the need to resort to the M&A market is an indication of at least some degree of failure in internal control mechanisms.

## ALTERNATIVE GOVERNANCE SYSTEMS

In German and Japanese corporate governance, two major differences from the American-British systems are observed. Commercial banks have large ownership shares in industrial firms and are major lenders as well. In addition, industrial firms own shares in each other. Groups of firms become tied together by cross-shareholdings (Kaplan, 1994).

In theory, this large ownership position of owners-lenders with business expertise and large financial stakes will lead to effective monitoring of business performance. In a survey of corporate governance, the *Economist* (January 29, 1994) presented material raising doubts about the effectiveness of the German and Japanese corporate governance models. The article cited studies that indicate that the banks have not monitored closely the firms to which they have provided both equity and debt capital. These studies suggest that the banks have become active only when their client firms experience substantial difficulties.

The *Economist* also argued that German and Japanese governance appeared to be good only because the earlier economic environment was so favorable. With growing economies, favorable productivity improvements, high employment, and rising exports, stock prices were moving continuously upward. In favorable economies, commitments could be made to provide employees with lifetime employment. Cross-holdings of common stocks lead to an increase in trust among partners. The system works well if all parties have the same long-term interests and goals.

The downturns in the economies of Germany and Japan that have continued into the mid-1990s have created some conflicts of interest. Competition for business relationships and financing has increased. Business transactions between group firms in Japan have dropped to 10% of sales (p. 11). Smaller shareholders are pushing for better treatment from managers. Managers are pushed to reassess their trade-offs of shareholder interests in relation to the interests of employees and other stakeholders. If the economic growth of the two economies slows over the longer term, these conflicts of interest are likely to be exacerbated.

The supervisory boards, in Germany particularly, did not seem to meet often enough. They appeared to act slowly. An incompetent manager was usually permitted to complete his standard five-year contract before being replaced. The chairman of the board was often the outgoing leader of the executive board and not as independent minded as an outsider would be. Supervisory boards were often not adequately informed.

The *Economist,* in completing its survey of corporate governance, concluded that the increased activism of pension funds in the United States helped make that system work better. An active market for corporate control in the form of mergers and takeovers provides a marketplace test of performance. The strength of the American-British systems of shareholder control is that they are ultimately market based. In the long run, this is held to be superior to the direct supervision and judgments of the large banking corporations, which have their own governance problems.

---

## Summary

Because there is a substantial literature on corporate governance, this summary provides a logical framework for the subject. Traditionally, corporate governance focused on conflicts of interest between managers and owners. It is increasingly recognized that conflicts of interest occur across a wide range of stakeholders: owners with a small number of shares, owners with large ownership positions, creditors, managers, employees, consumers, government, and society as a whole. To date, most of the literature discusses problems of the separation of ownership and control. Historically, in the United States, the main form of corporate ownership was small ownership stakes diffused among a large number of individual investors. The advantages were limited liability, broad diversification of investments, small monitoring requirements, and easy purchase or sale of ownership rights. But increasingly, several forms of agency problems became recognized. Managements may act in their own self-interest.

Compensation arrangements and competition among managers provide internal control mechanisms. In addition, poor stock price performance is likely to cause changes in management. In theory, the board of directors monitors management. In practice, boards tend to be dominated by management insiders. The use of outside directors provides for greater independence but does not solve the problem of effective monitoring of managers. The increased activism of large institutional holders of equity such as pension funds has demonstrated increased effectiveness in monitoring corporate managers and their performance.

Increased stock ownership by management has been proposed as a method of reducing conflicts of interest between owners and managers. Some studies suggest that performance improves with rising management ownership share in the 0 to 5% range; deteriorates in the 5 to 25% range; improves above 25%. Large block purchases have had positive event returns. When the shareholdings of a group are large, monitoring is increased. In addition, large blockholders are more likely to monitor management.

The holding of voting stock that achieves control of the firm commands a price premium. Because control is valued by the capital markets, dual-class recapitalizations are employed by majority owners to further consolidate their control position. Larger managerial holdings can have incentive effects. The voting rights premium may also result from the possibility that in a takeover, superior voting rights will receive a higher price.

Proxy contests represent another method of improving managerial performance. In most studies, the initiation of proxy contests is associated with substantial positive event returns. The challenge of a proxy contest may be sufficient to cause incumbent management to improve policies. Minority board representation enables dissidents to have a continuing impact. A strong link has been found between proxy contests and subsequent takeover activity. The positive event returns associated with proxy contests reflect the increased likelihood of improved performance or the eventual sale of the firm at a premium. Mergers and acquisitions represent an important external control mechanism.

Executive compensation plans have been suggested as another mechanism for influencing managerial performance. The elasticity of management **compensation** in relation to changes in the value of the firm is apparently small. But the elasticity of **wealth** changes of managers to changes in the value of the firm may be substantial. The increased ownership share of managers and LBOs in the early 1980s demonstrated strong motivational influences. Proposals to improve the influence of executive pay on corporate performance have been made. One is to base bonus, stock, and option plans on benchmark stock price changes. The benchmarks can be based on the stock price performance of close competitors, wider peer groups, broader stock market indexes, or other criteria. Another proposal is to adopt policies that result in substantial stock holdings by executives so that they think more like owners. Also, the bonus and stock ownership arrangements with executives should cause their wealth positions to increase with good performance and to deteriorate with poor performance. These arrangements should be appropriately benchmarked and related to the long-range planning processes of the firm.

Finally, it has been proposed that the alternative governance systems of Germany and Japan provide a better model for improving corporate governance. In these alternative governance systems, commercial banks hold large ownership shares in industrial firms and are major lenders as well. Also, groups of firms become tied together by cross-shareholdings. But some observers state that the alternative governance systems worked well when the general macroeconomic framework was favorable. With reduced economic growth, tensions and conflicts of interest have also arisen in the German and Japanese governance systems. Furthermore, even under favorable macroeconomic conditions, there were strains in the system. Monitoring by the large banking corporations with their own governance problems often was not effective. The strength of the American-British systems of shareholder control is that they are ultimately market based.

## Questions

19.1 What conclusions can you draw from the empirical evidence on the value of corporate control?

19.2 What are the effects of the size of the fraction of equity share ownership by top management on:
   a. q-ratio?
   b. Agency problems?
   c. Probability of a hostile bid?
   d. Level of premium required for a takeover bid to succeed?

19.3 What is the stock market's general response to recapitalizations providing for dual classes of stock? Why?

19.4 Why would any investor purchase an inferior-vote class of stock?

19.5 What characteristics are typical of firms with dual classes of stock?

19.6 What effect do proxy contests have on shareholder returns?

------------------------------------ C A S E    19–1 ------------------------------------

# Chrysler Corporation Versus Tracinda Corporation—A Struggle for Control

The control struggle between Kirk Kerkorian and the Chrysler Corporation continued over the period from early April 1995 until early February 1996 when a compromise agreement was reached. The battles and skirmishes reflected a number of twists and turns in strategies that involved many episodes. Here is a time line of events:

4/11/95   Robert Eaton, chairman of Chrysler, receives a phone call from Kirk Kerkorian that he and former Chrysler chairman Lee Iacocca were planning a takeover bid of $55 a share totaling $22.8 billion. The stock reaction was a 24% increase, closing at $48.75 on the announcement date, 4/12/95. Kerkorian charged that Chrysler was too conservative in holding cash reserves of $7.5 billion.

4/24/95   Chrysler formally rejected the Kerkorian bid, saying it did not want to gamble with Chrysler's future.

5/31/95   Kerkorian withdrew his bid due to lack of financing but stated that he would continue his efforts to help Chrysler management improve the value of its common stock. Kerkorian hired the investment banking firm Wasserstein Perella & Co. to develop a full range of possible options.

6/26/95   Kerkorian announced his intention to buy 14 million Chrysler shares at $50 each to raise his stake to 13.6%.

7/1/95   Chrysler's board adopted golden parachutes for its 30 highest ranking officers.

7/15/95   Chrysler moved to prevent Iacocca from exercising his Chrysler stock options because he had violated the prohibition from taking actions "which adversely affect the Chrysler Corporation."

8/25/95   Kerkorian achieved his goal of increasing his ownership of Chrysler to 13.6%.

9/5/95   Kerkorian announced that he had hired Jerome York, the CFO of IBM, and before that the treasurer of Chrysler, to be his main strategist.

9/7/95   Chrysler's board announced that it would double its share repurchase program to $2 billion.

9/10/95   York stated that Tracinda Corporation was considering a proxy fight. He criticized Chrysler's management for holding too much cash, stating that $4.5 billion would be an ample reserve rather than $7.5 billion. He also stated that $2.5 billion of Chrysler assets were "non-core."

9/20/95   Tracinda hired Ralph Whitworth, widely regarded as an expert on corporate governance and an influential shareholder activist.

10/1/95   Chrysler began a publicity campaign against York's criticisms and called attention to Chrysler's earnings and product successes.

10/25/95   York met with Chrysler's CFO and general counsel, requesting a seat on the board for himself and the addition of two independent members.

11/6/95   Iacocca filed a suit over his Chrysler stock options. Tracinda agreed to cover up to $2 million of his legal fees and make up the difference between $42 million and his award.

11/20/95   Tracinda announced that it would file preliminary proxy soliciting materials with the SEC including a proposal to replace board member Joseph Antonini with Jerome York.

11/23/95   Antonini announced that he would resign from the Chrysler board.

12/7/95   Chrysler announced a 20% dividend increase, its fifth dividend increase in two years.

1/19/96   Chrysler announced strong fourth quarter earnings.

2/7/96   Chrysler announced that it would recommend for membership on its board John R. Neff, a respected asset manager who had retired in the previous year as manager of the $4.5 billion Windsor Fund.

2/8/96   The two sides agreed to a five-year truce in the form of a five-year standstill agreement. Kerkorian would reserve a board seat to be occupied by James Aljian, a Tracinda executive in return for agreeing not to launch a proxy fight or to increase his shareholdings during the five-year period. Within 30 days, Kerkorian would also terminate his arrangements with Wasserstein Perella, with

Ralph Whitworth, and with D. F. King & Co., a proxy soliciting firm. Chrysler would add another billion to its share repurchase program and would continue its efforts to sell its nonautomotive units. Chrysler would increase the accountability of its board by switching from cash to stock compensation. In exchange for Iacocca's agreement to terminate his position as consultant to Tracinda and to refrain from publicly criticizing Chrysler for the

five-year period, Iacocca's stock option lawsuits would be settled; Chrysler would pay Iacocca $21 million and Tracinda would contribute $32 million.

5/17/96   Chrysler announced a dividend increase of 17% and a 2-for-1 stock split. The stock closed up $2.25 to $67.125 compared with its price in the low 40s in May 1995, about one year earlier.

## Question on Case Study C19.1

C19.1.1   What are the lessons from the Kerkorian Chrysler case?

## References

Agrawal, Anup, and Charles R. Knoeber, "Firm Performance and Mechanisms to Control Agency Problems between Managers and Shareholders," *Journal of Financial and Quantitative Analysis,* 31, September 1996, pp. 377–397.

Alchian, A. A., "Property Rights, Specialization and the Firm," chapter 1 in J. Fred Weston and Michael E. Granfield, eds., *Corporate Enterprise in a New Environment,* New York: KCG Productions, Inc., 1982, pp. 11–36.

———, and S. Woodward, "The Firm Is Dead: Long Live the Firm: A Review of Oliver E. Williamson's *The Economic Institutions of Capitalism,*" *Journal of Economic Literature,* 26, March 1988, pp. 65–79.

Amihud, Yakov, B. Lev, and N. G. Travlos, "Corporate Control & the Choice of Investment Financing," *Journal of Finance,* 45, June 1990, pp. 603–616.

Bagnani, Elizabeth Strock, Nikolaos T. Milonas, Anthony Saunders, and Nickolaos G. Travlos, "Managers, Owners, and the Pricing of Risky Debt: An Empirical Analysis," *Journal of Finance,* 49, June 1994, pp. 453–477.

Barclay, Michael J., and C. G. Holderness, "Negotiated Block Trades and Corporate Control," *Journal of Finance,* 46, July 1991, pp. 861–878.

Berle, A. A., Jr., and G. C. Means, *The Modern Corporation and Private Property,* New York: Macmillan, 1932.

Borokhovich, Kenneth A., Robert Parrino, and Teresa Trapani, "Outside Directors and CEO Selection," *Journal of Financial and Quantitative Analysis,* 31, September 1996, pp. 337–355.

Borstadt, Lisa F., and T. J. Zwirlein, "The Efficient Monitoring of Proxy Contests: An Empirical Analysis of Post-Contest Control Changes and Firm Performance," *Journal of Financial Management,* 21, Autumn 1992, pp. 22–34.

Bradley, Michael, Anand Desai, and E. Han Kim, "The Rationale Behind Interfirm Tender Offers: Information or Synergy," *Journal of Financial Economics,* 11, April 1983, pp. 183–206.

Byrne, John A., "The Best & Worst Boards," *Business Week,* November 25, 1996, pp. 82–106.

Chew, Donald H., ed., *Studies in International Corporate Finance and Governance Systems,* New York: Oxford University Press, 1997.

Copeland, Thomas E., and J. Fred Weston, *Financial Theory and Corporate Policy,* Reading, MA: Addison-Wesley Publishing Company, 1988.

Cornell, Bradford, and Alan Shapiro, "Corporate Stakeholders and Corporate Finance," *Financial Management,* 16, Spring 1987, pp. 5–14.

Coughlan, A. T., and R. M. Schmidt, "Executive Compensation, Managerial Turnover, and Firm Performance: An Empirical Investigation," *Journal of Accounting and Economics,* 7, 1985, pp. 43–66.

DeAngelo, Harry, and Linda DeAngelo, "Proxy Contests and the Governance of Publicly Held Corporations," *Journal of Financial Economics,* 23, 1989, pp. 29–60.

Demsetz, H., and K. Lehn, "The Structure of Corporate Ownership," *Journal of Political Economy,* 93, 1985, pp. 1155–1177.

Denis, David J., and Diane K. Denis, "Performance Changes Following Top Management Dismissals," *Journal of Finance,* 50, September 1995, pp. 1029–1057.

Dodd, Peter, and Jerold B. Warner, "On Corporate Governance: A Study of Proxy Contests," *Journal of Financial Economics,* 11, 1983, pp. 401–438.

*The Economist,* "A Survey of Corporate Governance," January 29, 1994, special supplement, pp. 1–18.

Fama, E. F., "Agency Problems and the Theory of the Firm," *Journal of Political Economy,* 88, 1980, pp. 288–307.

———, and Michael C. Jensen, "Separation of Ownership and Control," *The Journal of Law and Economics,* 26, June 1983a, pp. 301–325.

———, "Agency Problems and Residual Claims," *The Journal of Law and Economics,* 26, June 1983b, pp. 327–349.

Haubrich, Joseph G., "Risk Aversion, Performance Pay, and the Principal-Agent Problem," *Journal of Political Economy,* 102, April 1994, pp. 258–276.

Holderness, C. G., and D. P. Sheehan, "The Role of Majority Shareholders in Publicly Held Corporations: An Exploratory Analysis," *Journal of Financial Economics,* 20, 1988, pp. 317–346.

Ikenberry, David, and Josef Lakonishok, "Corporate Governance Through the Proxy Contest: Evidence and Implications," *Journal of Business,* 66, July 1993, pp. 405–435.

Jensen, Michael C., "Agency Costs of Free Cash Flow, Corporate Finance, and Takeovers," *American Economic Review,* Papers and Proceeedings, 76, May 1986, pp. 323–329.

———, and W. H. Meckling, "Theory of the Firm: Managerial Behavior, Agency Costs and Ownership Structure," *Journal of Financial Economics,* 3, 1976, pp. 305–360.

Jensen, Michael C., and Kevin J. Murphy, "Performance Pay and Top-Management Incentives," *Journal of Political Economy,* 98, April 1990, pp. 225–264.

Jensen, Michael C., and Richard S. Ruback, eds., "Symposium on the Structure and Governance of Enterprise," *Journal of Financial Economics,* 27, Part I, September 1990, Part II, October 1990.

Jensen, Michael C., and Jerold B. Warner, eds., "Symposium on the Distribution of Power Among Corporate Managers, Shareholders, and Directors," *Journal of Financial Economics,* 20, January/March 1988.

Kaplan, Steven N., "Top Executive Rewards and Firm Performance: A Comparison of Japan and the United States," *Journal of Political Economy,* 102, June 1994, pp. 510–546.

Mitchell, Mark L., and J. Harold Mulherin, "The Impact of Industry Shocks on Takeover and Restructuring Activity," *Journal of Financial Economics,* 41, 1996, pp. 193–229.

Monks, Robert A. G., and Nell Minow, *Corporate Governance,* Cambridge, MA: Blackwell Publishers, 1995.

Morck, R., A. Shleifer, and R. W. Vishny, "Management Ownership and Market Valuation: An Empirical Analysis," *Journal of Financial Economics,* 20, 1988, pp. 293–315.

———, "Alternative Mechanisms for Corporate Control," *American Economic Review,* 79, 1989, pp. 842–852.

Pound, John, "Proxy Contests and the Efficiency of Shareholder Oversight," *Journal of Financial Economics,* 20, 1988, pp. 237–265.

Rappaport, Alfred, *Creating Shareholder Value,* New York: The Free Press, 1986.

Rosenstein, Stuart, and J. G. Wyatt, "Outside Directors, Board Independence, and Shareholder Wealth," *Journal of Financial Economics,* 26, 1990, pp. 175–191.

Schwert, G. William, "Markup Pricing in Mergers and Acquisitions," *Journal of Financial Economics,* 41, 1996, pp. 153–192.

Scism, Leslie, "Labor Unions Increasingly Initiate Proxy Proposals," *The Wall Street Journal,* March 1, 1994, pp. C1, C16.

Shleifer, A., and R. W. Vishny, "A Survey of Corporate Governance," ms., September 1995.

Slovin, Myron B., and Marie E. Sushka, "Ownership Concentration, Corporate Control Activity, and Firm Value: Evidence from the Death of Inside Blockholders," *Journal of Finance,* 48, September 1993, pp. 1293–1321.

Sridharan, Uma V., and M. R. Reinganum, "Determinants of the Choice of the Hostile Takeover Mechanism: An Empirical Analysis of Tender Offers and Proxy Contests," *Financial Management,* 24, Spring 1995, pp. 57–67.

Strickland, Deon, Kenneth W. Wiles, and Marc Zenner, "A Requiem for the USA—Is Small Shareholder Monitoring Effective?" *Journal of Financial Economics,* 40, February 1996, pp. 319–338.

Stulz, R. M., "Managerial Control of Voting Rights: Financing Policies and the Market for Corporate Control," *Journal of Financial Economics,* 20, 1988, pp. 25–54.

Wahal, Sunil, "Pension Fund Activism and Firm Performance," *Journal of Financial and Quantitative Analysis,* 31, March 1996, pp. 1–23.

Warner, J. B., R. L. Watts, and K. H. Wruck, "Stock Prices and Top Management Changes," *Journal of Financial Economics,* 20, 1988, pp. 461–492.

Weisbach, M., "Outside Directors and CEO Turnover," *Journal of Financial Economics,* 20, 1988, pp. 431–460.

CHAPTER

# 20

-------------------------------------------------- -----------------------------------

# Takeover Defenses

A detailed study of poison pills was published by Ryngaert (1988). A later comprehensive study of takeover defenses was made by Comment and Schwert (1995), who calculated that by 1991, 87% of exchange-listed firms had adopted a poison pill or had been protected by some type of antitakeover statute (p. 4). More than 1,500 firms had adopted some type of antitakeover plan during the second half of the 1980s. There were 27 examples between 1985 and 1990 in which a court upheld a poison pill challenged by a bidder (p. 36). Nevertheless, only 11 of the 27 remained independent one year after the decision; the other 16 were acquired by the bidder-plaintiff or some other firm.

Hostile takeovers have become respectable and increasing in both numbers and dollar amounts (Bagli, 1997). Takeover defenses and antitakeover measures have added to the types of strategies employed by business firms in their long-range strategic planning processes. Takeover defenses are so numerous and varied that we provide a road map in Table 20.1. Some of the items have multiple purposes and effects. For example, share repurchases, which was the subject matter of chapter 18, have several effects. One is to signal that the firm is undervalued by prevailing market prices. But share repurchases are a takeover defense because they increase the ownership percentage of the insider group and can result in higher reservation prices by the remaining shareholders. Other strategies discussed in earlier chapters are also included in the outline of topics to be discussed in this chapter from the standpoint of their roles as takeover defenses.

The outline in Table 20.1 guides us through the many kinds of takeover defenses that have been developed.

## DUTY OF DIRECTORS

It is the duty of directors to approve only a transaction that is fair to the public shareholders and is the best transaction available. Directors have the burden of proof to demonstrate that the best interests of the shareholders have been served.

If the directors reject a takeover offer and choose to remain independent, they must demonstrate to the courts that they have sound business reasons for doing so. For example, when Time was completing its merger, a $200 per share offer from Paramount was rejected. Time Warner argued that a much greater value per share would be produced from the Time Warner merger over a longer period planning horizon. The courts upheld the rejection of Paramount's apparently higher bid, as consistent with the business judgment rule. (See full case in the next chapter.)

When a target company agrees to an acquisition, the directors must demonstrate that the price was fair to shareholders and was the best offer that could be obtained. The courts have elaborated this view in a series of cases. For example, in 1994 the Delaware Supreme Court enjoined the acquisition of Lynch Communication Systems by Alcatel,

**TABLE 20.1**   An Overview of Takeover Defenses

A.  Duty of directors
B.  Greenmail
    1.  Wealth effects of greenmail
    2.  Antigreenmail developments
C.  Financial defensive measures
D.  Strategic actions
    1.  Pac Man defense
    2.  White knight
    3.  White squire
E.  Defensive corporate restructuring and reorganization
    1.  Reorganization of assets
    2.  Other strategies
F.  Antitakeover amendments
    1.  Supermajority amendments
    2.  Fair-price amendments—to avoid two-tier offers
    3.  Staggered or classified board of directors
    4.  Create new classes of securities whose approval is required for a takeover
    5.  Other antitakeover amendments
    6.  Antitakeover amendments and shareholder returns
G.  Poison pills—rights to purchase securities at low prices
    1.  Types of plans
    2.  Case studies
    3.  Effects on shareholder returns
H.  Poison puts—permit bondholders to put (sell) bonds to the issuer in the event of a takeover
 I.  Golden parachutes
    1.  Rationale
    2.  Silver and tin parachutes
    3.  Returns to shareholders and golden parachutes

a French company. One of the Lynch shareholders, Kahn, alleged that Alcatel as a controlling shareholder of Lynch had dictated the terms of the merger and had paid an unfair price. The court held that Lynch had not fully explored independent competitive offers.

A fairness opinion from an investment banking firm on the price received is useful evidence, but it is not sufficient. Examples abound of firms that announce auctions and even encourage multiple rounds of bidding to establish that the best possible price has been obtained.

# GREENMAIL

In one sense, greenmail says to the bidder, "Here is some money, now go away." More formally, greenmail represents a targeted repurchase of a large block of stock from specified shareholders at a premium. The purpose of the premium buyback presumably is to end a hostile takeover threat by the large blockholder or greenmailer. The term **greenmail** connotes blackmail and both payers and receivers of greenmail have received negative publicity. Proponents of antigreenmail charter amendments or legislation that would prohibit targeted repurchases argue that damages to shareholders are caused by greenmailers. In this view, the large block investors are corporate "raiders" who expropriate corporate assets to the detriment of other shareholders. Allegedly, raiding takes the form of using the raiders' corporate voting power to accord themselves excessive compensation and perquisites, receiving on their shares a substantial premium over the market price through greenmail, or "looting" the corporate treasury in some unspecified manner (Holderness and Sheehan, 1985).

An alternative view is that the large block investors involved in greenmail help bring about management changes, either changes in corporate personnel or changes in corporate policy, or have superior skills at evaluating potential takeover targets (Holderness and Sheehan, 1985). In this view, proposals to prohibit targeted repurchases are antitakeover proposals in disguise (Jensen, 1988). Jensen (1988, p. 41) argued that "management can easily prohibit greenmail without legislation; it need only announce a policy that prohibits the board or management from making such payments." He suggested that managers made greenmail payments to protect themselves from competition in the corporate control market.

Often in connection with targeted repurchases, a standstill agreement is written. A standstill agreement is a voluntary contract in which the stockholder who is bought out agrees not to make further investments in the target company during a specified period of time (for example, ten years). When a standstill agreement is made without a repurchase, the large blockholder simply agrees not to increase his or her ownership, which presumably would put him or her in an effective control position.

The St. Regis Paper Company provides an example of greenmail. When an investor group led by Sir James Goldsmith acquired an 8.6% stake in St. Regis and expressed interest in taking over the paper concern, the company agreed to repurchase the shares at a premium. Goldsmith's group acquired the shares for an average price of $35.50 a share, a total of $109 million. It sold its stake at $52 a share, netting a profit of $51 million. Shortly after the payoff in March 1984, St. Regis became the target of publisher Rupert Murdoch. St. Regis turned to Champion International and agreed to a $1.84 billion takeover. Murdoch tendered his 5.6% stake in St. Regis to the Champion offer for a profit.

### Wealth Effects of Greenmail

The announcement of a greenmail transaction by a company generally results in a negative abnormal return to shareholders of about 2 to 3%, which is statistically significant (Bradley and Wakeman, 1983; Dann and DeAngelo, 1983; Mikkelson and Ruback, 1991). But further analysis is required. Consider a number of possibilities. When the large blockholder starts buying the shares that provide him with a threatening position, the price of the company stock is likely to increase. Other empirical studies find that when these initial stock purchases are taken into account, positive abnormal returns are earned both during the initial period when the foothold is being established and in the full "purchase-to-repurchase" period (Holderness and Sheehan, 1985; Klein and Rosenfeld, 1988; Mikkelson and Ruback, 1985, 1991).

But even at the announcement of a greenmail repurchase a decline in stock prices generally does not occur unless the greenmail is associated with a standstill agreement or preceded by a control contest (Mikkelson and Ruback, 1991). The standstill agreements may be viewed as reducing the probability of a subsequent takeover. Nevertheless, even with standstill agreements, about 40% of the firms experience a subsequent control change within three years of the greenmail.

We should not read the empirical results without thinking about some real-world possibilities, such as the hostile bid for Disney in 1984 by Saul Steinberg and his associates. Among other things, Disney paid Steinberg greenmail in the amount of about $50 million, but it was widely recognized that Disney needed some top management changes (Taylor, 1987). After fending off the Steinberg group, a new management team was brought in headed by Michael D. Eisner. Taking into account stock splits, the Disney stock increased from about $6 in 1984 to $34 by 1989, representing a compound rate of increase in the common stock price for shareholders of 41.5%. From 1989 to 1996, Disney stock increased to $60 a share, representing a further compound annual rate of increase of 8.5%. The initial jump in stock prices reflected the ability of Disney directors to make the top management changes needed. The slower rate of growth in stock prices after 1989 may have contributed to the Disney acquisition of Cap Cities/ABC in August 1995.

The moral of this story is that the impact of greenmail can be different depending on the circumstances. If it gives the directors time to work out a better solution, then the market reaction could be positive rather than negative.

## Antigreenmail Developments

The negative view of greenmail resulted in efforts to restrict its use. In 1986 Congress included in the tax law changes a provision in Section 5881 of the Internal Revenue Code that imposes a 50% excise tax on the recipient of greenmail payments. In addition, antigreenmail charter amendments began to be enacted by companies.

Antigreenmail charter amendments prohibit or discourage the targeted repurchase by requiring management to obtain the approval of a majority or supermajority of nonparticipating shareholders prior to a repurchase. Proxy statements proposing antigreenmail amendments typically state that greenmailers pressure the company for a premium buyback with "threats of disruption" including proxy contests and tender offers, that greenmail is inherently unfair to the nonparticipating shareholders, and that the decision-making power for any targeted repurchases should be properly transferred to the hands of those most affected by the repurchase decision. According to Bhagat and Jefferis (1991), proxy statements proposing antigreenmail amendments frequently include one or more of (other) antitakeover amendment proposals. Among a sample of 52 NYSE-listed firms proposing antigreenmail amendments in the 1984–1985 period, 40 firms also offered one or more antitakeover amendments in the proxy material. In 29 cases, shareholders had to approve or reject the antitakeover provisions and antigreenmail amendment jointly.

For a subsample in which the antigreenmail amendments are not associated with other antitakeover proposals, the antigreenmail amendment itself does not decrease shareholder wealth. Eckbo (1990) demonstrated the complexity of the effects of greenmail prohibitions. He found that the average market reaction to charter amendments prohibiting greenmail payments was weakly negative, indicating some value to retaining managerial flexibility. He found, however, that for a subsample of firms with an abnormal stock price runup over the three months prior to the mailing of a proxy providing for greenmail prohibitions, the market reaction was strongly positive. This was particularly true if the prior runup was associated with evidence or rumors of takeover activity. The logic here is that the prohibition against greenmail would remove a barrier to a takeover with positive gains to shareholders. It would follow that greenmail payments themselves would be value decreasing. Eckbo suggested that the possibility of alternative methods for remunerating takeover entrepreneurs would reduce the valuation effect of the greenmail prohibition.

# FINANCIAL DEFENSIVE MEASURES

It is often proposed that the best defense is for a firm to be highly efficient, its sales growth favorable, and its profitability margins to be high. This is said to provide a defense against a takeover. However, such a firm may become a takeover target by another firm seeking to benefit from an association with such an efficient firm. In addition, if it has long-range investment plans whose payoffs are not reflected in its current stock price, the firm may be viewed as undervalued.

Other characteristics that make a firm vulnerable to a takeover include:

- A low stock price in relation to the replacement cost of assets or their potential earning power (a low q-ratio).
- A highly liquid balance sheet with large amounts of excess cash, a valuable securities portfolio, and significant unused debt capacity.
- Good cash flow relative to current stock prices.
- Subsidiaries or properties that could be sold off without significantly impairing cash flow.
- Relatively small stockholdings under the control of incumbent management.

A combination of these factors can simultaneously make a firm an attractive investment opportunity and facilitate its financing. The firm's assets act as collateral for an acquirer's borrowings, and the target's cash flows from operations and divestitures can be used to repay the loans.

A firm fitting the above description would do well to take at least some of the following steps. Debt should be increased, with borrowed funds used to repurchase equity, thus concentrating management's percentage holdings while using up debt capacity. Dividends on remaining shares should be increased. Loan covenants can be structured to force acceleration of repayment in the event of takeover. Securities portfolios should be liquidated and excess cash drawn down. Continuing cash flow from operations should be invested in positive net present value projects or returned to shareholders. Some of the excess liquidity might be used to acquire other firms. Subsidiaries that can be eliminated without impairing cash flow should be divested, perhaps through spin-offs to avoid large sums of cash flowing in. The profitability of all operations should be analyzed in depth to get at the true picture beneath such accounting devices as transfer pricing and overhead allocation; low-profit operations should be divested. The true value of undervalued assets should be realized by selling them off or restructuring.

# STRATEGIC ACTIONS

Firms can employ several other types of strategies to resist a particular bidder. These include the Pac Man defense, the use of a white knight, and resort to a white squire.

## Pac Man Defense

Making a counterbid for the bidder is similar to the video game from which it gets its name. The Pac Man defense in essence involves the target counteroffering for the bidder. This severe defense is rarely used and in fact is usually designed not to be used. The defense is more likely to be effective if the target is much larger than the bidder, a phenomenon more common in the 1980s than today. The risk of using the defense is that it implies that the target finds combining the two firms is desirable but would like control of the resulting entity. The user of the Pac Man essentially gives up using antitrust issues as a defense.

In most takeovers, target managements that resist maintain that the combination is undesirable. If the Pac Man defense is used, it is extremely costly and could have devastating financial effects for both firms involved. If both firms employ a large amount of debt to buy each other's stock, the resulting entity may be crippled by the combined debt load. Also, there is a risk that under state law, should both firms buy substantial stakes in each other, each would be ruled as subsidiaries of the other and be unable to vote its shares against the corporate parent. Curiously, the severity of the defense may lead the bidder to disbelieve the target will actually employ the defense.

The famous example of the use of the Pac Man defense involves Bendix and Martin Marietta, among others. On August 25, 1982, Bendix Corporation announced a previously rumored tender offer for Martin Marietta of $43 a share. The case is noteworthy because Martin Marietta became the first firm to remain independent due to the Pac Man defense. Marietta, with the advice of its investment banker, announced a $75 a share countertender for half of Bendix, with a $55 back-end price. Although Marietta announced its tender offer after Bendix and would only be able to buy Bendix shares after Bendix could purchase Marietta shares, it believed that it might have been able to gain control first due to differences in state laws concerning the calling of a special meeting to approve a merger. United Technologies, a large defense contractor that was interested in the complementary fit of Bendix's automotive business and Bendix's consumer electronics business, later joined Marietta and agreed to tender for half of Bendix for $75 a share, and a $50 back-end price.

Efforts to convince Bendix of the seriousness of the counterbid were not effective in getting Bendix to back down. On September 17, Bendix bought 70% of Marietta shares for $48 a share. On September 23, Marietta purchased 42.4% of Bendix shares despite news that Allied Corporation and Bendix would merge. Allied, whose main businesses were oil and gas production and chemicals, had been searching for a profitable company to enable it to use its over $100 million in U.S. federal income tax credits and to reduce its dependence on gas and oil profits.

After Marietta declined Allied's offer to buy both Bendix and Marietta, the two sides agreed to a stock swap at cost. Marietta reacquired some of its shares, but Allied retained possession of a 39% stake in Marietta. Allied signed a ten-year standstill agreement. Due to the purchase of Bendix stock, Marietta had a debt-to-equity ratio of 85%, and the new debt of $930 million raised total debt to $1.3 billion. To raise funds it sold stock, businesses, plants, and other assets. The restructuring included the divestiture of its chemicals, cement, and aggregates businesses. In late 1983 Marietta bought back all its shares held by Allied for $345 million.

## White Knight

The white knight defense involves choosing another company with which the target prefers to be combined. An alternative company may be preferred by the target because it sees greater compatibility. Or the new bidder may promise not to break up the target or engage in massive employee dismissals.

Examples of the use of white knights abound. Frequently, T. Boone Pickens would make an offer for a company on behalf of his Mesa Petroleum. For example, in 1982, Mesa made a bid for the Cities Service Oil Company. Cities Service responded with a Pac Man defense. Then Cities Service invited Gulf Oil to make a bid. Gulf made a bid, but when the Federal Trade Commission raised antitrust objections, Gulf dropped out. Ultimately, Cities Service was purchased by Occidental Petroleum. In 1984 Mesa bid for Gulf Oil. Gulf responded by holding an auction. Chevron (then SOCAL) ultimately won the bidding contest.

### White Squire

The white squire is a modified form of a white knight, the difference being that the white squire does not acquire control of the target. In a white squire transaction, the target sells a block of its stock to a third party it considers to be friendly. The white squire sometimes is required to vote its shares with target management. These transactions are often accompanied by a standstill agreement that limits the amount of additional target stock the white squire can purchase for a specified period of time, and restricts the sale of its target stock, usually giving the right of first refusal to the target. In return, the white squire often receives a seat on the target board, generous dividends, and/or a discount on the target shares. Preferred stock enables the board to tailor the characteristics of that stock to fit the transaction and so is usually used in white squire transactions.

Here is a famous example of a white squire investment. Although Champion International did not face a direct takeover threat, the company became concerned about the possibility of an attempted takeover following the first hostile takeover in the paper industry, that of Georgia Pacific for Great Northern Nekoosa in 1989. Champion's management approached Warren Buffett about investing in the company. In December 1989 Buffett purchased $300 million of new Champion convertible preferred stock that carried a 9.25% annual dividend rate. This was about $6 million a year over the market rate of 7% for investment grade convertible preferred stock. Buffett held an 8% voting equity stake, one that he was allowed to raise to 18%.

## DEFENSIVE CORPORATE RESTRUCTURING AND REORGANIZATION

In the literature, both academic journals and business magazines, the topics on corporate restructuring and reorganization to increase value have been kept separate from the topics on defensive corporate restructuring and reorganization. After reading both types of literature, the insight came to us that this is really one subject, not two. We will review the topics of value-increasing activities and then show their application and extension in defensive programs. In Table 20.2, we modify Table 11.1 from chapter 11, which had outlined the value-increasing topics. From looking at the table, it is clear that four sections taken together are the headings for chapters 11 to 18. In the initial treatment of chapters 11 to 18, the emphasis was on the development of value-increasing strategies. Here we use the same framework to demonstrate how the entire panoply of activities can be employed as takeover defenses. We shall cover each of the four major topics.

### Reorganization of Assets

In the earlier discussion, the acquisition of assets was to extend the firm's capabilities. But asset acquisitions can also be used to block takeovers. In 1984 Disney bought the Arvida real estate firm with equity to dilute the ownership position as a defense against Saul Steinberg and his Reliance Group. Acquisitions can also be used to create antitrust problems for the bidder. The Marshall Field department store used this defense several times. For example, when Carter Hawley Hale (CHH) made a tender offer, Field's directors expanded into the Galleria in Houston and acquired five Liberty House stores in the Northwest. Because CHH was active in these areas, on February 22, 1978, it withdrew its tender offer, citing the impact of Field's expansion plan.

In chapter 11 we described how sell-offs and divestitures could be used to move resources to their higher valued uses, creating values for both the seller and buyer. To

**TABLE 20.2** Defensive Corporate Restructuring and Reorganization

1. Reorganization of assets (chapter 11)
   a. Acquisitions
   b. Sell-offs or divestitures
2. Creating new ownership relationships (chapter 12)
   a. Spin-offs
   b. Split-ups
   c. Equity carve-outs
3. Reorganizing financial claims (chapter 13)
   a. Exchange offers
   b. Dual-class recapitalizations
   c. Leveraged recapitalizations
   d. Financial reorganization (bankruptcy)
   e. Liquidation
4. Other strategies
   a. Joint ventures (chapter 14)
   b. ESOPs and MLPs (chapter 15)
   c. Going-private transactions (LBOs) (chapter 16)
   d. Using international markets (chapter 17)
   e. Share repurchase programs (chapter 18)

block a tender offer, however, a firm may dispose of those segments of its business in which the bidder is most interested. This is called "selling off the crown jewels."

In chapter 12 we described how spin-offs, split-ups, and equity carve-outs were used to create more value. These can also involve the "crown jewels" segment of the company, thereby representing takeover defenses.

In chapter 13 we discussed reorganizing financial claims. By using exchange offers, a firm can either increase or decrease leverage. A debt-for-equity expansion may be used to increase leverage to levels that would be unacceptable to the bidder. Dual-class recapitalizations can be used to increase the voting powers of an insider group to levels that would enable them to block a tender offer. Leveraged recapitalizations can be used to unlock potential values for the company. But a firm may also incur huge amounts of debt, using the proceeds to pay a large cash dividend and increase the ownership position of insiders. This tactic has been called a "scorched-earth" policy. The crown jewel and scorched-earth actions can be combined. The firm sells off attractive segments of the company and adds large amounts of debt, using the cash for a large dividend that may even exceed the tender offer price from the bidder.

### Other Strategies

In chapter 14 we described how joint ventures can be used to extend the capabilities of the firm. Joint ventures can also be used to block a takeover. A close involvement with other firms could represent liaisons that the potential bidder might prefer to avoid.

In chapter 15 we explained how ESOPs are often used to block takeovers, and we described the famous example of Polaroid and Shamrock Holdings. Chapter 16 discussed MBOs and LBOs, which are widely used as a defense against an outside tender offer. Sometimes the financing of the MBO or LBO comes from financial institutions. Sometimes the competitive bidder is an LBO specialist firm such as KKR. One of the incentives management may have for turning to the LBO specialist firm is that its stock ownership position may thereby be increased more than in the outside tender offer.

In chapter 17 we discussed how international liaisons and other transactions can be used to defend against unwanted takeovers. A domestic bidder may not offer as large potentials for augmenting the firm's capabilities and growth as an international partner.

In chapter 18 we discussed share repurchase programs. A theory of share repurchase programs is to signal that the current price of the stock represents undervaluation. But share repurchase programs are widely used to defend against takeovers. They increase the ownership of insiders. With respect to outside shareholders, the low reservation price investors are bought out in a share repurchase program. The tender offer price to succeed, therefore, is higher than it otherwise would be.

Another strategy to avoid a takeover is by a proxy contest as discussed in chapter 19. The aim is to change the control group and to make performance improvements (Dodd and Warner, 1983).

We have demonstrated that corporate restructuring and reorganization programs can be used to unlock values and/or defend against takeovers. Therefore, we can predict what studies of event returns are likely to find. When the restructuring represents a scorched-earth policy of some type, it predictably will have undesirable effects and result in CARs that are negative.

## ANTITAKEOVER AMENDMENTS

Other defense mechanisms are referred to as antitakeover amendments to a firm's corporate charter. These are often called "shark repellents." As with all charter amendments, antitakeover amendments must be voted on and approved by shareholders. Although 95% of antitakeover amendments proposed by management are ratified by shareholders, this may be because a planned amendment may not be introduced if management is unsure of its success (Brickley, Lease, and Smith, 1988). Failure to pass might be taken as a vote of no confidence in incumbent management and may provide a platform for a proxy fight or takeover attempt where none had existed before. The evidence provided by Brickley, Lease, and Smith (1988) indicated that institutional shareholders such as banks and insurance companies were more likely to vote with management on antitakeover amendments than others such as mutual funds and college endowments. Note that the former institutions generally have ongoing business relationships with management and thus are more likely to be influenced by management. Brickley, Lease, and Smith also found that blockholders more actively participate in voting than non-blockholders and may oppose proposals that appear to harm shareholders. This result is consistent with Jarrell and Poulsen (1987) who found that those amendments having the most negative effect on stock price (amendments other than fair-price amendments) are adopted by firms with the lowest percentage of institutional holdings and the highest percentage of insider holdings. Jarrell and Poulsen suggested that these results helped explain how harmful amendments receive approval by shareholders. The evidence also suggested that blockholders do play a monitoring role. Institutional holders are sophisticated and well informed so that they vote in accordance with their economic interest more consistently than less informed small investors.

Antitakeover amendments generally impose new conditions on the transfer of managerial control of the firm through a merger, tender offer, or by replacement of the board of directors. There are four major types of antitakeover amendments:

### Supermajority Amendments

These amendments require shareholder approval by at least two-thirds vote and sometimes as much as 90% of the voting power of outstanding capital stock for all transactions involving change of control. In most existing cases, however, the supermajority provisions have a board-out clause that provides the board with the power to determine when and if the supermajority provisions will be in effect. Pure supermajority provisions would seriously limit the management's flexibility in takeover negotiations.

### Fair-Price Amendments

These are supermajority provisions with a board-out clause and an additional clause waiving the supermajority requirement if a fair price is paid for all purchased shares. The fair price is commonly defined as the highest price paid by the bidder during a specified period and is sometimes required to exceed an amount determined relative to accounting earnings or book value of the target. Thus, fair-price amendments defend against two-tier tender offers that are not approved by the target's board. A uniform offer for all shares to be purchased in a tender offer and in a subsequent cleanup merger or tender offer will avoid the supermajority requirement. Because the two-tier tender offer is not essential in successful hostile takeovers, the fair-price amendment is the least restrictive among the class of supermajority amendments.

### Classified Boards

Another major type of antitakeover amendment provides for **staggered,** or **classified,** boards of directors to delay effective transfer of control in a takeover. Management's purported rationale in proposing a staggered board is to assure continuity of policy and experience. For example, a nine-member board might be divided into three classes, with only three members standing for election to a three-year term each year. Thus, a new majority shareholder would have to wait at least two annual meetings to gain control of the board of directors. Effectiveness of cumulative voting is reduced under the classified-board scheme because a greater shareholder vote is required to elect a single director. Variations on antitakeover amendments relating to the board of directors include provisions prohibiting the removal of directors except for cause, and provisions fixing the number of directors allowed to prevent "packing" the board.

### Authorization of Preferred Stock

The board of directors is authorized to create a new class of securities with special voting rights. This security, typically preferred stock, may be issued to friendly parties in a control contest. Thus, this device is a defense against hostile takeover bids, although historically it was used to provide the board of directors with flexibility in financing under changing economic conditions. Creation of a poison pill security could be included in this category, but is generally considered to be a different defensive device. (We examine the poison pill defense in the following section.)

### Other Antitakeover Amendments

Other amendments that management may propose as a takeover defense include:

1. Abolition of cumulative voting where it is not required by state law.
2. Reincorporation in a state with more accommodating antitakeover laws.

3. Provisions with respect to the scheduling of shareholder meetings and introduction of agenda items, including nomination of candidates to the board of directors.

The list is not inclusive. Another refinement is the passage of **lock-in amendments** making it difficult to void previously passed antitakeover amendments by requiring, for example, supermajority approval for a change. Shareholders may propose antigreenmail amendments that restrict a company's freedom to buy back a raider's shares at a premium.

## Antitakeover Amendments and Shareholder Returns

A substantial literature has studied the effects of antitakeover amendments on shareholder returns (Dodd and Leftwich, 1980; McWilliams, 1990; Pound, 1987; Romano, 1985, 1987, 1993; Ryngaert and Netter, 1988). The first edition of this book presented a review of the effects of several individual antitakeover measures in painstaking detail. Fortunately, a definitive, up-to-date analysis of the subject by Comment and Schwert (1995) enables us to compress our present discussion.

The literature predicts possible positive and negative effects of takeover amendments. Positive effects could result from the announcement of an antitakeover measure as a signal of the increased likelihood of a takeover with gains in value to shareholders of the order of magnitude of 30 to 50%. DeAngelo and Rice (1983) noted that shark repellents may have positive benefits in helping shareholders respond in unison (through management) to takeover bids. Negative effects of antitakeover amendments could result from discouraging or deterring takeovers because managers seek to prevent control changes. This is the management entrenchment hypothesis. Let us look at a review of the evidence.

The prior studies reviewed by Comment and Schwert showed a "typical decline" of less than 1% for most types of antitakeover measures and often under one-half of 1% (Jarrell and Poulsen, 1987; Karpoff and Malatesta, 1989; Malatesta and Walkling, 1988; Romano, 1993; Ryngaert, 1988). Two other studies found no statistically significant negative effects from the adoption of antitakeover charter amendments (DeAngelo and Rice, 1983; Linn and McConnell, 1983). Furthermore, another recent study showed that corporate governance efforts through shareholder-initiated proposals to repeal antitakeover amendments had no statistically significant effects (Karpoff, Malatesta, and Walkling, 1996). The finding that the repeal of antitakeover amendments is a nonevent further buttresses the likelihood of little effect when they were announced in the first place.

Counterevidence is provided by Mahoney and Mahoney (1993). They found that while antitakeover amendments had no significant effects for the period 1974–1979, they did for the period 1980–1988. However, they studied only classified board amendments and the supermajority provision. For 1980–1988 the effects of supermajority provisions were not statistically significant, but they were for the adoption of a classified board of directors. These results were the reverse of what logic would suggest. Supermajority provisions could be used to block takeovers by managers with some equity ownership. The effects of time-staggering fractions of director elections would be expected to be somewhat attenuated.

It is difficult to disentangle a number of influences operating. For example, if antitakeover amendments are adopted after a takeover is already under way, the purpose may be to help management obtain a better deal for the shareholders. Similarly, if a takeover is rumored. Also, if one takeover has occurred in an industry, there may be contagion effects. When one takeover is completed, often the financial press observes that other takeovers in that industry are likely to occur. If the positive runup in abnormal returns prior to the announcement of antitakeover amendments is considered, then a possible 1% decline in shareholder wealth should be netted against the prior positive returns. The 1% decline could be viewed as a reflection of the reduced probability of the takeover being completed. If 30% is taken as the average positive wealth effect of mergers and takeovers of all types, a wealth decline on the adoption of antitakeover amendments of 1% would mean a decrease in the probability of the takeover by 3.3% (0.01/0.30). If the event effect is a −0.5%, the decline in the probability of the takeover would be 1.67%. We concur with the Comment and Schwert judgment that these relationships suggest that even small negative event returns from the announcement of antitakeover measures would have little power to deter takeovers.

# POISON PILLS

Poison pills represent the creation of securities carrying special rights exercisable by a triggering event. The triggering event could be the accumulation of a specified percentage of target shares (like 20%) or the announcement of a tender offer. These rights take many forms. But they all make it more costly to acquire control of the target firm. Poison pills can be adopted by the board of directors without shareholder approval. While not required, directors will often submit poison pill adoptions to shareholders for ratification.

## Types of Plans

There is considerable jargon involved. The basic distinction is between flip-over and flip-in plans. As an oversimplification, flip-over plans provide for a bargain purchase of the *bidder's* shares at some trigger point. The flip-in plans provide for a bargain purchase of the *target's* shares at some trigger point. Flip-in plans became more widely used after the weakness of the flip-over plans was demonstrated in the Crown Zellerbach case in 1984–1985. Crown Zellerbach was a paper and forest products company. Because the market price of Crown Zellerbach did not fully reflect the value of its forest lands, it was vulnerable to a takeover. Crown Zellerbach adopted a flip-over poison pill plan that enabled its shareholders to buy $200 worth of stock in the merged firm for $100. The pill was in the form of rights that would be triggered when either (1) an acquirer bought 20% of its stock, or (2) a bidder made a tender offer for 30% of its stock. The rights or calls became exercisable when the bidder obtained 100% of the company stock.

Goldsmith purchased just over 50% of Crown Zellerbach stock in order to achieve control. The rights were issued when Goldsmith's purchasing program brought him to over 20% of the stock. But the rights never became exercisable because he did not plan to complete the purchase of the company until after the flip-over rights had expired. Crown Zellerbach continued to resist but ultimately agreed to the takeover by Goldsmith.

The ownership flip-in provision allows the rights holder to purchase shares of the target at a discount if an acquirer exceeds a shareholding limit. The rights of the bidder who has triggered the pill become void. Some plans waive the flip-in provision if the acquisition is a cash tender offer for all outstanding shares (to defend against two-tier offers).

## Case Studies

The nature of ownership flip-in shareholder rights plans can be illustrated by a case study of the Bank of New York (BONY) pursuit of the Irving Bank Corporation (IB). On September 25, 1987, BONY launched an unsolicited cash bid of $80 a share for 47.4% of IB's shares. The remaining shares would receive 1.9 shares of BONY per IB share. On October 9, 1987, IB rejected the BONY offer as inadequate and adopted a flip-in poison pill. The poison pill rights to the IB shareholders when triggered would permit them to purchase $400 of IB stock for $200. The IB shares held by BONY would be excluded from the rights distribution. The Bank of New York challenged the pill's legality. On October 4, 1988, the appellate division of the New York State Supreme Court upheld a lower court ruling. This ruling held that the flip-in provision violated New York law that shares of the same class should be treated equally. The court held that BONY should be allowed to buy shares at half price as well. On October 5, 1988, IB accepted BONY's offer. Irving Bank shareholders would receive $15 cash, 1.675 BONY shares, and a warrant to purchase BONY stock. The offer was valued at $77.15 a share. States subsequently modified their antitakeover statutes to exclude the discriminatory effect of flip-in poison pills.

On May 17, 1985, the Delaware Court upheld a discriminatory self-tender offer that was essentially a triggered back-end pill employed by UNOCAL against a bid by Mesa Petroleum. The court noted that Mesa had proposed a grossly inadequate coercive two-tier offer. The standard employed by the court was the "business judgment rule." The court stated that unless it could be shown that the directors' decisions were primarily based on perpetuating themselves in office or some other breach of judiciary duty, the court would not substitute its judgment for that of the board. The court's decision drew criticisms, and in 1986 the Securities and Exchange Commission changed its rules to prevent discriminatory tender offers of the kind that UNOCAL had employed.

Later in the year on November 19, 1985, the Delaware Supreme Court in *Moran v. Household International,* again upheld the adoption of the poison pill. It noted that any such defense by the directors must be justified on the basis of protection to the corporation and its stockholders. In 1986 the courts blocked a poison pill adopted by the CTS Corporation. The court held that the board had inadequately considered the bidders' offer and acted without adequate outside consultation. CTS formed a special committee of outside directors and solicited advice from investment bankers and legal counsel. It then adopted another poison pill that was upheld by the courts.

This brief review of court decisions demonstrates that the use of poison pills requires justification. Directors must establish that they were adopted not for their own entrenchment but in the best interests of the shareholders of the corporation. Thus, there remains some ambiguity whether the adoption of a poison pill will be effective and also whether it will be upheld by the courts.

## Effects of Poison Pills on Shareholder Returns

The early event studies of the wealth effect of poison pills found about a 2% negative impact (Malatesta and Walkling, 1988; Ryngaert, 1988). Comment and Schwert (1995) observed that these studies covered only the earlier one-fourth of adopted pills. The Comment and Schwert paper updated the earlier studies by using the entire population of 1,577 poison pills adopted from 1983 through December 1991. They observed that the wealth effect of a poison pill adoption reflected a number of elements. The possibility that managers may wait to adopt pills until they know that an offer is likely to be made may cause the pill to be viewed as a signal that the probability of a takeover attempt had increased. This would cause the event return to be positive. Also, the poison pill may enable managers to obtain a better price in negotiations with bidders. This also would have a positive influence. But if poison pills deterred takeovers, there would be a negative influence representing the expected present value of future takeover premiums lost. Accordingly, the Comment and Schwert analysis considered several influences using the familiar cumulative abnormal return (CAR) measure and a regression analysis. One variable takes into account whether rumors of a bid or an actual takeover bid made it likely that a control premium was built into the issuer's stock price at the time of the announcement of a poison pill. The wealth effect was about $-2\%$. Another variable measures whether merger and acquisition news was announced at the same time as the pill. This resulted in a positive wealth effect of about 3 to 4%. Dummy variables for the year of adoption distinguished the early pills from the later ones. In the year-by-year results, only 1984 had a negative wealth effect of between 2.3 and 2.9%. For the later seven years, the wealth effect was usually positive by about 1% or less, but significant only for the year 1988.

Comment and Schwert performed various sensitivity analyses, but the main thrusts of their findings remained unchanged. They observed that there were individual cases where potential takeovers were likely to have been deterred by poison pills. But their systematic evidence indicated small deterrence effects. They observed that only the earliest pills (before 1985) were associated with large declines in shareholder wealth. Their new evidence indicated that takeover premiums were higher when target firms were protected by state antitakeover laws or by poison pills. Thus, the gains to targets were increased, raising the cost to bidders. This suggested some deterrence, but they also found that target shareholders gained even after taking into account deals that were not completed because of poison pills.

A major emphasis of the Comment and Schwert study was to evaluate whether the decline in the level of takeover activity that took place in 1991 and 1992 was primarily due to the effectiveness of antitakeover legislation and defensive measures by targets. Their empirical analysis led them to the conclusion that it was more general economic factors that caused the decline in takeover activity, not the widespread use of antitakeover measures adopted by governments and firms. Their conclusion was supported by the evidence we presented in chapter 6. Our data established that by 1995, M&A activity measured in constant dollars had risen even above the previous peak level reached in 1988. Thus, the carefully reasoned analysis of Comment and Schwert successfully predicted the resurgence in M&A activity as the economic environment changed after 1993.

## POISON PUTS

Poison puts, or event risk covenants, give bondholders the right to put (sell) target bonds in the event of a change in control at an exercise price usually set at 100 to 101% of the bond's face amount. This poison put feature seeks to protect against risk of takeover-related deterioration of target bonds, at the same time placing a potentially large cash demand on the new owner, thus raising the cost of an acquisition. Merger and acquisition activity in general has had negative impacts on bondholder wealth. This was particularly true when leverage increases were substantial. As a consequence, poison put provisions began to be included in bond covenants beginning in 1986.

Cook and Easterwood (CE) (1994) analyzed the economic role of poison put bonds. They observed that poison puts could be included in corporate debt for three possible reasons. First, the entrenchment hypothesis was that the puts made firms less attractive as takeover targets. Second, the bondholder protection hypothesis was that the poison puts protect bondholders from wealth transfers associated with debt-financed takeovers and leveraged recapitalizations. If the poison puts had this purpose, their use would not reduce the probability of all takeovers, only those involving wealth transfers from bondholders to shareholders. If puts and related covenants did not increase the protection to existing debt, the bondholder protection hypothesis predicted no effect on the price of the firm's outstanding debt.

The impact on stock returns would be the net of two opposite influences. Takeovers motivated primarily by wealth transfers were deterred, which represented a negative influence on shareholder returns. Debt with event risk covenants could be issued at an interest cost lower than unprotected debt. If interest cost savings outweighed the forgone wealth transfers, there would be a nonnegative stock price reaction to the sale of protected debt.

The bondholder protection hypothesis had been tested in two ways. One looked at the difference in yield spreads at the offering date for samples of protected and unprotected bonds. Two empirical studies suggested that the inclusion of event risk protection reduced the required yields on protected bonds by 25 to 50 basis points; there was no effect in a third study. A second type of test analyzed wealth transfers from bondholders in leveraged buyouts. One study found no evidence of bondholder losses (Marais, Schipper, and Smith, 1989). Another by Warga and Welch (1993) found small losses. Other studies showed that whether bondholders lose depends on the covenant protection. Protected bonds did not experience losses while unprotected debt experienced significant losses. These findings were evidence that alternative contracting technologies could substitute for the use of poison puts.

The third hypothesis was the mutual interest hypothesis. This postulated that both managers and bondholders sought to prevent hostile debt-financed takeovers. The managers sought to protect their control positions, while the bondholders sought to avoid losses from deterioration in credit ratings. Under this hypothesis, stock price reactions would be negative while the effects on the price of existing debt would be positive. The wealth effects for debt and equity would be negatively correlated because more protective puts would make the price response for existing debt more positive and more negative for stock prices. These three alternatives are summarized in Table 20.3.

In their empirical analysis, CE found that the issuance of bonds with poison puts caused negative returns to shareholders and positive returns to outstanding bondholders. A control sample of straight bond issues without poison puts had no effect on stock prices. Note that the finding of no stock price effect of straight bond issues is different

| **TABLE 20.3**   Effects of Poison Puts on Shareholder and Debt Holder Returns | | | |
|---|---|---|---|
| | *Managerial Entrenchment Hypothesis* | *Bondholder Protection Hypothesis* | *Mutual Interest Hypothesis* |
| Effect on shareholder returns | − | 0 | − |
| Effect on outstanding debt | 0 | 0 | + |

from earlier studies and may be related to the economic environment that prevailed in 1988 and 1989, the years covered by their sample. A cross-sectional regression for the put sample showed a strong negative relation between the returns for stocks versus the returns for outstanding bonds. This relation was not found for the nonput sample. The study concluded that the empirical results were consistent with the mutual interest hypothesis, which holds that the use of poison put bonds protects managers from hostile takeovers and bondholders from event risk while lowering returns to shareholders.

## GOLDEN PARACHUTES

Golden parachutes (GPs) refer to separation provisions of an employment contract that compensate managers for the loss of their jobs under a change-of-control clause. The provision usually calls for a lump-sum payment or payment over a specified period at full or partial rates of normal compensation. This type of severance contract has been increasingly used even by the largest Fortune 500 firms as M&A activity intensified in the 1980s and these firms have become susceptible to hostile takeover.

A brief case study will convey the role of golden parachutes. On May 23, 1983, Diamond Shamrock Corporation launched a hostile tender offer for Natomas Company. The offer at $23 a share represented a 25% premium over the closing price of Natomas on May 20, 1983. Natomas began arranging bank financing to defend itself. It also adopted golden parachutes that would give its top four executives a $10.2 million severance payment if they decided to quit within six months after the merger. These four top executives had received $1.3 million in compensation and benefits in 1982. Diamond Shamrock had been in the process of transforming itself from a chemical company into an energy company under W. H. Bricker, its chairman. It was seeking additional oil reserves to feed its refineries. The oil reserves of Natomas in the Pacific Basin were especially attractive to Diamond. On May 29, 1983, a merger agreement was reached between Diamond and Natomas. The new terms were 1.05 shares of Diamond per share of Natomas. Diamond would retain the Natomas management with Dorman Commons remaining as chairman of Natomas and becoming vice chairman of Diamond. Kenneth Reed would remain president of Natomas. The combination was completed in August 1983. In October 1983 Commons and Reed resigned, departing the company with the severance payments provided by the golden parachutes.

Extreme cases of golden parachutes have created a stir among the public and were often viewed as "rewards for failure."[1] An example is the payment of $23.5 million to six officers of Beatrice Companies in connection with its leveraged buyout in 1985. One of the officers received a $2.7 million package even though he had been with the company only 13 months. Another received a $7 million package after being recalled from retirement only seven months before. Also in 1985, the chairman of Revlon received a $35 million package consisting of severance pay and stock options. Even in these extreme cases, the golden parachutes were small when compared to the total acquisition prices of $6.2 billion in the Beatrice LBO and $1.74 billion in the Revlon acquisition. Indeed, the cost of golden parachutes is estimated to be less than 1% of the total cost of a takeover in most cases.[2] For this reason, golden parachutes are not considered to be an effective takeover defense.

[1]See, for example, *The New York Times,* "Golden Chutes Under Attack," November 4, 1985, p. D1.
[2]*Fortune,* "Those Executive Bailout Deals," December 13, 1982, p. 86.

The excess use of GPs appears to be infrequent and a new tax law now imposes specific limits. The Deficit Reduction Act of 1984 denies corporate tax deductions for parachute payments in excess of three times the base amount on a present-value basis, where the base amount is the executive's average annual compensation over the five years prior to takeover. An executive has to pay an additional 20% income tax on "excess parachute payments." To be legally binding, the golden parachutes have to be entered into at least one year prior to the date of control change for the entire corporation or a significant portion of the corporation. In many employment contracts, the severance payment is triggered either when the manager is terminated by the acquiring firm or when the manager resigns voluntarily after a change of control. Coffee (1988, p. 131) reported several cases in which the court invalidated or granted preliminary injunctions against the exercise of golden parachutes especially when the payment could be triggered at the recipient's own election.

### Rationale

The use of golden parachutes has been defended by some (Coffee, 1988; Jensen, 1988; Knoeber, 1986). One argument is based on the concept of *implicit contracts* for managerial compensation. In general, managers' real contribution to the firm cannot be evaluated exactly in the current period, but can be estimated better as time passes and more information becomes available on the firm's long-term profitability and value. In this situation, an optimal contract between managers and shareholders will include deferred compensation (Knoeber, 1986). Seniority-based compensation and internal promotion partly reflect this deferred compensation process. Because detailing all the future possibilities and contingent payments in a written contract is costly and very likely futile, a long-term deferred contract will largely be implicit. Another argument presumes existence of firm-specific investments by managers. When the likelihood of an unexpected transfer of control and the loss of their job is high, managers will not be willing to invest in firm-specific skills and knowledge. A related argument is that the increased risk of losing one's job through a takeover may result in managers' focusing unduly on the short-term or even taking unduly high risks (Eisenberg, 1988).

Another rationale for golden parachutes is that they encourage managers to accept changes of control that would bring shareholder gains, and thus reduce the conflict of interest between managers and shareholders and the transaction costs resulting from managerial resistance. Berkovitch and Khanna (1991) further analyzed the role of golden parachutes in takeover markets in which the bidder had a choice between a merger and a tender offer. In their model, a tender offer was more desirable for target shareholders as more information was released in tender offers and this frequently led to an auction in which potential acquirers compete for the target. Excessive payment will tend to motivate managers to sell the firm at too low a gain. By tying the payment to synergy gains in the case of mergers, the firm can avoid the misuse of golden parachutes. Stock options that are exercisable in the event of a change of control are an appropriate solution, and in general increased stock ownership by management will tend to reduce the conflict of interest (Jensen, 1988).

### Silver and Tin Parachutes

The terms **silver parachutes** and **tin parachutes** have also been employed. Silver parachutes provide less generous severance payments to executives. Tin parachutes extend relatively modest severance payments to a wider coverage of managers including middle management, and in some cases, cover all salaried employees. Tin parachutes were employed by General American Oil of Texas when it faced a takeover threat from T. Boone Pickens in 1982. It adopted tin parachutes that would give all employees at least three months' pay whether they were terminated or chose to leave after any adverse changes in their pay or duties. Workers would be entitled to at least four weeks' pay for each year of service.

There is disagreement on the number of employees to be covered. Focusing on the conflict of interest problem in control-related situations, Jensen (1988) argued that the contract should cover only those members of the top-level management team who would be involved in negotiating and implementing any transfer of control. On the other hand, Coffee (1988) emphasized the implicit contract for deferred payments and the incentive for managers to make investments in firm-specific human capital. This led Coffee to propose that the control-related severance contracts should be extended to members of middle management as well as top management.

### Golden Parachutes and Returns to Shareholders

Mogavero and Toyne (1995) formulated three central hypotheses to be tested by the empirical evidence: (1) The **alignment hypothesis:** prearranged severance agreements reduced conflicts of interest between managers and shareholders. Golden parachutes will make executives more willing to support takeover offers beneficial to the firm's shareholders. (2) The **wealth transfer hypothesis** predicts that GPs reduce stock values by shifting gains from shareholders to managers. By increasing costs to bidders, GPs reduced the probability of takeover bids. By providing some insulation from the market for corporate control, GPs reduced the incentives for executives to manage firms efficiently. In addition, GPs may also indicate a level of influence over boards exercised by management that may increase the potential for other forms of executive benefit consumption. (3) Adoption of GPs may *signal* the likelihood of a future takeover, which would be associated with positive gains to shareholders. Alternatively, GPs may signal the decline of management influence over boards, which would have negative implications.

The empirical study by Lambert and Larcker (LL) (1985) covered the period 1975–1982. They found that the adoption of GPs resulted in abnormal positive returns to shareholders of about 3%. This finding was consistent with the alignment hypothesis, suggesting that the cost of reducing conflicts of interest between management and shareholders was low relative to potential gains from takeover premiums. Alternatively, the signaling hypothesis might be supported in that from 1975 to 1982 relatively few firms had adopted GPs, so that GPs could be taken as signals of a likely takeover bid. The study by Born, Trahan, and Faria (1993) looked at two samples for the period 1979–1989. One sample contained firms that announced GPs while in the process of being acquired. Hence, there should be no takeover signal effect. If alignment of interests, the returns should be positive; if wealth transfer, the returns should be negative. But no significant abnormal stock returns were found. The second sample from 1979 through 1984 contained firms not in the process of a takeover when the GPs were adopted. They found positive stock returns. The authors argued that the combined evidence is consistent with a takeover signaling hypothesis but not with an alignment hypothesis.

The study by Mogavero and Toyne (1995) was a sample of 41 large firms with adoption dates from 1982 through 1990. For their full sample, the CAR was −0.5% but not statistically significant. They divided their sample into 18 observations from 1982 to 1985 for which the CAR was +2.3% but not statistically significant. The second subsample of 23 observations covered the years 1986 through 1990. The CAR was −2.7% and statistically significant at the 1% level. This finding was consistent with a wealth transfer hypothesis. The authors noted that the stock returns associated with GPs changed from positive for the 1975–1982 period of the LL study to negative for the 1986–1990 period of their study. This change was associated with the initiation of legislative restraints on GPs that may have encouraged boards to adopt them to avoid further restrictions. Thus, shareholders in the later years may have perceived GP adoptions as unfavorable signals of management's ability to control directors in management's interest at the expense of shareholder interest.

---

## Summary

Takeover defenses and antitakeover measures have become part of management's long-range strategic planning for the firm. One view justifies these actions based on the desirability of creating an auction for the target, preventing coercive tender offers, and increasing management's ability to obtain better transaction terms in the bargaining process. Opposing views emphasize the increased cost of takeovers and the resulting inefficiency in the market for corporate control.

Just saying no to a takeover is not that simple. There must be a sound business reason by the target directors that the shareholders will gain more by not accepting the takeover offer. Even if the target company agrees to an acquisition, directors must demonstrate that the price is fair to shareholders and is the best offer that could be obtained.

In greenmail transactions, the target firm repurchases a large block of its shares at a premium price from large blockholders to end a hostile takeover threat. A standstill agreement may be included to prevent the greenmailer from making other takeover efforts for a specified period of time. The view that greenmail damages shareholders has prompted tax law penalties and antigreenmail charter amendments to discourage or prohibit its use. Antigreenmail amendments do not seem to decrease shareholder wealth, but appear to remove a barrier to takeovers with positive gains to shareholders.

A firm may be vulnerable to takeovers because of its financial characteristics. The firm's stock price may be low in relation to the replacement cost of assets or its potential earning power. It may possess a large amount of excess cash or unused debt capacity. Such characteristics make it an attractive investment opportunity and facilitate the financing of the takeover. The firm can take defensive adjustments to make itself less attractive. For example, it could sell assets, increase debt, and use its excess cash to increase cash dividends or share repurchases.

A target may counteroffer for the bidder in a Pac Man defense. This is a costly defense and rarely used. Another defense strategy is for the target to seek a white knight as an appropriate company for the combination. Alternatively, in a white squire transaction, the target could sell a block of its stock to a third party it considers friendly.

Corporate restructuring and reorganizations that increase a firm's value are also extensions to a defensive program. Acquisitions of assets are used to extend a firm's capabilities, to block a takeover by diluting the ownership position of the pursuer, or to create antitrust issues. Sell-offs and divestitures move resources to their higher valued uses, but can also involve selling off the "crown jewel." Spin-offs, split-ups, and equity carve-outs can be used to clarify organization structures and to increase managerial incentives, motivations, and performance.

The target firm can also reorganize its financial claims to make itself less attractive. Exchange offers such as debt-for-equity offers can increase leverage to unattractive levels. Dual-class recapitalizations can increase the voting power of target insiders to levels that make tender offers less likely to succeed. "Scorched-earth" tactics, such as leveraged recapitalizations may incur a huge amount of debt and increase the ownership position of insiders. Joint ventures could represent liaisons that potential bidders might prefer to avoid. Employee stock ownership plans can prevent a successful tender offer by making it difficult to meet supermajority requirements. Management buyouts and LBOs are other leverage increasing defenses favorable to managers' stock ownership position. Share repurchase can be used to pay premium prices to shareholders to compete with takeover bids. Low reservation price shareholders will tender, leaving high reservation price shareholders who with the increased ownership position of insiders will require higher tender offer prices.

Antitakeover amendments or "shark repellents" impose new conditions on the transfer of managerial control. Supermajority amendments require shareholders' approval of takeover negotiations by a two-thirds vote or higher. Fair-price amendments hinder two-tier tenders by requiring the bidder to pay the "fair" price to all purchased shares. A staggered, or classified, board of directors can delay effective transfer of control. New securities with special voting rights may be issued to friendly parties in a takeover contest. Previously enacted antitakeover measures can be reinforced with lock-in amendments, making them difficult to void.

The empirical literature on antitakeover amendments is extensive but difficult to interpret because multiple influences are operating. In general, positive returns will result if the announcement of the antitakeover amendment is interpreted as a signal of an increased likelihood of a takeover, or is associated with management's intention to obtain a better price in negotiations or a better solution. Negative effects could result if the amendment is interpreted as a management entrenchment tactic. Studies find small declines of about 1%, but no statistical significance.

Poison pills are securities carrying special rights exercisable by a triggering event such as the announcement of a tender offer or a specified ownership position in the firm's stock. Poison pills make it more costly to acquire control of the firm and can be adopted without shareholders' approval. But the adoption of poison pills requires justification that they are in the best interests of the shareholders for them to be upheld by the courts. Studies by Comment and Schwert find small deterrence effects of poison pills. Takeover premiums are higher when target firms are protected by state antitakeover laws or by poison pills. Even the decline in the level of takeover activity in 1991 and 1992 is attributable to general economic factors and not to antitakeover measures.

Poison puts or event risk covenants give bondholders the right to sell target bonds in the event of takeover at a price set at the bond's face value or higher. This feature seeks to protect bondholders' wealth and at the same time place potentially large requirements on the new owner. The negative returns found by Cook and Easterwood are consistent with the mutual interest hypothesis in which bondholders and managers gain at the expense of shareholders.

Golden parachutes (GPs) are severance contracts that compensate managers for losing their jobs after a takeover. Extreme cases of golden parachutes were often viewed as a reward for failure, but GPs are estimated to be less than 1% of the total cost of a takeover. For this reason, they are not considered to be a strong takeover defense. The rationale for their use is the reduction in the agency problem between managers and shareholders. This reduced conflict or alignment hypothesis is supported by the positive returns found by Lambert and Larcker. But the golden parachute adoption could also be interpreted as a signal of future takeovers. The study by Mogavero and Toyne finds negative returns for the 1986–1990 period, indicating a level of influence over boards exercised by managements, increasing the potentials for wealth transfers from shareholders to managers.

-----------------------------------------------------------------------------------

## Questions

20.1 What are three types of antitakeover amendments and how do they work to defend a target from an unwelcome takeover?

20.2 What is the effect of the passage of antitakeover amendments on stock price?

20.3 What is the role of litigation against a bidder in takeover contests?

20.4 Under what circumstances are share repurchase and exchange offers useful as anti-takeover measures?

20.5 How can legislation and regulation serve as merger defenses?

------------------------------------ C A S E   20–1 ------------------------------------

# Carter Hawley Hale Versus Marshall Field & Co.

In 1977 the president of Marshall Field & Co. died unexpectedly and was replaced by Angelo R. Arena, the former head of Carter Hawley Hale's (CHH) Neiman-Marcus division. Carter Hawley Hale, which had long been interested in Field, then approached Marshall Field with the idea of a merger and continued to pursue the idea despite Field's lack of interest. On December 10, 1977, Philip Hawley, the CEO of CHH, gave Marshall Field an ultimatum—either Field's directors agree to merger negotiations by December 12 or he would make a public exchange proposal. Arena was unwilling to enter into negotiations and Field directors rejected the $36 a share CHH offer, saying the merger would not be in the best interests of Field stockholders, employees, and customers, and the price was inadequate. Field filed an antitrust suit.

Carter Hawley Hale was the nation's eighth largest department store group and Field was the largest of the department store independents. Carter Hawley Hale, which had grown through acquisitions, sought to further expand by taking over Field. Field owned valuable real estate, was established in the Chicago market, possessed large cash reserves, and had a conservative debt-to-equity ratio of 28% even with lease capitalization. Carter Hawley Hale had been looking to break into the Chicago market and believed it could bring operating improvements to Field. The takeover battle drew attention to CHH's highly leveraged position. Carter Hawley Hale had a debt-to-equity ratio of 42% or 113% with lease capitalization, and was planning to finance the merger on the strength of Field's balance sheet.

Field had previously been targeted for takeover by Associated Dry Goods in 1969, Federated Department Stores in 1975, and Dayton-Hudson in 1976. In each battle, Field used the antitrust defense and/or made a major acquisition. Under the advice of lawyer Joseph Flom, Field believed expansion would help the firm remain independent. In 1976 CHH had sales of $1.4 billion compared with Field's sales of $610 million. At the time of the offer, Field shares, which had a book value of $27, were trading at $23. In the prior five years, Field earnings per share had fallen by 20% as it struggled with declining profit margins and shrinking market share.

In early February 1978 CHH announced a tender offer of $42 in cash and CHH stock for each share of Field stock tendered. Field's board continued to oppose the merger and agreed to expand into the Galleria in Houston and to acquire five Liberty House stores in the Northwest. The two transactions would total $34 million. Carter Hawley Hale already had a store in the Galleria, Neiman Marcus. Field had considered acquiring the Liberty House stores in the context of another takeover battle but at the time Field's vice president of corporate development judged the earnings potential to be minimal. It was rumored that CHH had also planned to expand to the Northwest. Field had the ambitious vision of becoming a national retailer. On February 22 CHH withdrew its proposed tender offer, citing doubts of the impact of Field's expansion plan. Through the expansion program, Field increased its debt, making it less attractive to CHH. Upon announcement of the withdrawal of CHH's offer, Field shares plummeted to $19.

Field's directors were sued by some of its shareholders for resisting the CHH offer regardless of shareholders' interests and breaching their fiduciary duty as directors. The court found that the plaintiffs failed to show there was a breach of fiduciary duty and the directors were protected by the business judgment rule.

Under Arena, the number of Field stores tripled and the firm took on $120 million in debt. Problems continued to plague Field and by 1981, share price had fallen to under $20 a share. In February 1982 Field came under attack by Carl Icahn. Icahn continued to purchase Field stock despite lawsuits filed against him. Field turned to a white knight, Batus Inc., the American subsidiary of B.A.T. Industries of London. Batus owned the nation's third largest tobacco company as well as Gimbel's and Saks Fifth Avenue. Other bidders included CHH and May Department Stores. Although Batus's initial offer was $25.50 a share, it eventually paid $30 a share for the front and back ends of the offer. Icahn walked away with a profit of $30 million.

--------------------------------------------------------

## Questions on Case Study C20.1

C20.1.1 What defensive actions did Marshall Field take in response to Carter Hawley Hale's interest?

C20.1.2 Why did Carter Hawley Hale want to acquire Marshall Field?

C20.1.3 Over the years, which defense did Marshall Field employ several times?

C20.1.4 Which characteristics attracted Marshall Field's suitors to bid for the company?

C20.1.5 Who was Marshall Field's white knight?

-------------------------------- C A S E 20–2 --------------------------------

# Mattel-Hasbro*

After some preliminary discussions on January 24, 1996, Mattel made an unsolicited proposal to buy the second largest toy company, Hasbro Inc. Their proposal indicated a fundamental reorganization in the toy industry. The *Financial Times* (January 27, 1996) stated, "Barbie fluttered her eyelashes at GI Joe and all the hearts in Toy Town skipped a beat!" Mattel was strong in dolls with its market leaders Barbie and Ken and was developing joint products with Disney and others. Hasbro was strong in toys for boys such as GI Joe and Tonka trucks, as well as in board games. Hasbro's reaction was to cry, "Monopoly" (one of its board games). Both firms had gaps in creating electronic toys in which foreign competitors such as Nintendo and Sony were leaders.

The preannouncement price of Mattel was $32 per share and for Hasbro it was $30.625. The Mattel offer of 1.67 shares for one share of Hasbro placed a value of $53.44 per share on Hasbro, representing a premium of 74%. Because Hasbro objected immediately, the Hasbro price never went above $40. The price of Mattel moved up by about $1. With 225 million shares, the wealth of Mattel shareholders increased about $225 million. For Hasbro, with 97 million shares outstanding, shareholder wealth increased by almost $1 billion.

Negotiations continued but Hasbro continued to raise antitrust objections. Finally, on February 3, 1996, it was announced that Mattel would withdraw its offer for Hasbro. John Amerman, the Mattel chairman, stated that in a friendly deal the antitrust barriers could have been resolved in about five months (*Wall Street Journal,* February 8, 1996, p. B8). But with the obstacles thrown up by Hasbro, the legal compli-

---

*This case was written by J. F. Weston, Aaron Cheatham, and Girish Kulai.

cations would have continued for as long as two years. Mr. Amerman stated that at the end of three years the earnings per share for Mattel would have been unchanged from current projections. He concluded by stating, "So why raise our risks?"

The Hasbro stock dropped back to $34.625. The Mattel stock stayed at about $33, about $1 above its prebid price. Mattel said that the costs related to the failed bid would lower their earnings per share for 1996 by about 1¢.

---

## Questions on Case Study C20.2

C20.2.1   What would have been the business advantages of the combination?

C20.2.2   Would the combination have created market power in production and distribution of toys?

C20.2.3   From the standpoint of U.S. public policy, evaluate the desirability of the combination.

---

## References

Bagli, Charles, V., "A New Breed of Wolf at the Corporate Door: It's the Era of the Civilized Hostile Takeover," *New York Times,* March 19, 1997, pp. C1, C4.

Berkovitch, E., and N. Khanna, "A Theory of Acquisition Markets: Mergers Versus Tender Offers, and Golden Parachutes," *Review of Financial Studies,* 4, 1991, pp. 149–174.

Bhagat, S., and R. H. Jefferis, "Voting Power in the Proxy Process: The Case of Antitakeover Charter Amendments," *Journal of Financial Economics,* 30, 1991, pp. 193–225.

Born, Jeffery A., Emery A. Trahan, and Hugo J. Faria, "Golden Parachutes: Incentive Aligners, Management Entrenchers, or Takeover Bid Signals?" *Journal of Financial Research,* 16, Winter 1993, pp. 299–308.

Bradley, M., and L. Wakeman, "The Wealth Effects of Targeted Share Repurchases," *Journal of Financial Economics,* 11, 1983, pp. 301–328.

Brickley, J. A., R. C. Lease, and C. W. Smith, Jr., "Ownership Structure and Voting on Antitakeover Amendments," *Journal of Financial Economics,* 20, 1988, pp. 267–292.

Coffee, J. C., "Shareholders Versus Managers: The Strain in the Corporate Web," chapter 6 in J. C. Coffee, L. Lowenstein, and S. Rose-Ackerman, eds., *Knights, Raiders, and Targets,* New York: Oxford University Press, 1988, pp. 77–134.

Comment, Robert, and G. William Schwert, "Poison or Placebo? Evidence on the Deterrence and Wealth Effects of Modern Antitakeover Measures," *Journal of Financial Economics,* 39, 1995, pp. 3–43.

Cook, Douglas O., and John C. Easterwood, "Poison Put Bonds: An Analysis of Their Economic Role," *Journal of Finance,* 49, December 1994, pp. 1905–1920.

Dann, Larry Y., and Harry DeAngelo, "Standstill Agreements, Privately Negotiated Stock Repurchases, and the Market for Corporate Control," *Journal of Financial Economics,* 11, 1983, pp. 275–300.

DeAngelo, Harry, and Edward M. Rice, "Antitakeover Charter Amendments and Stockholder Wealth," *Journal of Financial Economics,* 11, April 1983, pp. 329–359.

Dodd, P. R., and R. Leftwich, "The Market for Corporate Control: 'Unhealthy Competition' Versus Federal Regulation," *Journal of Business,* 53, 1980, pp. 259–283.

Dodd, P. R., and J. B. Warner, "On Corporate Governance: A Study of Proxy Contests," *Journal of Financial Economics,* 11, 1983, pp. 401–438.

Eckbo, B. Espen, "Valuation Effects of Greenmail Prohibitions," *Journal of Financial and Quantitative Analysis,* 25, December 1990, pp. 491–505.

Eisenberg, M. A., "Comment: Golden Parachutes and the Myth of the Web," chapter 9 in J. C. Coffee, L. Lowenstein, and S. Rose-Ackerman, eds., *Knights, Raiders, and Targets,* New York: Oxford University Press, 1988, pp. 155–158.

Holderness, C. G., and D. P. Sheehan, "Raiders or Saviors? The Evidence on Six Controversial Investors," *Journal of Financial Economics,* 14, 1985, pp. 555–579.

Jarrell, G. A., and A. Poulsen, "Shark Repellents and Stock Prices: The Effects of Antitakeover Amendments Since 1980," *Journal of Financial Economics,* 19, 1987, pp. 127–168.

Jensen, Michael C., "Takeovers: Their Causes and Consequences," *Journal of Economic Perspectives,* 2, Winter 1988, pp. 21–48.

Karpoff, Jonathan M., and Paul H. Malatesta, "The Wealth Effects of Second Generation State Takeover Legislation, *Journal of Financial Economics,* 25, 1989, pp. 291–322.

———, and Ralph A. Walkling, "Corporate Governance and Shareholder Initiatives: Empirical Evidence," *Journal of Financial Economics,* 42, 1996, pp. 365–395.

Klein, A., and J. Rosenfeld, "The Impact of Targeted Share Repurchases on the Wealth of Non-Participating Shareholders," *Journal of Financial Research,* 11, Summer 1988, pp. 89–97.

Knoeber, C. R., "Golden Parachutes, Shark Repellents, and Hostile Tender Offers," *American Economic Review,* 76, March 1986, pp. 155–167.

Lambert, R., and D. Larcker, "Golden Parachutes, Executive Decision-Making, and Shareholder Wealth," *Journal of Accounting and Economics,* 7, April 1985, pp. 179–204.

Linn, S. C., and J. J. McConnell, "An Empirical Investigation of the Impact of Antitakeover Amendments on Common Stock Prices," *Journal of Financial Economics,* 11, April 1983, pp. 361–399.

Mahoney, James M., and Joseph T. Mahoney, "An Empirical Investigation of the Effect of Corporate Charter Antitakeover Amendments on Stockholder Wealth," *Strategic Management Journal,* 14, 1993, pp. 17–31.

Malatesta, Paul H., and Ralph A. Walkling, "Poison Pill Securities: Stockholder Wealth, Profitability, and Ownership Structure," *Journal of Financial Economics,* 20, 1988, pp. 347–376.

Marais, L., K. Schipper, and A. Smith, "Wealth Effects of Going Private for Senior Securities," *Journal of Financial Economics,* 23, 1989, pp. 151–191.

McWilliams, V. B., "Managerial Share Ownership and the Stock Price Effects of Antitakeover Amendment Proposals," *Journal of Finance,* 45, 1990, pp. 1627–1640.

Mikkelson, W. H., and R. S. Ruback, "An Empirical Analysis of the Interfirm Equity Investment Process," *Journal of Financial Economics,* 14, 1985, pp. 523–553.

———, "Targeted Repurchases and Common Stock Returns," *The RAND Journal of Economics,* 22, Winter 1991, pp. 544–561.

Mogavero, Damian J., and Michael F. Toyne, "The Impact of Golden Parachutes on Fortune 500 Stock Returns: A Reexamination of the Evidence," *Quarterly Journal of Business and Economics,* 34, 1995, pp. 30–38.

*Moran v. Household International, Inc.,* Del. Ch. 490 A. 2d 1059, 1985.

Pound, J., "The Effects of Antitakeover Amendments on Takeover Activity: Some Direct Evidence," *Journal of Law and Economics,* 30, October 1987, pp. 353–367.

Romano, Roberta, "Law as a Product: Some Pieces of the Incorporation Puzzle," *Journal of Law, Economics and Organization,* 1, 1985, pp. 225–269.

———, "The Political Economy of Takeover Statutes," *Virginia Law Review,* 73, 1987, pp. 111–199.

————, "Competition for Corporate Charters and the Lesson of Takeover Statutes," *Fordham Law Review,* 61, 1993, pp. 843–864.

Ryngaert, Michael, "The Effect of Poison Pill Securities on Shareholder Wealth," *Journal of Financial Economics,* 20, 1988, pp. 377–417.

————, and J. M. Netter, "Shareholder Wealth Effects of the Ohio Antitakeover Law," *Journal of Law, Economics and Organization,* 4, Fall 1988, pp. 373–384.

Taylor, John, *Storming the Magic Kingdom,* New York: Ballantine Books, 1987.

Warga, A., and I. Welch, "Bondholder Losses in Leveraged Buyouts," *Review of Financial Studies,* 6, 1993, pp. 959–982.

C H A P T E R

# 21

# Case Studies
# of M&A Activity

This chapter presents case studies of general aspects of M&A activity, and discusses some factors that are not usually covered in the broader statistical studies that constitute the bulk of the M&A literature. We illustrate the application of concepts, test the validity of concepts and theories, and review the experiences of individual companies, all of which provides a guide to formulating sound public policy. The discussion may spark additional ideas for the reader that will be valuable to managers engaged in M&A activity.

In previous chapters on empirical aspects of M&A activity, we have cited the Mitchell and Mulherin (1996) study, which demonstrates the industry influence on M&A activity. They note that for the period 1993–1994, seven industries accounted for 51.5% of total takeover value. A similar analysis in the *Mergers & Acquisitions* magazine, March–April 1996, p. 45, shows that for 1995, 10 industries accounted for 52.6% to total M&A value. Industry definitions are somewhat artificial. In another analysis, *Mergers & Acquisitions* observes that three groupings accounted for 56.2% of takeover value. Nonfinancial services (mainly entertainment, leisure, and media) accounted for 27.8%, financial services (commercial banks, S&Ls, insurance firms, investment bankers, real estate companies) accounted for 18.2%, and telecommunications (television and related communications companies) accounted for 10.2%.

## A FRAMEWORK FOR CASE STUDIES

Several forces explain the high industry concentration of M&A activity. Usually some major impact, shock, or change requires a redefinition or realignment of firms, causing restructuring in which M&A activities perform a role. These forces include regulatory changes, technological changes, international influences, and major changes in managerial technology.

The processes and forces transforming industries help explain the restructuring activities that take place and the related roles of M&As. When the basic business economic forces of an industry change, individual firms must readjust and become realigned in the process. Thus, restructuring and M&A activity represent part of the adjustment processes whereby firms seek to realign themselves to their changing environments. This proposition is consistent with our emphasis on viewing M&A activity as a part of the long-range planning processes of firms.

M&A activity is relatively low in industries in which environments and competitive interactions have been relatively stable. But even when restructuring or an M&A event takes place in an industry with relatively little activity, it can best be understood in terms of the basic underlying economic processes taking place in that industry.

The above generalizations can be illustrated by reference to the telecommunications and media industries. We begin with a summary of the Telecommunications Act of February 8, 1996, presented in Table 21.1. This new law and the changes in regulatory policies it calls for reflect the many changes in technology and competitive processes that have taken place in recent decades. In turn, it will unleash new forces in the decades to come. In anticipation of and in response to the act, a number of strategic adjustments in the telecommunications and information industries have been taking place:

1. Proposed merger between Bell Atlantic and cable company Tele-Communications Inc. (TCI) canceled (February 1994).

2. A major joint phone-cable venture between SBC Communications Inc. and Cox Communications Inc. canceled (April 1994).

3. The three largest cable operators, TCI, Comcast Corporation, and Cox Communications Inc., revised their contract with Sprint to give themselves more flexibility (January 1996). The original plan was to market cable TV, local telephone and wireless service in one package with Sprint. The original agreement was an exclusive contract for 15 years. They revised the contract to permit them to market local phone services with any partner they choose.

4. AT&T Corporation (1995) plans a split into three separate companies by the end of 1996. Plans to compete against the regional Bells in both long distance and local telephone service.

5. TV networks merged with other media companies. Westinghouse acquired CBS. Walt Disney acquired Capital Cities/ABC. Time Warner announced (August 30, 1995) that it would acquire Turner broadcasting.

6. Merger talks between the regional Bell companies. In particular, NYNEX and Bell Atlantic discussing a merger that would provide local telephone and cellular systems from Virginia to Maine (April 2, 1996).

---

**TABLE 21.1** Summary of the Telecommunications Act of February 8, 1996

A. Long distance—seven regional Bell companies can enter.
B. Local markets—opened to new competitors such as AT&T, MCI, Sprint, and cable companies.
C. Cable—eliminates rate regulations in three years. New powers to resell phone services.
D. Video by phone or by satellite.
E. Cross-ownership—prohibition between cable and telephone eliminated.
F. Universal service—guaranteed. FCC and states to decide how to pay.
G. Broadcast—national TV station ownership cap raised from 25 to 35%. Blocking device on TV sets.
H. Spectrum—advanced TV qualifies for new broadcast spectrum free of charge.
I. Internet—crime to transmit indecent material to minors.

7. U S West agrees to acquire Continental Cablevision for $5.3 billion plus assumption of $5.5 billion in debt (February 27, 1996).

8. AT&T launched an Internet service that for the first year provides its long-distance customers with five free hours a month of access (February 27, 1996).

To provide further detail on the kinds of events that have been taking place in the information industries, we will describe seven takeovers as listed below with the dates that news stories first appeared.

1. Time Warner (March 4, 1989)

2. Paramount-QVC-Viacom (February 15, 1994)

3. SBC-Pac Tel, Bell South Alliance (April 2, 1996)

4. NYNEX-Bell Atlantic (April 22, 1996)

5. Disney-Capital Cities/ABC (July 31, 1995)

6. Time Warner-Turner Broadcasting (August 30, 1995)

7. Westinghouse-CBS (August 7, 1995)

We first discuss the Time Warner transaction because of its continuing impact on subsequent transactions.

## TIME WARNER

On March 4, 1989, Time and Warner announced a merger through an exchange of stock. On June 7, 1989, Paramount (previously Gulf & Western Industries) announced an offer to buy the common stock of Time. On July 14, 1989, the Delaware Chancery Court rejected Paramount's suit to prevent Time from buying Warner. On July 24, 1989, the Delaware Supreme Court affirmed the Chancery Court decision and Time purchased 100 million Warner shares at $70 each on the same day. Paramount withdrew its hostile offer for Time.

We observe here the impacts of rapidly changing technology and globalization. We see the convergence and expansion of industry segments and their interactions. Newspaper companies move into magazines and books in all their dimensions. Movies see increased revenues from TV broadcasting, videocassettes, and sales abroad. Cable systems become increasingly important parts of the delivery systems. Programming and software become critical activities. Entertainment and publishing now involve a large number of segments of the broader information industry. Industry segments increasingly overlap and compete with one another. Here is a significant case study of the dynamics of industry change in an important sector of the economy.

The legal issues involve primarily the dynamics of company control and the nature and theory of the firm. These interrelate with managers' responsibilities and relationships with shareholders. The assessments of the formulation and evolution of corporate strategies in changing environments are also involved.

The Time-Warner-Paramount struggles illustrate the impact of evolving industries, increased competition between industries and their segments, all moving to a setting of international markets. While the facts of this individual case are interesting in themselves, their broader implications make the subject a matter for serious analytical study.

## Brief Chronology of Events

We now recount the events beginning with the original Time-Warner merger announcement.

*March 4, 1989:* Time Inc. and Warner Communications, Inc. announce plans to merge.

*Terms:* Stock-for-stock swap.
Each of Warner's 177.2 million shares would be exchanged for 0.465 shares of Time. Based on Time's closing price on Friday, March 3, 1989 of $109.125, Warner would receive $50.74 in value per share. Warner's closing price on Friday, March 3, 1989 was $45.875.

*Stock price effects:*

|  | *Monday, February 27* | *Friday, March 3* | *Monday, March 6* |
|---|---|---|---|
| Time | $104.50 | $109.125 | $107.25 |
| Warner | $ 41.25 | $ 45.875 | $ 48.25 |

*Discussion:* The total value of the transaction would amount to $8.8 billion, a new record for stock swaps. The transaction would be a tax-free merger of equals using "pooling of interests" accounting and thus involve no goodwill. No new debt would be required, so that the combined firm would have only $3 billion in debt, and relatively high debt capacity for the future. No asset sales would be required to finance the transaction. Although Time's name would be first in the name of the combined firm, the former Warner shareholders would end up owning nearly 60% of the new entity. (Time had about 56.6 million shares outstanding.) Initially, Time's chairman J. Richard Munro and Warner's chairman Steven J. Ross would be co-chairmen and co–chief executive officers, but it was planned that eventually Time's president N. J. Nicholas, Jr. would take control. The merger was approved unanimously by the boards of both firms with the exception of an abstention on the Warner board by Herbert Siegel of Chris-Craft Industries.

 The only drawback seemed to be the length of time necessary to complete a stock-for-stock transaction, during which time both firms would be vulnerable to outside bids. As a defense, the merger terms included a stock-swap (a "lock-up") agreement between Time and Warner to swap blocks of each other's *newly issued* shares in the event of a hostile bid for either firm. The swap would result in Warner owning 11.1% of Time's shares outstanding and Time owning 8.7% of Warner's. It would be triggered if a hostile bidder sought to acquire more than 25% of Time before the completion of the merger. Although the merger was announced on Saturday, March 4, a report on the deal already appeared Saturday morning in the *Los Angeles Times.* Most media stocks increased in price on Monday, presumably due to the market's expectation that other mergers among media companies might be forthcoming.

*May 22, 1989:* Herbert Siegel of Chris-Craft Industries resigns from Warner board as Warner and Chris-Craft reach an accord to settle their dispute.

*Stock price effects:*
Time shares rose $2 to $126.75.
Warner shares rose $1 to $51.375.
Implied value of Warner shares under merger terms = $58.94.

*Discussion:* The increase in share price seems to indicate that the market assessed a higher probability that the merger would actually go through with the resignation of Siegel.

*May 23, 1989:* Release of proxy materials for Time's June 23 meeting at which shareholders would be asked to approve merger.

*Stock price effects:*
Time shares fell $0.25 to $125.25.
Warner shares rose $0.50 to $51.875.

*Discussion:* The proxy materials included statements that Time had paid fees to banks in exchange for agreements not to finance hostile bids for up to one year. A group of banks were lined up to provide up to $5 billion in case it was necessary for Time to make a friendly cash bid for Warner. The three investment bankers involved in the proposed merger will receive $36 million in fees if it is completed.

*June 7, 1989:* Paramount Communications Inc. (which changed its name from Gulf & Western in June) begins cash tender offer at $175 per share for all outstanding Time shares. (The bid was announced on June 6 after the close of trading.)

*Stock price effects:*
Time shares rose $44.00 to $170.00.
Warner shares rose $1.75 to $53.50.
Paramount shares rose $0.75 to $54.75.

*Discussion:* Total value of the cash offer was $10.7 billion. The bid represents a 60% premium over the price of Time's stock before the Time Warner merger announcement. Citibank had pledged $1 billion, and Paramount was confident of being able to line up senior bank financing for the remainder. Warner sued Citibank for its pledge to the Paramount takeover attempt. Paramount filed a suit to challenge the stock-swap (lock-up) defense in the original Time Warner merger agreement and to invalidate a poison pill allowing Time shareholders to buy additional Time shares at half-price if a hostile bidder acquires more than 20% of its stock. Paramount's chairman and CEO, Martin S. Davis, stated that Time had always refused friendly merger talks, wanting to remain independent, but "put themselves in play" by agreeing to a merger with Warner.

*June 16, 1989:* Time makes $14 billion cash bid for Warner. Warner would receive $70 cash for 50% of its shares plus a combination of cash plus stock or debt securities worth $70 for the remaining shares.

*Stock price effects:*
Time shares fell $5.625 to $156.875.
Warner shares rose $0.375 to $59.625.
Paramount shares rose $2.375 to $60.50.

*Discussion:* Under the terms of this new offer, the total debt of the combined Time Warner would rise from $3 billion to $17 billion, resulting in high interest payments, reduced future flexibility, and possible asset sales. The high purchase price would also necessitate a large amount of goodwill, which would be a drag on the earnings of the combined firm for 40 years. The combined Time Warner would be larger and more difficult to take over.

*June 21, 1989:* Paramount files a revised suit in Delaware Chancery Court to block Time's acquisition of Warner.

*Stock price effects:*
Time shares fell $4.375 to $152.50
Warner shares fell $0.125 to $59.50.
Paramount shares fell $1.125 to $53.375.

*Discussion:* The new suit adds allegations and requests to the original suit. It argues that Time put itself up for sale when it agreed in March to merge with Warner. The Delaware courts previously ruled that once a board of directors has determined that a company is for sale, it must conduct a fair auction process. The suit also argues that Time directors breached their fiduciary duty to shareholders by not seriously considering the Paramount bid and that they failed to exercise sound business judgment because they approved a tender offer for Warner that can only be stopped by the court or in extraordinary situations.

*June 23, 1989:* Paramount raises its offer for Time to $200 per share, increasing the total value of the offer to $12.2 billion.

*Stock price effects (Friday, June 23):*
Time shares rose $10.50 to $165.875.
Warner shares fell $0.50 to $58.625.
Paramount shares fell $0.50 to $58.00.

*Discussion:* Paramount admitted it was not yet able to finance the increased offer and perhaps would not be able to do so by the expiration date of July 7, 1989. Although the bid was announced after the close of trading on June 23, share prices reacted (speculatively) to a page 1 story in *USA Today,* June 23, 1989, that reported the forthcoming increase in the bid. It appears that the market was assigning a low probability to the success of Paramount's bid as the $25 increase in bid caused the stock price to rise only $10.50.

*June 26, 1989:* Time's board of directors rejects Paramount's $200 offer. Rumors circulated that a hostile bidder might surface for Paramount.

*Stock price effects:*
Time shares fell $1.875 to $164.00.
Warner shares rose $0.25 to $58.875.
Paramount shares rose $2.375 to $60.375.

*Discussion:* Paramount disclosed to the SEC the financing details for $15.6 billion, and it was thought they would have difficulty coming up with much more than that.

*June 28, 1989:* Delaware Chancery Court declines to postpone Time's annual meeting rescheduled for June 30, 1989. Renewed rumors circulated on a possible hostile bid for Paramount that might derail Paramount's bid for Time.

*Stock price effects:*
Time shares fell $6.00 to $157.25.
Warner shares rose $1.625 to $60.75.
Paramount shares rose $3.375 to $62.875.

*June 30, 1989:* Time holds annual meeting of shareholders.

*Stock price effects:*
Time shares fell $0.50 to $155.25.
Warner shares rose $0.375 to $60.375.
Paramount shares fell $1.375 to $59.50.

*Discussion:* No vote on the merger took place at the meeting. Three Time executives and one outside director were reelected to terms on the board of directors. Voting on a staggered board provision showed somewhat more support for moving away from a staggered board than at the previous annual meeting. Warner's share price increase may have been fueled by rumors that Marvin Davis (formerly of Twentieth Century-Fox) might bid for the company.

*July 11, 1989:* Paramount amends its $200-a-share offer to include 9% interest a year for any delays that might occur in completing the transaction due to regulatory approvals related to cable licenses.

*July 14, 1989:* The Delaware Chancery Court refused to block Time's purchase of Warner as sought by Paramount.

*Stock price effects:*
Time shares fell $4.75 to $145.25. (Had plunged $12 but recovered before closing.)
Warner shares rose $2.00 to $64.25.
Paramount shares fell $0.125 to $57.50.

*Discussion:* The decision was interpreted as pro-management, affirming the right of corporate directors to run the firm without necessarily taking a shareholder vote on every issue. The timing of the merger agreement was held to be important; because Time had agreed to merge with Warner three months before the Paramount bid, the court did not view Time's purchase of Warner as primarily defensive. The Delaware Supreme Court ruling affirmed that stock-swap transactions do not obligate companies to put themselves up for auction.

*July 24, 1989:* The Delaware Supreme Court refused to block the Time-Warner transaction. Paramount terminated its $12.2 billion offer to buy Time.

*Stock price effects:*
Time shares fell $1 to $137.50.
Warner shares climbed $1.625 to close at $67.125.
Paramount shares rose $1.875 to close at $59.375.

*Discussion:* Time bought 100 million Warner shares at $70 each just after 5 P.M. EDT. Including the 17 million shares that Time already owned, Time now holds a 58% stake in Warner. By declining to block Time's purchase of Warner, the Delaware Supreme Court affirmed the power of corporate directors to make major business decisions without a shareholder vote.

## Central Legal Issues

Paramount's lawyers argued that on March 4, 1989, when the Time-Warner merger agreement had been announced, Time had effectively put itself into play. Time was subject to be bought by the highest bidder. By the time of the suit, Paramount was bidding $200 a share for Time. It was widely argued that if the merger of Time and Warner were completed, the resulting price would be in the $120 to $140 range. But the board of directors of Time argued that the intrinsic value of the Time-Warner combination is $250.

A number of complex legal and valuation issues are raised by these numbers. Gregg Jarrell (1989) posed the question in the following terms. "Why is there this enormous difference of opinion between Time insiders and the marketplace about the economic value of Paramount's bid relative to Time post-Warner?" Jarrell suggests that most lawyers would answer the question by observing that Paramount's bid is short term while the value of Time combined with Warner is longer term. He then develops examples to demonstrate that, "This short-term argument is easily shown to be nonsense." He assumes a 10% discount rate and then considers the present value of the $250 depending on whether it is achieved in one year or in five years. The present value if achieved in one year is $227, which is superior to tendering at $200. But if the $250 is achieved in five years, its present value is only $155, which is far less than the Paramount bid of $200. Jarrell concludes that, "Time's directors and management cannot justify on any viable economic grounds denying their shareholders a legitimate choice between Paramount's offer (or a negotiated one) and the proposed takeover of Warner."

The Delaware Chancery Court speaking through William T. Allen disagreed. Chancellor Allen stated, "The corporation law does not operate on the theory that directors, in exercising their powers to manage the firm, are obligated to follow the wishes of a majority of shares. In fact, directors, not shareholders, are charged with the duty to manage the firm" (Hilder, 1989).

Aside from the numbers, the court argued that it is the fundamental responsibility and right of the board of directors to make such decisions on the basis of their long-run benefit for shareholders. Their judgments are based on experience and their best strategies for the future of the company. In an uncertain world such judgments cannot be wholly based on historical data. They are based on business experience and strategic planning processes. This is said to be the economic basis for the legal "business judg-ment rule."

But in later cases, the courts have moved closer to the views expressed by the financial economist, Jarrell (1989). The courts have emphasized the need for the board to consider and even elicit multiple bids to ensure that the best possible sales price has been obtained for the shareholders.

## PARAMOUNT VERSUS QVC NETWORK

When Paramount failed to acquire Time, it sought another entry into the cable televi-sion industry. Paramount negotiated a merger with Viacom. The arrangement included a no-shop provision, a termination fee, and a lock-up option for Viacom. Newspaper articles referred to the Paramount-Viacom merger as a completed transaction. But bids and counterbids by Viacom and QVC took place.

The courts held that Paramount had tried to favor Viacom and that QVC had made a higher bid. After further bidding and counterbids, Viacom ultimately acquired Paramount on February 15, 1994. Viacom chairman, Sumner Redstone, commented that the intervention by QVC had raised the price to Viacom by about $2 billion. But, of course, this was the objective of the court in requiring that the Paramount board shop around to get the best possible price for its shareholders.

## SBC AND PAC TEL

On April 2, 1996, SBC Communications Inc. (Texas based) announced the acquisition of the Pacific Telesis Group for $16.7 billion. The merged company would carry the SBC name. A major objective was to enable the two to compete more effectively in the long distance markets permitted by the act of February 8, 1996. Shortly thereafter it was announced that Bell South would join the alliance in pursuing opportunities in long dis-tance. Pac Tel had expertise in new services such as Internet access. SBC was the nation's number two wireless provider.

Using April 1, 1996, as the event date and employing a window of five days before through 10 days after, the market value of the Pacific Telesis Group stock increased by about $2.5 billion. Over the same period, the market value of SBC dropped by about the same amount.

## BELL ATLANTIC AND NYNEX

On April 22, 1996, after months of discussion, Bell Atlantic and NYNEX announced a merger of equals with a combined market value of $50 billion. The new company would be known as Bell Atlantic and would be majority owned by Bell Atlantic shareholders. This reduced the number of regional Bell companies to five from the original eight. Bell Atlantic had, in October 1993, planned to acquire TCI for $21.7 billion. The acquisition was based on the theory that cable television and telephone networks were converging into an information highway for transporting video, voice, and data. Later, however, the FCC reduced cable rates and the deal was not completed. A lengthy article discussed whether cable and television companies were a good combination (Landler, 1996).

The initial event returns, using April 22, 1996, as the reference point with a win-dow of −5 to +10 days, reflected a gain in the market value of Bell Atlantic of about

$550 million with a decline for NYNEX of about $1.5 billion. It is interesting that the market seemed to have second thoughts about the potentials for economies or improvements because extending the postevent window 10 additional days resulted in a negative event return for Bell Atlantic of $651 million and a negative event return for NYNEX of about $2.8 billion.

## DISNEY–CAPITAL CITIES/ABC

The acquisition by Disney of Capital Cities/ABC for $19 billion was announced on July 31, 1995. In the previous full year 1994, Disney reported total revenues of $10.06 billion of which 45% came from filmed entertainment, 35% from theme parks and resorts, and the remaining 18% from consumer products. Capital Cities/ABC had revenues of $6.38 billion with 83% from broadcasting and 17% from publishing. The ABC radio networks service more than 3,400 stations. The central argument for the combination was that there would be benefits of combining the programming capabilities of Disney with the distribution facilities of Capital Cities/ABC. Some question whether there are real synergies in combining programming with distribution. Television stations want to get the best possible product to achieve the best possible ratings. If the programming is good, it will have no problem finding distribution outlets.

The initial reaction of the market to the Disney–Capital Cities combination using July 31, 1995, as the event date was a gain of $2.0 billion for Walt Disney shareholders and an increase in market wealth for Capital Cities/ABC of $2.3 billion.

## TIME WARNER–TURNER BROADCASTING

The newspapers of September 23, 1995, headlined that Time Warner would buy the 82% of Turner it did not already own in a stock deal worth $7.5 billion. The articles commented that this ended a tumultuous five-week period of negotiations. A newspaper account of August 30, 1995, made a similar set of announcements, stating that Turner shareholders would receive between 0.7 and 0.8 of one share of Time Warner for each share of Turner. Time Warner's share price at the time was $42.375, which would value the Turner shares at about $35, representing a 48% premium over Turner's closing price of $23.625 on August 29, 1995. As of late May 1996, this transaction had not yet been completed. In fact, newspaper articles during May 1996 indicated that the staff of the Federal Trade Commission was raising antitrust objections to the Time Warner–Turner combination.

Turner had long been seeking to expand his TV and broadcasting networks. Some commented that the Disney acquisition of Capital Cities/ABC (announced July 31, 1995) caused a rethinking by entertainment executives of the media chain. It is said that Turner believed that even if he acquired a network, his debt burden would be so heavy that his company would remain a second-tier competitor in relation to the Disney giant. Time Warner had concluded that buying Turner would provide many of the distribution and programming benefits of owning a network. Before the merger, 40% of Time Warner's cash flow was from programming and 60% from cable. After the Turner deal, that mix would be reversed.

Using August 30, 1995, as the event date and with a window of five days before and 20 days after for measurement, the market value effect of the combination has been calculated. It represented a $2.4 billion loss for the shareholders of Time Warner and a gain of about a billion for the Turner shareholders.

## WESTINGHOUSE ACQUISITION OF CBS

The acquisition by Westinghouse of CBS was announced on August 7, 1995. For many years, CBS (founded by William Paley), was the number one radio and TV network. In the 1960s and 1970s, it diversified into a wide range of activities including book publishing, the New York Yankees, and record producers. In September 1986 Lawrence A. Tisch became the CEO of CBS. He initiated a series of divestitures to reduce debt and made an effort to improve profit margins. Competition with NBC and ABC for sports programming reduced margins for all three. In May 1994 the Fox network was able to acquire eight of the 208 affiliated stations of CBS. Further affiliate defections were rumored.

In June 1994 CBS and QVC agreed to merge. However, Comcast made a bid for QVC on July 12, 1994. The complications involved prevented the deal with CBS.

On April 18, 1985, Turner Broadcasting (TBS) offered $5.41 billion for CBS. Much of the payment would be in the form of high-risk, high-yield securities. On April 22, 1985, CBS rejected the Turner bid and filed a lawsuit claiming that TBS had overstated its earnings for 1983 and 1984.

It had been long viewed that CBS was up for sale. Finally, in early July, it was announced that Westinghouse Electric was negotiating with CBS. By July 18, 1995, it appeared that Westinghouse would succeed in its bid of $5.4 billion for CBS. A *Business Week* article was headlined "Six Months After Westinghouse Took Over, the Network May Be Waking Up" (Lesly, 1996). The event return analysis, using a window of five days before and 20 days after, indicated a decline in Westinghouse shareholder wealth of about $500 million and an increase in the wealth of CBS shareholders of about $800 million.

## WHAT'S AHEAD FOR THE INFORMATION INDUSTRY?

The Telecommunications Act of February 8, 1996, reflected many developments. In turn, it stimulated further changes. Many issues have been raised. Some see telecommunications moving into all aspects of the information industry. Some see a convergence of computers, telecommunications, radio broadcasting, TV broadcasting, etc.

Some have emphasized the issue of programming or content versus distribution. Some see the Internet and the personal computer as changing the whole world of telecommunications and broadcasting. Clearly, technological change is exploding in this area. The ultimate answers have not yet been found.

But changes and potential changes have stimulated restructuring and redefining firms and industries. The case studies of M&A activity in the telecommunications and information industries illustrate the broad influences that impact the restructuring and M&A activities of individual firms and industries.

We next turn to case studies of other industries and companies. We begin with some analytical approaches.

## RUBACK CASE STUDIES

Richard Ruback (1982, 1983) builds on empirical event studies of takeover activity, but focuses on individual cases rather than averaging across many events. Thus, he can examine in detail the abnormal returns of all takeover participants in response to a series of announcement dates preceding the final outcome. He uses this technique to verify the consistency of stock price reactions with the results of the empirical studies, to provide evidence of their predictive ability, and to test alternative theories. His approach also permits examination of more complex takeover scenarios (including multiple bidders, buybacks, and stand-still agreements) that are often eliminated from the samples of event studies to avoid confusion.

## Conoco

Ruback (1982) chronicled DuPont's successful pursuit of Conoco in a multibidder takeover battle in 1981. Throughout the takeover process, DuPont's returns were consistently negative. However, there were two other competing bidders: Seagram, which initiated the contest, and Mobil, which entered about midway through the bidding war.

Seagram's initial bids (June 19, 1981, starting at $70 per share for a 25% interest) produced significant positive abnormal returns for both firms, suggesting that the market viewed the combination as value increasing, in spite of Conoco's opposition. Conoco's search for other bidders brought DuPont into the contest; on July 6, 1981, Conoco and DuPont announced an agreement in which DuPont would buy 40% of Conoco for cash ($87.50 per share), trading DuPont shares for the remainder. The agreement included a nine-month option giving DuPont the right to buy 15.9 million Conoco shares at $87.50, simultaneously increasing the probability that the merger would succeed while providing a hedge against its failure. Even so, the market responded with significant negative abnormal returns for DuPont (−8.05%). Seagram stock also suffered at the announcement, confirming the earlier positive market response; the agreement between DuPont and Conoco meant that a good investment opportunity for Seagram had probably been lost, or would at the least become more expensive. A bidding war between Seagram and DuPont followed, and on July 17, 1981, Mobil entered the battle with a $90 per share offer for 50% of Conoco (with $90 of Mobil securities for the remainder). However, Mobil's offer was met with no more enthusiasm than DuPont's. Throughout the rest of July and into August, all three bidders continued to revise their offers. The Department of Justice entered the scene, approving a DuPont-Conoco merger (pending the elimination of a joint venture between Conoco and Monsanto), but requesting more information from Mobil, thus delaying a Mobil purchase and raising the possibility of antitrust problems.

The contest ended on August 5, 1981 with DuPont's announcement that it had received tenders for 55% of Conoco stock. (The final offer stood at $98 per share for 48% with 1.7 DuPont shares for each remaining share.) A summary of the market's responses to that final announcement, and over the entire period, with Ruback's interpretations follows.

### Conoco

The final announcement caused a small negative reaction, indicating that the market may have been hoping for even higher bids. Overall, Conoco earned significant positive abnormal returns (71% from June 17 through August 5, 1981, for an increase in equity value of $3.2 billion); the result is consistent with the broader empirical studies of target returns, although larger than average because of the competing bidders.

### DuPont

The final announcement produced a small positive reaction; in light of earlier negative responses, the end of the battle at least meant that DuPont would not be making further bids that were even more unprofitable. For the entire period, DuPont had negative abnormal returns (−9.9%, for a loss in equity value of $789 million).

The empirical evidence on the returns to bidding firms with rival bidders is generally negative.

### Mobil

Mobil responded positively to the end of the contest. Consistent with negative responses to its earlier bids, the failure was good news. For the entire period, Mobil had significant abnormal losses of −3.05% (or $400 million). These losses are too big to be explained by transactions costs alone. This contest may have raised the possibility of antitrust problems in future takeover attempts.

### Seagram

Seagram stock responded negatively to the final announcement, consistent with initial positive reactions. The end of the contest indicated Seagram had irrevocably lost a profitable investment opportunity. However, over the entire period, Seagram realized a market adjusted positive, but small, return of 1.13%.

Finally, Ruback (1982) attempts to explain the significant revaluation of Conoco, and why DuPont pursued so vigorously what the market perceived to be a negative net present value investment.

### Synergy (Vertical Integration, Economies of Scale, Monopolization of Product Markets)

The raw materials produced by Conoco and used by DuPont are sold in competitive markets offering few, if any, gains from vertical integration. Besides, some of the gains from vertical integration would have gone to DuPont. The market was aware of the vertical integration aspects of the merger, and still responded negatively. And furthermore, DuPont could have acquired any oil company if vertical integration were the goal, so why the aggressive pursuit of Conoco, especially when its price continued escalating? Economies of scale were not a major factor, because no explicit combination of assets was contemplated, and the two firms were in different industries. Economies in generic management areas would not have been sufficient to explain the magnitude of the premiums. Monopolization of product markets is also rejected as an explanation, because there were no antitrust objections from the Department of Justice.

### Managerialism (Managerial Departure from Shareholder Wealth Maximization)

Conoco did not have a reputation as being badly managed, nor were Conoco's managers replaced after the merger. If it were DuPont's managers who were departing from wealth maximization, they should have benefited at their shareholders' expense. But on the contrary, DuPont's managers at best stayed even throughout the transaction, and may even have lost money.

### New Information

Some appraisals of Conoco had gone as high as $160 per share, indicating that DuPont got a real bargain. But other natural resource companies were equally undervalued, so why pursue Conoco so vigorously? Besides, if the natural resources were the goal, *control* would not have been necessary; an investment position could have been obtained without paying such a high premium. Also, the market was aware of the $160 appraisal, and continued to value Conoco at less than DuPont offered (that is, the investment was a negative net present value investment for DuPont).

### Inside Information

Ruback concluded (somewhat unsatisfactorily) that DuPont must have had access to inside information not available to the market that led it to value Conoco more highly than the market. Such information must not have been specific to DuPont (that is, any bidder could have exploited the information), thus it could not be released publicly by either DuPont or Conoco without increasing still further the cost of the acquisition. To support this hypothesis, Ruback (1982) noted that Conoco allowed DuPont access to inside information. And further, on the day DuPont shareholders voted to approve the merger (August 18), DuPont had significant positive abnormal returns, indicating that DuPont management may have released enough information to cause the market partially to reevaluate the wisdom of the merger.

## Cities Service

In another case study, Ruback (1983) calculated the abnormal returns to participants in the Cities Service takeover of 1982. The contest began on May 28, 1982, with several weeks of offers and counteroffers between Cities Service and Mesa Petroleum bidding for each other. Mesa initially offered a friendly merger at $50 per share for half of Cities Service stock with Mesa securities for the remainder. Cities Service closing stock price was $35.50, so the bid represented a 41% premium. Cities Service's counterbid of $17 for 51% of Mesa represented only a 1.5% premium and was taken to have little chance of success. A second hostile offer by Mesa at $45 per share for only 15% of Cities Service stock indicated Mesa's inability or reluctance to obtain financing for a larger offer. Cities Service countered with a friendly bid of $21 per share for 51% of Mesa with Cities Service stock worth $16.31 for each remaining share, and recountered with a hostile bid at $21 for 51%.

Gulf's bid for Cities Service on June 17, 1982 ($63 per share for 51% plus $63 in fixed income securities for the remainder) effectively put Mesa out of the picture. Gulf's bid was followed by a premium buyback and standstill agreement in which Cities Service repurchased its stock from Mesa and Mesa agreed not to attempt a hostile takeover for five years. Contrary to empirical studies, Cities Service shareholders had no abnormal returns in response to the repurchase (the studies would have predicted negative returns), while Mesa shareholders suffered significant negative abnormal returns of −15.83%. This may be due to the fact that while the agreement put an end to Mesa's pursuit of Cities Service, it also ended Cities Service's pursuit of Mesa.

However, a temporary restraining order from the Federal Trade Commission in turn put an end to Gulf's attempt. Cities Service began to actively solicit other takeover bids, and even considered liquidation, when Occidental Petroleum entered the fray with a friendly offer (at $50 per share for 50% plus preferred stock and zero-coupon notes for the remainder), followed by revised bids: a hostile offer for 49% of Cities Service at $50 per share, and another friendly offer with a $52 per share cash component. Meanwhile, it was becoming evident that no other bidders would materialize. Mobil decided not to bid after being allowed to examine confidential information, and Amerada Hess was supposedly considering an offer, but none was forthcoming. On August 28, 1982, Cities Service accepted a revised Occidental bid ($55 per share for 45% with preferred stock and zero-coupon notes for the remainder), and the contest ended.

Cities Service enjoyed significant positive abnormal returns of 12.5%, or $352 million over the entire period, consistent with the results of empirical event studies. Occidental Petroleum, the eventual successful bidder, had zero abnormal returns, also consistent with several empirical studies. The market appeared to judge the acquisition as a zero net present value investment. Gulf Oil experienced significant negative abnormal returns of 17.6%, representing a loss of $1.1 billion. Most of these losses occurred on the day Gulf announced its bid for Cities Service; the offer's cancellation offset some of the initial loss, but not all of it, probably because of a $3 billion lawsuit brought by Cities Service for breach of contract, alleging that Gulf had not tried to resolve the FTC objections. The abnormal returns to Mesa Petroleum are more difficult to interpret, because Mesa was both a target and an unsuccessful bidder in the contest. Overall, Mesa had a 5.9% loss, which is puzzling, particularly because they had a gain of $80 million in the premium buyback, but the loss appeared not to be directly related to the Cities Service takeover episode.

# CASE STUDIES OF INDIVIDUAL FIRMS

Case studies of individual firms abound in the financial press, which reports repeated sagas of highly dramatic and often innovative stories. We have used these throughout the book. Here individual case studies are summarized from other published sources (see Rock, 1987).

## IC Industries

IC Industries originated as the Illinois Central Railroad, chartered in 1851. Its main line was from Chicago to New Orleans, with about 6,500 route miles in 12 states. A decision to diversify was made in the early 1960s. The goal was to enter businesses that would be less capital intensive, less labor intensive, less cyclical, less government regulated, and with better growth potentials. Because federal law prohibits railroads from owning unrelated businesses, a holding company was organized in 1962 and adopted the name IC Industries, Inc. in 1975.

In 1966 IC Industries developed its first strategic plan. It had four objectives:

1. Modernize the railroad.
2. Merge with another railroad to make IC more efficient and to enable it to expand its service in the growing industrial areas of the South.
3. Develop the company's large real estate holdings.
4. Diversify.

The Illinois Central merged with the Gulf, Mobile and Ohio Railroad reaching agreement in 1966 and obtaining final approval by the Interstate Commerce Commission and the courts in 1972. In 1965 a small builder of heavy electrical equipment was acquired and in 1968 a small manufacturer of precision castings and corrosion-resistant pumps and pumping systems was acquired. In 1968 IC Industries acquired ABEX Corp., a $275 million manufacturer of automotive products, specialty castings, hydraulic equipment, and rail products. The acquisition of ABEX doubled the size of IC Industries.

These three acquisitions were mostly in cyclical markets. To seek stability of earnings, in 1970 IC Industries acquired Pepsi-Cola General Bottlers, which had a six-state distribution franchise and sales of $100 million. With this as a base, Dad's Root Beer was acquired in 1971, Bubble-Up Company in 1973, and other Pepsi franchise operations during the 1970s and 1980s.

With further diversification as its goal, in 1972 Midas International, a Chicago-based franchiser of automotive service shops, was acquired (sales of $100 million). In 1982 the cyclical recreational vehicle manufacturing operations of Midas were divested.

IC began building a financial services group in the early 1970s, which made of small financial and life insurance companies. Subsequent developments i cial services industries indicated that a very large company was required ana tnat competition would be very strong. By 1979 IC divested all its financial service companies.

The second stage of IC's strategic program was to develop further in consumer products and to sell the railroad. In 1978 IC approached Pet, Inc., a nearly $1 billion company that marketed packaged foods and produced food store equipment under the Hussmann name. Pet management initially resisted, but finally agreed to be acquired in a cash tender offer that cost IC $406 million. Between 1978 and 1984 Pet divested 14 businesses that were viewed as "low potential" and made acquisitions of companies in baking and specialty goods and in specialty packaged foods. Eighty percent of Pet's remaining key product lines held the number one or number two position in their markets.

Stage three of IC's strategic plan was announced in 1981. It was focused on technology and market penetration. In 1982 William A. Underwood, a maker of meat spreads and baked beans, was acquired. This was an example of market penetration. Underwood also brought a strong foothold in foreign markets to be used by other food product operations in IC. In October 1984 IC acquired Pneumo Corporation. This was a $1.3 billion company producing aircraft landing gear and sophisticated flight control systems.

The main goals of IC Industries were said to have been reached with these acquisitions. IC saw itself as strong in three basic areas: specialty foods (Pet), consumer services (Midas), and commercial products (Pneumo). IC Industries felt that it had achieved growth with stability. Subsequently, in August 1988 Pneumo-ABEX was sold to the Henley Group and Wasserstein Perella. The railroad was spun off. The remaining parts of IC Industries consisted of consumer products. To emphasize this, the name was changed to Whitman Corporation in December 1988.

A review of the stock price performance of IC Industries indicates that it has indeed achieved success in its diversification program. However, some basic questions need to be raised. IC Industries appears to have violated a number of the key principles of strategy emphasized both by the Boston Consulting Group and the Porter approach. IC emphasized growth and stability. Their acquisitions did not appear to make them leaders in terms of production volume or experience or in achieving a balance of cash inflow and cash outflow activities. Furthermore, they seem to have violated the Porter emphasis on going into industries where entry barriers were high. Certainly the emphasis on diversification from a core into related activities was violated. IC Industries had virtually no experience in the three new major areas into which they moved. They did, however, appear to expand from a base into specialty foods in which they had established their initial position through the acquisition of Pet, a leader in many individual product lines.

In conclusion, IC Industries appears to have violated all of the rules but to have succeeded. This case study suggests that while the general principles would appear to be good guides most of the time, they can be violated and yet achieve a successful diversification and M&A program.

## ARA Services

ARA Services started with vending food products in 1936. Their initial product line was relatively narrow (peanuts). From very small beginnings, mergers and acquisitions played an important role in developing ARA Services into a company that by its 1984 fiscal year had revenues of $3.4 billion. In the process they completed more than 300 acquisitions.

ARA Services started with food service from vending machines. This led to a broader range of food and refreshment services for people on the job. These services were extended to students at schools and colleges, hospital patients and staff, senior citizens at community centers, air travelers, and then people engaged in leisure pursuits at parks, stadiums, resorts, and high-level restaurants. It was recognized that food services involved warehousing, inventory control, packing for shipment, distribution (routing trucks), fleet maintenance, and tight accounting and financial controls. With these basic functions, it was a natural extension of capabilities to move into magazines and book distribution. In 1984, ARA served 25,000 retail outlets providing food to hospital patients. This experience led to health care services through institutional long-term care facilities for the chronically ill and aged. A related activity is medical systems, which provide medical services for inmates in 16 correctional facilities in more than five states. Still another application is its National Child Care Centers, Inc., which manages 100 child care centers in 10 states.

Similar functions were involved in moving into various types of business services. This includes renting, maintaining, and delivering personalized work apparel and environmental control items. A related activity is managing building maintenance and inspection control programs for institutions and industry. Also, ground services are provided at 15 major airports.

The considerable warehousing and distribution activities led to a transfer division that specializes in less-than-truckload shipments and warehousing for 50,000 clients in 37 states. A fleet services division provides fleet maintenance for local governments and operates a remanufacturing center for ARA and client vehicles.

The central theme of ARA expansion was selecting the service area as a large and fast-growing economic sector. From a core of management functions ARA moved into areas in which basic functions such as distribution, warehousing, and transportation were all involved. None of these activities represent large-scale manufacturing activities of an assembly-line type. It is necessary for ARA to have a large group of qualified professional personnel. Because a large number of expert professional executives are involved, it is clear that management is an important ingredient in ARA operations. A large number of managers must be involved. It is not surprising, therefore, that in 1984 ARA engaged in an $882 million leveraged buyout. Its activities involved steady cash flows; its method of operations required involvement and motivation of a large number of managers. As we discussed in chapter 16 on LBOs, these are precisely the situations in which firms are likely to be stimulated to engage in LBOs.

## Merrill Lynch

Merrill Lynch had a clear concept of how to begin with a classification of types of acquisitions:

1. Operating acquisitions—related businesses that are bought rather than expanded from within.
2. Building block acquisitions—to acquire expertise in target areas to stimulate future internal growth.
3. Diversification acquisitions—to help move into new lines of business.
4. Networking—to combine the capabilities of two or more partners through joint ventures or through operating agreements.
5. Research and development (R&D) investments—to make investments in companies engaged in new areas as a limited-risk way to study and keep abreast of advanced technology at an early stage.

Merrill Lynch itself was formed through major mergers in the early 1940s, reflected in its early name of Merrill Lynch, Pierce, Fenner & Beane. A critical acquisition took place in 1964 when C. J. Devine, a leading government securities dealer, was purchased. This was a building block acquisition that enabled subsequent expansion into a wide variety of debt and money market instruments.

In 1968 Merrill Lynch acquired Hubbard, Westervelt & Mottelay, a specialist in net lease financing of real estate. This provided a bridge into general real estate financing and other services. It ultimately led to a Merrill Lynch realty business.

In 1969 Merrill Lynch acquired the financial management and economic consulting firm, Lionel D. Edie. This led to Merrill Lynch Asset Management, a leading sponsor and advisor of mutual funds. It also led to the development of major money market funds. Merrill Lynch Economics provides in-house economic analysis support in addition to its external consulting business.

In 1976 Merrill Lynch began to offer its securities-processing services to other firms through a separate subsidiary, Broadcort Capital Corporation. A year later it developed Cash Management Accounts through a networking arrangement with Bank One of Columbus, Ohio. In 1984 Merrill Lynch and IBM formed International MarketNet to offer an information distribution and office automation system that includes market data services, enhanced communications, software, minicomputers, and desktop computers.

As an example of R&D investments, Merrill Lynch acquired an interest in Institutional Networks (InstiNet), which operates a direct securities trading market with automated order execution. It invested in Financial News Network, which offers financial information via cable TV systems. It also invested in Comp-U-Card, a computerized buying service.

The goal of the acquisition program of Merrill Lynch was to move from a central core using a basic body of expertise into a wide range of financial services. This illustrates a standard and widely accepted philosophy of strategic diversification.

## A FRAMEWORK FOR EVALUATING M&As

From the principles set forth in previous chapters, and from a review of individual case studies, we have the basis for a framework for evaluating mergers or acquisitions. As each merger or takeover is announced, we can evaluate it by reference to the following points:

1. Is total value increased by this merger or acquisition or is total value decreased? This question uses the data on the initial market reaction to the transaction. Systematic research establishes that, on average, the initial market reaction is a good predictor of the subsequent performance of a merger or acquisition. By initial market reaction, we mean the change in market price per common share of the target company multiplied by the number of shares outstanding plus the change in market price of the acquiring company multiplied by the number of shares outstanding. This sum can be positive or negative. If the market prices of the common shares of acquiring and acquired companies all increase, total value will increase. The market value of the acquired company almost always increases because of the premium paid. So whether total value increases depends on by how much the market value per share of the acquiring firm decreases.

2. If the total market value is increased by the transaction, determine the potential sources of the value increases. Revenues may be increased, asset management may be improved, and other efficiencies may achieve cost savings. Or revenues may be increased by improved marketing or by product improvements. In mergers among financial institutions, savings may be achieved by better utilization of large investments in computer systems. Or economies may be achieved by eliminating overlapping activities. In the merger between

Boeing and McDonnell Douglas, Boeing augmented its capabilities of maintaining military business. McDonnell Douglas had excess capacity and capability for producing commercial aircraft, which could be utilized in Boeing's expanding commercial sales.

To summarize the first two questions, was value increased, and what was the source of these value increases? Are the reasons for the value gains plausible in relation to the business economics of the industry?

3. What are the obstacles that are likely to be encountered and can they be managed effectively? Are the cultures of the two companies different? How will cultural differences be managed over time? Are the cultural differences respected? What plans have been made to adjust to or assimilate cultural differences?

4. Will the companies allocate the requisite resources for successful implementation of combining the companies to achieve the potentials for cost savings and/or revenue enhancement?

These are the central issues involved in evaluating an individual merger or acquisition. Many other factors need to be taken into account as described in the detailed checklist presented in Table 22.1 in the following chapter.

---

## Summary

Sound M&A decisions take place within the broader framework of a firm's long-range planning process. Restructuring and M&A activity reflect the changing financial, economic, and competitive forces impacting industries and firms. Many of these shocks or new developments impact some industries more than others. More than 50% of M&A activity in a given time period takes place in 7 to 10 industries. The case study materials were consistent with the proposition that M&A activity is a part of the adjustment processes used by firms in the effort to realign themselves to their changing environments.

The case studies in these chapters, along with the many clinical studies of M&As that have appeared in the published literature, provide a framework for evaluating M&A decisions. This framework provides the basis for a research design for doing clinical studies of M&A transactions. It is also the framework that decision makers should employ in the analysis of whether to engage in a restructuring or in an M&A transaction as well as for use in their design and implementation. This analysis provides the basis for a prediction as to whether the total shareholder wealth effects of a restructuring or M&A transaction will be positive or negative.

Some key considerations formulated in the form of questions are:

1. Is there an opportunity for a turnaround and are the requisite managerial capabilities and incentive systems available to accomplish it?

2. Are operating synergies likely? What forms of the economies of scale or scope are likely? Are there complementarities with respect to both general management functions such as innovation, planning and control, as well as the specific management functions such as production and marketing?

3. Will there be financial synergies? Will the future cash flows of the combined firms exhibit greater stability and growth than the historical patterns of the component firms? Will debt capacity for target or optimal capital structures provide savings in financing costs and taxes?

4. Are the planning, control, and operating systems to be employed applicable to each component or segment of the combined firm? Do product characteristics, production requirements, and marketing strategies require different system designs for different segments?

5. Can the incentive systems of the component firms be harmonized? Do the incentive systems need to be different for different segments of the combined firms? Can the incentive systems employed effectively relate to the history of each segment and relate to critical requirements for motivation in the individual segments?

6. Each segment of the combined firm has a history as a sociological organization. Each segment has created its own individual cultural personality. Will these cultural differences be respected as the component firms are joined? Can the organizational structure of the combined firm accommodate the different cultural histories and patterns? Will management assign the requisite executive capabilities and talent to work toward harmonizing the cultural differences over time, preserving and developing strengths and first accommodating, then muting disharmonies?

7. Will the new organization structures preserve the diverse strengths and organization systems required for product and process innovation in changing environments? Will executive capabilities be assigned to monitor the changing economic, financial, and competitive environments? Will the information, feedback, and adjustment processes in the firm produce an environment that creates and exploits new opportunities for superiorities and new growth opportunities?

8. Will the new organization assign the requisite executive capabilities for effective implementation of the restructuring, combining, divesting, and reorganizing decisions? A merger or takeover is not completed when all the legal steps have been completed. This represents only the first step of many that must follow for completing the implementation of the decisions made. This applies equally to new programs and reorganizations that take place internally. A well-conceived organization change including a takeover or merger can fail if not effectively implemented.

9. Have other approaches to value improvements been explored? Could the firm achieve corporate renewal from internal transformations? Have the critical needs of the firm been identified? Effective management is the key to organization success if the existing management team is not achieving results. Downsizing should start with the top management team. Does it contain deadwood? Does it have the right combination of diverse skills and personalities? Have the requisite steps for improvement been identified? Which of the existing executives should be replaced? Has the best qualified executives for each management design been identified? Have efforts been made to hire the best executive talent whether from our competitors or firms in related industries or simply the best in the business world? Have all potential cost cutting efforts been pursued? Has the emphasis on efficiency and competence been extended through all levels of the organization? Can purchasing costs be reduced by changing the number and types of suppliers? Can inventory costs be reduced by innovations such as "just in time" inventory methods? Have effective quality control standards been worked out with suppliers? Can some inventories be obtained on a consignment basis? Can the number of items carried in stock be reduced by improved design and manufacturing processes? Could costs be significantly decreased by reducing the number and type of products without substantial loss of revenues? Have all sources of product definition and design been effectively explored? Has the firm optimized on its product family with respect to cost efficiency and market penetration? Have all types of outlays been evaluated with respect to their contributions to performance? Has this type of review included corporate jets, executive cars, club memberships, and subscriptions? Have consultant services contributed to a coherent long-term corporate strategy and have they made contributions to improved performance? Would the strengthening of the management team make consultant services unnecessary?

10. Having considered all of the forgoing, will the premium paid for another firm or the costs involved in a restructuring or reorganization yield sufficient savings or future cash flow improvements to make these positive net present value investments? Will the net improvement in future cash flows be sufficient to yield positive returns from the investment outlays required at the applicable cost of capital?

These and other questions should be analyzed in evaluating a prospective investment program whether internal or external. They are applicable to restructuring, reorganizing, new product or investment programs, as well as to external mergers and takeovers. This checklist of questions reflects the core of the key topics discussed in the previous 20 chapters of the book. The earlier in-depth analysis of the individual subjects has provided the basis for the key considerations for sound strategic and operating decisions. In this chapter we have used case studies to formulate and frame the key issues in the form of questions. In the concluding chapter that follows, we organize the materials in the form of management guidelines developed from rigorous studies of individual subject areas as well as in the individual clinical studies.

## Questions

21.1  Why is industry important in influencing the pace of M&A activity?

21.2  In evaluating an individual merger or takeover, why is it useful to start with an analysis of the business economics of the industry?

21.3  What does the Telecommunications Act of February 8, 1996 imply for M&A activity?

21.4  What was the motive for the original Time-Warner merger?

21.5  Why was Paramount interested in joining with Viacom?

21.6  Why are the regional Bell operating companies beginning to combine?

21.7  What was the reason for the Disney acquisition of Capital Cities/ABC?

21.8  What was the logic behind the DuPont acquisition of Conoco?

21.9  What is significant about the diversification program of the former Illinois Central Railroad?

21.10  Compare the long-range planning philosophy of ARA Services with that of IC Industries.

## References

Hilder, David B., "Court Refuses to Block Time's Plan to Buy Warner, Dealing a Blow to Paramount," *The Wall Street Journal,* July 17, 1989, p. A3.

Jarrell, Gregg A., "A Present-Value Lesson for the Lawyers," *The Wall Street Journal,* July 13, 1989, p. A10.

Landler, Mark, "A Sticking-to-Their-Knitting Deal," *New York Times,* April 23, 1996, pp. C1, C5.

Lesly, Elizabeth, "Six Months After Westinghouse Took Over, the Network May Be Waking Up," *Business Week,* June 3, 1996, pp. 32–34.

*Mergerstat Review,* 1986.

Mitchell, Mark L., and J. Harold Mulherin, "The Impact of Industry Shocks on Takeover and Restructuring Activity," *Journal of Financial Economics,* 41, June 1996, pp. 193–229.

Rock, Milton L., ed., *The Mergers & Acquisitions Handbook,* New York: McGraw-Hill Book Company, 1987.

Ruback, Richard S., "The Conoco Takeover and Stockholder Returns," *Sloan Management Review,* 23, Winter 1982, pp. 13–33.

———, "The Cities Service Takeover: A Case Study," *Journal of Finance,* 38, May 1983, pp. 319–330.

# CHAPTER

## 22

# Management Guides for M&As and Strategies

Any organization or individual is subject to continuing changes. The economic, political, cultural, and international environments are turbulent. Technologies and processes advance. Interactions with competitors, suppliers, customers, complementary firms, and a wide range of stakeholders must be adjusted. Sometimes the adjustments required are massive, sometimes they represent only fine-tuning. But continuous adjustments are necessary for both organizations and individuals.

## M&As IN A STRATEGIC LONG-RANGE PLANNING FRAMEWORK

Sometimes M&A activities can help a firm in improving its capabilities and performance; but sometimes M&A activities would represent a diversion from the fundamental adjustments that must be made. M&A planning must fit into the framework of the firm's overall strategic planning processes (Chung and Weston, 1982; Weston, 1970).

### Goals and Objectives

General goals may be formulated with respect to size, growth, stability, flexibility, and technological breadth. Size objectives are established in order to use effectively the fixed factors the firm owns or buys. Size objectives have also been expressed in terms of critical mass. Critical mass refers to the size a firm must achieve in order to attain cost levels that will enable the firm to operate profitably at market prices.

Growth objectives may be expressed in terms of sales, total assets, earnings per share, or the market price of the firm's stock. These are related to two valuation objectives. One is to attain a favorable price/earnings multiple for the firm's shares. A second is to increase the ratio of the market value of a firm's common stock to its book value.

Three major forms of instability can be distinguished. The first is exemplified by the defense market, which is subject to large, erratic fluctuations in its total size and abrupt shifts in individual programs. Another form of instability is the cyclical instability that characterizes producers of both industrial and consumer durable goods. Other instabilities are major discontinuities of the type that have taken place in the computer and media industries.

The goal of flexibility refers to the firm's ability to adjust to a wide variety of changes. Such flexibility may require a breadth of research, manufacturing, or marketing capabilities. Of increased interest in recent years is technological breadth. With the increased pace of technological change in the U.S. economy, a firm may consider it important to possess capabilities in the rapidly advancing technologies.

Goals may be stated in general or specific terms, but both are subject to quantification. For example, growth objectives may be expressed in relationship to the growth of the economy or the firm's industry. Specific objectives may be expressed in terms of percentage of sales in specified types of markets. The quantification of goals facilitates comparisons of goals with forecasts of the prospects for the firm. If it is necessary for the firm to alter its product-market mix or range of capabilities to reduce or close the planning gap, a diversification strategy may be formulated.

Efforts to achieve multiple goals suggest a broader range of variables in the decision processes of the firm. Decisions involve trade-offs and judgments of the nature of future environments, the policies of other firms with respect to the dimensions described, and new missions, technologies, and capabilities. In short, to the requirements of operating efficiency and optimal output adjustments has been added the increased importance of the planning processes (Weston, 1972; Weston and Copeland, 1992).

## The Role of Strategy

The literature views long-range planning and strategic planning as essentially synonymous (Steiner, 1979). The emphasis of strategic planning is on areas related to the firm's environments and constituencies, not just operating decisions (Summer, 1980). In our view, the modern literature on long-range planning indicates that long-range strategic planning involves at least the following elements:

1. Environmental reassessment.
2. A consideration of capabilities, missions, and environmental interaction from the standpoint of the firm and its divisions.
3. An emphasis on process rather than particular goals or objectives.
4. An emphasis on iteration and on an iterative feedback process as a methodology for dealing with ill-structured problems.
5. A recognition of the need for coordination and consistency in the resulting long-range planning processes with respect to individual divisions, product-market activities, and optimization from the standpoint of the firms as a whole.
6. A recognition of needs to relate effectively to the firm's changing environment and constituencies.
7. Integration of the planning process into a reward and penalty or incentive system, taking a long-range time perspective.

Earlier, the emphasis of long-range strategic planning was on doing something about the so-called gap. When it is necessary to take action to close a prospective gap between the firm's objectives and its potential based on its present capabilities, difficult choices must be made. For example, shall the firm attempt to change its environment or capabilities? What will be the costs of such changes? What are the risks and unknowns? What are the rewards if successful? What are the penalties of failure? Because the stakes are large, the iterative process is employed. A tentative decision is made. The process is repeated, perhaps from a different management function orientation, and at some point the total enterprise point of view is brought to bear on the problem. At some point, decisions are made and must involve entrepreneurial judgments.

Alternatively, the emphasis may be on broader orientations to the effective alignment of the firm with its environments and constituencies. Different approaches may be emphasized. One approach seeks to choose products related to the needs or missions of the customer that will provide large markets. A second approach focuses on technological bottlenecks or barriers, the solution of which may create new markets. A third strategy chooses to be at the frontiers of technological capabilities on the theory that attractive product fallout will result from such competence. A fourth approach emphasizes economic criteria including attractive growth prospects and appropriate stability.

Other things being equal, a preferred strategy is to move into a diversification program from the base of existing capabilities or organizational strengths. Guidance may be obtained by answers to the following questions: Is there strength in the general management functions? Can the company provide staff expertise in a wide range of areas? Does the firm's financial planning and control effectiveness have a broad carry-over? Are there specific capabilities such as research, marketing, and manufacturing that the firm is seeking to spread over a wider arena?

The firm should be clear on its strengths, its limitations, and the changing environments in which it operates. To remedy weaknesses, the firm should clearly define the specific new capabilities it is seeking to obtain. If the firm does not possess a sufficient breadth of capability to use as a basis for moving into other areas, an alternative strategy may be employed, one that would establish a beachhead of capabilities in one or more selected areas. The firm is then in a position to develop concentrically from each of these nuclei.

Changing product requirements and changing product-market opportunities require new technologies and new combinations of technologies. To illustrate, the aircraft industry moved through stages in which the critical competence shifted from structures, to engine and other propulsion methods, to guidance, and finally to the interaction of structures, propulsion, and guidance as reflected in the concept of aerospace systems. Similarly, in office equipment, products have moved from manual operation to electromechanical, to electric, to electronic, and to the interactions of specialized units in systems. Electronics technology has moved from electron tube to semiconductors to integrated circuitry, involving a fusion with chemistry and metallurgy. Competitive factors caused Intel to drop its production of memory chips and to focus its resources on microprocessors.

In the consumer nondurable-goods industries, product changes have characteristically been labeled product differentiation, with the unfavorable connotation that fundamental characteristics of products have not altered. Yet even in these industries, fluctuations in consumer income patterns and tastes have created needs and opportunities for basic changes. For example, the need to understand the nature of the impact of foods on people has increased the requirements for competence in the chemical and biological sciences in food industries.

## The Role of Planning

A number of misconceptions are held with respect to the significance of planning in the firm. The misconceptions range between two extremes. One view holds that we have always planned, that planning is nothing new, as the practice antedates biblical times. This view misses the real significance of modern planning, however. Certainly business firms have been planning for decades, with accounting and financial budgeting activities representing one kind of planning. But the important developments that set the new managerial technology of planning apart from its predecessor activities are (1) coordinating research, sales, production, marketing, facilities, personnel, and financial plans, making them consistent with one another, and resolving them into comprehensive planning for the enterprise as a whole; (2) a feedback system; and

(3) integration with a reward and penalty (incentive) system. Some U.S. firms developed and practiced such integrated and coordinated planning by the 1920s, but the broad extension of the practice did not occur until after World War II, with substantial gaps still persisting in the understanding and implementation of effective planning among a large number of firms.

The other erroneous view about business planning holds that the heavy investments of capital by large corporations have led them to devise methods for controlling demand and that planning has replaced the market mechanism. Such a view has led one author to sweeping generalizations, unsupported by systematic evidence, such as the following: "It is a feature of all planning that, unlike the market, it incorporates within itself no mechanism by which demand is accommodated to supply and the reverse" (Galbraith, 1967, p. 35).

This statement represents a basic misconception. Those with experience with purposive organization planning processes recognize that the development of integrated planning is an effort to adapt more responsively to increasingly dynamic environments. Planning and management controls do not remove the uncertainty of market influences; rather, they seek to help the firm adjust more sensitively to change, to new threats, and to opportunities.

## Managerial Capabilities Perspective

The capabilities concept encompasses important management technologies including planning, information sciences, computerization of information flows, formal decision models, problem-solving methodologies, and behavioral sciences. Thus, managerial capabilities include competence in the general management functions of planning, organizing, directing, and controlling, as well as in the specific management functions of research, production, personnel, marketing, and finance. In addition, they include a range of technological capabilities. Another important dimension is coordinating and achieving an effective organization system.

The development of such a range of capabilities requires substantial investments in the training and experience of people. This includes investments required to hold organizations together during periods of depressed sales. Market demand and supply forces place a high value on executive talent and staff expertise. Their importance in the competitive performance of firms leads to new forms of fixed investment in managerial organizations. The effective utilization of augmented fixed factors leads to firms of larger size and increased diversification. (Fixed factors are investments in plant and equipment or costs of specialist executives.)

The theory of the firm set forth by Coase (1937) predicts these developments. In explaining the role of firms in relation to markets, Coase identified two functions as determinants of the scope and size of firms. One was the relative efficiency of effecting transactions within the firm compared to transactions conducted in the external marketplace. The other was the effectiveness with which the elements of the firm were coordinated or managed. Coase described possible developments that would affect the size of firms compared to the relative scope of market transactions. Coase's model predicts that the broadening of capabilities encompassed by a firm and developments in managerial technology will result in both an increase in the absolute size of business firms and in the degree of their diversification with respect to capabilities, missions, and markets.

Potential competition has thus been enlarged. Industry boundaries defined by products become less meaningful than industries defined by the ability to perform the critical functions for meeting customers' needs or missions. The ease of entry is increased because the critical factor for success in changing environments may be a range of technologies, experience developed in international markets, or even more general organizational performance capabilities.

Because of the critical role of managerial capabilities some firms have emphasized hiring key executives rather than buying companies. While this policy may have some validity on theoretical grounds, it can also stir up ill will from the companies that have been raided. Companies that have succeeded in hiring new top executives with recognized capabilities have experienced an immediate increase in the market value of their common stock.

## A COMPREHENSIVE CHECKLIST FOR SOUND M&A DECISIONS

The implementation of the guidelines for sound M&A planning can usefully employ a checklist that takes into account the many factors involved in M&A activities. This checklist outlines the requirements for sound M&A transactions. It serves as a summary of the many topics discussed throughout the book.

We shall not review the checklist in Table 22.1 item by item. The main thrust is that a sound M&A transaction requires consideration of many factors.

Of central importance is the understanding that M&As should fit into the broad framework of the firm's overall strategic planning processes. The basic elements of strategic planning include an assessment of the firm's environment and an analysis of the firm's resources and capabilities as they relate to the environment. Goals are formulated, and adjustments, which may include mergers and acquisitions, are made to move the firm closer to these goals. The process is never complete, but rather performed iteratively as the firm's capabilities and environments change over time.

Increasingly, firms are defined less in terms of products and markets, and more as a range of capabilities. This creates both opportunities and increasing competitive threats in a dynamic economy. M&As provide a means of preserving the organization capital of those firms that have been less able to adapt to change. They allow more successful firms to acquire needed capabilities faster and with less risk than developing them internally. Even pure conglomerate M&As that start with transferability of only generic management capabilities provide an avenue for the eventual development of increased skills in specific management functions such as production and marketing.

Systematic studies of M&As enable us to draw a number of conclusions:

1. Value is created by mergers, takeovers, and restructuring; acquired firm shareholders gain 25 to 35% of equity value, on average, and acquiring firm shareholders do not lose, on average.
2. M&A profitability and activity is positively correlated with GNP growth and favorable investment opportunities.
3. The use of M&As to achieve firm goals is affected by the availability of alternative investment opportunities.
4. Financial variables (including relative costs of capital, monetary stringency, and risk premiums) are more important for pure conglomerate mergers than for product or market extension mergers.
5. Leverage generally increases following M&As.

M&A decisions involve the use of principles from finance, business economics, and strategy in a dynamic framework. It recognizes multiple dimensions of successful business operations. Operating activities must be efficient, but efficient operations must be a part of sound planning processes. The firm must continuously adjust to its changing

**TABLE 22.1**   Guides for Sound M&A Transactions

I. M&A program must be a part of long-range strategic planning. The framework:
1. What are the revolutionary challenges and opportunities potentially available to the firm?
2. Assessment of changes in the environments—competitive, technological, political.
3. Evaluation of company capabilities and limitations.
4. Assessment of expectations of stakeholders.
5. Analysis of company, competitors, industries, economies.
6. Relations with suppliers.
7. Relations with complementary firms.
8. Formulation of the missions, goals, and policies.
9. Development of sensitivity to critical possible changes.
10. Formulation of internal organization performance measurements.
11. Formulation of long-range and short-run strategies.
12. Organization and funding for implementation.
13. Information flow and feedback system for adjustments.

II. Rigorous search procedures.
1. What are our weaknesses and where do we have to improve?
2. What companies can help us or how can we help them?
3. How can we build a family of companies that will give strength to one another?

III. Either our company or our target needs some restructuring.
1. Consider research, production, marketing, resource management, product improvement, new products.
2. Be sure we are strong in the critical parts of the value chain.
3. Asset management.
4. Liability management.

IV. Financial engineering.
1. Improve the market for our equity stock.
2. Improve the sources and relationships for obtaining debt money—senior and mezzanine financing.

V. Management synergy.
1. Fill gaps in managerial capabilities and extend capabilities.
2. Augment our firm's resources in multiple dimensions.
3. Our management cultures must be harmonious in the long run.
4. Think through how the two management systems will fit together.
5. Maybe some managers or executives will have to come from other companies or go to other companies.
6. Will the acquired unit be worth more as a part of our firm than alone or with any other firm?
7. What are the new developments that will benefit our firm or require adjustments?

VI. Due diligence.
1. Examine all aspects of prospective partners.
2. Be sure there are no legal problems—pension funding, environmental or product liabilities.
3. Are the accounting records meaningful?
4. Has equipment been maintained properly?
5. Is our equipment modern enough and in sufficient quantity to be ahead of competition?
6. Can we control costs to be competitive?
7. Do we have quality products that people want?

**TABLE 22.1**   *(cont.)*

VII.   Valuation.
1. Consider future cash flows of acquiring and acquired firms separately and combined.
2. How will the cash flows change in quality and time patterns?
3. What does the nature of the cash flows imply for the appropriate discount or capitalization factor to apply?
4. Will value be increased by the combination?
5. Sources of value increase:
a. reduced costs
b. new products
c. better products.
6. Will the management group be stronger?
7. Valuation in relation to other recent transactions.
8. Valuation in relation to other groups of companies.

VIII.   Integration and implementation.
1. Postmerger coordination—a top management responsibility.
2. Give managers incentives to stay.
3. Continuously review how the implementation process is going.
4. Have our capabilities and resources been augmented?

IX.   Life after the merger.
1. What will our company look like?
2. How will it compare with its competitors?
3. Where are we in the value chain?
4. What is our management system for future improvements?
5. How can we stay alert to finding weaknesses and eliminating them?

---

economic, financial, political, and social environments. It must adjust to, as well as be proactive toward, potential competitors, suppliers, customers, and complementary firms. A successful firm must be a part of the processes that involve many change forces, such as changes in technology, changes in production processes, changes in product quality, new products, and changes in the organization of industry. It is within this broad framework that M&A decisions are made and contribute to increases in the value of organizations.

## THE RULES FOR SUCCESSFUL MERGERS

In his editorial page article in the *Wall Street Journal* of October 15, 1981, Peter F. Drucker set forth "The Five Rules for Successful Acquisition." He noted that the current merger movement in the United States paralleled the tremendous wave of acquisitions in Germany in 1920–1922, a period of chronic inflation that preceded the chaotic hyperinflation of 1923. He then went on to observe that during periods of severe inflation, fixed assets can be purchased by buying companies at market prices that are well below book value and even further below replacement costs. The low stock market valuations of companies over the past decade, he argued, were due in large part to sustained underdepreciation of assets because of tax regulations. The basic impetus driving increased merger activity under inflation was said to be the general flight by businesspersons and investors out of money and into hard assets.

### Drucker's Merger Rules

But although Drucker (1981) saw the stimulus for the most recent merger wave as primarily a financial one, he also argues that economically sensible mergers must follow the Drucker five commandments for successful acquisitions:

1. Acquirer must contribute something to the acquired company.
2. A common core of unity is required.
3. Acquirer must respect the business of the acquired company.
4. Within a year or so, acquiring company must be able to provide top management to the acquired company.
5. Within the first year of merger, managements in both companies should receive promotions across the entities.

Drucker supports his prescriptions by selected examples of successes and failures. The limitation of such a method of proof, of course, is that propositions derived from individual case studies often do not have general validity. There are, however, a large number of systematic empirical studies of mergers that have been performed during the last two decades. We found a consistency of their findings with Drucker's analysis and prescriptions for acquisitions.

The dollar value of merger and acquisition activity in the United States in recent years has averaged about 30% of new plant and equipment expenditures. This relationship, furthermore, is statistically significant. Thus, merger activity appears to be subject to the same influences as investment activity generally, and this suggests that there has been some economic rationale to merger activity in recent years in the United States. In short, mergers appear to be influenced by the availability of alternative investment opportunities and, more specifically, by the relative costs of merger as compared with direct internal expansion. These investment incentives, however, operate differently in different economic environments.

### Extending the Rules

Examination of the evidence, however, suggests that the Drucker rules may be unduly restrictive if interpreted too literally. In essence, the Drucker rules can be boiled down to two statements: (1) merging companies must have activities that are related in some way, and (2) well-structured incentives and rewards must be held out to the management of both firms to help make the merger work, although the acquiring firm should be prepared to cover the departure of the key management of acquired companies.

A less restrictive interpretation of these rules would include the following commentary on the Drucker pentalogue.

1. Relatedness is a necessary requirement, but complementarities are an even greater virtue. For example, combining a company strong in research but weak in marketing with a company strong in marketing but weak in research may bring blessings to both.
2. Relatedness or complementarities may apply to general management functions such as research, planning and control, and financial management as well as to the more firm-specific operating functions such as production and marketing. This perspective widely increases the basis for relatedness. Thus, companies with cash flows or managerial capabilities in excess of their investment opportunities or available capacity could effectively combine with companies lacking the financial or managerial resources to make the most of the prospects for growth and profits in their industries.
3. Even if the previous rules are followed, an acquiring firm will experience negative returns if it pays too much. It is difficult to fully and accurately evaluate another organization.

There may be great surprises on both sides after the marriage, and the problems of implementing complementarities may be substantial. The uncertainty associated with acquisitions is likely to be greater than the uncertainty attending internal investments made in product market areas more directly related to the firm's current activities. The external investments may appear to offer higher rates of return. But financial theory tells us that higher returns on average are associated with higher risks. The prospective high returns from a merger must be based on real economies, whether operating or financial, expected from the combination. Further, the expectation that a firm can improve the average risk-return relationship in an unfamiliar market or industry is likely to be disappointed.

Anslinger and Copeland (1996) suggest an alternative framework for making seemingly unrelated acquisitions. They studied in depth 21 successful acquirers of two types: diversified corporate acquirers and financial buyers such as leveraged buyout firms. These companies made a total of 829 acquisitions since the early 1980s. While many of the acquisitions seem to be unrelated in some respects, successful acquirers focused on a common theme. Clayton, Dubilier & Rice stockpiled management capabilities used to make turnarounds. Another financial buyer, Desai Capital Management, focused on retail-related industries. Emerson Electric Company looked for companies with a core competence in component manufacturing to exploit cost-control capabilities. Sara Lee used branding and retailing as its common thread.

Anslinger and Copeland identified the successful acquirers as those which substantially outperformed benchmarks such as the Standard & Poor's 500 and the Morgan Stanley capital international indices by almost 50% during a recent 10-year period. They appeared to employ seven key principles:

1. Acquire companies with a track record of innovative operating strategies.
2. Capable managerial talent is most important for creating values. If current executives are not capable of increasing value, look for managers within the organization who are not yet in leadership positions and/or hire outstanding talent from other firms.
3. Use strong incentive compensation systems such as stock purchase programs so that top managers have holdings in the company which represent a large part of their net worth.
4. Link compensation incentives to future changes in cash flow.
5. Push the pace of change to make turnarounds happen within the first two years of the takeover.
6. Develop information and feedback systems that promote continuing dynamic relationships among owners, managers, and the board.
7. Acquiring firms must use executives with expertise and demonstrated successful experience as deal makers. Their judgments are often critical to the success or failure of the transaction.

The above guidelines are consistent with themes that we have developed throughout this book. They provide useful inputs to the summary guidelines we now set forth.

## GENERAL GUIDELINES

Both the case studies and systematic empirical studies suggest the following guidelines for successful merger and acquisition activity:

1. The M&A program must be part of long-range strategic planning.
2. Recognize that in seeking new areas with higher growth potentials and improved opportunities for value enhancement, internal investments and restructuring can be used in conjunction with external investments and M&A activity.

3. Know the industry and its competitive environment as a basis for making projections for the future.

4. Be sure there is an element of relatedness, but don't be too restrictive in defining the scope of potential relatedness.

5. Combine firms that have relatively unique relationships that other firms cannot match, thus avoiding multiple bids that drive up the price of the target to excessively high levels. The acquired unit should be worth more as part of our firm than alone or with some other firm.

6. There is a time to buy. There is a time to sell. Sometimes a firm may seek to augment its position in an industry by acquiring related firms. If the prices received by sellers reflect overoptimistic expectations, it may make sense to reverse the strategy and become a seller rather than a buyer.

7. Top executives must be involved in M&A activity as well as other major investment programs.

8. Combining two companies is an activity involving substantial trauma and readjustment. Therefore, a strong emphasis on maintaining and enhancing managerial rewards and incentives is required in the postmerger period. The managements of all the companies combined in a merger must receive incentives to stay and to make contributions to the combined company.

9. Communicate as soon as possible when major investment and restructuring decisions are made.

10. Postmerger coordination must be another top management responsibility. This does not happen automatically. Top executives must be involved as well as all members of the organization.

11. For future promotions, distinctions based on employment in different segments of the company should disappear. If employees have to be separated, it should be done in an enlightened way as possible including assistance with insurance coverages and placement activities. This is ethically sound behavior and has an important impact on the future morale and culture of the firm.

12. Managing the integration of cultures and coordinating all the systems and informal processes of the combining firms are absolute musts. Cultural integration usually works best when the combining firms have similar cultures. When cultures are greatly different, each should be respected for its values. Initially, each component company may be encouraged to operate within its own culture. As each component learns to appreciate the strengths and weaknesses of cultural differences, a blended culture may develop over time.

13. The risk of mistakes stemming from wishful thinking are especially great in mergers. The planning may be sound from the standpoint of business or financial complementarities or relatedness. But if the aquiring firm pays too much, the result will be a negative net present value investment.

14. The restructuring and renewal requirements for an organization represent a continuing challenge to be addressed in the firm's strategic planning processes.

---

## Questions

22.1 What are the basic principles to keep in mind in mergers and acquisitions planning?

22.2 According to Coase, what are the determinants of the scope and size of firms?

22.3 How can the comprehensive checklist in Table 22.1 be used in implementing sound M&A decisions?

22.4 What are Drucker's rules for successful mergers?

22.5 List and discuss general guidelines for successful M&A planning and implementation.

------------------------------------ C A S E   22–1 ------------------------------------

# Analysis and Evaluation of Dean Witter Discover's Merger with Morgan Stanley*

## OVERVIEW OF DEAL TERMS

In a friendly bid on February 5, 1997, Dean Witter Discover & Co. ("DWD" or "the bidder") announced that it would be merging with Morgan Stanley Group Inc. ("MS" or "the target"), creating a leading global financial services firm with a market capitalization above $23 billion and leading positions in three businesses: securities, asset management, and credit services. The new company will be named Morgan Stanley, Dean Witter, Discover & Company. This transaction will knock Merrill Lynch from the number one spot in market capitalization and assets under management. The new entity will have a total of $270 billion in assets under management including mutual funds and individual accounts, the most of any securities firm.

### Expected Completion Date

The combination is expected to be completed in mid-1997. However, joint research efforts on 2,000 stocks had begun even before the merger became final.

### Price and Tax Treatment

DWD will make a tax-free exchange of 1.65 of its shares for each MS share. Many believe that DWD got a good deal, paying 11 times MS's 1996 profits and about two times book value. Regional banks have fetched as much as 15 times profits or three times book value, while Banc One paid about 18 times profits for First USA, a credit-card company.

### Accounting

The merger will be accounted for as a pooling of interests.

### Management

Richard B. Fisher, Morgan Stanley's chairman, will become chairman of the executive committee of the new firm's board of 14 directors, half drawn from DWD and half from MS. Phillip J. Purcell, DWD's top executive, will become chairman and chief executive of the combined company. His number two will be John J. Mack, now MS's president.

The merger is expected to be accretive to earnings per share (EPS) for the merged company. Each company has also granted the other an option to acquire shares representing 19.9% of its outstanding shares if a higher bidder comes along, in addition to a $250 million breakup fee. The deal, which was two years in the making, is the biggest ever between two Wall Street firms.

## COMPARISON OF MS's AND DWD's BUSINESSES

### MS

Morgan Stanley is a major international securities brokerage firm. Its principal businesses include securities underwriting, distribution, and trading; merchant banking; mergers and acquisitions; stock brokerage and research services; asset management; real estate; and trading of futures, options, foreign exchange, and commodities. Its foreign operations account for about 50% of its net revenues. It concentrates on serving very wealthy investors and underwriting securities for big corporations.

### DWD

Dean Witter Discover is a diversified financial services organization operating in three main businesses: full-service brokerage, credit services and asset management. Its Discover card is used by roughly 36.1 million accounts and 2.5 million merchants. Additionally, it is a full-service brokerage firm with about $80 billion under administration, servicing primarily retail clients.

---

*This case was written with Angela Zvinakis in early March, 1997. The merger was completed on May 28, 1997, but we will retain the write-up we developed shortly after the merger plan was announced.

The table below contrasts the companies' businesses:

| | Capital | Retail Brokers | Institutional Brokers | Domestic Offices | International Offices | Customer Accounts |
|---|---|---|---|---|---|---|
| MS | $15.7 B | 402 | 268 | 10 | 25 | 70,000 |
| DWD | $ 1.6 B | 8,406 | 169 | 353 | 1 | 3.1 million |

Source: USA Today, February 6, 1997.

## HISTORY OF THE DEAL

Morgan Stanley had been interested in a merger for a while. Three years earlier, it discussed and then dropped a possible merger with S.G. Warburg & Company, the London merchant bank. The history between MS and DWD is also an extended one. Morgan Stanley helped take DWD public in June 1993 and also advised Sears when it reorganized and spun off the brokerage firm. Moreover, MS and DWD had discussed working together intermittently during the last three years. They had also discussed how to structure contractual relationships in which securities underwritten by MS bankers could be sold by DWD brokers. This was the true precursor to the merger.

## THE FINANCIAL SERVICES INDUSTRY "SHAKE OUT"

The securities brokerage industry has performed remarkably well in 1996. See Table 22.2 for some key statistics on brokerages and investment banks in 1996. Continued pressure for superior performance in the financial services industry has led to an increase in merger activity, especially in the banking sector. No wonder DWD eyed MS in the wake of its impressive 1996 performance. Several factors explain the recent surge in merger activity in the industry:

- The growing power of the retail market, particularly led by the postwar baby-boom generation, has caught the attention of Wall Street. This sector is where much of the growth will come from in the future. The common belief is that greater profits can be achieved by putting under one roof the underwriting of stocks and bonds for corporate clients and the sale of stocks, bonds, and mutual funds to individual investors.

- Competition will intensify when commercial banks gain a bigger foothold in the securities industry as the rules on underwriting are loosened this year. (Elements of the Depression-era Glass-Steagall Act will be further relaxed later in 1997.) The Federal Reserve has decided to raise the proportion of revenues that banks can derive from a securities subsidiary from 10 to 25%.

- As the market becomes more globalized, Wall Street now believes that the key is to join a well-run distrib-

| TABLE 22.2 | 1996 Performance of Selected Brokerages and Investment Banks, for the Twelve Months Ended 12/31/96 |
|---|---|

| Company | ROE | Sales Growth | EPS Growth | Sales ($mm) | Net Income ($mm) | Profit Margin |
|---|---|---|---|---|---|---|
| Schwab | 33.20% | 33.60% | 31.50% | 2,167 | 217 | 10.00% |
| Raymond James | 24.30% | 30.30% | 40.80% | 722 | 66 | 9.10% |
| Alex. Brown | 29.30% | 45.40% | 71.40% | 1,042 | 150 | 14.40% |
| A.G. Edwards | 18.20% | 26.30% | 39.20% | 1,603 | 201 | 12.50% |
| Merrill Lynch | 23.00% | 14.50% | 56.80% | 23,703 | 1,478 | 6.20% |
| Bear Stearns | 19.20% | 27.60% | 79.70% | 5,126 | 505 | 9.90% |
| MS* | 20.90% | 17.40% | 178.70% | 12,720 | 980 | 7.70% |
| Paine Webber | 21.20% | 12.60% | N/A | 5,611 | 332 | 5.90% |
| Salomon Brothers | 20.20% | 13.30% | 500.0+% | 9,165 | 847 | 9.20% |
| Lehman Bros. | 8.60% | 11.10% | 74.20% | 14,061 | 357 | 2.50% |

Source: Forbes, January 13, 1997.

*Before any consideration of merger with DWD.

ution network with an investment bank in order to distribute successfully globally.

- Several analysts also believe that the industry is currently suffering from overcrowding. For the level of returns available, there is too much capital in the business.

## Possible Future Targets

Many believe that Paine Webber Group, Lehman Brothers, and Salomon Brothers must find partners if they want to compete against the full-service giants that are coming to dominate the financial services industry. Another potential target is the Equitable Companies' Donaldson, Lufkin & Jenrette unit. Additionally, investment banks or commercial banks might also consider A.G. Edwards with its fifth largest retail network in the country.

Goldman, Sachs & Company is rumored to be partnering with Citicorp in the near future. Other commercial banks, like Chase Manhattan, may buy brokerage houses as the regulatory barriers come down. Prudential Securities may even be put up for sale to take advantage of the high prices currently being offered in the industry.

## Recent Industry Developments

- Salomon Brothers announced an alliance in January 1997 with Fidelity Investments. Fidelity will gain access to Salomon's stock offerings, whereas Salomon can now reach a retail network with 6.1 million customers.
- Citicorp and American Express discussed a merger late in 1996 and then disregarded the idea.
- PIMCO recently opened 12 of its mutual funds to individual investors.
- Brown Bros. Harriman announced that it would sell its stock funds through the mutual-fund supermarkets.

## FINANCIAL ANALYSIS OF THE MERGER

### Stock Market's Reaction to the Merger

The table below details the stock market's reaction to the announcement on February 5, 1997, and the combined equity values of the new entity:

| | MS Close | DWD Close | MS Shares | DWD Shares | MS Equity Value | DWD Equity Value | Total |
|---|---|---|---|---|---|---|---|
| Feb. 4, 1997 | $57.375 | $38.625 | 152,428,000 | 321,514,000 | 8,745,556,500 | 12,418,478,250 | 21,164,034,750 |
| Feb 5, 1997 | $65.250 | $40.625 | 152,428,000 | 321,514,000 | 9,945,927,000 | 13,061,506,250 | 23,007,433,250 |
| Value created | | | | | $1,200,370,500 | $643,028,000 | $1,843,398,500 |

The new company will have a stock market value of $23 billion, as seen in the table above. On February 5, 1997, DWD's shareholders, in aggregate, gained approximately $600 million. MS's shareholders gained approximately $1.2 billion! Combined, $1.8 billion was created in market value on February 5, 1997, from this announcement. The table above also shows how the market prices of the individual stocks adjusted in order to reflect the exchange ratio proposed by DWD: 1.65 shares of DWD for each share of MS. On February 5, 1.65 shares of DWD were valued at $67.03, and 1 share of MS shot up to $65.25. Thus, the values were almost equated. MS's stock did not adjust fully (to $67.03) because there still remained the possibility that the deal would not go through.

### Shareholder Returns

In Table 22.3 and Figure 22.1 are calculated the returns for MS shareholders and DWD shareholders for the 30 days preceding the merger announcement and the 12 days after the merger announcement. The findings are summarized in the table below:

| | MS: Target | DWD: Bidder | S&P 500 |
|---|---|---|---|
| 44-day total return: from −30 to 12 | 16.65% | 20.37% | 8.48% |
| Runup: Return from −30 to −1 | 0.22% | 14.44% | 5.57% |
| Announcement day return: Return from −1 to 0 | 13.73% | 5.18% | −1.39% |
| Markup: Return from 0 to 12 | 2.35% | 0.00% | 4.11% |
| Cumulative abnormal return | 8.44% | 10.91% | N/A |

**TABLE 22.3**   Returns to MS and DWD Shareholders and to the S&P 500 Index

| Day | | Price | *MS* Actual | Predicted* | Residual | Price | *DWD* Actual | Predicted* | Residual | *S&P 500* Level | Return |
|---|---|---|---|---|---|---|---|---|---|---|---|
| | −30 | 57.2500 | | | | 33.7500 | | | | 746.92 | |
| | −29 | 58.3750 | 1.97% | 0.55% | 1.41% | 33.8750 | 0.37% | 0.55% | −0.18% | 751.03 | 0.55% |
| | −28 | 59.0000 | 1.07% | 0.64% | 0.43% | 33.6875 | −0.55% | 0.64% | −1.19% | 755.82 | 0.64% |
| | −27 | 58.8750 | −0.21% | 0.13% | −0.34% | 33.6250 | −0.19% | 0.13% | −0.31% | 756.79 | 0.13% |
| | −26 | 58.8750 | 0.00% | −0.39% | 0.39% | 33.8125 | 0.56% | −0.39% | 0.95% | 753.85 | −0.39% |
| | −25 | 57.1250 | −2.97% | −1.74% | −1.23% | 33.1250 | −2.03% | −1.74% | −0.29% | 740.74 | −1.74% |
| | −24 | 56.1250 | −1.75% | −0.50% | −1.25% | 33.1250 | 0.00% | −0.50% | 0.50% | 737.01 | −0.50% |
| | −23 | 56.3750 | 0.45% | 1.50% | −1.05% | 33.8125 | 2.08% | 1.50% | 0.58% | 748.03 | 1.50% |
| | −22 | 56.5000 | 0.22% | −0.05% | 0.27% | 33.8125 | 0.00% | −0.05% | 0.05% | 747.65 | −0.05% |
| | −21 | 56.0000 | −0.88% | 0.75% | −1.63% | 34.0000 | 0.55% | 0.75% | −0.19% | 753.23 | 0.75% |
| | −20 | 56.0000 | 0.00% | −0.64% | 0.64% | 33.6250 | −1.10% | −0.64% | −0.46% | 748.41 | −0.64% |
| | −19 | 55.8750 | −0.22% | 0.86% | −1.08% | 34.0625 | 1.30% | 0.86% | 0.44% | 754.85 | 0.86% |
| | −18 | 55.3750 | −0.89% | 0.62% | −1.51% | 33.8750 | −0.55% | 0.62% | −1.17% | 759.50 | 0.62% |
| | −17 | 54.3750 | −1.81% | 0.00% | −1.81% | 34.2500 | 1.11% | 0.00% | 1.11% | 759.51 | 0.00% |
| | −16 | 55.5000 | 2.07% | 1.23% | 0.84% | 35.1250 | 2.55% | 1.23% | 1.32% | 768.86 | 1.23% |
| | −15 | 55.1250 | −0.68% | −0.22% | −0.46% | 34.2500 | −2.49% | −0.22% | −2.28% | 767.20 | −0.22% |
| | −14 | 54.6250 | −0.91% | 0.25% | −1.16% | 34.6250 | 1.09% | 0.25% | 0.84% | 769.15 | 0.25% |
| | −13 | 56.5000 | 3.43% | 0.91% | 2.52% | 35.5000 | 2.53% | 0.91% | 1.61% | 776.17 | 0.91% |
| | −12 | 57.3750 | 1.55% | 0.07% | 1.48% | 36.5000 | 2.82% | 0.07% | 2.75% | 776.70 | 0.07% |
| | −11 | 57.2500 | −0.22% | 0.78% | −0.99% | 37.1250 | 1.71% | 0.78% | 0.94% | 782.72 | 0.78% |
| | −10 | 57.2500 | 0.00% | 0.45% | −0.45% | 38.0000 | 2.36% | 0.45% | 1.91% | 786.23 | 0.45% |
| | −9 | 57.2500 | 0.00% | −1.10% | 1.10% | 37.5000 | −1.32% | −1.10% | −0.21% | 777.56 | −1.10% |
| | −8 | 57.3750 | 0.22% | −0.91% | 1.12% | 37.2500 | −0.67% | −0.91% | 0.24% | 770.52 | −0.91% |
| | −7 | 56.6250 | −1.31% | −0.71% | −0.59% | 37.0000 | −0.67% | −0.71% | 0.04% | 765.02 | −0.71% |
| | −6 | 56.2500 | −0.66% | 0.00% | −0.66% | 36.6250 | −1.01% | 0.00% | −1.01% | 765.02 | 0.00% |
| | −5 | 56.5000 | 0.44% | 0.98% | −0.53% | 36.8750 | 0.68% | 0.98% | −0.30% | 772.50 | 0.98% |
| | −4 | 56.6250 | 0.22% | 1.51% | −1.29% | 37.7500 | 2.37% | 1.51% | 0.86% | 784.17 | 1.51% |
| | −3 | 57.1250 | 0.88% | 0.25% | 0.63% | 38.1250 | 0.99% | 0.25% | 0.74% | 786.16 | 0.25% |
| | −2 | 57.1250 | 0.00% | 0.07% | −0.07% | 38.3750 | 0.66% | 0.07% | 0.58% | 786.73 | 0.07% |
| | −1 | 57.3750 | 0.44% | 0.32% | 0.12% | 38.6250 | 0.65% | 0.32% | 0.33% | 789.26 | 0.32% |
| 5-Feb-97 | 0 | 65.2500 | 13.73% | −1.39% | 15.12% | 40.6250 | 5.18% | −1.39% | 6.57% | 778.28 | −1.39% |
| | 1 | 66.5000 | 1.92% | 0.24% | 1.68% | 41.1250 | 1.23% | 0.24% | 0.99% | 780.15 | 0.24% |
| | 2 | 67.3750 | 1.32% | 1.21% | 0.11% | 42.0000 | 2.13% | 1.21% | 0.92% | 789.56 | 1.21% |
| | 3 | 67.8750 | 0.74% | −0.52% | 1.27% | 41.8750 | −0.30% | −0.52% | 0.23% | 785.43 | −0.52% |
| | 4 | 67.5000 | −0.55% | 0.53% | −1.08% | 41.6250 | −0.60% | 0.53% | −1.13% | 789.59 | 0.53% |
| | 5 | 66.8750 | −0.93% | 1.67% | −2.60% | 40.8750 | −1.80% | 1.67% | −3.47% | 802.77 | 1.67% |
| | 6 | 68.8750 | 2.99% | 1.13% | 1.86% | 42.0000 | 2.75% | 1.13% | 1.62% | 811.82 | 1.13% |
| | 7 | 68.7500 | −0.18% | −0.41% | 0.23% | 42.3750 | 0.89% | −0.41% | 1.30% | 808.48 | −0.41% |
| | 8 | 70.8750 | 3.09% | 0.97% | 2.12% | 43.5000 | 2.65% | 0.97% | 1.69% | 816.29 | 0.97% |
| | 9 | 71.8750 | 1.41% | −0.47% | 1.88% | 43.7500 | 0.57% | −0.47% | 1.04% | 812.49 | −0.47% |
| | 10 | 69.8750 | −2.78% | −1.19% | −1.59% | 42.5000 | −2.86% | −1.19% | −1.66% | 802.80 | −1.19% |
| | 11 | 67.6250 | −3.22% | −0.13% | −3.09% | 41.2500 | −2.94% | −0.13% | −2.81% | 801.77 | −0.13% |
| 24-Feb-97 | 12 | 66.7813 | −1.25% | 1.06% | −2.31% | 40.6250 | −1.52% | 1.06% | −2.58% | 810.28 | 1.06% |
| 44 trading day total return | | 16.65% | | | | 20.37% | | | | 8.48% | |
| Average daily return | | 0.38% | | | | 0.46% | | | | 0.19% | |
| Return from −30 to −1 | | 0.22% | | | | 14.44% | | | | 5.67% | |
| Return from −1 to 0 | | 13.73% | | | | 5.18% | | | | −1.39% | |
| Return from 0 to 12 | | 2.35% | | | | 0.00% | | | | 4.11% | |
| Cumulative abnormal return | | | | | 8.44% | | | | 10.91% | | |

*Used the market adjusted return model, in which the predicted return for a firm for a day is just the return on the market index for that day.

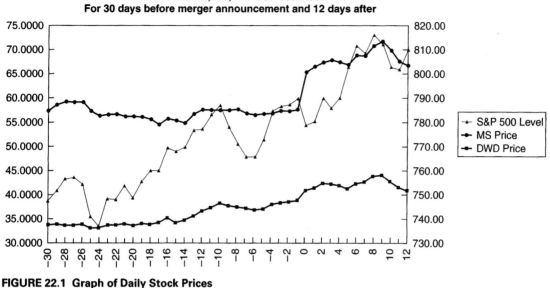

**FIGURE 22.1  Graph of Daily Stock Prices**

Amazingly, over this 44-day period, *MS's stock rose by less than DWD stock.* This is strange because historically the target's stock experiences a positive return, while the return to the bidder is small or even negative. In support of empirical evidence, however, we do see that *the target stock gained more on the announcement date versus the bidder's stock.* Another interesting fact is that *the runup,* the return from day -30 to day -1, *is seen in the bidder's stock.* So far, *there has also been little cumulative markup in this deal.* As a proxy for the market return, the S&P 500 index is used. Additionally, to calculate the **cumulative abnormal returns (CAR)** over the period, the "market adjusted return method" is used. Once again, DWD's shareholders were better off than MS's shareholders during this 44-day period. *DWD's CAR was 10.91%, whereas MS's CAR was 8.44%.*

**Valuation of MS**

The following two valuations of MS were done "premerger," ignoring any possible synergies that would occur from the merger with DWD, such as reduced operating expenses.

1. *Spreadsheet/formula approach:* The value of the firm is $147,992 million ($9,413 million in equity and $138,579 million in debt). All of the historical drivers are used for the value going forward and temporary supernormal growth for five years, then no growth. Five years was more applicable than 10, given the cyclicality and riskiness in the investment banking industry. Also, the company's growth in EBIT over the last five years has only been 8.8% annually. The valuation can be viewed in Table 22.4.

2. *Comparable companies approach:* Morgan Stanley premerger is valued by comparing it to other investment banks, using price/book, price/sales, and price/net income ratios. The total value of MS's equity was $7,226 million using this method. The valuation can be viewed in Table 22.5.

**Results**

The table below details the results of the two approaches and compares them to the market value of MS's equity on February 4, one day before the merger announcement:

|  | *Value of MS's Equity* |
| --- | --- |
| Formula approach | $9,413 million |
| Comparable companies approach | $7,226 million |
| Equity value of MS on February 4, 1997 | $8,746 million |

The results are mixed. We cannot say is MS was being undervalued or overvalued by the markets. The comparable companies approach gave the lowest results because some of the companies in the pool, such as Bear Stearns and Salomon Bros., are not

Free CF - after Inter/tax ↑ in w/c Investments

**TABLE 22.4** Valuation of Morgan Stanley (Premerger) Using the Formula Approach, 1988–1995

| | (1) Current Assets Total | (2) Marketable Securities | (3) Current Liabilities Total | (4) Debt in Current Liabilities | (5) Pretax Income | (6) Income Taxes Total | (7) Interest Expense | (8) Property, Plant, and Equipment Total (Net) | (9) Net Working Capital $(1-2)-(3-4)$ | (10) Total Capital $(8+9)$ | (11) Investment (Delta 10) | (12) EBIT $(5+7)$ |
|---|---|---|---|---|---|---|---|---|---|---|---|---|
| 1988 | $ 39,312 | $24,504 | $ 36,951 | $ 32,561 | $ 637 | $ 242 | $1,905 | $ 238 | $10,419 | $10,657 | | $ 2,541 |
| 1989 | $ 52,366 | $24,877 | $ 49,565 | $ 44,252 | $ 738 | $ 295 | $3,378 | $ 268 | $22,175 | $22,442 | $11,785 | $ 4,117 |
| 1990 | $ 53,009 | $15,836 | $ 49,201 | $ 41,580 | $ 470 | $ 200 | $3,711 | $ 385 | $29,553 | $29,938 | $ 7,495 | $ 4,181 |
| 1991 | $ 62,951 | $17,892 | $ 57,314 | $ 47,966 | $ 772 | $ 297 | $3,925 | $ 544 | $35,711 | $36,255 | $ 6,317 | $ 4,697 |
| 1992 | $ 79,610 | $23,170 | $ 72,896 | $ 61,357 | $ 793 | $ 283 | $4,362 | $ 552 | $44,902 | $45,454 | $ 9,199 | $ 5,156 |
| 1993 | $ 96,127 | $29,370 | $ 86,305 | $ 70,627 | $1,200 | $ 414 | $5,020 | $ 778 | $51,079 | $51,857 | $ 6,403 | $ 6,220 |
| 1994 | $115,168 | $38,029 | $103,926 | $ 86,762 | $ 594 | $ 199 | $5,875 | $1,061 | $59,975 | $61,036 | $ 9,179 | $ 6,469 |
| 1995 | $141,841 | $47,225 | $128,813 | $101,470 | $ 883 | $ 283 | $5,501 | $1,286 | $67,273 | $68,559 | $ 7,523 | $ 6,384 |
| Totals | | | | | $6,088 | $2,213 | | | | | $57,902 | $39,765 |

| | Historicals | Projected | |
|---|---|---|---|
| $X_0 =$ | $6,384 | $6,384 | |
| $T =$ | 36.36% | 36.36% | |
| $b =$ | 228.79% | 228.79% | Assumed same drivers for future. Used $n$ of 5. |
| $r =$ | 4.22% | 4.22% | Valuation: |
| $g =$ | 9.66% | 9.66% | |
| $n =$ | | 5 | 1st term $= X_0(1-T)(1-b)\sum_{t=1}^{n}\left(\dfrac{1+g}{1+k}\right)^t =$ $\quad$ $-$31,375$ $(-21.2\%)$ |
| $k =$ | 3.34% | 3.34% | |
| $(1+h)=(1+g)/(1+k)=$ | 1.061 | 1.061 | |
| $p =$ inflation rate $=$ | 0.00% | 0.00% | 2nd term $= \dfrac{X_0(1-T)(1-z)}{k-p}\left(\dfrac{1+g}{1+k}\right)^n(1+g) =$ \$179,367 $(121.2\%)$ |
| $z =$ reinvestment rate $=$ | 0.00% | 0.00% | |
| Risk free rate | 5.40% | 5.40% | Total value of FIRM = $\qquad$ $147,992$ $(100.0\%)$ |
| Market return | 12.70% | 12.70% | Debt in current liabilities $\qquad$ $101,470 |
| Beta | 1.49 | 1.49 | Long-term debt $\qquad$ $ 9,171 |
| Cost of equity | 16.28% | 16.28% | Other liabilities $\qquad$ $ 27,938 |
| Cost of debt[1] | 3.97% | 3.97% | Implied Equity Value $\qquad$ $ 9,413 |
| After tax cost of debt | 2.53% | 2.53% | |
| $S/B + S$ | 5.94% | 5.94% | |
| $B/B + S$ | 94.06% | 94.06% | |

Note: Data for 1985–1987 was eliminated because Compustat did not separate out marketable securities. Calculations may not compute due to rounding.

[1]Interest expense/total liabilities (for 1995).

[2]Based on market value of equity of $8.745 billion and total debt of $138.579 billion.

*Source:* Compustat.

highly valued by the market. The formula approach gives a higher value because it assumes growth higher than MS's growth for the last five years. Based on the 1.65 exchange ratio on February 4, 1997, (DWD share price = $38.625), DWD was offering MS shareholders $9,714 million. This price would go higher as the stock market reacted. This does not necessarily mean that DWD overpaid. This price included a control premium for MS shareholders, and it also took into account possible synergies and cost savings which would result from the merger.

## DEAL SYNERGIES

Although many feel that DWD and MS operate at two opposite spectrums of the securities business, the market believed that the merger contained many synergies and was a positive move for both parties. According to DWD's CEO, the deal is "based on powerful franchises, high profitability and opportunities for accelerated growth."

- In securities, it combines MS's strengths in investment banking and institutional sales and trading with

**TABLE 22.5**   Comparables Valuation for MS: Premerger

| Comparable Companies | Market/Sales[1] | Market/Book[2] | P/E = Market/Net Income[3] |
|---|---|---|---|
| Bear Stearns | 0.91 | 1.43 | 7.75 |
| A.G. Edwards | 1.65 | 1.97 | 11.60 |
| Lehman Bros. | 0.28 | 1.03 | 10.69 |
| Merrill Lynch | 0.87 | 2.64 | 11.66 |
| Salomon Brothers | 0.68 | 1.43 | 7.22 |
| Paine Webber | 0.64 | 2.06 | 9.48 |
| Average | 0.84 | 1.76 | 9.73 |
| | *Sales* | *Book Value* | *Net Income* |
| Morgan Stanley | 9,124 | 4,653 | 600 |
| | *Market/Sales* | *Market/Book* | *PE = Market/Net Income* |
| Equity valuation based on averages (in Million) | $7,648.95 | $8,189.28 | $5,840.00 |
| Average Equity Valuation | $7,226.08 | (In Million) | |

*Source:* Bloomberg Investor Services.

Note: Market values are current values as of February 24, 1997.

[1]Sales are the latest available fiscal year end sales.

[2]Book value is from the latest quarter available.

[3]Net income is from the latest 12 months available.

DWD's in retail distribution and asset gathering. In asset management, the new entity will manage more than $270 billion, the largest of any securities firm. In credit services, MS's global presence will create opportunities for expansion. Cross-selling of Discover cards to MS clientele may occur.

- The deal creates an entity with unmatched origination and distribution skills and a global presence among both providers and users of capital.

- The deal will enable both firms "to do far more together than either could have done separately," in the words of MS's chairman.

- It enhances the value drivers in this business: preeminent brands, quality professionals, proprietary distribution, multiple channels, broad customer relationships, global platform, size, and scale.

- The deal includes complementary origination and distribution. (1) Morgan Stanley can supply its product through DWD's distribution channels, including its top-ranked research, underwritten equity and fixed income securities, and its global products. (2) The entity's retail distribution will be strengthened, as account executives' productivity and growth is enhanced. (3) The entity's origination capability is enhanced, leading to increased lead management in underwritings and enhanced corporate relationships.

- The deal builds a powerful asset management platform. Multiple channels and brands are created, the product mix is more balanced, strengths can be leveraged across brands (DWD's mutual funds have not been stellar performers), and the business can expand globally with MS's global presence in Europe and emerging markets. Cost savings are also involved, as much of the trading, research, and back-office operations can be merged.

- In general, cost savings of $250 million are expected, and a loss of 600 jobs has occurred. (On February 24, 1997, DWD fired 600 employees in its New York headquarters.) The savings would come in the merging of data-processing systems and reduced employment—in traders, institutional salespeople, research analysts, and back-office support personnel.

## REASONS FOR THE DEAL AND DEAL CHALLENGES

### Reasons from Both Parties' Perspective

Inevitably, this merger has the potential to create various synergies, including cutting capacity and costs, as duplicate functions at the two firms are erased. This could be one reason why the market reacted so positively. However, DWD's chairman stated: "[Cost savings is] not what we want you to walk away thinking about. The message we're giving you is a message of growth and revenues, not cost savings" (*USA Today,* February 6, 1997).

### Reasons from MS's Perspective

MS favored the merger because:

- it saw DWD as the perfect pipeline from Wall Street to Main Street.
- it wanted to increase its access to millions of Americans who have been lured to the stock market in recent years; the importance of the retail customer was a key factor in this merger.
- it eyed mutual funds, credit cards, and other retail business as a way to soften the rough cycles of the institutional brokerage business.
- it saw a higher growth potential among small retail investors.
- it saw wider profit margins in the retail business than in the investment banking business.

### Reasons from DWD's Perspective

DWD favored the merger because:

- its customers would have access to many new investment choices from MS's stock and bond factory.
- it would be able to use the prestige of the MS name to attract money from ordinary investors.

- it could build its credit business globally with MS's global presence.

### Challenges

First, integrating Morgan Stanley's aristocratic culture (although analysts say that "it is one of substance over appearance") with the "meat and potatoes" environment at DWD will prove to be challenging. The firms will mainly steer clear of conflict by their autonomy. Next, mergers of equals are usually very difficult to carry out and often one party emerges as the dominant force. Dean Witter Discover will have to manage the egos of MS's executives. Finally, retail brokerages might be less inclined to push MS's mutual funds since the funds are now "associated" with competing broker DWD.

### CONCLUSION

Overall, the market reacted very positively to this merger. The price paid by DWD was judged to be quite fair. There are many potential synergies and cost savings to be realized. The question remains: Can retail and institutional houses be successful under one roof? So far, only Merrill Lynch has been successful. Additionally, the health of the combined entity still depends greatly on the health of the financial markets.

---

## Questions on Case Study C22.1

C22.1.1 What were the key financial industry developments that provided a background for the Dean Witter–Morgan Stanley merger?

C22.1.2 Was the total market value of the two companies increased or decreased at the announcement of the proposed merger?

C22.1.3 What are the business and financial factors involved that explain the market reaction to the proposed merger?

C22.1.4 What are the main implementation challenges that will have to be managed well if the merger is to achieve its objectives?

C22.1.5 From the data provided in the case, present your judgment of whether Dean Witter paid too much for Morgan Stanley.

---

### References

Anslinger, Patricia L., and Thomas E. Copeland, "Growth Through Acquisitions: A Fresh Look," Harvard Business Review, 74, January–February 1996, pp. 126–135.

Chung, Kwang S., and J. Fred Weston, "Diversification and Mergers in a Strategic Long-Range-Planning Framework," chapter 13 in M. Keenan and L. J. White, eds., *Mergers and Acquisitions,* Lexington, MA: D. C. Heath & Co., 1982, pp. 315–347.

Coase, Ronald H., "The Nature of the Firm," *Economica,* 4, November 1937, pp. 386–405.

Drucker, Peter F., "Five Rules for Successful Acquisition," *The Wall Street Journal,* October 15, 1981, p. 28.

Galbraith, John K., *The New Industrial State,* Boston: Houghton Mifflin, 1967.

Steiner, George A., *Strategic Planning,* New York: Free Press, 1979.

Summer, Charles E., *Strategic Behavior in Business and Government,* Boston: Little, Brown and Company, 1980.

Weston, J. Fred, "Mergers and Acquisitions in Business Planning," *Rivista Internazionale di Scienze Economiche e Commerciali,* 17, April 1970, pp. 309–320.

———, "ROI Planning and Control," *Business Horizons,* 15, August 1972, pp. 35–42.

———, "The Rules for Successful Mergers," *Midland Corporate Finance Journal,* 1, Winter 1983, pp. 47–50.

———, and Thomas E. Copeland, *Managerial Finance,* 9th ed., Fort Worth, TX: The Dryden Press, 1992.

# Glossary*

**Abnormal return** In event studies, the part of the return that is not predicted; the change in value caused by the event.

**Acquisition** The purchase of a controlling interest in a firm, generally via a tender offer for the target shares.

**Acquisition MLP** Also called start-up master limited partnership; the assets of an existing entity are transferred to an MLP, and the business is henceforth conducted as an MLP. The Boston Celtics' conversion into an MLP is an example.

**ACR** See *Macroconcentration.*

**Adverse selection** Without a basis for buyers to identify good products, bad products will always be offered at the same price as good products; said to be a characteristic of the used-car market in which the buyer has to consider the probability that he is being offered a lemon.

**Agency problem** The conflict of interest between principal (e.g., shareholders) and agent (e.g., managers) in which the agent has an incentive to act in his own self-interest because he bears less than the total costs of his actions.

**Anergy** Negative synergy. Instead of a "2 + 2 = 5" effect, anergy implies "2 + 2 = 3." Business units actively interfere with each other and may have more value if separated.

**Announcement date** In event studies, typically, the day information becomes public.

**Antigreenmail amendment** Corporate charter amendment which prohibits targeted share repurchases at a premium from an unwanted acquirer without the approval of nonparticipating shareholders.

**Antitakeover amendment** A corporate charter amendment which is intended to make it more difficult for an unwanted acquirer to take over the firm.

**Any-or-all offer** A tender offer which does not specify a maximum number of shares to be purchased, but none will be purchased if the conditions of the offer are not met.

**Appraisal right** The right of minority shareholders to obtain an independent valuation of their shares to determine the appropriate back-end value in a two-tier tender offer.

**APT** See *Arbitrage pricing theory.*

**Arbitrage** The purchase of an asset for near-term resale at a higher price. In the context of M&As, risk arbitrage refers to investing in the stock of takeover targets for short-term resale to capture a portion of the gains which typically accrue to target shareholders.

**Arbitrage pricing theory** A general approach to asset pricing which allows for the possibility that multiple factors may be used to explain asset returns, as opposed to the capital asset pricing model in which the market return is the sole explanatory factor.

**Atomistic competition** Numerous small sellers and buyers, none of which have the power to influence market prices or output.

**Atomistic shareholders** Each shareholder has only a small amount of stock. Small shareholders

---

*Technical terms used in explanations are defined in their alphabetical position.

have less incentive to monitor management than large block shareholders.

**Auction** Two or more bidders competing for a single target. An auction increases the price target shareholders receive.

**Back-end value** The amount paid to remaining shareholders in the second stage of a two-tier or partial tender offer.

**Bear hug** A takeover strategy in which the acquirer, without previous warning, mails the directors of the target a letter announcing the acquisition proposal and demanding a quick decision.

**Benchmark** A company, group of companies, or portfolio used as a standard of performance.

**Beta** In the capital asset pricing model, the systematic risk of the asset; the variability of the asset's return in relation to the return on the market.

**Bidder** The acquiring firm in a tender offer.

**Blended price** The weighted average price in a two-tier tender offer. The front-end price is weighted by the percent of shares purchased in the first step of the transaction, and the lower, back-end price is weighted by the percent of shares purchased to complete the transaction.

**Blockholder** The holder of a significant percentage of the ownership shares.

**Board-out clause** A provision in most supermajority antitakeover amendments which gives the board of directors the power to decide when and if the supermajority provision will be in effect.

**Bootstrap transaction** A highly leveraged transaction (HLT).

**Bottom-up** An approach to firm strategy formulation based on the aggregation of segment forecasts.

**Bounded rationality** Refers to the limited capacity of the human mind to deal with complexity.

**Brand-name capital** Firm reputation; the result of nonsalvageable investment which provides customers with an implicit guarantee of product quality for which they are willing to pay a premium.

**Breach of trust** Unilaterally changing the terms of a contract.

**Business judgment rule** A legal doctrine which holds that the board of directors is acting in the best interests of shareholders unless it can be proven by a preponderance of the evidence that the board is acting in its own interest or is in breach of its fiduciary duty.

**Bust-up takeover** An acquisition followed by the divestiture of some or all of the operating units of the acquired firm which can be sold at prices greater than their current value.

**Buyback** See *Share repurchase.*

**Calls** Options to buy an asset at a specified price for a specified period of time.

**Capital asset pricing model** Calculates the required return on an asset as a function of the risk-free rate plus the market risk premium times the asset's beta.

**Capital budgeting** The process of planning expenditures whose returns extend over a period of time.

**Capital intensity** In economics, the ratio of investment required per dollar of sales. In finance, the sales to investment ratio. The steel industry and manufacturing generally are more capital intensive than the wholesale or retail industries.

**CAPM** See *Capital asset pricing model.*

**CAR** See *Cumulative abnormal return.*

**Cash cows** A Boston Consulting Group term for business segments which have a high market share in low-growth product markets and thus throw off more cash flow than needed for reinvestment.

**Chinese wall** The imaginary barrier separating investment banking and other activities within a financial intermediary.

**Classified board** Also called a staggered board. An antitakeover measure which divides a firm's board of directors into several classes, only one of which is up for election in any given year, thus delaying effective transfer of control to a new owner in a takeover.

**Clayton Act** Federal antitrust law originally passed in 1914 and strengthened in 1950 by the Celler-Kefauver amendment. Section 7 gives the Federal Trade Commission (FTC) power to prohibit the acquisition of one company by another if adverse effects on competition would result, or if the FTC perceived a trend which might ultimately lead to decreased competition.

**Clean-up merger** Also called a take-out merger. The consolidation of the acquired firm into the acquiring firm after the acquirer has obtained control.

**Clientele effect** A dividend theory which states that high-tax bracket shareholders will prefer to hold stock in firms with low dividend payout rates and low-tax bracket shareholders will prefer the stock of firms with high payouts.

**Coercive tender offer** Any tender offer which puts pressure on target shareholders to tender by offering a higher price to those who tender early.

**Coinsurance effect** The combination of two firms whose cash flows are not perfectly correlated will result in cash flows of less variability for the merged firm, thus decreasing the risk to lenders to the firm and thereby increasing its debt capacity.

**Collateral restraints** Agreements between the parties to a joint venture to limit competition between themselves in certain areas.

**Collusion** Illegal coordination or cooperation among competitors with respect to price or output.

**Complementarity** The strengths of one firm offset the weaknesses of another firm with which it combines. For example, one firm strong in marketing combines with one strong in research.

**Concentration** Measures of the percentage of total industry sales accounted for by a specified number of firms, such as 4, 8, or 20.

**Concentric merger** A merger in which there is carry-over in *specific* management functions (e.g., marketing) or complementarity in relative strengths among *specific* management functions rather than carry-over/complementarities in only generic management functions (e.g., planning).

**Conglomerate** A combination of unrelated firms; any combination that is not vertical or horizontal.

**Conjectural variation** The reaction of rival firms as one firm, Firm A, restricts output or raises prices. Ranges from −1 to +1; a negative conjectural variation indicates competitive behavior, i.e., Firm A's action is offset by the reactions of competing rival firms.

**Contingent voting rights** Rights to vote in corporate elections which become exercisable upon the occurrence of a particular event. Examples: Preferred stockholders may win the right to vote if preferred dividends are missed; convertible debt may be viewed as having voting rights contingent upon conversion.

**Convergence of interests hypothesis** Predicts a positive relationship between the proportion of management stock ownership and the market's valuation of the firm's assets.

**Cost leadership** A business strategy based on achieving lower costs than rivals.

**Covenant** See *Indenture*.

**Crown jewels** The most valuable segments of a company; the parts most wanted by an acquirer.

**Cumulative abnormal return (CAR)** In event studies, the sum of daily abnormal returns over a period relative to the event.

**Cumulative voting** Instead of one vote per candidate selected, shareholders can vote (the number of shares they hold times the number of directors to be elected) for one candidate or divide the total votes among a desired number of candidates. Example: A shareholder has 100 shares; six directors are to be elected. With cumulative voting the shareholder has 600 votes to distribute among six candidates however he or she chooses.

**DCF** See *Discounted cash flow valuation*.

**Decision control** Fundamental ownership rights of shareholders to select management, monitor management, and to determine reward/incentive arrangements.

**Decision management** Decision functions related to day-to-day operations which may be delegated to managers. Includes initiation and implementation of policies and procedures.

**Defensive diversification** Entering new product markets to offset the limitations of the firm's existing product-market areas.

**Defined benefit plan** A pension plan which specifies in advance the amount beneficiaries will receive based on compensation, years of service, and so on.

**Defined contribution plan** A pension plan in which the annual contributions are specified in advance. Benefits upon retirement depend on the performance of the assets in which the contributions are invested.

**Delphi technique** An information-gathering technique in which questionnaires are sent to informed individuals. The responses are summarized into a feedback report and used to generate subsequent questionnaires to probe more deeply into the issue under study.

**De novo entry** Entry into an industry by forming a new company as opposed to combining with an existing firm in the industry.

**Differential managerial efficiency hypothesis** A theory which hypothesizes that more efficient managements take over firms with less efficient managements and achieve gains by improving the efficiency of the target.

**Discounted cash flow valuation (DCF)** The application of an appropriate cost of capital to a future stream of cash flows.

**Discriminatory poison pill** Antitakeover plans which penalize acquirers who exceed a given shareholding percentage (the kick-in or trigger point).

**Dissident** A shareholder, or group of shareholders, who disagrees with incumbent management and seeks to make changes via a proxy contest to gain representation on the board of directors.

**Diversification** Holding assets whose returns are not perfectly correlated.

**Divestiture** Sale of a segment of a company (assets, a product line, a subsidiary) to a third party for cash and/or securities.

**Dividend growth valuation model** The application of an appropriate discount factor to a future stream of dividends.

**Dividend method dual-class recapitalization** Most widely used method of converting to dual-class stock ownership. A stock split or dividend is used to distribute new inferior voting stock. The previously existing common stock is redesignated as superior-vote class B stock.

**Dogs** A Boston Consulting Group term for business segments characterized by low market shares in product markets with low growth rates.

**Dual-class recapitalization** Corporate restructuring used to create two classes of common stock with the superior-vote stock concentrated in the hands of management.

**Dual-class stock** Two (or more) classes of common stock with equal rights to cash flows, but with unequal voting rights.

**DuPont system** A financial planning and control system focusing on return on investment by relating asset turnover (effective asset management) to profit margin on sales (effective cost control).

**Dutch auction repurchases (DARs)** Shareholders are permitted to put their shares to the company within a range of prices; at a price at which the company's target level of shares is reached, all shares offered receive that price.

**Dynamic competition theory** A model of industrial organization theory which extends the traditional models of price and output decisions of firms in a static environment to decisions on product quality, innovation, promotion, marketing, and so on in changing environments.

**Dynamic oligopoly** Although an industry may be dominated by a few large firms (oligopoly), recognized interdependence does not occur because decisions must be made on so many factors that actions and reactions of rivals cannot be predicted or coordinated.

**Empirical test** Systematic examination of data to check the consistency of evidence with alternative theories.

**Employee Retirement Income Security Act (ERISA)** 1974 federal legislation regulating pension plans including some ESOPs. Sets vesting requirements, fiduciary standards, minimum funding standards. Established Pension Benefit Guarantee Corporation (PBGC) to guarantee pensions.

**Employee stock ownership plan (ESOP)** Defined contribution pension plan (stock bonus and/or money purchase) designed to invest primarily in the stock of the employer firm.

**End of regulation** A theory hypothesizing that takeovers occur following deregulation of an industry as a result of increased competition which exposes management inefficiency which may have been masked by regulation.

**Entrenchment** See *Managerial entrenchment.*

**Equity carve-out** A transaction in which a parent firm offers *some* of a subsidiary's common stock to the general public, to bring in a cash infusion to the parent without loss of control.

**ERISA** See *Employee Retirement Income Security Act.*

**ERISA-type ESOP** Employee stock ownership plans other than tax-credit ESOPs; i.e., includes leveraged, leveragable, and nonleveraged ESOPs recognized under ERISA rather than under the Tax Reduction Act of 1975.

**ESOP** See *Employee stock ownership plan.*

**Event returns** A measure of the stock price reaction to the announcement of significant new information such as a takeover or some type of restructuring.

**Event study** An empirical test of the effect of an event (e.g., a merger, divestiture) on stock returns. The event is the reference date from which analysis of returns is made regardless of the calendar timing of the occurrences in the sample of firms.

**Excess return** See *Abnormal return.*

**Exchange method dual-class recapitalization** Means of converting to a dual-class stock corporate structure. High-vote stock is issued to insiders in exchange for their currently outstanding (low-vote) stock. The remaining low-vote stock, in the hands of outside shareholders, generally receives a higher dividend.

**Exchange offer** A transaction which provides one class (or more) of securities with the right or option to exchange part or all of their holdings for a different class of the firm's securities, e.g., an exchange of debt for common stock. Enables a change in capital structure with no change in investment.

**Exit-type firm** In Jensen's free cash flow hypothesis, a firm with positive free cash flows. The theory predicts that for such a firm, stock prices will increase with unexpected increases in payout.

**Extra merger premium hypothesis** The possibility that a higher price will be paid for superior-vote shares if a dual-class stock firm becomes a takeover target causes the price of superior-vote stock to be higher even in the absence of a takeover bid.

**Failing firm defense** A defense against a merger challenge alleging that in the absence of the merger, the firm(s) would fail. The 1982 Merger Guidelines spell out the conditions under which this defense will be acceptable.

**Fair-price amendment** An antitakeover charter amendment which waives the supermajority approval requirement for a change of control if a fair price is paid for all purchased shares. Defends against two-tier offers which do not have board approval.

**Fallen angel** A bond issued at investment grade whose rating is subsequently dropped to below investment grade, below BBB.

**Financial conglomerates** Conglomerate firms in which corporate management provides a flow of funds to operating segments, exercises control and strategic planning functions, and is the ulti-

mate financial risk taker, but does *not* participate in operating decisions.

**Financial Institutions Reform, Recovery, and Enforcement Act (FIRREA)** A 1989 law changing the regulatory rules for savings and loan companies as well as other financial institutions.

**Financial synergy** A theory which suggests a financial motive for mergers, especially between firms with high internal cash flows (but poor investment opportunities) and firms with low internal cash flows (and high investment opportunities which, absent merger, would require costly external financing). Also includes increased debt capacity or coinsurance effect, and economies of scale in flotation and transaction costs of securities.

**Fixed price tender offers (FPTs)** A method of share repurchase in which a put price is specified for a specified number of company shares.

**Flip-in poison pill plan** Shareholders of the target firm are issued rights to acquire stock in the target at a substantial discount when a bidder has reached a designated percentage ownership trigger point.

**Flip-over poison pill plan** Shareholders of the target firm are issued rights to purchase the common stock of the acquirer at a premium until a trigger point is reached; after which the price flips over to a substantial discount—a deep in the money call option.

**Formula approach** A discounted cash flow valuation in which key variables or value drivers are used to calculate the net present value of a project or firm.

**Four-firm concentration ratio** The sum of the shares of sales, value added, assets, or employees held by the largest four firms in an industry. A measure of competitiveness, according to the structural theory.

**Free cash flow** Cash flows in excess of positive net present value investment opportunities available.

**Free cash flow hypothesis** Jensen's theory of how the payout of free cash flows helps resolve the agency problem between managers and shareholders. Holds that bonding payout of current (and future) free cash flows reduces the power of management as well as subjecting them more frequently to capital market scrutiny.

**Free-rider problem** Atomistic shareholder reasons that its decision has no impact on the outcome of the tender offer and refrains from tendering to free-ride on the value increase resulting from the merger, thus causing the bid to fail.

**Front-end loading** A tender offer in which the offer price is greater than the value of any unpurchased shares. Resolves the free-rider problems by providing an incentive to tender early.

**Full ex post settling up** A manager's compensation is frequently adjusted over the course of his or her career to fully reflect his or her performance, thus eliminating an incentive to shirk.

**Gambler's ruin** An adverse string of losses which could lead to bankruptcy, although the long-run cash flows could be positive.

**Game theory** An analysis of the behavior (actions and reactions) of participants under specified rules, information, and strategies.

**General Utilities doctrine** An IRS rule which allowed firms to not recognize gains on the distribution of appreciated property in redemption of its shares (e.g., in a "legal" liquidation). Repealed by the Tax Reform Act of 1986.

**Generic management functions** Those functions that are not industry specific and are thus transferrable even in conglomerate mergers. Include planning, organizing, directing, and controlling.

**Going-concern value** The value of the firm as a whole over and above the sum of the values of each of its parts; the value of organization learning and reputation.

**Going private** The transformation of a public corporation into a privately-held firm (often via a leveraged buyout or a management buyout).

**Golden parachute** Provision in the employment contracts of top management providing for compensation for loss of jobs following a change of control.

**Goodwill** The excess of the purchase price paid for a firm over the book value received. Recorded on the acquirer's balance sheet, to be amortized over not more than 40 years (amortization not tax deductible).

**Greenmail** The premium over the current market price of stock paid to buy back the holdings accumulated by an unwanted acquirer to avoid a takeover.

**Gross present value** An appropriately discounted stream of future cash flows before the deduction of investment costs.

**Growth/share matrix** A guide to strategy formulation which emphasizes attainment of high market share in industries with favorable growth rates.

**Harassment hypothesis** Ellert's theory that Federal Trade Commission antitrust complaints are brought against firms with abnormally good stock price performance, at the instigation of the firms' competitors who are threatened by their superior performance.

**Hart-Scott-Rodino Antitrust Improvements Act of 1976** Expands power of Department of Justice in antitrust investigations; provides for waiting period (15 days for tender offers, 30 days for mergers) following submission of information to Department of Justice and Federal Trade Commission before transaction can be completed; expands power of state attorneys general to institute triple damage antitrust lawsuits on behalf of their citizens.

**Herfindahl-Hirschman Index (HHI)** The measure of concentration under the 1982 Merger Guidelines, defined as the sum of the *squares* of the market shares of *all* the firms in the industry.

**HHI** See *Herfindahl-Hirschman Index.*

**Hidden equity** Undervalued assets whose market value exceeds their depreciated book value, but is not reflected in stock price.

**Highly leveraged transaction (HLT)** Use of debt in relation to equity in excess of average industry ratios.

**High-yield bond** See *Junk bond.*

**Holding company** An organization whose primary function is to hold the stock of other corporations, but which has no operating units of its own. Similar to the multidivisional organization which has profit centers and a single central headquarters. However, the segments owned by the holding company are separate legal entities which in practice are controlled by the holding company.

**Holdup** Whenever a resource is dependent on (specialized to) the rest of the firm, there may be a temptation for others to try to expropriate the quasi-rent of the dependent resource by withholding their complementary resources; this is holdup. However, each resource in the team (firm) may be dependent on all the others, and thus all are vulnerable to expropriation.

**Horizontal merger** A combination of firms operating in the same business activity.

**Hostile takeover** A tender offer which proceeds even after it has been opposed by the management of the target.

**Hubris hypothesis** (Winner's curse) Roll's theory that acquiring firm managers commit errors of overoptimism in evaluating merger opportunities (due to excessive pride, animal spirits), and end up paying too high a price for acquisitions.

**IAA** See *Investment Advisers Act of 1940.*

**ICA** See *Investment Company Act of 1940.*

**Implicit claim** A tacit rather than contractual promise of continuing service and delivery of expected quality to customers and job security to employees.

**Incentive stock option (ISO)** An executive compensation plan to align the interests of managers with stockholders. Executives are issued options whose exercise price is equal to or greater than the stock price at the time of issue and thus have value only if the stock price rises, giving managers incentives to take actions to maximize stock price.

**Increased debt capacity hypothesis** A theory that postmerger financial leverage increases are the result of increased debt capacity (as opposed to the firms involved having been underleveraged before the merger) due to reduced expected bankruptcy costs.

**Indenture** The contract between a firm and its bondholders which sets out the terms and conditions of the borrowing, and the rights and obligations of each party (covenants).

**Industry life cycle** A conceptual model of the different stages of an industry's development. (1) Development stage—new product, high investment needs, losses; (2) Growth stage—consumer acceptance, expanding sales, high profitability, ease of entry; (3) Maturity stage—sales growth slows, excess capacity, prices and profits decline—key period for merger strategy; (4) Decline stage—substitute products emerge, sales growth declines, pressure for mergers to survive.

**Inferior-vote stock** In dual-class stock firms, the class of common stock which has less voting power, e.g., may be able to elect only a minority on the board of directors; may be compensated with higher dividends.

**Information asymmetry** A game or decisions in which one party has more information than other players.

**Initial public offering (IPO)** The first offering to the public of common stock (e.g., of a former privately-held firm) or a portion of the common stock of a hitherto wholly-owned subsidiary.

**In play** Because of a bid or rumors of a bid, the financial community regards the company as receptive or vulnerable to takeover bids.

**Insider trading** Some parties take action based on information not available to outside investors.

**Internal rate of return (IRR)** A capital budgeting method which finds the discount rate (the IRR) which equates the present value of cash inflows and investment outlays. The IRR must equal or exceed the relevant risk-adjusted cost of capital for the project to be acceptable.

**Investment Advisers Act of 1940 (IAA)** Federal securities legislation providing for registration and regulation of investment advisers.

**Investment Company Act of 1940 (ICA)** Federal securities legislation regulating publicly-owned companies in the business of investing and trading in securities; subjects them to SEC rules. Amended in 1970 to place more controls on management compensation and sales charges.

**Investment requirements ratio** A firm's investment expenditures (or opportunities) in relation to after-tax cash flows.

**IPO** See *Initial public offering.*

**IRR** See *Internal rate of return.*

**ISO** See *Incentive stock option.*

**Joint production** Production using complementary inputs in which the output cannot be unambiguously attributed to any single input; and in which the output is greater than the sum of the inputs (i.e., synergy). Problems in assigning returns may arise if the inputs are not owned by the same entity.

**Joint venture** A combination of subsets of assets contributed by two (or more) business entities for a specific business purpose and a limited duration. Each of the venture partners continues to exist as a separate firm, and the joint venture represents a new business enterprise.

**Junk bond** High-yield bonds that are below investment grade when issued; that is, rated below

BBB (Standard & Poor's) or below Baa3 (Moody's).

**Kick-in or trigger point** The level of share ownership by an acquiring firm which activates a poison-pill antitakeover defense plan.

**Kick-in-the-pants hypothesis** Attributes the increase in a takeover target's stock price to the impetus given by the bid to target management to implement a higher-valued strategy.

**Latent debt capacity hypothesis** A theory that postmerger increases in financial leverage are due to underleverage in the premerger period.

**LBO** See *Leveraged buyout.*

**LCO** Leveraged cash-out. See *Leveraged recapitalization.*

**Learning-by-doing** A means of transferring knowledge which is complex, or embedded in a complex set of technological and/or organizational circumstances, and thus difficult or impossible to transfer in a classroom setting. May motivate knowledge-acquisition joint ventures.

**Learning curve** An approach to strategy formulation which hypothesizes that costs decline with cumulative volume experience, resulting in competitive advantage for the first entrants into an industry.

**Leveraged buyout (LBO)** The purchase of a company by a small group of investors, financed largely by debt. Usually entails going private.

**Leveraged cash-out (LCO)** See *Leveraged recapitalization.*

**Leveraged ESOP** An employee stock ownership plan recognized under ERISA in which the ESOP borrows funds to purchase employer securities. (Banks have tax incentives to make loans to ESOPs.) The employer then makes tax-deductible contributions to the ESOP sufficient to cover both principal repayment and interest on the loan.

**Leveraged recapitalization** A defensive reorganization of the firm's capital structure in which outside shareholders receive a large one-time cash dividend, and inside shareholders receive new shares of stock instead. The cash dividend is largely financed with newly borrowed funds, leaving the firm highly leveraged and with a greater proportional ownership share in the hands of management. Also called leveraged cash-out.

**Life cycle model of firm ownership** A theory which suggests firms will attract different shareholder clienteles (high or low tax bracket investors) over different periods of firm development depending on changing investment needs and profitability.

**Line and staff** An organizational form characterized by the separation of support activities (staff) from operations (line).

**Liquidation** Divestiture of all the assets of a firm so that the firm ceases to exist.

**Liquidation MLP** The complete liquidation of a corporation into a master limited partnership.

**Lock-in amendment** A corporate charter amendment which makes it more difficult to void previously passed (antitakeover) amendments, e.g., by requiring supermajority approval for a change.

**Lock-up option** An option to buy a large block of newly issued shares which target management may grant to a favored bidder, thus virtually guaranteeing that the favored bidder will succeed. Target management's ability to grant a lock-up option induces bidders to negotiate.

**Logical incrementalism** A process of effecting major changes in strategy via a series of relatively small (incremental) changes.

**M-form** See *Multidivisional corporation.*

**Macroconcentration** An overall measure of the share of sales or value added by a specified number of firms; their share is the aggregate concentration ratio (ACR).

**Management buyout (MBO)** A going-private transaction led by the incumbent managers of the formerly public firm.

**Managerial conglomerates** Conglomerate firms which provide managerial expertise, counsel, and interaction on decisions to operating units. Based on the transferability of generic management skills even across nonrelated businesses.

**Managerial entrenchment hypothesis** A theory that antitakeover efforts are motivated by managers' self-interests in keeping their jobs rather than in the best interests of shareholders.

**Managerialism** A theory that managers pursue mergers and acquisitions to increase the size of the organizations they control and thus increase their compensation.

**Marginal cost of capital (MCC)** The relevant discount factor for a current decision.

**Market-adjusted return** The return for a firm for a period is its actual return less the return on the market index for that period.

**Market-extension merger** A combination of firms whose operations had previously been conducted in nonoverlapping geographic areas.

**Market model** In event studies, the most widely used method of calculating the return predicted if no event took place. In this method, a clean period (with no events) is chosen, and a regression is run of firm returns against the market index return over the clean period. The regression coefficient and intercept are then used with the market index return for the day of interest in the event period to predict what the return for the firm would have been on that day had no event taken place.

**Market value rule** The principle that all decisions of a corporation should be judged solely by their contribution to the market value of the firm's stock.

**Mark-to-market accounting** At statement dates, assets and liabilities are restated to measures of their current market values.

**Markup return** The event return measured from the announcement date to various designated dates thereafter.

**Master limited partnership (MLP)** An organizational form in which limited partnership interests are publicly traded (like shares of corporate stock), while retaining the tax attributes of a partnership.

**Maximum limit offer** A stock repurchase tender offer in which all tendered shares will be purchased if the offer is undersubscribed; but if the offer is oversubscribed, shares may be purchased only on a pro rata basis.

**MBO** See *Management buyout.*

**Mean adjusted return** The actual return for a period less the average (mean) return calculated for a time segment before, after, or both in relation to the event.

**Merger** Any transaction that forms one economic unit from two or more previous units.

**Mezzanine financing** Subordinated debt issued in connection with leveraged buyouts. Sometimes carries payment-in-kind (PIK) provisions, in which debt holders receive more of the same kind of debt securities in lieu of cash payments under specified conditions.

**Microconcentration** A measure of the market share of individual firms or groups such as the four-firm concentration ratio or a measure of inequality of market shares such as the HHI.

**Minority squeeze-out** The elimination by controlling shareholders of noncontrolling (minority) shareholders.

**Misappropriation doctrine** A rationale for insider trading prosecution of outsiders who trade on the basis of information which they have "misappropriated," e.g., stolen from their employers or obtained by fraud.

**MLP** See *Master limited partnership.*

**MNE** See *Multinational enterprise.*

**Money purchase plan** A defined contribution pension plan in which the firm contributes a specified annual amount of cash as opposed to stock bonus plans in which the firm contributes stock, and profit-sharing plans in which the amount of the annual cash contribution depends on profitability.

**Monopoly** A single seller.

**Moral hazard** One party (principal) relies on the behavior of another (agent) and it is costly to observe information or action. Opportunistic behavior in which success benefits one party and failure injures another, e.g., high leverage benefits equity holders under success and injures creditors under failure.

**Muddling through** An approach to strategy formulation in which policy makers focus only on those alternatives which differ incrementally (i.e., only a little) from existing policies rather than considering a wider range of alternatives.

**Multidivisional corporation (M-form)** An organizational form to achieve greater efficiency via profit centers to reduce the need for information flow across divisions and to guide resource allocation to the highest-valued uses. Benefits from large fixed investment in general management expertise (especially strategic planning, monitoring, and control) spread over a number of individual decentralized operations (at which level decision making on specific management functions takes place).

**Multinational enterprise (MNE)** A business organization with operations in more than one country, beyond import/export operations.

**NAAG** See *National Association of Attorneys General.*

**NASDAQ** Stock quotation system of the National Association of Securities Dealers for stocks which trade over the counter as opposed to on an organized exchange.

**National Association of Attorneys General (NAAG)** An organization of state attorneys general.

**Negotiated share repurchase** Refers to buying back the stock of a large blockholder (an unwanted acquirer) at a premium over market price (greenmail).

**Net operating loss carry-over** Tax provision allowing firms to use net operating losses to offset taxable income over a period of years before and after the loss. Available to firms which acquire a loss firm only under strictly specified conditions.

**Net present value (NPV)** Capital budgeting criterion which compares the present value of cash inflows of a project discounted at the risk-adjusted cost of capital to the present value of investment outlays (discounted at the risk-adjusted cost of capital).

**Niche opportunities** A business strategy which aims at meeting the needs or interests of specific consumer groups.

**NOL carry-over** See *Net operating loss carry-over.*

**Nolo contendere** A legal plea in which a defendant, without admitting guilt, declines to contest allegations of wrongdoing.

**Nondiscriminatory poison pill** Antitakeover defense plans which do not penalize acquirers exceeding a given shareholding limit. Include flip-over plans, preferred stock plans, and ownership flip-in plans which permit cash offers for all shares.

**Nonleveraged ESOP** An employee stock ownership plan recognized under ERISA which does not provide for borrowing by the ESOP. Essentially the same as stock bonus plans.

**Normal return** In event studies, the predicted return if no event took place, the reference point for the calculation of abnormal, or excess, return attributable to the event.

**No-shop agreement** The target agrees not to consider other offers while negotiating with a particular bidder.

**NPV** See *Net present value.*

**Oligopoly** A small number (few) of sellers.

**Omnibus Budget Reconciliation Act of 1993 (OBRA)** A tax law which included the conditions under which the excess purchase price over the accounting value of a target could be amortized as a tax deductible expense.

**Open corporations** Fama and Jensen's term for large corporations whose residual claims (common stock) are least restricted. They identify the following characteristics: (1) They have property rights in net cash flows for an indefinite horizon; (2) Stockholders are not required to hold any other role in the organization; (3) Common stock is alienable (transferrable, saleable) without restriction.

**Open-market share repurchase** Refers to a corporation's buying its own shares on the open market at the going price just as any other investor might buy the corporation's shares; as opposed to a tender offer for share repurchase or a negotiated repurchase.

**Operating synergy** Combining two or more entities results in gains in revenues or cost reductions because of complementarities or economies of scale or scope.

**Opportunism** Self-interest seeking with guile, including shirking, cheating.

**Organization capital** Firm-specific informational assets which accumulate over time to enhance productivity. Includes information used in assigning employees to appropriate tasks, and forming teams of employees, and the information each employee acquires about other employees and the organization. Alternatively, defined by Cornell and Shapiro as the current market value of all future implicit claims the firm expects to sell.

**Organization culture** An organization's "style" or approach to problem solving, relations with employees, customers and other stakeholders.

**Organization learning** The improvement in skills and abilities of individuals or groups (teams) of employees through learning by experience within the firm. Includes managerial learning (generic, as well as industry specific) and nonmanagerial labor learning.

**Original plan poison pill** Also called preferred stock plan. An early poison pill antitakeover defense in which the firm issues a dividend of convertible preferred stock to its common stockholders. If an acquiring firm passes a trigger point of share ownership, preferred stockholders (other than the large blockholder) can put the preferred stock to the target firm (force the firm to redeem it) at the highest price paid by the acquiring firm for the target's common or preferred stock during the past year. If the acquirer merges with the target, the preferred can be converted into acquirer voting stock with a market value no less than the redemption value at the trigger point.

**Ownership flip-in plan** A poison pill antitakeover defense often included as part of a flip-over plan. Target stockholders are issued rights to purchase target shares at a discount if an acquirer passes a specified level of share ownership. The acquirer's rights are void, and his or her ownership interest becomes diluted.

**Pac Man defense** The target makes a counterbid for the acquirer.

**Parking** A securities law violation in which traders attempt to hide the extent of their share ownership (to avoid the 5% trigger requiring disclosure of takeover intentions and keep down the price of target stock) by depositing, or parking, shares with an accomplice broker until a later date, e.g., when the takeover attempt is out in the open.

**Partial tender offer** A tender offer for less than all target shares; specifies a maximum number of shares to be accepted, but does not announce bidder's plans with respect to the remaining shares.

**Payment-in-kind provision (PIK)** A clause which provides for issuance of more of the same type of securities to bondholders in lieu of cash interest payments.

**Payroll-based ESOP (PAYSOP)** A type of employee stock ownership plan in which employers could take a tax credit of 0.5% of ESOP-covered payroll. Repealed by the Tax Reform Act of 1986.

**Pension plan** A fund established by an organization to provide for benefits to plan participants (e.g., employees) after their retirement.

**Perfect competition** Set of assumptions for an idealized economic model: (1) Large numbers of buyers and sellers so none can influence market prices or output; (2) Economies of scale exhausted at relatively small size and cost efficiencies are the same for all companies; (3) No significant barriers to entry; (4) Constant innovation, new product development; (5) Complete knowledge of all aspects of input/output markets is costlessly available.

**PIK provision** See *Payment-in-kind provision.*

**Plasticity** (Alchian and Woodward) Resources are considered plastic when a wide range of discretionary uses can be employed by the user. If monitoring costs are high, moral hazard problems are likely to develop.

**Poison pill** Any antitakeover defense which creates securities that provide their holders with special rights (e.g., to buy target or acquiring firm shares) exercisable only after a triggering event (e.g., a tender offer for or the accumulation of a specified percentage of target shares). Exercise of the rights would make it more difficult and/or costly for an acquirer to take over the target against the will of its board of directors.

**Poison put** A provision in some new bond issues designed to protect bondholders against takeover-related credit deterioration of the issuer. Following a triggering event, bondholders may put their bonds to the corporation at an exercise price of 100 to 101% of the bond's face amount.

**Pooling of interest accounting** Assets and liabilities of each firm are combined based solely on their previous accounting values.

**Portfolio balance strategy** A balance in business segments based on market-growth/market-share criteria. Combine high-growth/high-market-share (stars), low-growth/high-market-share (cash cows), low-growth/low-market-share (dogs) segments to achieve favorable overall growth, profitability, and sufficient internal cash flows to finance positive NPV investment opportunities.

**Potential competition** Firms not in an industry at the present time, but which could enter.

**Predatory behavior** A theory which holds that a dominant firm may price below cost or build excess capacity to inflict economic harm on existing firms and to deter potential entrants.

**Premium buyback** Refers to repurchasing the stock of a large blockholder (an unwanted acquirer) at a premium over market price (greenmail).

**Price-cost margin (PCM)** Defined as (Price minus Marginal Cost) divided by Price. That is, operating profit as a percentage of price. A zero PCM reflects perfect competition, i.e., Price = Marginal Cost.

**Price pressure** A theory that the demand curve for the securities of an individual company is downward sloping and that this causes negative stock price effects of large supply increases such as large block offerings.

**Price trader** Outside investors who trade in response to price changes in securities regardless of whether or not they understand the cause of the price change.

**Product breadth** Carry-over of organizational capabilities to new products.

**Product differentiation** The development of a variety of product configurations to appeal to a variety of consumer tastes.

**Product-extension merger** A type of conglomerate merger; a combination between firms in related business activities that broadens the product lines of the firms; also called concentric mergers.

**Product life cycle** A conceptual model of the stages through which products or lines of business pass. Includes development, growth, maturity, and decline. Each stage presents its own threats and opportunities.

**Production knowledge** A form of organization learning; entrepreneurial or managerial ability to organize and maintain complex production processes economically.

**Profit-sharing plan** A defined contribution pension plan in which the firm's annual contributions to the plan are based on the firm's profitability.

**Proxy contest** An attempt by a dissident group of shareholders to gain representation on a firm's board of directors.

**Public Utilities Holding Company Act of 1935** Federal securities legislation to correct abuses in financing and operation of gas and electric utility holding company systems.

**Purchase accounting** The total assets of the combined firm reflects the purchase price of the target.

**Pure conglomerate merger** A combination of firms in nonrelated business activities that is neither a product-extension nor a geographic-extension merger.

**Puts** An option to sell an asset at a specified price for a designated period of time.

**q-ratio** (Tobin's q-ratio) The ratio of the market value of a firm's securities to the replacement costs of its physical assets.

**Quasi-rent** The excess return to an asset above the return necessary to maintain its current service flow.

**Racketeer Influenced and Corrupt Organizations Act of 1970 (RICO)** Federal legislation which provides for seizure of assets upon accusation and triple damages upon conviction for companies which conspire to defraud consumers, investors, and so on.

**Recap** See *Leveraged recapitalization.*

**Recapture of depreciation** The amount of prior depreciation which becomes taxable as ordinary income when an asset is sold for more than its tax basis.

**Redistribution hypothesis** A theory that value increases in mergers represent wealth shifts among stakeholders (e.g., a wealth transfer from bondholders to shareholders) rather than real increases in value.

**Residual analysis** The examination of asset returns to determine if a particular event has caused the return to deviate from a normal or predicted return which would have resulted if the event had not taken place. The difference between the actual return and the predicted return is the residual.

**Residual claims** The right of owners of an organization to cash flows not otherwise committed.

**Restricted vote stock** In dual-class stock firms, the stock with inferior voting rights.

**Restructuring** Significant changes in the strategies and policies relating to asset composition, liability and equity patterns, as well as operations.

**Retention ratio** The percentage of free cash flows retained in the firm.

**Reverse LBOs** Firms, or divisions of firms, which go public again after having been taken private in a leveraged buyout transaction.

**Reverse mergers** The uncombining of firms via spin-offs, divestitures, and so on.

**RICO** See *Racketeer Influenced and Corrupt Organizations Act of 1970.*

**Risk-free rate** The return on an asset with no risk of default. In theory, the return on short-term government securities.

**Risk premium** The differential of the required return on an asset in excess of the risk-free rate.

**Roll-out MLP** Also called spin-off MLP. A corporation transfers some of its assets to an MLP to avoid double taxation, for example. MLP units are initially distributed to corporate shareholders, and corporate management serves as the general partner.

**Roll-up MLP** The combination of several ordinary limited partnerships into a master limited partnership.

**Royalty trust** An organizational form used by firms which would otherwise be taxed heavily (due to declining depreciation and increasing pre-tax cash flows) to transfer ownership to investors in low tax brackets.

**Runup return** The event return measured for some period ending with the announcement date.

**Sample selection bias** Criteria for sample may exclude some relevant categories. Examples: Completed spin-offs will not include spin-offs announced, but not completed. Measures of industry profitability will not include firms that have failed. Studies of leveraged buyouts that have a subsequent public offering will represent the most successful and exclude the failures or less successful.

**Saturday night special** A hostile tender offer with a short time for response.

**Scale economies** The reduction in per-unit costs achievable by spreading fixed costs over a higher level of production.

**Schedule 13D** The form which must be filed with the SEC within ten days of acquiring 5% or more of a firm's stock; discloses the acquirer's identity and business intentions toward the target. Applies to all large stock acquisitions.

**Schedule 14D** The form which must be filed with the SEC by *any* group or individual making solicitations or recommendations which would result in its owning more than 5% of the target's stock. Applies to public tender offers only.

**Scorched-earth defenses** Actions to make the target less attractive to the acquiring firm and which may also leave the target in weakened condition. Examples are sale of best segments (crown jewels) and incurring high levels of debt to pay a large dividend or to engage in substantial share repurchase.

**Secondary initial public offering (SIPO)** The reoffering to the public of common stock in a company which had initially been public, but had then been taken private (e.g., in an LBO).

**Second-step transaction** Typically the merger of an acquired firm into the acquirer after control has been obtained.

**Securities Act of 1933 (SA)** First of the federal securities laws of the 1930s. Provides for federal regulation of the sale of securities to the public and registration of public offerings of securities.

**Securities Exchange Act of 1934 (SEA)** Federal legislation which established the Securities and Exchange Commission (SEC) to administer securities laws and to regulate practices in the purchase and sale of securities.

**Securities Investor Protection Act of 1970 (SIPA)** Federal legislation which established the Securities Investor Protection Corporation empowered to supervise the liquidation of bankrupt securities firms and to arrange for payments to their customers.

**Securities parking** An arrangement in which a second party holds ownership of assets to avoid identification of the actual owner in order to avoid rules and regulations related to securities trading.

**Sell-off** General term for divestiture of part or all of a firm by any one of a number of means, e.g., sale, liquidation, spin-off, and so on.

**Shareholder interest hypothesis** The theory that shareholder benefits of antitakeover defenses outweigh management entrenchment motives and effects.

**Share repurchase** A public corporation buys its own shares, by tender offer, on the open market, or in a negotiated buyback from a large block-holder.

**Shark repellent** Any of a number of takeover defenses designed to make a firm less attractive and less vulnerable to unwanted acquirers.

**Shark watcher** A firm (usually a proxy solicitation firm) which monitors trading activity in its clients' stock to detect early accumulations by an unwanted acquirer before the 5% disclosure threshold.

**Shelf registration** The federal securities law provision in Rule 415 which allows firms to register at one time the total amount of debt or equity they plan to sell over a two-year period. Securities can then be sold with no further delays whenever market conditions are most favorable.

**Sherman Act of 1890** Early antitrust legislation. Section 1 prohibits contracts, combinations, conspiracies in restraint of trade. Section 2 is directed against actual or attempted monopolization.

**Short-swing trading rule** Federal regulation under Section 16 of the Securities Exchange Act which prohibits designated corporate insiders from retaining the profits on any purchase and sale of their own firms' securities within a six-month period.

**SIC** See *Standard Industrial Classification.*

**Signaling** An action which conveys information to other players; for example, seasoned new equity issues signal that the stock is overvalued.

**Silver parachutes** Extending reduced golden parachute provisions to a wider range of managers.

**SIPO** See *Secondary initial public offering.*

**Sitting-on-a-gold-mine hypothesis** Attributes the increase in a takeover target's stock price to information disclosed during the takeover process that the target's assets are undervalued by the market.

**Small numbers problem** When the number of bidders is large, rivalry among bidders renders opportunistic behavior ineffectual. When the number of bidders is small, each party seeks terms most favorable to it through opportunistic representations and haggling.

**Specialized asset** An asset whose use is complementary to other assets. For example, a pipeline from producing fields to a cluster of refineries near large consumption markets.

**Specificity** The degree to which an asset or resource is specialized to and thus dependent on the rest of the firm or organization.

**Spin-off** A transaction in which a company distributes on a pro rata basis all of the shares it owns in a subsidiary to its own shareholders. Creates a new public company with (initially) the same proportional equity ownership as the parent company.

**Split-off** A transaction in which some, but not all, parent company shareholders receive shares in a subsidiary in return for relinquishing their parent company shares.

**Split-up** A transaction in which a company spins off all of its subsidiaries to its shareholders and ceases to exist.

**Spreadsheet approach** Analysis of data over a number of past and projected time periods.

**Squeeze-out** The elimination of minority shareholders by a controlling shareholder.

**Staggered board** Also called a classified board. An antitakeover measure which divides a firm's board of directors into several classes only one of which is up for election in any given year, thus delaying effective transfer of control to a new owner in a takeover.

**Stakeholder** Any individual or group who has an interest in a firm; in addition to shareholders and bondholders, includes labor, consumers, suppliers, the local community, and so on.

**Stake-out investment** Preliminary investment for a foothold in anticipation of the future possibility of a larger investment.

**Standard Industrial Classification (SIC)** The Census Bureau's system of categorizing industry groups, mainly product or process oriented.

**Standstill agreement** A voluntary contract by a large block shareholder (or former large blockholder bought out in a negotiated repurchase) not to make further investments in the target company for a specified period of time.

**Start-up MLP** Also called acquisition MLP; the assets of an existing entity are transferred to a master limited partnership, and the business is henceforth conducted as an MLP. The Boston Celtics' conversion into an MLP is an example.

**Stepped-up asset basis** The provision allowing asset purchasers to use the price paid for an asset as the starting point for future depreciation rather than the asset's depreciated book value in the hands of the seller.

**Stock appreciation right (SAR)** Part of executive compensation programs to align managers' interests with those of shareholders. SARs are issued to managers giving them the right to purchase stock on favorable terms; the exercise price can be as low as 50% of the stock price at issuance; maximum life is ten years.

**Stock bonus plan** A defined contribution pension plan in which the firm contributes a specified number of shares to the plan annually. The benefits to plan beneficiaries depend on the stock performance.

**Stock lockup** An option to buy some fraction of the target stock at the first bidder's initial offer when a rival bidder wins.

**Strategy** The long-range planning process for an organization. A succession of plans (with provisions for implementation) for the future of a firm.

**Strip financing** A type of financing, often used in leveraged buyouts in which all claimants hold approximately the same proportion of each security (except for management incentive shares and the most senior bank debt).

**Structural theory** An approach to industrial organization that argues that higher concentration in an industry causes less competition due to tacit coordination or overt collusion among the largest companies.

**Stub** New shares issued in exchange for old shares in a leveraged recapitalization.

**Subchapter S corporation** A form of business organization which provides the limited liability feature of the corporate form while allowing business income to be taxed at the personal tax rates of the business owners.

**Superior-vote stock** In dual-class stock firms, the class of stock which has more power to elect directors; usually concentrated in the hands of management.

**Supermajority** A requirement in many anti-takeover charter amendments that a change of control (for example) must be approved by more than a simple majority of shareholders; at least 67 to 90% approval may be required.

**Supernormal growth** Growth due to a profitability rate above the cost of capital.

**Swaps** Exchanges of one class of securities for another.

**SWOT** Acronym for Strengths, Weaknesses, Opportunities, and Threats; an approach to formulating firm strategy via assessments of firm capabilities in relation to the environment.

**Synergy** The "2 + 2 = 5" effect. The output of a combination of two entities is greater than the sum of their individual outputs.

**Take-out merger** The second-step transaction which merges the acquired firm into the acquirer and thus "takes out" the remaining target shares

which were not purchased in the initial (partial) tender offer.

**Takeover** A general term which includes both mergers and tender offers (acquisitions).

**Takeover defenses** Methods employed by targets to prevent the success of bidders' efforts.

**Target** The object of takeover efforts.

**Targeted share repurchase** Refers to repurchasing the stock of a large blockholder (an unwanted acquirer) at a premium over market price (greenmail).

**Tax credit ESOP (TRASOP, PAYSOP)** An employee stock ownership plan which allowed employers to take a credit against their tax liability for contributions up to a specified amount, based on qualified investment in plant and equipment (TRASOP) and/or covered payroll (PAYSOP). Repealed by the Economic Recovery Tax Act of 1981 and the Tax Reform Act of 1986.

**Tax-free reorganization** A takeover transaction in which the primary consideration paid to obtain the voting stock or assets of the target must be the voting stock of the acquiring firm. (In fact, tax is only deferred until target shareholders sell the stock received.)

**Team effects** A form of organization capital; information which helps assign employees for an efficient match of capabilities to tasks and which helps to match managers and other employees to form efficient teams.

**Team production** Alchian and Demsetz's distinguishing characteristic of a firm. Team output is greater than the sum of outputs of individual team members working independently (synergy); increased output cannot be unambiguously attributed to any individual team member.

**Tender offer** A method of effecting a takeover via a public offer to target firm shareholders to buy their shares.

**Termination fee** The payment or consolation prize to unsuccessful bidders.

**Third market** Trading off the organized securities exchanges by institutional investors.

**Time trader** Investors who buy or sell because of events unrelated to stock price fluctuations, e.g., for portfolio adjustment needs.

**Tin parachutes** Payments to a wide range of the target's employees for terminations resulting from a takeover.

**Tobin's q** The ratio of the current market value of the firm's securities to the current replacement costs of its assets; used as a measure of management performance.

**Toehold** The initial fraction of a target firm's shares acquired by a bidder.

**Top-down planning** An approach to overall firm strategy based on company-wide forecasts from top management, versus aggregation of segment forecasts.

**Total capitalization** The sum of total debt, preferred stock, and equity.

**Total capital requirements** A firm's financing requirements. Two alternative measures: (1) Total capital = Current Assets minus Noninterest-Bearing Debt plus Net Fixed Assets; (2) Total Capital = Interest-Bearing Debt plus Shareholders' Equity.

**TPRs** See *Transferable put rights.*

**Transaction cost** The cost of transferring a good or service across economic units or agents.

**Transferable put rights (TPRs)** A share repurchase plan in which puts for a limited time period issued to current shareholders can be resold to others.

**TRASOP** See *Tax credit ESOP.*

**Trigger point** The level of share ownership by a bidder at which provisions of a poison pill antitakeover defense plan are activated.

**Trust Indenture Act of 1939 (TIA)** Federal securities regulation of public issues of debt securities of $5 million or more. Specifies requirements to be included in the indenture (the agreement between the borrower and lenders) and sets out the responsibilities of the indenture trustee.

**Two-tier tender offer** Tender offers in which the bidder offers a superior first-tier price (e.g., higher or all cash) for a specified maximum number of shares it will accept and simultaneously announces its intentions to acquire remaining shares at a second-tier price (lower and/or securities rather than cash).

**Type A, B, C reorganization** Forms of tax-free reorganizations. Type A—statutory mergers (target merged into acquirer) and consolidations (new entity created). Type B—Stock-for-stock transaction in which target is liquidated into acquirer or maintained as separate operating entity. Type C—Stock-for-asset transaction in which at least 80% of fair market value of target's property is acquired; target then dissolves.

**Undervaluation** A firm's securities are selling for less than their intrinsic, or potential, or long-run value for one or more reasons.

**Underwritten offerings** Public securities issues which are sold by a firm to an investment banker at a negotiated price; the investment banker then bears the risk of price fluctuations before the securities are sold to the general public.

**Value additivity principle (VAP)** A quality of the NPV method of capital budgeting which enables managers to consider each project independently. The sum of project NPVs represents the value added to the corporation by taking them on.

**Value chain** An approach to strategy which analyzes the steps or chain of activities in the firm to find opportunities for reducing cost outlays while adding product characteristics valued by customers.

**Value drivers** Operating measures which have a major influence on the value of a firm.

**Vertical merger** A combination of firms which operate in different levels or stages of the same industry; e.g., a toy manufacturer merges with a chain of toy stores (forward integration); an auto manufacturer merges with a tire company (backward integration).

**Voting plan** A poison pill antitakeover defense plan which issues voting preferred stock to target firm shareholders. At a trigger point, preferred stockholders (other than the bidder for the target) become entitled to supervoting privileges, making it difficult for the bidder to obtain voting control.

**Voting trust** A device by means of which shareholders retain cash flow rights to their shares while giving the right to vote those shares to another entity.

**WACC** See *Weighted average marginal cost of capital.*

**Wealth transfer** The gain of one type of stakeholder in relation to the associated losses of other stakeholders.

**Weighted average marginal cost of capital (WACC)** The relevant discount rate or investment hurdle rate based on targeted capital structure proportions.

**White knight**  A more acceptable merger partner sought out by the target of a hostile bidder.

**White squire**  A third party friendly to management who helps a company avoid an unwanted takeover without taking over the company on its own.

**Williams Act of 1968**  Federal legislation designed to protect target shareholders from swift and secret takeovers in three ways: (1) Generating more information during the takeover process; (2) Requiring minimum period for tender offer to remain open; (3) Authorizing targets to sue bidders.

**Winner's curse**  The tendency that in a bidding contest or in some types of auctions, the winner is the bidder with the highest (overoptimistic) estimate of value. This explains the high frequency of negative returns to acquiring firms in takeovers with multiple bidders.

**WOTS UP**  Acronym for Weaknesses, Opportunities, Threats, and Strengths; a technique to identify these key elements as part of the iterative process used to develop strategy.

# Author Index

# Subject Index